THIS anthology provides a selection of science-fiction tales from the close of the 'Romantic' period to the end of the First World War. It gathers together classic short stories, from Edgar Allan Poe's playful hoaxes to Gertrude Barrows Bennett's feminist fantasy. The collection shows the vitality and literary diversity of the field, and also expresses something of the potent appeal of the visionary, the fascination with science, and the allure of an imagined future that characterized this period. An excellent resource for those interested in science fiction, and also an essential volume for understanding the development of the genre.

In his introduction, Michael Newton draws together literary influences from Jonathan Swift to Mary Shelley, the interest in the irrational and dreaming mind, and the relation of the tales to the fact of Empire and the discoveries made by anthropology. He also considers how the figure of the alien and non-human 'other' complicated contemporary definitions of the human being.

MICHAEL NEWTON is the author of *Savage Girls and Wild Boys: A History of Feral Children* (2002) and *Age of Assassins: A History of Conspiracy and Political Violence, 1865–1981* (2012). On the subject of cinema, he has written *Show People: A History of the Film Star* (2019) and books on *Kind Hearts and Coronets* (2003) and *Rosemary's Baby* (2020) for the BFI Film Classics series. He has edited Edmund Gosse's *Father and Son* and *Victorian Fairy Tales* for Oxford World's Classics, and Joseph Conrad's *The Secret Agent* and *The Penguin Book of Ghost Stories* for Penguin Classics, and co-edited the anthology, *Literature and Science, 1660–1834: Science as Polite Culture* (Pickering & Chatto). He teaches literature and film at Leiden University.

OXFORD WORLD'S CLASSICS

*For over 100 years Oxford World's Classics have brought
readers closer to the world's great literature. Now with over 700
titles—from the 4,000-year-old myths of Mesopotamia to the
twentieth century's greatest novels—the series makes available
lesser-known as well as celebrated writing.*

*The pocket-sized hardbacks of the early years contained
introductions by Virginia Woolf, T. S. Eliot, Graham Greene,
and other literary figures which enriched the experience of reading.
Today the series is recognized for its fine scholarship and
reliability in texts that span world literature, drama and poetry,
religion, philosophy, and politics. Each edition includes perceptive
commentary and essential background information to meet the
changing needs of readers.*

OXFORD WORLD'S CLASSICS

MICHAEL NEWTON

The Origins of Science Fiction

From Mary Shelley to W. E. B. Dubois

Edited with an Introduction and Notes by
MICHAEL NEWTON

OXFORD
UNIVERSITY PRESS

OXFORD

UNIVERSITY PRESS

Great Clarendon Street, Oxford, OX2 6DP,
United Kingdom

Oxford University Press is a department of the University of Oxford.
It furthers the University's objective of excellence in research, scholarship,
and education by publishing worldwide. Oxford is a registered trade mark of
Oxford University Press in the UK and in certain other countries

First published 2022
First published as Oxford World's Classics paperback in 2023

Published in the United States of America by Oxford University Press
198 Madison Avenue, New York, NY 10016, United States of America

British Library Cataloguing in Publication Data

Data available

Library of Congress Control Number: 2023931644

ISBN 978–0–19–889194–9

Printed and bound in the UK by
Clays Ltd, Elcograf S.p.A.

ACKNOWLEDGEMENTS

My thanks go to Luciana O'Flaherty, for inviting me to make the proposal in the first place, and to Christina Fleischer and Rebecca Darley at OUP for their help and support. I would like to thank the Society of Authors, and particularly Sarah Baxter, for their generous permission to print here E. M. Forster's prescient story, 'The Machine Stops'. Thanks to Richard Hamblyn and Jo Lynch, for the hospitality and the loan of the Poe, and to Gregory Dart for sharing the delights and difficulties of editing. I am especially grateful to Lena, for helping me to work on this book, particularly during the dystopian days of the Covid-19 lockdown, and for all her generosity, affection, and care. I dedicate my work on this book first of all to my daughters, Alice and Hannah, who are time-travelling bravely into an unimaginable future; may it be a beautiful one. And I also dedicate this book to my scholarly colleague, neighbour, and friend, Evert Jan van Leeuwen, whose enthusiasm for science fiction has always been gloriously contagious.

CONTENTS

INTRODUCTION

'Thou hast fallen into fearful hands!': Naming Science Fiction

WHEN in the 1890s, reviewers considered H. G. Wells' series of 'scientific romances', at least one critic greeted them with both praise and puzzlement, bewailing the fact that rather than write straight scientific philosophy, he had chosen to '"tell horrible little stories about monsters"'. Yet it was clear that Wells was busy perfecting a novel kind of story, one that would combine the fantastic and the scientific, giving us 'a fairy tale with a plausible scientific justification'.[1] This new form of writing would by the 1940s seem a ubiquitous feature of 'juvenile' fiction, purveying visions of the future for boys. In 1940, examining 'boys' weeklies', George Orwell noted: 'The one theme that is really new is the scientific one. Death-rays, Martians, invisible men, robots, helicopters and interplanetary rockets figure largely . . . Whereas the *Gem* and *Magnet* derive from Dickens and Kipling, the *Wizard, Champion, Modern Boy*, etc., owe a great deal to H. G. Wells, who, rather than Jules Verne, is the father of "Scientification." Naturally it is the magical, Martian aspect of science that is most exploited'.[2] In a little over forty years, the type of writing that Wells was practising had transformed from being something idiosyncratic and more or less nameless, to being sharply defined, mildly contemptible, and pointedly 'fathered' by the author.

Every writer who discusses science fiction rapidly stumbles into the perilous territory of definition. Despite Orwell's claims regarding Wells' paternity, science fiction remains a form with more than one origin story. Some point to Mary Shelley, to others everything flows from the genius of Edgar Allan Poe, or finds its roots in Jules Verne, or in Wells, described in 1906 as 'that flamingo of letters who for the last decade or so has been a wonder to our island birds'.[3] Otherwise,

---

[1] Clement Shorter, 'Review in *Bookman*', October 1897, in Patrick Parrinder (ed.), *H. G. Wells: The Critical Heritage* (London and Boston: Routledge & Kegan Paul, 1972), pp. 58–9.

[2] George Orwell, 'Boys' Weeklies', *The Collected Essays, Journalism and Letters* (London: Penguin Books, 1970), Vol. 1, p. 521.

[3] W. H. Hudson, 'Introduction', *A Crystal Age* (London: T. Fisher Unwin, 1906), p. vi.

science fiction can seem an antique progeny, taking first tentative steps in Lucian of Samoasta's *True History* (written in the second century CE.), or making new strides in Johannes Kepler's *Somnium* (1634) or Jonathan Swift's *Gulliver's Travels* (1726), or discovering its true mother in *Frankenstein* (1818). Alternatively it can be seen as having a specifically late Victorian birth, in an era that saw the foundation of a series of literary genres established in the context of industrial modernity: detective fiction, the horror story, the Imperial romance, the boys' book, or the literary ghost story. Elements of all these kinds converge in this collection of tales. As literary critic Peter Keating writes: 'As all of these sub-genres began to establish their own traditions and inspirational texts, the narrative skills became more self-consciously adventurous: they were able to exist within a frame of reference created by their own conventions'.[4] In the last decades of the nineteenth century, rules of play were forming that could be riffed on, subverted, and developed. Particularly in the period from *Frankenstein* to Jules Verne's *Vingt mille lieues sous les mers* (1870), the tropes were still in flux and the conventions unfixed. Hence the tales in this book might seem a disparate bunch, a collection, but perhaps not a homogeneity. Then again that is how things should be, for the origins of science fiction were simply not homogeneous. (Indeed, I have sometimes felt that the most telling connection that unites the writers in this anthology is that nearly all endured some form of childhood trauma—whether abandonment, the death of one or both parents, or a family bankruptcy.) Otherwise what we find gathered in this book are the fertile grounds out of which science fiction grew, a shared set of subjects and themes, of motifs and figures, with a neighbourly attachment to utopian fiction, to fairy tale and fantasy, to Gothic, to the Imperialist yarn, and even to the realist nineteenth-century novel. The themes and subjects of these stories form a recognisable heritage, an array of concerns that would be picked up in twentieth and twenty-first-century works: mad scientists and overreachers; apocalypses; alien encounters; time-travellers; dystopian and utopian visions; the power of machines and the estrangements of new technologies; the fallible, bewildered self. Up to around 1890, the stories in this collection are perhaps only equivocally

---

[4] Peter Keating, *The Haunted Study: A Social History of the English Novel, 1875–1914* (1989) (London: Fonanta Press, 1991), p. 342.

categorizable as science fiction, and then suddenly that label does not feel debatable anymore. Something new had come to light.

The late nineteenth century saw a the formation of a myriad new genres, a confusion of possibilities, where a writer must position themselves in the marketplace as the purveyor of a certain kind of fiction: Kipling's Indian tales, Arthur Conan Doyle's Holmes stories, or Sarah Orne Jewett's fictions of New England domesticities. Writers could, of course, have more than one string to their bow, and Henry James or Mary Wilkins Freeman could swerve from realism to the ghost story, and back again. In these new kinds, and particularly in the nameless field where science fiction would grow, a writer could feel unburdened by the greatness of past practitioners, with no Shakespeare or Cervantes, no Homer or Scott, to vie with or out-do. Thinking of science fiction or 'fantasy', both Adam Roberts and Neil Gaiman have argued that over the twentieth century, these experimental forms became increasingly familiar, comforting, as sealed in conventional certainty as any Sunday evening police procedural. Contrariwise, at the time of their publication the tales in this anthology were genuinely new, and more or less uncategorizable.

It is curious to trace just how contemporaries tried to describe and name the stories collected here. Contemporary reviews of Eliot's 'The Lifted Veil' find it hard to pin down precisely what kind of story it is. It's a tale 'of morbid interest', a not very interesting 'autobiography', 'a strange story, metaphysical and unnatural', or 'a strange wild story', 'a curious revelation', or 'a somewhat mystical, yet highly interesting story'.[5] The term 'strange stories' was picked up by Grant Allen and for a collection of stories by Wells in 1898 (*Thirty Strange Stories*); in an article on 'Arsenic Eaters', F. W. Clarke begins by talking of Hawthorne's 'strange story', 'Rappaccini's Daughter'.[6] However, the designation, 'strange', was also felt to be equally suitable for Lafcadio Hearn's book of Japanese ghost stories, *Kwaidan* (1904) or for an anthology of E. T. A. Hoffmann's tales. Stockton's 'The Water-Devil' is both an 'ingenious yarn' and 'an

---

[5] From reviews in: *Nottinghamshire Guardian*, July 7 1859, p. 3; The *Elgin Courier* July 8 1859, p. 4; *Boston Daily Advertiser*, July 30 1859, p. 2; *Westmorland Gazette*, July 2 1859, p. 3; *Blackburn Standard* July 6 1859, p. 4; *Newcastle Journal* July 9 1859, p. 2.

[6] In *Appleton's Journal of Literature, Science and Art*, Feb 10 1872, 7/150: 158.

amusing story'.[7] Grant Allen's 'Pausodyne' gives 'another turn to the Rip van Winkle style of tale' and proves a 'capital extravaganza'.[8] In a review of H. G. Wells' *The Country of the Blind and other Stories*, the *Daily Mirror* writes: 'There are stories of all types here—the humbler character studies contrasting with ghost-tales, or with those weird mechanical inventions and adaptations of scientific possibility that first made Mr. Wells famous'.[9] In each of these cases, it remains clear that reviewers sense that there is something odd about the stories in question, though they cannot quite pin down wherein that oddity consists.

Before Wells, to the best of my knowledge, no-one put together an anthology of short stories that might all, or might predominantly, be described now as 'science fiction'. This is very unlike the contemporary situation with ghost stories, detective fiction, or the literary fairy tale, all of which could form the linking generic premise for a book. This absence of such a thing as a 'science fiction' collection would suggest that even in the 1890s there was not a significant sense of such stories forming a category in themselves. There is instead a tentativeness regarding the tales in this book: George Eliot does not put 'The Lifted Veil' in a volume for twenty years; Mary Shelley leaves 'The Mortal Immortal' uncollected; and Mary Wilkins Freeman does not find a place in any book for 'The Hall Bedroom'. Other stories do appear in collections, but are not marked out as being in essence a different kind of thing. A writer such as Poe or Kipling mingled all kinds of diverse tales in their volumes. In any case, in terms of genre, diversity is as cogent a fact in the tale itself, as in the books that frame them. Few tales are a pure entity, but live instead as a site where several genres cross: to take a much later example, one might think of *Star Wars* (1977) with its simultaneous indebtedness to the western, the *Buck Rogers* Saturday-morning serial, the samurai film, and the war movie. So it is that the tales here merge with other modes or

---

[7] *The Literary World* 22/1 Jan 3 1891 calls 'The Water-Devil' an 'ingenious yarn' (13); on on the story's conclusion, it wrote (22/3 Jan 31 1891, 'Mr. Stockton's story, "The Water Devil" comes to an ingenious end, showing how one of the marines can relate, as well as accept, the marvelous' (44).The *Christian Advocate* 66/7 Feb 12 1891 calls it 'his amusing story' (112).

[8] *Derbyshire Times ad Chesterfield Herald*, Dec 3 1881, p. 8; *Illustrated London News* 79/2223 December 10 1881: 20.

[9] *Daily Mirror*, August 19 1911, p. 7.

genres: romance, detection, satire, pastoral, and so on. Given as they are to the investigation of scientific experimentation, these tales are themselves experiments, forays into unknown territory.

Yet, for all the diversity, an indebtedness to one literary kind is particularly evident: again and again, these stories seem to be adopting the procedures of Gothic. Indeed, the novelist and critic, Brian Aldiss has strongly argued for the Gothic roots of science fiction, that it was 'born from the Gothic mode'.[10] The essentially hybrid nature of these early stories (with that hybridity perhaps passed on to their descendants) renders it perhaps futile to disentangle the Gothic from the proto-science-fictional. And yet, for all their shared fascination with the dreamed-up landscapes of the fantastic, there is a difference between the staging and strategies of the two kinds of story. Reading Freeman's 'The Hall Bedroom' or Kipling's ' "Wireless" ', it may feel legitimate to describe them both as a form of ghost story. However, in ' "Wireless" ', the radio set significantly does not actually channel the spirit of John Keats; rather the shared condition of the two men produce the same result, one conducted through the novel mechanical apparatus. In 'The Hall Bedroom', the possibility of its being a spiritual fantasy suddenly moves elsewhere, with the evocation of a putative, scientifically-imagined space, a 'fifth dimension'. What stands out in both cases, as in all the stories in this book, is that, counter to the methods of the ghost story, the tales move towards explication, and not towards uncanny bafflement, to hesitancies in interpretation. Indeed, for all the stress on enchantment in the tales here, what ultimately defines them as something distinct and new is this concern with elucidation. Mystery here becomes a problem in need of a solution. Therefore, though all definitions are fallible, I would suggest that in its origins, science fiction begins as a mode in which either the characters or the readers are non-plussed, and are therefore busy with the work of explanation, and that when explanation comes, it has a scientific basis. The certainty that a mystery may be explained (however, far-fetched the rationalization) lies at the root of science-fiction. Like Gothic, like the detective story, it is a form of and for the curious. In this sense, all these three genres honed by Edgar Allan Poe are predicated

---

[10] Brian Aldiss, *Billion Year Spree: The History of Science Fiction* (London: Weidenfeld and Nicholson, 1973), p. 18.

on the desire to know, and on the sense that curiosity may be fatal or forbidden.

Moreover, unlike Gothic and the nineteenth-century ghost story, in the tales in this volume, the sense of 'hauntedness' by the historical past is tellingly absent. Though some of the stories ('The Moral Immortal' and 'Pausodyne') describe emissaries from another century, they're strikingly practical figures, living survivors into a present, and not the baffling residue of history. In Hawthorne, too, the tale may be set in the past, and it enjoys some of the glamour cast by that distance, but 'pastness' itself is far from being the freight of that story. It is equally striking how infrequently these particular stories are tales of the future; only really 'The Machine Stops' and 'Friend Island' are exceptions to this rule. Elsewhere the interest in utopias and, later, dystopias, brought in accounts of a future realm (though both Samuel Butler's *Erewhon* (1872) and Bulwer Lytton's *The Coming Race* (1871) proffer societies contemporaneous to our own). More usually what preoccupies these tales is what is jarring and astonishing now, the future already present in the nineteenth-century world.

'Overburthened With The Majesty Of All Things': *Fantasies of Science*

In annotating these stories, it quickly becomes clear just how profoundly they intermingle real science and invented fantasy. Alongside their imagined figures, they cite contemporary scientists in the field. In Fitz-James O'Brien's 'The Diamond Lens', in Grant Allen's 'Pausodyne', in H. G. Well's *The War of the Worlds*, hypotheses take root in the real. Actual science fires the imagination in the tales in these books, responding to genuine hypothetical possibilities. They pursue certain ideas, imagining the scientific bent as a source of dread or an unsettled, surprising joy. The journals in which the stories in this anthology were first published customarily mixed science and the arts, natural philosophy and fiction. When in 1897 *Pearson's Magazine* serialized Wells' *The War of the Worlds*, the Martian invaders jostled alongside journalistic articles that speculated on a scientific basis for a greatly expanded life-span, detailed new electrical inventions, or celebrated 'The Greatest Telescope on Earth', so that a close-up of the moon was only a page or so distant from a Tripod flailing its way to Chertsey. Such juxtapositions were intrinsic to nineteenth-century periodical culture. Indeed, it is central to the understanding of Poe's 'The Facts in the Case of M. Valdemar' that in context it might prove hard to tell if that account were fiction or fact. However, science does not just pervade the pages of these journals, it seeps through the tales themselves. Regarding George Eliot's 'The Lifted Veil', its provenance as proto-Science Fiction depends upon the story's concerns with genuine science and pseudo-science, with blood transfusion and phrenology. Among other matters, it is this profound engagement with scientific discoveries and theories that positions the fictions in this volume as science-fictional, melding as Wells would do, 'the emotions of an artist and the intellectual imagination of a scientific investigator'.[11]

Despite this strong interest in the scientific, it remains the case that the stories gathered together in this volume are as attuned to the fantastic and the anomalous. Indeed, these tales take their place in an ongoing conflict in the nineteenth century between 'realism' and 'romance'. Edward Bulwer Lytton set out a literary landscape in which a dusty, pedestrian realism confronted an 'idealism' that turned to ideas, to myth and fable as a surer path to 'the inward signification'.[12] This was a war with hostages held by both sides. For instance, Émile Zola and the naturalists were the fiercest opponents of 'the idealists'. They deliberately set out to ground their work in science— both evolutionary and sociological—and in their strong interest in science they occupy a border territory with the more scientifically minded of the romancers. In the proto-science-fictional stories in the volume, we find a complex interaction between these two modes, with realism in approach, and romance in the subject matter, the archetypal versus the documentary. Science fiction provides an approach to the romantic via the empirical. Its speculative 'what ifs' ground themselves on extrapolated possibilities, no matter how remote. The late Victorian category of the 'scientific romance' gives us a productive oxymoron, reminding us that the science itself might be seen as romantic or yearning. Robert Chambers' *Vestiges of the Natural*

[11] Chalmers Mitchell, 'Review in *Saturday Review*', April 11 1896, in Patrick Parrinder (ed.), *H. G. Wells: The Critical Heritage* (London and Boston: Routledge & Kegan Paul, 1972), p. 43.

[12] See Sir Edward Bulwer Lytton, 'On Certain Principles of Art in Works of Imagination', in *Caxtoniana: A Series of Essays on Life, Literature and Manners* (New York: Harper Brothers, 1863), 318.

History of Creation (1844) had been itself described by hostile reviewers as a 'scientific romance', that is, untrue, and the phrase first
applied to apparently implausible speculation, and only later to a text
that deliberately indulged in such speculations in order to create a literary fiction. So it was that critics were as apt to see Robert Louis
Stevenson as being as much of an influence on H. G. Wells, as Swift
and Defoe. The first stories set in outer space envisioned the distant
planet as a kind of fairyland, kin to the fabulous islands visited by
Odysseus or Prospero.

So it is that Wells was hailed in a letter sent by Joseph Conrad as,
'O realist of the fantastic!'[13] Similarly, as another fan, the journalist
and editor, W. T. Stead declared: 'He has caught the trick of describing events which only exist in his imagination with the technical
precision of a newspaper reporter.'[14] One aspect of this narrative
approach was an estranging aloofness, an absence of affect that reveals
much about how science fiction was developing. In *The War of the
Worlds* and other of his 'scientific romances', Wells describes violence
and destruction with a matter-of-fact blankness. He not only delin-
eates the marvellous with pragmatic clarity, but he also detaches himself from emotional engagement with the deaths of others. There is
a clue here both to Wells' approach, but, as I shall suggest later, to the
core of much of science fiction itself.

As unveiled in the tales in this anthology, science fiction finds its
origins in a romantic impulse performed anti-romantically. Wonder
expresses itself in dissection, analysis, and intrusion into secret
realms. As opposed to the perception of a living truth the tales probe
what they with regularity name 'the facts'. In Poe's inquiry into
M. Valdemar, in the conclusion to Wells' 'The Crystal Egg' the same
insistence on the fact presents itself, a clinging to the observable data.

The creative tension of these stories resides in a perceived conflict
between the poetic vision of truth and the observation of the empirical
real. In a letter, Mary Wilkins Freeman declared that 'most of my own
work is not really the kind I myself like. I want more symbolism, more
mysticism. I left that out, because it struck me people did not want it,

---

[13] Sent December 4 1898, and quoted in Patrick Parrinder (ed.), *H. G. Wells:
The Critical Heritage* (London and Boston: Routledge & Kegan Paul, 1972), p. 60.
[14] From a review published in *Review of Reviews* in April 1898 (ibid., p. 62).

and I was forced to consider selling qualities'.[15] The connection and the disparity between the scientist and the poet, the romancer and the realist, melds the imaginative frame of these fictions. They invite the giving of oneself to the marvellous, to the visionary intensity of the tale, where it may prove equally extraordinary if the force that works against you is a water-devil or an enormous magnetized undersea cable. Science fiction comes into being as the productive battleground for these concerns, perpetually held in view and perpetually unresolved. In Eliot's 'The Lifted Veil', Latimer's responses are those of a poet, though his Keatsian self is perverted by the will of the father into becoming scientific. He loses himself, just as Fitz-James O'Brien's narrator does, in the 'microscopic vision'. In Wordsworth's *The Prelude*, the disillusioning gaze is the 'microscopic' one (XII, 91). In Wells' 'The Crystal Egg', Mr Cave wonders, while his scientific collaborator, Mr Wace, measures. In Poe, in Hawthorne, in Eliot, in O'Brien, the poet stands as an opposite type to the scientist, delineating two separate and yet interrelated modes of understanding the world—wonder against analysis, gratitude contra curiosity. Such is the perversity of these men. The range of allusion in O'Brien's story shifts from science to poetry and myth when the feminine swims into view. In 'The Diamond Lens', O'Brien's protagonist, Linley, embodies a fantasy of the solitary scientist, yet the fabric of allusion in the tale shows both poetry and science to be collaborative ventures—hence the pertinency of the plagiarism charge brought at the time against O'Brien.

These stories enact the difficulty of believing in things, including believing in stories. E. M. Forster's 'The Machine Stops' immediately invites you to imagine, and then abruptly informs you in fact the world here outstrips your facility to do so. Stockton's 'The Water-Devil' asks constantly what should go into a story, what is the 'real' part. It presents a process by which what happens is 'fact-checked' even as the narrator recounts it. As in the ghost story, many other of the fictions here play with the possibility that you may disbelieve what you are told. Poe's 'Valdemar' was a contraption designed to trap you into belief. H. G. Wells' 'The Crystal Egg' plays with curious insistence on the 'circumstantial' nature of the story, linking its methods to the evidential, the reliability or otherwise of another man's vision. Yet

---

[15] Letter to Fred Lewis Pattee, 5 September 1919, quoted in Leah Blatt Glasser, *In a Closet Hidden: The Life and Work of Mary E. Wilkins Freeman* (Amherst, MA: University of Massachusetts Press, 1996), p. 219.

Wells knows too the importance of imagination as such, the desire of his dowdy protagonist for a realm beyond the fustiness and oppressions of a drab London life, a forbidden garden of masculine freedom away from a wife's demands.

A need for another space, for the potentialities of dreaming finds room here. An extreme of realism is not poetic enough to render the complexities of life. Perhaps the note of wonder is strikingly rare— maybe only 'Rappaccini's Daughter', 'The Water-Devil', 'The Hall Bedroom', and ' "Wireless" ' strike it, and then mutedly, sighingly. Wonder means more often the desire to gaze, and to look at and to look into. Yet, the science itself can be 'fantastic', experimental and searching. A scientific hypothesis resembles a dream in search of its observable fulfilment. Jules Verne's *An Antarctic Mystery* (*Le Sphinx des glaces*) (1897) responds to and endeavours to complete Edgar Allan Poe's *The Narrative of Arthur Gordon Pym* (1837). In doing so, it attempts the futile task of bringing rationality and logic to a narrative that lacks either. Again in this curious attempt, we find the same fault-line within science fiction, a form of writing that cherishes a fantasy of the machine, of the industrial age, and that therefore incorporates a kind of deathliness, and yet nonetheless enshrines a space for dreaming, for the fabled, for the promptings of life. In several tales, the figures of myth, the naiads, the monsters, even the cherubs of legend, reveal themselves to be realities elsewhere. Behind the myth lives the actual thing.

'Was this, then, his dark tower?': The Literature of Discovery

The tales in this anthology and early science fiction novels in general have many ancestors, and we have already traced their lineage back to Gothic. Perhaps of equal impact was the long-standing literature of exploration and discovery. Books such as Samuel Butler's *Erewhon* or tales like Bennett's 'Friend Island' and London's 'The Red One' look across to such colonial accounts. The same sense of the strangeness of an earthly elsewhere runs through Mary Shelley's *Frankenstein* or Poe's *Arthur Gordon Pym*. The worldly voyager is something of a space-traveller too, encountering otherness in unexplored regions of the globe, or under the sea, or beneath the earth's crust. Such stories enact the finding of a realm, either in a geographical elsewhere or in a distant future, a place to be understood as a negation or an exaggeration of trends in our everyday world.

So it is that colonialist desires and anxieties pervade nineteenth- and early twentieth-century proto-science fiction. Kipling's '"Wireless"' touches on the argosies of the mercantile seas, with drugs derived from India or Java, borne by sea and trade coming to the marketplace of a chill English shop. Samuel Butler's *Erewhon* and Anthony Trollope's curious fantasy, *The Fixed Period* (1882) similarly involve the relation between the home nation and the colony (in both cases with New Zealand clearly in view). Gustave Doré's engraving, 'The New Zealander' (1872), the book that inspired it, Henry O'Neill's *Two Thousand Years Hence* (1867), and Thomas Babington Macaulay's evocation in 1840 of a visitor from New Zealand in the far future gazing out at the ruins of St. Paul's, all express fears of a destroyed Europe and a resurgent Pacific colony.[16]

As such, as also through the indebtedness to the archetypes of romance narrative, these early science fiction works align themselves alongside a literary move towards 'extroversion', adventure, towards plot and the concept as the basis of the tale. At the same time, they lose interest in the dramas of the inner life. Poe, Hawthorne or Eliot, in their very different ways are still writing dramas of consciousness, but the inner life of Wells' characters or London's is a startlingly unreflective affair. An interest in identity remains, but identity becomes something exposed by the surface of plot, or tied up in the exploration of a hypothesis.

In the early science fiction tale's interest in the journey of exploration, as in the strong connections that link science fiction to utopian narratives, we can detect the mark of the newly developing social sciences. If science fiction concerns 'science', then the sciences that were perhaps most decisive were anthropology and sociology. Like an anthropologist, like a sociologist, the protagonists (and the reader) must decode an unfamiliar system of rules. Being an alien or a stranger to the future, or the hidden realm, they look on from outside. The empirical processes of some of our stories, and of many of the 'scientific romances' of the period, derive from the mapping of a colonial elsewhere,

[16] Thomas Babington Macaulay, 'Ranke's History of the Popes', in *Critical and Historical Essays, Contributed to The Edinburgh Review* (London: Longman, Brown, Green, and Longmans, 1854): Vol. II, 128.

as voyagers from 'here' attempt to interpret the rules and modes of being 'there'. In 'The Country of the Blind', for instance, the narrative taps out an empirical process, with the narrative driven by the explorer's success (and initial failure) at interpreting the society he finds. These 'romances' often entail the outsider's reading of a strange society, repeating the colonial experience with its pragmatic interest in social and anthropological organization as such, as well as the disorientation of contact, both for the intruders and for those intruded upon. Society itself, the form of culture, becomes the burden of the tale. So it is that traces of other forms of 'alienness' in social forms enter into the tales, as in the glancing preoccupation in Poe, O'Brien, and Eliot with the place of the Jews in New York or European society.

These 'sociological' and 'anthropological elements in the tale were modish, and leave their impression on these stories precisely at the moment in which they are being formed as academic disciplines. Pertinently, George Eliot's review of Riehl's volumes on 'The Natural History of German Life' (1856) helped to focus what would be her sociological approach to the novel, while W. E. B. Du Bois was both an author of a striking science fiction tale and an innovative academic sociologist. The idea of 'sociology' as a science might be traced back to Giambattista Vico (1668–1744), but effectively comes in with August Comte and then via Herbert Spencer. The word 'sociology' was first used in English in 1842; 'sociologist' first appears one year later; the first courses in sociology at Yale were offered from 1876 onwards, taught by William Graham Sumner (1840–1910), and in 1894 at Columbia, Franklin Giddings (1855–1931) became the first full professor of sociology. Similarly, 'anthropology' in our modern understanding of it as the scientific study of human culture is effectively also a nineteenth-century invention—in 1863, the 'Anthropological Society of London' was formed—with 'cultural anthropology' or 'social anthropology' being later nineteenth-century formulations. Though they have eighteenth-century roots, 'Ethnology' and 'Ethnography' are likewise disseminated widely in the nineteenth century. As the century progressed, Darwin's ideas acted as a galvanizing force in these disciplines, and this indebtedness to biological fact was one thing that was supposed to ensure that they would be truly scientific.

In part through their anthropological bias, many tales of exploration (and later of space exploration), the imperialist urge comes under the microscope, that desire for relentless possession that made Cecil Rhodes lament, ' "I would annex the planets if I could" '.[17] A story like 'The Red One' re-enacts a version of the colonial shock, the destabilising encounter with others who may or may not be considered human, though the story only fully imagines one side of that encounter. In invasion narratives, like Wells' *The War of the Worlds*, comfortable, bourgeois Britons endure the genocidal violence that they themselves had sanctioned and perpetrated in Africa, Asia and the Pacific, with the people of Surrey and London forced to share the fate of the slaughtered Tasmanians, or even of the dodo. What historian and critic Tzvetan Todorov has named 'the culture of massacre' comes to Shepperton and Chalk Farm. The invading Martians' minds are essentially 'unsympathetic', perhaps both in the sense of being impervious to communication with us, but also in being separate, cold, beyond pity or compunction. This too closely resembles the colonists' gaze. In this looking-glass of otherness, Wells invites us to view ourselves.

Jack London's 'The Red One' offers its reader the conjunction of racist discourse about the 'savage' and an idea of the holy, the numinous, as disturbing and primeval, and essentially shared. This tale's simultaneous sense of community and of estrangement, of complicity and disgust, runs through many of the fantastic texts of our period. In Wells' *The First Men in the Moon*, the Selenites repel the narrator simply by being so other to himself, 'an insect that has somehow contrived to mock humanity', separated by uncrossable distances, where 'our resemblances were not going to bridge our differences'.[18] And yet the human explorers' expedition is itself 'inhuman', a journey of discovery that exceeds the bounds of human capacities.[19]

In Wells' novel of lunar exploration an intriguing question arises, one already familiar to plundering colonists across our own globe: why is it not murder to kill a Selenite? In *The War of the Worlds*, someone suggests that ' "It ain't no murder killing beasts like that" '.[20]

---

[17] Sarah Gertrude Millin, *Rhodes* (London: Chatto & Windus, 1933), p 138, quoted in Hannah Arendt, *The Origins of Totalitarianism* (1951) (San Diego, New York and London: Harcourt Brace Jovanovich, 1979), p. 124, 170.

[18] H. G. Wells, *The First Men in the Moon* (London: George Newnes, Limited, 1901), p. 295.

[19] Ibid., p. 161.

[20] H. G. Wells, *The War of the Worlds* (London: William Heinemann, 1898), p. 59.

The shade of colonial violence falls over many of those early science-fiction texts that draw upon the romance of exploration. In *The First Men in the Moon*, the narrator's desire is to return to the moon with more guns, and on his return to earth he shows remarkably scant remorse for his lost companion, Cavor, or for a boy launched accidentally to a lonely death from starvation or suffocation in space. Indeed, a profound indifference to the suffering of other people lingers through all of Wells' scientific romances. They make themselves 'hard'. Weakness finds its punishment; only the tough survive. In *The Time Machine*, the class distinctions of the 1890s become an absolute racial distinction, an actual species difference. The symbiotic society of cannibalistic Morlock and effete Eloi turns class war on its head, and yet the feeling that the ruling classes related to the oppressed much as colonial rulers did to their subject peoples was of long-standing. In this sense too, the world of science fiction was only the nineteenth-century world rendered with disconcerting clarity.

'The Names and Uses of the Mechanism': Technologies of the Tale

In Edith Wharton's novel of irony and lament, *The Age of Innocence* (1920), two would-be lovers kept apart by social rules imagine the science-fiction technologies of the future, drawing on Edgar Allan Poe and Jules Verne to play with fantasies of a society so connected that one day people might converse from a distance, even ('incredible dream!') from one town to another.[21] The reader, naturally, is on the joke that the impossible communication technology whimsically described by the pair of them will in their own lifetime come to pass. They live, without knowing it, in a world already in the process of being transformed by technologies, and what seems ideas from science fiction describe the near-future that they themselves will live into.

In a diary entry, in January 1908, E. M. Forster noted that 'a man—named Farman—flew a ¾ mile circuit in 1½ minutes . . . It really is a new civilisation. I have been born at the end of the age of peace and can't expect to feel anything but despair. Science, instead of freeing man . . . is enslaving him to machines. . . . Man may get a new and perhaps a greater soul for the new conditions. But such a soul as mine

---

[21] Edith Wharton, *The Age of Innocence* (New York: D. Appleton and Company, 1920), p. 135.

will be crushed out.'[22] This was not only reactionary frailty, it was prescience. Born in the mid-1960s, at the end of the century I should have realized that with the coming of the internet my analog world of phone booths and record players was as suddenly gone as Forster's had been, and now that I had to live on into the indescribable. Witnesses in Regency England had felt similarly about the advent of steam engines and spinning Jennies. Indeed, the apparently exponential development of machine-knowledge has meant that every generation must live through such a moment of alienation, and face the fact that technologies frame the social realm.

The new machinery of the century were already surpassing the capacity of the human imagination to assimilate it. Edgar Allan Poe's 'The Thousand-and-Second Tale of Scheherazade' (1845) shows existing technology outstripping fantasy, and, in consequence, unveils the fantastic nature of that technology. Forster's 'The Machine Stops' is the most famous of all the early engagements here with the technical world. In Forster's dystopia, the personal dwindles to the impersonal, as selves mediated through the machine become texts. Kipling's '"Wireless"' investigates the same territory. With its double-quote marks, the story's title already places the word as second-hand, a jargon coinage, merely what other people call such things. Here, the modern self exists caught up in the language of quotation, in a story that draws together trade names, advertising slogans, and the rich ore of poetry in Keats's verse. Kipling suggests that we are, in D. H. Lawrence's phrase, 'transmitters', and receivers too, repetitions of other selves. Like the machine itself, the person reproduces something, becomes themselves an expression of an age of mechanical reproduction. In his spiritual communication, Kipling's Shaynor becomes himself 'machine-like'; in a letter to H. Rider Haggard, Kipling declared, 'we are only telephone wires'.[23] A language of repetitions pervades the tale—'as it is written in the book—as it is written in the book'—even as one person's words echo, or falter in echoing, another's. Around the time of writing the story, Kipling's sister, Alice Kipling, was involved in experiments with automatic writing, under the scientific

[22] Diary, 27 January 1908, quoted in Oliver Stallybrass, 'Editor's Introduction', *Howard's End* (Harmondsworth: Penguin Books, 1973), p. 10.

[23] Quoted in M. Cohen (ed), *Rudyard Kipling to Rider Haggard: The Record of a Friendship* (London: Hutchinson, 1965), p. 100.

(or pseudo-scientific) aegis of F. W. H. Myers' 'Society for Psychical Research'. Yet the story describes an act of clairvoyance—or 'clairouïe' ('clear-hearing')—and not automatic writing. The story's apothecary poet is not even a poet, he's an instrument operating under the same conditions—imbued with Keats' specific training as an apothecary (and medical student), like Keats mortally ill, like Keats hopelessly in love. His poem is no 'vile chromo' of Keats' original, but the same poem traced back from the point of its own origin. Like causes lead to like effects, he tells us—as though the human being must work, like a machine, in predictable ways, a determined creature in a deterministic world, behaving and never acting of its own free will. The mystery of poetic imagination and creation metamorphoses into something predictable, experimental, a matter of cause and effect bound to laws as 'inevitable as induction'. Yet, as Kipling writes down the process of writing, still one person enters into the space of another. If W. H. Auden is right, and Kipling's theme is besiegement, then in '"Wireless"' the other is inside the gates, dwelling in a benign, though uneasy possession.

Anxiety about machines runs through these tales. In her essay, "Shadows of the Coming Race', George Eliot expresses her uneasy thought that machines might transcend and supersede us, as in time they 'evolve conditions of self-supply, self-repair, and reproduction'.[24] Samuel Butler's utopian fantasy, *Erewhon* plays with the same apprehensions, bringing Darwinian thought to the world of the mechanical, reducing consciousness to a very paltry thing (potatoes likely enjoy it too), and thereby simplifying human beings themselves to another kind of mere machine: 'Man's very soul is due to the machines; it is a machine-made thing: he thinks as he thinks, and feels as he feels, through the work that machines have wrought upon him, and their existence is quite as much a *sine quâ non* for his, as his for theirs.'[25]

These proto-science fiction stories offered New Worlds, it was true, located in a far elsewhere. However, their strongest intuition was that the quotidian modern nineteenth-century world was itself being rendered strange by urbanisation, industrialisation, technology. The

[24] George Eliot, *Impressions of Theophrastus Such* (Edinburgh and London: William Blackwood and Sons, 1879), p. 302.
[25] Samuel Butler, *Erewhon or Over the Range* (London: Trübner & Co., 1872), p. 200.

world was becoming new, and identity was changing in relation to it. Kipling's fantasies of the 1900s—'They', 'Mrs Bathurst', '"Wireless"'—place the insubstantial human being against or within the machine, ghosts come upon on a car-ride, a fleeting image on a cinema screen, a voice. These fragile traces of the self stand beleaguered in the material world. The strange tales presented in this volume were likewise markers of this newness, of this modernity. Butler's living machines, his mechanical people, can be read as sardonic versions of doubts and anxieties about the effects of industrialisation, the dread that human life was becoming automatic, unfree. The critic, Darko Suvin has controversially suggested that science fiction re-emerged in the 1870s, due to a sense of social values being in flux, brought on by the turmoil of the Franco-Prussian War and the commune, an upswell of political radicalism and collective uncertainty.[26] While it is indeed hard to quantify such uncertainties, or to unravel how and why they might lead to treatment in this particular form of the fantastic, it is, of course, the case that social anxieties find their expression in these early science-fiction tales. One of the clearest ways in which this manifests itself is through how such stories handle the relations between men and women, and, often in strongly connected terms, in the imagining of another ordering of society altogether, that utopian impulse so central to the literature of the period.

'This Beautiful Being Was Forever Imprisoned':
Relations of the Future

In so far as romance and the fiction of adventure proliferated in the emerging forms of fantasy, so too did a concept of masculinity. These forms were synonymous with dramas of maleness, where notions of being a 'man' predominate. It is a curious feature of the tales collected in this book that all of them, including those written by women, have male narrators, and all, bar Barrows Bennett's 'Friend Island', feature male protagonists too. It is significant that Bennett's story is the outlier here, offering a rather different Pacific world than that sold us by Jack London's 'The Red One'. Bennett names her male sailor, Nelson, and then sweetly 'feminises' that name as 'Nelly'. Nelson, of course, stands

---

[26] Darko Suvin, *Victorian Science Fiction in the UK: The Discourses of Knowledge and Power* (Boston: G. K. Hall, 1983), pp. 14, 315–25.

in for the archetypal heroic male sailor, a type no longer required here. More customarily, male knowledge and masculine heroism (and anti-heroism) can be seen to form the actual subject of these stories. Stockton's 'The Water Devil' is in part a story about what women can know or not know, that is still told primarily with a silent female audience in mind. In 'The Mortal Immortal', Mary Shelley, the ageing widow to a husband who had died in youth, projects herself into her husband's position, irritated and saddened by the woman who drags upon him. In Eliot's 'The Lifted Veil', opposing ways of being masculine are offered to us, the sporty or the sensitive, the scientific or the poetic. All filters through the perceptions of its narrator, Latimer, and the reader, like him, becomes a mirror, seeing scenes that Latimer sees, entering a man's mind, predicting a future that can be corroborated by flicking onward through the pages of book.

That chilly gaze with which Wells' invading Martians regard us proves to be only one of the possibilities raised in the stories in this book when it comes to that first encounter with an other form of life. Women are apt to be looked over in these tales. In 'The Diamond Lens', when Linley regards Animula through the microscope's lens, he falls into an unrequitable desire. The stories play out such notions of longing, such ways of framing and forging the object of yearning. Hawthorne's poisoned, and poisonous Beatrice is a young woman without a mother, fathered only she is 'the offspring of his science', the creation of an experiment.

Above all, the relations between men and women form a key element in how Victorian and Edwardian writers imagined alternative societies, their wished-for, improbable utopias. In utopian fictions such as W. H. Hudson's *The Crystal Age* (1887), Lytton's *The Coming Race* and even William Morris' *News From Nowhere* (1890), desire between men and women is disruptive, a poisoned draught that spoils the social equilibrium. In the beehive world of the future, unsexed and therefore free of conflict, the sexual selection described by Darwin becomes the source of the conflict that provokes development, but also that brings suffering and strife. Behind Barrows Bennett's female-led future were single-sex utopias, such as Mary E. Bradley Lane's *Mizora: A Prophecy* (1881) or Charlotte Perkins Gilman's *Herland* (1915). Such texts were applying the insights of political science, as well as a desire to re-set social forms and bonds. Often, these utopian narratives are closer to fictionalised tracts and manifestoes than they are to the conventions of the nineteenth-century novel. In a period so dominated by the novel, it was inevitable perhaps that writers should turn to this loose form for their speculations. However, in the main these are fictions written by those without much taste, or talent, for fiction. Works like *Looking Backwards* or *Erewhon* or *Herland* push at the limits of the novel form. In Lytton, in Butler and in Hudson, the interest soon shifts from the narrative of discovery to the invention of a society, a dull parlour game descending from Gonzalo's fantasised commonwealth in Shakespeare's *The Tempest*. To this reader, at least, the static serenity of these dream worlds proves weirdly threatening, and the supposed claustrophobia of suburban bourgeois life can barely match the suffocation of such realised wisdom.

For some, then, there's an upswell of panic in considering those shiny schemes of utopian improvement. More consciously, it is striking how often, as the twentieth century begins, the warning voice is the tone struck in these tales. Do not live like this, do not let the world become this, they tell us with their prophetic strain. Visions of apocalypse and of social disintegration abound. In the early nineteenth century, dreams of the end of things began to proliferate, in Jean-Baptiste Cousin de Grainville's *Le Dernier homme* (1805), Byron's 'Darkness' (1816), and various attempts to trace the fate of the 'last man' by Thomas Campbell, Thomas Hood, and Mary Shelley. Later in our period, toxic purple clouds descend on the earth or poison belts thicken. With a naturalist's accuracy, Richard Jefferies' *After London* (1885) dreams of the modern urbanised world being swept aside by a return of a copious wilderness; the population dwindles, and England returns to a disorderly medievalised realm of robber barons. W. H. Hudson's *A Crystal Age* similarly envisions the far-future as pastoral utopia, agrarian, rustic, and green. For Jefferies, certainly, the future here lies in the past, just as a cyclical notion of history was becoming central, in particular, with regard to a sense of the brittleness of modern civilisation: 'Cities and Thrones and Powers Stand in Time's eye Almost as long as flowers, Which daily die . . .', Kipling gently, threateningly, informed his readers. The world was deemed apt to end with the coming of a comet, or the extinguishing of the sun, or the devastation of a plague. These would be 'natural' events, determined by the implacability of a natural world otherwise beguilingly open to exploitation in an age of industrialism and deforestation. For all the talk of progress, death, or simply the natural cycle of things, could not be evaded.

A taste for destruction breeds such longings. Lingering over scenes of violence had its instructively gruesome appeal, as in Théodore Géricault's *Le Radeau de la Méduse* ('The Raft of the Medusa') (1818–19). The social compact was perplexingly flimsy, and was exposed as such both in the Gothic fictions of the period and in these formative works of scientific fantasy. These were the disreputable siblings of the nineteenth-century novel, with its courting couples, its orphans and foundlings, its adulterers and adventurers, all threaded together in the social weave. The rise of the invasion novel, beginning with George Tomkyns Chesney's *The Battle of Dorking* (1871), also painted exposures of societal precariousness. A later invasion fantasy, Wells' *The War of the Worlds* turns the English crowd into a character, a maddened, desperate one. The masses are the subject of this novel of interplanetary invasion, and Wells clearly enjoys giving that fat, complacent entity a stiff whack.

Otherwise, the decay that came would be social in origin, a canker of the political body, and the dark counterpart to all those speculative dreams of progress. Jack London's *The Iron Heel*, R. H. Benson's *Lord of the World* and E. M. Forster's *The Machine Stops* all appeared in 1907–08, each imagining in its own way a dismal prospect for the future of mankind. As it turned out, we all now see how right each of these authors were to express unease; within thirty-five years of their writing, social experiments of an unprecedently cruel kind were to be brutally enacted across the breadth of Europe. These writers might be thought to be transmitters too, and in this sense the questioning of myths of progress intrinsic to so much of the best early science fiction (and later science fiction too) proves one of the great merits of the kind. This literature apparently so preoccupied by the future was precisely where questionings of the direction of society could most clearly come into focus.

The concept of progress naturally entailed a linked concept of the future, the domain to which we were supposedly progressing. Down the approaching avenue of years could be viewed the more rational, more compassionate, more perfect society that would follow ours. In W. H. Freeman and T. Jones's song, 'Three Hundred Years to Come' (1835), those in the future will look down on our inefficiency and inconsistency, and 'The World will be turned Topsy Turvey!' Development was the key nineteenth-century mode of thought; the reverse side of the historical imagination being conjecture about what we might develop into. This putative human of the future might yet be quite alien to ourselves. Wells lived out a complex relation to notions of progress, both adhering to them, and seeking to destroy them, in his scientific romances undermining, as he does, complacency and optimism. Wells' 'The Man of the Year Million' imagines a distant descendant of ourselves parallel to the repellent alien Martians pictured in *The War of the Worlds*.[27] *The Time Machine* too cooks up two future versions of the human being, both of which are remote enough from us, and yet also disturbingly akin. Just as curiously, in Grant Allen's 'Pausodyne', the future in which the protagonist is lost coincides with the reader's now, that distant year we were now living in of 1881.

Inextricably entwined in the model of progress, the future lives as the place of fulfilment, the insufficient moving towards the better. In some cases, as in Lytton's *The Coming Race* (1871), the rough beast that approaches is a model of a superman, the next evolutionary step pending. Out there, ahead of us (or in Lytton's case beneath us) broods a new kind of human being. These were reveries of racial purity, with the anxiety or the yearning expressed that humanity itself was something intended to be surpassed. Theories of the colonial encounter are in such notions, as Henry Rowe Schoolcraft theorised with the relation between the colonising European settlers and the native Americans, 'superior' races (or more advanced technologies) inevitably displace more primitive ones.[28] As Lytton put it:

The only important point is to keep in view the Darwinian proposition that a coming race is destined to supplant our races, that such a race would be very gradually formed, and be indeed a new species developing itself out of our old one, that this process would be invisible to our eyes, and therefore in some region unknown to us. And that in the course of this development, the coming race will have acquired some peculiarities so distinct from our

---

[27] First published in *Pall Mall Gazette* (9 November 1893), and quickly parodied in *Punch* (25 November 1893).

[28] As in, for instance, Henry Rowe Schoolcraft, *Oneota, or the Red Race of America* (New York: Burgess, Stringer & Co., 1844).

ways, that it could not be fused with us, and certain destructive powers which our science could not enable us to attain to, or cope with.[29]

Those supermen tend to resemble the strong heroes and implacable leaders so dear to the proto-fascist elements of the nineteenth- and early twentieth-century imagination.

It is an open question if these god-like denizens of the future will have much in common with fallible us. One only gets to the future by changing, by becoming different from the present. Therefore the question at stake in considering the future (outside utopian or dystopian political concerns) is one of identity: how do we know that the person of the future will be one like us, one with whom we can sympathize, when the very idea of the future depends upon on the sense that it will be changed, different, that it will be fractured from us. (This difference becomes really a concern particularly for those living in an industrial society; before then it was safely assumed that the future would pretty much repeat the past.)

And yet that different, unpicturable future, can only be fashioned from the viewpoint of the present. Considering the milky utopian novel he had published almost twenty years before, in September 1906, W. H. Hudson wrote of the 'perennial if mild interest' of 'romances of the future', born of 'a sense of dissatisfaction with the existing order of things, combined with a vague faith in or hope of a better one to come'. But the problem is, he immediately concedes, that in writing of the future we are in fact hemmed in by the mentality possible in the present: 'Our mental atmosphere surrounds and shuts us in like our own skins; no one can boast that he has broken out of that prison'.[30] So it was that his own book was coloured by 'the little cults and crazes, and modes of thought of the eighties of the last century'.[31] Fictions of the future, like historical fictions, most truly express and expose the faultlines and preoccupations of the present in which they are written.

---

[29] In a letter from Edward Bulwer Lytton to John Forster, March 15 1870, in Victor Alexander George Robert Bulwer-Lytton, *Life of Edward Bulwer, First Lord Lytton* (London: Macmillan and Co., 1913), Vol. II, p. 465.

[30] W. H. Hudson, 'Introduction', *A Crystal Age* (London: T. Fisher Unwin, 1906), p. v.

[31] Ibid., vii.

'*With Power in his Eyes and Ghostly Scepters Hovering
to his Grasp*': *The Sublime and the Global*

Like Gothic, science fiction finds its roots as an artform in the sublime, from Poe's cosmic vistas all the way to the cinematic spectacle of
Stanley Kubrick's *2001, A Space Odyssey*. The concern with the
future, the sense of evolutionary aeons, like the growing fascination
with distances, either microscopic or cosmic, all bring to the different
tales in this book, a boundlessness, a dizzying freedom from the
human condition. That freedom can seem to some writers to be
accursed, 'abnormal'; as such, it returns the human subject to little-
ness and fragility, though in any case the experience of such insignifi-
cance lies at the heart of the sublime.

The sublime shifted the human scale to the immeasurable. Above all,
in these collected tales, as in other of the new scientific romances that
appeared in those years, a new way of understanding a human life
comes into view, moving from the parochial to the global. Formerly the
sense of 'the world' a vast, single domain was largely religious, much as
apocalyptic fears were similarly understood in Biblical terms. The creation, Adam and Eve's fall, the flood, Christ's birth, and his second
coming were the only planetary events. Consequently, early utopias
were local, a far place you might visit—hidden in 'subterranean fields,
Or some secreted island'—only later, as the undiscovered areas of the
globe shrank, do they become global.[32] With its proud American hero,
Lytton's *The Coming Race* is a transitional text here, beginning locally,
but shifting to the titanic, the discovery of another inner Earth. Schemes
were become earthly, supranational. At the end of the nineteenth century, the tycoon and science-fiction author, King C. Gillette dreamt of
a World Corporation. The title of Wells' *The War of the Worlds* signals
the planetary scope of his tale, for all its dealings with Leatherhead and
Chobham. Indeed, in this text Wells coins 'interplanetary' to mean
communication between planets, as opposed to applying to the space
that lies between them. *The First Men in the Moon* conceives of a world
government, a science-fiction concept that ties into Wells' own belief in
the efficacies of a 'world state' (itself another idea that had passed from
Christian thinking to secular fancies).

[32] William Wordsworth, *The Prelude* (1850), XI, 140–1.

There had naturally enough always been a sense of the earthly mundane (from 'Aristotle's' *De Mundo* (350–200BC) to the first terrestrial globes, such as the one constructed in 1492, by Martin Behaim—the *Erdapfel*). Nonetheless, one may suggest that with a new intensification the eighteenth and nineteenth centuries witnessed the concoction of 'the world' as a self-contained entity that could be envisioned as a whole. The word 'global' itself only came to mean that which pertains to the whole world in the 1830s; from the 1850s on, one might think 'globally'; in 1831, the word 'planetary' was first applied to our planet; in 1836, 'world-wide' mutated into an adverb. This discovery could be linked to the consequence of Imperialism and the expansion of global trade and travel (in 1839, Charles Darwin was remarking that a well-stocked yacht could now circumnavigate the earth). Geological science likewise helped to foster the sense of the planet as an immense interconnected system, as did study of ocean currents (including the work done by Benjamin Franklin in the 1760s), and of George Hadley's model of the global circulation of the trade winds in the 1730s. In the 1820s, 'world-historical' entered English, via German; in the 1850s, the concept of a 'world language' (English, naturally) entered discourse; in the 1830s, Thomas Carlyle expressed his hopes for a 'world literature'. Just in the moment where we ceased to feel at home here, the world became an object that might be traversed, measured, a little round paced out from end to end. In 1873, the word 'globetrotter' is coined (in his book, *Heretics* (1905), G. K. Chesterton would condemn Kipling as one); in the late nineteenth century one might become a 'world-wanderer' or a 'world-traveller', and from the 1880s, 'world-cruises' were on offer. As markets expanded, the world grew smaller, and could become the field of narrative. From Mary Shelley's *The Last Man* to Du Bois' 'The Comet', the world itself (forming around Manhattan in the latter) makes the context of the tale.

Around the World in Eighty Days is perhaps Jules Verne's best science-fiction book, and science-fictional precisely in setting out the circling of the globe. In Stockton's 'The Water Devil', where the real wonders are facts, they face in the end not an autochthonous monster, but an international network, the confined story held between lines of communication, moving from the still point to the vast prospects of oceans. This might stand as a paradigm for the drift of the tales in this book as such. Over and over, the normalised world encounters the strange. In this confrontation, these tales again resemble Gothic. And yet Gothic is confined, personal, whereas, step by step, these early science fiction stories reach to the comprehensive and impersonal. They do not so much favour haunting (which is of the person) but global changes and invasion (which threaten all of us)—though it's the absence of human solidarity that the dystopian form and the apocalyptic mode exposes.

'And Where Was This Other World?': Connecting Spaces

Such tales as 'The Conversation of Eiros and Charmion', 'The Crystal Egg', 'The Hall Bedroom', or 'The Comet' all glance from the near at hand to the immense. In this way, separate spheres reveal themselves to be in communication, as in 'The Crystal Egg', Mars establishes an exchange with Covent Garden. Often, these are stories that play with the location of the story, disrupting the 'playing space' of narrative. In 'The Hall Bedroom', Freeman's treatment of respectability involves the dislocation of a failing woman, shifting from married respectability and village life to a boarding house existence in an urban centre, adjoined to the dissociation and alienation of her lodger. For her as for him, space exists within our space. We may live in two worlds at once, and those worlds belong *en rapport*, in association with each other. Concepts of *'rapport'* play on the equally porous relation between spiritualism and science in the period. Like 'science fiction' itself, 'science' may be thought as an entity with an ambiguous boundary.

This pattern of a permeable boundary, a rapport established, between the self and others, between one context and another, between science and the fantastic, repeats itself through many of the stories collected in this volume. The self stands vulnerable, penetrable, before the alien, the machine. For these are fantasies that are rooted in real property relations and economic conditions, that reimagine the social real through the distorting lens of the hypothesis. Sometimes our protagonists look on and observe from here the otherness elsewhere. For instance, O'Brien's 'The Diamond Lens' is a tale of failed communication and foiled intercourse with others, whether they be the spirits of the dead, a Jew, or microscopic creatures too distant really to meet. Like 'The Crystal Egg' or 'Rappaccini's Daughter', the tale can be read as a parable of voyeurism (even in the case of the Wells as a fable of cinema). These are stories of unrequitedness and of disconnection. O'Brien's microscopist hates to get close to another, hence the murder he commits, hence his revulsion for an actual woman, hence his longing for someone where immeasurable distance protects him from contact. Indeed it's a tale of two murders, as he goes on to kill Animula, with strange inadvertence, the experiment he has set up providing the context for her demise. O'Brien's narrator links himself to Hermaphroditus and Adonis, two men who say no to women. In each half of O'Brien's story, an isolated man comes close to another, and ends the connection by causing the death of that other. The narrator rejects actual human contact in favour of the fantastic, the dream of femininity, that which must be unattainable.

Often the stories are told (as in 'The Lifted Veil' or 'Pausodyne', or 'The Water-Devil' or 'The Terror of Blue John Gap') by and of someone who attempts to win our sympathy, to gain our credence. The other person is beyond us, living in another unreachable space. In 'The Lifted Veil', body and soul entwine and correlate, distinct and joined. The narrator's friend, Meunier, is curious about the 'psychological relations of diseases' and the physiological transfusion of blood, much as the story scrutinises that which passes from within one body to another, breaking the 'privacy of another soul'. Meanwhile, Eliot withholds information from the reader—playing with our distance, our curiosity, our need for suspense. Boundaries of the self blur even in the act of reading, as we absorb the language, the constructed identity, of another. Disrupted messages reach us, in communications akin to those in Kipling's ' "Wireless" '. Again, Wells' 'unsympathetic' aliens come to mind. In the 1890s, the English scientist, Sir Francis Galton considered the difficulties that might be involved in communicating with aliens, even more insurmountable, he deemed, than communicating with 'deaf mutes' or 'savages', as he wondered about the possibility of creating signals that could be intrinsically intelligible.[33] Again, one repeating motif in these tales becomes the problem of 'other minds'—and indeed at times the problem of understanding our own minds, porous and desperate and self-destructive as they might be. In 'The Terror of Blue John Gap', Conan Doyle's hero returns to 'the old primeval hunting-spirit', a good atavism in him set against the bad atavism of the creature itself.

[33] Sir Francis Galton, 'Intelligible Signals Between Neighbouring Stars', *Fortnightly Review* (November 1896) 60/359, pp. 657–64.

His regression is not 'degenerate' but regenerating, marking him out as an Erskine Childers-style hero saved (for a while) from ennui and illness by action and adventure—by being a man. Falling back into the condition of an ancient, this modern man finds the possibility of a makeshift renewal.

'The Poet's Sensibility Without His Voice': The Fausts of the Future

In our tales gathered here, in these once scattered origins of science fiction, we discern a disorientated and anguished subject, a wounded protagonist, adrift, plagued. The individual stands trapped between the finite little and the equally finite great, unable to believe in an infinite beyond, confined to the material realm.

Yet it is curious how often these stories evoke the possibility of comedy. In *Erewhon*, in *The Fixed Period*, in Wells' scientific romances too, the tone can shift unstably towards farce or irony. In 'Pausodyne' or 'Rappaccini's Daughter', the situations could be humorous, dwelling as the latter does on a confidence trick. However, the grotesque and fanciful instead draws upon the horrifying, as in both cases unreal situations threaten the reality of a life—and expose life's reality as provisional and tainted. In 'The Facts in the Case of M. Valdemar', Poe starts off by making sardonic jokes, about what is 'matter for wonder', what might 'have been a miracle' but was instead prosaically, scientifically appalling.

In one sense, our tales celebrate the figure of the scientist, that solitary hero, that intrepid adventurer into the unknown. Occult knowledge can be hard to tell apart from the discoveries of natural philosophy. Cornelius Agrippa, Valdemar's scientific friends, Dr. Rappaccini, all present an image of curious heartlessness. The patient—whether Valdemar or Beatrice—becomes a subject for experimentation, and not a 'person'. These stories resonate with moves in the period towards an understanding of the other in medicalised situations as mere materiality—an organic, material body, not as a person with a history. 'The Facts in the Case of M. Valdmar' describes an insult against the dignity of death; that is the horror of it—that death narrows to an opportunity for experimentation.

In 'The Lifted Veil' too, through a reimagining of the techniques of transfusions, we find the possibility of medically defeating death—proffering a materialist version of resurrection. As it blurs the boundary between death and life, the engagement with science becomes uncanny and terrifying. Death is the great subject here—an area of life coming under the purview of science, even as that science can only tell you about the dead, the inert, the material, that which can be dissected.

What scientific practices may appear to do, and what these proto-science-fiction stories certainly describe them as doing is to deny the other. Both O'Brien's and Jack London's stories touch on the erasure of personhood manifest in slavery, and there, as in Poe's or Hawthorne's stories, the person turns into money, or the possibility of acquired knowledge. Personhood degrades, and others become a means to an end, potential subjects, as in 'The Country of the Blind', or demands upon us that our desire for ease would repulse, as in 'The Machine Stops'. One irony of London's 'The Red One' is that 'civilization' entails slavery. A scepticism about civilization as such is in there, and in Forster too, where our end is brought about by our becoming over-civilized.

A questioning of the operations of power in civilised society tests these tales. The social situation that is the scientific experiment is merely an intense example of this. In both 'The Water Devil' and 'The Comet', danger shelves the conventional social pressures and distinctions, permitting romance. The emergency situation puts social separation in abeyance, for as long as the emergency lasts, and no longer. Adventures suspend social divisions (the stuff of realist fictions). Du Bois' tale long defers the use of names, and only at the end suddenly the woman becomes Julia ('a rose by any other name') and the man becomes Jim Davis, before being put down to the level of the racist slur that would, in social terms, erase his personhood. *Les préférences* reassert themselves, and the story ends.

The scientist as cultural figure seems to belong to the world of power and possibility, to all that human beings might achieve, all that they might come to know. Instead, the stories return their Faustian protagonists to their limitations. 'The Country of the Blind', for instance, moves from being a fantasy of power to a narrative about human isolation and fallibility.

As we have seen in 'The Lifted Veil', Eliot contrasts the poet and the philosopher—one concerned with wonder, the other with facts—one inventing, the other penetrating—one imaginative, the other ratiocinative. When Rappaccini is said to take a 'scientific interest in thee', the sinister implications of this interest are clear, and we know that this attention he pays you will be coldly curious, and not humane. The desire to know is the great sin here, where knowledge exceeds all other concerns. The notion arises that the scientist, the discoverer, is above morals, their crimes absolved by 'benefit of clergy'. Jack London's protagonist is also 'a scientist first, a humanist afterward'. His disgust at the people there on the Pacific island is distressingly tangible, though not necessarily intended to be endorsed by us. It's how that character sees things, caught up as he is in scientific curiosity, inhuman colonialism, and fastidious misogyny—an interconnected bundle of responses. He lives as a perfectly insidious melange of every racist and sexist, scientifically-backed, cliché of the period.

The heart stands against the intellect; that's London's protagonist's own distinction. The 'heart', that mysterious little organ, is something not much engaged in these stories. Love comes to life here in imagination and with 'no depth of root into the heart'. Here, our storytellers describe those who probe mysteries, turning the ineffable into a 'problem' to be solved. The observer, the experimenter, the reader, imagines themselves as placed in a realm where all that matters is the gaze that yearns for knowledge. The rights, the duties, imposed on us by that which we observe escapes their attention, until too late. Their gaze informs them that it has no limits. There is nothing that may not be found out.

They are wrong. Our authors know that the ultimate subject of these speculations is death, and that death is the terminus of such gazing. That includes the death of the world, a sublime version of our mortality (though mortality is already sublime). It is intriguing and puzzling how often a desire to go beyond the limits of death expresses itself in our stories here. There's an interesting literary aspiration evidenced in 'The Conversation of Eiros and Charmion' and 'The Lifted Veil', and otherwhere in Victorian fiction, to write in the first person of the experience of death. Hence Dickens' tale of the hanged man in *The Lazy Tour of Two Idle Apprentices*; hence those voices from 'beyond the veil' at those spiritualist séances; hence Valdemar's impossibly oxymoronic statement, 'I am dead', those words that cannot be spoken, for the 'I' is precisely what death ends. To write of death from within is to confront the problem of first-person narration (where is it told?) and a problem of consciousness, that all we can know of death is what we can become conscious of, and death circumscribes consciousness.[34] The great anxiety and the great hope in these stories is the survival of the human spirit (and equally often the actual survival of a particular human in danger). Faced with that which would destroy the human—whether a human enemy, a machine, a society, an alien—still something lingers. The man vanishes into the picture in the hall bedroom; the survivors of an apocalypse meet and converse; Keats' voice merges with another's; the free stargazing rebel goes to the forbidden outside—and yet they all leave traces of themselves, a remnant of a human voice, a word, a tale.

You can tell that science fiction is unfixed and elusive as a 'genre' because it has no defined way to end. The courtship novel ends in marriage, the foundling novel in the discovery of kin, a tragedy in death, and detective fiction in a solution. How does a science fiction story end? The palpable absence of a telos show us that we are dealing with a literary form that is infinitely adaptable, an evolving, unstable mode. These stories signpost various paths that writers after them might tread, setting out tropes and patterns, motifs and archetypes. They were discovering worlds, with visionary foresight mapping routes that other travellers would follow.

---

[34] I am indebted here to Daniel Heller-Roazen's discussion of Poe's story in *Echolalias: On the Forgetting of Language* (New York: Zone Books, 2005: 154–161.

NOTES ON THE TEXTS

As far as possible, I have elected to base each copy-text in this edition on the stories' first appearance in volume form. However, in some cases, it has been better to make use of the initial periodical publication as the basis for the text in this volume. A full description of each copy-text appears in the explanatory notes. On some occasions, where the first edition was impossible to locate or too frail to use, or where there are good editorial reasons for doing so, a later edition was taken as the basis for the text. In the majority of cases, I have compared the copy-text used with the text as it appeared in the periodical publication, and also with other competing versions of the text overseen by the authors.

Several guiding principles are behind the selection of stories for this anthology. First of all, and most subjectively, I have chosen those stories from the period 1830–1920 that I consider the most interesting and entertaining, the most illuminating and complex. Others will disagree with me, but I have found each of these stories to be one that repays close reading, and that after many re-readings remains fresh. I also selected stories on account of their representative nature, with the thought that they would provide the reader with a sense of the various kinds of fiction that fed into the formation of science fiction. It was a conscious decision therefore to include examples of the following types of tale: utopian and dystopian fictions; stories where Gothic touches on scientific speculation; tales of obsessive scientists and of haunted technologies; stories of encounter with aliens; time-travel narratives; scientific romances; tales where science fiction merges with fantasy; and apocalyptic accounts. Stories were similarly picked so that the most influential authors working in the field should be represented here, from Mary Shelley to Jack London. There are two stories each from Edgar Allan Poe and H. G. Wells. This reflects the fact that in my estimation (and that of many other critics) these authors are the most seminal in the development of SF. In the case of Poe, it was also because his range is so great that one tale alone can hardly do justice to the different approaches to the fantastic in his work.

I have not shied away from choosing stories that are likely to be already familiar to those engaged with the genre. There are few anthologies available of such stories, and those that do exist are sometimes hard to track down. For this reason, among others, I felt that a range of the best possible stories for reading and for study was a useful and not a superfluous task. On the other hand, some of the most interesting tales in the field have not been much anthologized, and I am happy in that regard to include here such stories as Frank R. Stockton's 'The Water-Devil', Mary E. Wilkins Freeman's 'The Hall Bedroom' and Gertrude Barrows Bennett's 'Friend Island'. Finally, I was particularly interested to break down the demarcation lines between the North American, Irish and British canons, and this book is a purposively trans-Atlantic volume. Poe influenced British (and French) writers as deeply as he did Americans, and Wells fostered imitators in the USA as much as he did at home. Fitz-James O'Brien is my great exemplar here, as an Irishman, who after a ruinous sojourn in London, established his career in New York City, before dying fighting in America's civil war. Likewise, Grant Allen has links to Canada, Ireland, Scotland, the USA and England, and Kipling was born in India, resided in Vermont, and wrote the story " 'Wireless' " in Sussex. These English-language authors transcend, pertinently enough, the narrow limits of a strictly national canon.

The only constraint on inclusion were length (though there are some longer stories here, such as Eliot's 'The Lifted Veil'). I would have loved to include longer tales by Barrows Bennett or Jack London; but limits of space meant that it was not possible to do so. This is also the reason why there is nothing here from Edgar Rice Burroughs, certainly one of the most vital writers in the development of SF, but someone whose best work tends to be in novel or novella form.

The only other constraint was the difficulty of reproducing all the original illustrations that accompanied these tales. I have, however, included instead an account of the accompanying illustrations in my individual notes on the text for each story.

As far as possible, the texts printed here reproduce their first appearance in book form. Definite errors in the original text have been silently corrected, and certain typographic conventions have been regularized to conform to modern practice: substituting single quotation marks for double ones, and placing punctuation marks outside rather than inside closing quotation marks with single words and short phrases. Otherwise the oddities of the originals are retained.

SELECT BIBLIOGRAPHY

Anthologies of Nineteenth and Early Twentieth Century Science Fiction

Ashley, Mike (ed.), *Menace of the Machine: The Rise of AI in Classic Science Fiction* (London: The British Library, 2019).

Ashely, Mike (ed.), *Moonrise: The Golden Age of Lunar Adventures* (London: The British Library, 2019).

Franklin, H. Bruce, *Future Perfect: American Science Fiction of the Nineteenth Century* (Revised Edition) (London, Oxford and New York: Oxford University Press, 1976).

Moorcock, Michael (ed.), *Before Armageddon: An Anthology of Victorian and Edwardian Imaginative Fiction Published Before 1914* (London: W. H. Allen, 1975).

Rabkin, Eric (ed.), *Science Fiction: A Historical Anthology* (New York: Oxford University Press, 1983).

Shippey, Tom (ed.), *The Oxford Book of Science Fiction Stories* (Oxford: Oxford University Press, 2006).

On the History of Science Fiction and on Science Fiction in General

Aldiss, Brian, *Billion Year Spree: The History of Science Fiction* (London: Weidenfeld & Nicholson, 1973).

Amis, Kingsley, *New Maps of Hell* (New York: Harcourt, Brace, 1960).

Armitt, Lucie (ed.), *Where No Man Has Gone Before: Women and Science Fiction* (London and New York: Routledge, 1991).

Barr, Marleen S., *Alien to Femininity: Speculative Fiction and Feminist Theory* (Westport, Connecticut: Greenwood Press, 1987).

Boskovich, Desirina, *Lost Transmissions: The Secret History of Science Fiction and Fantasy* (New York: Abrams Image, 2019).

Bould, Mark; Butler, Andrew M.; Roberts, Adam; and Vint, Sheryll (eds.), *The Routledge Companion to Science Fiction* (Oxford: Routledge, 2009).

Clute, John, and Nicholls, Peter (eds.), The *Encyclopedia of Science Fiction* (London: Orbit, 1993).

Donawerth, Jane, and Kolmerten, Carol A. (eds) *Utopian and Science Fiction by Women: Worlds of Difference* (Liverpool: Liverpool University Press, 1994).

Freedman, Carl, *Critical Theory and Science Fiction* (Middletown, Connecticut: Wesleyan University Press, 2000).

Hubble, Nick, and Mousoutzanis. Aris (eds.), *The Science Fiction Handbook* (London: Bloomsbury Academic, 2013).

James, Edward, and Mendlesohn, Farah (eds.), *The Cambridge Companion to Science Fiction* (Cambridge: Cambridge University Press, 2003).

Jameson, Frederic, *Archaeologies of the Future: The Desire Called Utopia and Other Science Fictions* (London and New York: Verso, 2005).

Latham, Rob (ed.), *The Oxford Companion of Science Fiction* (Oxford: Oxford University Press, 2014).

Latham, Rob (ed.), *Science Fiction Criticism: An Anthology of Essential Writings* (London: Bloomsbury, 2017).

Le Guin, Ursula, *The Language of the Night: Essays on Fantasy and Science Fiction* (London: Women's Press, 1989).

Lefanu, Sarah, *In the Chinks of the World Machine: Feminism and Science Fiction* (London: Women's Press, 1988).

Luckhurst, Roger, *Science Fiction* (Cambridge: Polity, 2005).

Luckhurst, Roger (ed.), *Science Fiction: A Literary History* (London: The British Library, 2017).

Manlove, Colin, *Science Fiction: Ten Explorations* (Kent, Ohio: Kent State University Press, 1986).

Merril, Judith, 'What Do You Mean: Science? Fiction?' [1966], *SF: The Other Side of Realism: Essays on Modern Science Fiction and Fantasy* (ed. Thomas D. Clareson) (Bowling Green, Ohio: Bowling Green University Press, 1971), 53–95.

Parrinder, Patrick, *Science Fiction: A Critical Guide* (London: Longman, 1979).

Roberts, Adam, *The History of Science Fiction* (London: Palgrave and Macmillan, 2006).

Roberts, Adam, *Science Fiction* (Second Edition) (London and New York: Routledge, 2006).

Seed, David, *Science Fiction: A Very Short Introduction* (Oxford: Oxford University Press, 2011).

Stableford, Brian, *The Plurality of Imaginary Worlds: The Evolution of French Roman Scientifique* (Encino, California: Black Coat Press, 2016).

Stockwell, Peter, *The Poetics of Science Fiction* (Harlow: Longman, 2000).

Suvin, Darko, *Metamorphoses of Science Fiction: On the Poetics and History of a Literary Genre* (New Haven, Connecticut: Yale University Press, 1979).

Westfahl, Gary, *The Mechanics of Wonder: The Creation of the Idea of Science Fiction* (Liverpool: Liverpool University Press, 1998).

On Periodical Culture, the Profession of Writing, and Early Science Fiction

Ashley, Mike, *The Age of the Storytellers: British Popular Fiction Magazines 1880–1950* (London: British Library and Oak Knoll Press, 2006).

Bleiler, Everett F., *Science-fiction, the Early Years: A Full Description of More Than 3,000 Science-fiction Stories from Earliest Times to the Appearance of the Genre Magazines in 1930: With Author, Title, and Motif Indexes* (Kent, Ohio: Kent State University Press, 1990).

Keating, Peter, *The Haunted Study: A Social History of the English Novel, 1875–1914* (1989) (London: Fontana Press, 1991).

Pound, Reginald, *The Strand Magazine, 1891–1950* (London: Heinemann, 1966).

Biographical Works

Ashton, Rosemary, *George Eliot: A Life* (London: Hamish Hamilton, 1996).

Carrington, Charles, *Rudyard Kipling: His Life and Work* (London: Macmillan, 1955).

Doyle, Arthur Conan, *Memories and Reflections* (London: Hodder & Stoughton, 1924).

Du Bois, W. E. B., *The Autobiography of W. E. B. Du Bois* (New York: International Publishers, 1968).

Furbank, P. N., *E. M. Forster: A Life – Vol. One: The Growth of the Novelist* (London: Martin Secker & Warburg, 1977).

Glasser, Leah Blatt, *In a Closet Hidden: The Life and Work of Mary E. Wilkins Freeman* (Amherst, MA: University of Massachusetts Press, 1996).

Griffin, Martin I. J., *Frank R. Stockton: A Critical Biography* (Philadelphia: University of Pennsylvania Press, 1939).

Haight, Gordon, *George Eliot: A Biography* (Oxford: The Clarendon Press, 1968).

Hoppenstand, Gary C., "The Woman Who Invented Dark Fantasy", in Francis Stevens, *The Nightmare and Other Tales of Dark Fantasy* (Lincoln, Nebraska and London: University of Nebraska Press, 2004), ix–xxv.

Kipling, Rudyard, *Something of Myself* (London: Macmillan, 1937).

Labor, Earle, *Jack London: An American Life* (New York: Farrar, Straus and Giroux, 2013).

Lewis, David Levering, *W. E. B. Du Bois: A Biography 1868–1963* (New York: Henry Holt and Co;, 2009).

Lycett, Andrew, *Conan Doyle: The Man Who Created Sherlock Holmes* (London: Weidenfeld & Nicholson, 2007).

Mackenzie, Norman and Jeanne Mackenzie, *The Time Traveller: The Life of H. G.Wells* (2nd Edn.) (London: The Hogarth Press, 1987).

Miller, Edwin Holland, *Salem Is My Dwelling Place: A Life of Nathaniel Hawthorne* (Iowa City: University of Iowa Press, 1991).

Moffat, Wendy, *E. M. Forster: A New Life* (London: Bloomsbury, 2011).

Quinn, Arthur Hobson, *Edgar Allan Poe: A Critical Biography* (New York and London: D. Appleton Century Company, 1941).

Sampson, Fiona, *In Search of Mary Shelley: The Girl Who Wrote Frankenstein* (London: Profile, 2018).

Seymour, Miranda, *Mary Shelley* (London: Simon & Schuster, 2018).

Sherborne, Michael, *H. G. Wells: Another Kind of Life* (London: Michael Owen, 2010).

Sinclair, Andrew, *Jack: A Biography of Jack London* (New York: Harper, 1977).

Wells, H. G., *Experiment in Autobiography* (2 vols.) (London: Gollancz and Cresset Press, 1934).

Woole, Francis, *Fitz-James O'Brien: A Literary Bohemian of the Eighteen-Fifties* (Boulder, Colorado: University of Colorado Press, 1944).

Background Works on Nineteenth-Century Science

Beer, Gillian, *Darwin's Plots: Evolutionary Narrative in Darwin, George Eliot, and Nineteenth-Century Fiction* (London: Routledge and Kegan Paul, 1983).

Beer, Gillian, *Open Fields: Science in Cultural Encounter* (New York: Oxford University Press, 1996).

Christie, John, and Shuttleworth, Sally (eds.), *Nature Transfigured: Science and Literature, 1700–1900* (New York: St. Martin's, 1989).

Coslett, Tess, *The 'Scientific Movement' and Victorian Literature* (Brighton: Harvester; New York: St. Martin's, 1982).

Ellenberger, Henri F., *The Discovery of the Unconscious: The History and Evolution of Dynamic Psychiatry* (New York: Basic Books, 1970).

Haynes, Roslynn D., *From Faust to Strangelove: Representations of the Scientist in Western Literature* (Baltimore: John Hopkins University Press, 1994).

Holmes, Richard, *The Age of Wonder: How the Romantic Generation Discovered the Beauty and Terror of Science* (London: HarperPress, 2008).

Levine, George, *Darwin and the Novelists: Patterns of Science in Victorian Fiction* (Chicago: University of Chicago Press, 1988).

Lightman, Bernard (ed.), *Victorian Science in Context* (Chicago: University of Chicago Press, 1997).

Marvin, Carolyn, *When Old Technologies Were New: Thinking about Electric Communication in the Late Nineteenth Century* (New York: Oxford University Press, 1988).

Otis, Laura, *Membranes: Metaphors of Invasion in Nineteenth-Century Literature, Science, and Politics* (Baltimore: John Hopkins University Press, 1999).

Pick, Daniel, *Faces of Degeneration: A European Disorder, c. 1848–1918* (Cambridge: Cambridge University Press, 1989).

Robinson, Michael F., *The Coldest Crucible: Arctic Exploration and American Culture* (Chicago: University of Chicago Press, 2006).

Shuttleworth, Sally, *George Eliot and Nineteenth-Century Science: The Make-Believe of a Beginning* (Cambridge: Cambridge University Press, 1984).

Winter, Alison, *Mesmerized: Powers of Mind in Victorian Britain* (Chicago: University of Chicago Press, 1998).

Critical Monographs and Essays on Nineteenth and Early Twentieth Century Science Fiction

Alkon, Paul K., *Origins of Futuristic Fiction* (Athens, Georgia: University of Georgia Press, 1987).

Alkon, Paul K., *Science Fiction Before 1900: Imagination Discovers Technology* (London: Routledge, 1994).

Angenot, Marc, 'Science Fiction Before Verne', *Science Fiction Studies*, 5/1 (1978), 58–66.

Bailey, J. O., *Pilgrims through Space and Time: Trends and Patterns in Scientific and Utopian Fiction* (New York: Argus Books, 1947).

Beaumont, Matthew, *Utopia Ltd.: Ideologies for Social Dreaming in England, 1870–1900* (London: Haymarket, 2009).

Beaumont, Matthew, *The Spectre of Utopia: Utopian and Science Fictions at the Fin de Siècle* (Oxford: Peter Lang, 2012).

Clarke, I. F., *Voices Prophesying War: Future Wars, 1763–1984* (2nd edn.) (Oxford: Oxford University Press, 1992).

Clarke, I. F. (ed.), *British Future Fiction* (London: Pickering and Chatto, 2001).

Disch, Thomas M., *The Dreams Our Stuff Is Made Of: How Science Fiction Conquered the World* (New York: Simon & Schuster, 1998).

Evans, Arthur B., 'Nineteenth-century SF', *The Routledge Companion to Science Fiction* (eds. Bould, Mark; Butler, Andrew M,; Roberts, Adam; and Vint, Sheryll), (Oxford: Routledge, 2009), 13–22.

Evans, Arthur B, 'The Beginnings: Early Forms of Science Fiction', *Science Fiction: A Literary History* (ed. Roger Luckhurst) (London: The British Library, 2017), 11–43.

Gove, Philip Babcock, *The Imaginary Voyage in Prose Fiction* (New York: Columbia University Press, 1941).

Luckhurst, Roger, 'From Scientific Romance to Science Fiction: 1870–1914', *Science Fiction: A Literary History* (ed. Roger Luckhurst) (London: The British Library, 2017), 44–71.

Mazzeno, Laurence W. and Ronald D. Morrison (eds.), *Victorian Environmental Nightmares* (Cham, Switzerland: Palgrave Macmillan, 2019).

Moskowitz, Sam, *Explorers of the Infinite: Shapers of Science Fiction* (Cleveland: World Publishing Co., 1963).

Mousoutzanis, Aris, *Fin-de-Siècle Fictions, 1890s/1990s: Apocalypse, Technoscience, Empire* (New York: Palgrave Macmillan, 2014).

Page, Michael R., *The Literary Imagination from Erasmus Darwin to H. G. Wells: Science, Evolution and Ecology* (London and New York: Routledge, 2012).

Parrett, Aaron, 'Alternative Worlds of the Nineteenth Century', *Science Fiction Studies*, 30/3 (Greencastle, Indiana: 2003), 500–503.

Parrington, Vernon Louis, *American Dreams: A Study of American Utopias* (Providence: Brown University Press, 1947).

Rabkin, Eric, Greenberg, Martin H., and Olander (eds.), *No Place Else: Explorations in Utopian and Dystopian Fiction* (Carbondale: Southern Illinois University Press, 1983).

Rieder, John, *Colonialism and the Emergence of Science Fiction* (Middletown, Connecticut: Wesleyan University Press, 2009).

Seed, David, 'Introduction' to Edward Bulwer-Lytton, *The Coming Race* (1871) (Middletown, Connecticut: Wesleyan University Press, 2005), xiii–liii.

Stableford, Brian, 'Marriage of Science and Fiction: The Emergence of a New Fiction', *Encyclopedia of Science Fiction* (ed. Robert Holdstock) (London: Octopus Books, 1978), 18–27.

Stableford, Brian, *Scientific Romance in Britain, 1890–1950* (New York: St. Martin's Press, 1985).

Stableford, Brian, 'Science Fiction Before the Genre', *Cambridge Companion to Science Fiction* (eds. Edward James and Farah Mendlesohn) (Cambridge: Cambridge University Press, 2003), 15–31.

Stafford, Fiona J., *The Last of the Race: The Growth of a Myth from Milton to Darwin* (Oxford: Clarendon Press, 1994).

Suvin, Darko, *Victorian Science Fiction in the UK: The Discourses of Knowledge and Power* (Boston: G. K. Hall, 1983).

Wagar, Warren W., *Terminal Visions: The Literature of Last Things* (Bloomington, Indiana: Indiana University Press, 1982).

Williams, Raymond, 'Utopia and Science Fiction', in *Science Fiction: A Critical Guide* (ed. Patrick Parrinder) (London: Longman, 1979), 52–66.

Critical Works on Individual Authors

Roland Barthes, Roland, 'Textual Analysis of a Tale by Edgar Poe,' (1973) (translated by Donald G. Marshall), *Poe Studies* 10/1 (1977), 1–12.

Beherec, Marc A., 'The Devil, The Terror, and the Horror: The Whateley Twins' Further Debts to Folklore and Fiction', *Lovecraft Studies* ; 2004; 44 23–25.

Bergonzi, Bernard, *The Early H. G. Wells* (Manchester: Manchester University Press, 1961).

Blacklock, Mark, 'Higher Spatial Form in Weird Fiction' [on Mary Wilkins Freeman's 'The Hall Bedroom'], *Textual Process*, 31/6 (2017), 1101–1116

Busch, Justin E. A., *The Utopian Vision of H. G. Wells* (Jefferson, North Carolina: McFarland & Co., 2009).

Dillingham, William B., 'Eavesdropping on Eternity: Kipling's "Wireless" ', *English Literature in Transition, 1880–1920*, 55/2 (2012), 131–154.

Draper, Michael, *H. G. Wells* (Basingstoke: Macmillan, 1987).

Uroff, M. D., 'The Doctors in "Rappaccini's Daughter', *Nineteenth-Century Fiction*, 27/1 (1972), 61–70.

Evans, Arthur B., *Jules Verne Rediscovered: Didacticism and the Scientific Novel* (Westport, Connecticut: Greenwood Press, 1988).

Fielding, Heather, 'Kipling's Wireless Impressionism: Telecommunication and Narration in Early Modernist Narrative', *MFS Modern Fiction Studies* 61/1 (Spring 2015), 24–46.

Flint, Kate, 'Blood, Bodies, and *The Lifted Veil*', *Nineteenth-Century Literature*, 51/4 (1997), 455–73.

Golemba, Henry L., *Frank R. Stockton* (Boston: Twayne Publishers, 1981).

Gray, B. M., 'Pseudoscience and George Eliot's "The Lifted Veil" ', *Nineteenth-Century Fiction*, 66/4 (1982), 407–23.

Haynes, Roslynn D., *H. G. Wells: Discoverer of the Future* (London and Basingstoke: Macmillan, 1980).

Hoeveler, Diane Long, 'Mary Shelley and Gothic Feminism: The Case of "The Mortal Immortal" ', Conger, Syndy M., Frank, Frederick S., O'Dea, Gregory, and Yocum, Jennifer (eds.) *Iconoclastic Departures: Mary Shelley after Frankenstein: Essays in Honor of the Bicentenary of Mary Shelley's Birth* (Madison, NJ: Fairleigh Dickinson University Press; 1997), 150–63.

Huntington, John, *The Logic of Fantasy: H. G. Wells and Science Fiction* (New York: Columbia University Press, 1982).

James, Simon J., *Maps of Utopia: H. G. Wells, Modernity and the End of Culture* (Oxford: Oxford University Press, 2012).

Jonsson, Emelie, ' "Man is the Measure": Forster's Evolutionary Conundrum', *Style: A Quarterly Journal of Aesthetics, Poetics Stylistics, and Literary Criticism*, 46/2 (Summer 2012), 161–176.

Kemp, Peter, *H. G. Wells and the Culminating Ape: Biological Themes and Imaginative Obsessions* (London and Basingstoke: Macmillan, 1982).

Klein, Sascha, 'Subversions and Intensifications of Race, Class, and Gender Divisions on the Post-Apocalyptic Urban Frontier in the Early-Twentieth Century American Science Fiction Short Story', [on Du Bois' 'The Comet'], Brasch, Ilka, Mayer, Ruth (eds.), *Modernities and*

Modernization in North America (Heidelberg, Germany: Universitätsverlag Winter GmbH; 2018), 249–269.

Laverty, Carroll D., *Science and Pseudo-Science in the Writings of Poe* (Duke University, PhD thesis, 1951).

Murray, Brian, *H. G. Wells* (New York: Continuum, 1990).

Murray, Hannah Lauren, '"I Say To You That I Am Dead!": Medical Experiments and the Limits of Personhood in Edgar Allan Poe's "The Facts in the Case of M. Valdemar"', *Irish Journal of Gothic and Horror Studies*, 16 (Autumn 2017), 22–40.

Nattermann, Udo, 'Mundane Boundaries: Eco-Political Elements in Three Science Fiction Stories' [on 'The Machine Stops'] *Isle: Interdisciplinary Studies in Literature and Environment*, 20/1 (Winter 2013), 112–124.

Pafford, Mark, 'Romance and Death in "Wireless"', *Kipling Journal*, 90/364 (2016), 30–38.

Parrinder, Patrick (ed.), *H. G. Wells: The Critical Heritage* (London: Routledge, 1972).

Parrinder, Patrick, *Shadows of the Future: H. G. Wells Science Fiction and Prophecy* (Liverpool: Liverpool University Press, 1995).

Partington, John S., *Building Cosmopolis: The Political Thought of H. G. Wells* (Aldershot: Ashgate, 2003).

Pordzik, Ralph, 'Closet Fantasies and the Future of Desire in E. M. Forster's "The Machine Stops", *English Literature in Transition 1880–1920* 53/1 (2010), 54–74.

Robinson, Douglas, 'Poe's Mini-Apocalypse', *Studies in Short Fiction*, 19/4 (Fall 1982), 329–337.

Rosenberry, Edward H., 'Hawthorne's Allegory of Science: "Rappaccini's Daughter"', *American Literature: A Journal of Literary History, Criticism, and Bibliography*, 32/1 (1960), 39–46.

Seabury, Marcia Bundy, 'Images of a Networked Society: E. M. Forster's "The Machine Stops"', *Studies in Short Fiction*, 34/1 (Winter 1997), 61–71.

Small, Helen, 'Introduction' to *The Lifted Veil* and *Brother Jacob* (Oxford: Oxford University Press, 1999), ix–xxx.

Swift, John N., 'Jack London's "The Unparalleled Invasion": Germ Warfare, Eugenics, and Cultural Hygiene', *American Literary Realism*, 35/1 (2002), 59–71.

Taylor, Matthew A., 'Ghost Humanism: or, Specters of Materialism' [on 'The Diamond Lens] *The Journal of Nineteenth-Century Americanists* ½ (Fall 2013), 416–422.

Tresch, John, 'Extra! Extra! Poe Invents Science Fiction!', *Cambridge Companion to Edgar Allan Poe*, ed. Hayes, Kevin J., (Cambridge: Cambridge University Press, 2007): 113–32.

Wagar, W. Warren, *H. G. Wells and the World State* (New Haven: Yale University Press, 1961).

Ware, Tracy, 'The "Salutary Discomfort" in the Case of M. Valdemar', *Studies in Short Fiction*, 31/3 (Summer 1994), 471–80.

The journals, *Science Fiction Studies* (De Pauw University, Indiana, 1973–), *Extrapolation* (Liverpool University Press, 1959-), and *Foundations: The International Review of Science Fiction* (Science Fiction Foundation, 1972–) are all great resources in the study of science fiction. Also highly recommended is *The Wellsian: The Journal of the H. G. Wells Society* (1976–).

Further Reading in Oxford World's Classics

Du Bois, W. E. B., *The Souls of Black Folk*, ed. Brent Hayes Edwards.

Kipling, Rudyard, *Stories and Poems*, ed. Daniel Karlin.

London, Jack, *The Call of the Wild, White Fang, and Other Stories*, eds. Earle Labor and Robert C. Leitz.

Morris, William, *News From Nowhere*, ed. David Leopold.

Otis, Laura (ed.), *Literature and Science in the Nineteenth Century: An Anthology*.

Shelley, Mary, *Frankenstein, or the Modern Prometheus*, ed. M. K. Joseph.

Shelley, Mary, *The Last Man*, ed. Morton D. Paley.

Verne, Jules, *Journey to the Centre of the Earth*, trans. and ed. William Butcher.

Verne, Jules, *Twenty Thousand Leagues under the Seas*, trans. and ed. William Butcher.

Wells, H. G., *The First Men in the Moon*, ed. Simon J. James.

Wells, H. G., *The Invisible Man*, ed. Matthew Beaumont.

Wells, H. G., *The Island of Doctor Moreau*, ed. Darryl Jones.

Wells, H. G., *The Time Machine*, ed. Roger Luckhurst.

Wells, H. G., *The War of the Worlds*, ed. Darryl Jones.

A CHRONOLOGY OF SCIENCE FICTION FROM THE BIRTH OF MARY SHELLEY TO THE DEATH OF E. M. FORSTER

1797 Birth of Mary Wollstonecraft Godwin in London. The population of the city at that point was approximately one million people.

1800 Sir William Herschel, *On the Power of Penetrating into Space by Telescopes*; Xavier Bichat, *Recherches physiologiques sur la vie et la mort* (*Physiological Researches upon Life and Death*). Alessandro Volta develops the battery.

1802 William Herschel coins the word 'asteroids' to describe the minute planetary bodies orbiting the sun between Mars and Jupiter.

1803 Luke Howard, *On the Modifications of Clouds*.

1804 Nathaniel Hawthorne born in Salem, Massachusetts.

1805 Jean-Baptiste Cousin de Grainville, *Le Dernier homme* (*The Last Man*).

1809 Edgar Allan Poe born in Boston, Massachusetts; Charles Darwin born in Shrewsbury, Shropshire.

1815 Battle of Waterloo.

1816 At the Villa Diodati near Lake Geneva, Mary Wollstonecraft Godwin has the waking dream that inspires the novel, *Frankenstein*; Lord Byron writes the apocalyptic poem, 'Darkness', in this 'year without a summer'.

1818 Mary Shelley, *Frankenstein; or, the Modern Prometheus*.

1819 George Eliot (Mary Ann Evans) born in Warwickshire; The Peterloo Massacre.

1820 'Adam Seaborn', *Symzonia*.

1822 Charles Babbage completes his Difference Engine, a mechanical calculator that is an ancestor of the computer.

1823 Thomas Campbell, 'The Last Man' (poem).

1824 Sadi Carnot, *Réflexions sur la puissance motrice du feu et sur les machines propres à développer cette puissance* (*Reflections on the Motive Power of Fire and on Machines Fitted to Develop that Power*), a key work in the development of thermodynamics. In the *Transactions of the Geological Society*, William Buckland publishes an account of what he names a 'megalosaurus'.

1825 In County Durham, the opening of the first public railway line.

1826 Thomas Hood, 'The Last Man' (poem) collected in *Whims and Oddities*; Mary Shelley, *The Last Man*; Johann Gaspar Spurzheim, *Phrenology, in Connection with the Study of Physiognomy*.

1827 Jane Webb, *The Mummy! A Tale of the Twenty-Second Century*.

1828 Fitz-James O'Brien born in Cork, Ireland; Jules Verne born at Île Feydeau in Nantes.

1830 Charles Babbage, *Reflections on the Decline of Science in England*; Sir Charles Lyell, *Principles of Geology* (to 1833). The first major railway line opened between Liverpool and Manchester; in the USA, under President Andrew Jackson, the Indian Removal Act is passed, leading to the forced relocation of many thousands of Native Americans over the next twenty years.

1831 John Ayrton Paris, *The Life of Sir Humphry Davy*. Cholera arrives in Britain.

1832 In Great Britain, the passing of the Great Reform Act, extending the franchise to middle-class property holders.

1833 Mary Shelley, 'The Mortal Immortal'. Founding of the Great Western Railway; Charles Babbage and Ada Lovelace meet for the first time.

1834 Frank Stockton born in Philadelphia; slavery abolished in the British Empire; in a 'Review of *On the Connexion of the Physical Sciences* by Mrs Somerville', William Whewell coins the word, 'scientist'.

1835 Edgar Allan Poe, 'The Unparalleled Adventure of One Hans Pfaal'.

1836 Mary Griffith, *Three Hundred Years Hence*.

1837 Nathaniel Hawthorne, *Twice-Told Tales*; William Whewell, *History of the Inductive Sciences*. Accession of Victoria.

1838 Edgar Allan Poe, *The Narrative of Arthur Gordon Pym of Nantucket*. The population of New York is around 327 000 people; the "People's Charter", the beginning of Chartist movement.

1839 Edgar Allan Poe, 'The Conversation of Eiros and Charmion'; S. Austin, Jr., 'The Comet'; Michael Faraday, *Experimental Researches in Electricity* (to 1855).

1841 Richard Owen coins the word 'dinosaur'; Henry Fox Talbot patents his photographic Process.

1842 Edward Bulwer-Lytton, *Zanoni*; Sir Edwin Chadwick, *An Inquiry into the Sanitary Condition of the Labouring Population of Great Britain*. The Coal Mines Act forbids the employment of children under the age of 10 and of women in underground coal mines.

1843 John Elliotson, *Numerous Cases of Surgical Operations Without Pain in the Mesmeric State*. Ada Lovelace publishes an algorithm for Charles Babbage's Analytical Engine, producing what is effectively the first computer program; Samuel Morse sends the first official telegraph message (writing 'What hath God wrought!').

1844 Nathaniel Hawthorne, 'Writings of Aubépine:—Rappaccini's Daughter'; Robert Chambers, *Vestiges of the Natural History of Creation*.

1845 Edgar Allan Poe, 'The Thousand-and-Second Tale of Scheherazade', his collection, *Tales*, and 'The Facts in the Case of M. Valdemar'. The United States Coast Survey begins study of the Gulf Stream; Jean Foucault and Armand Fizeau take detailed photographs of the surface of the sun; famine begins in Ireland (to 1850, with the worst year being 1847); approximately one million people die, and another million are forced to emigrate.

1846 Nathaniel Hawthorne, *Mosses from an Old Manse*; Émile Souvestre, *Le Monde tel qu'il sera (The World As It Will Be)*. Using calculations made by Urbain Le Verrier, on September 23 Johann Gottfried Galle identifies the planet Neptune.

1847 James Y. Simpson demonstrates that chloroform can be used as an anaesthetic during surgery or labour.

1848 Edgar Allan Poe, *Eureka: A Prose Poem* Grant Allen born in Kingston, Ontario; the year of revolutions across continental Europe; Karl Marx and Friedrich Engels, *The Communist Manifesto;* the Pre-Raphaelite Brotherhood founded.

1849 Poe dies in Baltimore; John Martin's painting 'The Last Man' is first exhibited; Sir John Herschel, *Outlines of Astronomy*.

1851 Mary Shelley dies; the critic, William Wilson issues an appeal that fiction be used to popularise science; the Great Exhibition held in London.

1852 Birth of Mary E. Wilkins Freeman; Herbert Spencer, 'The Development Hypothesis'.

1854 The beginning of the Crimean War.

1855 Matthew Fontaine Maury, *The Physical Geography of the Sea*.

1856 William Morris, 'The Hollow Land'. In *The Westminster Review*, George Eliot's essay, 'The Natural History of German Life' makes an appeal for greater realism in fiction; Eunice Foote's paper, 'Circumstances affecting the heat of the sun's rays' argues that the proportion of carbon dioxide in the atmosphere would raise global temperatures; the end of the Crimean War.

1857 The Indian Mutiny.

1858 Fitz-James O'Brien, 'The Diamond Lens'; George MacDonald, *Phantastes*. Isambard Kingdom Brunel's steamship, 'Great Eastern' launched; Britain proclaims permanent British rule of India by the Crown (as opposed to the East India Company).

1859 George Eliot, 'The Lifted Veil' published in the July edition of *Blackwood's Magazine*; George Henry Lewes, *The Physiology of Common Life;* Fitz-James O'Brien, 'The Wondersmith'; Charles Darwin, *On the Origin of Species by Means of Natural Selection*. Birth of Arthur Conan Doyle in Edinburgh.

1860 William Morris founds Morris, Marshall, Faulkner & Co.

1861 The American Civil War begins.

1862 William Thomson, Lord Kelvin, *On the Age of the Sun's Heat*. In West Virginia, Fitz-James O'Brien dies of his wounds, following a skirmish at Bloomery Gap; President Abraham Lincoln issues the Emancipation Proclamation, ending slavery in the U.S.A.

1863 Thomas Henry Huxley, *Evidence as to Man's Place in Nature*. The Union army wins at the Battle of Gettysburg, the bloodiest battle of the War; the underground railway opens in London.

1864 Jules Verne, *Voyage au centre de la terre* (translated into English in 1871). Nathaniel Hawthorne dies in Concord, Massachusetts; the Sand Creek Massacre, where the U.S. Army wipe out a village of Cheyenne and Arapaho; a Confederate submarine sinks the USS Housatonic; Louis Pasteur perfects 'pasteurization', as a way to kill microbes (initially) in wine.

1865 Jules Verne, *De la Terre à la lune* (translated into English in 1867); Achille Eyraud, *Voyage à Vénus*; Camille Flammarion, *Les Mondes imaginaires et les mondes réels* (*Real and Imaginary Worlds*); Sir Francis Galton, 'Hereditary Talent and Character'. Birth of Rudyard Kipling; the Union North defeat the Southern Confederacy in the American Civil War; in Washington D.C., Edwin Booth, an actor, assassinates President Abraham Lincoln; in the UK, the first Women's Suffrage Committee founded; James Clerk Maxwell, 'A Dynamical Theory of the Electromagnetic Field', posits that electric and magnetic fields travel through space as waves, moving at the speed of light.

1866 Herbert George Wells born in Bromley; Alfred Nobel invents dynamite; Gregor Mendel publishes his discoveries regarding the laws of heredity—though the significance of his work remains unrecognised until 1900.

1867   Henry O'Neill, *Two Thousand Years Hence*; Sir Joseph Lister, *Illustrations of the Antiseptic System of Treatment in Surgery*; Henry Maudsley, *The Physiology and Pathology of Mind*. James Clerk Maxwell's thought-experiment, known as 'Maxwell's Demon', that a demon might violate the Second Law of Thermodynamics.

1868   Edward S. Ellis, *The Steam Man of the Prairies*. William Edward Burghardt Du Bois born in Massachusetts.

1869   Friedrich Miescher is the first person to isolate DNA; founding of Girton College for women; from the *HMS Porcupine*, Wyville Thomas dredges marine life from 2,435 fathoms down.

1870   Jules Verne, *Vingt mille lieues sous les mers* (translated into English in 1873). John Tyndall lectures to the British Association at Liverpool on 'The Scientific Use of the Imagination'; Franco-Prussian War (to 1871); Married Women's Property Act; W. E. Forster's Education Act.

1871   Edward Bulwer-Lytton, *The Coming Race*; Colonel George Tomkyns Chesney, *The Battle of Dorking*; Charles Darwin, *The Descent of Man, and Selection in Relation to Sex*; James Clerk Maxwell, *Theory of Heat*. The Paris Commune; founding of Newnham College for women.

1872   Samuel Butler, *Erewhon*. The American astronomer, Henry Draper photographs the spectrum of a star; Sir William Thomson invents a tide-predicting machine, a forerunner of the computer.

1873   Invention of the typewriter.

1874   Frank Stockton, 'The Water-Devil. A Marine Tale'; Ernst Haeckel, *Anthropogenie, oder Entwickelungsgeschichte des Menschen* (in English, as *The Evolution of Man* (1876)).

1875   Edgar Rice Burroughs born in Chicago.

1876   Cesare Lombroso, *L'uomo delinquente* (*Criminal Man*). Jack London born in San Francisco; Queen Victoria named Empress of India; The Challenger expedition, led by Wyville Thomson, completes the circumnavigation of the world; Alexander Graham Bell invents the telephone; King Leopold II of Belgium sets up the International Association for the Exploration and Civilisation of the Congo; the Great Famine begins in India (to 1878)—approximately 5.5 million die.

1877   Samuel Butler, *Life and Habit*. Thomas Edison patents the phonograph.

1878   In Connecticut, publication of the first telephone directory.

1879 George Eliot, 'Shadows of the Coming Race'. Birth of Edward Morgan Forster in Dorset Square, London; birth of Albert Einstein in Ulm; first electric street lighting in London.

1880 Percy Greg, *Across the Zodiac*; Charles Howard Hinton, 'What is the Fourth Dimension?' Thomas Henry Huxley gives the address, 'Science and Culture' at the opening of Sir Josiah Mason's Science College in Birmingham; George Eliot dies.

1881 Grant Allen, 'Pausodyne: A Great Chemical Discovery' and *The Evolutionist At Large*; Anon., *The Great Romance* published in New Zealand; Mary E. Bradley Lane, *Mizora: A Prophecy*; Matthew Arnold gives the Rede Lecture at Cambridge on 'Literature and Science'; William Delisle Hay, *Three Hundred Years Hence: or, a Voice from Posterity*; Sir James Paget, *Vivisection: Its Pains and Its Uses*.

1882 Frank Stockton, *The Great War Syndicate* and 'The Lady, or the Tiger'; Ignatius, Donnelly, *Atlantis: The Antediluvian World*. Charles Darwin dies; the German microbiologist, Robert Koch identifies the tuberculosis bacillus; the Phoenix Park Murders in Ireland; Second Married Women's Property Act.

1883 Ismar Thuisen (John Macnie), *The Diothas: or, a Far Look Ahead*. In his *Inquiries into Human Faculty and Its Development* Sir Francis Galton coins the word 'eugenics'; the Swiss surgeon, Theodor Kocher performs the first organ transplant surgery, implanting thyroid tissue; in Chicago, first skyscraper is built (ten stories high).

1884 Grant Allen, *Strange Stories* (including 'Pausodyne', 'The Child of the Phalanstery', and 'Our Scientific Observations of a Ghost'); Edwin Abbott Abbott, *Flatland: A Romance of Many Dimensions*. Gertrude Barrows born in Minneapolis (some say in 1883); the International Meredian Conference establishes local time at Greenwich, London as the base reference for world time; Sir Hiram Stevens Maxim invents the machine gun; at the Berlin Conference (1884–5) launches the colonial 'Scramble for Africa'; Leopold II sets up the Congo Free State.

1885 H. Rider Haggard, *King Solomon's Mines*; Richard Jefferies, *After London*. Criminal Law Amendment Act—among other provisions, it raises age of consent from 13 to 16, and also re-criminalizes sexual contact (or "gross indecency") between men.

1886 Marie Corelli, *A Romance of Two Worlds*; Robert Louis Stevenson, *The Strange Case of Doctor Jekyll and Mister Hyde*; H. Rider Haggard, *She*.

1887 Camille Flammarion, *Lumen*; W. H. Hudson, *A Crystal Age*; Albert Robida, *La Guerre au vingtième siècle*. Thomas Edison patents the Kinetoscope.

1888 George John Romanes, *Mental Evolution in Man: Origin of Human Faculty*; Edward Bellamy, *Looking Backward: 2000–1887*; Charles Howard Hinton, *A New Era of Thought*. 'Bloody Sunday'—violence breaks out between police and radical demonstrators in Trafalgar Square.

1889 Elizabeth Corbett, *New Amazonia*; Marie Corelli, *Ardath: The Story of a Dead Self*; August Weismann, *Essays Upon Heredity and Kindred Biological Problems*.

1890 Albert Robida, *Le Vingtième siècle. La vie électrique*; William James, *The Principles of Psychology*; Arthur Machen, 'The Great God Pan' published in *The Whirlwind*. William Morris founds the Kelmscott Press—he publishes the utopian fiction, *News From Nowhere*; George Newnes' periodical, *The Strand* begins publication; the Battle of Wounded Knee; the U.S. Census announces the closure of the American frontier.

1891 Edwin Lester Arnold, *The Wonderful Adventures of Phra the Phoenician*; William Dean Howells, *A Traveler from Altruria* begins publication in *The Cosmopolitan*. Death of the Irish politician, Charles Stewart Parnell; in the UK, The Assisted Education Act establishes the right to free elementary schooling.

1893 Rudyard Kipling, 'A Matter of Fact' in *Many Inventions* (1893); George Griffith, *The Angel of the Revolution*; Thomas Henry Huxley, *The Romanes Lecture: Evolution and Ethics*; Addison Peale Russell, *Sub-Coelum: A Sky-Built Human World*. At the Battle of the Shangani, British troops use Maxim guns against Matabele troops.

1894 John Jacob Astor IV, *A Journey in Other Worlds*; Camille Flammarion, *La Fin du monde* (translated as *Omega: The Last Days of the World*); George Griffith, *Olga Romanoff*; William Le Queux, *The Great War in England in 1897*; Gustavus W. Pope, *Journey to Mars the Wonderful World*. The invention of radio.

1895 H. G. Wells, *The Time Machine*; Grant Allen, *The British Barbarians*; King C. Gillette, *The Human Drift*; Percival Jones, *Mars*. Auguste and Louis Lumière screen the first-ever film of 'moving pictures'; William Roentgen publishes a report on his discovery of the existence of X-rays, including an x-ray photograph of his wife's hand.

1896 H. G. Wells, *The Island of Doctor Moreau*; William Morris, *The Well at the World's End*. Henri Becquerel discovers radioactivity.

1897 H. G. Wells, 'The Crystal Egg' and *The Invisible Man*; Kurd Lasswitz, *Auf zwei Planeten* (*On Two Planets*). In the UK, the 'Wireless Telegraph and Signal Company' (from 1900, 'Marconi's Wireless Telegraph Company) is established.

1898 H. G. Wells, *The War of the Worlds*; Alexander Craig, *Ionia: Land of Wise Men and Women*; M. P. Shiel, *The Yellow Danger*. Marie and Pierre Curie discover polonium and radium.

1899 Charles Willing Beale, *The Secret of the Earth*; W. E. B. Du Bois, *The Philadelphia Negro*; C. J. Cutcliffe Hyne, *The Lost Continent*; Bradford Peck, *The World a Department Store: A Story of Life Under a Coöperative System*. Grant Allen dies in Hindhead, Surrey.

1900 Robert William Cole, *The Struggle for Empire: A Story of the Year 2236*. During the Second Boer War, the British set up concentration camps in South Africa.

1901 H. G. Wells, *The First Men in the Moon*; Joseph Conrad and Ford Madox Ford, *The Inheritors: An Extravagant Story*; M. P. Shiel, *The Purple Cloud* serialised in *Royal Magazine;* Alexander Taylor, *Intermere* Death of Queen Victoria; accession of Edward VII; the Oldsmobile becomes the first mass-produced car; Ivan Pavlov develops the theory of the 'conditional reflex'.

1902 Rudyard Kipling, 'Wireless' appears in *Scribner's Magazine*; Georges Méliès's film, *Le voyage dans la lune* Frank R. Stockton dies in Washington D.C.

1903 Mary Wilkins Freeman, 'The Hall Bedroom' appears in *Collier's* magazine; H. G. Wells, 'The Country of the Blind' published in *The Strand;* W. E. B. Du Bois, *The Souls of Black Folk*. The Wright Brothers' first successful powered flight; Ford Motor Company founded.

1904 Georges Méliès's film, *Le voyage à travers l'impossible*.

1905 Edwin Lester Arnold, *Lieut. Gullivar Jones: His Vacation*; Rudyard Kipling 'With the Night Mail: A Story of 2000 A.D.'. Jules Verne dies in Amiens; Frank Munsey's periodical, *The All-Story Magazine* begins publication; in a series of four scientific papers, Alfred Einstein describes the Theory of Relativity.

1906 H. G. Wells, *In the Days of the Comet*.

1907 Jack London, *Before Adam*; Robert Hugh Benson, *Lord of the World*. Albert Einstein publishes "On the Relativity Principle and the Conclusions Drawn from It".

1908 E. M. Forster, 'The Machine Stops'; Jack London, *The Iron Heel*; William Hope Hodgson, *The House on the Borderland*. The Ford Model T automobile is first produced.

1909 In Paris, Georges Rignoux and A. Fournier demonstrate the live transmission of images, a vital step in the development of television.

1910 Sir Arthur Conan Doyle, 'The Terror of Blue John Gap'; Jack London, 'The Unparalleled Invasion' published in *McClure's Magazine*; C. J. Cutcliffe Hyne, *The Empire of the World*; Theodore Roosevelt, *Biological Analogies in History*; J.-H. Rosny aîné, *La Mort de la terre* (*The Death of the Earth*). The Scottish astronomer, Willamina Fleming publishes an account regarding her discovery of a 'white dwarf'.

1911 H. G. Wells, *The Country of the Blind and Other Stories*; Sir Arthur Conan Doyle, *The Last Galley*; J. D. Beresford, *The Hampdenshire Wonder*; Hugo Gernsback, *Ralph 124C 41 +* serialised in *Modern Electrics* magazine. The population of London has grown from one million in 1800 to just over seven million; Ernest Rutherford proposes a model of the atom; in Libya, the Italians launch the first-ever air-raid.

1912 Sir Arthur Conan Doyle, *The Lost World*; Rudyard Kipling, 'As Easy as A.B.C.'; Jack London, *The Scarlet Plague*; Edgar Rice Burroughs, *A Princess of Mars* and *Tarzan of the Apes*; William Hope Hodgson, *The Night Land*. Karl Pearson, *The Problem of Practical Eugenics*, a lecture given at The Francis Galton Eugenics Laboratory at University College London; the sinking of 'The Titanic'.

1913 Sir Arthur Conan Doyle, *The Poison Belt* and 'The Horror of the Heights'; J.-H. Rosny aîné, *La Force Mystérieuse* (*The Mysterious Force*); Niels Bohr improves on Rutherford's model of the atom.

1914 Edgar Rice Burroughs, *At the Earth's Core* Beginning of the First World War; in August, Zeppelins carry out an air-raid over Antwerp; in September, during the Battle of the Marne, around half a million men are killed.

1915 Jack London, *The Star Rover*; Edgar Rice Burroughs, *Pellucidar*; Charlotte Perkins Gilman, *Herland*. The German army first uses poison gas against French colonial troops at Ypres.

1916 Cleveland Moffett, *The Conquest of America: A Romance of Disaster and Recovery*; the first part of Otto Rippert's film, *Homunculus* plays in Germany; in Denmark, August Blom's film, *Verdens Undergang* ('The End of the World') appears; Madison Grant, *The Passing of the Great Race*. Death of Jack London; on 1 July 1916, the Battle of the Somme begins—on that first day, 19 240 British troops are killed; in September, for the first time, the British army deploy tanks against the German lines.

1917 G. K. Chesterton, *Eugenics and Other Evils*. Ernest Rutherford makes the first observation of a nuclear reaction; the U.S.A. declares war on Germany; the Russian Revolution begins.

1918   Gertrude Barrows Bennett ('Francis Stevens'), 'Friend Island' pub-
       lished in *All-Story Weekly*; Jack London, *The Red One*; Edgar Rice
       Burroughs, *The Land That Time Forgot* published in *Blue Book
       Magazine*; Abraham Merrit, 'The Moon Pool' in *All-Story Weekly*;
       Holger-Madsen's film, *Himmelskibet* ('A Trip to Mars') is released.
       The end of the First World War.

1919   Gertrude Barrows Bennett ('Francis Stevens'), 'The Heads of
       Cerberus' serialized in *The Thrill Book*; H. Rider Haggard, *When
       the Earth Shook*. John Alcock and Arthur Brown make the first non-
       stop transatlantic flight.

1920   Gertrude Barrows Bennett ('Francis Stevens'), 'Serapion';
       W. E. B. Du Bois, *Darkwater: Voices From Within the Veil* (including
       the story, 'The Comet'); Karel Čapek, *R.U.R.* (*Rossum's Universal
       Robots*); David Lindsay, *Voyage to Arcturus*; Henry Ford, *The
       International Jew*. John B. Watson and Rosalie Rayner conduct the
       'Little Albert' experiment, designed to show the effects of psychological
       conditioning, by inducing a phobia in a nine-month old baby; the
       population of New York in this year is around 7,798,000 people.

1922   Foundation of the Irish Free State.

1924   The Society for Studies of Interplanetary Travel is founded in
       Moscow.

1925   Harry O. Hoyt's film adaptation of Doyle's *The Lost World* is
       released—this same year it becomes the first ever in-flight movie; in
       Selfridge's Department Store in London, John Logie Baird demon-
       strates television.

1926   Edgar Wallace, *The Day of Uniting*. Hugo Gernsback founds *Amazing
       Stories* magazine.

1927   Fritz Lang's film, *Metropolis*. Werner Heisenberg sets out the
       'uncertainty principle'.

1928   Henrik Galeen's film *Alraune* ('A Daughter of Destiny') appears;
       Buck Rogers makes his first appearance in *Amazing Stories*.
       Alexander Fleming discovers penicillin.

1929   Fritz Lang's film, *Die Frau im Mond*. Edwin Hubble discovers that
       the universe is expanding; the Wall Street Crash starts off an inter-
       national economic depression that lasts through the next decade.

1930   Olaf Stapledon, *Last and First Men*. Sir Arthur Conan Doyle dies;
       death of Mary E. Wilkins Freeman.

1931   Aldous Huxley, *Brave New World*; Charles Williams, *Many Dimensions*.
       Georges Lemaître posits 'the Big Bang theory'.

1932 Erle C. Kenton's *Island of Lost Souls* (with a script by Philip Wylie), an adaptation of *The Island of Doctor Moreau*. Over this year, and the next, around 7–10 million Ukrainians die in a famine created by the policies of the Soviet state; James Chadwick discovers the neutron.

1934 The Flash Gordon comic strip begins publication.

1935 The Nazi government in Germany pass the Nuremberg Laws, enshrining anti-Semitism in statutes.

1936 William Cameron Menzies' film, *Things to Come*, produced by Alexander Korda, and written by H. G. Wells. Rudyard Kipling dies; Stalin starts the Great Terror; it lasts until 1938, and leads to the execution of around one million people.

1937 Katharine Burdekin (under the pseudonym, Murray Constantine), *Swastika Night*.

1938 On October 30, CBS Radio broadcasts Orson Welles' adaptation of *The War of the Worlds*; experiments by Otto Hahn, Lise Meltner and Fritz Strassmann achieve nuclear fission.

1939 John Carnell becomes editor of the British SF magazine, *New Worlds* Germany invades Poland. Beginning of the Second World War; the Swiss scientist, Paul Hermann Müller discovers the insecticidal properties of DDT; Leó Szilárd with other refugee scientists, including Einstein, write a letter to President Franklin Delano Roosevelt warning of the potentially catastrophic consequences of a nuclear fission chain reaction.

1940 Crematoria are constructed at Auschwitz.

1942 The Nazis begin the mass gassing of Jews and other minority groups in concentration camps across Europe.

1943 C. S. Lewis, *Perelandra*. Famine in Bengal, a catastrophe significantly worsened by British government inaction; The young physician, Josef Mengele becomes the chief medical officer at Auschwitz; the Manhattan Project is set up in the U.S.A., charged with producing a workable atomic bomb.

1944 The U.S. Air Force drops napalm incendiary bombs on Berlin; in September, the Germans begin the bombardment Britain with V-2 Rockets, the first guided ballistic missiles.

1945 The bombing of Dresden; in Berlin, Hitler commits suicide as Russian troops surround him; the war in Europe ends; President Truman approves the dropping of atomic bombs on the Japanese cities of Hiroshima and Nagasaki; the end of the war in the Pacific; in *Wireless World*, Arthur C. Clarke publishes an article, 'Extra-Terrestrial Relays—Can Rocket Stations Give Worldwide Radio Coverage?', arguing for the use of geostationary satellites.

1946 A. E. Van Vogt, *Slan*. Death of H. G. Wells in London.

1947 The 'Roswell Incident', in which either a US Air Force balloon comes to earth near a ranch in Roswell, New Mexico, or otherwise an alien craft crashes there, and its dead alien crew are secretly found; fruit flies become the first animals to leave the earth's atmosphere.

1948 B. F. Skinner, *Walden Two*. Gertrude Barrows Bennett dies in California.

1949 George Orwell, *Nineteen Eighty-Four*.

1950 Isaac Asimov, *I, Robot*, including the 'Three Laws of Robotics'; Judith Merril, *Shadow on the Hearth*. Edgar Rice Burroughs dies in California.

1951 John Wyndham, *The Day of the Triffids*; Robert Wise's film, *The Day the Earth Stood Still*.

1952 Alfred Hershey and Martha Chase confirm DNA's role in heredity; under the supervision of Rosalind Franklin, Raymond Gosling takes an X-ray diffraction image of DNA, a photograph that is passed on to Francis Crick and James Watson at the Cavendish Laboratory in Cambridge.

1953 Ray Bradbury, *Fahrenheit 451*; Arthur C. Clarke, *Childhood's End*; Byron Haskin's film of *The War of the Worlds*, produced by George Pal. The US Air Force coins the term 'Unidentified Flying Object'; in February, Crick and Watson complete the first model of the double-helix structure of DNA.

1954 Richard Matheson, *I Am Legend*; J. R. R. Tolkien, *The Lord of the Rings* (Volume III in 1955); the BBC adaptation of *Nineteen Eighty-Four*, adapted by Nigel Kneale.

1955 William Golding, *The Inheritors*; John Wyndham, *The Chrysalids*.

1956 Alfred Bester, *The Stars My Destination*; John Christopher, *The Death of Grass*; Fred M. Wilcox's film, *Forbidden Planet*; Don Siegel's movie, *Invasion of the Body Snatchers*.

1957 Jack Arnold's film, *The Incredible Shrinking Man*. Launch of the Sputnik satellite; Laika becomes the first dog in space.

1958 Nigel Kneale's *Quatermass and the Pit* begins on the BBC.

1959 Richard Condon, *The Manchurian Candidate*; Walter M. Miller, Jr., *A Canticle for Leibowitz*.

1960 George Pal's film, *The Time Machine*.

1961 Robert A. Heinlein, *Stranger in a Strange Land*; Stanislaw Lem, *Solaris*. President John F. Kennedy authorises the use of the herbicide, Agent Orange, in Vietnam; on September 19 in New Hampshire, Barney and Betty Hill are, they later claim, kidnapped by aliens; Yuri Gagarin becomes the first man in space.

1962 Anthony Burgess, *A Clockwork Orange*; J. G. Ballard, *The Drowned World*; Philip K. Dick, *The Man in the High Castle*; Rachel Carson, *Silent Spring*. In a speech at Rice University, President Kennedy declares, 'we choose to go to the moon'.

1963 Walter Tevis, *The Man Who Fell to Earth* W. E. B. Du Bois dies in Ghana; President Kennedy is assassinated in Dallas, Texas; the following day, the first episode of *Doctor Who* is screened by the BBC; the American artist, Andy Warhol declares, 'I want to be a machine.'

1964 Michael Moorcock becomes editor of *New Worlds*.

1966 In an episode of the BBC's *Out of the Unknown*, an adaptation of Forster's 'The Machine Stops' is screened; Gene Roddenberry's *Star Trek* begins on NBC. Under the leadership of Mao Zedong, the Cultural Revolution is launched in China.

1967 Jocelyn Bell Burnell and Antony Hewish detect the first pulsar; The Beatles play 'All You Need Is Love' on a globally-transmitted satellite broadcast.

1968 Philip K. Dick, *Do Androids Dream of Electric Sheep?*; Stanley Kubrick's film, *2001, A Space Odyssey* (with a script by Arthur C. Clarke). In the U.S.A., both civil rights leader, Martin Luther King and Presidential candidate, Robert Kennedy are assassinated.

1969 Angela Carter, *Heroes and Villains*; Ursula Le Guin, *The Left Hand of Darkness*; Kurt Vonnegut, *Slaughterhouse-Five*. On 20 July, Apollo 11, piloted by Neil Armstrong and Buzz Aldrin, becomes the first manned flight to land on the moon.

1970 Gerry Anderson's TV series, *UFO* begins on ITV. E. M. Forster dies in Warwickshire.

MARY WOLLSTONECRAFT SHELLEY

THE MORTAL IMMORTAL

JULY 16, 1833.—This is a memorable anniversary for me; on it I complete my three hundred and twenty-third year!

The Wandering Jew?*—certainly not. More than eighteen centuries have passed over his head. In comparison with him, I am a very young Immortal.

Am I, then, immortal? This is a question which I have asked myself, by day and night, for now three hundred and three years, and yet cannot answer it. I detected a grey hair amidst my brown locks this very day that surely signifies decay. Yet it may have remained concealed there for three hundred years—for some persons have become entirely white-headed before twenty years of age.

I will tell my story, and my reader shall judge for me. I will tell my story, and so contrive to pass some few hours of a long eternity, become so wearisome to me. For ever! Can it be? to live for ever! I have heard of enchantments, in which the victims were plunged into a deep sleep, to wake, after a hundred years, as fresh as ever: I have heard of the Seven Sleepers*—thus to be immortal would not be so burthensome: but, oh! the weight of never-ending time—the tedious passage of the still-succeeding hours! How happy was the fabled Nourjahad!*—But to my task.

All the world has heard of Cornelius Agrippa.* His memory is as immortal as his arts have made me. All the world has also heard of his scholar, who, unawares, raised the foul fiend during his master's absence, and was destroyed by him. The report, true or false, of this accident, was attended with many inconveniences to the renowned philosopher. All his scholars at once deserted him—his servants disappeared. He had no one near him to put coals on his ever-burning fires while he slept, or to attend to the changeful colours of his medicines while he studied. Experiment after experiment failed, because one pair of hands was insufficient to complete them: the dark spirits laughed at him for not being able to retain a single mortal in his service.

I was then very young—very poor—and very much in love. I had been for about a year the pupil of Cornelius, though I was absent when this accident took place. On my return, my friends implored me not to return to the alchymist's abode. I trembled as I listened to the dire tale they told; I required no second warning; and when Cornelius came and offered me a purse of gold if I would remain under his roof, I felt as if Satan himself tempted me. My teeth chattered my hair stood on end;—I ran off as fast as my trembling knees would permit.

My failing steps were directed whither for two years they had every evening been attracted,—a gently bubbling spring of pure living water, beside which lingered a dark-haired girl, whose beaming eyes were fixed on the path I was accustomed each night to tread. I cannot remember the hour when I did not love Bertha; we had been neighbours and playmates from infancy,—her parents, like mine, were of humble life, yet respectable,—our attachment had been a source of pleasure to them. In an evil hour, a malignant fever carried off both her father and mother, and Bertha became an orphan. She would have found a home beneath my paternal roof, but, unfortunately, the old lady of the near castle, rich, childless, and solitary, declared her intention to adopt her. Henceforth Bertha was clad in silk—inhabited a marble palace—and was looked on as being highly favoured by fortune. But in her new situation among her new associates, Bertha remained true to the friend of her humbler days; she often visited the cottage of my father, and when forbidden to go thither, she would stray towards the neighbouring wood, and meet me beside its shady fountain.

She often declared that she owed no duty to her new protectress equal in sanctity to that which bound us. Yet still I was too poor to marry, and she grew weary of being tormented on my account. She had a haughty but an impatient spirit, and grew angry at the obstacles that prevented our union. We met now after an absence, and she had been sorely beset while I was away; she complained bitterly, and almost reproached me for being poor. I replied hastily,—

'I am honest, if I am poor!—were I not, I might soon become rich!'

This exclamation produced a thousand questions. I feared to shock her by owning the truth, but she drew it from me; and then, casting a look of disdain on me, she said,—

'You pretend to love, and you fear to face the Devil for my sake!'

I protested that I had only dreaded to offend her;—while she dwelt on the magnitude of the reward that I should receive. Thus encouraged—shamed by her—led on by love and hope, laughing at my late fears, with quick steps and a light heart, I returned to accept the offers of the alchymist, and was instantly installed in my office.

A year passed away. I became possessed of no insignificant sum of money. Custom had banished my fears. In spite of the most painful vigilance, I had never detected the trace of a cloven foot; nor was the studious silence of our abode ever disturbed by demoniac howls. I still continued my stolen interviews with Bertha, and Hope dawned on me—Hope—but not perfect joy; for Bertha fancied that love and security were enemies, and her pleasure was to divide them in my bosom. Though true of heart, she was somewhat of a coquette in manner; and I was jealous as a Turk. She slighted me in a thousand ways, yet would never acknowledge herself to be in the wrong. She would drive me mad with anger, and then force me to beg her pardon. Sometimes she fancied that I was not sufficiently submissive, and then she had some story of a rival, favoured by her protectress. She was surrounded by silk-clad youths—the rich and gay. What chance had the sad-robed scholar of Cornelius compared with these?

On one occasion, the philosopher made such large demands upon my time, that I was unable to meet her as I was wont. He was engaged in some mighty work, and I was forced to remain, day and night, feeding his furnaces and watching his chemical preparations. Bertha waited for me in vain at the fountain. Her haughty spirit fired at this neglect; and when at last I stole out during the few short minutes allotted to me for slumber, and hoped to be consoled by her, she received me with disdain, dismissed me in scorn, and vowed that any man should possess her hand rather than he who could not be in two places at once for her sake. She would be revenged! And truly she was. In my dingy retreat I heard that she had been hunting, attended by Albert Hoffer. Albert Hoffer was favoured by her protectress, and the three passed in cavalcade before my smoky window. Methought that they mentioned my name; it was followed by a laugh of derision, as her dark eyes glanced contemptuously towards my abode.

Jealousy, with all its venom and all its misery, entered my breast. Now I shed a torrent of tears, to think that I should never call her mine; and, anon, I imprecated a thousand curses on her inconstancy. Yet, still I must stir the fires of the alchymist, still attend on the changes of his unintelligible medicines.

Cornelius had watched for three days and nights, nor closed his eyes. The progress of his alembics* was slower than he expected: in spite of his anxiety, sleep weighed upon his eyelids. Again and again he threw off drowsiness with more than human energy; again and again it stole away his senses. He eyes his crucibles wistfully. 'Not ready yet,' he murmured; 'will another night pass before the work is accomplished? Winzy, you are vigilant—you are faithful—you have slept, my boy—you slept last night. Look at that glass vessel. The liquid it contains is of a soft rose-colour: the moment it begins to change its hue, awaken me—till then I may close my eyes. First, it will turn white, and then emit golden flashes; but wait not till then; when the rose-colour fades, rouse me.' I scarcely heard the last words, muttered, as they were, in sleep. Even then he did not quite yield to nature. 'Winzy, my boy,' he again said, 'do not touch the vessel do not put it to your lips; it is a philter—a philter to cure love; you would not cease to love your Bertha—beware to drink!'

And he slept. His venerable head sunk on his breast, and I scarce heard his regular breathing. For a few minutes I watched the vessel the rosy hue of the liquid remained unchanged. Then my thoughts wandered—they visited the fountain, and dwelt on a thousand charming scenes never to be renewed—never! Serpents and adders were in my heart as the word 'Never!' half formed itself on my lips. False girl! false and cruel! Never more would she smile on me as that evening she smiled on Albert. Worthless, detested woman! I would not remain unrevenged—she should see Albert expire at her feet—she should die beneath my vengeance. She had smiled in disdain and triumph—she knew my wretchedness and her power. Yet what power had she?—the power of exciting my hate—my utter scorn—my—oh, all but indifference! Could I attain that—could I regard her with care-less eyes, transferring my rejected love to one fairer and more true, that were indeed a victory!

A bright flash darted before my eyes. I had forgotten the medicine of the adept; I gazed on it with wonder: flashes of admirable beauty, more bright than those which the diamond emits when the sun's rays are on it, glanced from the surface of the liquid; an odour the most fragrant and grateful stole over my sense; the vessel seemed one globe of living radiance, lovely to the eye, and most inviting to the taste. The first thought, instinctively inspired by the grosser sense, was, I will—I must drink. I raised the vessel to my lips. 'It will cure me of love—of torture!' Already I had quaffed half of the most delicious liquor ever tasted by the palate of man, when the philosopher stirred.

I started—I dropped the glass—the fluid flamed and glanced along the floor, while I felt Cornelius's gripe at my throat, as he shrieked aloud, 'Wretch! you have destroyed the labour of my life!'

The philosopher was totally unaware that I had drunk any portion of his drug. His idea was, and I gave a tacit assent to it, that I had raised the vessel from curiosity, and that, frighted at its brightness, and the flashes of intense light it gave forth, I had let it fall. I never undeceived him. The fire of the medicine was quenched—the fragrance died away—he grew calm, as a philosopher should under the heaviest trials, and dismissed me to rest.

I will not attempt to describe the sleep of glory and bliss which bathed my soul in paradise during the remaining hours of that memorable night. Words would be faint and shallow types of my enjoyment, or of the gladness that possessed my bosom when I woke. I trod air—my thoughts were in heaven. Earth appeared heaven, and my inheritance upon it was to be one trance of delight. 'This it is to be cured of love,' I thought; 'I will see Bertha this day, and she will find her lover cold and regardless; too happy to be disdainful, yet how utterly indifferent to her!'

The hours danced away. The philosopher, secure that he had once succeeded, and believing that he might again, began to concoct the same medicine once more. He was shut up with his books and drugs, and I had a holiday. I dressed myself with care; I looked in an old but polished shield, which served me for a mirror; methought my good looks had wonderfully improved. I hurried beyond the precincts of the town, joy in my soul, the beauty of heaven and earth around me. I turned my steps towards the castle—I could look on its lofty turrets with lightness of heart, for I was cured of love. My Bertha saw me afar off, as I came up the avenue. I know not what sudden impulse animated her bosom, but at the sight, she sprung with a light fawn-like bound down the marble steps, and was hastening towards me. But I had been perceived by another person. The old high-born hag, who called herself her protectress, and was her tyrant, had seen me also; she hobbled, panting, up the terrace; a page, as ugly as herself, held up her train, and fanned her as she hurried along, and stopped my fair girl with a 'How, now, my bold mistress? whither so fast? Back to your cage—hawks are abroad!'

Bertha clasped her hands—her eyes were still bent on my approaching figure. I saw the contest. How I abhorred the old crone who checked the kind impulses of my Bertha's softening heart. Hitherto, respect for her rank had caused me to avoid the lady of the castle; now I disdained such trivial considerations. I was cured of love, and lifted above all human fears; I hastened forwards, and soon reached the terrace. How lovely Bertha looked! her eyes flashing fire, her cheeks glowing with impatience and anger, she was a thousand times more graceful and charming than ever. I no longer loved—Oh no!—I adored— worshipped—idolized her!

She had that morning been persecuted, with more than usual vehemence, to consent to an immediate marriage with my rival. She was reproached with the encouragement that she had shown him—she was threatened with being turned out of doors with disgrace and shame. Her proud spirit rose in arms at the threat; but when she remembered the scorn that she had heaped upon me, and how, perhaps, she had thus lost one whom she now regarded as her only friend, she wept with remorse and rage. At that moment I appeared. 'Oh, Winzy!' she exclaimed, 'take me to your mother's cot; swiftly let me leave the detested luxuries and wretchedness of this noble dwelling— take me to poverty and happiness.'

I clasped her in my arms with transport. The old dame was speechless with fury, and broke forth into invective only when we were far on our road to my natal cottage. My mother received the fair fugitive, escaped from a gilt cage to nature and liberty, with tenderness and joy; my father, who loved her, welcomed her heartily; it was a day of rejoicing, which did not need the addition of the celestial potion of the alchymist to steep me in delight.

Soon after this eventful day, I became the husband of Bertha. I ceased to be the scholar of Cornelius, but I continued his friend. I always felt grateful to him for having, unawares, procured me that delicious draught of a divine elixir, which, instead of curing me of love (sad cure! solitary and joyless remedy for evils which seem blessings to the memory), had inspired me with courage and resolution, thus winning for me an inestimable treasure in my Bertha.

I often called to mind that period of trance-like inebriation with wonder. The drink of Cornelius had not fulfilled the task for which he affirmed that it had been prepared, but its effects were more potent and blissful than words can express. They had faded by degrees, yet they lingered long—and painted life in hues of splendour. Bertha often wondered at my lightness of heart and unaccustomed gaiety; for, before, I had been rather serious, or even sad, in my disposition. She loved me the better for my cheerful temper, and our days were winged by joy.

Five years afterwards I was suddenly summoned to the bedside of the dying Cornelius. He had sent for me in haste, conjuring my instant presence. I found him stretched on his pallet, enfeebled even to death; all of life that yet remained animated his piercing eyes, and they were fixed on a glass vessel, full of a roseate liquid.

'Behold,' he said, in a broken and inward voice, 'the vanity of human wishes! a second time my hopes are about to be crowned, a second time they are destroyed. Look at that liquor—you remember five years ago I had prepared the same, with the same success;—then, as now, my thirsting lips expected to taste the immortal elixir—you dashed it from me! and at present it is too late.'

He spoke with difficulty, and fell back on his pillow. I could not help saying,—

'How, revered master, can a cure for love restore you to life?'

A faint smile gleamed across his face as I listened earnestly to his scarcely intelligible answer.

'A cure for love and for all things the Elixir of Immortality. Ah! if now I might drink, I should live for ever!'

As he spoke, a golden flash gleamed from the fluid; a well-remembered fragrance stole over the air; he raised himself, all weak as he was strength seemed miraculously to re-enter his frame—he stretched forth his hand—a loud explosion startled me, a ray of fire shot up from the elixir, and the glass vessel which contained it was shivered to atoms! I turned my eyes towards the philosopher; he had fallen back—his eyes were glassy—his features rigid—he was dead!

But I lived, and was to live for ever! So said the unfortunate alchymist, and for a few days I believed his words. I remembered the glorious intoxication that had followed my stolen draught. I reflected on the change I had felt in my frame—in my soul. The bounding elasticity of the one—the buoyant lightness of the other. I surveyed myself in a mirror, and could perceive no change in my features during the space of the five years which had elapsed. I remembered the radiant hues and grateful scent of that delicious beverage—worthy the gift it was capable of bestowing—I was, then, IMMORTAL!

A few days after I laughed at my credulity. The old proverb, that 'a prophet is least regarded in his own country,'* was true with respect to me and my defunct master. I loved him as a man—I respected him as a sage—but I derided the notion that he could command the powers of darkness, and laughed at the superstitious fears with which he was regarded by the vulgar. He was a wise philosopher, but had no acquaintance with any spirits but those clad in flesh and blood. His science was simply human; and human science, I soon persuaded myself, could never conquer nature's laws so far as to imprison the soul for ever within its carnal habitation. Cornelius had brewed a soul-refreshing drink—more inebriating than wine—sweeter and more fragrant than any fruit: it possessed probably strong medicinal powers, imparting gladness to the heart and vigour to the limbs; but its effects would wear out; already were they diminished in my frame. I was a lucky fellow to have quaffed health and joyous spirits, and perhaps long life, at my master's hands; but my good fortune ended there: longevity was far different from immortality.

I continued to entertain this belief for many years. Sometimes a thought stole across me—Was the alchymist indeed deceived? But my habitual credence was, that I should meet the fate of all the children of Adam at my appointed time—a little late, but still at a natural age. Yet it was certain that I retained a wonderfully youthful look. I was laughed at for my vanity in consulting the mirror so often, but I consulted it in vain—my brow was untrenched—my cheeks—my eyes—my whole person continued as untarnished as in my twentieth year.

I was troubled. I looked at the faded beauty of Bertha—I seemed more like her son. By degrees our neighbours began to make similar observations, and I found at last that I went by the name of the Scholar bewitched. Bertha herself grew uneasy. She became jealous and peevish, and at length she began to question me. We had no children; we were all in all to each other; and though, as she grew older, her vivacious spirit became a little allied to ill-temper, and her beauty sadly diminished, I cherished her in my heart as the mistress I had idolized, the wife I had sought and won with such perfect love.

At last our situation became intolerable: Bertha was fifty—I twenty years of age. I had, in very shame, in some measure adopted the habits of a more advanced age; I no longer mingled in the dance among the young and gay, but my heart bounded along with them while I restrained my feet; and a sorry figure I cut among the Nestors of our village.* But before the time I mention, things were altered—we were universally shunned; we were—at least, I was—reported to have kept up an iniquitous acquaintance with some of my former master's supposed friends. Poor Bertha was pitied, but deserted. I was regarded with horror and detestation.

What was to be done? we sat by our winter fire—poverty had made itself felt, for none would buy the produce of my farm; and often I had been forced to journey twenty miles, to some place where I was not known, to dispose of our property. It is true, we had saved something for an evil day—that day was come.

We sat by our lone fireside the old-hearted youth and his antiquated wife. Again Bertha insisted on knowing the truth; she recapitulated all she had ever heard said about me, and added her own observations. She conjured me to cast off the spell; she described how much more comely grey hairs were than my chestnut locks; she descanted on the reverence and respect due to age—how preferable to the slight regard paid to mere children: could I imagine that the despicable gifts of youth and good looks outweighed disgrace, hatred, and scorn? Nay, in the end I should be burnt as a dealer in the black art, while she, to whom I had not deigned to communicate any portion of my good fortune, might be stoned as my accomplice. At length she insinuated that I must share my secret with her, and bestow on her like benefits to those I myself enjoyed, or she would denounce me—and then she burst into tears.

Thus beset, methought it was the best way to tell the truth. I revealed it as tenderly as I could, and spoke only of a *very long life*, not of immortality—which representation, indeed, coincided best with my own ideas. When I ended, I rose and said,—

'And now, my Bertha, will you denounce the lover of your youth? —You will not, I know. But it is too hard, my poor wife, that you should suffer from my ill-luck and the accursed arts of Cornelius. I will leave you—you have wealth enough, and friends will return in my absence. I will go; young as I seem, and strong as I am, I can work and gain my bread among strangers, unsuspected and unknown. I loved you in youth; God is my witness that I would not desert you in age, but that your safety and happiness require it.'

I took my cap and moved towards the door; in a moment Bertha's arms were round my neck, and her lips were pressed to mine. 'No, my husband, my Winzy,' she said, 'you shall not go alone—take me with you; we will remove from this place, and, as you say, among strangers we shall be unsuspected and safe. I am not so very old as quite to shame you, my Winzy; and I daresay the charm will soon wear off, and, with the blessing of God, you will become more elderly-looking, as is fitting; you shall not leave me.'

I returned the good soul's embrace heartily. 'I will not, my Bertha; but for your sake I had not thought of such a thing. I will be your true, faithful husband while you are spared to me, and do my duty by you to the last.'

The next day we prepared secretly for our emigration. We were obliged to make great pecuniary sacrifices—it could not be helped. We realized a sum sufficient, at least, to maintain us while Bertha lived; and, without saying adieu to any one, quitted our native country to take refuge in a remote part of western France.

It was a cruel thing to transport poor Bertha from her native village, and the friends of her youth, to a new country, new language, new customs. The strange secret of my destiny rendered this removal immaterial to me; but I compassionated her deeply, and was glad to perceive that she found compensation for her misfortunes in a variety of little ridiculous circumstances. Away from all tell-tale chroniclers, she sought to decrease the apparent disparity of our ages by a thousand feminine arts—rouge, youthful dress, and assumed juvenility of manner. I could not be angry. Did not I myself wear a mask? Why quarrel with hers, because it was less successful? I grieved deeply when I remembered that this was my Bertha, whom I had loved so fondly, and won with such transport—the dark-eyed, dark-haired girl, with smiles of enchanting archness and a step like a fawn—this mincing, simpering, jealous old woman. I should have revered her grey locks and withered cheeks; but thus!—It was my work, I knew; but I did not the less deplore this type of human weakness.

Her jealousy never slept. Her chief occupation was to discover that, in spite of outward appearances, I was myself growing old. I verily believe that the poor soul loved me truly in her heart, but never had woman so tormenting a mode of displaying fondness. She would discern wrinkles in my face and decrepitude in my walk, while I bounded along in youthful vigour, the youngest looking of twenty youths. I never dared address another woman. On one occasion, fancying that the belle of the village regarded me with favouring eyes, she brought me a grey wig. Her constant discourse among her acquaintances was, that though I looked so young, there was ruin at work within my frame; and she affirmed that the worst symptom about me was my apparent health. My youth was a disease, she said, and I ought at all times to prepare, if not for a sudden and awful death, at least to awake some morning white-headed and bowed down with all the marks of advanced years. I let her talk—I often joined in her conjectures. Her warnings chimed in with my never-ceasing speculations concerning my state, and I took an earnest, though painful, interest in listening to all that her quick wit and excited imagination could say on the subject.

Why dwell on these minute circumstances? We lived on for many long years. Bertha became bedrid and paralytic; I nursed her as a mother might a child. She grew peevish, and still harped upon one string—of how long I should survive her. It has ever been a source of consolation to me, that I performed my duty scrupulously towards her. She had been mine in youth, she was mine in age; and at last, when I heaped the sod over her corpse, I wept to feel that I had lost all that really bound me to humanity.

Since then how many have been my cares and woes, how few and empty my enjoyments! I pause here in my history—I will pursue it no further. A sailor without rudder or compass, tossed on a stormy sea—a traveller lost on a widespread heath, without landmark or stone to guide him—such have I been: more lost, more hopeless than either. A nearing ship, a gleam from some far cot, may save them; but I have no beacon except the hope of death.

Death! mysterious, ill-visaged friend of weak humanity! Why alone of all mortals have you cast me from your sheltering fold? Oh, for the peace of the grave! the deep silence of the iron-bound tomb! that thought would cease to work in my brain, and my heart beat no more with emotions varied only by new forms of sadness!

Am I immortal? I return to my first question. In the first place, is it not more probable that the beverage of the alchymist was fraught rather with longevity than eternal life? Such is my hope. And then be it remembered, that I only drank *half* of the potion prepared by him. Was not the whole necessary to complete the charm? To have drained half the Elixir of Immortality is but to be half-immortal—my Forever is thus truncated and null.

But again, who shall number the years of the half of eternity? I often try to imagine by what rule the infinite may be divided. Sometimes I fancy age advancing upon me. One grey hair I have found. Fool! do I lament? Yes, the fear of age and death often creeps coldly into my heart; and the more I live, the more I dread death, even while I abhor life. Such an enigma is man—born to perish—when he wars, as I do, against the established laws of his nature.

But for this anomaly of feeling surely I might die: the medicine of the alchymist would not be proof against fire—sword—and the strangling waters. I have gazed upon the blue depths of many a placid lake, and the tumultuous rushing of many a mighty river, and have said, peace inhabits those waters; yet I have turned my steps away, to live yet another day. I have asked myself, whether suicide would be a crime in one to whom thus only the portals of the other world could be opened. I have done all, except presenting myself as a soldier or duellist, an object of destruction to my—no, *not* my fellow-mortals, and therefore I have shrunk away. They are not my fellows. The inextinguishable power of life in my frame, and their ephemeral existence, places us wide as the poles asunder. I could not raise a hand against the meanest or the most powerful among them.

Thus I have lived on for many a year—alone, and weary of myself—desirous of death, yet never dying—a mortal immortal. Neither ambition nor avarice can enter my mind, and the ardent love that gnaws at my heart, never to be returned—never to find an equal on which to expend itself—lives there only to torment me.

This very day I conceived a design by which I may end all—without self-slaughter, without making another man a Cain*—an expedition, which mortal frame can never survive, even endued with the youth and strength that inhabits mine. Thus I shall put my immortality to the test, and rest for ever—or return, the wonder and benefactor of the human species.*

Before I go, a miserable vanity has caused me to pen these pages. I would not die, and leave no name behind. Three centuries have passed since I quaffed the fatal beverage; another year shall not elapse before, encountering gigantic dangers—warring with the powers of frost in their home—beset by famine, toil, and tempest—I yield this body, too tenacious a cage for a soul which thirsts for freedom, to the destructive elements of air and water; or, if I survive, my name shall be recorded as one of the most famous among the sons of men; and, my task achieved, I shall adopt more resolute means, and, by scattering and annihilating the atoms that compose my frame, set at liberty the life imprisoned within, and so cruelly prevented from soaring from this dim earth to a sphere more congenial to its immortal essence.

EDGAR ALLAN POE

THE CONVERSATION OF EIROS AND CHARMION*

Πυρ σοι προσισω
I will bring fire to thee.

Euripides—*Androm:**

EIROS.

Why do you call me Eiros?

CHARMION.

So henceforward will you always be called. You must forget, too, *my* earthly name, and speak to me as Charmion.

EIROS.

This is indeed no dream!

CHARMION.

Dreams are with us no more;—but of these mysteries anon. I rejoice to see you looking life-like and rational. The film of the shadow has already passed from off your eyes. Be of heart, and fear nothing. Your allotted days of stupor have expired; and, to-morrow, I will myself induct you into the full joys and wonders of your novel existence.

EIROS.

True—I feel no stupor—none at all. The wild sickness and the terrible darkness have left me, and I hear no longer that mad, rushing, horrible sound, like the 'voice of many waters.'* Yet my senses are bewildered, Charmion, with the keenness of their perception of *the new*.

CHARMION.

A few days will remove all this;—but I fully understand you, and feel for you. It is now ten earthly years since I underwent what you undergo—yet the remembrance of it hangs by me still. You have now suffered all of pain, however, which you will suffer in Aidenn.*

EIROS.

In Aidenn?

CHARMION.

In Aidenn.

EIROS.

Oh God!—pity me, Charmion!—I am overburthened with the majesty of all things—of the unknown now known—of the speculative Future merged in the august and certain Present.

CHARMION.

Grapple not now with such thoughts. To-morrow we will speak of this. Your mind wavers, and its agitation will find relief in the exercise of simple memories. Look not around, nor forward—but back. I am burning with anxiety to hear the details of that stupendous event which threw you among us. Tell me of it. Let us converse of familiar things, in the old familiar language of the world which has so fearfully perished.

EIROS.

Most fearfully, fearfully!—this is indeed no dream.

CHARMION.

Dreams are no more. Was I much mourned, my Eiros?

EIROS.

Mourned, Charmion?—oh deeply. To that last hour of all, there hung a cloud of intense gloom and devout sorrow over your household.

CHARMION.

And that last hour—speak of it. Remember that, beyond the naked fact of the catastrophe itself, I know nothing. When, coming out from among mankind, I passed into Night through the Grave—at that period, if I remember aright, the calamity which overwhelmed you was utterly unanticipated. But, indeed, I knew little of the speculative philosophy of the day.

EIROS.

The individual calamity was, as you say, entirely unanticipated; but analogous misfortunes had been long a subject of discussion with astronomers. I need scarce tell you, my friend, that, even when you left us, men had agreed to understand those passages in the most holy writings which speak of the final destruction of all things by fire,* as having reference to the orb of the earth alone. But in regard to the immediate agency of the ruin, speculation had been at fault from that epoch in astronomical knowledge in which the comets were divested of the terrors of flame. The very moderate density of these bodies had been well established. They had been observed to pass among the satellites of Jupiter, without bringing about any sensible alteration either in the masses or in the orbits of these secondary planets. We had long regarded the wanderers as vapory creations of inconceivable tenuity, and as altogether incapable of doing injury to our substantial globe, even in the event of contact. But contact was not in any degree dreaded; for the elements of all the comets were accurately known. That among *them* we should look for the agency of the threatened fiery destruction had been for many years considered an inadmissible idea. But wonders and wild fancies had been, of late days, strangely rife among mankind; and, although it was only with a few of the ignorant that actual apprehension prevailed, upon the announcement by astronomers of a *new* comet,* yet this announcement was generally received with I know not what of agitation and mistrust.

The elements of the strange orb were immediately calculated, and it was at once conceded by all observers, that its path, at perihelion,* would bring it into very close proximity with the earth. There were two or three astronomers, of secondary note, who resolutely maintained that a contact was inevitable. I cannot very well express to you the effect of this intelligence upon the people. For a few short days they would not believe an assertion which their intellect, so long employed among worldly considerations, could not in any manner grasp. But the truth of a vitally important fact soon makes its way into the understanding of even the most stolid. Finally, all men saw that astronomical knowledge lied not, and they awaited the comet. Its approach was not, at first, seemingly rapid; nor was its appearance of very unusual character. It was of a dull red, and had little perceptible train. For seven or eight days we saw no material increase in its apparent diameter, and but a partial alteration in its color. Meantime, the ordinary affairs of men were discarded, and all interests absorbed in a growing discussion, instituted by the philosophic, in respect to the cometary nature. Even the grossly ignorant aroused their sluggish capacities to such considerations. The learned *now* gave their intellect—their soul—to no such points as the allaying of fear, or to the sustenance of loved theory. They sought—they panted for right views. They groaned for perfected knowledge. *Truth* arose in the purity of her strength and exceeding majesty, and the wise bowed down and adored.

That material injury to our globe or to its inhabitants would result from the apprehended contact, was an opinion which hourly lost ground among the wise; and the wise were now freely permitted to rule the reason and the fancy of the crowd. It was demonstrated, that the density of the comet's *nucleus* was far less than that of our rarest gas; and the harmless passage of a similar visitor among the satellites of Jupiter was a point strongly insisted upon, and which served greatly to allay terror. Theologists, with an earnestness fear-enkindled, dwelt upon the biblical prophecies, and expounded them to the people with a directness and simplicity of which no previous instance had been known. That the final destruction of the earth must be brought about by the agency of fire, was urged with a spirit that enforced every where conviction; and that the comets were of no fiery nature (as all men now knew) was a truth which relieved all, in a great measure, from the apprehension of the great calamity foretold. It is noticeable that the popular prejudices and vulgar errors in regard to pestilences and wars—errors which were wont to prevail upon every appearance of a comet—were now altogether unknown. As if by some sudden convulsive exertion, reason had at once hurled superstition from her throne. The feeblest intellect had derived vigor from excessive interest.

What minor evils might arise from the contact were points of elaborate question. The learned spoke of slight geological disturbances, of probable alterations in climate, and consequently in vegetation; of possible magnetic and electric influences. Many held that no visible or perceptible effect would in any manner be produced. While such discussions were going on, their subject gradually approached, growing larger in apparent diameter, and of a more brilliant lustre. Mankind grew paler as it came. All human operations were suspended.

There was an epoch in the course of the general sentiment when the comet had attained, at length, a size surpassing that of any previously recorded visitation. The people now, dismissing any lingering hope that the astronomers were wrong, experienced all the certainty of evil. The chimerical aspect of their terror was gone. The hearts of the stoutest of our race beat violently within their bosoms. A very few days sufficed, however, to merge even such feelings in sentiments more unendurable. We could no longer apply to the strange orb any *accustomed* thoughts. Its *historical* attributes had disappeared. It oppressed us with a hideous *novelty* of emotion. We saw it not as an astronomical phenomenon in the heavens, but as an incubus upon our hearts, and a shadow upon our brains. It had taken, with inconceivable rapidity, the character of a gigantic mantle of rare flame, extending from horizon to horizon.

Yet a day, and men breathed with greater freedom. It was clear that we were already within the influence of the comet; yet we lived. We even felt an unusual elasticity of frame and vivacity of mind. The exceeding tenuity of the object of our dread was apparent; for all heavenly objects were plainly visible through it. Meantime, our vegetation had perceptibly altered; and we gained faith, from this predicted circumstance, in the foresight of the wise. A wild luxuriance of foliage, utterly unknown before, burst out upon every vegetable thing.

Yet another day—and the evil was not altogether upon us. It was now evident that its nucleus would first reach us. A wild change had come over all men; and the first sense of *pain* was the wild signal for general lamentation and horror. This first sense of pain lay in a rigorous constriction of the breast and lungs, and an insufferable dryness of the skin. It could not be denied that our atmosphere was radically affected; the conformation of this atmosphere and the possible modifications to which it might be subjected, were now the topics of discussion. The result of investigation sent an electric thrill of the intensest terror through the universal heart of man.

It had been long known that the air which encircled us was a compound of oxygen and nitrogen gases, in the proportion of twenty-one measures of oxygen, and seventy-nine of nitrogen, in every one hundred of the atmosphere.* Oxygen, which was the principle of combustion, and the vehicle of heat, was absolutely necessary to the support of animal life, and was the most powerful and energetic agent in nature. Nitrogen, on the contrary, was incapable of supporting either animal life or flame. An unnatural excess of oxygen would result, it had been ascertained, in just such an elevation of the animal spirits as we had latterly experienced. It was the pursuit, the extension of the idea, which had engendered awe. What would be the result of *a total extraction of the nitrogen?* A combustion irresistible, all-devouring, omni-prevalent, immediate;—the entire fulfillment, in all their minute and terrible details, of the fiery and horror-inspiring denunciations of the prophecies of the Holy Book.*

Why need I paint, Charmion, the now disenchained frenzy of mankind? That tenuity in the comet which had previously inspired us with hope, was now the source of the bitterness of despair. In its impalpable gaseous character we clearly perceived the consummation of Fate. Meantime a day again passed—bearing away with it the last shadow of Hope. We gasped in the rapid modification of the air. The red blood bounded tumultuously through its strict channels. A furious delirium possessed all men; and, with arms rigidly outstretched towards the threatening heavens, they trembled and shrieked aloud.

But the nucleus of the destroyer was now upon us;—even here in Aidenn, I shudder while I speak. Let me be brief—brief as the ruin that overwhelmed. For a moment there was a wild lurid light alone, visiting and penetrating all things. Then—let us bow down, Charmion, before the excessive majesty of the great God!—then, there came a shouting and pervading sound, as if from the mouth itself of HIM; while the whole incumbent mass of ether in which we existed, burst at once into a species of intense flame, for whose surpassing brilliancy and all-fervid heat even the angels in the high Heaven of pure knowledge have no name. Thus ended all.

NATHANIEL HAWTHORNE

RAPPACCINI'S DAUGHTER

A YOUNG man, named Giovanni Guasconti, came, very long ago, from the more southern region of Italy, to pursue his studies at the University of Padua.* Giovanni, who had but a scanty supply of gold ducats in his pocket, took lodgings in a high and gloomy chamber of an old edifice, which looked not unworthy to have been the palace of a Paduan noble, and which, in fact, exhibited over its entrance the armorial bearings of a family long since extinct. The young stranger, who was not unstudied in the great poem of his country, recollected that one of the ancestors of this family, and perhaps an occupant of this very mansion, had been pictured by Dante as a partaker of the immortal agonies of his Inferno.* These reminiscences and associations, together with the tendency to heart-break natural to a young man for the first time out of his native sphere, caused Giovanni to sigh heavily, as he looked around the desolate and ill-furnished apartment.

'Holy Virgin, signor,' cried old dame Lisabetta, who, won by the youth's remarkable beauty of person, was kindly endeavoring to give the chamber a habitable air, 'what a sigh was that to come out of a young man's heart! Do you find this old mansion gloomy? For the love of heaven, then, put your head out of the window, and you will see as bright sunshine as you have left in Naples.'

Guasconti mechanically did as the old woman advised, but could not quite agree with her that the Lombard sunshine was as cheerful as that of southern Italy. Such as it was, however, it fell upon a garden beneath the window, and expended its fostering influences on a variety of plants, which seemed to have been cultivated with exceeding care.

'Does this garden belong to the house?' asked Giovanni.

'Heaven forbid, signor!—unless it were fruitful of better pot-herbs than any that grow there now,' answered old Lisabetta. 'No: that garden is cultivated by the own hands of Signor Giacomo Rappaccini, the famous Doctor, who, I warrant him, has been heard of as far as Naples. It is said that he distils these plants into medicines that are as potent as a charm. Oftentimes you may see the signor Doctor at work, and perchance the signora his daughter, too, gathering the strange flowers that grow in the garden.'

The old woman had now done what she could for the aspect of the chamber, and, commending the young man to the protection of the saints, took her departure.

Giovanni still found no better occupation than to look down into the garden beneath his window. From its appearance, he judged it to be one of those botanic gardens, which were of earlier date in Padua than elsewhere in Italy, or in the world.* Or, not improbably, it might once have been the pleasure-place of an opulent family; for there was the ruin of a marble fountain in the centre, sculptured with rare art, but so wofully shattered that it was impossible to trace the original design from the chaos of remaining fragments. The water, however, continued to gush and sparkle into the sunbeams as cheerfully as ever. A little gurgling sound ascended to the young man's window, and made him feel as if a fountain were an immortal spirit, that sung its song unceasingly, and without heeding the vicissitudes around it; while one century embodied it in marble, and another scattered the perishable garniture on the soil. All about the pool into which the water subsided, grew various plants, that seemed to require a plentiful supply of moisture for the nourishment of gigantic leaves, and, in some instances, flowers gorgeously magnificent. There was one shrub in particular, set in a marble vase in the midst of the pool, that bore a profusion of purple blossoms, each of which had the lustre and richness of a gem; and the whole together made a show so resplendent that it seemed enough to illuminate the garden, even had there been no sunshine. Every portion of the soil was peopled with plants and herbs, which, if less beautiful, still bore tokens of assiduous care; as if all had their individual virtues, known to the scientific mind that fostered them. Some were placed in urns, rich with old carving, and others in common garden-pots; some crept serpent-like along the ground, or climbed on high, using whatever means of ascent was offered them. One plant had wreathed itself round a statue of Vertumnus,* which was thus quite veiled and shrouded in a drapery of hanging foliage, so happily arranged that it might have served a sculptor for a study.

While Giovanni stood at the window, he heard a rustling behind a screen of leaves, and became aware that a person was at work in the garden. His figure soon emerged into view, and showed itself to be that of no common laborer, but a tall, emaciated, sallow, and sickly-looking man, dressed in a scholar's garb of black. He was beyond the middle term of life, with grey hair, a thin grey beard, and a face singularly marked with intellect and cultivation, but which could never, even in his more youthful days, have expressed much warmth of heart.

Nothing could exceed the intentness with which this scientific gardener examined every shrub which grew in his path; it seemed as if he was looking into their inmost nature, making observations in regard to their creative essence, and discovering why one leaf grew in this shape, and another in that, and wherefore such and such flowers differed among themselves in hue and perfume. Nevertheless, in spite of the deep intelligence on his part, there was no approach to intimacy between himself and these vegetable existences. On the contrary, he avoided their actual touch, or the direct inhaling of their odors, with a caution that impressed Giovanni most disagreeably; for the man's demeanor was that of one walking among malignant influences, such as savage beasts, or deadly snakes, or evil spirits, which, should he allow them one moment of license, would wreak upon him some terrible fatality. It was strangely frightful to the young man's imagination, to see this air of insecurity in a person cultivating a garden, that most simple and innocent of human toils, and which had been alike the joy and labor of the unfallen parents of the race. Was this garden, then, the Eden of the present world?—and this man, with such a perception of harm in what his own hands caused to grow, was he the Adam?*

The distrustful gardener, while plucking away the dead leaves or pruning the too luxuriant growth of the shrubs, defended his hands with a pair of thick gloves. Nor were these his only armor. When, in his walk through the garden, he came to the magnificent plant that hung its purple gems beside the marble fountain, he placed a kind of mask over his mouth and nostrils, as if all this beauty did but conceal a deadlier malice. But finding his task still too dangerous, he drew back, removed the mask, and called loudly, but in the infirm voice of a person affected with inward disease:

'Beatrice!—Beatrice!'

'Here am I, my father! What would you?' cried a rich and youthful voice from the window of the opposite house; a voice as rich as a tropical sunset, and which made Giovanni, though he knew not why, think of deep hues of purple or crimson, and of perfumes heavily delectable.—'Are you in the garden!'*

'Yes, Beatrice,' answered the gardener, 'and I need your help.'

Soon there emerged from under a sculptured portal the figure of a young girl, arrayed with as much richness of taste as the most splendid of the flowers, beautiful as the day, and with a bloom so deep and vivid that one shade more would have been too much. She looked redundant with life, health, and energy; all of which attributes were bound down and compressed, as it were, and girdled tensely, in their luxuriance, by her virgin zone. Yet Giovanni's fancy must have grown morbid, while he looked down into the garden; for the impression which the fair stranger made upon him was as if here were another flower, the human sister of those vegetable ones, as beautiful as they—more beautiful than the richest of them—but still to be touched only with a glove, nor to be approached without a mask. As Beatrice came down the garden-path, it was observable that she handled and inhaled the odor of several of the plants, which her father had most sedulously avoided.

'Here, Beatrice,' said the latter,—'see how many needful offices require to be done to our chief treasure. Yet, shattered as I am, my life might pay the penalty of approaching it so closely as circumstances demand. Henceforth, I fear, this plant must be consigned to your sole charge.'

'And gladly will I undertake it,' cried again the rich tones of the young lady, as she bent towards the magnificent plant, and opened her arms as if to embrace it. 'Yes, my sister, my splendor, it shall be Beatrice's task to nurse and serve thee; and thou shalt reward her with thy kisses and perfume breath, which to her is as the breath of life!'

Then, with all the tenderness in her manner that was so strikingly expressed in her words, she busied herself with such attentions as the plant seemed to require; and Giovanni, at his lofty window, rubbed his eyes, and almost doubted whether it were a girl tending her favorite flower, or one sister performing the duties of affection to another. The scene soon terminated. Whether Doctor Rappaccini had finished his labors in the garden, or that his watchful eye had caught the stranger's face, he now took his daughter's arm and retired. Night was already closing in; oppressive exhalations seemed to proceed from the plants, and steal upward past the open window; and Giovanni, closing the lattice, went to his couch, and dreamed of a rich flower and beautiful girl. Flower and maiden were different and yet the same, and fraught with some strange peril in either shape.

But there is an influence in the light of morning that tends to rectify whatever errors of fancy, or even of judgment, we may have incurred during the sun's decline, or among the shadows of the night, or in the less wholesome glow of moonshine. Giovanni's first movement on starting from sleep, was to throw open the window, and gaze down into the garden which his dreams had made so fertile of mysteries. He was surprised, and a little ashamed, to find how real and matter-of-fact an affair it proved to be, in the first rays of the sun, which gilded the dew-drops that hung upon leaf and blossom, and, while giving a brighter beauty to each rare flower, brought everything within the limits of ordinary experience. The young man rejoiced, that, in the heart of the barren city, he had the privilege of overlooking this spot of lovely and luxuriant vegetation. It would serve, he said to himself, as a symbolic language, to keep him in communion with nature. Neither the sickly and thought-worn Doctor Giacomo Rappaccini, it is true, nor his brilliant daughter, were now visible; so that Giovanni could not determine how much of the singularity which he attributed to both, was due to their own qualities, and how much to his wonder-working fancy. But he was inclined to take a most rational view of the whole matter.

In the course of the day, he paid his respects to Signor Pietro Baglioni, professor of medicine in the University, a physician of eminent repute, to whom Giovanni had brought a letter of introduction. The Professor was an elderly personage, apparently of genial nature, and habits that might almost be called jovial; he kept the young man to dinner, and made himself very agreeable by the freedom and liveliness of his conversation, especially when warmed by a flask or two of Tuscan wine. Giovanni, conceiving that men of science, inhabitants of the same city, must needs be on familiar terms with one another, took an opportunity to mention the name of Dr. Rappaccini. But the Professor did not respond with so much cordiality as he had anticipated.

'Ill would it become a teacher of the divine art of medicine,' said Professor Pietro Baglioni, in answer to a question of Giovanni, 'to withhold due and well-considered praise of a physician so eminently skilled as Rappaccini. But, on the other hand, I should answer it but scantily to my conscience, were I to permit a worthy youth like yourself, Signor Giovanni, the son of an ancient friend, to imbibe erroneous ideas respecting a man who might hereafter chance to hold your life and death in his hands. The truth is, our worshipful Doctor Rappaccini has as much science as any member of the faculty—with perhaps one single exception—in Padua, or all Italy. But there are certain grave objections to his professional character.'

'And what are they?' asked the young man.

'Has my friend Giovanni any disease of body or heart, that he is so inquisitive about physicians?' said the Professor, with a smile. 'But as for Rappaccini, it is said of him—and I, who know the man well, can answer for its truth—that he cares infinitely more for science than for mankind. His patients are interesting to him only as subjects for some new experiment. He would sacrifice human life, his own among the rest, or whatever else was dearest to him, for the sake of adding so much as a grain of mustard-seed to the great heap of his accumulated knowledge.'

'Methinks he is an awful man, indeed,' remarked Guasconti, mentally recalling the cold and purely intellectual aspect of Rappaccini. 'And yet, worshipful Professor, is it not a noble spirit? Are there many men capable of so spiritual a love of science?'

'God forbid,' answered the Professor, somewhat testily—'at least, unless they take sounder views of the healing art than those adopted by Rappaccini. It is his theory, that all medicinal virtues are comprised within those substances which we term vegetable poisons. These he cultivates with his own hands, and is said even to have produced new varieties of poison, more horribly deleterious than Nature, without the assistance of this learned person, would ever have plagued the world with. That the Signor Doctor does less mischief than might be expected, with such dangerous substances, is undeniable. Now and then, it must be owned, he has effected—or seemed to effect—a marvellous cure. But, to tell you my private mind, Signor Giovanni, he should receive little credit for such instances of success—they being probably the work of chance—but should be held strictly accountable for his failures, which may justly be considered his own work.'

The youth might have taken Baglioni's opinions with many grains of allowance, had he known that there was a professional warfare of long continuance between him and Doctor Rappaccini, in which the latter was generally thought to have gained the advantage. If the reader be inclined to judge for himself, we refer him to certain black-letter tracts on both sides, preserved in the medical department of the University of Padua.

'I know not, most learned Professor,' returned Giovanni, after musing on what had been said of Rappaccini's exclusive zeal for science— 'I know not how dearly this physician may love his art; but surely there is one object more dear to him. He has a daughter.'

'Aha!' cried the Professor with a laugh. 'So now our friend Giovanni's secret is out. You have heard of this daughter, whom all the young men in Padua are wild about, though not half a dozen have ever had the good hap to see her face. I know little of the Signora Beatrice, save that Rappaccini is said to have instructed her deeply in his science, and that, young and beautiful as fame reports her, she is already qualified to fill a professor's chair. Perchance her father destines her for mine! Other absurd rumors there be, not worth talking about, or listening to. So now, Signor Giovanni, drink off your glass of Lacryma.'*

Guasconti returned to his lodgings somewhat heated with the wine he had quaffed, and which caused his brain to swim with strange fantasies in reference to Doctor Rappaccini and the beautiful Beatrice. On his way, happening to pass by a florist's, he bought a fresh bouquet of flowers.

Ascending to his chamber, he seated himself near the window, but within the shadow thrown by the depth of the wall, so that he could look down into the garden with little risk of being discovered. All beneath his eye was a solitude. The strange plants were basking in the sunshine, and now and then nodding gently to one another, as if in acknowledgment of sympathy and kindred. In the midst, by the shattered fountain, grew the magnificent shrub, with its purple gems clustering all over it; they glowed in the air, and gleamed back again out of the depths of the pool, which thus seemed to overflow with colored radiance from the rich reflection that was steeped in it. At first, as we have said, the garden was a solitude. Soon, however,—as Giovanni had half-hoped, half-feared, would be the case,—a figure appeared beneath the antique sculptured portal, and came down between the rows of plants, inhaling their various perfumes, as if she were one of those beings of old classic fable, that lived upon sweet odors. On again beholding Beatrice, the young man was even startled to perceive how much her beauty exceeded his recollection of it; so brilliant, so vivid in its character, that she glowed amid the sunlight, and, as Giovanni whispered to himself, positively illuminated the more shadowy intervals of the garden path. Her face being now more revealed than on the former occasion, he was struck by its expression of simplicity and sweetness; qualities that had not entered into his idea of her character, and which made him ask anew, what manner of mortal she might be. Nor did he fail again to observe, or imagine, an analogy between the beautiful girl and the gorgeous shrub that hung its gem-like flowers over the fountain; a resemblance which Beatrice seemed to have indulged a fantastic humor in heightening, both by the arrangement of her dress and the selection of its hues.

Approaching the shrub, she threw open her arms, as with a passionate ardor, and drew its branches into an intimate embrace; so intimate, that her features were hidden in its leafy bosom, and her glistening ringlets all intermingled with the flowers.

'Give me thy breath, my sister,' exclaimed Beatrice; 'for I am faint with common air! And give me this flower of thine, which I separate with gentlest fingers from the stem, and place it close beside my heart.'

With these words, the beautiful daughter of Rappaccini plucked one of the richest blossoms of the shrub, and was about to fasten it in her bosom. But now, unless Giovanni's draughts of wine had bewildered his senses, a singular incident occurred. A small orange-colored reptile, of the lizard or chameleon species, chanced to be creeping along the path, just at the feet of Beatrice. It appeared to Giovanni—but, at the distance from which he gazed, he could scarcely have seen anything so minute—it appeared to him, however, that a drop or two of moisture from the broken stem of the flower descended upon the lizard's head. For an instant, the reptile contorted itself violently, and then lay motionless in the sunshine. Beatrice observed this remarkable phenomenon, and crossed herself, sadly, but without surprise; nor did she therefore hesitate to arrange the fatal flower in her bosom. There it blushed, and almost glimmered with the dazzling effect of a precious stone, adding to her dress and aspect the one appropriate charm, which nothing else in the world could have supplied. But Giovanni, out of the shadow of his window, bent forward and shrank back, and murmured and trembled.

'Am I awake? Have I my senses?' said he to himself. 'What is this being?—beautiful, shall I call her?—or inexpressibly terrible?'

Beatrice now strayed carelessly through the garden, approaching closer beneath Giovanni's window, so that he was compelled to thrust his head quite out of its concealment, in order to gratify the intense and painful curiosity which she excited. At this moment, there came a beautiful insect over the garden wall; it had perhaps wandered through the city and found no flowers nor verdure among those antique haunts of men, until the heavy perfumes of Doctor Rappaccini's shrubs had lured it from afar. Without alighting on the flowers, this winged brightness seemed to be attracted by Beatrice, and lingered in the air and fluttered about her head. Now here it could not be but that Giovanni Guasconti's eyes deceived him. Be that as it might, he fancied that while Beatrice was gazing at the insect with childish delight, it grew faint and fell at her feet!—its bright wings shivered! it was dead!—from no cause that he could discern, unless it were the atmosphere of her breath. Again Beatrice crossed herself and sighed heavily, as she bent over the dead insect.

An impulsive movement of Giovanni drew her eyes to the window. There she beheld the beautiful head of the young man—rather a Grecian than an Italian head,* with fair, regular features, and a glistening of gold among his ringlets—gazing down upon her like a being that hovered in mid-air. Scarcely knowing what he did, Giovanni threw down the bouquet which he had hitherto held in his hand.

'Signora,' said he, 'there are pure and healthful flowers. Wear them for the sake of Giovanni Guasconti!'

'Thanks, Signor,' replied Beatrice, with her rich voice, that came forth as it were like a gush of music; and with a mirthful expression half childish and half woman-like. 'I accept your gift, and would fain recompense it with this precious purple flower; but if I toss it into the air, it will not reach you. So Signor Guasconti must even content himself with my thanks.'

She lifted the bouquet from the ground, and then as if inwardly ashamed at having stepped aside from her maidenly reserve to respond to a stranger's greeting, passed swiftly homeward through the garden. But, few as the moments were, it seemed to Giovanni when she was on the point of vanishing beneath the sculptured portal, that his beautiful bouquet was already beginning to wither in her grasp. It was an idle thought; there could be no possibility of distinguishing a faded flower from a fresh one, at so great a distance.

For many days after this incident, the young man avoided the window that looked into Doctor Rappaccini's garden, as if something ugly and monstrous would have blasted his eye-sight, had he been betrayed into a glance. He felt conscious of having put himself, to a certain extent, within the influence of an unintelligible power, by the

communication which he had opened with Beatrice. The wisest
course would have been; if his heart were in any real danger, to quit
his lodgings and Padua itself, at once; the next wiser, to have accustomed himself, as far as possible, to the familiar and day-light view of
Beatrice; thus bringing her rigidly and systematically within the
limits of ordinary experience. Least of all, while avoiding her sight,
should Giovanni have remained so near this extraordinary being, that
the proximity and possibility even of intercourse, should give a kind
of substance and reality to the wild vagaries which his imagination ran
riot continually in producing. Guasconti had not a deep heart—or at
all events, its depths were not sounded now—but he had a quick
fancy, and an ardent southern temperament, which rose every instant
to a higher fever-pitch. Whether or no Beatrice possessed those terrible attributes—that fatal breath—the affinity with those so beautiful and deadly flowers—which were indicated by what Giovanni had
witnessed, she had at least instilled a fierce and subtle poison into his
system. It was not love, although her rich beauty was a madness to
him; nor horror, even while he fancied her spirit to be imbued with
the same baneful essence that seemed to pervade her physical frame;
but a wild offspring of both love and horror that had each parent in it,
and burned like one and shivered like the other. Giovanni knew not
what to dread; still less did he know what to hope; yet hope and dread
kept a continual warfare in his breast, alternately vanquishing one
another and starting up afresh to renew the contest. Blessed are all
simple emotions, be they dark or bright! It is the lurid intermixture
of the two that produces the illuminating blaze of the infernal regions.

Sometimes he endeavored to assuage the fever of his spirit by
a rapid walk through the streets of Padua, or beyond its gates; his
footsteps kept time with the throbbings of his brain, so that the walk
was apt to accelerate itself to a race. One day, he found himself
arrested; his arm was seized by a portly personage who had turned
back on recognizing the young man, and expended much breath in
overtaking him.

'Signor Giovanni!—stay, my young friend!' cried he. 'Have you
forgotten me? That might well be the case, if I were as much altered
as yourself.'

It was Baglioni, whom Giovanni had avoided, ever since their first
meeting, from a doubt that the professor's sagacity would look too
deeply into his secrets. Endeavoring to recover himself, he stared

forth wildly from his inner world into the outer one, and spoke like a man in a dream.

'Yes; I am Giovanni Guasconti. You are Professor Pietro Baglioni. Now let me pass!'

'Not yet—not yet, Signor Giovanni Guasconti,' said the Professor, smiling, but at the same time scrutinizing the youth with an earnest glance.—'What; did I grow up side by side with your father, and shall his son pass me like a stranger, in these old streets of Padua? Stand still, Signor Giovanni; for we must have a word or two before we part.'

'Speedily, then, most worshipful Professor, speedily!' said Giovanni, with feverish impatience. 'Does not your worship see that I am in haste?'

Now, while he was speaking, there came a man in black along the street, stooping and moving feebly, like a person in inferior health. His face was all overspread with a most sickly and sallow hue, but yet so pervaded with an expression of piercing and active intellect, that an observer might easily have overlooked the merely physical attributes, and have seen only this wonderful energy. As he passed, this person exchanged a cold and distant salutation with Baglioni, but fixed his eyes upon Giovanni with an intentness that seemed to bring out whatever was within him worthy of notice. Nevertheless, there was a peculiar quietness in the look, as if taking merely a speculative, not a human interest, in the young man.

'It is Doctor Rappaccini!' whispered the Professor, when the stranger had passed.—'Has he ever seen your face before?'

'Not that I know,' answered Giovanni, starting at the name.

'He *has* seen you!—he must have seen you!' said Baglioni, hastily. 'For some purpose or other, this man of science is making a study of you. I know that look of his! It is the same that coldly illuminates his face, as he bends over a bird, a mouse, or a butterfly, which, in pursuance of some experiment, he has killed by the perfume of a flower;— a look as deep as nature itself, but without nature's warmth of love. Signor Giovanni, I will stake my life upon it, you are the subject of one of Rappaccini's experiments!'

'Will you make a fool of me?' cried Giovanni, passionately. '*That*, Signor Professor, were an untoward experiment.'

'Patience, patience!' replied the imperturbable Professor.—'I tell thee, my poor Giovanni, that Rappaccini has a scientific interest in thee. Thou hast fallen into fearful hands! And the Signora Beatrice? What part does she act in this mystery?'

But Guasconti, finding Baglioni's pertinacity intolerable, here broke away, and was gone before the Professor could again seize his arm. He looked after the young man intently, and shook his head.

'This must not be,' said Baglioni to himself. 'The youth is the son of my old friend, and shall not come to any harm from which the arcana of medical science can preserve him. Besides, it is too insufferable an impertinence in Rappaccini thus to snatch the lad out of my own hands, as I may say, and make use of him for his infernal experiments. This daughter of his! It shall be looked to. Perchance, most learned Rappaccini, I may foil you where you little dream of it!'

Meanwhile, Giovanni had pursued a circuitous route, and at length found himself at the door of his lodgings. As he crossed the threshold, he was met by old Lisabetta, who smirked and smiled, and was evidently desirous to attract his attention; vainly, however, as the ebullition of his feelings had momentarily subsided into a cold and dull vacuity. He turned his eyes full upon the withered face that was puckering itself into a smile, but seemed to behold it not. The old dame, therefore, laid her grasp upon his cloak.

'Signor!—Signor!' whispered she, still with a smile over the whole breadth of her visage, so that it looked not unlike a grotesque carving in wood, darkened by centuries—'Listen, Signor! There is a private entrance into the garden!'

'What do you say?' exclaimed Giovanni, turning quickly about, as if an inanimate thing should start into feverish life.—'A private entrance into Doctor Rappaccini's garden!'

'Hush! hush!—not so loud!' whispered Lisabetta, putting her hand over his mouth. 'Yes; into the worshipful Doctor's garden, where you may see all his fine shrubbery. Many a young man in Padua would give gold to be admitted among those flowers.'

Giovanni put a piece of gold into her hand.

'Show me the way,' said he.

A surmise, probably excited by his conversation with Baglioni, crossed his mind, that this interposition of old Lisabetta might perchance be connected with the intrigue, whatever were its nature, in which the Professor seemed to suppose that Doctor Rappaccini was involving him. But such a suspicion, though it disturbed Giovanni, was inadequate to restrain him. The instant he was aware of the possibility of approaching Beatrice, it seemed an absolute necessity of his existence to do so. It mattered not whether she were angel or demon;

he was irrevocably within her sphere, and must obey the law that whirled him onward, in ever lessening circles, towards a result which he did not attempt to foreshadow. And yet, strange to say, there came across him a sudden doubt, whether this intense interest on his part were not delusory—whether it were really of so deep and positive a nature as to justify him in now thrusting himself into an incalculable position—whether it were not merely the fantasy of a young man's brain, only slightly, or not at all, connected with his heart!

He paused—hesitated—turned half about—but again went on. His withered guide led him along several obscure passages, and finally undid a door, through which, as it was opened, there came the sight and sound of rustling leaves, with the broken sunshine glimmering among them. Giovanni stepped forth, and forcing himself through the entanglement of a shrub that wreathed its tendrils over the hidden entrance, he stood beneath his own window, in the open area of Doctor Rappaccini's garden.

How often is it the case, that, when impossibilities have come to pass, and dreams have condensed their misty substance into tangible realities, we find ourselves calm, and even coldly self-possessed, amid circumstances which it would have been a delirium of joy or agony to anticipate! Fate delights to thwart us thus. Passion will choose his own time to rush upon the scene, and lingers sluggishly behind, when an appropriate adjustment of events would seem to summon his appearance. So was it now with Giovanni. Day after day, his pulses had throbbed with feverish blood, at the improbable idea of an interview with Beatrice, and of standing with her, face to face, in this very garden, basking in the oriental sunshine of her beauty, and snatching from her full gaze the mystery which he deemed the riddle of his own existence. But now there was a singular and untimely equanimity within his breast. He threw a glance around the garden to discover if Beatrice or her father were present, and perceiving that he was alone, began a critical observation of the plants.

The aspect of one and all of them dissatisfied him; their gorgeousness seemed fierce, passionate, and even unnatural. There was hardly an individual shrub which a wanderer, straying by himself through a forest, would not have been startled to find growing wild, as if an unearthly face had glared at him out of the thicket. Several, also, would have shocked a delicate instinct by an appearance of artificialness, indicating that there had been such commixture, and, as it were, adultery of various vegetable species, that the production was no longer of God's making, but the monstrous offspring of man's depraved fancy, glowing with only an evil mockery of beauty. They were probably the result of experiment, which, in one or two cases, had succeeded in mingling plants individually lovely into a compound possessing the questionable and ominous character that distinguished the whole growth of the garden. In fine, Giovanni recognized but two or three plants in the collection, and those of a kind that he well knew to be poisonous. While busy with these contemplations, he heard the rustling of a silken garment, and turning, beheld Beatrice emerging from beneath the sculptured portal.

Giovanni had not considered with himself what should be his deportment; whether he should apologize for his intrusion into the garden, or assume that he was there with the privity, at least, if not by the desire, of Doctor Rappaccini or his daughter. But Beatrice's manner placed him at his ease, though leaving him still in doubt by what agency he had gained admittance. She came lightly along the path, and met him near the broken fountain. There was surprise in her face, but brightened by a simple and kind expression of pleasure.

'You are a connoisseur in flowers, Signor,' said Beatrice with a smile, alluding to the bouquet which he had flung her from the window. 'It is no marvel, therefore, if the sight of my father's rare collection has tempted you to take a nearer view. If he were here, he could tell you many strange and interesting facts as to the nature and habits of these shrubs, for he has spent a life-time in such studies, and this garden is his world.'

'And yourself, lady'—observed Giovanni—'if fame says true—you, likewise, are deeply skilled in the virtues indicated by these rich blossoms, and these spicy perfumes. Would you deign to be my instructress, I should prove an apter scholar than under Signor Rappaccini himself.'

'Are there such idle rumors?' asked Beatrice, with the music of a pleasant laugh. 'Do people say that I am skilled in my father's science of plants? What a jest is there! No; though I have grown up among these flowers, I know no more of them than their hues and perfume; and sometimes, methinks I would fain rid myself of even that small knowledge. There are many flowers here, and those not the least brilliant, that shock and offend me, when they meet my eye. But, pray, Signor, do not believe these stories about my science. Believe nothing of me save what you see with your own eyes.'

'And must I believe all that I have seen with my own eyes?' asked
Giovanni pointedly, while the recollection of former scenes made
him shrink. 'No, Signora, you demand too little of me. Bid me believe
nothing, save what comes from your own lips.'

It would appear that Beatrice understood him. There came
a deep flush to her cheek; but she looked full into Giovanni's eyes,
and responded to his gaze of uneasy suspicion with a queen-like
haughtiness.

'I do so bid you, Signor!' she replied. 'Forget whatever you may
have fancied in regard to me. If true to the outward senses, still it may
be false in its essence. But the words of Beatrice Rappaccini's lips are
true from the heart outward. Those you may believe!'

A fervor glowed in her whole aspect, and beamed upon Giovanni's
consciousness like the light of truth itself. But while she spoke, there
was a fragrance in the atmosphere around her rich and delightful,
though evanescent, yet which the young man, from an indefinable
reluctance, scarcely dared to draw into his lungs. It might be the odor
of the flowers. Could it be Beatrice's breath, which thus embalmed
her words with a strange richness, as if by steeping them in her heart?
A faintness passed like a shadow over Giovanni, and flitted away; he
seemed to gaze through the beautiful girl's eyes into her transparent
soul, and felt no more doubt or fear.

The tinge of passion that had colored Beatrice's manner vanished;
she became gay, and appeared to derive a pure delight from her communion with the youth, not unlike what the maiden of a lonely island*
might have felt, conversing with a voyager from the civilized world.
Evidently her experience of life had been confined within the limits
of that garden. She talked now about matters as simple as the daylight or summer-clouds, and now asked questions in reference to the
city, or Giovanni's distant home, his friends, his mother, and his sisters; questions indicating such seclusion, and such lack of familiarity
with modes and forms, that Giovanni responded as if to an infant.
Her spirit gushed out before him like a fresh rill, that was just catching its first glimpse of the sunlight, and wondering at the reflections of earth and sky which were flung into its bosom. There came
thoughts, too, from a deep source, and fantasies of a gem-like brilliancy, as if diamonds and rubies sparkled upward among the bubbles
of the fountain. Ever and anon, there gleamed across the young man's
mind a sense of wonder, that he should be walking side by side with

the being who had so wrought upon his imagination—whom he had idealized in such hues of terror—in whom he had positively witnessed such manifestations of dreadful attributes—that he should be conversing with Beatrice like a brother, and should find her so human and so maiden-like. But such reflections were only momentary; the effect of her character was too real, not to make itself familiar at once.

In this free intercourse, they had strayed through the garden, and now, after many turns among its avenues, were come to the shattered fountain, beside which grew the magnificent shrub with its treasury of glowing blossoms. A fragrance was diffused from it, which Giovanni recognized as identical with that which he had attributed to Beatrice's breath, but incomparably more powerful. As her eyes fell upon it, Giovanni beheld her press her hand to her bosom, as if her heart were throbbing suddenly and painfully.

'For the first time in my life,' murmured she, addressing the shrub, 'I had forgotten thee!'

'I remember, Signora,' said Giovanni, 'that you once promised to reward me with one of these living gems for the bouquet, which I had the happy boldness to fling to your feet. Permit me now to pluck it as a memorial of this interview.'

He made a step towards the shrub, with extended hand. But Beatrice darted forward, uttering a shriek that went through his heart like a dagger. She caught his hand, and drew it back with the whole force of her slender figure. Giovanni felt her touch thrilling through his fibres.

'Touch it not!' exclaimed she, in a voice of agony. 'Not for thy life! It is fatal!'

Then, hiding her face, she fled from him, and vanished beneath the sculptured portal. As Giovanni followed her with his eyes, he beheld the emaciated figure and pale intelligence of Doctor Rappaccini, who had been watching the scene, he knew not how long, within the shadow of the entrance.

No sooner was Guasconti alone in his chamber, than the image of Beatrice came back to his passionate musings, invested with all the witchery that had been gathering around it ever since his first glimpse of her, and now likewise imbued with a tender warmth of girlish womanhood. She was human: her nature was endowed with all gentle and feminine qualities; she was worthiest to be worshipped; she was capable, surely, on her part, of the height and heroism of love. Those tokens, which he had hitherto considered as proofs of a frightful peculiarity in her physical and moral system, were now either forgotten, or, by the subtle sophistry of passion, transmuted into a golden crown of enchantment, rendering Beatrice the more admirable, by so much as she was the more unique. Whatever had looked ugly, was now beautiful; or, if incapable of such a change, it stole away and hid itself among those shapeless half-ideas, which throng the dim region beyond the daylight of our perfect consciousness. Thus did Giovanni spend the night, nor fell asleep, until the dawn had begun to awake the slumbering flowers in Doctor Rappaccini's garden, whither his dreams doubtless led him. Up rose the sun in his due season, and flinging his beams upon the young man's eyelids, awoke him to a sense of pain. When thoroughly aroused, he became sensible of a burning and tingling agony in his hand—in his right hand—the very hand which Beatrice had grasped in her own, when he was on the point of plucking one of the gem-like flowers. On the back of that hand there was now a purple print, like that of four small fingers, and the likeness of a slender thumb upon his wrist.

Oh, how stubbornly does love—or even that cunning semblance of love which flourishes in the imagination, but strikes no depth of root into the heart—how stubbornly does it hold its faith, until the moment come, when it is doomed to vanish into thin mist! Giovanni wrapt a handkerchief about his hand, and wondered what evil thing had stung him, and soon forgot his pain in a reverie of Beatrice.

After the first interview, a second was in the inevitable course of what we call fate. A third; a fourth; and a meeting with Beatrice in the garden was no longer an incident in Giovanni's daily life, but the whole space in which he might be said to live; for the anticipation and memory of that ecstatic hour made up the remainder. Nor was it otherwise with the daughter of Rappaccini. She watched for the youth's appearance, and flew to his side with confidence as unreserved as if they had been playmates from early infancy—as if they were such playmates still. If, by any unwonted chance, he failed to come at the appointed moment, she stood beneath the window, and sent up the rich sweetness of her tones to float around him in his chamber, and echo and reverberate throughout his heart—'Giovanni! Giovanni! Why tarriest thou? Come down!'—And down he hastened into that Eden of poisonous flowers.

But, with all this intimate familiarity, there was still a reserve in Beatrice's demeanor, so rigidly and invariably sustained, that the idea of infringing it scarcely occurred to his imagination. By all appreciable signs, they loved; they had looked love, with eyes that conveyed the holy secret from the depths of one soul into the depths of the other, as if it were too sacred to be whispered by the way; they had even spoken love, in those gushes of passion when their spirits darted forth in articulated breath, like tongues of long-hidden flame; and yet there had been no seal of lips, no clasp of hands, nor any slightest caress, such as love claims and hallows. He had never touched one of the gleaming ringlets of her hair; her garment—so marked was the physical barrier between them—had never been waved against him by a breeze. On the few occasions when Giovanni had seemed tempted to overstep the limit, Beatrice grew so sad, so stern, and withal wore such a look of desolate separation, shuddering at itself, that not a spoken word was requisite to repel him. At such times, he was startled at the horrible suspicions that rose, monster-like, out of the caverns of his heart, and stared him in the face; his love grew thin and faint as the morning-mist; his doubts alone had substance. But when Beatrice's face brightened again, after the momentary shadow, she was transformed at once from the mysterious, questionable being, whom he had watched with so much awe and horror; she was now the beautiful and unsophisticated girl, whom he felt that his spirit knew with a certainty beyond all other knowledge.

A considerable time had now passed since Giovanni's last meeting with Baglioni. One morning, however, he was disagreeably surprised by a visit from the Professor, whom he had scarcely thought of for whole weeks, and would willingly have forgotten still longer. Given up, as he had long been, to a pervading excitement, he could tolerate no companions, except upon condition of their perfect sympathy with his present state of feeling. Such sympathy was not to be expected from Professor Baglioni.

The visitor chatted carelessly, for a few moments, about the gossip of the city and the University, and then took up another topic.

'I have been reading an old classic author lately,' said he, 'and met with a story that strangely interested me.* Possibly you may remember it. It is of an Indian prince, who sent a beautiful woman as a present to Alexander the Great.* She was as lovely as the dawn, and gorgeous as the sunset; but what especially distinguished her was a certain rich perfume in her breath—richer than a garden of Persian roses. Alexander, as was natural to a youthful conqueror, fell in love at first sight with this magnificent stranger. But a certain sage physician, happening to be present, discovered a terrible secret in regard to her.'

'And what was that?' asked Giovanni, turning his eyes downward to avoid those of the Professor.

'That this lovely woman,' continued Baglioni, with emphasis, 'had been nourished with poisons from her birth upward, until her whole nature was so imbued with them, that she herself had become the deadliest poison in existence. Poison was her element of life. With that rich perfume of her breath, she blasted the very air. Her love would have been poison!—her embrace death! Is not this a marvellous tale?'

'A childish fable,' answered Giovanni, nervously starting from his chair. 'I marvel how your worship finds time to read such nonsense, among your graver studies.'

'By the bye,' said the Professor, looking uneasily about him, 'what singular fragrance is this in your apartment? Is it the perfume of your gloves? It is faint, but delicious, and yet, after all, by no means agreeable. Were I to breathe it long, methinks it would make me ill. It is like the breath of a flower—but I see no flowers in the chamber.'

'Nor are there any,' replied Giovanni, who had turned pale as the Professor spoke; 'nor, I think, is there any fragrance, except in your worship's imagination. Odors, being a sort of element combined of the sensual and the spiritual, are apt to deceive us in this manner. The recollection of a perfume—the bare idea of it—may easily be mistaken for a present reality.'

'Aye; but my sober imagination does not often play such tricks,' said Baglioni; 'and were I to fancy any kind of odor, it would be that of some vile apothecary drug, wherewith my fingers are likely enough to be imbued. Our worshipful friend Rappaccini, as I have heard, tinctures his medicaments with odors richer than those of Araby.* Doubtless, likewise, the fair and learned Signora Beatrice would minister to her patients with draughts as sweet as a maiden's breath. But wo to him that sips them!'

Giovanni's face evinced many contending emotions. The tone in which the Professor alluded to the pure and lovely daughter of Rappaccini was a torture to his soul; and yet, the intimation of a view of her character, opposite to his own, gave instantaneous distinctness to a thousand dim suspicions, which now grinned at him like so many demons. But he strove hard to quell them, and to respond to Baglioni with a true lover's perfect faith.

'Signor Professor,' said he, 'you were my father's friend—perchance, too, it is your purpose to act a friendly part towards his son. I would fain feel nothing towards you save respect and deference. But I pray you to observe, Signor, that there is one subject on which we must not speak. You know not the Signora Beatrice. You cannot, therefore, estimate the wrong—the blasphemy, I may even say—that is offered to her character by a light or injurious word.'

'Giovanni!—my poor Giovanni!' answered the Professor, with a calm expression of pity, 'I know this wretched girl far better than yourself. You shall hear the truth in respect to the poisoner Rappaccini, and his poisonous daughter. Yes; poisonous as she is beautiful! Listen; for even should you do violence to my grey hairs, it shall not silence me. That old fable of the Indian woman has become a truth, by the deep and deadly science of Rappaccini, and in the person of the lovely Beatrice!'

Giovanni groaned and hid his face.

'Her father,' continued Baglioni, 'was not restrained by natural affection from offering up his child, in this horrible manner, as the victim of his insane zeal for science. For—let us do him justice—he is as true a man of science as ever distilled his own heart in an alembic.* What, then, will be your fate? Beyond a doubt, you are selected as the material of some new experiment. Perhaps the result is to be death—perhaps a fate more awful still! Rappaccini, with what he calls the interest of science before his eyes, will hesitate at nothing.'

'It is a dream!' muttered Giovanni to himself, 'surely it is a dream!'

'But,' resumed the professor, 'be of good cheer, son of my friend! It is not yet too late for the rescue. Possibly, we may even succeed in bringing back this miserable child within the limits of ordinary nature, from which her father's madness has estranged her. Behold this little silver vase! It was wrought by the hands of the renowned Benvenuto Cellini,* and is well worthy to be a love-gift to the fairest dame in Italy. But its contents are invaluable. One little sip of this antidote would have rendered the most virulent poisons of the Borgias* innocuous. Doubt not that it will be as efficacious against those of Rappaccini. Bestow the vase, and the precious liquid within it, on your Beatrice, and hopefully await the result.'

Baglioni laid a small, exquisitely wrought silver phial on the table, and withdrew, leaving what he had said to produce its effect upon the young man's mind.

'We will thwart Rappaccini yet!' thought he, chuckling to himself, as he descended the stairs. 'But, let us confess the truth of him, he is a wonderful man!—a wonderful man indeed! A vile empiric,* however, in his practice, and therefore not to be tolerated by those who respect the good old rules of the medical profession!'

Throughout Giovanni's whole acquaintance with Beatrice, he had occasionally, as we have said, been haunted by dark surmises as to her character. Yet, so thoroughly had she made herself felt by him as a simple, natural, most affectionate and guileless creature, that the image now held up by Professor Baglioni, looked as strange and incredible, as if it were not in accordance with his own original conception. True, there were ugly recollections connected with his first glimpses of the beautiful girl; he could not quite forget the bouquet that withered in her grasp, and the insect that perished amid the sunny air, by no ostensible agency save the fragrance of her breath. These incidents, however, dissolving in the pure light of her character, had no longer the efficacy of facts, but were acknowledged as mistaken fantasies, by whatever testimony of the senses they might appear to be substantiated. There is something truer and more real, than what we can see with the eyes, and touch with the finger. On such better evidence, had Giovanni founded his confidence in Beatrice, though rather by the necessary force of her high attributes, than by any deep and generous faith on his part. But, now, his spirit was incapable of sustaining itself at the height to which the early enthusiasm of passion had exalted it; he fell down, grovelling among earthly doubts, and defiled therewith the pure whiteness of Beatrice's image. Not that he gave her up; he did but distrust. He resolved to institute some decisive test that should satisfy him, once for all, whether there were those dreadful peculiarities in her physical nature, which could not be supposed to exist without some corresponding monstrosity of soul. His eyes, gazing down afar, might have deceived him as to the lizard, the insect, and the flowers. But if he could witness, at the distance of a few paces, the sudden blight of one fresh and healthful flower in Beatrice's hand, there would be room for no further question. With this idea, he hastened to the florist's, and purchased a bouquet that was still gemmed with the morning dew-drops.

It was now the customary hour of his daily interview with Beatrice. Before descending into the garden, Giovanni failed not to look at his figure in the mirror; a vanity to be expected in a beautiful young man, yet, as displaying itself at that troubled and feverish moment, the token of a certain shallowness of feeling and insincerity of character. He did gaze, however, and said to himself, that his features had never before possessed so rich a grace, nor his eyes such vivacity, nor his cheeks so warm a hue of superabundant life.

'At least,' thought he, 'her poison has not yet insinuated itself into my system. I am no flower to perish in her grasp!'

With that thought, he turned his eyes on the bouquet, which he had never once laid aside from his hand. A thrill of indefinable horror shot through his frame, on perceiving that those dewy flowers were already beginning to droop; they wore the aspect of things that had been fresh and lovely, yesterday. Giovanni grew white as marble, and stood motionless before the mirror, staring at his own reflection there, as at the likeness of something frightful. He remembered Baglioni's remark about the fragrance that seemed to pervade the chamber. It must have been the poison in his breath! Then he shuddered—shuddered at himself! Recovering from his stupor, he began to watch, with curious eye, a spider that was busily at work, hanging its web from the antique cornice of the apartment, crossing and re-crossing the artful system of interwoven lines, as vigorous and active a spider as ever dangled from an old ceiling. Giovanni bent towards the insect, and emitted a deep, long breath. The spider suddenly ceased its toil; the web vibrated with a tremor originating in the body of the small artizan. Again Giovanni sent forth a breath, deeper, longer, and imbued with a venomous feeling out of his heart; he knew not whether he were wicked or only desperate. The spider made a convulsive gripe with his limbs, and hung dead across the window.

'Accursed! Accursed!' muttered Giovanni, addressing himself. 'Hast thou grown so poisonous, that this deadly insect perishes by thy breath?'

At that moment, a rich, sweet voice came floating up from the garden:—

'Giovanni! Giovanni! It is past the hour! Why tarriest thou! Come down!'

'Yes,' muttered Giovanni again. 'She is the only being whom my breath may not slay! Would that it might!'

He rushed down, and in an instant, was standing before the bright and loving eyes of Beatrice. A moment ago, his wrath and despair had been so fierce that he could have desired nothing so much as to wither her by a glance. But, with her actual presence, there came influences which had too real an existence to be at once shaken off; recollections of the delicate and benign power of her feminine nature, which had so often enveloped him in a religious calm; recollections of many a holy and passionate outgush* of her heart, when the pure fountain had been unsealed from its depths, and made visible in its transparency to his mental eye; recollections which, had Giovanni known how to estimate them, would have assured him that all this ugly mystery was but an earthly illusion, and that, whatever mist of evil might seem to have gathered over her, the real Beatrice was a heavenly angel. Incapable as he was of such high faith, still her presence had not utterly lost its magic. Giovanni's rage was quelled into an aspect of sullen insensibility. Beatrice, with a quick spiritual sense, immediately felt that there was a gulf of blackness between them, which neither he nor she could pass. They walked on together, sad and silent, and came thus to the marble fountain, and to its pool of water on the ground, in the midst of which grew the shrub that bore gem-like blossoms. Giovanni was affrighted at the eager enjoyment—the appetite, as it were—with which he found himself inhaling the fragrance of the flowers.

'Beatrice,' asked he abruptly, 'whence came this shrub?'

'My father created it,' answered she, with simplicity.

'Created it! created it!' repeated Giovanni. 'What mean you, Beatrice?'

'He is a man fearfully acquainted with the secrets of nature,' replied Beatrice; 'and, at the hour when I first drew breath, this plant sprang from the soil, the offspring of his science, of his intellect, while I was but his earthly child. Approach it not!' continued she, observing with terror that Giovanni was drawing nearer to the shrub. 'It has qualities that you little dream of. But I, dearest Giovanni,—I grew up and blossomed with the plant, and was nourished with its breath. It was my sister, and I loved it with a human affection: for—alas! hast thou not suspected it? there was an awful doom.'

Here Giovanni frowned so darkly upon her that Beatrice paused and trembled. But her faith in his tenderness reassured her, and made her blush that she had doubted for an instant.

'There was an awful doom,' she continued,— 'the effect of my father's fatal love of science—which estranged me from all society of my kind. Until Heaven sent thee, dearest Giovanni, Oh! how lonely was thy poor Beatrice!'

'Was it a hard doom?' asked Giovanni, fixing his eyes upon her.

'Only of late have I known how hard it was,' answered she tenderly. 'Oh, yes; but my heart was torpid, and therefore quiet.'

Giovanni's rage broke forth from his sullen gloom like a lightning-flash out of a dark cloud.

'Accursed one!' cried he, with venomous scorn and anger. 'And finding thy solitude wearisome, thou hast severed me, likewise, from all the warmth of life, and enticed me into thy region of unspeakable horror!'

'Giovanni!' exclaimed Beatrice, turning her large bright eyes upon his face. The force of his words had not found its way into her mind; she was merely thunder-struck.

'Yes, poisonous thing!' repeated Giovanni, beside himself with passion. 'Thou hast done it! Thou hast blasted me! Thou hast filled my veins with poison! Thou hast made me as hateful, as ugly, as loathsome and deadly a creature as thyself,—a world's wonder of hideous monstrosity! Now—if our breath be happily as fatal to ourselves as to all others—let us join our lips in one kiss of unutterable hatred, and so die!'

'What has befallen me?' murmured Beatrice, with a low moan out of her heart. 'Holy Virgin pity me, a poor heart-broken child!'

'Thou! Dost thou pray?' cried Giovanni, still with the same fiendish scorn. 'Thy very prayers, as they come from thy lips, taint the atmosphere with death. Yes, yes; let us pray! Let us to church, and dip our fingers in the holy water at the portal! They that come after us will perish as by a pestilence. Let us sign crosses in the air! It will be scattering curses abroad in the likeness of holy symbols!'

'Giovanni,' said Beatrice calmly, for her grief was beyond passion, 'why dost thou join thyself with me thus in those terrible words? I, it is true, am the horrible thing thou namest me. But thou!—what hast thou to do, save with one other shudder at my hideous misery, to go forth out of the garden and mingle with thy race, and forget that there ever crawled on earth such a monster as poor Beatrice?'

'Dost thou pretend ignorance?' asked Giovanni, scowling upon her. 'Behold! This power have I gained from the pure daughter of Rappaccini!'

There was a swarm of summer-insects flitting through the air, in search of the food promised by the flower-odors of the fatal garden. They circled round Giovanni's head, and were evidently attracted towards him by the same influence which had drawn them, for an instant, within the sphere of several of the shrubs. He sent forth a breath among them, and smiled bitterly at Beatrice, as at least a score of the insects fell dead upon the ground.

'I see it! I see it!' shrieked Beatrice. 'It is my father's fatal science? No, no, Giovanni; it was not I! Never, never! I dreamed only to love thee, and be with thee a little time, and so to let thee pass away, leaving but thine image in mine heart. For, Giovanni—believe it—though my body be nourished with poison, my spirit is God's creature, and craves love as its daily food. But my father!—he has united us in this fearful sympathy. Yes; spurn me!—tread upon me!—kill me! Oh, what is death, after such words as thine? But it was not I! Not for a world of bliss would I have done it!'

Giovanni's passion had exhausted itself in its outburst from his lips. There now came across him a sense, mournful, and not without tenderness, of the intimate and peculiar relationship between Beatrice and himself. They stood, as it were, in an utter solitude, which would be made none the less solitary by the densest throng of human life. Ought not, then, the desert of humanity around them to press this insulated pair closer together? If they should be cruel to one another, who was there to be kind to them? Besides, thought Giovanni, might there not still be a hope of his returning within the limits of ordinary nature, and leading Beatrice—the redeemed Beatrice—by the hand? Oh, weak, and selfish, and unworthy spirit, that could dream of an earthly union and earthly happiness as possible, after such deep love had been so bitterly wronged as was Beatrice's love by Giovanni's blighting words! No, no; there could be no such hope. She must pass heavily, with that broken heart, across the borders—she must bathe her hurts in some fount of Paradise, and forget her grief in the light of immortality—and *there* be well!

But Giovanni did not know it.

'Dear Beatrice,' said he, approaching her, while she shrank away, as always at his approach, but now with a different impulse—'dearest Beatrice, our fate is not yet so desperate. Behold! There is a medicine, potent, as a wise physician has assured me, and almost divine in its efficacy. It is composed of ingredients the most opposite to those by which thy awful father has brought this calamity upon thee and me. It is distilled of blessed herbs. Shall we not quaff it together, and thus be purified from evil?'

'Give it me!' said Beatrice, extending her hand to receive the little silver phial which Giovanni took from his bosom. She added, with a peculiar emphasis: 'I will drink—but do thou await the result.'

She put Baglioni's antidote to her lips; and, at the same moment, the figure of Rappaccini emerged from the portal, and came slowly towards the marble fountain. As he drew near, the pale man of science seemed to gaze with a triumphant expression at the beautiful youth and maiden, as might an artist who should spend his life in achieving a picture or a group of statuary, and finally be satisfied with his success. He paused—his bent form grew erect with conscious power, he spread out his hand over them, in the attitude of a father imploring a blessing upon his children. But those were the same hands that had thrown poison into the stream of their lives! Giovanni trembled. Beatrice shuddered very nervously, and pressed her hand upon her heart.

'My daughter,' said Rappaccini, 'thou art no longer lonely in the world! Pluck one of those precious gems from thy sister shrub, and bid thy bridegroom wear it in his bosom. It will not harm him now! My science, and the sympathy between thee and him, have so wrought within his system, that he now stands apart from common men, as thou dost, daughter of my pride and triumph, from ordinary women. Pass on, then, through the world, most dear to one another, and dreadful to all besides!'

'My father,' said Beatrice, feebly—and still, as she spoke, she kept her hand upon her heart—'wherefore didst thou inflict this miserable doom upon thy child?'

'Miserable!' exclaimed Rappaccini. 'What mean you, foolish girl? Dost thou deem it misery to be endowed with marvellous gifts, against which no power nor strength could avail an enemy? Misery, to be able to quell the mightiest with a breath? Misery, to be as terrible as thou art beautiful? Wouldst thou, then, have preferred the condition of a weak woman, exposed to all evil, and capable of none?'

'I would fain have been loved, not feared,' murmured Beatrice, sinking down upon the ground. 'But now it matters not; I am going, father, where the evil, which thou hast striven to mingle with my being, will pass away like a dream—like the fragrance of these poisonous flowers, which will no longer taint my breath among the flowers of Eden. Farewell, Giovanni! Thy words of hatred are like lead within my heart—but they, too, will fall away as I ascend. Oh, was there not, from the first, more poison in thy nature than in mine?'

To Beatrice—so radically had her earthly part been wrought upon by Rappaccini's skill—as poison had been life, so the powerful antidote was death. And thus the poor victim of man's ingenuity and of thwarted nature, and of the fatality that attends all such efforts of perverted wisdom, perished there, at the feet of her father and Giovanni. Just at that moment. Professor Pietro Baglioni looked forth from the window, and called loudly, in a tone of triumph mixed with horror, to the thunder-stricken man of science:—

'Rappaccini! Rappaccini! And is *this* the upshot of your experiment?'

EDGAR ALLAN POE

*THE FACTS IN THE CASE OF M. VALDEMAR**

OF course I shall not pretend to consider it any matter for wonder, that the extraordinary case of M. Valdemar has excited discussion. It would have been a miracle had it not—especially under the circumstances. Through the desire of all parties concerned, to keep the affair from the public, at least for the present, or until we had farther opportunities for investigation—through our endeavors to effect this—a garbled or exaggerated account made its way into society, and became the source of many unpleasant misrepresentations, and, very naturally, of a great deal of disbelief.

It is now rendered necessary that I give the *facts*—as far as I comprehend them myself. They are, succinctly, these:

My attention, for the last three years, had been repeatedly drawn to the subject of Mesmerism; and, about nine months ago, it occurred to me, quite suddenly, that in the series of experiments made hitherto, there had been a very remarkable and most unaccountable omission:—no person had as yet been mesmerized *in articulo mortis.** It remained to be seen, first, whether, in such condition, there existed in the patient any susceptibility to the magnetic influence; secondly, whether, if any existed, it was impaired or increased by the condition; thirdly, to what extent, or for how long a period, the encroachments of Death might be arrested by the process. There were other points to be ascertained, but these most excited my curiosity—the last in especial, from the immensely important character of its consequences.

In looking around me for some subject by whose means I might test these particulars, I was brought to think of my friend, M. Ernest Valdemar, the well-known compiler of the 'Bibliotheca Forensica,' and author (under the *nom de plume* of Issachar Marx) of the Polish versions of 'Wallenstein' and 'Gargantua.'* M. Valdemar, who has resided principally at Harlaem, N. Y.,* since the year 1839, is (or was) particularly noticeable for the extreme spareness of his person—his lower limbs much resembling those of John Randolph;* and, also, for the whiteness of his whiskers, in violent contrast to the blackness of his hair—the latter, in consequence, being very generally mistaken for a wig. His temperament was markedly nervous, and rendered him a good subject for mesmeric experiment. On two or three occasions I had put him to sleep with little difficulty, but was disappointed in other results which his peculiar constitution had naturally led me to anticipate. His will was at no period positively, or thoroughly, under my control, and in regard to *clairvoyance*, I could accomplish with him nothing to be relied upon. I always attributed my failure at these points to the disordered state of his health. For some months previous to my becoming acquainted with him, his physicians had declared him in a confirmed phthisis.* It was his custom, indeed, to speak calmly of his approaching dissolution, as of a matter neither to be avoided nor regretted.

When the ideas to which I have alluded first occurred to me, it was of course very natural that I should think of M. Valdemar. I knew the steady philosophy of the man too well to apprehend any scruples from *him*; and he had no relatives in America who would be likely to interfere. I spoke to him frankly upon the subject; and, to my surprise, his interest seemed vividly excited. I say to my surprise; for, although he had always yielded his person freely to my experiments, he had never before given me any tokens of sympathy with what I did. His disease was of that character which would admit of exact calculation in respect to the epoch of its termination in death; and it was finally arranged between us that he would send for me about twenty-four hours before the period announced by his physicians as that of his decease.

It is now rather more than seven months since I received, from M. Valdemar himself, the subjoined note:

MY DEAR P——,
You may as well come *now*. D——and F——* are agreed that I cannot hold out beyond to-morrow midnight; and I think they have hit the time very nearly.
VALDEMAR.

I received this note within half an hour after it was written, and in fifteen minutes more I was in the dying man's chamber. I had not seen him for ten days, and was appalled by the fearful alteration which the brief interval had wrought in him. His face wore a leaden hue; the eyes were utterly lustreless; and the emaciation was so extreme that the skin had been broken through by the cheek-bones. His expectoration was excessive. The pulse was barely perceptible. He retained, nevertheless, in a very remarkable manner, both his mental power and a certain degree of physical strength. He spoke with distinctness—took some palliative medicincs without aid—and, when I entered the room, was occupied in penciling memoranda in a pocket-book.* He was propped up in the bed by pillows. Doctors D——and F——were in attendance.

After pressing Valdemar's hand, I took these gentlemen aside, and obtained from them a minute account of the patient's condition. The left lung had been for eighteen months in a semi-osseous or cartilaginous state, and was, of course, entirely useless for all purposes of vitality. The right, in its upper portion, was also partially, if not thoroughly, ossified, while the lower region was merely a mass of purulent tubercles, running one into another. Several extensive perforations existed; and, at one point, permanent adhesion to the ribs had taken place. These appearances in the right lobe were of comparatively recent date. The ossification had proceeded with very unusual rapidity; no sign of it had been discovered a month before, and the adhesion had only been observed during the three previous days. Independently of the phthisis, the patient was suspected of aneurism of the aorta; but on this point the osseous symptoms rendered an exact diagnosis impossible. It was the opinion of both physicians that M. Valdemar would die about midnight on the morrow (Sunday). It was then seven o'clock on Saturday evening.

On quitting the invalid's bed-side to hold conversation with myself, Doctors D——and F——had bidden him a final farewell. It had not been their intention to return; but, at my request, they agreed to look in upon the patient about ten the next night.

When they had gone, I spoke freely with M. Valdemar on the subject of his approaching dissolution, as well as, more particularly, of the experiment proposed. He still professed himself quite willing and even anxious to have it made, and urged me to commence it at once. A male and a female nurse were in attendance; but I did not feel myself altogether at liberty to engage in a task of this character with no more reliable witnesses than these people, in case of sudden accident, might prove. I therefore postponed operations until about eight the next night, when the arrival of a medical student with whom I had some acquaintance, (Mr. Theodore L——l,)* relieved me from farther embarrassment. It had been my design, originally, to wait for the physicians; but I was induced to proceed, first, by the urgent entreaties of M. Valdemar, and secondly, by my conviction that I had not a moment to lose, as he was evidently sinking fast.

Mr. L——l was so kind as to accede to my desire that he would take notes of all that occurred; and it is from his memoranda that what I now have to relate is, for the most part, either condensed or copied *verbatim*.

It wanted about five minutes of eight when, taking the patient's hand, I begged him to state, as distinctly as he could, to Mr. L——l, whether he (M. Valdemar) was entirely willing that I should make the experiment of mesmerizing him in his then condition.

He replied feebly, yet quite audibly, 'Yes, I wish to be mesmerized'— adding immediately afterwards, 'I fear you have deferred it too long.'

While he spoke thus, I commenced the passes* which I had already found most effectual in subduing him. He was evidently influenced with the first lateral stroke of my hand across his forehead; but although I exerted all my powers, no farther perceptible effect was induced until some minutes after ten o'clock, when Doctors D——and F——called, according to appointment. I explained to them, in a few words, what I designed, and as they opposed no objection, saying that the patient was already in the death agony, I proceeded without hesitation—exchanging, however, the lateral passes for downward ones, and directing my gaze entirely into the right eye of the sufferer.

By this time his pulse was imperceptible and his breathing was stertorous, and at intervals of half a minute.

This condition was nearly unaltered for a quarter of an hour. At the expiration of this period, however, a natural although a very deep sigh escaped the bosom of the dying man, and the stertorous breathing ceased—that is to say, its stertorousness was no longer apparent; the intervals were undiminished. The patient's extremities were of an icy coldness.

At five minutes before eleven I perceived unequivocal signs of the mesmeric influence. The glassy roll of the eye was changed for that expression of uneasy *inward* examination which is never seen except in cases of sleep-waking,* and which it is quite impossible to mistake. With a few rapid lateral passes I made the lids quiver, as in incipient sleep, and with a few more I closed them altogether. I was not satisfied, however, with this, but continued the manipulations vigorously, and with the fullest exertion of the will, until I had completely stiffened the limbs of the slumberer, after placing them in a seemingly easy position. The legs were at full length; the arms were nearly so, and reposed on the bed at a moderate distance from the loins. The head was very slightly elevated.

When I had accomplished this, it was fully midnight, and I requested the gentlemen present to examine M. Valdemar's condition. After a few experiments, they admitted him to be in an unusually perfect state of mesmeric trance. The curiosity of both the physicians was greatly excited. Dr. D——resolved at once to remain with the patient all night, while Dr. F——took leave with a promise to return at day-break. Mr. L——l and the nurses remained.

We left M. Valdemar entirely undisturbed until about three o'clock in the morning, when I approached him and found him in precisely the same condition as when Dr. F——went away—that is to say, he lay in the same position; the pulse was imperceptible; the breathing was gentle (scarcely noticeable, unless through the application of a mirror to the lips); the eyes were closed naturally; and the limbs were as rigid and as cold as marble. Still, the general appearance was certainly not that of death.

As I approached M. Valdemar I made a kind of half effort to influence his right arm into pursuit of my own, as I passed the latter gently to and fro above his person. In such experiments with this patient I had never perfectly succeeded before, and assuredly I had little thought of succeeding now; but to my astonishment, his arm very readily, although feebly, followed every direction I assigned it with mine. I determined to hazard a few words of conversation.

'M. Valdemar,' I said, 'are you asleep?' He made no answer, but I perceived a tremor about the lips, and was thus induced to repeat the question, again and again. At its third repetition, his whole frame was agitated by a very slight shivering; the eye-lids unclosed themselves so far as to display a white line of the ball; the lips moved sluggishly, and from between them, in a barely audible whisper, issued the words:

'Yes;—asleep now. Do not wake me!—let me die so!'

I here felt the limbs and found them as rigid as ever. The right arm, as before, obeyed the direction of my hand. I questioned the sleep-waker again:

'Do you still feel pain in the breast, M. Valdemar?'

The answer now was immediate, but even less audible than before:

'No pain—I am dying.'

I did not think it advisable to disturb him farther just then, and nothing more was said or done until the arrival of Dr. F——, who came a little before sunrise, and expressed unbounded astonishment at finding the patient still alive. After feeling the pulse and applying a mirror to the lips, he requested me to speak to the sleep-waker again. I did so, saying:

'M. Valdemar, do you still sleep?'

As before, some minutes elapsed ere a reply was made; and during the interval the dying man seemed to be collecting his energies to speak. At my fourth repetition of the question, he said very faintly, almost inaudibly:

'Yes; still asleep—dying.'

It was now the opinion, or rather the wish, of the physicians, that M. Valdemar should be suffered to remain undisturbed in his present apparently tranquil condition, until death should supervene—and this, it was generally agreed, must now take place within a few minutes. I concluded, however, to speak to him once more, and merely repeated my previous question.

While I spoke, there came a marked change over the countenance of the sleep-waker. The eyes rolled themselves slowly open, the pupils disappearing upwardly; the skin generally assumed a cadaverous hue, resembling not so much parchment as white paper; and the circular hectic spots which, hitherto, had been strongly defined in the centre of each cheek, *went out* at once. I use this expression, because the suddenness of their departure put me in mind of nothing so much as the extinguishment of a candle by a puff of the breath. The upper lip, at the same time, writhed itself away from the teeth, which it had previously covered completely; while the lower jaw fell with an audible jerk, leaving the mouth widely extended, and disclosing in full view the swollen and blackened tongue. I presume that no member of the party then present had been unaccustomed to death-bed horrors; but so hideous beyond conception was the appearance of M. Valdemar at this moment, that there was a general shrinking back from the region of the bed.

I now feel that I have reached a point of this narrative at which every reader will be startled into positive disbelief. It is my business, however, simply to proceed.

There was no longer the faintest sign of vitality in M. Valdemar; and concluding him to be dead, we were consigning him to the charge of the nurses, when a strong vibratory motion was observable in the tongue. This continued for perhaps a minute. At the expiration of this period, there issued from the distended and motionless jaws a voice—such as it would be madness in me to attempt describing. There are, indeed, two or three epithets which might be considered as applicable to it in part; I might say, for example, that the sound was harsh, and broken and hollow; but the hideous whole is indescribable, for the simple reason that no similar sounds have ever jarred upon the ear of humanity. There were two particulars, nevertheless, which I thought then, and still think, might fairly be stated as characteristic of the intonation—as well adapted to convey some idea of its unearthly peculiarity. In the first place, the voice seemed to reach our ears—at least mine—from a vast distance, or from some deep cavern within the earth. In the second place, it impressed me (I fear, indeed, that it will be impossible to make myself comprehended) as gelatinous or glutinous matters impress the sense of touch.

I have spoken both of 'sound' and of 'voice.' I mean to say that the sound was one of distinct—of even wonderfully, thrillingly distinct—syllabification. M. Valdemar *spoke*—obviously in reply to the question I had propounded to him a few minutes before. I had asked him, it will be remembered, if he still slept. He now said:

'Yes;—no;—I *have been* sleeping—and now—now—*I am dead*.'

No person present even affected to deny, or attempted to repress, the unutterable, shuddering horror which these few words, thus uttered, were so well calculated to convey. Mr. L——l (the student) swooned. The nurses immediately left the chamber, and could not be induced to return. My own impressions I would not pretend to render intelligible to the reader. For nearly an hour, we busied ourselves, silently—without the utterance of a word—in endeavors to revive Mr. L——l. When he came to himself, we addressed ourselves again to an investigation of M. Valdemar's condition.

It remained in all respects as I have last described it, with the exception that the mirror no longer afforded evidence of respiration. An attempt to draw blood from the arm failed. I should mention, too, that this limb was no farther subject to my will. I endeavored in vain to make it follow the direction of my hand. The only real indication, indeed, of the mesmeric influence, was now found in the vibratory movement of the tongue, whenever I addressed M. Valdemar a question. He seemed to be making an effort at reply, but had no longer sufficient volition. To queries put to him by any other person than myself he seemed utterly insensible—although I endeavored to place each member of the company in mesmeric *rapport** with him. I believe that I have now related all that is necessary to an understanding of the sleep-waker's state at this epoch. Other nurses were procured; and at ten o'clock I left the house in company with the two physicians and Mr. L——l.

In the afternoon we all called again to see the patient. His condition remained precisely the same. We had now some discussion as to the propriety and feasibility of awakening him; but we had little difficulty in agreeing that no good purpose would be served by so doing. It was evident that, so far, death (or what is usually termed death) had been arrested by the mesmeric process. It seemed clear to us all that to awaken M. Valdemar would be merely to insure his instant, or at least his speedy dissolution.

From this period until the close of last week—*an interval of nearly seven months*—we continued to make daily calls at M. Valdemar's house, accompanied, now and then, by medical and other friends. All this time the sleep-waker remained *exactly* as I have last described him. The nurses' attentions were continual.

It was on Friday last that we finally resolved to make the experiment of awakening, or attempting to awaken him; and it is the (perhaps) unfortunate result of this latter experiment which has given rise to so much discussion in private circles—to so much of what I cannot help thinking unwarranted popular feeling.

For the purpose of relieving M. Valdemar from the mesmeric trance, I made use of the customary passes. These, for a time, were unsuccessful. The first indication of revival was afforded by a partial descent of the iris. It was observed, as especially remarkable, that this lowering of the pupil was accompanied by the profuse out-flowing of a yellowish ichor (from beneath the lids) of a pungent and highly offensive odor.

It now was suggested that I should attempt to influence the patient's arm, as heretofore. I made the attempt and failed. Dr. F——then intimated a desire to have me put a question. I did so as follows:

'M. Valdemar, can you explain to us what are your feelings or wishes now?'

There was an instant return of the hectic circles on the cheeks; the tongue quivered, or rather rolled violently in the mouth (although the jaws and lips remained rigid as before;) and at length the same hideous voice which I have already described, broke forth:

'For God's sake!—quick!—quick!—put me to sleep—or, quick!—waken me!—quick!—*I say to you that I am dead!*'

I was thoroughly unnerved, and for an instant remained undecided what to do. At first I made an endeavor to re-compose the patient; but, failing in this through total abeyance of the will, I retraced my steps and as earnestly struggled to awaken him. In this attempt I soon saw that I should be successful—or at least I soon fancied that my success would be complete—and I am sure that all in the room were prepared to see the patient awaken.

For what really occurred, however, it is quite impossible that any human being could have been prepared.

As I rapidly made the mesmeric passes, amid ejaculations of 'dead! dead!' absolutely *bursting* from the tongue and not from the lips of the sufferer, his whole frame at once—within the space of a single minute, or even less, shrunk—crumbled—absolutely *rotted* away beneath my hands. Upon the bed, before that whole company, there lay a nearly liquid mass of loathsome—of detestable putridity.

FITZ-JAMES O'BRIEN

THE DIAMOND LENS

I. THE BENDING OF THE TWIG

FROM a very early period of my life the entire bent of my inclinations had been towards microscopic investigations. When I was not more than ten years old, a distant relative of our family, hoping to astonish my inexperience, constructed a simple microscope for me, by drilling in a disk of copper a small hole, in which a drop of pure water was sustained by capillary attraction.* This very primitive apparatus, magnifying some fifty diameters, presented, it is true, only indistinct and imperfect forms, but still sufficiently wonderful to work up my imagination to a preternatural state of excitement.

Seeing me so interested in this rude instrument, my cousin explained to me all that he knew about the principles of the microscope, related to me a few of the wonders which had been accomplished through its agency, and ended by promising to send me one regularly constructed, immediately on his return to the city. I counted the days, the hours, the minutes, that intervened between that promise and his departure.

Meantime I was not idle. Every transparent substance that bore the remotest resemblance to a lens I eagerly seized upon, and employed in vain attempts to realize that instrument, the theory of whose construction I as yet only vaguely comprehended. All panes of glass containing those oblate spheroidal knots familiarly known as 'bull's-eyes'* were ruthlessly destroyed, in the hope of obtaining lenses of marvellous power. I even went so far as to extract the crystalline humor from the eyes of fishes and animals, and endeavored to press it into the microscopic service. I plead guilty to having stolen the glasses from my Aunt Agatha's spectacles, with a dim idea of grinding them into lenses of wondrous magnifying properties,—in which attempt it is scarcely necessary to say that I totally failed.

At last the promised instrument came. It was of that order known as Field's simple microscope,* and had cost perhaps about fifteen dollars. As far as educational purposes went, a better apparatus could not have been selected. Accompanying it was a small treatise on the microscope,—its history, uses, and discoveries. I comprehended then for the first time the 'Arabian Nights' Entertainments.'* The dull veil of ordinary existence that hung across the world seemed suddenly to roll away, and to lay bare a land of enchantments. I felt towards my companions as the seer might feel towards the ordinary masses of men. I held conversations with nature in a tongue which they could not understand. I was in daily communication with living wonders, such as they never imagined in their wildest visions. I penetrated beyond the external portal of things, and roamed through the sanctuaries. Where they beheld only a drop of rain slowly rolling down the window-glass, I saw a universe of beings animated with all the passions common to physical life, and convulsing their minute sphere with struggles as fierce and protracted as those of men. In the common spots of mould, which my mother, good housekeeper that she was, fiercely scooped away from her jam pots, there abode for me, under the name of mildew, enchanted gardens, filled with dells and avenues of the densest foliage and most astonishing verdure, while from the fantastic boughs of these microscopic forests hung strange fruits glittering with green, and silver, and gold.

It was no scientific thirst that at this time filled my mind. It was the pure enjoyment of a poet to whom a world of wonders has been disclosed. I talked of my solitary pleasures to none. Alone with my microscope, I dimmed my sight, day after day and night after night, poring over the marvels which it unfolded to me. I was like one who, having discovered the ancient Eden still existing in all its primitive glory, should resolve to enjoy it in solitude, and never betray to mortal the secret of its locality. The rod of my life was bent at this moment. I destined myself to be a microscopist.

Of course, like every novice, I fancied myself a discoverer. I was ignorant at the time of the thousands of acute intellects engaged in the same pursuit as myself, and with the advantage of instruments a thousand times more powerful than mine. The names of Leeuwenhoek, Williamson, Spencer, Ehrenberg, Schultz, Dujardin, Schact, and Schleiden* were then entirely unknown to me, or if known, I was ignorant of their patient and wonderful researches. In every fresh specimen of cryptogamia* which I placed beneath my instrument I believed that I discovered wonders of which the world was as yet ignorant. I remember well the thrill of delight and admiration that shot through me the first time that I discovered the common wheel animalcule (*Rotifera vulgaris*)* expanding and contracting its flexible spokes, and seemingly rotating through the water. Alas! as I grew older, and obtained some works treating of my favorite study, I found that I was only on the threshold of a science to the investigation of which some of the greatest men of the age were devoting their lives and intellects.

As I grew up, my parents, who saw but little likelihood of anything practical resulting from the examination of bits of moss and drops of water through a brass tube and a piece of glass, were anxious that I should choose a profession. It was their desire that I should enter the counting-house of my uncle, Ethan Blake, a prosperous merchant, who carried on business in New York. This suggestion I decisively combated. I had no taste for trade; I should only make a failure; in short, I refused to become a merchant.

But it was necessary for me to select some pursuit. My parents were staid New England people, who insisted on the necessity of labor; and therefore, although, thanks to the bequest of my poor Aunt Agatha, I should, on coming of age, inherit a small fortune sufficient to place me above want, it was decided that, instead of waiting for this, I should act the nobler part, and employ the intervening years in rendering myself independent.

After much cogitation I complied with the wishes of my family, and selected a profession. I determined to study medicine at the New York Academy.* This disposition of my future suited me. A removal from my relatives would enable me to dispose of my time as I pleased without fear of detection. As long as I paid my Academy fees, I might shirk attending the lectures if I chose; and, as I never had the remotest intention of standing an examination, there was no danger of my being 'plucked.' Besides, a metropolis was the place for me. There I could obtain excellent instruments, the newest publications, intimacy with men of pursuits kindred with my own, in short, all things necessary to insure a profitable devotion of my life to my beloved science. I had an abundance of money, few desires that were not bounded by my illuminating mirror on one side and my object-glass on the other; what, therefore, was to prevent my becoming an illustrious investigator of the veiled worlds! It was with the most buoyant hope that I left my New England home and established myself in New York.

II. THE LONGING OF A MAN OF SCIENCE

My first step, of course, was to find suitable apartments. These I obtained, after a couple of days' search, in Fourth Avenue; a very pretty second-floor unfurnished, containing sitting-room, bedroom, and a smaller apartment which I intended to fit up as a laboratory. I furnished my lodgings simply, but rather elegantly, and then devoted all my energies to the adornment of the temple of my worship. I visited Pike, the celebrated optician,* and passed in review his splendid collection of microscopes,—Field's Compound, Hingham's, Spencer's, Nachet's Binocular, (that founded on the principles of the stereoscope,) and at length fixed upon that form known as Spencer's Trunnion Microscope,* as combining the greatest number of improvements with an almost perfect freedom from tremor. Along with this I purchased every possible accessory,—draw-tubes, micrometers, a *camera-lucida*, lever-stage, achromatic condensers, white cloud illuminators, prisms, parabolic condensers, polarizing apparatus, forceps, aquatic boxes, fishing-tubes,* with a host of other articles, all of which would have been useful in the hands of an experienced microscopist, but, as I afterwards discovered, were not of the slightest present value to me. It takes years of practice to know how to use a complicated microscope. The optician looked suspiciously at me as I made these wholesale purchases. He evidently was uncertain whether to set me down as some scientific celebrity or a madman. I think he inclined to the latter belief. I suppose I was mad. Every great genius is mad upon the subject in which he is greatest. The unsuccessful madman is disgraced and called a lunatic.

Mad or not, I set myself to work with a zeal which few scientific students have ever equalled. I had everything to learn relative to the delicate study upon which I had embarked,—a study involving the most earnest patience, the most rigid analytic powers, the steadiest hand, the most untiring eye, the most refined and subtile manipulation.

For a long time half my apparatus lay inactively on the shelves of my laboratory, which was now most amply furnished with every possible contrivance for facilitating my investigations. The fact was that I did not know how to use some of my scientific implements, never having been taught microscopies, and those whose use I understood theoretically were of little avail, until by practice I could attain the necessary delicacy of handling. Still, such was the fury of my ambition, such the untiring perseverance of my experiments, that, difficult of credit as it may be, in the course of one year I became theoretically and practically an accomplished microscopist.

During this period of my labors, in which I submitted specimens of every substance that came under my observation to the action of my lenses, I became a discoverer,—in a small way, it is true, for I was very young, but still a discoverer. It was I who destroyed Ehrenberg's theory that the *Volvox globator* was an animal, and proved that his 'monads'* with stomachs and eyes were merely phases of the formation of a vegetable cell, and were, when they reached their mature state, incapable of the act of conjugation, or any true generative act, without which no organism rising to any stage of life higher than vegetable can be said to be complete. It was I who resolved the singular problem of rotation in the cells and hairs of plants into ciliary attraction, in spite of the assertions of Mr. Wenham* and others, that my explanation was the result of an optical illusion.

But notwithstanding these discoveries, laboriously and painfully made as they were, I felt horribly dissatisfied. At every step I found myself stopped by the imperfections of my instruments. Like all active microscopists, I gave my imagination full play. Indeed, it is a common complaint against many such, that they supply the defects of their instruments with the creations of their brains. I imagined depths beyond depths in nature which the limited power of my lenses prohibited me from exploring. I lay awake at night constructing imaginary microscopes of immeasurable power, with which I seemed to pierce through all the envelopes of matter down to its original atom. How I cursed those imperfect mediums which necessity through ignorance compelled me to use! How I longed to discover the secret of some perfect lens, whose magnifying power should be limited only by the resolvability of the object, and which at the same time should be free from spherical and chromatic aberrations,* in short from all the obstacles over which the poor microscopist finds himself continually stumbling! I felt convinced that the simple microscope, composed of a single lens of such vast yet perfect power was possible of construction. To attempt to bring the compound microscope up to such a pitch would have been commencing at the wrong end; this latter being simply a partially successful endeavor to remedy those very defects of the simple instrument, which, if conquered, would leave nothing to be desired.

It was in this mood of mind that I became a constructive microscopist. After another year passed in this new pursuit, experimenting on every imaginable substance, glass, gems, flints, crystals, artificial crystals formed of the alloy of various vitreous materials, in short, having constructed as many varieties of lenses as Argus had eyes,* I found myself precisely where I started, with nothing gained save an extensive knowledge of glass-making. I was almost dead with despair. My parents were surprised at my apparent want of progress in my medical studies, (I had not attended one lecture since my arrival in the city,) and the expenses of my mad pursuit had been so great as to embarrass me very seriously.

I was in this frame of mind one day, experimenting in my laboratory on a small diamond,—that stone, from its great refracting power, having always occupied my attention more than any other,—when a young Frenchman, who lived on the floor above me, and who was in the habit of occasionally visiting me, entered the room.

I think that Jules Simon was a Jew. He had many traits of the Hebrew character: a love of jewelry, of dress, and of good living. There was something mysterious about him. He always had something to sell, and yet went into excellent society. When I say sell, I should perhaps have said peddle; for his operations were generally confined to the disposal of single articles, a picture, for instance, or a rare carving in ivory, or a pair of duelling-pistols, or the dress of a Mexican *caballero*.* When I was first furnishing my rooms, he paid me a visit, which ended in my purchasing an antique silver lamp, which he assured me was a Cellini,* it was—handsome enough even for that,—and some other knickknacks for my sitting-room. Why Simon should pursue this petty trade I never could imagine. He apparently had plenty of money, and had the *entrée* of the best houses in the city,—taking care, however, I suppose, to drive no bargains within the enchanted circle of the Upper Ten.* I came at length to the conclusion that this peddling was but a mask to cover some greater object, and even went so far as to believe my young acquaintance to be implicated in the slave-trade. That, however, was none of my affair.

On the present occasion, Simon entered my room in a state of considerable excitement.

'*Ah! mon ami!*' he cried, before I could even offer him the ordinary salutation, 'it has occurred to me to be the witness of the most astonishing things in the world. I promenade myself to the house of

Madame—How does the little animal—*le renard**—name himself in the Latin?'

'Vulpes,' I answered.

'Ah! yes,—Vulpes. I promenade myself to the house of Madame Vulpes.'

'The spirit medium!'

'Yes, the great medium. Great heavens! what a woman! I write on a slip of paper many of questions concerning affairs the most secret,—affairs that conceal themselves in the abysses of my heart the most profound; and behold! by example! what occurs? This devil of a woman makes me replies the most truthful to all of them. She talks to me of things that I do not love to talk of to myself. What am I to think? I am fixed to the earth!'

'Am I to understand you, M. Simon, that this Mrs. Vulpes replied to questions secretly written by you, which questions related to events known only to yourself?'

'Ah! more than that, more than that,' he answered, with an air of some alarm. 'She related to me things—But,' he added, after a pause, and suddenly changing his manner, 'why occupy ourselves with these follies? It was all the biology, without doubt. It goes without saying that it has not my credence. But why are we here, *mon ami*? It has occurred to me to discover the most beautiful thing as you can imagine,—a vase with green lizards on it, composed by the great Bernard Palissy.* It is in my apartment; let us mount. I go to show it to you.'

I followed Simon mechanically; but my thoughts were far from Palissy and his enamelled ware, although I, like him, was seeking in the dark a great discovery. This casual mention of the spiritualist, Madame Vulpes, set me on a new track. What if this spiritualism should be really a great fact? What if, through communication with more subtle organisms than my own, I could reach at a single bound the goal, which perhaps a life of agonizing mental toil would never enable me to attain?

While purchasing the Palissy vase from my friend Simon, I was mentally arranging a visit to Madame Vulpes.

III. THE SPIRIT OF LEEUWENHOEK

Two evenings after this, thanks to an arrangement by letter and the promise of an ample fee, I found Madame Vulpes awaiting me at her residence alone. She was a coarse-featured woman, with keen and rather cruel dark eyes, and an exceedingly sensual expression about her mouth and under jaw. She received me in perfect silence, in an apartment on the ground floor, very sparely furnished. In the centre of the room, close to where Mrs. Vulpes sat, there was a common round mahogany table. If I had come for the purpose of sweeping her chimney, the woman could not have looked more indifferent to my appearance. There was no attempt to inspire the visitor with awe. Everything bore a simple and practical aspect. This intercourse with the spiritual world was evidently as familiar an occupation with Mrs. Vulpes as eating her dinner or riding in an omnibus.

'You come for a communication, Mr. Linley?' said the medium, in a dry, business-like tone, of voice.

'By appointment,—yes.'

'What sort of communication do you want?—a written one?'

'Yes,—I wish for a written one.'

'From any particular spirit?'

'Yes.'

'Have you ever known this spirit on this earth?'

'Never. He died long before I was born. I wish merely to obtain from him some information which he ought to be able to give better than any other.'

'Will you seat yourself at the table, Mr. Linley,' said the medium, 'and place your hands upon it?'

I obeyed,—Mrs. Vulpes being seated opposite to me, with her hands also on the table. We remained thus for about a minute and a half, when a violent succession of raps came on the table, on the back of my chair, on the floor immediately under my feet, and even on the window-panes. Mrs. Vulpes smiled composedly.

'They are very strong to-night,' she remarked. 'You are fortunate.' She then continued, 'Will the spirits communicate with this gentleman?'

Vigorous affirmative.

'Will the particular spirit he desires to speak with communicate?'

A very confused rapping followed this question.

'I know what they mean,' said Mrs. Vulpes, addressing herself to me; 'they wish you to write down the name of the particular spirit that you desire to converse with. Is that so?' she added, speaking to her invisible guests.

That it was so was evident from the numerous affirmatory responses. While this was going on, I tore a slip from my pocket-book, and scribbled a name, under the table.

'Will this spirit communicate in writing with this gentleman?' asked the medium once more.

After a moment's pause, her hand seemed to be seized with a violent tremor, shaking so forcibly that the table vibrated. She said that a spirit had seized her hand and would write. I handed her some sheets of paper that were on the table, and a pencil. The latter she held loosely in her hand, which presently began to move over the paper with a singular and seemingly involuntary motion. After a few moments had elapsed, she handed me the paper, on which I found written, in a large, uncultivated hand, the words, 'He is not here, but has been sent for.' A pause of a minute or so now ensued, during which Mrs. Vulpes remained perfectly silent, but the raps continued at regular intervals. When the short period I mention had elapsed, the hand of the medium was again seized with its convulsive tremor, and she wrote, under this strange influence, a few words on the paper, which she handed to me. They were as follows:

'I am here. Question me.

'LEEUWENHOEK.'

I was astounded. The name was identical with that I had written beneath the table, and carefully kept concealed. Neither was it at all probable that an uncultivated woman like Mrs. Vulpes should know even the name of the great father of microscopies. It may have been biology;* but this theory was soon doomed to be destroyed. I wrote on my slip—still concealing it from Mrs. Vulpes—a series of questions, which, to avoid tediousness, I shall place with the responses, in the order in which they occurred:—

I.—Can the microscope be brought to perfection?

SPIRIT.—Yes.

I.—Am I destined to accomplish this great task?

SPIRIT.—You are.

I.—I wish to know how to proceed to attain this end. For the love which you bear to science, help me!

SPIRIT.—A diamond of one hundred and forty carats, submitted to electro-magnetic currents for a long period, will experience a rearrangement of its atoms inter se, and from that stone you will form the universal lens.

I.—Will great discoveries result from the use of such a lens?

SPIRIT.—So great that all that has gone before is as nothing.

I.—But the refractive power of the diamond is so immense, that the image will be formed within the lens. How is that difficulty to be surmounted?

SPIRIT.—Pierce the lens through its axis, and the difficulty is obviated. The image will be formed in the pierced space, which will itself serve as a tube to look through. Now I am called. Good night.

I cannot at all describe the effect that these extraordinary communications had upon me. I felt completely bewildered. No biological theory could account for the *discovery* of the lens. The medium might, by means of biological *rapport** with my mind, have gone so far as to read my questions, and reply to them coherently. But biology could not enable her to discover that magnetic currents would so alter the crystals of the diamond as to remedy its previous defects, and admit of its being polished into a perfect lens. Some such theory may have passed through my head, it is true; but if so, I had forgotten it. In my excited condition of mind there was no course left but to become a convert, and it was in a state of the most painful nervous exaltation that I left the medium's house that evening. She accompanied me to the door, hoping that I was satisfied. The raps followed us as we went through the hall, sounding on the balusters, the flooring, and even the lintels of the door. I hastily expressed my satisfaction, and escaped hurriedly into the cool night air. I walked home with but one thought possessing me,—how to obtain a diamond of the immense size required. My entire means multiplied a hundred times over would have been inadequate to its purchase. Besides, such stones are rare, and become historical. I could find such only in the regalia of Eastern or European monarchs.

IV. THE EYE OF MORNING

There was a light in Simon's room as I entered my house. A vague impulse urged me to visit him. As I opened the door of his sitting-room unannounced, he was bending, with his back toward me, over a carcel lamp,* apparently engaged in minutely examining some object which he held in his hands. As I entered, he started suddenly, thrust his hand into his breast pocket, and turned to me with a face crimson with confusion.

'What!' I cried, 'poring over the miniature of some fair lady? Well, don't blush so much; I won't ask to see it.'

Simon laughed awkwardly enough, but made none of the negative protestations usual on such occasions. He asked me to take a seat.

'Simon,' said I, 'I have just come from Madame Vulpes.'

This time Simon turned as white as a sheet, and seemed stupefied, as if a sudden electric shock had smitten him. He babbled some incoherent words, and went hastily to a small closet where he usually kept his liquors. Although astonished at his emotion, I was too preoccupied with my own idea to pay much attention to anything else.

'You say truly when you call Madame Vulpes a devil of a woman,' I continued. 'Simon, she told me wonderful things to-night, or rather was the means of telling me wonderful things. Ah! if I could only get a diamond that weighed one hundred and forty carats!'

Scarcely had the sigh with which I uttered this desire died upon my lips, when Simon, with the aspect of a wild beast, glared at me savagely, and, rushing to the mantelpiece, where some foreign weapons hung on the wall, caught up a Malay creese,* and brandished it furiously before him.

'No!' he cried in French, into which he always broke when excited. 'No! you shall not have it! You are perfidious! You have consulted with that demon, and desire my treasure! But I will die first! Me! I am brave! You cannot make me fear!'

All this, uttered in a loud voice trembling with excitement, astounded me. I saw at a glance that I had accidentally trodden upon the edges of Simon's secret, whatever it was. It was necessary to reassure him.

'My dear Simon,' I said, 'I am entirely at a loss to know what you mean. I went to Madame Vulpes to consult with her on a scientific problem, to the solution of which I discovered that a diamond of the size I just mentioned was necessary. You were never alluded to during the evening, nor, so far as I was concerned, even thought of. What can be the meaning of this outburst? If you happen to have a set of valuable diamonds in your possession, you need fear nothing from me. The diamond which I require you could not possess; or, if you did possess it, you would not be living here.'

Something in my tone must have completely reassured him; for his expression immediately changed to a sort of constrained merriment, combined, however, with a certain suspicious attention to my movements. He laughed, and said that I must bear with him; that he was at certain moments subject to a species of vertigo, which betrayed itself in incoherent speeches, and that the attacks passed off as rapidly as they came. He put his weapon aside while making this explanation, and endeavored, with some success, to assume a more cheerful air.

All this did not impose on me in the least. I was too much accustomed to analytical labors to be baffled by so flimsy a veil. I determined to probe the mystery to the bottom.

'Simon,' I said, gayly, 'let us forget all this over a bottle of Burgundy. I have a case of Lausseure's *Clos Vougeot* down-stairs, fragrant with the odors and ruddy with the sunlight of the Côte d'Or.* Let us have up a couple of bottles. What say you?'

'With all my heart,' answered Simon, smilingly.

I produced the wine and we seated ourselves to drink. It was of a famous vintage, that of 1848,* a year when war and wine throve together, and its pure but powerful juice seemed to impart renewed vitality to the system. By the time we had half finished the second bottle, Simon's head, which I knew was a weak one, had begun to yield, while I remained calm as ever, only that every draught seemed to send a flush of vigor through my limbs. Simon's utterance became more and more indistinct. He took to singing French *chansons** of a not very moral tendency. I rose suddenly from the table just at the conclusion of one of those incoherent verses, and, fixing my eyes on him with a quiet smile, said: 'Simon, I have deceived you. I learned your secret this evening. You may as well be frank with me. Mrs. Vulpes, or rather one of her spirits, told me all.'

He started with horror. His intoxication seemed for the moment to fade away, and he made a movement towards the weapon that he had a short time before laid down. I stopped him with my hand.

'Monster!' he cried, passionately, 'I am ruined! What shall I do? You shall never have it! I swear by my mother!'

'I don't want it,' I said; 'rest secure, but be frank with me. Tell me all about it.'

The drunkenness began to return. He protested with maudlin earnestness that I was entirely mistaken,—that I was intoxicated; then asked me to swear eternal secrecy, and promised to disclose the mystery to me. I pledged myself, of course, to all. With an uneasy look in his eyes, and hands unsteady with drink and nervousness, he drew a small case from his breast and opened it. Heavens! How the mild lamp-light was shivered into a thousand prismatic arrows, as it fell upon a vast rose-diamond that glittered in the case! I was no judge of diamonds, but I saw at a glance that this was a gem of rare size and purity. I looked at Simon with wonder, and—must I confess it?—with envy. How could he have obtained this treasure? In reply to my questions, I could just gather from his drunken statements (of which, I fancy, half the incoherence was affected) that he had been superintending a gang of slaves engaged in diamond-washing in Brazil; that he had seen one of them secrete a diamond, but, instead of informing his employers, had quietly watched the negro until he saw him bury his treasure; that he had dug it up and fled with it, but that as yet he was afraid to attempt to dispose of it publicly,—so valuable a gem being almost certain to attract too much attention to its owner's antecedents,—and he had not been able to discover any of those obscure channels by which such matters are conveyed away safely. He added, that, in accordance with oriental practice, he had named his diamond with the fanciful title of 'The Eye of Morning.'

While Simon was relating this to me, I regarded the great diamond attentively. Never had I beheld anything so beautiful. All the glories of light, ever imagined or described, seemed to pulsate in its crystalline chambers. Its weight, as I learned from Simon, was exactly one hundred and forty carats. Here was an amazing coincidence. The hand of destiny seemed in it.

On the very evening when the spirit of Leeuwenhoek communicates to me the great secret of the microscope, the priceless means which he directs me to employ start up within my easy reach! I determined, with the most perfect deliberation, to possess myself of Simon's diamond.

I sat opposite to him while he nodded over his glass, and calmly revolved the whole affair. I did not for an instant contemplate so foolish an act as a common theft, which would of course be discovered, or at least necessitate flight and concealment, all of which must interfere with my scientific plans. There was but one step to be taken,—to kill Simon. After all, what was the life of a little peddling Jew, in comparison with the interests of science? Human beings are taken every day from the condemned prisons to be experimented on by surgeons. This man, Simon, was by his own confession a criminal, a robber, and I believed on my soul a murderer. He deserved death quite as much as any felon condemned by the laws: why should I not, like government, contrive that his punishment should contribute to the progress of human knowledge?

The means for accomplishing everything I desired lay within my reach. There stood upon the mantel-piece a bottle half full of French laudanum. Simon was so occupied with his diamond, which I had just restored to him, that it was an affair of no difficulty to drug his glass. In a quarter of an hour he was in a profound sleep.

I now opened his waistcoat, took the diamond from the inner pocket in which he had placed it, and removed him to the bed, on which I laid him so that his feet hung down over the edge. I had possessed myself of the Malay creese, which I held in my right hand, while with the other I discovered as accurately as I could by pulsation the exact locality of the heart. It was essential that all the aspects of his death should lead to the surmise of self-murder. I calculated the exact angle at which it was probable that the weapon, if levelled by Simon's own hand, would enter his breast; then with one powerful blow I thrust it up to the hilt in the very spot which I desired to penetrate. A convulsive thrill ran through Simon's limbs. I heard a smothered sound issue from his throat, precisely like the bursting of a large air-bubble, sent up by a diver, when it reaches the surface of the water; he turned half round on his side, and, as if to assist my plans more effectually, his right hand, moved by some mere spasmodic impulse, clasped the handle of the creese, which it remained holding with extraordinary muscular tenacity. Beyond this there was no apparent struggle. The laudanum, I presume, paralyzed the usual nervous action. He must have died instantly.

There was yet something to be done. To make it certain that all suspicion of the act should be diverted from any inhabitant of the house to Simon himself, it was necessary that the door should be found in the morning *locked on the inside*. How to do this, and afterwards escape myself? Not by the window; that was a physical impossibility. Besides, I was determined that the windows *also* should be found bolted. The solution was simple enough. I descended softly to my own room for a peculiar instrument which I had used for holding small slippery substances, such as minute spheres of glass, etc. This instrument was nothing more than a long slender hand-vice, with a very powerful grip, and a considerable leverage, which last was accidentally owing to the shape of the handle. Nothing was simpler than, when the key was in the lock, to seize the end of its stem in this vice, through the keyhole, from the outside, and so lock the door. Previously, however, to doing this, I burned a number of papers on Simon's hearth. Suicides almost always burn papers before they destroy themselves. I also emptied some more laudanum into Simon's glass,—having first removed from it all traces of wine,—cleaned the other wineglass, and brought the bottles away with me. If traces of two persons drinking had been found in the room, the question naturally would have arisen, Who was the second? Besides, the wine-bottles might have been identified as belonging to me. The laudanum I poured out to account for its presence in his stomach, in case of a *post-mortem* examination. The theory naturally would be, that he first intended to poison himself, but, after swallowing a little of the drug, was either disgusted with its taste, or changed his mind from other motives, and chose the dagger. These arrangements made, I walked out, leaving the gas burning, locked the door with my vice, and went to bed.

Simon's death was not discovered until nearly three in the afternoon. The servant, astonished at seeing the gas burning,—the light streaming on the dark landing from under the door,—peeped through the keyhole and saw Simon on the bed. She gave the alarm. The door was burst open, and the neighborhood was in a fever of excitement.

Every one in the house was arrested, myself included. There was an inquest; but no clew to his death beyond that of suicide could be obtained. Curiously enough, he had made several speeches to his friends the preceding week, that seemed to point to self-destruction. One gentleman swore that Simon had said in his presence that 'he was tired of life.' His landlord affirmed that Simon, when paying him his last month's rent, remarked that 'he should not pay him rent much longer.' All the other evidence corresponded,—the door locked inside, the position of the corpse, the burnt papers. As I anticipated, no one knew of the possession of the diamond by Simon, so that no motive was suggested for his murder. The jury, after a prolonged examination, brought in the usual verdict, and the neighborhood once more settled down into its accustomed quiet.

V. ANIMULA*

The three months succeeding Simon's catastrophe I devoted night and day to my diamond lens. I had constructed a vast galvanic battery, composed of nearly two thousand pairs of plates,*—a higher power

I dared not use, lest the diamond should be calcined. By means of this enormous engine I was enabled to send a powerful current of electricity continually through my great diamond, which it seemed to me gained in lustre every day. At the expiration of a month I commenced the grinding and polishing of the lens, a work of intense toil and exquisite delicacy. The great density of the stone, and the care required to be taken with the curvatures of the surfaces of the lens, rendered the labor the severest and most harassing that I had yet undergone.

At last the eventful moment came; the lens was completed. I stood trembling on the threshold of new worlds. I had the realization of Alexander's famous wish* before me. The lens lay on the table, ready to be placed upon its platform. My hand fairly shook as I enveloped a drop of water with a thin coating of oil of turpentine, preparatory to its examination,—a process necessary in order to prevent the rapid evaporation of the water. I now placed the drop on a thin slip of glass under the lens, and throwing upon it, by the combined aid of a prism and a mirror, a powerful stream of light, I approached my eye to the minute hole drilled through the axis of the lens. For an instant I saw nothing save what seemed to be an illuminated chaos, a vast luminous abyss. A pure white light, cloudless and serene, and seemingly limitless as space itself, was my first impression. Gently, and with the greatest care, I depressed the lens a few hair's-breadths. The wondrous illumination still continued, but as the lens approached the object a scene of indescribable beauty was unfolded to my view.

I seemed to gaze upon a vast space, the limits of which extended far beyond my vision. An atmosphere of magical luminousness permeated the entire field of view. I was amazed to see no trace of animalculous life. Not a living thing, apparently, inhabited that dazzling expanse.

I comprehended instantly that, by the wondrous power of my lens, I had penetrated beyond the grosser particles of aqueous matter, beyond the realms of infusoria and protozoa, down to the original gaseous globule,* into whose luminous interior I was gazing, as into an almost boundless dome filled with a supernatural radiance.

It was, however, no brilliant void into which I looked. On every side I beheld beautiful inorganic forms, of unknown texture, and colored with the most enchanting hues. These forms presented the appearance of what might be called, for want of a more specific definition, foliated clouds of the highest rarity; that is, they undulated and broke into vegetable formations, and were tinged with splendors compared with which the gilding of our autumn woodlands is as dross compared with gold. Far away into the illimitable distance stretched long avenues of these gaseous forests, dimly transparent, and painted with prismatic hues of unimaginable brilliancy. The pendent branches waved along the fluid glades until every vista seemed to break through half-lucent ranks of many-colored drooping silken pennons. What seemed to be either fruits or flowers, pied with a thousand hues, lustrous and ever varying, bubbled from the crowns of this fairy foliage. No hills, no lakes, no rivers, no forms animate or inanimate, were to be seen, save those vast auroral copses that floated serenely in the luminous stillness, with leaves and fruits and flowers gleaming with unknown fires, unrealizable by mere imagination.

How strange, I thought, that this sphere should be thus condemned to solitude! I had hoped, at least, to discover some new form of animal life,—perhaps of a lower class than any with which we are at present acquainted, but still, some living organism. I found my newly discovered world, if I may so speak, a beautiful chromatic desert.

While I was speculating on the singular arrangements of the internal economy of Nature, with which she so frequently splinters into atoms our most compact theories, I thought I beheld a form moving slowly through the glades of one of the prismatic forests. I looked more attentively, and found that I was not mistaken. Words cannot depict the anxiety with which I awaited the nearer approach of this mysterious object. Was it merely some inanimate substance, held in suspense in the attenuated atmosphere of the globule? or was it an animal endowed with vitality and motion? It approached, flitting behind the gauzy, colored veils of cloud-foliage, for seconds dimly revealed, then vanishing. At last the violet pennons that trailed nearest to me vibrated; they were gently pushed aside, and the form floated out into the broad light.

It was a female human shape. When I say human, I mean it possessed the outlines of humanity, but there the analogy ends. Its adorable beauty lifted it illimitable heights beyond the loveliest daughter of Adam.

I cannot, I dare not, attempt to inventory the charms of this divine revelation of perfect beauty. Those eyes of mystic violet, dewy and serene, evade my words. Her long, lustrous hair following her glorious head in a golden wake, like the track sown in heaven by a falling star, seems to quench my most burning phrases with its splendors. If all the bees of Hybla* nestled upon my lips, they would still sing but hoarsely the wondrous harmonies of outline that enclosed her form.

She swept out from between the rainbow-curtains of the cloud-trees into the broad sea of light that lay beyond. Her motions were those of some graceful naiad,* cleaving, by a mere effort of her will, the clear, unruffled waters that fill the chambers of the sea. She floated forth with the serene grace of a frail bubble ascending through the still atmosphere of a June day. The perfect roundness of her limbs formed suave and enchanting curves. It was like listening to the most spiritual symphony of Beethoven the divine,* to watch the harmonious flow of lines. This, indeed, was a pleasure cheaply purchased at any price. What cared I, if I had waded to the portal of this wonder through another's blood? I would have given my own to enjoy one such moment of intoxication and delight.

Breathless with gazing on this lovely wonder, and forgetful for an instant of everything save her presence, I withdrew my eye from the microscope eagerly,—alas! As my gaze fell on the thin slide that lay beneath my instrument, the bright light from mirror and from prism sparkled on a colorless drop of water! There, in that tiny bead of dew, this beautiful being was forever imprisoned. The planet Neptune* was not more distant from me than she. I hastened once more to apply my eye to the microscope.

Animula (let me now call her by that dear name which I subsequently bestowed on her) had changed her position. She had again approached the wondrous forest, and was gazing earnestly upwards. Presently one of the trees—as I must call them—unfolded a long ciliary process, with which it seized one of the gleaming fruits that glittered on its summit, and, sweeping slowly down, held it within reach of Animula. The sylph* took it in her delicate hand and began to eat. My attention was so entirely absorbed by her, that I could not apply myself to the task of determining whether this singular plant was or was not instinct with volition.

I watched her, as she made her repast, with the most profound attention. The suppleness of her motions sent a thrill of delight through my frame; my heart beat madly as she turned her beautiful eyes in the direction of the spot in which I stood. What would I not have given to have had the power to precipitate myself into that luminous ocean, and float with her through those groves of purple and gold! While I was thus breathlessly following her every movement, she suddenly started, seemed to listen for a moment, and then cleaving the brilliant ether in which she was floating, like a flash of light, pierced through the opaline forest, and disappeared.

Instantly a series of the most singular sensations attacked me. It seemed as if I had suddenly gone blind. The luminous sphere was still before me, but my daylight had vanished. What caused this sudden disappearance? Had she a lover or a husband? Yes, that was the solution! Some signal from a happy fellow-being had vibrated through the avenues of the forest, and she had obeyed the summons.

The agony of my sensations, as I arrived at this conclusion, startled me. I tried to reject the conviction that my reason forced upon me. I battled against the fatal conclusion,—but in vain. It was so. I had no escape from it. I loved an animalcule!

It is true that, thanks to the marvellous power of my microscope, she appeared of human proportions. Instead of presenting the revolting aspect of the coarser creatures, that live and struggle and die, in the more easily resolvable portions of the water-drop, she was fair and delicate and of surpassing beauty. But of what account was all that? Every time that my eye was withdrawn from the instrument, it fell on a miserable drop of water, within which, I must be content to know, dwelt all that could make my life lovely.

Could she but see me once! Could I for one moment pierce the mystical walls that so inexorably rose to separate us, and whisper all that filled my soul, I might consent to be satisfied for the rest of my life with the knowledge of her remote sympathy. It would be something to have established even the faintest personal link to bind us together,—to know that at times, when roaming through those enchanted glades, she might think of the wonderful stranger, who had broken the monotony of her life with his presence, and left a gentle memory in her heart!

But it could not be. No invention of which human intellect was capable could break down the barriers that nature had erected. I might feast my soul upon her wondrous beauty, yet she must always remain ignorant of the adoring eyes that day and night gazed upon her, and, even when closed, beheld her in dreams. With a bitter cry of anguish I fled from the room, and, flinging myself on my bed, sobbed myself to sleep like a child.

VI. THE SPILLING OF THE CUP

I arose the next morning almost at daybreak, and rushed to my microscope. I trembled as I sought the luminous world in miniature that contained my all. Animula was there. I had left the gas-lamp, surrounded by its moderators, burning, when I went to bed the night before. I found the sylph bathing, as it were, with an expression of pleasure animating her features, in the brilliant light which surrounded her. She tossed her lustrous golden hair over her shoulders with innocent coquetry. She lay at full length in the transparent medium, in which she supported herself with ease, and gambolled with the enchanting grace that the nymph Salmacis might have exhibited when she sought to conquer the modest Hermaphroditus.* I tried an experiment to satisfy myself if her powers of reflection were developed. I lessened the lamp-light considerably. By the dim light that remained, I could see an expression of pain flit across her face. She looked upward suddenly, and her brows contracted. I flooded the stage of the microscope again with a full stream of light, and her whole expression changed. She sprang forward like some substance deprived of all weight. Her eyes sparkled and her lips moved. Ah! if science had only the means of conducting and reduplicating sounds, as it does the rays of light, what carols of happiness would then have entranced my ears! what jubilant hymns to Adonaïs* would have thrilled the illumined air!

I now comprehended how it was that the Count de Gabalis* peopled his mystic world with sylphs,—beautiful beings whose breath of life was lambent fire, and who sported forever in regions of purest ether and purest light. The Rosicrucian had anticipated the wonder that I had practically realized.

How long this worship of my strange divinity went on thus I scarcely know. I lost all note of time. All day from early dawn, and far into the night, I was to be found peering through that wonderful lens. I saw no one, went nowhere, and scarce allowed myself sufficient time for my meals. My whole life was absorbed in contemplation as rapt as that of any of the Romish saints. Every hour that I gazed upon the divine form strengthened my passion,—a passion that was always overshadowed by the maddening conviction, that, although I could gaze on her at will, she never, never could behold me!

At length, I grew so pale and emaciated, from want of rest, and continual brooding over my insane love and its cruel conditions, that

I determined to make some effort to wean myself from it. 'Come,' I said, 'this is at best but a fantasy. Your imagination has bestowed on Animula charms which in reality she does not possess. Seclusion from female society has produced this morbid condition of mind. Compare her with the beautiful women of your own world, and this false enchantment will vanish.'

I looked over the newspapers by chance. There I beheld the advertisement of a celebrated *danseuse* who appeared nightly at Niblo's.* The Signorina Caradolce* had the reputation of being the most beautiful as well as the most graceful woman in the world. I instantly dressed and went to the theatre.

The curtain drew up. The usual semicircle of fairies in white muslin were standing on the right toe around the enamelled flower-bank, of green canvas, on which the belated prince was sleeping. Suddenly a flute is heard. The fairies start. The trees open, the fairies all stand on the left toe, and the queen enters. It was the Signorina. She bounded forward amid thunders of applause, and, lighting on one foot, remained poised in air. Heavens! was this the great enchantress that had drawn monarchs at her chariot-wheels? Those heavy muscular limbs, those thick ankles, those cavernous eyes, that stereotyped smile, those crudely painted cheeks! Where were the vermeil blooms, the liquid expressive eyes, the harmonious limbs of Animula?

The Signorina danced. What gross, discordant movements! The play of her limbs was all false and artificial. Her bounds were painful athletic efforts; her poses were angular and distressed the eye. I could bear it no longer; with an exclamation of disgust that drew every eye upon me, I rose from my seat in the very middle of the Signorina's *pas-de-fascination*,* and abruptly quitted the house.

I hastened home to feast my eyes once more on the lovely form of my sylph. I felt that henceforth to combat this passion would be impossible. I applied my eye to the lens. Animula was there,—but what could have happened? Some terrible change seemed to have taken place during my absence. Some secret grief seemed to cloud the lovely features of her I gazed upon. Her face had grown thin and haggard; her limbs trailed heavily; the wondrous lustre of her golden hair had faded. She was ill!—ill, and I could not assist her! I believe at that moment I would have gladly forfeited all claims to my human birthright, if I could only have been dwarfed to the size of an animalcule, and permitted to console her from whom fate had forever divided me.

I racked my brain for the solution of this mystery. What was it that afflicted the sylph? She seemed to suffer intense pain. Her features contracted, and she even writhed, as if with some internal agony. The wondrous forests appeared also to have lost half their beauty. Their hues were dim and in some places faded away altogether. I watched Animula for hours with a breaking heart, and she seemed absolutely to wither away under my very eye. Suddenly I remembered that I had not looked at the water-drop for several days. In fact, I hated to see it; for it reminded me of the natural barrier between Animula and myself. I hurriedly looked down on the stage of the microscope. The slide was still there,—but, great heavens! the water-drop had vanished! The awful truth burst upon me; it had evaporated, until it had become so minute as to be invisible to the naked eye; I had been gazing on its last atom, the one that contained Animula,—and she was dying!

I rushed again to the front of the lens, and looked through. Alas! the last agony had seized her. The rainbow-hued forests had all melted away, and Animula lay struggling feebly in what seemed to be a spot of dim light. Ah! the sight was horrible: the limbs once so round and lovely shrivelling up into nothings; the eyes—those eyes that shone like heaven—being quenched into black dust; the lustrous golden hair now lank and discolored. The last throe came. I beheld that final struggle of the blackening form—and I fainted.

When I awoke out of a trance of many hours, I found myself lying amid the wreck of my instrument, myself as shattered in mind and body as it. I crawled feebly to my bed, from which I did not rise for months.

They say now that I am mad; but they are mistaken. I am poor, for I have neither the heart nor the will to work; all my money is spent, and I live on charity. Young men's associations that love a joke invite me to lecture on Optics before them, for which they pay me, and laugh at me while I lecture. 'Linley, the mad microscopist,' is the name I go by. I suppose that I talk incoherently while I lecture. Who could talk sense when his brain is haunted by such ghastly memories, while ever and anon among the shapes of death I behold the radiant form of my lost Animula!

GEORGE ELIOT

*THE LIFTED VEIL**

> Give me no light, great Heaven, but such as turns
> To energy of human fellowship;
> No powers beyond the growing heritage
> That makes completer manhood.*

CHAPTER I

THE time of my end approaches. I have lately been subject to attacks of *angina pectoris*;* and in the ordinary course of things, my physician tells me, I may fairly hope that my life will not be protracted many months. Unless, then, I am cursed with an exceptional physical constitution, as I am cursed with an exceptional mental character, I shall not much longer groan under the wearisome burthen of this earthly existence. If it were to be otherwise—if I were to live on to the age most men desire and provide for—I should for once have known whether the miseries of delusive expectation can outweigh the miseries of true prevision. For I foresee when I shall die, and everything that will happen in my last moments.

Just a month from this day, on the 20th of September 1850, I shall be sitting in this chair, in this study, at ten o'clock at night, longing to die, weary of incessant insight and foresight, without delusions and without hope. Just as I am watching a tongue of blue flame rising in the fire, and my lamp is burning low, the horrible contraction will begin at my chest. I shall only have time to reach the bell, and pull it violently, before the sense of suffocation will come. No one will answer my bell. I know why. My two servants are lovers, and will have quarrelled. My housekeeper will have rushed out of the house in a fury, two hours before, hoping that Perry will believe she has gone to drown herself. Perry is alarmed at last, and is gone out after her. The little scullery-maid is asleep on a bench: she never answers the bell; it does not wake her. The sense of suffocation increases: my lamp goes out with a horrible stench: I make a great effort, and snatch at the bell again. I long for life, and there is no help. I thirsted for the unknown: the thirst is gone. O God, let me stay with the known, and be weary of it: I am content. Agony of pain and suffocation—and all the while the earth, the fields, the pebbly brook at the bottom of the rookery, the fresh scent after the rain, the light of the morning through my chamber-window, the warmth of the hearth after the frosty air—will darkness close over them for ever?

Darkness—darkness—no pain—nothing but darkness: but I am passing on and on through the darkness: my thought stays in the darkness, but always with a sense of moving onward. . . .

Before that time comes, I wish to use my last hours of ease and strength in telling the strange story of my experience. I have never fully unbosomed myself to any human being; I have never been encouraged to trust much in the sympathy of my fellow-men. But we have all a chance of meeting with some pity, some tenderness, some charity, when we are dead: it is the living only who cannot be forgiven—the living only from whom men's indulgence and reverence are held off, like the rain by the hard east wind. While the heart beats, bruise it—it is your only opportunity; while the eye can still turn towards you with moist timid entreaty, freeze it with an icy unanswering gaze; while the ear, that delicate messenger to the inmost sanctuary of the soul, can still take in the tones of kindness, put it off with hard civility, or sneering compliment, or envious affectation of indifference; while the creative brain can still throb with the sense of injustice, with the yearning for brotherly recognition—make haste— oppress it with your ill-considered judgments, your trivial comparisons, your careless misrepresentations. The heart will by-and-by be still—*ubi sæva indignatio ulterius cor lacerare nequit;*[1] the eye will cease to entreat; the ear will be deaf; the brain will have ceased from all wants as well as from all work. Then your charitable speeches may find vent; then you may remember and pity the toil and the struggle and the failure; then you may give due honour to the work achieved; then you may find extenuation for errors, and may consent to bury them.

That is a trivial schoolboy text; why do I dwell on it? It has little reference to me, for I shall leave no works behind me for men to honour. I have no near relatives who will make up, by weeping over my grave, for the wounds they inflicted on me when I was among them. It is only the story of my life that will perhaps win a little more

---

[1] Inscription on Swift's tombstone.

sympathy from strangers when I am dead, than I ever believed it would obtain from my friends while I was living.

My childhood perhaps seems happier to me than it really was, by contrast with all the after-years. For then the curtain of the future was as impenetrable to me as to other children: I had all their delight in the present hour, their sweet indefinite hopes for the morrow; and I had a tender mother: even now, after the dreary lapse of long years, a slight trace of sensation accompanies the remembrance of her caress as she held me on her knee—her arms round my little body, her cheek pressed on mine. I had a complaint of the eyes that made me blind for a little while, and she kept me on her knee from morning till night. That unequalled love soon vanished out of my life, and even to my childish consciousness it was as if that life had become more chill. I rode my little white pony with the groom by my side as before, but there were no loving eyes looking at me as I mounted, no glad arms opened to me when I came back. Perhaps I missed my mother's love more than most children of seven or eight would have done, to whom the other pleasures of life remained as before; for I was certainly a very sensitive child. I remember still the mingled trepidation and delicious excitement with which I was affected by the tramping of the horses on the pavement in the echoing stables, by the loud resonance of the grooms' voices, by the booming bark of the dogs as my father's carriage thundered under the archway of the courtyard, by the din of the gong as it gave notice of luncheon and dinner. The measured tramp of soldiery which I sometimes heard—for my father's house lay near a county town where there were large barracks—made me sob and tremble; and yet when they were gone past, I longed for them to come back again.

I fancy my father thought me an odd child, and had little fondness for me; though he was very careful in fulfilling what he regarded as a parent's duties. But he was already past the middle of life, and I was not his only son. My mother had been his second wife, and he was five-and-forty when he married her. He was a firm, unbending, intensely orderly man, in root and stem a banker, but with a flourishing graft of the active landholder, aspiring to county influence: one of those people who are always like themselves from day to day, who are uninfluenced by the weather, and neither know melancholy nor high spirits. I held him in great awe, and appeared more timid and sensitive in his presence than at other times; a circumstance which, perhaps, helped to confirm him in the intention to educate me on a different plan from the prescriptive one with which he had complied in the case of my elder brother, already a tall youth at Eton.* My brother was to be his representative and successor; he must go to Eton and Oxford, for the sake of making connections, of course: my father was not a man to underrate the bearing of Latin satirists or Greek dramatists on the attainment of an aristocratic position. But, intrinsically, he had slight esteem for 'those dead but sceptred spirits';* having qualified himself for forming an independent opinion by reading Potter's 'Æschylus', and dipping into Francis's 'Horace'.* To this negative view he added a positive one, derived from a recent connection with mining speculations; namely, that a scientific education was the really useful training for a younger son. Moreover, it was clear that a shy, sensitive boy like me was not fit to encounter the rough experience of a public school. Mr Letherall had said so very decidedly. Mr Letherall was a large man in spectacles, who one day took my small head between his large hands, and pressed it here and there in an exploratory, suspicious manner—then placed each of his great thumbs on my temples, and pushed me a little way from him, and stared at me with glittering spectacles. The contemplation appeared to displease him, for he frowned sternly, and said to my father, drawing his thumbs across my eyebrows—

'The deficiency is there, sir—there; and here,' he added, touching the upper sides of my head, 'here is the excess. That must be brought out, sir, and this must be laid to sleep.'

I was in a state of tremor, partly at the vague idea that I was the object of reprobation, partly in the agitation of my first hatred—hatred of this big, spectacled man, who pulled my head about as if he wanted to buy and cheapen it.

I am not aware how much Mr Letherall had to do with the system afterwards adopted towards me, but it was presently clear that private tutors, natural history, science, and the modern languages, were the appliances by which the defects of my organisation were to be remedied. I was very stupid about machines, so I was to be greatly occupied with them; I had no memory for classification, so it was particularly necessary that I should study systematic zoology and botany; I was hungry for human deeds and human emotions, so I was to be plentifully crammed with the mechanical powers, the elementary bodies, and the phenomena of electricity and magnetism. A better-constituted boy would certainly have profited under my intelligent tutors, with their scientific apparatus; and would, doubtless, have found the phenomena of electricity and magnetism as fascinating as I was, every Thursday, assured they were. As it was, I could have paired off, for ignorance of whatever was taught me, with the worst Latin scholar that was ever turned out of a classical academy. I read Plutarch, and Shakspere, and Don Quixote* by the sly, and supplied myself in that way with wandering thoughts, while my tutor was assuring me that 'an improved man, as distinguished from an ignorant one, was a man who knew the reason why water ran down-hill.' I had no desire to be this improved man; I was glad of the running water; I could watch it and listen to it gurgling among the pebbles, and bathing the bright green water-plants, by the hour together. I did not want to know *why* it ran; I had perfect confidence that there were good reasons for what was so very beautiful.

There is no need to dwell on this part of my life. I have said enough to indicate that my nature was of the sensitive, unpractical order, and that it grew up in an uncongenial medium, which could never foster it into happy, healthy development. When I was sixteen I was sent to Geneva* to complete my course of education; and the change was a very happy one to me, for the first sight of the Alps, with the setting sun on them, as we descended the Jura,* seemed to me like an entrance into heaven; and the three years of my life there were spent in a perpetual sense of exaltation, as if from a draught of delicious wine, at the presence of Nature in all her awful loveliness. You will think, perhaps, that I must have been a poet, from this early sensibility to Nature. But my lot was not so happy as that. A poet pours forth his song and *believes* in the listening ear and answering soul, to which his song will be floated sooner or later. But the poet's sensibility without his voice—the poet's sensibility that finds no vent but in silent tears on the sunny bank, when the noonday light sparkles on the water, or in an inward shudder at the sound of harsh human tones, the sight of a cold human eye—this dumb passion brings with it a fatal solitude of soul in the society of one's fellow-men. My least solitary moments were those in which I pushed off in my boat, at evening, towards the centre of the lake; it seemed to me that the sky, and the glowing mountain-tops, and the wide blue water, surrounded me with a cherishing love such as no human face had shed on me since my mother's love had vanished out of my life. I used to do as Jean Jacques did*—lie down in my boat and let it glide where it would, while I looked up at the departing glow leaving one mountain-top after the other, as if the prophet's chariot of fire* were passing over them on its way to the home of light. Then, when the white summits were all sad and corpse-like, I had to push homeward, for I was under careful surveillance, and was allowed no late wanderings. This disposition of mine was not favourable to the formation of intimate friendships among the numerous youths of my own age who are always to be found studying at Geneva. Yet I made *one* such friendship; and, singularly enough, it was with a youth whose intellectual tendencies were the very reverse of my own. I shall call him Charles Meunier; his real surname—an English one, for he was of English extraction—having since become celebrated. He was an orphan, who lived on a miserable pittance while he pursued the medical studies for which he had a special genius. Strange! that with my vague mind, susceptible and unobservant, hating inquiry and given up to contemplation, I should have been drawn towards a youth whose strongest passion was science. But the bond was not an intellectual one; it came from a source that can happily blend the stupid with the brilliant, the dreamy with the practical: it came from community of feeling. Charles was poor and ugly, derided by Genevese *gamins*,* and not acceptable in drawing-rooms. I saw that he was isolated, as I was, though from a different cause, and, stimulated by a sympathetic resentment, I made timid advances towards him. It is enough to say that there sprang up as much comradeship between us as our different habits would allow; and in Charles's rare holidays we went up the Salève together, or took the boat to Vevay,* while I listened dreamily to the monologues in which he unfolded his bold conceptions of future experiment and discovery. I mingled them confusedly in my thought with glimpses of blue water and delicate floating cloud, with the notes of birds and the distant glitter of the glacier. He knew quite well that my mind was half absent, yet he liked to talk to me in this way; for don't we talk of our hopes and our projects even to dogs and birds, when they love us? I have mentioned this one friendship because of its connection with a strange and terrible scene which I shall have to narrate in my subsequent life.

This happier life at Geneva was put an end to by a severe illness, which is partly a blank to me, partly a time of dimly-remembered suffering, with the presence of my father by my bed from time to time. Then came the languid monotony of convalescence, the days gradually breaking into variety and distinctness as my strength enabled me to take longer and longer drives. On one of these more vividly remembered days, my father said to me, as he sat beside my sofa—

'When you are quite well enough to travel, Latimer, I shall take you home with me. The journey will amuse you and do you good, for I shall go through the Tyrol and Austria, and you will see many new places. Our neighbours, the Filmores, are come; Alfred will join us at Basle, and we shall all go together to Vienna, and back by Prague'*...

My father was called away before he had finished his sentence, and he left my mind resting on the word *Prague*, with a strange sense that a new and wondrous scene was breaking upon me: a city under the broad sunshine, that seemed to me as if it were the summer sunshine of a long-past century arrested in its course—unrefreshed for ages by the dews of night, or the rushing rain-cloud; scorching the dusty, weary, time-eaten grandeur of a people doomed to live on in the stale repetition of memories, like deposed and superannuated kings in their regal gold-inwoven tatters. The city looked so thirsty that the broad river seemed to me a sheet of metal; and the blackened statues, as I passed under their blank gaze, along the unending bridge, with their ancient garments and their saintly crowns, seemed to me the real inhabitants and owners of this place, while the busy, trivial men and women, hurrying to and fro, were a swarm of ephemeral visitants infesting it for a day. It is such grim, stony beings as these, I thought, who are the fathers of ancient faded children, in those tanned time-fretted dwellings that crowd the steep before me; who pay their court in the worn and crumbling pomp of the palace which stretches its monotonous length on the height; who worship wearily in the stifling air of the churches, urged by no fear or hope, but compelled by their doom to be ever old and undying, to live on in the rigidity of habit, as they live on in perpetual mid-day, without the repose of night or the new birth of morning.

A stunning clang of metal suddenly thrilled through me, and I became conscious of the objects in my room again: one of the fire-irons had fallen as Pierre opened the door to bring me my draught. My heart was palpitating violently, and I begged Pierre to leave my draught beside me; I would take it presently.

As soon as I was alone again, I began to ask myself whether I had been sleeping. Was this a dream—this wonderfully distinct vision—minute in its distinctness down to a patch of rainbow light on the pavement, transmitted through a coloured lamp in the shape of a star—of a strange city, quite unfamiliar to my imagination? I had seen no picture of Prague: it lay in my mind as a mere name, with vaguely-remembered historical associations—ill-defined memories of imperial grandeur and religious wars.

Nothing of this sort had ever occurred in my dreaming experience before, for I had often been humiliated because my dreams were only saved from being utterly disjointed and commonplace by the frequent terrors of nightmare. But I could not believe that I had been asleep, for I remembered distinctly the gradual breaking-in of the vision upon me, like the new images in a dissolving view, or the growing distinctness of the landscape as the sun lifts up the veil of the morning mist. And while I was conscious of this incipient vision, I was also conscious that Pierre came to tell my father Mr Filmore was waiting for him, and that my father hurried out of the room. No, it was not a dream; was it—the thought was full of tremulous exultation—was it the poet's nature in me, hitherto only a troubled yearning sensibility, now manifesting itself suddenly as spontaneous creation? Surely it was in this way that Homer saw the plain of Troy, that Dante saw the abodes of the departed, that Milton saw the earthward flight of the Tempter.* Was it that my illness had wrought some happy change in my organisation—given a firmer tension to my nerves—carried off some dull obstruction? I had often read of such effects—in works of fiction at least. Nay; in genuine biographies I had read of the subtilising or exalting influence of some diseases on the mental powers. Did not Novalis feel his inspiration intensified under the progress of consumption?*

When my mind had dwelt for some time on this blissful idea, it seemed to me that I might perhaps test it by an exertion of my will. The vision had begun when my father was speaking of our going to Prague. I did not for a moment believe it was really a representation of that city; I believed—I hoped it was a picture that my newly-liberated genius had painted in fiery haste, with the colours snatched from lazy memory. Suppose I were to fix my mind on some other place—Venice, for example, which was far more familiar to my imagination than Prague: perhaps the same sort of result would follow. I concentrated my thoughts on Venice; I stimulated my imagination with poetic memories, and strove to feel myself present in Venice, as I had felt myself present in Prague. But in vain. I was only colouring the Canaletto* engravings that hung in my old bedroom at home; the picture was a shifting one, my mind wandering uncertainly in search of more vivid images; I could see no accident of form or shadow without conscious labour after the necessary conditions. It was all prosaic effort, not rapt passivity, such as I had experienced half an hour before. I was discouraged; but I remembered that inspiration was fitful.

For several days I was in a state of excited expectation, watching for a recurrence of my new gift. I sent my thoughts ranging over my world of knowledge, in the hope that they would find some object which would send a reawakening vibration through my slumbering genius. But no; my world remained as dim as ever, and that flash of strange light refused to come again, though I watched for it with palpitating eagerness.

My father accompanied me every day in a drive, and a gradually lengthening walk as my powers of walking increased; and one evening he had agreed to come and fetch me at twelve the next day, that we might go together to select a musical box, and other purchases rigorously demanded of a rich Englishman visiting Geneva. He was one of the most punctual of men and bankers, and I was always nervously anxious to be quite ready for him at the appointed time. But, to my surprise, at a quarter past twelve he had not appeared. I felt all the impatience of a convalescent who has nothing particular to do, and who has just taken a tonic in the prospect of immediate exercise that would carry off the stimulus.

Unable to sit still and reserve my strength, I walked up and down the room, looking out on the current of the Rhone, just where it leaves the dark-blue lake; but thinking all the while of the possible causes that could detain my father.

Suddenly I was conscious that my father was in the room, but not alone: there were two persons with him. Strange! I had heard no footstep, I had not seen the door open; but I saw my father, and at his right hand our neighbour Mrs Filmore, whom I remembered very well, though I had not seen her for five years. She was a commonplace middle-aged woman, in silk and cashmere; but the lady on the left of my father was not more than twenty, a tall, slim, willowy figure, with luxuriant blond hair, arranged in cunning braids and folds that looked almost too massive for the slight figure and the small-featured, thin-lipped face they crowned. But the face had not a girlish expression:

the features were sharp, the pale grey eyes at once acute, restless, and sarcastic. They were fixed on me in half-smiling curiosity, and I felt a painful sensation as if a sharp wind were cutting me. The pale-green dress, and the green leaves that seemed to form a border about her pale blond hair, made me think of a Water-Nixie,—for my mind was full of German lyrics,* and this pale, fatal-eyed woman, with the green weeds, looked like a birth from some cold sedgy stream, the daughter of an aged river.

'Well, Latimer, you thought me long,' my father said. . . .

But while the last word was in my ears, the whole group vanished, and there was nothing between me and the Chinese painted folding-screen that stood before the door. I was cold and trembling; I could only totter forward and throw myself on the sofa. This strange new power had manifested itself again. . . . But *was* it a power? Might it not rather be a disease—a sort of intermittent delirium, concentrating my energy of brain into moments of unhealthy activity, and leaving my saner hours all the more barren? I felt a dizzy sense of unreality in what my eye rested on; I grasped the bell convulsively, like one trying to free himself from nightmare, and rang it twice. Pierre came with a look of alarm in his face.

'Monsieur ne se trouve pas bien?'* he said, anxiously.

'I'm tired of waiting, Pierre,' I said, as distinctly and emphatically as I could, like a man determined to be sober in spite of wine; 'I'm afraid something has happened to my father—he's usually so punctual. Run to the Hôtel des Bergues* and see if he is there.'

Pierre left the room at once, with a soothing 'Bien, Monsieur'; and I felt the better for this scene of simple, waking prose. Seeking to calm myself still further, I went into my bedroom, adjoining the salon, and opened a case of eau-de-Cologne; took out a bottle; went through the process of taking out the cork very neatly, and then rubbed the reviving spirit over my hands and forehead, and under my nostrils, drawing a new delight from the scent because I had procured it by slow details of labour, and by no strange sudden madness. Already I had begun to taste something of the horror that belongs to the lot of a human being whose nature is not adjusted to simple human conditions.

Still enjoying the scent, I returned to the *salon*, but it was not unoccupied, as it had been before I left it. In front of the Chinese folding-screen there was my father, with Mrs Filmore on his right hand, and on his left—the slim blond-haired girl, with the keen face and the keen eyes fixed on me in half-smiling curiosity.

'Well, Latimer, you thought me long,' my father said. . . .

I heard no more, felt no more, till I became conscious that I was lying with my head low on the sofa, Pierre and my father by my side. As soon as I was thoroughly revived, my father left the room, and presently returned, saying—

'I've been to tell the ladies how you are, Latimer. They were waiting in the next room. We shall put off our shopping expedition to-day.'

Presently he said, 'That young lady is Bertha Grant, Mrs Filmore's orphan niece. Filmore has adopted her, and she lives with them, so you will have her for a neighbour when we go home—perhaps for a near relation; for there is a tenderness between her and Alfred, I suspect, and I should be gratified by the match, since Filmore means to provide for her in every way as if she were his daughter. It had not occurred to me that you knew nothing about her living with the Filmores.'

He made no further allusion to the fact of my having fainted at the moment of seeing her, and I would not for the world have told him the reason: I shrank from the idea of disclosing to any one what might be regarded as a pitiable peculiarity, most of all from betraying it to my father, who would have suspected my sanity ever after.

I do not mean to dwell with particularity on the details of my experience. I have described these two cases at length, because they had definite, clearly traceable results in my after-lot.

Shortly after this last occurrence—I think the very next day— I began to be aware of a phase in my abnormal sensibility, to which, from the languid and slight nature of my intercourse with others since my illness, I had not been alive before. This was the obtrusion on my mind of the mental process going forward in first one person, and then another, with whom I happened to be in contact: the vagrant, frivolous ideas and emotions of some uninteresting acquaintance— Mrs Filmore, for example—would force themselves on my consciousness like an importunate, ill-played musical instrument, or the loud activity of an imprisoned insect. But this unpleasant sensibility was fitful, and left me moments of rest, when the souls of my companions were once more shut out from me, and I felt a relief such as silence brings to wearied nerves. I might have believed this importunate insight to be merely a diseased activity of the imagination, but that my prevision of incalculable words and actions proved it to have a fixed relation to the mental process in other minds. But this super-added consciousness, wearying and annoying enough when it urged on me the trivial experience of indifferent people, became an intense pain and grief when it seemed to be opening to me the souls of those who were in a close relation to me—when the rational talk, the grace-ful attentions, the wittily-turned phrases, and the kindly deeds, which used to make the web of their characters, were seen as if thrust asun-der by a microscopic vision,* that showed all the intermediate frivol-ities, all the suppressed egoism, all the struggling chaos of puerilities, meanness, vague capricious memories, and indolent make-shift thoughts, from which human words and deeds emerge like leaflets covering a fermenting heap.

At Basle we were joined by my brother Alfred, now a handsome self-confident man of six-and-twenty—a thorough contrast to my fragile, nervous, ineffectual self. I believe I was held to have a sort of half-womanish, half-ghostly beauty; for the portrait-painters, who are thick as weeds at Geneva, had often asked me to sit to them, and I had been the model of a dying minstrel in a fancy picture. But I thoroughly disliked my own *physique*, and nothing but the belief that it was a condition of poetic genius would have reconciled me to it. That brief hope was quite fled, and I saw in my face now nothing but the stamp of a morbid organisation, framed for passive suffering—too feeble for the sublime resistance of poetic production. Alfred, from whom I had been almost constantly separated, and who, in his present stage of character and appearance, came before me as a perfect stranger, was bent on being extremely friendly and brother-like to me. He had the superficial kindness of a good-humoured, self-satisfied nature, that fears no rivalry, and has encountered no contrarieties. I am not sure that my disposition was good enough for me to have been quite free from envy towards him, even if our desires had not clashed, and if I had been in the healthy human condition which admits of generous confidence and charitable construction. There must always have been an antipathy between our natures. As it was, he became in a few weeks an object of intense hatred to me; and when he entered the room, still more when he spoke, it was as if a sensation of grating metal had set my teeth on edge. My diseased consciousness was more intensely and continually occupied with his thoughts and emotions, than with those of any other person who came in my way.

I was perpetually exasperated with the petty promptings of his conceit and his love of patronage, with his self-complacent belief in Bertha Grant's passion for him, with his half-pitying contempt for me—seen not in the ordinary indications of intonation and phrase and slight action, which an acute and suspicious mind is on the watch for, but in all their naked skinless complication.

For we were rivals, and our desires clashed, though he was not aware of it. I have said nothing yet of the effect Bertha Grant produced in me on a nearer acquaintance. That effect was chiefly determined by the fact that she made the only exception, among all the human beings about me, to my unhappy gift of insight. About Bertha I was always in a state of uncertainty: I could watch the expression of her face, and speculate on its meaning; I could ask for her opinion with the real interest of ignorance; I could listen for her words and watch for her smile with hope and fear: she had for me the fascination of an unravelled destiny. I say it was this fact that chiefly determined the strong effect she produced on me: for, in the abstract, no womanly character could seem to have less affinity for that of a shrinking, romantic, passionate youth than Bertha's. She was keen, sarcastic, unimaginative, prematurely cynical, remaining critical and unmoved in the most impressive scenes, inclined to dissect all my favourite poems, and especially contemptuous towards the German lyrics which were my pet literature at that time. To this moment I am unable to define my feeling towards her: it was not ordinary boyish admiration, for she was the very opposite, even to the colour of her hair, of the ideal woman who still remained to me the type of loveliness; and she was without that enthusiasm for the great and good, which, even at the moment of her strongest dominion over me, I should have declared to be the highest element of character. But there is no tyranny more complete than that which a self-centred negative nature exercises over a morbidly sensitive nature perpetually craving sympathy and support. The most independent people feel the effect of a man's silence in heightening their value for his opinion—feel an additional triumph in conquering the reverence of a critic habitually captious and satirical: no wonder, then, that an enthusiastic self-distrusting youth should watch and wait before the closed secret of a sarcastic woman's face, as if it were the shrine of the doubtfully benignant deity who ruled his destiny. For a young enthusiast is unable to imagine the total negation in another mind of the emotions which are stirring his own: they may be feeble, latent, inactive, he thinks, but they are there—they may be called forth; sometimes, in moments of happy hallucination, he believes they may be there in all the greater strength because he sees no outward sign of them. And this effect, as I have intimated, was heightened to its utmost intensity in me, because Bertha was the only being who remained for me in the mysterious seclusion of soul that renders such youthful delusion possible. Doubtless there was another sort of fascination at work—that subtle physical attraction which delights in cheating our psychological predictions, and in compelling the men who paint sylphs,* to fall in love with some *bonne et brave femme*,* heavy-heeled and freckled.

. Bertha's behaviour towards me was such as to encourage all my illusions, to heighten my boyish passion, and make me more and more dependent on her smiles. Looking back with my present wretched knowledge, I conclude that her vanity and love of power were intensely gratified by the belief that I had fainted on first seeing her purely from the strong impression her person had produced on me. The most prosaic woman likes to believe herself the object of a violent, a poetic passion; and without a grain of romance in her, Bertha had that spirit of intrigue which gave piquancy to the idea that the brother of the man she meant to marry was dying with love and jealousy for her sake. That she meant to marry my brother, was what at that time I did not believe; for though he was assiduous in his attentions to her, and I knew well enough that both he and my father had made up their minds to this result, there was not yet an understood engagement—there had been no explicit declaration; and Bertha habitually, while she flirted with my brother, and accepted his homage in a way that implied to him a thorough recognition of its intention, made me believe, by the subtlest looks and phrases—feminine nothings which could never be quoted against her—that he was really the object of her secret ridicule; that she thought him, as I did, a coxcomb, whom she would have pleasure in disappointing. Me she openly petted in my brother's presence, as if I were too young and sickly ever to be thought of as a lover; and that was the view he took of me. But I believe she must inwardly have delighted in the tremors into which she threw me by the coaxing way in which she patted my curls, while she laughed at my quotations. Such caresses were always given in the presence of our friends; for when we were alone together, she affected a much greater distance towards me, and now and then took the opportunity, by words or slight actions, to stimulate my foolish timid hope that she really preferred me. And why should she not follow her inclination? I was not in so advantageous a position as my brother, but I had fortune, I was not a year younger than she was, and she was an heiress, who would soon be of age to decide for herself.

The fluctuations of hope and fear, confined to this one channel, made each day in her presence a delicious torment. There was one deliberate act of hers which especially helped to intoxicate me. When we were at Vienna her twentieth birthday occurred, and as she was very fond of ornaments, we all took the opportunity of the splendid jewellers' shops in that Teutonic Paris to purchase her a birthday present of jewellery. Mine, naturally, was the least expensive; it was an opal ring—the opal was my favourite stone, because it seems to blush and turn pale as if it had a soul. I told Bertha so when I gave it her, and said that it was an emblem of the poetic nature, changing with the changing light of heaven and of woman's eyes. In the evening she appeared elegantly dressed, and wearing conspicuously all the birthday presents except mine. I looked eagerly at her fingers, but saw no opal. I had no opportunity of noticing this to her during the evening; but the next day, when I found her seated near the window alone, after breakfast, I said, 'You scorn to wear my poor opal. I should have remembered that you despised poetic natures, and should have given you coral, or turquoise, or some other opaque unresponsive stone.' 'Do I despise it?' she answered, taking hold of a delicate gold chain which she always wore round her neck and drawing out the end from her bosom with my ring hanging to it; 'it hurts me a little, I can tell you,' she said, with her usual dubious smile, 'to wear it in that secret place; and since your poetical nature is so stupid as to prefer a more public position, I shall not endure the pain any longer.'

She took off the ring from the chain and put it on her finger, smiling still, while the blood rushed to my cheeks, and I could not trust myself to say a word of entreaty that she would keep the ring where it was before.

I was completely fooled by this, and for two days shut myself up in my own room whenever Bertha was absent, that I might intoxicate myself afresh with the thought of this scene and all it implied.

I should mention that during these two months—which seemed a long life to me from the novelty and intensity of the pleasures and pains I underwent—my diseased participation in other people's consciousness continued to torment me; now it was my father, and now my brother, now Mrs Filmore or her husband, and now our German courier, whose stream of thought rushed upon me like a ringing in the ears not to be got rid of, though it allowed my own impulses and ideas to continue their uninterrupted course. It was like a preternaturally heightened sense of hearing, making audible to one a roar of sound where others find perfect stillness.* The weariness and disgust of this involuntary intrusion into other souls was counteracted only by my ignorance of Bertha, and my growing passion for her; a passion enormously stimulated, if not produced, by that ignorance. She was my oasis of mystery in the dreary desert of knowledge. I had never allowed my diseased condition to betray itself, or to drive me into any unusual speech or action, except once, when, in a moment of peculiar bitterness against my brother, I had forestalled some words which I knew he was going to utter—a clever observation, which he had prepared beforehand. He had occasionally a slightly-affected hesitation in his speech, and when he paused an instant after the second word, my impatience and jealousy impelled me to continue the speech for him, as if it were something we had both learned by rote. He coloured and looked astonished, as well as annoyed; and the words had no sooner escaped my lips than I felt a shock of alarm lest such an anticipation of words—very far from being words of course, easy to divine—should have betrayed me as an exceptional being, a sort of quiet energumen,* whom every one, Bertha above all, would shudder at and avoid. But I magnified, as usual, the impression any word or deed of mine could produce on others; for no one gave any sign of having noticed my interruption as more than a rudeness, to be forgiven me on the score of my feeble nervous condition.

While this superadded consciousness of the actual was almost constant with me, I had never had a recurrence of that distinct prevision which I have described in relation to my first interview with Bertha; and I was waiting with eager curiosity to know whether or not my vision of Prague would prove to have been an instance of the same kind. A few days after the incident of the opal ring, we were paying one of our frequent visits to the Lichtenberg Palace.* I could never look at many pictures in succession; for pictures, when they are at all powerful, affect me so strongly that one or two exhaust all my capability of contemplation. This morning I had been looking at Giorgione's picture of the cruel-eyed woman, said to be a likeness of Lucrezia Borgia.* I had stood long alone before it, fascinated by the terrible reality of that cunning, relentless face, till I felt a strange poisoned sensation, as if I had long been inhaling a fatal odour, and was just beginning to be conscious of its effects. Perhaps even then I should not have moved away, if the rest of the party had not returned to this room, and announced that they were going to the Belvedere Gallery* to settle a bet which had arisen between my brother and Mr Filmore about a portrait. I followed them dreamily, and was hardly alive to what occurred till they had all gone up to the gallery, leaving me below; for I refused to come within sight of another picture that day. I made my way to the Grand Terrace, since it was agreed that we should saunter in the gardens when the dispute had been decided. I had been sitting here a short space, vaguely conscious of trim gardens, with a city and green hills in the distance, when, wishing to avoid the proximity of the sentinel, I rose and walked down the broad stone steps, intending to seat myself farther on in the gardens. Just as I reached the gravel-walk, I felt an arm slipped within mine, and a light hand gently pressing my wrist. In the same instant a strange intoxicating numbness passed over me, like the continuance or climax of the sensation I was still feeling from the gaze of Lucrezia Borgia. The gardens, the summer sky, the consciousness of Bertha's arm being within mine, all vanished, and I seemed to be suddenly in darkness, out of which there gradually broke a dim firelight, and I felt myself sitting in my father's leather chair in the library at home. I knew the fireplace—the dogs for the wood-fire*—the black marble chimney-piece with the white marble medallion of the dying Cleopatra* in the centre. Intense and hopeless misery was pressing on my soul; the light became stronger, for Bertha was entering with a candle in her hand—Bertha, my wife—with cruel eyes, with green jewels and green leaves on her white ball-dress; every hateful thought within her present to me. . . . 'Madman, idiot! why don't you kill yourself, then?' It was a moment of hell. I saw into her pitiless soul—saw its barren worldliness, its scorching hate—and felt it clothe me round like an air I was obliged to breathe. She came with her candle and stood over me with a bitter smile of contempt; I saw the great emerald brooch on her bosom, a studded serpent with diamond eyes. I shuddered—I despised this woman with the barren soul and mean thoughts; but I felt helpless before her, as if she clutched my bleeding heart, and would clutch it till the last drop of life-blood ebbed away. She was my wife, and we hated each other. Gradually the hearth, the dim library, the candle-light disappeared—seemed to melt away into a background of light, the green serpent with the diamond eyes remaining a dark image on the retina. Then I had a sense of my eyelids quivering, and the living daylight broke in upon me; I saw gardens, and heard voices; I was seated on the steps of the Belvedere Terrace, and my friends were round me.

The tumult of mind into which I was thrown by this hideous vision made me ill for several days, and prolonged our stay at Vienna. I shud-dered with horror as the scene recurred to me; and it recurred con-stantly, with all its minutiæ, as if they had been burnt into my memory; and yet, such is the madness of the human heart under the influence of its immediate desires, I felt a wild hell-braving joy that Bertha was to be mine; for the fulfilment of my former prevision concerning her first appearance before me, left me little hope that this last hideous glimpse of the future was the mere diseased play of my own mind, and had no relation to external realities. One thing alone I looked towards as a possible means of casting doubt on my terrible convic-tion—the discovery that my vision of Prague had been false—and Prague was the next city on our route.

Meanwhile, I was no sooner in Bertha's society again, than I was as completely under her sway as before. What if I saw into the heart of Bertha, the matured woman—Bertha, my wife? Bertha, the girl, was a fascinating secret to me still: I trembled under her touch; I felt the witchery of her presence; I yearned to be assured of her love. The fear of poison is feeble against the sense of thirst. Nay, I was just as jealous of my brother as before—just as much irritated by his small patron-ising ways; for my pride, my diseased sensibility, were there as they had always been, and winced as inevitably under every offence as my eye winced from an intruding mote. The future, even when brought within the compass of feeling by a vision that made me shudder, had still no more than the force of an idea, compared with the force of present emotion—of my love for Bertha, of my dislike and jealousy towards my brother.

It is an old story, that men sell themselves to the tempter, and sign a bond with their blood,* because it is only to take effect at a distant day; then rush on to snatch the cup their souls thirst after with an impulse not the less savage because there is a dark shadow beside them for evermore. There is no short cut, no patent tram-road,* to wisdom: after all the centuries of invention, the soul's path lies through the thorny wilderness which must be still trodden in solitude, with bleeding feet, with sobs for help, as it was trodden by them of old time.

My mind speculated eagerly on the means by which I should become my brother's successful rival, for I was still too timid, in my ignorance of Bertha's actual feeling, to venture on any step that would urge from her an avowal of it. I thought I should gain confidence even for this, if my vision of Prague proved to have been veracious; and yet, the horror of that certitude! Behind the slim girl Bertha, whose words and looks I watched for, whose touch was bliss, there stood continually that Bertha with the fuller form, the harder eyes, the more rigid mouth,—with the barren selfish soul laid bare; no longer a fascinating secret, but a measured fact, urging itself perpetually on my unwilling sight. Are you unable to give me your sympathy—you who read this? Are you unable to imagine this double consciousness* at work within me, flowing on like two parallel streams which never mingle their waters and blend into a common hue? Yet you must have known something of the presentiments that spring from an insight at war with passion; and my visions were only like presentiments intensified to horror. You have known the powerlessness of ideas before the might of impulse; and my visions, when once they had passed into memory, were mere ideas—pale shadows that beckoned in vain, while my hand was grasped by the living and the loved.

In after-days I thought with bitter regret that if I had foreseen something more or something different—if instead of that hideous vision which poisoned the passion it could not destroy, or if even along with it I could have had a foreshadowing of that moment when I looked on my brother's face for the last time, some softening influence would have been shed over my feeling towards him: pride and hatred would surely have been subdued into pity, and the record of those hidden sins would have been shortened. But this is one of the vain thoughts with which we men flatter ourselves. We try to believe that the egoism within us would have easily been melted, and that it was only the narrowness of our knowledge which hemmed in our generosity, our awe, our human piety, and hindered them from submerging our hard indifference to the sensations and emotions of our fellow. Our tenderness and self-renunciation seem strong when our egoism has had its day—when, after our mean striving for a triumph that is to be another's loss, the triumph comes suddenly, and we shudder at it, because it is held out by the chill hand of death.

Our arrival in Prague happened at night, and I was glad of this, for it seemed like a deferring of a terribly decisive moment, to be in the city for hours without seeing it. As we were not to remain long in Prague, but to go on speedily to Dresden, it was proposed that we should drive out the next morning and take a general view of the place, as well as visit some of its specially interesting spots, before the heat became oppressive—for we were in August, and the season was hot and dry. But it happened that the ladies were rather late at their morning toilet, and to my father's politely-repressed but perceptible annoyance, we were not in the carriage till the morning was far advanced. I thought with a sense of relief, as we entered the Jews' quarter, where we were to visit the old synagogue,* that we should be kept in this flat, shut-up part of the city, until we should all be too tired and too warm to go farther, and so we should return without seeing more than the streets through which we had already passed. That would give me another day's suspense—suspense, the only form in which a fearful spirit knows the solace of hope. But, as I stood under the blackened, groined arches of that old synagogue, made dimly visible by the seven thin candles in the sacred lamp, while our Jewish cicerone* reached down the Book of the Law, and read to us in its ancient tongue,—I felt a shuddering impression that this strange building, with its shrunken lights, this surviving withered remnant of medieval Judaism, was of a piece with my vision. Those darkened dusty Christian saints, with their loftier arches and their larger candles, needed the consolatory scorn with which they might point to a more shrivelled death-in-life than their own.

As I expected, when we left the Jews' quarter the elders of our party wished to return to the hotel. But now, instead of rejoicing in this, as I had done beforehand, I felt a sudden overpowering impulse to go on at once to the bridge, and put an end to the suspense I had been wishing to protract. I declared, with unusual decision, that I would get out of the carriage and walk on alone; they might return without me. My father, thinking this merely a sample of my usual 'poetic nonsense', objected that I should only do myself harm by walking in the heat; but when I persisted, he said angrily that I might follow my own absurd devices, but that Schmidt (our courier) must go with me. I assented to this, and set off with Schmidt towards the bridge. I had no sooner passed from under the archway of the grand old gate leading on to the bridge, than a trembling seized me, and I turned cold under the mid-day sun; yet I went on; I was in search of something—a small detail which I remembered with special intensity as part of my vision. There it was—the patch of rainbow light on the pavement transmitted through a lamp in the shape of a star.

CHAPTER II

Before the autumn was at an end, and while the brown leaves still stood thick on the beeches in our park, my brother and Bertha were engaged to each other, and it was understood that their marriage was to take place early in the next spring. In spite of the certainty I had felt from that moment on the bridge at Prague, that Bertha would one day be my wife, my constitutional timidity and distrust had continued to benumb me, and the words in which I had sometimes premeditated a confession of my love, had died away unuttered. The same conflict had gone on within me as before—the longing for an assurance of love from Bertha's lips, the dread lest a word of contempt and denial should fall upon me like a corrosive acid. What was the conviction of a distant necessity to me? I trembled under a present glance, I hungered after a present joy, I was clogged and chilled by a present fear. And so the days passed on: I witnessed Bertha's engagement and heard her marriage discussed as if I were under a conscious nightmare—knowing it was a dream that would vanish, but feeling stifled under the grasp of hard-clutching fingers.

When I was not in Bertha's presence—and I was with her very often, for she continued to treat me with a playful patronage that wakened no jealousy in my brother—I spent my time chiefly in wandering, in strolling, or taking long rides while the daylight lasted, and then shutting myself up with my unread books; for books had lost the power of chaining my attention. My self-consciousness was heightened to that pitch of intensity in which our own emotions take the form of a drama which urges itself imperatively on our contemplation, and we begin to weep, less under the sense of our suffering than at the thought of it. I felt a sort of pitying anguish over the pathos of my own lot: the lot of a being finely organised for pain, but with hardly any fibres that responded to pleasure—to whom the idea of future evil robbed the present of its joy, and for whom the idea of future good did not still the uneasiness of a present yearning or a present dread. I went dumbly through that stage of the poet's suffering, in which he feels the delicious pang of utterance, and makes an image of his sorrows.

I was left entirely without remonstrance concerning this dreamy wayward life: I knew my father's thought about me: 'That lad will never be good for anything in life: he may waste his years in an insignificant way on the income that falls to him: I shall not trouble myself about a career for him.'

One mild morning in the beginning of November, it happened that I was standing outside the portico patting lazy old Cæsar, a Newfoundland* almost blind with age, the only dog that ever took any notice of me—for the very dogs shunned me, and fawned on the happier people about me—when the groom brought up my brother's horse which was to carry him to the hunt, and my brother himself appeared at the door, florid, broad-chested, and self-complacent, feeling what a good-natured fellow he was not to behave insolently to us all on the strength of his great advantages.

'Latimer, old boy,' he said to me in a tone of compassionate cordiality, 'what a pity it is you don't have a run with the hounds now and then! The finest thing in the world for low spirits!'

'Low spirits!' I thought bitterly, as he rode away; 'that is the sort of phrase with which coarse, narrow natures like yours think to describe experience of which you can know no more than your horse knows. It is to such as you that the good of this world falls: ready dulness, healthy selfishness, good-tempered conceit—these are the keys to happiness.'

The quick thought came, that my selfishness was even stronger than his—it was only a suffering selfishness instead of an enjoying one. But then, again, my exasperating insight into Alfred's self-complacent soul, his freedom from all the doubts and fears, the unsatisfied yearnings, the exquisite tortures of sensitiveness, that had made the web of my life, seemed to absolve me from all bonds towards him. This man needed no pity, no love; those fine influences would have been as little felt by him as the delicate white mist is felt by the rock it caresses. There was no evil in store for *him*: if he was not to marry Bertha, it would be because he had found a lot pleasanter to himself.

Mr Filmore's house lay not more than half a mile beyond our own gates, and whenever I knew my brother was gone in an another direction,* I went there for the chance of finding Bertha at home. Later on in the day I walked thither. By a rare accident she was alone, and we walked out in the grounds together, for she seldom went on foot beyond the trimly-swept gravel-walks. I remember what a beautiful sylph she looked to me as the low November sun shone on her blond hair, and she tripped along teasing me with her usual light banter, to which I listened half fondly, half moodily; it was all the sign Bertha's mysterious inner self ever made to me. To-day perhaps the moodiness predominated, for I had not yet shaken off the access of jealous hate which my brother had raised in me by his parting patronage. Suddenly I interrupted and startled her by saying, almost fiercely, 'Bertha, how can you love Alfred?'

She looked at me with surprise for a moment, but soon her light smile came again, and she answered sarcastically, 'Why do you suppose I love him?'

'How can you ask that, Bertha?'

'What! your wisdom thinks I must love the man I'm going to marry? The most unpleasant thing in the world. I should quarrel with him; I should be jealous of him; our *ménage* would be conducted in a very ill-bred manner. A little quiet contempt contributes greatly to the elegance of life.'

'Bertha, that is not your real feeling. Why do you delight in trying to deceive me by inventing such cynical speeches?'

'I need never take the trouble of invention in order to deceive you, my small Tasso'*—(that was the mocking name she usually gave me). 'The easiest way to deceive a poet is to tell him the truth.'

She was testing the validity of her epigram in a daring way, and for a moment the shadow of my vision—the Bertha whose soul was no secret to me—passed between me and the radiant girl, the playful sylph whose feelings were a fascinating mystery. I suppose I must have shuddered, or betrayed in some other way my momentary chill of horror.

'Tasso!' she said, seizing my wrist, and peeping round into my face, 'are you really beginning to discern what a heartless girl I am? Why, you are not half the poet I thought you were; you are actually capable of believing the truth about me.'

The shadow passed from between us, and was no longer the object nearest to me. The girl whose light fingers grasped me, whose elfish charming face looked into mine—who, I thought, was betraying an interest in my feelings that she would not have directly avowed,—this warm-breathing presence again possessed my senses and imagination like a returning syren melody* which had been overpowered for an instant by the roar of threatening waves. It was a moment as delicious to me as the waking up to a consciousness of youth after a dream of middle age. I forgot everything but my passion, and said with swimming eyes—

'Bertha, shall you love me when we are first married? I wouldn't mind if you really loved me only for a little while.'

Her look of astonishment, as she loosed my hand and started away from me recalled me to a sense of my strange, my criminal indiscretion.

'Forgive me,' I said, hurriedly, as soon as I could speak again; 'I did not know what I was saying.'

'Ah, Tasso's mad fit has come on, I see,' she answered quietly, for she had recovered herself sooner than I had. 'Let him go home and keep his head cool. I must go in, for the sun is setting.'

I left her—full of indignation against myself. I had let slip words which, if she reflected on them, might rouse in her a suspicion of my abnormal mental condition—a suspicion which of all things I dreaded. And besides that, I was ashamed of the apparent baseness I had committed in uttering them to my brother's betrothed wife. I wandered home slowly, entering our park through a private gate instead of by the lodges. As I approached the house, I saw a man dashing off at full speed from the stable-yard across the park. Had any accident happened at home? No; perhaps it was only one of my father's peremptory business errands that required this headlong haste. Nevertheless I quickened my pace without any distinct motive, and was soon at the house. I will not dwell on the scene I found there. My brother was dead—had been pitched from his horse, and killed on the spot by a concussion of the brain.

I went up to the room where he lay, and where my father was seated beside him with a look of rigid despair. I had shunned my father more than any one since our return home, for the radical antipathy between our natures made my insight into his inner self a constant affliction to me. But now, as I went up to him, and stood beside him in sad silence, I felt the presence of a new element that blended us as we had never been blent before. My father had been one of the most successful men in the money-getting world: he had had no sentimental sufferings, no illness. The heaviest trouble that had befallen him was the death of his first wife. But he married my mother soon after; and I remember he seemed exactly the same, to my keen childish observation, the week after her death as before. But now, at last, a sorrow had come—the sorrow of old age, which suffers the more from the crushing of its pride and its hopes, in proportion as the pride and hope are narrow and prosaic. His son was to have been married soon—would probably have stood for the borough at the next election. That son's existence was the best motive that could be alleged for making new purchases of land every year to round off the estate. It is a dreary thing to live on doing the same things year after year, without knowing why we do them. Perhaps the tragedy of disappointed youth and passion is less piteous than the tragedy of disappointed age and worldliness.

As I saw into the desolation of my father's heart, I felt a movement of deep pity towards him, which was the beginning of a new affection—an affection that grew and strengthened in spite of the strange bitterness with which he regarded me in the first month or two after my brother's death. If it had not been for the softening influence of my compassion for him—the first deep compassion I had ever felt—I should have been stung by the perception that my father transferred the inheritance of an eldest son to me with a mortified sense that fate had compelled him to the unwelcome course of caring for me as an important being. It was only in spite of himself that he began to think of me with anxious regard. There is hardly any neglected child for whom death has made vacant a more favoured place, who will not understand what I mean.

Gradually, however, my new deference to his wishes, the effect of that patience which was born of my pity for him, won upon his affection, and he began to please himself with the endeavour to make me fill my brother's place as fully as my feebler personality would admit. I saw that the prospect which by-and-by presented itself of my becoming Bertha's husband was welcome to him, and he even contemplated in my case what he had not intended in my brother's—that his son and daughter-in-law should make one household with him. My softened feeling towards my father made this the happiest time I had known since childhood;—these last months in which I retained the delicious illusion of loving Bertha, of longing and doubting and hoping that she might love me. She behaved with a certain new consciousness and distance towards me after my brother's death; and I too was under a double constraint—that of delicacy towards my brother's memory, and of anxiety as to the impression my abrupt words had left on her mind. But the additional screen this mutual reserve erected between us only brought me more completely under her power: no matter how empty the adytum,* so that the veil be thick enough. So absolute is our soul's need of something hidden and uncertain for the maintenance of that doubt and hope and effort which are the breath of its life, that if the whole future were laid bare to us beyond to-day, the interest of all mankind would be bent on the hours that lie between; we should pant after the uncertainties of our one morning and our one afternoon; we should rush fiercely to the Exchange for our last possibility of speculation, of success, of disappointment; we should have a glut of political prophets foretelling a crisis or a no-crisis within the only twenty-four hours left open to prophecy. Conceive the condition of the human mind if all propositions whatsoever were self-evident except one, which was to become self-evident at the close of a summer's day, but in the meantime might be the subject of question, of hypothesis, of debate. Art and philosophy, literature and science, would fasten like bees on that one proposition which had the honey of probability in it, and be the more eager because their enjoyment would end with sunset. Our impulses, our spiritual activities, no more adjust themselves to the idea of their future nullity, than the beating of our heart, or the irritability of our muscles.

Bertha, the slim, fair-haired girl, whose present thoughts and emotions were an enigma to me amidst the fatiguing obviousness of the other minds around me, was as absorbing to me as a single unknown to-day—as a single hypothetic proposition to remain problematic till sunset; and all the cramped, hemmed-in belief and disbelief, trust and distrust, of my nature, welled out in this one narrow channel.

And she made me believe that she loved me. Without ever quitting her tone of *badinage** and playful superiority, she intoxicated me with the sense that I was necessary to her, that she was never at ease unless I was near her, submitting to her playful tyranny. It costs a woman so little effort to besot us in this way! A half-repressed word, a moment's unexpected silence, even an easy fit of petulance on our account, will serve us as *hashish** for a long while. Out of the subtlest web of scarcely perceptible signs, she set me weaving the fancy that she had always unconsciously loved me better than Alfred, but that, with the ignorant fluttered sensibility of a young girl, she had been imposed on by the charm that lay for her in the distinction of being admired and chosen by a man who made so brilliant a figure in the world as my brother. She satirised herself in a very graceful way for her vanity and ambition. What was it to me that I had the light of my wretched prevision on the fact that now it was I who possessed at least all but the personal part of my brother's advantages? Our sweet illusions are half of them conscious illusions, like effects of colour that we know to be made up of tinsel, broken glass, and rags.

We were married eighteen months after Alfred's death, one cold, clear morning in April, when there came hail and sunshine both together; and Bertha, in her white silk and pale-green leaves, and the pale hues of her hair and face, looked like the spirit of the morning. My father was happier than he had thought of being again: my marriage, he felt sure, would complete the desirable modification of my character, and make me practical and worldly enough to take my place in society among sane men. For he delighted in Bertha's tact and acuteness, and felt sure she would be mistress of me, and make me what she chose: I was only twenty-one, and madly in love with her. Poor father! He kept that hope a little while after our first year of marriage, and it was not quite extinct when paralysis came and saved him from utter disappointment.

I shall hurry through the rest of my story, not dwelling so much as I have hitherto done on my inward experience. When people are well known to each other, they talk rather of what befalls them externally, leaving their feelings and sentiments to be inferred.

We lived in a round of visits for some time after our return home, giving splendid dinner-parties, and making a sensation in our neighbourhood by the new lustre of our equipage, for my father had reserved this display of his increased wealth for the period of his son's marriage; and we gave our acquaintances liberal opportunity for remarking that it was a pity I made so poor a figure as an heir and a bridegroom. The nervous fatigue of this existence, the insincerities and platitudes which I had to live through twice over—through my inner and outward sense—would have been maddening to me, if I had not had that sort of intoxicated callousness which came from the delights of a first passion. A bride and bridegroom, surrounded by all the appliances of wealth, hurried through the day by the whirl of society, filling their solitary moments with hastily-snatched caresses, are prepared for their future life together as the novice is prepared for the cloister—by experiencing its utmost contrast.

Through all these crowded excited months, Bertha's inward self remained shrouded from me, and I still read her thoughts only through the language of her lips and demeanour: I had still the human interest of wondering whether what I did and said pleased her, of longing to hear a word of affection, of giving a delicious exaggeration of meaning to her smile. But I was conscious of a growing difference in her manner towards me; sometimes strong enough to be called haughty coldness, cutting and chilling me as the hail had done that came across the sunshine on our marriage morning; sometimes only perceptible in the dexterous avoidance of a *tête-à-tête** walk or dinner to which I had been looking forward. I had been deeply pained by this—had even felt a sort of crushing of the heart, from the sense that my brief day of happiness was near its setting; but still I remained dependent on Bertha, eager for the last rays of a bliss that would soon be gone for ever, hoping and watching for some after-glow more beautiful from the impending night.

I remember—how should I not remember?—the time when that dependence and hope utterly left me, when the sadness I had felt in Bertha's growing estrangement became a joy that I looked back upon with longing, as a man might look back on the last pains in a paralysed limb. It was just after the close of my father's last illness, which had necessarily withdrawn us from society and thrown us more upon each other. It was the evening of my father's death. On that evening the veil which had shrouded Bertha's soul from me—had made me find in her alone among my fellow-beings the blessed possibility of mystery, and doubt, and expectation—was first withdrawn. Perhaps it was the first day since the beginning of my passion for her, in which that passion was completely neutralised by the presence of an absorbing feeling of another kind. I had been watching by my father's deathbed: I had been witnessing the last fitful yearning glance his soul had cast back on the spent inheritance of life—the last faint consciousness of love he had gathered from the pressure of my hand. What are all our personal loves when we have been sharing in that supreme agony? In the first moments when we come away from the presence of death, every other relation to the living is merged, to our feeling, in the great relation of a common nature and a common destiny.

In that state of mind I joined Bertha in her private sitting-room. She was seated in a leaning posture on a settee, with her back towards the door; the great rich coils of her pale blond hair surmounting her small neck, visible above the back of the settee. I remember, as I closed the door behind me, a cold tremulousness seizing me, and a vague sense of being hated and lonely—vague and strong, like a presentiment. I know how I looked at that moment, for I saw myself in Bertha's thought as she lifted her cutting grey eyes, and looked at me: a miserable ghost-seer, surrounded by phantoms in the noon-day, trembling under a breeze when the leaves were still, without appetite for the common objects of human desire, but pining after the moon-beams. We were front to front with each other, and judged each other. The terrible moment of complete illumination had come to me, and I saw that the darkness had hidden no landscape from me, but only a blank prosaic wall; from that evening forth, through the sickening years which followed, I saw all round the narrow room of this woman's soul—saw petty artifice and mere negation where I had delighted to believe in coy sensibilities and in wit at war with latent feeling—saw the light floating vanities of the girl defining themselves into the systematic coquetry, the scheming selfishness, of the woman—saw repulsion and antipathy harden into cruel hatred, giving pain only for the sake of wreaking itself.

For Bertha too, after her kind, felt the bitterness of disillusion. She had believed that my wild poet's passion for her would make me her slave; and that, being her slave, I should execute her will in all things. With the essential shallowness of a negative, unimaginative nature, she was unable to conceive the fact that sensibilities were anything else than weaknesses. She had thought my weaknesses would put me in her power, and she found them unmanageable forces. Our positions were reversed. Before marriage she had completely mastered my imagination, for she was a secret to me; and I created the unknown thought before which I trembled as if it were hers. But now that her soul was laid open to me, now that I was compelled to share the privacy of her motives, to follow all the petty devices that preceded her words and acts, she found herself powerless with me, except to produce in me the chill shudder of repulsion—powerless, because I could be acted on by no lever within her reach. I was dead to worldly ambitions, to social vanities, to all the incentives within the compass of her narrow imagination, and I lived under influences utterly invisible to her.

She was really pitiable to have such a husband, and so all the world thought. A graceful, brilliant woman, like Bertha, who smiled on morning callers, made a figure in ball-rooms, and was capable of that light repartee which, from such a woman, is accepted as wit, was secure of carrying off all sympathy from a husband who was sickly, abstracted, and, as some suspected, crack-brained. Even the servants in our house gave her the balance of their regard and pity. For there were no audible quarrels between us; our alienation, our repulsion from each other, lay within the silence of our own hearts; and if the mistress went out a great deal, and seemed to dislike the master's society, was it not natural, poor thing? The master was odd. I was kind and just to my dependants, but I excited in them a shrinking, half-contemptuous pity; for this class of men and women are but slightly determined in their estimate of others by general considerations, or even experience, of character. They judge of persons as they judge of coins, and value those who pass current at a high rate.

After a time I interfered so little with Bertha's habits, that it might seem wonderful how her hatred towards me could grow so intense and active as it did. But she had begun to suspect, by some involuntary betrayals of mine, that there was an abnormal power of penetration in me—that fitfully, at least, I was strangely cognisant of her thoughts and intentions, and she began to be haunted by a terror of me, which alternated every now and then with defiance. She meditated continually how the incubus could be shaken off her life—how she could be freed from this hateful bond to a being whom she at once despised as an imbecile, and dreaded as an inquisitor. For a long while she lived in the hope that my evident wretchedness would drive me to the commission of suicide; but suicide was not in my nature. I was too completely swayed by the sense that I was in the grasp of unknown forces, to believe in my power of self-release. Towards my own destiny I had become entirely passive; for my one ardent desire had spent itself, and impulse no longer predominated over knowledge. For this reason I never thought of taking any steps towards a complete separation, which would have made our alienation evident to the world. Why should I rush for help to a new course, when I was only suffering from the consequences of a deed which had been the act of my intensest will? That would have been the logic of one who had desires to gratify, and I had no desires. But Bertha and I lived more and more aloof from each other. The rich find it easy to live married and apart.

That course of our life which I have indicated in a few sentences filled the space of years. So much misery—so slow and hideous a growth of hatred and sin, may be compressed into a sentence! And men judge of each other's lives through this summary medium. They epitomise the experience of their fellow-mortal, and pronounce judgment on him in neat syntax, and feel themselves wise and virtuous—conquerors over the temptations they define in well-selected predicates. Seven years of wretchedness glide glibly over the lips of the man who has never counted them out in moments of chill disappointment, of head and heart throbbings, of dread and vain wrestling, of remorse and despair. We learn *words* by rote, but not their meaning; *that* must be paid for with our life-blood, and printed in the subtle fibres of our nerves.

But I will hasten to finish my story. Brevity is justified at once to those who readily understand, and to those who will never understand.

Some years after my father's death, I was sitting by the dim fire-light in my library one January evening—sitting in the leather chair that used to be my father's—when Bertha appeared at the door, with a candle in her hand, and advanced towards me. I knew the ball-dress she had on—the white ball-dress, with the green jewels, shone upon by the light of the wax candle which lit up the medallion of the dying Cleopatra on the mantelpiece. Why did she come to me before going out? I had not seen her in the library, which was my habitual place, for months. Why did she stand before me with the candle in her hand, with her cruel contemptuous eyes fixed on me, and the glittering serpent, like a familiar demon, on her breast? For a moment I thought this fulfilment of my vision at Vienna marked some dreadful crisis in my fate, but I saw nothing in Bertha's mind, as she stood before me, except scorn for the look of overwhelming misery with which I sat before her. . . . 'Fool, idiot, why don't you kill yourself, then?'—that was her thought. But at length her thoughts reverted to her errand, and she spoke aloud. The apparently indifferent nature of the errand seemed to make a ridiculous anticlimax to my prevision and my agitation.

'I have had to hire a new maid. Fletcher is going to be married, and she wants me to ask you to let her husband have the public-house and farm at Molton. I wish him to have it. You must give the promise now, because Fletcher is going to-morrow morning—and quickly, because I'm in a hurry.'

'Very well; you may promise her,' I said, indifferently, and Bertha swept out of the library again.

I always shrank from the sight of a new person, and all the more when it was a person whose mental life was likely to weary my reluctant insight with worldly ignorant trivialities. But I shrank especially from the sight of this new maid, because her advent had been announced to me at a moment to which I could not cease to attach some fatality: I had a vague dread that I should find her mixed up with the dreary drama of my life—that some new sickening vision would reveal her to me as an evil genius. When at last I did unavoidably meet her, the vague dread was changed into definite disgust. She was a tall, wiry, dark-eyed woman, this Mrs Archer, with a face handsome enough to give her coarse hard nature the odious finish of bold, self-confident coquetry. That was enough to make me avoid her, quite apart from the contemptuous feeling with which she contemplated me. I seldom saw her; but I perceived that she rapidly became a favourite with her mistress, and, after the lapse of eight or nine months, I began to be aware that there had arisen in Bertha's mind towards this woman a mingled feeling of fear and dependence, and that this feeling was associated with ill-defined images of candle-light scenes in her dressing-room, and the looking-up of something in Bertha's cabinet. My interviews with my wife had become so brief and so rarely solitary, that I had no opportunity of perceiving these images in her mind with more definiteness. The recollections of the past become contracted in the rapidity of thought till they sometimes bear hardly a more distinct resemblance to the external reality than the forms of an oriental alphabet to the objects that suggested them.

Besides, for the last year or more a modification had been going forward in my mental condition, and was growing more and more marked. My insight into the minds of those around me was becoming dimmer and more fitful, and the ideas that crowded my double consciousness became less and less dependent on any personal contact. All that was personal in me seemed to be suffering a gradual death, so that I was losing the organ through which the personal agitations and projects of others could affect me. But along with this relief from wearisome insight, there was a new development of what I concluded—as I have since found rightly—to be a prevision of external scenes. It was as if the relation between me and my fellow-men was more and more deadened, and my relation to what we call the inanimate was quickened into new life. The more I lived apart from society, and in proportion as my wretchedness subsided from the violent throb of agonised passion into the dulness of habitual pain, the more frequent and vivid became such visions as that I had had of Prague—of strange cities, of sandy plains, of gigantic ruins, of midnight skies with strange bright constellations, of mountain-passes, of grassy nooks flecked with the afternoon sunshine through the boughs: I was in the midst of such scenes, and in all of them one presence seemed to weigh on me in all these mighty shapes—the presence of something unknown and pitiless. For continual suffering had annihilated religious faith within me: to the utterly miserable—the unloving and the unloved— there is no religion possible, no worship but a worship of devils. And beyond all these, and continually recurring, was the vision of my death—the pangs, the suffocation, the last struggle, when life would be grasped at in vain.

Things were in this state near the end of the seventh year. I had become entirely free from insight, from my abnormal cognisance of any other consciousness than my own, and instead of intruding involuntarily into the world of other minds, was living continually in my own solitary future. Bertha was aware that I was greatly changed. To my surprise she had of late seemed to seek opportunities of remaining in my society, and had cultivated that kind of distant yet familiar talk which is customary between a husband and wife who live in polite and irrevocable alienation. I bore this with languid submission, and without feeling enough interest in her motives to be roused into keen observation; yet I could not help perceiving something triumphant and excited in her carriage and the expression of her face—something too subtle to express itself in words or tones, but giving one the idea that she lived in a state of expectation or hopeful suspense. My chief feeling was satisfaction that her inner self was once more shut out from me; and I almost revelled for the moment in the absent melancholy that made me answer her at cross purposes, and betray utter ignorance of what she had been saying. I remember well the look and the smile with which she one day said, after a mistake of this kind on my part: 'I used to think you were a clairvoyant, and that was the reason why you were so bitter against other clairvoyants, wanting to keep your monopoly; but I see now you have become rather duller than the rest of the world.'

I said nothing in reply. It occurred to me that her recent obtrusion of herself upon me might have been prompted by the wish to test my power of detecting some of her secrets; but I let the thought drop again at once: her motives and her deeds had no interest for me, and whatever pleasures she might be seeking, I had no wish to balk her. There was still pity in my soul for every living thing, and Bertha was living—was surrounded with possibilities of misery.

Just at this time there occurred an event which roused me somewhat from my inertia, and gave me an interest in the passing moment that I had thought impossible for me. It was a visit from Charles Meunier, who had written me word that he was coming to England for relaxation from too strenuous labour, and would like to see me. Meunier had now a European reputation; but his letter to me expressed that keen remembrance of an early regard, an early debt of sympathy, which is inseparable from nobility of character: and I too felt as if his presence would be to me like a transient resurrection into a happier pre-existence.

He came, and as far as possible, I renewed our old pleasure of making *tête-à-tête* excursions, though, instead of mountains and glaciers and the wide blue lake, we had to content ourselves with mere slopes and ponds and artificial plantations. The years had changed us both, but with what different result! Meunier was now a brilliant figure in society, to whom elegant women pretended to listen, and whose acquaintance was boasted of by noblemen ambitious of brains. He repressed with the utmost delicacy all betrayal of the shock which I am sure he must have received from our meeting, or of a desire to penetrate into my condition and circumstances, and sought by the utmost exertion of his charming social powers to make our reunion agreeable. Bertha was much struck by the unexpected fascinations of a visitor whom she had expected to find presentable only on the score of his celebrity, and put forth all her coquetries and accomplishments. Apparently she succeeded in attracting his admiration, for his manner towards her was attentive and flattering. The effect of his presence on me was so benignant, especially in those renewals of our old *tête-à-tête* wanderings, when he poured forth to me wonderful narratives of his professional experience, that more than once, when his talk turned on the psychological relations of disease, the thought crossed my mind that, if his stay with me were long enough, I might possibly bring myself to tell this man the secrets of my lot. Might there not lie some remedy for *me*, too, in his science? Might there not at least lie some comprehension and sympathy ready for me in his large and susceptible mind?

But the thought only flickered feebly now and then, and died out before it could become a wish. The horror I had of again breaking in on the privacy of another soul, made me, by an irrational instinct, draw the shroud of concealment more closely around my own, as we automatically perform the gesture we feel to be wanting in another.

When Meunier's visit was approaching its conclusion, there happened an event which caused some excitement in our household, owing to the surprisingly strong effect it appeared to produce on Bertha—on Bertha, the self-possessed, who usually seemed inaccessible to feminine agitations, and did even her hate in a self-restrained hygienic manner. This event was the sudden severe illness of her maid, Mrs Archer. I have reserved to this moment the mention of a circumstance which had forced itself on my notice shortly before Meunier's arrival, namely, that there had been some quarrel between Bertha and this maid, apparently during a visit to a distant family, in which she had accompanied her mistress. I had overheard Archer speaking in a tone of bitter insolence, which I should have thought an adequate reason for immediate dismissal. No dismissal followed; on the contrary, Bertha seemed to be silently putting up with personal inconveniences from the exhibitions of this woman's temper. I was the more astonished to observe that her illness seemed a cause of strong solicitude to Bertha; that she was at the bedside night and day, and would allow no one else to officiate as head-nurse. It happened that our family doctor was out on a holiday, an accident which made Meunier's presence in the house doubly welcome, and he apparently entered into the case with an interest which seemed so much stronger than the ordinary professional feeling, that one day when he had fallen into a long fit of silence after visiting her, I said to him—

'Is this a very peculiar case of disease, Meunier?'

'No,' he answered, 'it is an attack of peritonitis,* which will be fatal, but which does not differ physically from many other cases that have come under my observation. But I'll tell you what I have on my mind. I want to make an experiment on this woman, if you will give me permission. It can do her no harm—will give her no pain—for I shall not make it until life is extinct to all purposes of sensation. I want to try the effect of transfusing blood* into her arteries after the heart has ceased to beat for some minutes. I have tried the experiment again and again with animals that have died of this disease, with astounding results, and I want to try it on a human subject. I have the small tubes necessary, in a case I have with me, and the rest of the apparatus could be prepared readily. I should use my own blood—take it from my own arm. This woman won't live through the night, I'm convinced, and I want you to promise me your assistance in making the experiment. I can't do without another hand, but it would perhaps not be well to call in a medical assistant from among your provincial doctors. A disagreeable foolish version of the thing might get abroad.'

'Have you spoken to my wife on the subject?' I said, 'because she appears to be peculiarly sensitive about this woman: she has been a favourite maid.'

'To tell you the truth,' said Meunier, 'I don't want her to know about it. There are always insuperable difficulties with women in these matters, and the effect on the supposed dead body may be startling. You and I will sit up together, and be in readiness. When certain symptoms appear I shall take you in, and at the right moment we must manage to get every one else out of the room.'

I need not give our farther conversation on the subject. He entered very fully into the details, and overcame my repulsion from them, by exciting in me a mingled awe and curiosity concerning the possible results of his experiment.

We prepared everything, and he instructed me in my part as assistant. He had not told Bertha of his absolute conviction that Archer would not survive through the night, and endeavoured to persuade her to leave the patient and take a night's rest. But she was obstinate, suspecting the fact that death was at hand, and supposing that he wished merely to save her nerves. She refused to leave the sick-room. Meunier and I sat up together in the library, he making frequent visits to the sick-room, and returning with the information that the case was taking precisely the course he expected. Once he said to me, 'Can you imagine any cause of ill feeling this woman has against her mistress, who is so devoted to her?'

'I think there was some misunderstanding between them before her illness. Why do you ask?'

'Because I have observed for the last five or six hours—since, I fancy, she has lost all hope of recovery—there seems a strange prompting in her to say something which pain and failing strength forbid her to utter; and there is a look of hideous meaning in her eyes, which she turns continually towards her mistress. In this disease the mind often remains singularly clear to the last.'

'I am not surprised at an indication of malevolent feeling in her,' I said. 'She is a woman who has always inspired me with distrust and dislike, but she managed to insinuate herself into her mistress's favour.' He was silent after this, looking at the fire with an air of absorption, till he went up-stairs again. He stayed away longer than usual, and on returning, said to me quietly, 'Come now.'

I followed him to the chamber where death was hovering. The dark hangings of the large bed made a background that gave a strong relief to Bertha's pale face as I entered. She started forward as she saw me enter, and then looked at Meunier with an expression of angry inquiry; but he lifted up his hand as if to impose silence, while he fixed his glance on the dying woman and felt her pulse. The face was pinched and ghastly, a cold perspiration was on the forehead, and the eyelids were lowered so as almost to conceal the large dark eyes. After a minute or two, Meunier walked round to the other side of the bed where Bertha stood, and with his usual air of gentle politeness towards her begged her to leave the patient under our care—everything should be done for her—she was no longer in a state to be conscious of an affectionate presence. Bertha was hesitating, apparently almost willing to believe his assurance and to comply She looked round at the ghastly dying face, as if to read the confirmation of that assurance, when for a moment the lowered eyelids were raised again, and it seemed as if the eyes were looking towards Bertha, but blankly. A shudder passed through Bertha's frame, and she returned to her station near the pillow, tacitly implying that she would not leave the room.

The eyelids were lifted no more. Once I looked at Bertha as she watched the face of the dying one. She wore a rich *peignoir*,* and her blond hair was half covered by a lace cap: in her attire she was, as always, an elegant woman, fit to figure in a picture of modern aristocratic life: but I asked myself how that face of hers could ever have seemed to me the face of a woman born of woman, with memories of childhood, capable of pain, needing to be fondled? The features at that moment seemed so preternaturally sharp, the eyes were so hard and eager—she looked like a cruel immortal, finding her spiritual feast in the agonies of a dying race. For across those hard features there came something like a flash when the last hour had been breathed out, and we all felt that the dark veil had completely fallen. What secret was there between Bertha and this woman? I turned my eyes from her with a horrible dread lest my insight should return, and

I should be obliged to see what had been breeding about two unloving women's hearts. I felt that Bertha had been watching for the moment of death as the sealing of her secret: I thanked Heaven it could remain sealed for me.

Meunier said quietly, 'She is gone.' He then gave his arm to Bertha, and she submitted to be led out of the room.

I suppose it was at her order that two female attendants came into the room, and dismissed the younger one who had been present before. When they entered, Meunier had already opened the artery in the long thin neck that lay rigid on the pillow, and I dismissed them, ordering them to remain at a distance till we rang: the doctor, I said, had an operation to perform—he was not sure about the death. For the next twenty minutes I forgot everything but Meunier and the experiment in which he was so absorbed, that I think his senses would have been closed against all sounds or sights which had no relation to it. It was my task at first to keep up the artificial respiration in the body after the transfusion had been effected, but presently Meunier relieved me, and I could see the wondrous slow return of life; the breast began to heave, the inspirations became stronger, the eyelids quivered, and the soul seemed to have returned beneath them. The artificial respiration was withdrawn: still the breathing continued, and there was a movement of the lips.

Just then I heard the handle of the door moving: I suppose Bertha had heard from the women that they had been dismissed: probably a vague fear had arisen in her mind, for she entered with a look of alarm. She came to the foot of the bed and gave a stifled cry.

The dead woman's eyes were wide open, and met hers in full recognition—the recognition of hate. With a sudden strong effort, the hand that Bertha had thought for ever still was pointed towards her, and the haggard face moved. The gasping eager voice said—

'You mean to poison your husband . . . the poison is in the black cabinet . . . I got it for you . . . you laughed at me, and told lies about me behind my back, to make me disgusting . . . because you were jealous . . . are you sorry . . . now?'

The lips continued to murmur, but the sounds were no longer distinct. Soon there was no sound—only a slight movement: the flame had leaped out, and was being extinguished the faster. The wretched woman's heart-strings had been set to hatred and vengeance; the spirit of life had swept the chords for an instant, and was gone again for ever. Great God! Is this what it is to live again . . . to wake up with our unstilled thirst upon us, with our unuttered curses rising to our lips, with our muscles ready to act out their half-committed sins?

Bertha stood pale at the foot of the bed, quivering and helpless, despairing of devices, like a cunning animal whose hiding-places are surrounded by swift-advancing flame. Even Meunier looked paralysed; life for that moment ceased to be a scientific problem to him. As for me, this scene seemed of one texture with the rest of my existence: horror was my familiar, and this new revelation was only like an old pain recurring with new circumstances.

Since then Bertha and I have lived apart—she in her own neighbourhood, the mistress of half our wealth, I as a wanderer in foreign countries, until I came to this Devonshire nest to die. Bertha lives pitied and admired; for what had I against that charming woman, whom every one but myself could have been happy with? There had been no witness of the scene in the dying room except Meunier, and, while Meunier lived, his lips were sealed by a promise to me.

Once or twice, weary of wandering, I rested in a favourite spot, and my heart went out towards the men and women and children whose faces were becoming familiar to me: but I was driven away again in terror at the approach of my old insight—driven away to live continually with the one Unknown Presence revealed and yet hidden by the moving curtain of the earth and sky. Till at last disease took hold of me and forced me to rest here—forced me to live in dependence on my servants. And then the curse of insight—of my double consciousness, came again, and has never left me. I know all their narrow thoughts, their feeble regard, their half-wearied pity.

It is the 20th of September 1850. I know these figures I have just written, as if they were a long familiar inscription. I have seen them on this page in my desk unnumbered times, when the scene of my dying struggle has opened upon me. . . .

GRANT ALLEN

PAUSODYNE: A GREAT CHEMICAL DISCOVERY

WALKING along the Strand one evening last year towards Pall Mall, I was accosted near Charing Cross Station by a strange-looking, middle-aged man in a poor suit of clothes, who surprised and startled me by asking if I could tell him from what inn the coach usually started for York.*

'Dear me!' I said, a little puzzled. 'I didn't know there was a coach to York. Indeed, I'm almost certain there isn't one.'

The man looked puzzled and surprised in turn. 'No coach to York?' he muttered to himself, half inarticulately. 'No coach to York? How things have changed! I wonder whether nobody ever goes to York nowadays!'

'Pardon me,' I said, anxious to discover what could be his meaning; 'many people go to York every day, but of course they go by rail.'

'Ah, yes,' he answered softly, 'I see. Yes, of course, they go by rail. They go by rail, no doubt. How very stupid of me!' And he turned on his heel as if to get away from me as quickly as possible.

I can't exactly say why, but I felt instinctively that this curious stranger was trying to conceal from me his ignorance of what a railway really was. I was quite certain from the way in which he spoke that he had not the slightest conception what I meant, and that he was doing his best to hide his confusion by pretending to understand me. Here was indeed a strange mystery. In the latter end of this nineteenth century, in the metropolis of industrial England, within a stone's-throw of Charing Cross terminus, I had met an adult Englishman who apparently did not know of the existence of railways. My curiosity was too much piqued to let the matter rest there. I must find out what he meant by it. I walked after him hastily, as he tried to disappear among the crowd, and laid my hand upon his shoulder, to his evident chagrin.

'Excuse me,' I said, drawing him aside down the corner of Craven Street; 'you did not understand what I meant when I said people went to York by rail?'

He looked in my face steadily, and then, instead of replying to my remark, he said slowly, 'Your name is Spottiswood, I believe?'

Again I gave a start of surprise. 'It is,' I answered; 'but I never remember to have seen you before.'

'No,' he replied, dreamily; 'no, we have never met till now, no doubt; but I knew your father, I'm sure; or perhaps it may have been your grandfather.'

'Not my grandfather, certainly,' said I, 'for he was killed at Waterloo.'

'At Waterloo! Indeed! How long since, pray?'

I could not refrain from laughing outright. 'Why, of course,' I answered, 'in 1815. There has been nothing particular to kill off any large number of Englishmen at Waterloo since the year of the battle, I suppose.'

'True,' he muttered, 'quite true; so I should have fancied.' But I saw again from the cloud of doubt and bewilderment which came over his intelligent face that the name of Waterloo conveyed no idea whatsoever to his mind.

Never in my life had I felt so utterly confused and astonished. In spite of his poor dress, I could easily see from the clear-cut face and the refined accent of my strange acquaintance that he was an educated gentleman—a man accustomed to mix in cultivated society. Yet he clearly knew nothing whatsoever about railways, and was ignorant of the most salient facts in English history. Had I suddenly come across some Caspar Hauser,* immured for years in a private prison, and just let loose upon the world by his gaolers? Or was my mysterious stranger one of the Seven Sleepers of Ephesus,* turned out unexpectedly in modern costume on the streets of London? I don't suppose there exists on earth a man more utterly free than I am from any tinge of superstition, any lingering touch of a love for the miraculous; but I confess for a moment I felt half inclined to suppose that the man before me must have drunk the elixir of life, or must have dropped suddenly upon earth from some distant planet.

The impulse to fathom this mystery was irresistible. I drew my arm through his. 'If you knew my father,' I said, 'you will not object to come into my chambers and take a glass of wine with me.'

'Thank you,' he answered, half suspiciously; 'thank you very much. I think you look like a man who can be trusted, and I will go with you.'

We walked along the Embankment to Adelphi Terrace,* where I took him up to my rooms, and seated him in my easy-chair near the window. As he sat down, one of the trains on the Metropolitan line* whirred past the Terrace, snorting steam and whistling shrilly, after the fashion of Metropolitan engines generally. My mysterious stranger jumped back in alarm, and seemed to be afraid of some immediate catastrophe. There was absolutely no possibility of doubting it. The man had obviously never seen a locomotive before.

'Evidently,' I said, 'you do not know London. I suppose you are a colonist from some remote district, perhaps an Australian from the interior somewhere, just landed at the Tower?'*

'No, not an Austrian'—I noted his misapprehension—'but a Londoner born and bred.'

'How is it, then, that you seem never to have seen an engine before?'

'Can I trust you?' he asked in a piteously plaintive, half-terrified tone. 'If I tell you all about it, will you at least not aid in persecuting and imprisoning me?'

I was touched by his evident grief and terror. 'No,' I answered, 'you may trust me implicitly. I feel sure there is something in your history which entitles you to sympathy and protection.'

'Well,' he replied, grasping my hand warmly, 'I will tell you all my story; but you must be prepared for something almost too startling to be credible.'

'My name is Jonathan Spottiswood,' he began calmly.

Again I experienced a marvellous start; Jonathan Spottiswood was the name of my great-great-uncle, whose unaccountable disappearance from London just a century since had involved our family in so much protracted litigation as to the succession to his property. In fact, it was Jonathan Spottiswood's money which at that moment formed the bulk of my little fortune. But I would not interrupt him, so great was my anxiety to hear the story of his life.

'I was born in London,' he went on, 'in 1750. If you can hear me say that and yet believe that possibly I am not a madman, I will tell you the rest of my tale; if not, I shall go at once and for ever.'

'I suspend judgment for the present,' I answered. 'What you say is extraordinary, but not more extraordinary perhaps than the clear anachronism of your ignorance about locomotives in the midst of the present century.'

'So be it, then. Well, I will tell you the facts briefly in as few words as I can. I was always much given to experimental philosophy, and I spent most of my time in the little laboratory which I had built for myself behind my father's house in the Strand. I had a small independent fortune of my own, left me by an uncle who had made successful ventures in the China trade; and as I was indisposed to follow my father's profession of solicitor, I gave myself up almost entirely to the pursuit of natural philosophy, following the researches of the great Mr. Cavendish, our chief English thinker in this kind, as well as of Monsieur Lavoisier, the ingenious French chemist, and of my friend Dr. Priestley, the Birmingham philosopher, whose new theory of phlogiston* I have been much concerned to consider and to promulgate. But the especial subject to which I devoted myself was the elucidation of the nature of fixed air.* I do not know how far you yourself may happen to have heard respecting these late discoveries in chemical science, but I dare venture to say that you are at least acquainted with the nature of the body to which I refer.'

'Perfectly,' I answered with a smile, 'though your terminology is now a little out of date. Fixed air was, I believe, the old-fashioned name for carbonic acid gas.'*

'Ah,' he cried vehemently, 'that accursed word again! Carbonic acid has undone me, clearly. Yes, if you will have it so, that seems to be what they call it in this extraordinary century; but fixed air was the name we used to give it in our time, and fixed air is what I must call it, of course in telling you my story. Well, I was deeply interested in this curious question, and also in some of the results which I obtained from working with fixed air in combination with a substance I had produced from the essential oil of a weed known to us in England as lady's mantle, but which the learned Mr. Carl Linnæus describes in his system as *Alchemilla vulgaris.** From that weed I obtained an oil which I combined with a certain decoction of fixed air into a remarkable compound; and to this compound, from its singular properties, I proposed to give the name of Pausodyne.* For some years I was almost wholly engaged in investigating the conduct of this remarkable agent; and lest I should weary you by entering into too much detail, I may as well say at once that it possessed the singular power of entirely suspending animation in men or animals for several hours together. It is a highly volatile oil, like ammonia in smell, but much thicker in gravity; and when held to the nose of an animal, it causes immediate stoppage of the heart's action, making the body seem quite dead for long periods at a time. But the moment a mixture of the pausodyne with oil of vitriol and gum resin is presented to the nostrils, the animal instantaneously revives exactly as before, showing no sign of evil effects whatsoever from its temporary simulation of death. To the reviving mixture I have given the appropriate name of Anegeiric.*

'Of course you will instantly see the valuable medical applications which may be made of such an agent. I used it at first for experimenting upon the amputation of limbs and other surgical operations. It succeeded admirably. I found that a dog under the influence of pausodyne suffered his leg, which had been broken in a street accident, to be set and spliced without the slightest symptom of feeling or discomfort. A cat shot with a pistol by a cruel boy, had the bullet extracted without moving a muscle. My assistant, having allowed his little finger to mortify from neglect of a burn, permitted me to try the effect of my discovery upon himself; and I removed the injured joints while he remained in a state of complete insensibility, so that he could hardly believe afterwards in the actual truth of their removal. I felt certain that I had invented a medical process of the very highest and greatest utility.

'All this took place in or before the year 1781. How long ago that may be according to your modern reckoning I cannot say; but to me it seems hardly more than a few months since. Perhaps you would not mind telling me the date of the current year. I have never been able to ascertain it.'

'This is 1881,' I said, growing every moment more interested in his tale.

'Thank you. I gathered that we must now be somewhere near the close of the nineteenth century, though I could not learn the exact date with certainty. Well, I should tell you, my dear sir, that I had contracted an engagement about the year 1779 with a young lady of most remarkable beauty and attractive mental gifts, a Miss Amelia Spragg, daughter of the well-known General Sir Thomas Spragg, with whose achievements you are doubtless familiar. Pardon me, my friend of another age, pardon me, I beg of you, if I cannot allude to this subject without emotion after a lapse of time which to you doubtless seems like a century, but is to me a matter of some few months only at the utmost. I feel towards her as towards one whom I have but recently lost, though I now find that she has been dead for more than eighty years.' As he spoke, the tears came into his eyes profusely; and I could see that under the external calmness and quaintness of his eighteenth century language and demeanour his whole nature was profoundly stirred at the thought of his lost love.

'Look here,' he continued, taking from his breast a large, old-fashioned gold locket containing a miniature; 'that is her portrait, by Mr. Walker,* and a very truthful likeness indeed. They left me that when they took away my clothes at the Asylum, for I would not consent to part with it, and the physician in attendance observed that to deprive me of it might only increase the frequency and violence of my paroxysms. For I will not conceal from you the fact that I have just escaped from a pauper lunatic establishment.'

I took the miniature which he handed me, and looked at it closely. It was the picture of a young and beautiful girl, with the features and costume of a Sir Joshua.* I recognized the face at once as that of a lady whose portrait by Gainsborough* hangs on the walls of my uncle's dining-room at Whittingham Abbey. It was strange indeed to hear a living man speak of himself as the former lover of this, to me, historic personage.

'Sir Thomas, however,' he went on, 'was much opposed to our union, on the ground of some real or fancied social disparity in our positions; but I at last obtained his conditional consent, if only I could succeed in obtaining the Fellowship of the Royal Society,* which might, he thought, be accepted as a passport into that fashionable circle of which he was a member. Spurred on by this ambition, and by the encouragement of my Amelia, I worked day and night at the perfectioning of my great discovery, which I was assured would bring not only honor and dignity to myself, but also the alleviation and assuagement of pain to countless thousands of my fellow-creatures. I concealed the nature of my experiments, however, lest any rival investigator should enter the field with me prematurely, and share the credit to which I alone was really entitled. For some months I was successful in my efforts at concealment; but in March of this year—I mistake; of the year 1781, I should say—an unfortunate circumstance caused me to take special and exceptional precautions against intrusion.

'I was then conducting my experiments upon living animals, and especially upon the extirpation of certain painful internal diseases to which they are subject. I had a number of suffering cats in my laboratory, which I had treated with pausodyne, and stretched out on boards for the purpose of removing the tumors with which they were afflicted. I had no doubt that in this manner, while directly benefiting the animal creation, I should indirectly obtain the necessary skill to operate successfully upon human beings in similar circumstances. Already

I had completely cured several cats without any pain whatsoever, and I was anxious to proceed to the human subject. Walking one morning in the Strand, I found a beggar woman outside a gin-shop, quite drunk, with a small, ill-clad child by her side, suffering the most excruciating torments from a perfectly remediable cause. I induced the mother to accompany me to my laboratory, and there I treated the poor little creature with pausodyne, and began to operate upon her with perfect confidence of success.

'Unhappily, my laboratory had excited the suspicion of many ill-disposed persons among the low mob of the neighbourhood. It was whispered abroad that I was what they called a vivisectionist; and these people, who would willingly have attended a bull-baiting or a prize fight, found themselves of a sudden wondrous humane when scientific procedure was under consideration. Besides, I had made myself unpopular by receiving visits from my friend Dr. Priestley, whose religious opinions were not satisfactory to the strict orthodoxy of St. Giles's.* I was rumoured to be a philosopher, a torturer of live animals, and an atheist. Whether the former accusation were true or not, let others decide; the two latter, heaven be my witness, were wholly unfounded. However, when the neighbouring rabble saw a drunken woman with a little girl entering my door, a report got abroad at once that I was going to vivisect a Christian child. The mob soon collected in force, and broke into the laboratory. At that moment I was engaged, with my assistant, in operating upon the girl, while several cats, all completely anaestheticised, were bound down on the boards around, awaiting the healing of their wounds after the removal of tumours. At the sight of such apparent tortures the people grew wild with rage, and happening in their transports to fling down a large bottle of the anegeiric, or reviving mixture, the child and the animals all at once recovered consciousness, and began of course to writhe and scream with acute pain. I need not describe to you the scene that ensued. My laboratory was wrecked, my assistant severely injured, and I myself barely escaped with my life.

'After this *contretemps* I determined to be more cautious. I took the lease of a new house at Hampstead, and in the garden I determined to build myself a subterranean laboratory where I might be absolutely free from intrusion. I hired some laborers from Bath for this purpose, and I explained to them the nature of my wishes, and the absolute necessity of secrecy. A high wall surrounded the garden, and here the workmen worked securely and unseen. I concealed my design even from my dear brother—whose great-grandson I suppose you must be—and when the building was finished, I sent my men back to Bath, with strict injunctions never to mention the matter to any one. A trapdoor in the cellar, artfully concealed, gave access to the passage; a large oak portal, bound with iron, shut me securely in; and my air supply was obtained by means of pipes communicating through blank spaces in the brick wall of the garden with the outer atmosphere. Every arrangement for concealment was perfect; and I resolved in future, till my results were perfectly established, that I would dispense with the aid of an assistant.

'I was in high spirits when I went to visit my Amelia that evening, and I told her confidently that before the end of the year I expected to gain the gold medal of the Royal Society. The dear girl was pleased at my glowing prospects, and gave me every assurance of the delight with which she hailed the probability of our approaching union.

'Next day I began my experiments afresh in my new quarters. I bolted myself into the laboratory, and set to work with renewed vigour. I was experimenting upon an injured dog, and I placed a large bottle of pausodyne beside me as I administered the drug to his nostrils. The rising fumes seemed to affect my head more than usual in that confined space, and I tottered a little as I worked. My arm grew weaker, and at last fell powerless to my side. As it fell it knocked down the large bottle of pausodyne, and I saw the liquid spreading over the floor. That was almost the last thing that I knew. I staggered toward the door, but did not reach it; and then I remember nothing more for a considerable period.'

He wiped his forehead with his sleeve—he had no handkerchief—and then proceeded.

'When I woke up again the effects of the pausodyne had worn themselves out, and I felt that I must have remained unconscious for at least a week or a fortnight. My candle had gone out, and I could not find my tinderbox. I rose up slowly and with difficulty, for the air of the room was close and filled with fumes, and made my way in the dark towards the door. To my surprise, the bolt was so stiff with rust that it would hardly move. I opened it after a struggle, and found myself in the passage. Groping my way towards the trapdoor of the cellar, I felt it was obstructed by some heavy body. With an immense effort, for my strength seemed but feeble, I pushed it up, and discovered that a heap of sea-coals lay on top of it. I extricated myself into the cellar, and there a fresh surprise awaited me. A new entrance had been made into the front, so that I walked out at once upon the open road, instead of up the stairs into the kitchen. Looking up at the exterior of my house, my brain reeled with bewilderment when I saw that it had disappeared almost entirely, and that a different porch and wholly unfamiliar windows occupied its façade. I must have slept far longer than I at first imagined—perhaps a whole year or more. A vague terror prevented me from walking up the steps of my own home. Possibly my brother, thinking me dead, might have sold the lease; possibly some stranger might resent my intrusion into the house that was now his own. At any rate, I thought it safer to walk into the road. I would go towards London, to my brother's house in St. Mary le Bone.* I turned into the Hampstead Road, and directed my steps thitherward.

'Again, another surprise began to affect me with a horrible and ill-defined sense of awe. Not a single object that I saw was really familiar to me. I recognized that I was in the Hampstead Road, but it was not the Hampstead Road which I used to know before my fatal experiments. The houses were far more numerous, the trees were bigger and older. A year, nay, even a few years would not have sufficed for such a change. I began to fear that I had slept away a whole decade.

'It was early morning, and few people were yet abroad. But the costume of those whom I met seemed strange and fantastic to me. Moreover, I noticed that they all turned and looked after me with evident surprise, as though my dress caused them quite as much astonishment as theirs caused me. I was quietly attired in my snuff-colored suit of small-clothes, with silk stockings and simple buckle shoes, and I had of course no hat; but I gathered that my appearance caused universal amazement and concern, far more than could be justified by the mere accidental absence of headgear. A dread began to oppress me that I might actually have slept out my whole age and generation. Was my Amelia alive? and if so, would she be still the same Amelia I had known a week or two before? Should I find her an aged woman, still cherishing a reminiscence of her former love; or might she herself perhaps be dead and forgotten, while I remained, alone and solitary, in a world which knew me not?

'I walked along unmolested, but with reeling brain, through streets more and more unfamiliar, till I came near the St. Mary le Bone

Road. There, as I hesitated a little and staggered at the crossing, a man in a curious suit of dark blue clothes, with a grotesque felt helmet on his head, whom I afterwards found to be a constable, came up and touched me on the shoulder.

' "Look here," he said to me in a rough voice, "what are you a-doin' in this 'ere fancy-dress at this hour in the mornin'? You've lost your way home, I take it."

' "I was going," I answered, "to the St. Mary le Bone Road."

' "Why, you image," says he rudely, "if you mean Marribon, why don't you say Marribon?* What house are you a-lookin' for, eh?"

' "My brother lives," I replied, "at the Lamb, near St. Mary's Church, and I was going to his residence."

' "The Lamb!" says he, with a rude laugh; "there ain't no public of that name in the road. It's my belief," he goes on after a moment, "that you're drunk, or mad, or else you've stole them clothes. Any way, you've got to go along with me to the station, so walk it, will you?"

' "Pardon me," I said, "I suppose you are an officer of the law, and I would not attempt to resist your authority"—"You'd better not," says he, half to himself—"but I should like to go to my brother's house, where I could show you that I am a respectable person."

' "Well," says my fellow insolently, "I'll go along of you if you like, and if it's all right, I suppose you won't mind standing a bob?"

' "A what?" said I.

' "A bob," says he, laughing; "a shillin', you know."

'To get rid of his insolence for a while, I pulled out my purse and handed him a shilling. It was a George II. with milled edges,* not like the things I see you use now. He held it up and looked at it, and then he said again, "Look here, you know, this isn't good. You'd better come along with me straight to the station, and not make a fuss about it. There's three charges against you, that's all. One is, that you're drunk. The second is, that you're mad. And the third is, that you've been trying to utter false coin. Any one of 'em's quite enough to jus-tify me in takin' you into custody."

'I saw it was no use to resist, and I went along with him.

'I won't trouble you with the whole of the details, but the upshot of it all was, they took me before a magistrate. By this time I had begun to realize the full terror of the situation, and I saw clearly that the real danger lay in the inevitable suspicion of madness under which I must labor. When I got into the court I told the magistrate my story very shortly and simply, just as I have told it to you now. He listened to me without a word, and at the end he turned round to his clerk, and said, "This is clearly a case for Dr. Fitz-Jenkins, I think."

' "Sir," I said, "before you send me to a madhouse, which I suppose is what you mean by those words, I trust you will at least examine the evidences of my story. Look at my clothing, look at these coins, look at everything about me." And I handed him my purse to see for himself.

'He looked at it for a minute, and then he turned towards me very sternly. "Mr. Spottiswood," he said, "or whatever else your real name may be, if this is a joke, it is a very foolish and unbecoming one. Your dress is no doubt very well designed; your small collection of coins is interesting and well-selected; and you have got up your character remarkably well. If you are really sane, which I suspect to be the case, then your studied attempt to waste the time of this court and to make a laughing-stock of its magistrate, will meet with the punishment it deserves. I shall remit your case for consideration to our medical officer. If you consent to give him your real name and address, you will be liberated after his examination. Otherwise, it will be necessary to satisfy ourselves as to your identity. Not a word more, sir," he continued, as I tried to speak on behalf of my story. "Inspector, remove the prisoner."

'They took me away, and the surgeon examined me. To cut things short, I was pronounced mad, and three days later the commissioners passed me for a pauper asylum. When I came to be examined, they said I showed no recollection of most subjects of ordinary education.

' "I am a chemist," said I; "try me with some chemical questions. You will see that I can answer sanely enough."

' "How do you mix a gray powder?"* said the commissioner.

' "Excuse me," I said, "I mean a chemical philosopher, not an apothecary."

' "Oh, very well, then; what is carbonic acid?"

' "I never heard of it," I answered in despair. "It must be something which has come into use since—since I left off learning chemistry." For I had discovered that my only chance now was to avoid all reference to my past life and the extraordinary calamity which had thus unexpectedly overtaken me. "Please try me with something else."

' "Oh, certainly. What is the atomic weight of chlorine?"*

'I could only answer that I did not know.

' "This is a very clear case," said the commissioner. "Evidently he is a gentleman by birth and education, but he can give no very satisfactory account of his friends, and till they come forward to claim him we can only send him for a time to North Street."

' "For heaven's sake, gentlemen," I cried, "before you consign me to an asylum, give me one more chance. I am perfectly sane; I remember all I ever knew; but you are asking me questions about subjects on which I never had any information. Ask me anything historical, and see whether I have forgotten or confused any of my facts."

'I will do the commissioner the justice to say that he seemed anxious not to decide upon the case without full consideration. "Tell me what you can recollect," he said, " as to the reign of George IV."

' "I know nothing at all about it," I answered, terror-stricken, "but oh, do pray ask me anything up to the time of George III."

' "Then please say what you think of the French Revolution."

'I was thunderstruck. I could make no reply, and the commissioners shortly signed the papers to send me to North Street pauper asylum. They hurried me into the street, and I walked beside my captors towards the prison to which they had consigned me. Yet I did not give up all hope even so of ultimately regaining my freedom. I thought the rationality of my demeanor and the obvious soundness of all my reasoning powers would suffice in time to satisfy the medical attendant as to my perfect sanity. I felt sure that people could never long mistake a man so clear-headed and collected as myself for a madman.

'On our way, however, we happened to pass a churchyard where some workmen were engaged in removing a number of old tombstones from the crowded area. Even in my existing agitated condition, I could not help catching the name and date on one mouldering slab which a laborer had just placed upon the edge of the pavement. It ran something like this: "Sacred to the memory of Amelia, second daughter of the late Sir Thomas Spragg, knight, and beloved wife of Henry McAlister, Esq., by whom this stone is erected. Died May 20, 1799, aged 44 years." Though I had gathered already that my dear girl must probably have long been dead, yet the reality of the fact had not yet had time to fix itself upon my mind. You must remember, my dear sir, that I had but awaked a few days earlier from my long slumber, and that during those days I had been harassed and agitated by such a flood of incomprehensible complications, that I could not really grasp in all its fullness the complete isolation of my present position.

When I saw the tombstone of one whom, as it seemed to me, I had loved passionately but a week or two before, I could not refrain from rushing to embrace it, and covering the insensible stone with my boiling tears. "Oh, my Amelia, my Amelia," I cried, "I shall never again behold thee, then! I shall never again press thee to my heart, or hear thy dear lips pronounce my name!"

'But the unfeeling wretches who had charge of me were far from being moved to sympathy by my bitter grief. "Died in 1799," said one of them with a sneer. "Why, this madman's blubbering over the grave of an old lady who has been buried for about a hundred years!" And the workmen joined in their laughter as my gaolers tore me away to the prison where I was to spend the remainder of my days.

'When we arrived at the asylum, the surgeon in attendance was informed of this circumstance, and the opinion that I was hopelessly mad thus became ingrained in his whole conceptions of my case. I remained five months or more in the asylum, but I never saw any chance of creating a more favorable impression on the minds of the authorities. Mixing as I did only with other patients, I could gain no clear ideas of what had happened since I had taken my fatal sleep; and whenever I endeavored to question the keepers, they amused themselves by giving me evidently false and inconsistent answers, in order to enjoy my chagrin and confusion. I could not even learn the actual date of the present year, for one keeper would laugh and say it was 2001, while another would confidentially advise me to date my petition to the Commissioners, "Jan. I, A. D. one million." The surgeon, who never played me any such pranks, yet refused to aid me in any way, lest as he said, he should strengthen me in my sad delusion. He was convinced that I must be an historical student, whose reason had broken down through too close study of the eighteenth century; and he felt certain that sooner or later my friends would come to claim me. He is a gentle and humane man, against whom I have no personal complaint to make; but his initial misconception prevented him and everybody else from ever paying the least attention to my story. I could not even induce them to make inquiries at my house at Hampstead, where the discovery of the subterranean laboratory would have partially proved the truth of my account.

'Many visitors came to the asylum from time to time, and they were always told that I possessed a minute and remarkable acquaintance with the history of the eighteenth century. They questioned me about facts which are as vivid in my memory as those of the present month, and were much surprised at the accuracy of my replies. But they only thought it strange that so clever a man should be so very mad, and that my information should be so full as to past events, while my notions about the modern world were so utterly chaotic. The surgeon, however, always believed that my reticence about all events posterior to 1781 was a part of my insanity. I had studied the early part of the eighteenth century so fully, he said, that I fancied I had lived in it; and I had persuaded myself that I knew nothing at all about the subsequent state of the world.'

The poor fellow stopped a while, and again drew his sleeve across his forehead. It was impossible to look at him and believe for a moment that he was a madman.

'And how did you make your escape from the asylum?' I asked.

'Now, this very evening,' he answered; 'I simply broke away from the door and ran down toward the Strand, till I came to a place that looked a little like St. Martin's Fields, with a great column and some fountains, and near there I met you. It seemed to me that the best thing to do was to catch the York coach and get away from the town as soon as possible. You met me, and your look and name inspired me with confidence. I believe you must be a descendant of my dear brother.'

'I have not the slightest doubt,' I answered solemnly, 'that every word of your story is true, and that you are really my great-great-uncle. My own knowledge of our family history exactly tallies with what you tell me. I shall spare no endeavor to clear up this extraordinary matter, and to put you once more in your true position.'

'And you will protect me?' he cried, fervently, clasping my hand in both his own with intense eagerness. 'You will not give me up once more to the asylum people?'

'I will do everything on earth that is possible for you,' I replied.

He lifted my hand to his lips and kissed it several times, while I felt hot tears falling upon it as he bent over me. It was a strange position, look at it how you will. Grant that I was but the dupe of a madman, yet even to believe for a moment that I, a man of well-nigh fifty, stood there in face of my own great-grandfather's brother, to all appearance some twenty years my junior, was in itself an extraordinary and marvellous thing. Both of us were too overcome to speak. It was a few minutes before we said anything, and then a loud knock at the door made my hunted stranger rise up hastily in terror from his chair.

'Gracious heavens!' he cried, 'they have tracked me hither. They are coming to fetch me. Oh, hide me, hide me, anywhere from these wretches!'

As he spoke, the door opened, and two keepers with a policeman, entered my room.

'Ah, here he is!' said one of them, advancing towards the fugitive, who shrank away towards the window as he approached.

'Do not touch him,' I exclaimed, throwing myself in the way. 'Every word of what he says is true, and he is no more insane than I am.'

The keeper laughed a low laugh of vulgar incredulity. 'Why, there's a pair of you, I do believe,' he said. 'You're just as mad yourself as t'other one.' And he pushed me aside roughly to get at his charge.

But the poor fellow, seeing him come towards him, seemed suddenly to grow instinct with a terrible vigour, and hurled off the keeper with one hand, as a strong man might do with a little terrier. Then, before we could see what he was meditating, he jumped upon the ledge of the open window, shouted out loudly, 'Farewell, farewell!' and leapt with a spring on to the Embankment beneath.

All four of us rushed hastily down the three flights of steps to the bottom, and came below upon a crushed and mangled mass on the spattered pavement. He was quite dead. Even the policeman was shocked and horrified at the dreadful way in which the body had been crushed and mutilated in its fall, and at the suddenness and unexpectedness of the tragedy. We took him up and laid him out in my room; and from that room he was interred after the inquest, with all the respect which I should have paid to an undoubted relative. On his grave in Kensal Green Cemetery* I have placed a stone bearing the simple inscription, 'Jonathan Spottiswood. Died 1881.' The hint I had received from the keeper prevented me from saying anything as to my belief in his story, but I asked for leave to undertake the duty of his interment on the ground that he bore my own surname, and that no other person was forthcoming to assume the task. The parochial authorities were glad enough to rid the ratepayers of the expense.

At the inquest I gave my evidence simply and briefly, dwelling mainly upon the accidental nature of our meeting, and the facts as to his fatal leap. I said nothing about the known disappearance of Jonathan Spottiswood in 1781, nor the other points which gave credibility to his strange tale. But from this day forward I give myself up to proving the truth of his story, and realizing the splendid chemical discovery which promises so much benefit to mankind. For the first purpose, I have offered a large reward for the discovery of a trapdoor in a coal-cellar at Hampstead, leading into a subterranean passage and laboratory; since, unfortunately, my unhappy visitor did not happen to mention the position of his house. For the second purpose, I have begun a series of experiments upon the properties of the essential oil of alchemilla, and the possibility of successfully treating it with carbonic anhydride; since, unfortunately, he was equally vague as to the nature of his process and the proportions of either constituent. Many people will conclude at once, no doubt, that I myself have become infected with the monomania of my miserable namesake, but I am determined at any rate, not to allow so extraordinary an anæsthetic to go unacknowledged, if there be even a remote chance of actually proving its useful nature. Meanwhile, I say nothing even to my dearest friends with regard to the researches upon which I am engaged.

FRANK R. STOCKTON

THE WATER-DEVIL: A MARINE TALE

IN the village of Riprock there was neither tavern nor inn, for it was but a small place through which few travellers passed; but it could not be said to be without a place of entertainment, for if by chance a stranger—or two or three of them, for that matter—wished to stop at Riprock for a meal, or to pass the night, there was the house of blacksmith Fryker, which was understood to be always open to decent travellers.

The blacksmith was a prominent man in the village, and his house was a large one, with several spare bedrooms, and it was said by those who had had an opportunity of judging, that nobody in the village lived better than blacksmith Fryker and his family.

Into the village there came, late one autumn afternoon, a tall man, who was travelling on foot, with a small valise hanging from his shoulder. He had inquired for lodging for the night, had been directed to the blacksmith's house, had arranged to stop there, had had his supper, which greatly satisfied him, and was now sitting before the fire in the large living-room, smoking blacksmith Fryker's biggest pipe. This stranger was a red-haired man, with a cheery expression, and a pair of quick, bright eyes. He was slenderly but strongly built, and was a good fellow, who would stand by, with his hands in the pockets of his short pea-jacket, and right willingly tell one who was doing something how the thing ought to be done.

But the traveller did not sit alone before the crackling fire of logs, for the night being cool, a table was drawn near to one side of the fire-place, and by this sat Mistress Fryker and her daughter Joanna, both engaged in some sort of needle-work. The blacksmith sat between the corner of the fire-place and this table, so that when he had finished smoking his after-supper pipe, he might put on his spectacles and read the weekly paper by the light of the big lamp. On the other side of the stranger, whose chair was in front of the middle of the fire-place, sat the school-master, Andrew Cardly by name; a middle-aged man of sober and attentive aspect, and very glad when chance threw in his way a book he had not read, or a stranger who could reinforce his stock of information. At the other corner of the fire-place, in a cushioned chair, which was always given to him when he dropped in to spend an evening with the blacksmith, sat Mr. Harberry, an elderly man, a man of substance, and a man in whom all Riprock, not excluding himself, placed unqualified confidence as to his veracity, his financial soundness, and his deep insight into the causes, the influences, and the final issue of events and conditions.

'On a night like this,' said the stranger, stretching his long legs toward the blaze, 'there is nothing I like better than a fire of wood, except indeed it be the society of ladies who do not object to a little tobacco smoke,' and he glanced with a smile toward the table with a lamp upon it.

Now blacksmith Fryker was a prudent man, and he did not consider that the privileges of his hearthstone—always freely granted to a decent stranger—included an acquaintance with his pretty daughter; and so, without allowing his women-folk a chance to enter into the conversation, he offered the stranger a different subject to hammer upon.

'In the lower country,' said he, 'they don't need fires as early in the season as we do. What calling do you follow, sir? Some kind of trade, perhaps?'

'No,' said the traveller, 'I follow no trade; I follow the sea.'

At this the three men looked at him, as also the two women. His appearance no more suggested that he was a seaman than the appearance of Mr. Harberry suggested that he was what the village of Riprock believed him to be.

'I should not have taken you for a sailor,' said the blacksmith.

'I am not a sailor,' said the other; 'I am a soldier; a sea-soldier—in fact, a marine.'

'I should say, sir,' remarked the school-master, in a manner intended rather to draw out information than to give it, 'that the position of a soldier on a ship possessed advantages over that of a soldier on land. The former is not required to make long marches, nor to carry heavy baggage. He remains at rest, in fact, while traversing great distances. Nor is he called on to resist the charges of cavalry, nor to form hollow squares on the deadly battle-field.'

The stranger smiled. 'We often find it hard enough,' said he, 'to resist the charges made against us by our officers; the hollow squares form themselves in our stomachs when we are on short rations; and I have known many a man who would rather walk twenty miles than sail one, especially when the sea chops.'

'I am very sure, sir,' said school-master Cardly, 'that there is nothing to be said against the endurance and the courage of marines. We all remember how they presented arms, and went down with the *Royal George.*'*

The marine smiled.

'I suppose,' said the blacksmith, 'that you never had to do anything of that sort?'

The stranger did not immediately answer, but sat looking into the fire. Presently he said: 'I have done things of nearly every sort, although not exactly that; but I have thought my ship was going down with all on board, and that's the next worst thing to going down, you know.'

'And how was that?' inquired Fryker.

'Well,' said the other, 'it happened more times than I can tell you of, or even remember. Yes,' said he, meditatively, 'more times than I can remember.'

'I am sure,' said the school-master, 'that we should all like to hear some of your experiences.'

The marine shrugged his shoulders. 'These things,' said he, 'come to a man, and then if he lives through them, they pass on, and he is ready for the next streak of luck, good or bad. That's the way with us followers of the sea, especially if we happen to be marines, and have to bear, so to speak, the responsibility of two professions. But sometimes a mischance or a disaster does fix itself upon a man's mind so that he can tell about it if he is called upon; and just now there comes to my mind a very odd thing which once happened to me, and I can give you the points of that, if you like.'

The three men assured him that they would very much like it, and the two women looked as if they were of the same opinion.

Before he began the marine glanced about him, with a certain good-natured wistfulness which might have indicated, to those who understood the countenances of the sea-going classes, a desire to wet his whistle; but if this expression were so intended it was thrown away, for blacksmith Fryker took no spirits himself, nor furnished them to anybody else. Giving up all hope in this direction, the marine took a long pull at his pipe and began.

'It was in the winter of 1878 that I was on the Bay of Bengal, on my way to Calcutta,* and about five hundred miles distant from that city. I was not on my own ship, but was returning from a leave of absence on an American steamer from San Francisco to Calcutta, where my vessel, the United States frigate *Apache* was then lying. My leave of absence would expire in three days; but although the *General Brooks*, the vessel I was aboard of, was more of a freight than a passenger vessel, and was heavily laden, we would have been in port in good time if, two days before, something had not happened to the machinery. I am not a machinist myself, and don't know exactly what it was that was out of order, but the engine stopped, and we had to proceed under sail. That sounds like a slow business; but the *Brooks* was a clipper-built vessel with three masts and a lot of sails—square sails, fore-and-aft sails, jib sails,* and all that sort of thing. I am not a regular sailor myself, and don't know the names of all the sails; but whatever sails she could have she did have, and although she was an iron vessel, and heavily freighted, she was a good sailer. We had a strong, steady wind from the south, and the captain told me that at the rate we were going he didn't doubt that he would get me aboard my vessel before my leave ran out, or at least so soon afterward that it wouldn't make any difference.

'Well, as I said, the wind blew strong and steady behind us, the sails were full, and the spray dashed up at our bow in a way calculated to tickle the soul of any one anxious to get to the end of his voyage; and I was one of that sort, I can tell you.

'In the afternoon of the second day after our engine stopped, I was standing at the bow, and looking over, when suddenly I noticed that there wasn't any spray dashing up in front of the vessel. I thought we must have struck a sudden calm, but, glancing up, I saw the sails were full, and the wind blew fair in my face as I turned toward the stern. I walked aft to the skipper, and touching my cap, I said, "Captain, how is it that when a ship is dashing along at this rate she doesn't throw up any spray with her cutwater?"* He grinned a little, and said, "But she does, you know." "If you will come forward," said I, "I'll show you that she doesn't," and then we walked forward, and I showed him that she didn't. I never saw a man so surprised. At first he thought that somebody had been squirting oil in front, but even if that had been the case, there would have been some sort of a ripple on each side of the bow, and there wasn't anything of the kind. The skipper took off his cap and scratched his head. Then he turned and sang out, "Mr. Rogers, throw the log."

'Now the log,' said the marine, turning to Mrs. Fryker and her daughter, 'is a little piece of wood with a long line to it, that they throw out behind a vessel to see how fast she is going. I am not a regular Jack Tar myself, and don't understand the principle of the thing, but it tells you exactly how many miles an hour the ship is going.

'In about two minutes Mr. Rogers stepped up, with his eyes like two auger-holes, and said he, "Captain, we're makin' no knots an hour. We're not sailing at all."

' "Get out," roared the captain, "don't you see the sails? Don't you feel the wind? Throw that log again, sir."

'Well, they threw the log again, the captain saw it done, and sure enough Mr. Rogers was right. The vessel wasn't moving. With a wind that ought to have carried her spinning along, miles and miles in an hour, she was standing stock-still. The skipper here let out one of the strongest imprecations used in navigation, and said he, "Mr. Rogers, is it possible that there is a sand-bar in the middle of the Bay of Bengal, and that we've stuck on it? Cast the lead."

'I will just state to the ladies,' said the marine, turning toward the table, 'that the lead is a heavy weight that is lowered to the bottom of a body of water to see how deep it is, and this operation is called sounding. Well, they sounded and they sounded, but everywhere— fore, aft, and midship—they found plenty of water; in fact, not having a line for deep-sea sounding they couldn't touch bottom at all.

'I can tell you, ladies and gentlemen,' said the marine, looking from one to the other of the party, 'that things now began to feel creepy. I am not afraid of storms, nor fires at sea, nor any of the common accidents of the ocean; but for a ship to stand still with plenty of water under her, and a strong wind filling her sails, has more of the uncanny about it than I fancy. Pretty near the whole of the crew was on deck by this time, and I could see that they felt very much as I did, but nobody seemed to know what to say about it.

'Suddenly the captain thought that some unknown current was setting against us, and forcing the vessel back with the same power that the wind was forcing her forward, and he tried to put the ship about so as to have the wind on her starboard quarter; but as she hadn't any headway, or for some other reason, this didn't work. Then it struck him that perhaps one of the anchors had been accidentally dropped, but they were all in their places, and if one of them had dropped, its cable would not have been long enough to touch bottom.

'Now I could see that he began to look scared. "Mr. Browser," said he, to the chief engineer, "for some reason or other this ship does not make headway under sail. You must go to work and get the engine running." And for the rest of that day everybody on board who understood that sort of thing was down below, hard at work with the machinery, hammering and banging like good fellows.

'The chief officer ordered a good many of the sails to be taken in, for they were only uselessly straining the masts, but there were enough left to move her in case the power of the current, or whatever it was that stopped her, had slackened, and she steadily kept her position with the breeze abaft.*

'All the crew, who were not working below, were crowded together on deck, talking about this strange thing. I joined them, and soon found that they thought it was useless to waste time and labor on the machinery. They didn't believe it could be mended, and if it should be, how could an engine move a vessel that the wind couldn't stir?

'These men were of many nationalities—Dutch, Scandinavian, Spanish, Italian, South American, and a lot more. Like many other American vessels that sail from our ports, nearly all the officers and crew were foreigners. The captain was a Finlander, who spoke very good English. And the only man who called himself an American was the chief officer; and he was only half a one; for he was born in Germany, came to the United States when he was twenty years old, stayed there five years, which didn't count either way, and had now been naturalized for twenty years.

'The consequence of this variety in nationality was that the men had all sorts of ideas and notions regarding the thing that was happening. They had thrown over chips and bits of paper to see if the vessel had begun to move, and had found that she didn't budge an inch, and now they seemed afraid to look over the sides.

'They were a superstitious lot, as might be expected, and they all believed that, in some way or other, the ship was bewitched; and in fact I felt like agreeing with them, although I did not say so.

'There was an old Portuguese sailor on board, an ugly-looking, weather-beaten little fellow, and when he had listened to everything the others had to say, he shuffled himself into the middle of the group. "Look here, mates," said he, in good enough English, "it's no use talking no more about this. I know what's the matter; I've sailed these seas afore, and I've been along the coast of this bay all the way from Negapatam to Jellasore on the west coast, and from Chittagong to Kraw on the other;* and I have heard stories of the strange things that are in this Bay of Bengal, and what they do, and the worst of them all is the Water-devil—and he's got us!"

'When the old rascal said this, there wasn't a man on deck who didn't look pale, in spite of his dirt and his sunburn. The chief officer tried to keep his knees stiff, but I could see him shaking. "What's a Water-devil?" said he, trying to make believe he thought it all stuff and nonsense. The Portuguese touched his forelock. "Do you remember, sir," said he, "what was the latitude and longitude when you took your observation to-day?" "Yes," said the other, "it was 15° north and 90° east." The Portuguese nodded his head. "That's just about the spot, sir, just about. I can't say exactly where the spot is, but it's just about here, and we've struck it. There isn't a native sea-man on any of these coasts that would sail over that point if he knowed it and could help it, for that's the spot where the Water-devil lives."

'It made me jump to hear the grunt that went through that crowd when he said this, but nobody asked any questions, and he went on. "This here Water-devil," said he, "is about as big as six whales, and in shape very like an oyster without its shell, and he fastens himself to the rocks at the bottom with a million claws. Right out of the middle of him there grows up a long arm that reaches to the top of the water, and at the end of this arm is a fist about the size of a yawl-boat,* with fifty-two fingers to it, with each one of them covered with little suckers that will stick fast to anything—iron, wood, stone, or flesh. All that this Water-devil gets to eat is what happens to come swimmin' or sailin' along where he can reach it, and it doesn't matter to him whether it's a shark, or a porpoise, or a shipful of people, and when he takes a grab of anything, that thing never gets away."

'About this time there were five or six men on their knees saying their prayers, such as they were, and a good many others looked as if they were just about to drop.

' "Now, when this Water-devil gets hold of a ship," the old fellow went on, "he don't generally pull her straight down to the bottom, but holds on to it till he counts his claws, and sees that they are all fastened to the rocks; for if a good many of them wasn't fastened he might pull himself loose, instead of pulling the ship down, and then he'd be a goner, for he'd be towed away, and like as not put in a museum. But when he is satisfied that he is moored fast and strong, then he hauls on his arm, and down comes the ship, no matter how big she is. As the ship is sinkin' he turns her over, every now and then, keel uppermost, and gives her a shake, and when the people drop out, he sucks them into a sort of funnel, which is his mouth."

'"Does he count fast?" asked one of the men, this being the first question that had been asked.

'"I've heard," said the Portuguese, "that he's a rapid calculator, and the minute he's got to his millionth claw, and finds it's hooked tight and fast, he begins to haul down the ship."'

At this point the marine stopped and glanced around at the little group. The blacksmith's wife and daughter had put down their work, and were gazing at him with an air of horrified curiosity. The blacksmith held his pipe in his hand, and regarded the narrator with the steadiness and impassiveness of an anvil. The school-master was listening with the greatest eagerness. He was an enthusiast on Natural History and Mythology, and had written an article for a weekly paper on the reconciliation of the beasts of tradition with the fauna of to-day. Mr. Harberry was not looking at the marine. His eyes were fixed upon the school-master.

'Mr. Cardly,' said he, 'did you ever read of an animal like that?'

'I cannot say that I have,' was his reply; 'but it is certain that there are many strange creatures, especially in the sea, of which scientists are comparatively ignorant.'

'Such as the sea-serpent,' added the marine, quickly, 'and a great many other monsters who are not in the books, but who have a good time at the bottom of the sea, all the same. Well, to go on with my story, you must understand that, though this Portuguese spoke broken English, which I haven't tried to give you, he made himself perfectly plain to all of us, and I can assure you that when he got through talking there was a shaky lot of men on that deck.

'The chief officer said he would go below and see how the captain was getting on, and the crew huddled together in the bow, and began whispering among themselves, as if they were afraid the Water-devil would hear them. I turned to walk aft, feeling pretty queer, I can tell you, when I saw Miss Minturn just coming up from the cabin below.

'I haven't said anything about Miss Minturn, but she and her father, who was an elderly English gentleman and an invalid, who had never left his berth since we took him up at Singapore, were our only passengers, except, of course, myself. She was a beautiful girl, with soft blue eyes and golden hair, and a little pale from constantly staying below to nurse her father.

'Of course I had had little or nothing to say to her, for her father was a good deal of a swell and I was only a marine; but now she saw me standing there by myself, and she came right up to me. "Can you tell me, sir," she said, "if anything else has happened? They are making a great din in the engine-room. I have been looking out of our port, and the vessel seems to me to be stationary." She stopped at that, and waited to hear what I had to say, but I assure you I would have liked to have had her go on talking for half an hour. Her voice was rich and sweet, like that of so many Englishwomen, although, I am happy to say, a great many of my countrywomen have just as good voices; and when I meet any of them for the first time, I generally give them the credit of talking in soft and musical notes, even though I have not had the pleasure of hearing them speak.'

'Look here,' said the blacksmith, 'can't you skip the girl and get back to the Devil?'

'No,' said the marine, 'I couldn't do that. The two are mixed together, so to speak, so that I have to tell you of both of them.'

'You don't mean to say,' exclaimed Mrs. Fryker, speaking for the first time, and by no means in soft and musical tones, 'that he swallowed her?'

'I'll go on with the story,' said the marine; 'that's the best way, and everything will come up in its place. Now, of course, I wasn't going to tell this charming young woman, with a sick father, anything about the Water-devil, though what reason to give her for our standing still here I couldn't imagine; but of course I had to speak, and I said, "Don't be alarmed, miss, we have met with an unavoidable detention; that sort of thing often happens in navigation. I can't explain it to you, but you see the ship is perfectly safe and sound, and she is merely under sail instead of having her engines going."

'"I understood about that," said she, "and father and I were both perfectly satisfied; for he said that if we had a good breeze we would not be long in reaching Calcutta; but we seem to have a breeze, and yet we don't go." "You'll notice," said I, "that the sails are not all set, and for some reason the wind does not serve. When the engines are mended, we shall probably go spinning along." She looked as if she was trying to appear satisfied. "Thank you, sir," she said. "I hope we may shortly proceed on our way, but in the meantime I shall not say anything to my father about this detention. I think he has not noticed it." "That would be very wise," I replied, and as she turned toward the companionway I was wild to say to her that it would be a lot better for her to stay on deck, and get some good fresh air, instead of coop- ing herself up in that close cabin; but I didn't know her well enough for that.'

'Now that you are through with the girl,' said the blacksmith, 'what did the Devil do?'

'I haven't got to him yet,' said the marine, 'but after Miss Minturn went below I began to think of him, and the more I thought of him, the less I liked him. I think the chief officer must have told the men below about the Water-devil, for pretty soon the whole kit and boodle* of them left their work and came on deck, skipper and all. They told me they had given up the engine as a bad job, and I thought to myself that most likely they were all too nervous to rightly know what they were about. The captain threw out the log again, but it floated along- side like a cork on a fishing-line, and at this he turned pale and walked away from the ship's side, forgetting to pull it in again.

'It was now beginning to grow dark, and as nobody seemed to think about supper, I went below to look into that matter. It wouldn't do for Miss Minturn and her father to go without their regular meal, for that would be sure to scare them to death, and if I'm to have a big scare I like to take it on a good square meal, so I went below to see about it. But I wasn't needed, for Miss Minturn's maid, who was an elderly woman, and pretty sharp set in her temper, was in the cook's galley superintending supper for her people, and after she got through I superintended some for myself.

'After that I felt a good deal bolder, and I lighted a pipe and went on deck. There I found the whole ship's company, officers and crew, none of them doing anything, and most of them clustered together in little groups, whispering or grunting.

'I went up to the captain and asked him what he was going to do next. "Do?" said he; "there is nothing to do; I've done everything that I can do. I'm all upset; I don't know whether I am myself or some other man"; and then he walked away.

'I sat there and smoked and looked at them, and I can tell you the sight wasn't cheerful. There was the ship, just as good and sound, as far as anybody could see, as anything that floated on the ocean, and here were all her people, shivering and shaking and not speaking above their breath, looking for all the world, under the light of the stars and the ship's lamps, which some of them had had sense enough to light, as if they expected in the course of the next half-hour, to be made to walk the plank; and, to tell the truth, what they were afraid of would come to pretty much the same thing.'

'Mr. Cardly,' here interrupted Mr. Harberry, 'how long does it take to count a million?'

'That depends,' said the school-master, 'on the rapidity of the calculator; some calculators count faster than others. An ordinary boy, counting two hundred a minute, would require nearly three days and a half to count a million.'

'Very good,' said Mr. Harberry; 'please go on with your story, sir.'

'Of course,' said the marine, 'there is a great difference between a boy and a Water-devil, and it is impossible for anybody to know how fast the latter can count, especially as he may be supposed to be used to it. Well, I couldn't stand it any longer on deck, and having nothing else to do, I turned in and went to sleep.'

'To sleep! Went to sleep!' exclaimed Mrs. Fryker. 'I don't see how you could have done that.'

'Ah, madam,' said the marine, 'we soldiers of the sea are exposed to all sorts of dangers,—combination dangers, you might call them,—and in the course of time we get used to it; if we didn't we couldn't do our duty.

'As the ship had been in its present predicament for six or seven hours, and nothing had happened, there was no reason to suppose that things would not remain as they were for six or seven hours more, in which time I might get a good sleep, and be better prepared for what might come. There's nothing like a good meal and a good sleep as a preparation for danger.

'It was daylight when I awakened, and rapidly glancing about me, I saw that everything appeared to be all right. Looking out of the port-hole, I could see that the vessel was still motionless. I hurried on deck, and was greatly surprised to find nobody there—no one on watch, no one at the wheel, no one anywhere. I ran down into the fo'castle, which is the sailors' quarters, but not a soul could I see. I called, I whistled, I searched everywhere, but no one answered; I could find no one. Then I dashed up on deck, and glared around me. Every boat was gone.

'Now I knew what had happened: the cowardly rascals, from captain to cook, had deserted the ship in the night, and I had been left behind!

'For some minutes I stood motionless, wondering how men could be so unfeeling as to do such a thing. I soon became convinced, from what I had seen of the crew, that they had not all gone off together, that there had been no concerted action. A number of them had probably quietly lowered a boat and sneaked away; then another lot had gone off, hoping their mates would not hear them and therefore crowd into their boat. And so they had all departed, not one boat-load thinking of anybody but themselves; or if they thought at all about others, quieting their consciences by supposing that there were enough boats on the vessel, and that the other people were as likely to get off as they were.

'Suddenly I thought of the other passengers. Had they been left behind? I ran down below, and I had scarcely reached the bottom of the steps when I met Miss Minturn's maid. "It seems to me," she said, sharply, "that the people on this ship are neglecting their duty. There's nobody in the kitchen, and I want some gruel." "My good woman," said I, "who do you want it for?" "Who!" she replied; "why, for Mr. Minturn, of course; and Miss Minturn may like some, too."

'Then I knew that all the passengers had been left behind!

'"If you want any gruel," said I, "you will have to go into the galley and make it yourself"; and then in a low tone I told her what had happened, for I knew that it would be much better for me to do this than for her to find it out for herself. Without a word she sat right down on the floor, and covered her head with her apron. "Now don't make a row," said I, "and frighten your master and mistress to death; we're all right so far, and all you've got to do is to take care of Mr. and Miss Minturn, and cook their meals. The steamer is tight and sound, and it can't be long before some sort of a craft will come by and take us off." I left her sniffling with her apron over her head, but when I came back, ten minutes afterward, she was in the galley making gruel.

'I don't think you will be surprised, my friends,' continued the marine, 'when I tell you that I now found myself in a terrible state of mind. Of course I hadn't felt very jovial since the steamer had been so wonderfully stopped; but when the captain and all the crew were aboard, I had that sort of confidence which comes from believing that when there are people about whose duty it is to do things, when the time comes to do the things, they will do them; but now, practically speaking, there was nobody but me. The others on board were not to be counted, except as encumbrances. In truth, I was alone,—alone with the Water-devil!

'The moment I found no one to depend upon but myself, and that I was deserted in the midst of this lonely mass of water, in that moment did my belief in the Water-devil begin to grow. When I first heard of the creature, I didn't consider that it was my business either to believe in it, or not to believe in it, and I could let the whole thing drop out of my mind, if I chose; but now it was a different matter. I was bound to think for myself, and the more I thought, the more I believed in the Water-devil.

'The fact was, there wasn't anything else to believe in. I had gone over the whole question, and the skipper had gone all over it, and everybody else had gone all over it, and no one could think of anything but a Water-devil that could stop a steamer in this way in the middle of the Bay of Bengal, and hold her there hour after hour, in spite of wind and wave and tide. It could not be anything but the monster the Portuguese had told us of, and all I now could do was to wonder whether, when he was done counting his million claws, he would be able to pull down a vessel of a thousand tons, for that was about the size of the *General Brooks*.

'I think I should now have begun to lose my wits if it had not been for one thing, and that was the coming of Miss Minturn on deck. The moment I saw her lovely face I stiffened up wonderfully. "Sir," said she, "I would like to see the captain." "I am representing the captain, miss," I said, with a bow; "what is it that I can do for you?" "I want to speak to him about the steward," she said; "I think he is neglecting his duty." "I also represent the steward," I replied; "tell me what you wish of him." She made no answer to this, but looked about her in a startled way. "Where are all the men?" she said. "Miss Minturn," said I, "I represent the crew—in fact, I represent the whole ship's company except the cook, and his place must be taken by your maid." "What do you mean?" she asked, looking at me with her wide-opened, beautiful eyes.

'Then, as there was no help for it, I told her everything, except that I did not mention the Water-devil in connection with our marvellous stoppage. I only said that that was caused by something which nobody understood.

'She did not sit down and cover her head, nor did she scream or faint. She turned pale, but looked steadily at me, and her voice did not shake as she asked me what was to be done. "There is nothing to be done," I answered, "but to keep up good hearts, eat three meals a day, and wait until a ship comes along and takes us off."

'She stood silent for about three minutes. "I think," she then said, "that I will not yet tell my father what has happened"; and she went below.

'Now, strange to say, I walked up and down the deck with my hat cocked on one side and my hands in my pockets, feeling a great deal better. I did not like Water-devils any more than I did before, and I did not believe in this one any less than I did before, but, after all, there was some good about him. It seems odd, but the arm of this submarine monster, over a mile long for all that I knew, was a bond of union between the lovely Miss Minturn and me. She was a lady; I was a marine. So far as I knew anything about bonds of union, there wasn't one that could have tackled itself to us two, except this long, slippery arm of the Water-devil, with one end in the monstrous flob at the bottom, and the other fast to our ship.

'There was no doubt about it, if it hadn't been for that Water-devil she would have been no more to me than the Queen of Madagascar was; but under the circumstances, if I wasn't everything to her, who could be anything—that is, if one looked at the matter from a practical point of view?'

The blacksmith made a little movement of impatience. 'Suppose you cut all that,' said he. 'I don't care about the bond of union; I want to know what happened to the ship.'

'It is likely,' said the marine, 'if I could have cut the bond of union that I spoke of, that is to say, the Water-devil's arm, that I would have done it, hoping that I might safely float off somewhere with Miss Minturn; but I couldn't cut it then, and I can't cut it now. That bond is part of my story, and it must all go on together.

'I now set myself to work to do what I thought ought to be done under the circumstances, but, of course, that wasn't very much. I hoisted a flag upside down, and after considering the matter I concluded to take in all the sails that had been set. I thought that a steamer without smoke coming from her funnel, and no sails set, would be more likely to attract attention from distant vessels than if she appeared to be under sail.

'I am not a regular sailor, as I said before, but I got out on the yard, and cut the square sail loose and let it drop on the deck, and I let the jib come down on a run, and managed to bundle it up some way on the bowsprit. This sort of thing took all the nautical gymnastics that I was master of, and entirely occupied my mind, so that

I found myself whistling while I worked. I hoped Miss Minturn heard me whistle, because it would not only give her courage, but would let her see that I was not a man who couldn't keep up his spirits in a case like this.

'When that work was over, I began to wonder what I should do next, and then an idea struck me. "Suppose," thought I, "that we are not stationary, but that we are in some queer kind of a current, and that the water, ship and all are steadily moving on together, so that after a while* we shall come in sight of land, or into the track of vessels!"

'I instantly set about to find out if this was the case. It was about noon, and it so happened that on the day before, when the chief officer took his observation, I was seized with a desire to watch him and see how he did it. I don't see why I should have had this notion, but I had it, and I paid the strictest attention to the whole business, calculation part and all, and I found out exactly how it was done.

'Well, then, I went and got the quadrant,—that's the thing they do it with,—and I took an observation, and I found that we were in latitude 15° north, 90° east, exactly where we had been twenty-four hours before!

'When I found out this, I turned so faint that I wanted to sit down and cover up my head. The Water-devil had us, there was no mistake about it and no use trying to think of anything else. I staggered along the deck, went below, and cooked myself a meal. In a case like this there's nothing like a square meal to keep a man up.

'I know you don't like to hear her mentioned,' said the marine, turning to the blacksmith, 'but I am bound to say that in course of the afternoon Miss Minturn came on deck several times, to ask if anything new had happened, and if I had seen a vessel. I showed her all that I had done, and told her I was going to hang out lights at night, and did everything I could to keep her on deck as long as possible; for it was easy to see that she needed fresh air, and I needed company. As long as I was talking to her I didn't care a snap of my finger for the Water-devil. It is queer what an influence a beautiful woman has on a man, but it's so, and there's no use arguing about it. She said she had been puzzling her brains to find out what had stopped us, and she supposed it must be that we had run onto a shallow place and stuck fast in the mud, but thought it wonderful that there should be such a place so far from land. I agreed with her that it was wonderful, and added that that was probably the reason the captain and the crew had been seized with a panic. But sensible people like herself and her father, I said, ought not to be troubled by such an occurrence, especially as the vessel remained in a perfectly sound condition.

'She said that her father was busily engaged in writing his memoirs, and that his mind was so occupied, he had not concerned himself at all about our situation, that is, if he had noticed that we were not moving. "If he wants to see the steward, or anybody else," I said, "please call upon me. You know I represent the whole ship's company, and I shall be delighted to do anything for him or for you." She thanked me very much and went below.

'She came up again, after this, but her maid came with her, and the two walked on deck for a while. I didn't have much to say to them that time; but just before dark Miss Minturn came on deck alone, and walked forward, where I happened to be. "Sir," said she, and her voice trembled a little as she spoke, "if anything should happen, will you promise me that you will try to save my father?" You can't imagine how these touching words from this beautiful woman affected me. "My dear lady," said I, and I hope she did not take offence at the warmth of my expression, "I don't see how anything can happen; but I promise you, on the word of a sea-soldier, that if danger should come upon us, I will save not only your father, but yourself and your maid. Trust me for that."

'The look she gave me when I said these words, and especially the flash of her eye when I spoke of my being a sea-soldier, made me feel strong enough to tear that sea-monster's arm in twain, and to sail away with the lovely creature for whom my heart was beginning to throb.'

'It's a pity,' said the blacksmith, 'that you hadn't jumped into the water while the fit was on you, and done the tearing.'

'A man often feels strong enough to do a thing,' said the marine, 'and yet doesn't care to try to do it, and that was my case at that time; but I vowed to myself that if the time came when there was any saving to be done, I'd attend to Miss Minturn, even if I had to neglect the rest of the family.

'She didn't make any answer, but she gave me her hand; and she couldn't have done anything I liked better than that. I held it as long as I could, which wasn't very long, and then she went down to her father.'

'Glad of it,' said the blacksmith.

'When I had had my supper, and had smoked my pipe, and everything was still, and I knew I shouldn't see anybody any more that night, I began to have the quakes and the shakes. If even I had had the maid to talk to, it would have been a comfort; but in the way of faithfully attending to her employers that woman was a trump.* She cooked for them, and did for them, and stuck by them straight along, so she hadn't any time for chats with me.

'Being alone, I couldn't help all the time thinking about the Water-devil, and although it seems a foolish thing now that I look back on it, I set to work to calculate how long it would take him to count his feet. I made it about the same time as you did, sir,' nodding to the school-master, 'only I considered that if he counted twelve hours, and slept and rested twelve hours, that would make it seven days, which would give me a good long time with Miss Minturn, and that would be the greatest of joys to me, no matter what happened afterward.

'But then nobody could be certain that the monster at the bottom of the bay needed rest or sleep. He might be able to count without stopping, and how did I know that he couldn't check off four hundred claws a minute? If that happened to be the case, our time must be nearly up.

'When that idea came into my head, I jumped up and began to walk about. What could I do? I certainly ought to be ready to do something when the time came. I thought of getting life-preservers, and strapping one on each of us, so that if the Water-devil turned over the vessel and shook us out, we shouldn't sink down to him, but would float on the surface.

'But then the thought struck me that if he should find the vessel empty of live creatures, and should see us floating around on the top, all he had to do was to let go of the ship and grab us, one at a time. When I thought of a fist as big as a yawl-boat, clapping its fifty-two fingers on me, it sent a shiver through my bones. The fact was there wasn't anything to do, and so after a while I managed to get asleep, which was a great comfort.'

'Mr. Cardly,' said Mr. Harberry to the school-master, 'what reason can you assign why a sea-monster, such as has been described to us, should neglect to seize upon several small boats filled with men who were escaping from a vessel which it held in custody?'

'I do not precisely see,' answered Mr. Cardly, 'why these men should have been allowed this immunity, but I—'

'Oh, that is easily explained,' interrupted the marine, 'for of course the Water-devil could not know that a lot more people were not left in the ship, and if he let go his hold on her, to try and grab a boat that was moving as fast as men could row it, the steamer might get out of his reach, and he mightn't have another chance for a hundred years to make fast to a vessel. No, sir, a creature like that isn't apt to take any wild chances, when he's got hold of a really good thing. Anyway, we were held tight and fast, for at twelve o'clock the next day I took another observation, and there we were, in the same latitude and longitude that we had been in for two days. I took the captain's glass, and I looked all over the water of that bay, which, as I think I have said before, was all the same as the ocean, being somewhere about a thousand miles wide. Not a sail, not a puff of smoke could I see. It must have been a slack season for navigation, or else we were out of the common track of vessels; I had never known that the Bay of Bengal was so desperately lonely.

'It seems unnatural, and I can hardly believe it, when I look back on it, but it's a fact, that I was beginning to get used to the situation. We had plenty to eat, the weather was fine—in fact, there was now only breeze enough to make things cool and comfortable. I was head-man on that vessel, and Miss Minturn might come on deck at any moment, and as long as I could forget that there was a Water-devil fastened to the bottom of the vessel, there was no reason why I should not be perfectly satisfied with things as they were. And if things had stayed as they were, for two or three months, I should have been right well pleased, especially since Miss Minturn's maid, by order of her mistress, had begun to cook my meals, which she did in a manner truly first-class. I believed then, and I stand to it now, that there is no better proof of a woman's good feeling toward a man, than for her to show an interest in his meals. That's the sort of sympathy that comes home to a man, and tells on him, body and soul.'

As the marine made this remark, he glanced at the blacksmith's daughter; but that young lady had taken up her sewing and appeared to be giving it her earnest attention. He then went on with his story.

'But things did not remain as they were. The next morning, about half an hour after breakfast, I was walking up and down the upper deck, smoking my pipe, and wondering when Miss Minturn would be coming up to talk to me about the state of affairs, when suddenly I felt the deck beneath me move with a quick, sharp jerk, something like, I imagine, a small shock of an earthquake.

'Never, in all my life, did the blood run so cold in my veins; my legs trembled so that I could scarcely stand. I knew what had happened, the Water-devil had begun to haul upon the ship!

'I was in such a state of collapse that I did not seem to have any power over my muscles; but for all that, I heard Miss Minturn's voice at the foot of the companion-way, and knew that she was coming on deck. In spite of the dreadful awfulness of that moment, I felt it would never do for her to see me in the condition I was in, and so, shuffling and half-tumbling, I got forward, went below, and made my way to the steward's room, where I had already discovered some spirits, and I took a good dram; for although I am not by any means an habitual drinker, being principled against that sort of thing, there are times when a man needs the support of some good brandy or whiskey.

'In a few minutes I felt more like myself, and went on deck, and there was Miss Minturn, half-scared to death. "What is the meaning of that shock?" she said; "have we struck anything?" "My dear lady," said I, with as cheerful a front as I could put on, "I do not think we have struck anything. There is nothing to strike." She looked at me for a moment like an angel ready to cry, and clasping her hands, she said, "Oh, tell me, sir, I pray you, sir, tell me what has happened. My father felt that shock. He sent me to inquire about it. His mind is disturbed." At that moment, before I could make an answer, there was another jerk of the ship, and we both went down on our knees, and I felt as if I had been tripped. I was up in a moment, however, but she continued on her knees. I am sure she was praying, but very soon up she sprang. "Oh, what is it, what is it?" she cried; "I must go to my father."

'"I cannot tell you," said I; "I do not know, but don't be frightened; how can such a little shock hurt so big a ship?"

'It was all very well to tell her not to be frightened, but when she ran below she left on deck about as frightened a man as ever stood in shoes. There could be no doubt about it; that horrible beast was beginning to pull upon the ship. Whether or not it would be able to draw us down below, was a question which must soon be solved.

'I had had a small opinion of the maid, who, when I told her the crew had deserted the ship, had sat down and covered her head; but now I did pretty much the same thing; I crouched on the deck and pulled my cap over my eyes. I felt that I did not wish to see, hear, or feel anything.

'I had sat in this way for about half an hour, and had felt no more shocks, when a slight gurgling sound came to my ears. I listened for a moment, then sprang to my feet. Could we be moving? I ran to the side of the ship. The gurgle seemed to be coming from the stern. I hurried there and looked over. The wheel had been lashed fast, and the rudder stood straight out behind us. On each side of it there was a ripple in the quiet water. We were moving, and we were moving backward!

'Overpowered by horrible fascination, I stood grasping the rail, and looking over at the water beneath me, as the vessel moved slowly and steadily onward, stern foremost. In spite of the upset condition of my mind, I could not help wondering why the vessel should move in this way.

'There was only one explanation possible: The Water-devil was walking along the bottom, and towing us after him! Why he should pull us along in this way I could not imagine, unless he was making for his home in some dreadful cave at the bottom, into which he would sink, dragging us down after him.

'While my mind was occupied with these horrible subjects, some one touched me on the arm, and turning, I saw Miss Minturn. "Are we not moving?" she said. "Yes," I answered, "we certainly are." "Do you not think," she then asked, "that we may have been struck by a powerful current, which is now carrying us onward?" I did not believe this, for there was no reason to suppose that there were currents which wandered about, starting off vessels with a jerk, but I was glad to think that this idea had come into her head, and said that it was possible that this might be the case. "And now we are going somewhere," she said, speaking almost cheerfully. "Yes, we are," I answered, and I had to try hard not to groan as I said the words. "And where do you think we are going?" she asked. It was altogether out of my power to tell that sweet creature that in my private opinion she, at least, was going to heaven, and so I answered that I really did not know. "Well," she said, "if we keep moving, we're bound at last to get near land, or to some place where ships would pass near us."

'There is nothing in this world,' said the marine, 'which does a man so much good in time of danger as to see a hopeful spirit in a woman—that is, a woman that he cares about. Some of her courage comes to him, and he is better and stronger for having her alongside of him.'

Having made this remark, the speaker again glanced at the black-smith's daughter. She had put down her work and was looking at him with an earnest brightness in her eyes.

'Yes,' he continued, 'it is astonishing what a change came over me, as I stood by the side of that noble girl. She was a born lady, I was a marine, just the same as we had been before, but there didn't seem to be the difference between us that there had been. Her words, her spirits, everything about her, in fact, seemed to act on me, to elevate me, to fill my soul with noble sentiments, to make another man of me. Standing there beside her, I felt myself her equal. In life or death I would not be ashamed to say, "Here I am, ready to stand by you, whatever happens."'

Having concluded this sentiment, the marine again glanced toward the blacksmith's daughter. Her eyes were slightly moist, and her face was glowing with a certain enthusiasm.

'Look here,' said the blacksmith, 'I suppose that woman goes along with you into the very maw of the sunken Devil, but I do wish you could take her more for granted, and get on faster with the real part of the story.'

'One part is as real as another,' said the marine; 'but on we go, and on we did go for the whole of the rest of that day, at the rate of about half a knot an hour, as near as I could guess at it. The weather changed, and a dirty sort of fog came down on us, so that we couldn't see far in any direction.

'Why that Water-devil should keep on towing us, and where he was going to take us, were things I didn't dare to think about. The fog did not prevent me from seeing the water about our stern, and I leaned over the rail, watching the ripples that flowed on each side of the rudder, which showed that we were still going at about the same uniform rate.

'But toward evening the gurgling beneath me ceased, and I could see that the rudder no longer parted the quiet water, and that we had ceased to move. A flash of hope blazed up within me. Had the Water-devil found the ship too heavy a load, and had he given up the attempt to drag it to its under-ocean cave? I went below and had my supper; I was almost a happy man. When Miss Minturn came to ask me how we were getting along, I told her that I thought we were doing very well indeed. I did not mention that we had ceased to move, for she thought that a favorable symptom. She went back to her quarters greatly cheered up. Not so much, I think, from my words, as from my joyful aspect; for I did feel jolly, there was no doubt about it. If that Water-devil had let go of us, I was willing to take all the other chances that might befall a ship floating about loose on the Bay of Bengal.

'The fog was so thick that night that it was damp and unpleasant on deck, and so, having hung out and lighted a couple of lanterns, I went below for a comfortable smoke in the captain's room. I was puffing away here at my ease, with my mind filled with happy thoughts of two or three weeks with Miss Minturn on this floating paradise, where she was bound to see a good deal of me, and couldn't help liking me better, and depending on me more and more every day, when I felt a little jerking shock. It was the same thing that we had felt before. The Water-devil still had hold of us!

'I dropped my pipe, my chin fell upon my breast, I shivered all over. In a few moments I heard the maid calling to me, and then she ran into the room. "Miss Minturn wants to know, sir," she said, "if you think that shock is a sudden twist in the current which is carrying us on?" I straightened myself up as well as I could, and in the dim light I do not think she noticed my condition. I answered that I thought it was something of that sort, and she went away.

'More likely, a twist of the Devil's arm, I thought, as I sat there alone in my misery.

'In ten or fifteen minutes there came two shocks, not very far apart. This showed that the creature beneath us was at work in some way or another. Perhaps he had reached the opening of his den, and was shortening up his arm before he plunged down into it with us after him. I couldn't stay any longer in that room alone. I looked for the maid, but she had put out the galley light, and had probably turned in for the night.

'I went up, and looked out on deck, but everything was horribly dark and sticky and miserable there. I noticed that my lanterns were not burning, and then I remembered that I had not filled them. But this did not trouble me. If a vessel came along and saw our lights she would probably keep away from us, and I would have been glad to have a vessel come to us, even if she ran into us. Our steamer would probably float long enough for us to get on board the other one, and almost anything would be better than being left alone in this dreadful place, at the mercy of the Water-devil.

'Before I left the deck I felt another shock. This took out of me whatever starch was left, and I shuffled below and got to my bunk, where I tumbled in and covered myself up, head and all. If there had been any man to talk to, it would have been different, but I don't know when I ever felt more deserted than I did at that time.

'I tried to forget the awful situation in which I was; I tried to think of other things; to imagine that I was drilling with the rest of my company, with Tom Rogers on one side of me, and old Humphrey Peters on the other. You may say, perhaps, that this wasn't exactly the way of carrying out my promise of taking care of Miss Minturn and the others. But what was there to do? When the time came to do anything, and I could see what to do, I was ready to do it; but there was no use of waking them up now and setting their minds on edge, when they were all comfortable in their beds, thinking that every jerk of the Devil's arm was a little twist in the current that was carrying them to Calcutta or some other desirable port.

'I felt some shocks after I got into bed, but whether or not there were many in the night, I don't know, for I went to sleep. It was daylight when I awoke, and jumping out of my bunk I dashed on deck. Everything seemed pretty much as it had been, and the fog was as thick as ever. I ran to the stern and looked over, and I could scarcely believe my eyes when I saw that we were moving again, still stern foremost, but a little faster than before. That beastly Water-devil had taken a rest for the night, and had probably given us the shocks by turning over in his sleep, and now he was off again, making up for lost time.

'Pretty soon Miss Minturn came on deck, and bade me good morning, and then she went and looked over the stern. "We are still moving on," she said, with a smile, "and the fog doesn't seem to make any difference. It surely cannot be long before we get somewhere." "No, miss," said I, "it cannot be very long." "You look tired," she said, "and I don't wonder, for you must feel the heavy responsibility on you. I have told my maid to prepare breakfast for you in our cabin. I want my father to know you, and I think it is a shame that you, the only protector that we have, should be shut off so much by yourself; so after this we shall eat together." "After this," I groaned to myself, "we shall be eaten together." At that moment I did not feel that I wanted to breakfast with Miss Minturn.'

'Mr. Cardly,' said Mr. Harberry to the school-master, 'have you ever read, in any of your scientific books, that the Bay of Bengal is subject to heavy fogs that last day after day?'

'I cannot say,' answered the school-master, 'that my researches into the geographical distribution of fogs have resulted—'

'As to fogs,' interrupted the marine, 'you can't get rid of them, you know. If you had been in the habit of going to sea, you would know that you are likely to run into a fog at any time, and in any weather; and as to lasting, they are just as likely to last for days as for hours. It wasn't the fog that surprised me. I did not consider that of any account at all. I had enough other things to occupy my mind.' And having settled this little matter, he went on with his story.

'Well, my friends, I did not breakfast with Miss Minturn and her father. Before that meal was ready, and while I was standing alone at the stern, I saw coming out of the water, a long way off in the fog, which must have been growing thinner about this time, a dark and mysterious object, apparently without any shape or form. This sight made the teeth chatter in my head. I had expected to be pulled down to the Water-devil, but I had never imagined that he would come up to us!

'While my eyes were glued upon this apparition, I could see that we were approaching it. When I perceived this, I shut my eyes and turned my back—I could look upon it no longer. My mind seemed to forsake me; I did not even try to call out and give the alarm to the others. Why should I? What could they do?'

'If it had been me,' said Mrs. Fryker, in a sort of gasping whisper, 'I should have died right there.'

The marine turned his eyes in the direction of the blacksmith's daughter. She was engaged with her work, and was not looking at him.

'I cannot say,' he continued, 'that, had Miss Minturn been there at that moment, that I would not have declared that I was ready to die for her or with her; but there was no need of trying to keep up her courage, that was all right. She knew nothing of our danger. That terrible knowledge pressed on me alone. Is it wonderful that a human soul should sink a little under such an awful load?' Without turning to observe the effect of these last words, the marine went on. 'Suddenly I heard behind me a most dreadful sound. "Good Heavens," I exclaimed, "can a Water-devil bray?"

'The sound was repeated. Without knowing what I did, I turned. I heard what sounded like words; I saw in the fog the stern of a vessel, with a man above it, shouting to me through a speaking-trumpet.

'I do not know what happened next; my mind must have become confused. When I regained my senses, Miss Minturn, old Mr. Minturn, and the maid were standing by me. The man had stopped shouting from his trumpet, and a boat was being lowered from the other ship. In about ten minutes there were half-a-dozen men on board of us, all in the uniform of the British navy. I was stiff enough now, and felt myself from top to toe a regular marine in the service of my country. I stepped up to the officer in command and touched my cap.

'He looked at me and my companions in surprise, and then glancing along the deck, said, "What has happened to this vessel? Who is in command?" I informed him, that, strictly speaking, no one was in command, but that I represented the captain, officers, and crew of this steamer, the *General Brooks*, from San Francisco to Calcutta, and I then proceeded to tell him the whole story of our misfortunes; and concluded by telling the officer, that if we had not moved since his vessel had come in sight, it was probably because the Water-devil had let go of us, and was preparing to make fast to the other ship; and therefore it would be advisable for us all to get on board his vessel, and steam away as quickly as possible.

'The Englishmen looked at me in amazement. "Drunk!" ejaculated the officer I had addressed. "Cracked, I should say," suggested another. "Now," spoke up Mr. Minturn, "I do not understand what I have just heard," he said. "What is a Water-devil? I am astounded." "You never said a word of this to me!" exclaimed Miss Minturn. "You never told me that we were in the grasp of a Water-devil, and that that was the reason the captain and the crew ran away." "No," said I, "I never divulged the dreadful danger we were in. I allowed you to believe that we were in the influence of a current, and that the shocks we felt were the sudden twists of that current. The terrible truth I kept to myself. Not for worlds would I have made known to a tenderly nurtured lady, to her invalid father, and devoted servant, what might have crushed their souls, driven them to the borders of frenzy; in which case the relief which now has come to us would have been of no avail."

'The officer stood and steadily stared at me. "I declare," he said, "you do not look like a crazy man. At what time did this Water-devil begin to take you in tow?"

'"Yesterday morning," I answered. "And he stopped during last night?" he asked. I replied that that was the case. Then he took off his cap, rubbed his head, and stood silent for a minute. "We'll look into this matter!" he suddenly exclaimed, and turning, he and his party left us to ourselves. The boat was now sent back with a message to the English vessel, and the officers and men who remained scattered themselves over our steamer, examining the engine-room, hold, and every part of her.

'I was very much opposed to all this delay; for although the Englishmen might doubt the existence of the Water-devil, I saw no reason to do so, and in any case I was very anxious to be on the safe side by getting away as soon as possible; but, of course, British officers would not be advised by me, and as I was getting very hungry I went down to breakfast. I ate this meal alone, for my fellow-passengers seemed to have no desire for food.

'I cannot tell all that happened during the next hour, for, to tell the truth, I did not understand everything that was done. The boat passed several times between the two vessels, bringing over a number of men—two of them scientific fellows, I think. Another was a diver, whose submarine suit* and air-pumping machines came over with him. He was lowered over the side, and after he had been down about fifteen minutes he was hauled up again, and down below was the greatest hammering and hauling that ever you heard. The *General Brooks* was put in charge of an officer and some men; a sail was hoisted to keep her in hand, so that she wouldn't drift into the other ship; and in the midst of all the rowdy-dow we were told that if we liked we might go on board the English vessel immediately.

'Miss Minturn and her party instantly accepted this invitation, and although under ordinary circumstances I would have remained to see for myself what these people found out, I felt a relief in the thought of leaving that vessel which is impossible for me to express, and I got into the boat with the others.

'We were treated very handsomely on board the English vessel, which was a mail steamship, at that time in the employment of the English Government. I told my story at least half-a-dozen times, sometimes to the officers and sometimes to the men, and whether they believed me or not, I don't think any one ever created a greater sensation with a story of the sea.

'In an hour or so the officer in charge of the operations on the *General Brooks* came aboard. As he passed me on his way to the captain, he said, "We found your Water-devil, my man." "And he truly had us in tow?" I cried. "Yes, you are perfectly correct," he said, and went on to make his report to the captain.'

'Now, then,' said the blacksmith, 'I suppose we are going to get to the point. What did he report?'

'I didn't hear his report,' said the marine, 'but everybody soon knew what had happened to our unlucky vessel, and I can give you the whole story of it. The *General Brooks* sailed from San Francisco to Calcutta, with a cargo of stored electricity, contained in large, strongly made boxes. This I knew nothing about, not being in the habit of inquiring into cargoes. Well, in some way or other, which I don't understand, not being a scientific man myself, a magnetic connection was formed between these boxes, and also, if I got the story straight, between them and the iron hull of our vessel, so that it became, in fact, an enormous floating magnet, one of the biggest things of the kind on record. I have an idea that this magnetic condition was the cause of the trouble to our machinery; every separate part of it was probably turned to a magnet, and they all stuck together.'

'Mr. Cardly,' said Mr. Harberry to the school-master, 'I do not suppose you have given much attention to the study of commerce, and therefore are not prepared to give us any information in regard to stored electricity as an article of export from this country; but perhaps you can tell us what stored electricity is, and how it is put into boxes.'

'In regard to the transportation,' answered the school-master, speaking a little slowly, 'of encased electric potency, I cannot—'

'Oh, bless me!' interrupted the marine; 'that is all simple enough; you can store electricity and send it all over the world, if you like; in places like Calcutta, I think it must be cheaper to buy it than to make it. They use it as a motive power for sewing-machines, apple-parers, and it can be used in a lot of ways, such as digging post-holes and churning butter. When the stored electricity in a box is all used up, all you have to do is to connect a fresh box with your machinery, and there you are, ready to start again. There was nothing strange about our cargo. It was the electricity leaking out and uniting itself and the iron ship into a sort of conglomerate magnet that was out of the way.'

'Mr. Cardly,' said Mr. Harberry, 'if an iron ship were magnetized in that manner, wouldn't it have a deranging effect upon the needle of the compass?'

The marine did not give the school-master time to make answer. 'Generally speaking,' said he, 'that sort of thing would interfere with keeping the vessel on its proper course, but with us it didn't make any difference at all. The greater part of the ship was in front of the binnacle where they keep the compass, and so the needle naturally pointed that way, and as we were going north before a south wind, it was all right.

'Being a floating magnet, of course, did not prevent our sailing, so we went along well enough until we came to longitude 90°, latitude 15° north. Now it so happened that a telegraphic cable which had been laid down by the British Government to establish communication between Madras and Rangoon,* had broken some time before, and not very far from this point.

'Now you can see for yourselves that when an enormous mass of magnetic iron, in the shape of the *General Brooks*, came sailing along there, the part of that cable which lay under us was so attracted by such a powerful and irresistible force that its broken end raised itself from the bottom of the bay and reached upward until it touched our ship, when it laid itself along our keel, to which it instantly became fastened as firmly as if it had been bolted and riveted there. Then, as the rest of this part of the cable was on the bottom of the bay all the way to Madras, of course we had to stop; that's simple enough. That's the way the Water-devil held us fast in one spot for two days.

'The British Government determined not to repair this broken cable, but to take it up and lay down a better one; so they chartered a large steamer, and fitted her up with engines, and a big drum that they use for that sort of thing, and set her to work to wind up the Madras end of the broken cable. She had been at this business a good while before we were caught by the other end, and when they got near enough to us for their engines to be able to take up the slack from the bottom between us and them, then of course they pulled upon us, and we began to move. And when they lay to for the night, and stopped the winding business, of course we stopped, and the stretch of cable between the two ships had no effect upon us, except when the big mail steamer happened to move this way or that, as they kept her head to the wind; and that's the way we lay quiet all night except when we got our shocks.

'When they set the drum going again in the morning, it wasn't long before they wound us near enough for them to see us, which they would have done sooner if my lights hadn't gone out so early in the evening.'

'And that,' said the blacksmith, with a somewhat severe expression on his face, 'is all that you have to tell about your wonderful Water-devil!'

'All!' said the marine; 'I should say it was quite enough, and nothing could be more wonderful than what really happened. A Water-devil is one of two things: he is real, or he's not real. If he's not real, he's no more than an ordinary spook or ghost, and is not to be practically considered. If he's real, then he's an alive animal, and can be put in a class with other animals, and described in books, because even if nobody sees him, the scientific men know how he must be constructed, and then he's no more than a great many other wonderful things, which we can see alive, stuffed, or in plaster casts.

'But if you want to put your mind upon something really wonderful, just think of a snake-like rope of wire, five or six hundred miles long, lying down at the very bottom of the great Bay of Bengal, with no more life in it than there is in a ten-penny nail.

'Then imagine that long, dead wire snake to be suddenly filled with life, and to know that there was something far up above it, on the surface of the water, that it wants to reach up to and touch. Think of it lifting and flapping its broken end, and then imagine it raising yard after yard of itself up and up, through the solemn water, more and more of it lifting itself from the bottom, curling itself backward and forward as it rises higher and higher, until at last, with a sudden jump that must have ripped a mile or more of it from the bottom, it claps its end against the thing it wants to touch, and which it can neither see, nor hear, nor smell, but which it knows is there. Could there be anything in this world more wonderful than that?

'And then, if that isn't enough of a wonder, think of the Rangoon end of that cable squirming and wriggling and stretching itself out toward our ship, but not being able to reach us on account of a want of slack; just as alive as the Madras part of the cable, and just as savage and frantic to get up to us and lay hold of us; and then, after our vessel had been gradually pulled away from it, think of this other part getting weaker and weaker, minute by minute, until it falls flat on the bay, as dead as any other iron thing!'

The marine ceased to speak, and Mrs. Fryker heaved a sigh.

'It makes me shiver to think of all that down so deep,' she said; 'but I must say I am disappointed.'

'In what way?' asked the marine.

'A Water-devil,' said she, 'as big as six whales, and with a funnelly mouth to suck in people, is different; but, of course, after all, it was better as it was.'

'Look here,' said the blacksmith, 'what became of the girl? I wanted her finished up long ago, and you haven't done it yet.'

'Miss Minturn, you mean,' said the marine. 'Well, there is not much to say about her. Things happened in the usual way. When the danger was all over, when she had other people to depend upon besides me, and we were on board a fine steamer, with a lot of hand-somely dressed naval officers, and going comfortably to Madras, of course she thought no more of the humble sea-soldier who once stood between her and—nobody knew what. In fact, the only time she spoke to me after we got on board the English steamer, she made me feel, although she didn't say it in words, that she was not at all obliged to me for supposing that she would have been scared to death if I had told her about the Water-devil.'

'I suppose,' said the blacksmith, 'by the time you got back to your ship you had overstayed your leave of absence a good while. Did your captain let you off when you told him this story of the new-fashioned Water-devil?'

The marine smiled. 'I never went back to the *Apache*,' he said. 'When I arrived at Madras I found that she had sailed from Calcutta. It was, of course, useless for me to endeavor to follow her, and I there-fore concluded to give up the marine service for a time and go into another line of business, about which it is too late to tell you now.'

'Mr. Cardly,' said Mr. Harberry to the school-master, 'have you ever read that the British Government has a submarine cable from Madras to Rangoon?'

The marine took it upon himself to answer this question. 'The cable of which I spoke to you,' he said, 'was taken up, as I told you, and I never heard that another one was laid. But it is getting late, and I think I will go to bed; I have a long walk before me to-morrow.' So saying he rose, put his pipe upon the mantel-piece, and bade the company good night. As he did so, he fixed his eyes on the black-smith's daughter, but that young lady did not look at him; she was busily reading the weekly newspaper, which her father had left upon the table.

Mr. Harberry now rose, preparatory to going home; and as he but-toned up his coat, he looked from one to another of the little group, and remarked, 'I have often heard that marines are a class of men who are considered as fit subjects to tell tough stories to, but it strikes me that the time has come when the tables are beginning to be turned.'

H. G. WELLS

THE CRYSTAL EGG

THERE was, until a year ago, a little and very grimy-looking shop near Seven Dials,* over which, in weather-worn yellow lettering, the name of 'C. Cave, Naturalist and Dealer in Antiquities,' was inscribed. The contents of its window were curiously variegated. They comprised some elephant tusks and an imperfect set of chessmen, beads and weapons, a box of eyes, two skulls of tigers and one human, several moth-eaten stuffed monkeys (one holding a lamp), an old-fashioned cabinet, a fly-blown ostrich egg or so, some fishing-tackle, and an extraordinarily dirty, empty glass fish-tank. There was also, at the moment the story begins, a mass of crystal, worked into the shape of an egg and brilliantly polished. And at that two people who stood outside the window were looking, one of them a tall, thin clergyman, the other a black-bearded young man of dusky complexion and unobtrusive costume. The dusky young man spoke with eager gesticulation, and seemed anxious for his companion to purchase the article.

While they were there, Mr. Cave came into his shop, his beard still wagging with the bread and butter of his tea. When he saw these men and the object of their regard, his countenance fell. He glanced guiltily over his shoulder, and softly shut the door. He was a little old man, with pale face and peculiar watery blue eyes; his hair was a dirty grey, and he wore a shabby blue frock-coat, an ancient silk hat, and carpet slippers very much down at heel. He remained watching the two men as they talked. The clergyman went deep into his trouser pocket, examined a handful of money, and showed his teeth in an agreeable smile. Mr. Cave seemed still more depressed when they came into the shop.

The clergyman, without any ceremony, asked the price of the crystal egg. Mr. Cave glanced nervously towards the door leading into the parlour, and said five pounds. The clergyman protested that the price was high, to his companion as well as to Mr. Cave—it was, indeed, very much more than Mr. Cave had intended to ask when he had stocked the article—and an attempt at bargaining ensued. Mr. Cave stepped to the shop door, and held it open. 'Five pounds is my price,' he said, as though he wished to save himself the trouble of unprofitable discussion. As he did so, the upper portion of a woman's face appeared above the blind in the glass upper panel of the door leading into the parlour, and stared curiously at the two customers. 'Five pounds is my price,' said Mr. Cave, with a quiver in his voice.

The swarthy young man had so far remained a spectator, watching Cave keenly. Now he spoke. 'Give him five pounds,' he said. The clergyman glanced at him to see if he were in earnest, and when he looked at Mr. Cave again, he saw that the latter's face was white. 'It's a lot of money,' said the clergyman, and, diving into his pocket, began counting his resources. He had little more than thirty shillings, and he appealed to his companion, with whom he seemed to be on terms of considerable intimacy. This gave Mr. Cave an opportunity of collecting his thoughts, and he began to explain in an agitated manner that the crystal was not, as a matter of fact, entirely free for sale. His two customers were naturally surprised at this, and inquired why he had not thought of that before he began to bargain. Mr. Cave became confused, but he stuck to his story, that the crystal was not in the market that afternoon, that a probable purchaser of it had already appeared. The two, treating this as an attempt to raise the price still further, made as if they would leave the shop. But at this point the parlour door opened, and the owner of the dark fringe and the little eyes appeared.

She was a coarse-featured, corpulent woman, younger and very much larger than Mr. Cave; she walked heavily, and her face was flushed. 'That crystal *is* for sale,' she said. 'And five pounds is a good enough price for it. I can't think what you're about, Cave, not to take the gentleman's offer!'

Mr. Cave, greatly perturbed by the irruption, looked angrily at her over the rims of his spectacles, and, without excessive assurance, asserted his right to manage his business in his own way. An altercation began. The two customers watched the scene with interest and some amusement, occasionally assisting Mrs. Cave with suggestions. Mr. Cave, hard driven, persisted in a confused and impossible story of an inquiry for the crystal that morning, and his agitation became painful. But he stuck to his point with extraordinary persistence. It was the young Oriental who ended this curious controversy. He proposed that they should call again in the course of two days—so as to give the alleged inquirer a fair chance. 'And then we must insist,' said the clergyman. 'Five pounds.' Mrs. Cave took it on herself to apologise for her husband, explaining that he was sometimes 'a little odd,' and as the two customers left, the couple prepared for a free discussion of the incident in all its bearings.

Mrs. Cave talked to her husband with singular directness. The poor little man, quivering with emotion, muddled himself between his stories, maintaining on the one hand that he had another customer in view, and on the other asserting that the crystal was honestly worth ten guineas. 'Why did you ask five pounds?' said his wife. '*Do* let me manage my business my own way!' said Mr. Cave.

Mr. Cave had living with him a step-daughter and a step-son, and at supper that night the transaction was re-discussed. None of them had a high opinion of Mr. Cave's business methods, and this action seemed a culminating folly.

'It's my opinion he's refused that crystal before,' said the step-son, a loose-limbed lout of eighteen.

'But *Five Pounds*!' said the step-daughter, an argumentative young woman of six-and-twenty.

Mr. Cave's answers were wretched; he could only mumble weak assertions that he knew his own business best. They drove him from his half-eaten supper into the shop, to close it for the night, his ears aflame and tears of vexation behind his spectacles. Why had he left the crystal in the window so long? The folly of it! That was the trouble closest in his mind. For a time he could see no way of evading sale.

After supper his step-daughter and step-son smartened themselves up and went out and his wife retired upstairs to reflect upon the business aspects of the crystal, over a little sugar and lemon and so forth in hot water. Mr. Cave went into the shop, and stayed there until late, ostensibly to make ornamental rockeries for gold-fish cases, but really for a private purpose that will be better explained later. The next day Mrs. Cave found that the crystal had been removed from the window, and was lying behind some second-hand books on angling. She replaced it in a conspicuous position. But she did not argue further about it, as a nervous headache disinclined her from debate. Mr. Cave was always disinclined. The day passed disagreeably. Mr. Cave was, if anything, more absent-minded than usual, and uncommonly irritable withal. In the afternoon, when his wife was taking her customary sleep, he removed the crystal from the window again.

The next day Mr. Cave had to deliver a consignment of dog-fish* at one of the hospital schools, where they were needed for dissection. In his absence Mrs. Cave's mind reverted to the topic of the crystal, and the methods of expenditure suitable to a windfall of five pounds. She had already devised some very agreeable expedients, among others a dress of green silk for herself and a trip to Richmond,* when a jangling of the front door bell summoned her into the shop. The customer was an examination coach who came to complain of the non-delivery of certain frogs asked for the previous day. Mrs. Cave did not approve of this particular branch of Mr. Cave's business, and the gentleman, who had called in a somewhat aggressive mood, retired after a brief exchange of words—entirely civil, so far as he was concerned. Mrs. Cave's eye then naturally turned to the window; for the sight of the crystal was an assurance of the five pounds and of her dreams. What was her surprise to find it gone!

She went to the place behind the locker on the counter, where she had discovered it the day before. It was not there; and she immediately began an eager search about the shop.

When Mr. Cave returned from his business with the dog-fish, about a quarter to two in the afternoon, he found the shop in some confusion, and his wife, extremely exasperated and on her knees behind the counter, routing among his taxidermic material. Her face came up hot and angry over the counter, as the jangling bell announced his return, and she forthwith accused him of 'hiding it.'

'Hid *what?*' asked Mr. Cave.

'The crystal!'

At that Mr. Cave, apparently much surprised, rushed to the window. 'Isn't it here?' he said. 'Great Heavens! what has become of it?'

Just then Mr. Cave's step-son re-entered the shop from the inner room—he had come home a minute or so before Mr. Cave—and he was blaspheming freely. He was apprenticed to a second-hand furniture dealer down the road, but he had his meals at home, and he was naturally annoyed to find no dinner ready.

But when he heard of the loss of the crystal, he forgot his meal, and his anger was diverted from his mother to his step-father. Their first idea, of course, was that he had hidden it. But Mr. Cave stoutly denied all knowledge of its fate, freely offering his bedabbled affidavit in the matter—and at last was worked up to the point of accusing, first, his wife and then his step-son of having taken it with a view to a private sale. So began an exceedingly acrimonious and emotional discussion, which ended for Mrs. Cave in a peculiar nervous condition midway between hysterics and amuck,* and caused the step-son to be half-an-hour late at the furniture establishment in the afternoon. Mr. Cave took refuge from his wife's emotions in the shop.

In the evening the matter was resumed, with less passion and in a judicial spirit, under the presidency of the step-daughter. The supper passed unhappily and culminated in a painful scene. Mr. Cave gave way at last to extreme exasperation, and went out banging the front door violently. The rest of the family, having discussed him with the freedom his absence warranted, hunted the house from garret to cellar, hoping to light upon the crystal.

The next day the two customers called again. They were received by Mrs. Cave almost in tears. It transpired that no one *could* imagine all that she had stood from Cave at various times in her married pilgrimage. . . . She also gave a garbled account of the disappearance. The clergyman and the Oriental laughed silently at one another, and said it was very extraordinary. As Mrs. Cave seemed disposed to give them the complete history of her life they made to leave the shop. Thereupon Mrs. Cave, still clinging to hope, asked for the clergyman's address, so that, if she could get anything out of Cave, she might communicate it. The address was duly given, but apparently was afterwards mislaid. Mrs. Cave can remember nothing about it.

In the evening of that day the Caves seem to have exhausted their emotions, and Mr. Cave, who had been out in the afternoon, supped in a gloomy isolation that contrasted pleasantly with the impassioned controversy of the previous days. For some time matters were very badly strained in the Cave household, but neither crystal nor customer reappeared.

Now, without mincing the matter, we must admit that Mr. Cave was a liar. He knew perfectly well where the crystal was. It was in the rooms of Mr. Jacoby Wace, Assistant Demonstrator at St. Catherine's Hospital, Westbourne Street.* It stood on the sideboard partially covered by a black velvet cloth, and beside a decanter of American whisky. It is from Mr. Wace, indeed, that the particulars upon which this narrative is based were derived. Cave had taken off the thing to the hospital hidden in the dog-fish sack, and there had pressed the young investigator to keep it for him. Mr. Wace was a little dubious at first. His relationship to Cave was peculiar. He had a taste for singular characters, and he had more than once invited the old man to smoke and drink in his rooms, and to unfold his rather amusing views of life in general and of his wife in particular. Mr. Wace had encountered

Mrs. Cave, too, on occasions when Mr. Cave was not at home to attend to him. He knew the constant interference to which Cave was subjected, and having weighed the story judicially, he decided to give the crystal a refuge. Mr. Cave promised to explain the reasons for his remarkable affection for the crystal more fully on a later occasion, but he spoke distinctly of seeing visions therein. He called on Mr. Wace the same evening.

He told a complicated story. The crystal he said had come into his possession with other oddments at the forced sale of another curiosity dealer's effects, and not knowing what its value might be, he had ticketed it at ten shillings. It had hung upon his hands at that price for some months, and he was thinking of 'reducing the figure,' when he made a singular discovery.

At that time his health was very bad—and it must be borne in mind that, throughout all this experience, his physical condition was one of ebb—and he was in considerable distress by reason of the negligence, the positive ill-treatment even, he received from his wife and step-children. His wife was vain, extravagant, unfeeling, and had a growing taste for private drinking; his step-daughter was mean and over-reaching; and his step-son had conceived a violent dislike for him, and lost no chance of showing it. The requirements of his business pressed heavily upon him, and Mr. Wace does not think that he was altogether free from occasional intemperance. He had begun life in a comfortable position, he was a man of fair education, and he suffered, for weeks at a stretch, from melancholia and insomnia. Afraid to disturb his family, he would slip quietly from his wife's side, when his thoughts became intolerable, and wander about the house. And about three o'clock one morning, late in August, chance directed him into the shop.

The dirty little place was impenetrably black except in one spot, where he perceived an unusual glow of light. Approaching this, he discovered it to be the crystal egg, which was standing on the corner of the counter towards the window. A thin ray smote through a crack in the shutters, impinged upon the object, and seemed as it were to fill its entire interior.

It occurred to Mr. Cave that this was not in accordance with the laws of optics as he had known them in his younger days. He could understand the rays being refracted by the crystal and coming to a focus in its interior, but this diffusion* jarred with his physical conceptions. He approached the crystal nearly, peering into it and round it, with a transient revival of the scientific curiosity that in his youth had determined his choice of a calling. He was surprised to find the light not steady, but writhing within the substance of the egg, as though that object was a hollow sphere of some luminous vapour. In moving about to get different points of view, he suddenly found that he had come between it and the ray, and that the crystal none the less remained luminous. Greatly astonished, he lifted it out of the light ray and carried it to the darkest part of the shop. It remained bright for some four or five minutes, when it slowly faded and went out. He placed it in the thin streak of daylight, and its luminousness was almost immediately restored.

So far, at least, Mr. Wace was able to verify the remarkable story of Mr. Cave. He has himself repeatedly held this crystal in a ray of light (which had to be of a less diameter than one millimetre). And in a perfect darkness, such as could be produced by velvet wrapping, the crystal did undoubtedly appear very faintly phosphorescent. It would seem, however, that the luminousness was of some exceptional sort, and not equally visible to all eyes; for Mr. Harbinger—whose name will be familiar to the scientific reader in connection with the Pasteur Institute*—was quite unable to see any light whatever. And Mr. Wace's own capacity for its appreciation was out of comparison inferior to that of Mr. Cave's. Even with Mr. Cave the power varied very considerably: his vision was most vivid during states of extreme weakness and fatigue.

Now, from the outset, this light in the crystal exercised a curious fascination upon Mr. Cave. And it says more for his loneliness of soul than a volume of pathetic writing could do, that he told no human being of his curious observations. He seems to have been living in such an atmosphere of petty spite that to admit the existence of a pleasure would have been to risk the loss of it. He found that as the dawn advanced, and the amount of diffused light increased, the crystal became to all appearance non-luminous. And for some time he was unable to see anything in it, except at night-time, in dark corners of the shop.

But the use of an old velvet cloth, which he used as a background for a collection of minerals, occurred to him, and by doubling this, and putting it over his head and hands, he was able to get a sight of the luminous movement within the crystal even in the day-time. He was very cautious lest he should be thus discovered by his wife, and he practised this occupation only in the afternoons, while she was asleep upstairs, and then circumspectly in a hollow under the counter. And one day, turning the crystal about in his hands, he saw something. It came and went like a flash, but it gave him the impression that the object had for a moment opened to him the view of a wide and spacious and strange country; and turning it about, he did, just as the light faded, see the same vision again.

Now it would be tedious and unnecessary to state all the phases of Mr. Cave's discovery from this point. Suffice that the effect was this: the crystal, being peered into at an angle of about 137 degrees from the direction of the illuminating ray, gave a clear and consistent picture of a wide and peculiar country-side. It was not dream-like at all: it produced a definite impression of reality, and the better the light the more real and solid it seemed. It was a moving picture: that is to say, certain objects moved in it, but slowly in an orderly manner like real things, and, according as the direction of the lighting and vision changed, the picture changed also. It must, indeed, have been like looking through an oval glass at a view, and turning the glass about to get at different aspects.

Mr. Cave's statements, Mr. Wace assures me, were extremely circumstantial, and entirely free from any of that emotional quality that taints hallucinatory impressions. But it must be remembered that all the efforts of Mr. Wace to see any similar clarity in the faint opalescence of the crystal were wholly unsuccessful, try as he would. The difference in intensity of the impressions received by the two men was very great, and it is quite conceivable that what was a view to Mr. Cave was a mere blurred nebulosity to Mr. Wace.

The view, as Mr. Cave described it, was invariably of an extensive plain, and he seemed always to be looking at it from a considerable height, as if from a tower or a mast. To the east and to the west the plain was bounded at a remote distance by vast reddish cliffs, which reminded him of those he had seen in some picture; but what the picture was Mr. Wace was unable to ascertain. These cliffs passed north and south—he could tell the points of the compass by the stars that were visible of a night—receding in an almost illimitable perspective and fading into the mists of the distance before they met. He was nearer the eastern set of cliffs; on the occasion of his first vision the sun was rising over them, and black against the sunlight and pale against their shadow appeared a multitude of soaring forms that Mr. Cave regarded as birds. A vast range of buildings spread below him; he seemed to be looking down upon them; and as they approached the blurred and refracted edge of the picture they became indistinct. There were also trees curious in shape, and in colouring a deep mossy green and an exquisite grey, beside a wide and shining canal. And something great and brilliantly coloured flew across the picture. But the first time Mr. Cave saw these pictures he saw only in flashes, his hands shook, his head moved, the vision came and went, and grew foggy and indistinct. And at first he had the greatest difficulty in finding the picture again once the direction of it was lost.

His next clear vision, which came about a week after the first, the interval having yielded nothing but tantalising glimpses and some useful experience, showed him the view down the length of the valley. The view was different, but he had a curious persuasion, which his subsequent observations abundantly confirmed, that he was regarding the strange world from exactly the same spot, although he was looking in a different direction. The long façade of the great building, whose roof he had looked down upon before, was now receding in perspective. He recognised the roof. In the front of the façade was a terrace of massive proportions and extraordinary length, and down the middle of the terrace, at certain intervals, stood huge but very graceful masts, bearing small shiny objects which reflected the setting sun. The import of these small objects did not occur to Mr. Cave until some time after, as he was describing the scene to Mr. Wace. The terrace overhung a thicket of the most luxuriant and graceful vegetation, and beyond this was a wide grassy lawn on which certain broad creatures, in form like beetles but enormously larger, reposed. Beyond this again was a richly decorated causeway of pinkish stone; and beyond that, and lined with dense red weeds,* and passing up the valley exactly parallel with the distant cliffs, was a broad and mirror-like expanse of water. The air seemed full of squadrons of great birds, manœuvring in stately curves; and across the river was a multitude of splendid buildings, richly coloured and glittering with metallic tracery and facets, among a forest of moss-like and lichenous trees. And suddenly something flapped repeatedly across the vision, like the fluttering of a jewelled fan or the beating of a wing, and a face, or rather the upper part of a face with very large eyes, came as it were close to his own and as if on the other side of the crystal. Mr. Cave was so startled and so impressed by the absolute reality of these eyes that he drew his head back from the crystal to look behind it. He had become so absorbed in watching that he was quite surprised to find himself in the cool darkness of his little shop, with its familiar odour of methyl, mustiness, and decay. And as he blinked about him, the glowing crystal faded and went out.

Such were the first general impressions of Mr. Cave. The story is curiously direct and circumstantial. From the outset, when the valley first flashed momentarily on his senses, his imagination was strangely affected, and as he began to appreciate the details of the scene he saw, his wonder rose to the point of a passion. He went about his business listless and distraught, thinking only of the time when he should be able to return to his watching. And then a few weeks after his first sight of the valley came the two customers, the stress and excitement of their offer, and the narrow escape of the crystal from sale, as I have already told.

Now, while the thing was Mr. Cave's secret, it remained a mere wonder, a thing to creep to covertly and peep at, as a child might peep upon a forbidden garden. But Mr. Wace has, for a young scientific investigator, a particularly lucid and consecutive habit of mind. Directly the crystal and its story came to him, and he had satisfied himself, by seeing the phosphorescence with his own eyes, that there really was a certain evidence for Mr. Cave's statements, he proceeded to develop the matter systematically. Mr. Cave was only too eager to come and feast his eyes on this wonderland he saw, and he came every night from half-past eight until half-past ten, and sometimes, in Mr. Wace's absence, during the day. On Sunday afternoons, also, he came. From the outset Mr. Wace made copious notes, and it was due to his scientific method that the relation between the direction from which the initiating ray entered the crystal and the orientation of the picture were proved. And, by covering the crystal in a box perforated only with a small aperture to admit the exciting ray, and by substituting black holland for his buff blinds, he greatly improved the conditions of the observations; so that in a little while they were able to survey the valley in any direction they desired.

So having cleared the way, we may give a brief account of this visionary world within the crystal. The things were in all cases seen by Mr. Cave, and the method of working was invariably for him to watch the crystal and report what he saw, while Mr. Wace (who as a science student had learnt the trick of writing in the dark) wrote a brief note of his report. When the crystal faded, it was put into its box in the proper position and the electric light turned on. Mr. Wace asked questions, and suggested observations to clear up difficult points. Nothing, indeed, could have been less visionary and more matter-of-fact.

The attention of Mr. Cave had been speedily directed to the bird-like creatures he had seen so abundantly present in each of his earlier visions. His first impression was soon corrected, and he considered for a time that they might represent a diurnal species of bat.* Then he thought, grotesquely enough, that they might be cherubs. Their heads were round and curiously human, and it was the eyes of one of them that had so startled him on his second observation. They had broad, silvery wings, not feathered, but glistening almost as brilliantly as new-killed fish and with the same subtle play of colour, and these wings were not built on the plan of bird-wing or bat, Mr. Wace learned, but supported by curved ribs radiating from the body. (A sort of butterfly wing with curved ribs seems best to express their appearance.) The body was small, but fitted with two bunches of pre-hensile organs, like long tentacles, immediately under the mouth. Incredible as it appeared to Mr. Wace, the persuasion at last became irresistible that it was these creatures which owned the great quasi-human buildings and the magnificent garden that made the broad valley so splendid. And Mr. Cave perceived that the buildings, with other peculiarities, had no doors, but that the great circular windows, which opened freely, gave the creatures egress and entrance. They would alight upon their tentacles, fold their wings to a smallness almost rod-like, and hop into the interior. But among them was a multitude of smaller-winged creatures, like great dragon-flies and moths and flying beetles, and across the greensward brilliantly-coloured gigantic ground-beetles crawled lazily to and fro. Moreover, on the causeways and terraces, large-headed creatures similar to the greater winged flies, but wingless, were visible, hopping busily upon their hand-like tangle of tentacles.

Allusion has already been made to the glittering objects upon masts that stood upon the terrace of the nearer building. It dawned upon Mr. Cave, after regarding one of these masts very fixedly on one particularly vivid day that the glittering object there was a crystal exactly like that into which he peered. And a still more careful scrutiny convinced him that each one in a vista of nearly twenty carried a similar object.

Occasionally one of the large flying creatures would flutter up to one, and folding its wings and coiling a number of its tentacles about the mast, would regard the crystal fixedly for a space,—sometimes for as long as fifteen minutes. And a series of observations, made at the suggestion of Mr. Wace, convinced both watchers that, so far as this visionary world was concerned, the crystal into which they peered actually stood at the summit of the end-most mast on the terrace, and that on one occasion at least one of these inhabitants of this other world had looked into Mr. Cave's face while he was making these observations.

So much for the essential facts of this very singular story. Unless we dismiss it all as the ingenious fabrication of Mr. Wace, we have to believe one of two things: either that Mr. Cave's crystal was in two worlds at once, and that while it was carried about in one, it remained stationary in the other, which seems altogether absurd; or else that it had some peculiar relation of sympathy with another and exactly similar crystal in this other world, so that what was seen in the interior of the one in this world was, under suitable conditions, visible to an observer in the corresponding crystal in the other world; and *vice versa*. At present, indeed, we do not know of any way in which two crystals could so come *en rapport*,* but nowadays we know enough to understand that the thing is not altogether impossible. This view of the crystals as *en rapport* was the supposition that occurred to Mr. Wace, and to me at least it seems extremely plausible. . . .

And where was this other world? On this, also, the alert intelligence of Mr. Wace speedily threw light. After sunset, the sky darkened rapidly—there was a very brief twilight interval indeed—and the stars shone out. They were recognisably the same as those we see, arranged in the same constellations. Mr. Cave recognised the Bear, the Pleiades, Aldebaran, and Sirius; so that the other world must be somewhere in the solar system, and, at the utmost, only a few hundreds of millions of miles from our own. Following up this clue, Mr. Wace learned that the midnight sky was a darker blue even than our midwinter sky, and that the sun seemed a little smaller. *And there were two small moons!* 'like our moon* but smaller, and quite differently marked,' one of which moved so rapidly that its motion was clearly visible as one regarded it. These moons were never high in the sky, but vanished as they rose: that is, every time they revolved they were eclipsed because they were so near their primary planet. And all this answers quite completely, although Mr. Cave did not know it, to what must be the condition of things on Mars.

Indeed, it seems an exceedingly plausible conclusion that peering into this crystal Mr. Cave did actually see the planet Mars and its inhabitants. And if that be the case, then the evening star that shone so brilliantly in the sky of that distant vision was neither more nor less than our own familiar earth.

For a time the Martians—if they were Martians—do not seem to have known of Mr. Cave's inspection. Once or twice one would come to peer, and go away very shortly to some other mast, as though the vision was unsatisfactory. During this time Mr. Cave was able to watch the proceedings of these winged people without being disturbed by their attentions, and although his report is necessarily vague and fragmentary, it is nevertheless very suggestive. Imagine the impression of humanity a Martian observer would get who, after a difficult process of preparation and with considerable fatigue to the eyes, was able to peer at London from the steeple of St. Martin's Church* for stretches, at longest, of four minutes at a time. Mr. Cave was unable to ascertain if the winged Martians were the same as the Martians who hopped about the causeways and terraces, and if the latter could put on wings at will. He several times saw certain clumsy bipeds, dimly suggestive of apes, white and partially translucent, feeding among certain of the lichenous trees, and once some of these fled before one of the hopping, round-headed Martians. The latter caught one in its tentacles, and then the picture faded suddenly and left Mr. Cave most tantalisingly in the dark. On another occasion a vast thing, that Mr. Cave thought at first was some gigantic insect, appeared advancing along the causeway beside the canal with extraordinary rapidity. As this drew nearer Mr. Cave perceived that it was a mechanism of shining metals and of extraordinary complexity. And then, when he looked again, it had passed out of sight.

After a time Mr. Wace aspired to attract the attention of the Martians, and the next time that the strange eyes of one of them appeared close to the crystal Mr. Cave cried out and sprang away, and they immediately turned on the light and began to gesticulate in a manner suggestive of signalling. But when at last Mr. Cave examined the crystal again the Martian had departed.

Thus far these observations had progressed in early November, and then Mr. Cave, feeling that the suspicions of his family about the crystal were allayed, began to take it to and fro with him in order that, as occasion arose in the daytime or night, he might comfort himself with what was fast becoming the most real thing in his existence.

In December Mr. Wace's work in connection with a forthcoming examination became heavy, the sittings were reluctantly suspended for a week, and for ten or eleven days—he is not quite sure which—he saw nothing of Cave. He then grew anxious to resume these investigations, and, the stress of his seasonal labours being abated, he went down to Seven Dials. At the corner he noticed a shutter before a bird fancier's window, and then another at a cobbler's. Mr. Cave's shop was closed.

He rapped and the door was opened by the step-son in black. He at once called Mrs. Cave, who was, Mr. Wace could not but observe, in cheap but ample widow's weeds of the most imposing pattern. Without any very great surprise Mr. Wace learnt that Cave was dead and already buried. She was in tears, and her voice was a little thick. She had just returned from Highgate.* Her mind seemed occupied with her own prospects and the honourable details of the obsequies, but Mr. Wace was at last able to learn the particulars of Cave's death. He had been found dead in his shop in the early morning, the day after his last visit to Mr. Wace, and the crystal had been clasped in his stone-cold hands. His face was smiling, said Mrs. Cave, and the velvet cloth from the minerals lay on the floor at his feet. He must have been dead five or six hours when he was found.

This came as a great shock to Wace, and he began to reproach himself bitterly for having neglected the plain symptoms of the old man's ill-health. But his chief thought was of the crystal. He approached that topic in a gingerly manner, because he knew Mrs. Cave's peculiarities. He was dumfounded* to learn that it was sold.

Mrs. Cave's first impulse, directly Cave's body had been taken upstairs, had been to write to the mad clergyman who had offered five pounds for the crystal, informing him of its recovery; but after a violent hunt, in which her daughter joined her, they were convinced of the loss of his address. As they were without the means required to mourn and bury Cave in the elaborate style the dignity of an old Seven Dials inhabitant demands, they had appealed to a friendly fellow-tradesman in Great Portland Street. He had very kindly taken over a portion of the stock at a valuation. The valuation was his own, and the crystal egg was included in one of the lots. Mr. Wace, after a few suitable condolences, a little off-handedly proffered perhaps, hurried at once to Great Portland Street. But there he learned that the crystal egg had already been sold to a tall, dark man in grey. And there the material facts in this curious, and to me at least very suggestive, story come abruptly to an end. The Great Portland Street dealer did not know who the tall dark man in grey was, nor had he observed him with sufficient attention to describe him minutely. He did not even know which way this person had gone after leaving the shop. For a time Mr. Wace remained in the shop, trying the dealer's patience with hopeless questions, venting his own exasperation. And at last, realising abruptly that the whole thing had passed out of his hands, had vanished like a vision of the night, he returned to his own rooms, a little astonished to find the notes he had made still tangible and visible upon his untidy table.

His annoyance and disappointment were naturally very great. He made a second call (equally ineffectual) upon the Great Portland Street dealer, and he resorted to advertisements in such periodicals as were likely to come into the hands of a *bric-a-brac* collector. He also wrote letters to *The Daily Chronicle* and *Nature*,* but both those periodicals, suspecting a hoax, asked him to reconsider his action before they printed, and he was advised that such a strange story, unfortunately so bare of supporting evidence, might imperil his reputation as an investigator. Moreover, the calls of his proper work were urgent. So that after a month or so, save for an occasional reminder to certain dealers, he had reluctantly to abandon the quest for the crystal egg, and from that day to this it remains undiscovered. Occasionally, however, he tells me, and I can quite believe him, he has bursts of zeal, in which he abandons his more urgent occupation and resumes the search.

Whether or not it will remain lost for ever, with the material and origin of it, are things equally speculative at the present time. If the present purchaser is a collector, one would have expected the enquiries of Mr. Wace to have reached him through the dealers. He has been able to discover Mr. Cave's clergyman and 'Oriental'—no other than the Rev. James Parker and the young Prince of Bosso-Kuni in Java.* I am obliged to them for certain particulars. The object of the Prince was simply curiosity—and extravagance. He was so eager to buy because Cave was so oddly reluctant to sell. It is just as possible that the buyer in the second instance was simply a casual purchaser and not a collector at all, and the crystal egg, for all I know, may at the present moment be within a mile of me, decorating a drawing-room or serving as a paper-weight—its remarkable functions all unknown. Indeed, it is partly with the idea of such a possibility that I have thrown this narrative into a form that will give it a chance of being read by the ordinary consumer of fiction.

My own ideas in the matter are practically identical with those of Mr. Wace. I believe the crystal on the mast in Mars and the crystal egg of Mr. Cave's to be in some physical, but at present quite inexplicable, way *en rapport*, and we both believe further that the terrestrial crystal must have been—possibly at some remote date—sent hither from that planet, in order to give the Martians a near view of our affairs. Possibly the fellows to the crystals on the other masts are also on our globe. No theory of hallucination suffices for the facts.

RUDYARD KIPLING

'WIRELESS'

KASPAR'S SONG IN 'VARDA'*
(*From the Swedish of Stagnelius**)

Eyes aloft, over dangerous places,
    The children follow where Psyche flies,*
And, in the sweat of their upturned faces,
    Slash with a net at the empty skies.

So it goes they fall amid brambles,
    And sting their toes on the nettle-tops,
Till after a thousand scratches and scrambles
    They wipe their brows, and the hunting stops.

Then to quiet them comes their father
    And stills the riot of pain and grief,
Saying, 'Little ones, go and gather
    Out of my garden a cabbage leaf.

'You will find on it whorls and clots of
    Dull grey eggs that, properly fed,
Turn, by way of the worm, to lots of
    Radiant Psyches raised from the dead.'

'Heaven is beautiful, Earth is ugly,'
    The three-dimensioned preacher saith,
So we must not look where the snail and the slug lie
    For Psyche's birth . . . And that is our death!

'Wireless'

'It's a funny thing, this Marconi business,* isn't it?' said Mr. Shaynor, coughing heavily. 'Nothing seems to make any difference, by what they tell me—storms, hills, or anything; but if that's true we shall know before morning.'

'Of course it's true,' I answered, stepping behind the counter. 'Where's old Mr. Cashell?'

'He's had to go to bed on account of his influenza. He said you'd very likely drop in.'

'Where's his nephew?'

'Inside, getting the things ready. He told me that the last time they experimented they put the pole on the roof of one of the big hotels here, and the batteries electrified all the water-supply, and'—he giggled—'the ladies got shocks when they took their baths.'

'I never heard of that.'

'The hotel wouldn't exactly advertise it, would it? Just now, by what Mr. Cashell tells me, they're trying to signal from here to Poole,* and they're using stronger batteries than ever. But, you see, he being the guvnor's nephew and all that (and it will be in the papers too), it doesn't matter how they electrify things in this house. Are you going to watch?'

'Very much. I've never seen this game. Aren't you going to bed?'

'We don't close till ten on Saturdays. There's a good deal of influenza in town, too, and there'll be a dozen prescriptions coming in before morning. I generally sleep in the chair here. It's warmer than jumping out of bed every time. Bitter cold, isn't it?'*

'Freezing hard. I'm sorry your cough's worse.'

'Thank you. I don't mind cold so much. It's this wind that fair cuts me to pieces.' He coughed again hard and hackingly, as an old lady came in for ammoniated quinine.* 'We've just run out of it in bottles, madam,' said Mr. Shaynor, returning to the professional tone, 'but if you will wait two minutes, I'll make it up for you, madam.'

I had used the shop for some time, and my acquaintance with the proprietor had ripened into friendship. It was Mr. Cashell who revealed to me the purpose and power of Apothecaries' Hall what time a fellow-chemist had made an error in a prescription of mine, had lied to cover his sloth, and when error and lie were brought home to him had written vain letters.

'A disgrace to our profession,' said the thin, mild-eyed man, hotly, after studying the evidence. 'You couldn't do a better service to the profession than report him to Apothecaries' Hall.'*

I did so, not knowing what djinns* I should evoke, and the result was such an apology as one might make who had spent a night on the rack. I conceived great respect for Apothecaries' Hall, and esteem for Mr. Cashell, a zealous craftsman who magnified his calling. Until Mr. Shaynor came down from the North his assistants had by no means agreed with Mr. Cashell. 'They forget,' said he, 'that, first and foremost, the compounder is a medicine-man. On him depends the physician's reputation. He holds it literally in the hollow of his hand, Sir.'

Mr. Shaynor's manners had not, perhaps, the polish of the grocery and Italian warehouse next door, but he knew and loved his dispensary work in every detail. For relaxation he seemed to go no farther afield than the romance of drugs—their discovery, preparation, packing, and export—but it led him to the ends of the earth, and on this subject, and the Pharmaceutical Formulary,* and Nicholas Culpepper,* most confident of physicians, we met.

Little by little I grew to know something of his beginnings and his hopes—of his mother, who had been a school-teacher in one of the northern counties, and of his red-headed father, a small job-master at Kirby Moors,* who died when he was a child; of the examinations he had passed and of their exceeding and increasing difficulty; of his dreams of a shop in London; of his hate for the price-cutting Co-operative stores;* and, most interesting, of his mental attitude towards customers.

'There's a way you get into,' he told me, 'of serving them carefully, and I hope, politely, without stopping your own thinking. I've been reading Christie's *New Commercial Plants** all this autumn, and that needs keeping your mind on it, I can tell you. So long as it isn't a prescription, of course, I can carry as much as half a page of Christie in my head, and at the same time I could sell out all that window twice over, and not a penny wrong at the end. As to prescriptions, I think I could make up the general run of 'em in my sleep, almost.'

For reasons of my own, I was deeply interested in Marconi experiments at their outset in England; and it was of a piece with Mr. Cashell's unvarying thoughtfulness that, when his nephew the electrician appropriated the house for a long-range installation, he should, as I have said, invite me to see the result.

The old lady went away with her medicine, and Mr. Shaynor and I stamped on the tiled floor behind the counter to keep ourselves warm. The shop, by the light of the many electrics, looked like a Paris-diamond mine, for Mr. Cashell believed in all the ritual of his craft. Three superb glass jars—red, green, and blue—of the sort that led Rosamund to parting with her shoes*—blazed in the broad plate-glass windows, and there was a confused smell of orris, Kodak films, vulcanite,* tooth-powder, sachets, and almond-cream in the air. Mr. Shaynor fed the dispensary stove, and we sucked cayenne-pepper jujubes and menthol lozenges.* The brutal east wind had cleared the streets, and the few passers-by were muffled to their puckered eyes. In the Italian warehouse next door some gay feathered birds and game, hung upon hooks, sagged to the wind across the left edge of our window-frame.

'They ought to take these poultry in—all knocked about like that,' said Mr. Shaynor. 'Doesn't it make you feel fair perishing? See that old hare! The wind's nearly blowing the fur off him.'*

I saw the belly-fur of the dead beast blown apart in ridges and streaks as the wind caught it, showing bluish skin underneath. 'Bitter cold,' said Mr. Shaynor, shuddering. 'Fancy going out on a night like this! Oh, here's young Mr. Cashell.'

The door of the inner office behind the dispensary opened, and an energetic, spade-bearded man stepped forth, rubbing his hands.

'I want a bit of tin-foil, Shaynor,' he said. 'Good-evening. My uncle told me you might be coming.' This to me, as I began the first of a hundred questions.

'I've everything in order,' he replied. 'We're only waiting until Poole calls us up. Excuse me a minute. You can come in whenever you like—but I'd better be with the instruments. Give me that tin-foil. Thanks.'

While we were talking, a girl—evidently no customer—had come into the shop, and the face and bearing of Mr. Shaynor changed. She leaned confidently across the counter.

'But I can't,' I heard him whisper uneasily—the flush on his cheek was dull red, and his eyes shone like a drugged moth's.* 'I can't. I tell you I'm alone in the place.'

'No, you aren't. Who's *that*? Let him look after it for half an hour. A brisk walk will do you good. Ah, come now, John.'

'But he isn't—'

'I don't care. I want you to; we'll only go round by St. Agnes.* If you don't—'

He crossed to where I stood in the shadow of the dispensary counter, and began some sort of broken apology about a lady-friend.

'Yes,' she interrupted. 'You take the shop for half an hour—to oblige *me*, won't you?'

She had a singularly rich and promising voice that well matched her outline.

'All right,' I said. 'I'll do it—but you'd better wrap yourself up, Mr. Shaynor.'

'Oh, a brisk walk ought to help me. We're only going round by the church.' I heard him cough grievously as they went out together.

I refilled the stove, and, after reckless expenditure of Mr. Cashell's coal, drove some warmth into the shop. I explored many of the glass-knobbed drawers that lined the walls, tasted some disconcerting drugs, and, by the aid of a few cardamoms, ground ginger, chloric-ether, and dilute alcohol, manufactured a new and wildish drink, of which I bore a glassful to young Mr. Cashell, busy in the back office. He laughed shortly when I told him that Mr. Shaynor had stepped out—but a frail coil of wire held all his attention, and he had no word for me bewildered among the batteries and rods. The noise of the sea on the beach began to make itself heard as the traffic in the street ceased. Then briefly, but very lucidly, he gave me the names and uses of the mechanism that crowded the tables and the floor.

'When do you expect to get the message from Poole?' I demanded, sipping my liquor out of a graduated glass.*

'About midnight, if everything is in order. We've got our installation-pole fixed to the roof of the house. I shouldn't advise you to turn on a tap or anything to-night. We've connected up with the plumbing, and all the water will be electrified.' He repeated to me the history of the agitated ladies at the hotel at the time of the first installation.

'But what *is* it?' I asked. 'Electricity is out of my beat altogether.'

'Ah, if you knew *that* you'd know something nobody knows. It's just It—what we call Electricity, but the magic—the manifest-ations—the Hertzian waves*—are all revealed by *this*. The coherer,* we call it.'

He picked up a glass tube not much thicker than a thermometer, in which, almost touching, were two tiny silver plugs, and between them an infinitesimal pinch of metallic dust. 'That's all,' he said, proudly, as though himself responsible for the wonder. 'That is the thing that will reveal to us the Powers—whatever the Powers may be—at work—through space—a long distance away.'

Just then Mr. Shaynor returned alone and stood coughing his heart out on the mat.

'Serves you right for being such a fool,' said young Mr. Cashell, as annoyed as myself at the interruption. 'Never mind—we've all the night before us to see wonders.'

Shaynor clutched the counter, his handkerchief to his lips. When he brought it away I saw two bright red stains.

'I—I've got a bit of a rasped throat from smoking cigarettes,' he panted. 'I think I'll try a cubeb.'*

'Better take some of this I've been compounding while you've been away.' I handed him the brew.

''Twon't make me drunk, will it? I'm almost a teetotaller. My word! That's grateful and comforting.'*

He set down the empty glass to cough afresh.

'Brr! But it was cold out there! I shouldn't care to be lying in my grave a night like this. Don't *you* ever have a sore throat from smoking?' He pocketed the handkerchief after a furtive peep.

'Oh, yes, sometimes,' I replied, wondering, while I spoke, into what agonies of terror I should fall if ever I saw those bright-red danger-signals under my nose. Young Mr. Cashell among the batteries coughed slightly to show that he was quite ready to continue his scientific explanations, but I was thinking still of the girl with the rich voice and the significantly cut mouth, at whose command I had taken charge of the shop. It flashed across me that she distantly resembled the seductive shape on a gold-framed toilet-water advertisement whose charms were unholily heightened by the glare from the red bottle in the window. Turning to make sure, I saw Mr. Shaynor's eyes bent in the same direction, and by instinct recognised that the flamboyant thing was to him a shrine. 'What do you take for your—cough?' I asked.

'Well, I'm the wrong side of the counter to believe much in patent medicines. But there are asthma cigarettes and there are pastilles. To tell you the truth, if you don't object to the smell, which is very like incense, I believe, though I'm not a Roman Catholic, Blaudett's Cathedral Pastilles relieve me as much as anything.'

'Let's try.' I had never raided a chemist's shop before, so I was thorough. We unearthed the pastilles—brown, gummy cones of benzoin*—and set them alight under the toilet-water advertisement, where they fumed in thin blue spirals.

'Of course,' said Mr. Shaynor, to my question, 'what one uses in the shop for one's self comes out of one's pocket. Why, stock-taking in our business is nearly the same as with jewellers—and I can't say more than that. But one gets them'—he pointed to the pastille-box—'at trade prices.' Evidently the censing of the gay, seven-tinted wench with the teeth was an established ritual which cost something.

'And when do we shut up shop?'

'We stay like this all night. The guv—old Mr. Cashell—doesn't believe in locks and shutters as compared with electric light. Besides,

it brings trade. I'll just sit here in the chair by the stove and write
a letter, if you don't mind. Electricity isn't my prescription.'

The energetic young Mr. Cashell snorted within, and Shaynor settled himself up in his chair over which he had thrown a staring red,
black, and yellow Austrian jute blanket,* rather like a table-cover. I cast
about, amid patent-medicine pamphlets, for something to read, but
finding little, returned to the manufacture of the new drink. The
Italian warehouse took down its game and went to bed. Across the
street blank shutters flung back the gaslight in cold smears; the dried
pavement seemed to rough up in goose-flesh under the scouring of the
savage wind, and we could hear, long ere he passed, the policeman
flapping his arms to keep himself warm. Within, the flavours of cardamoms and chloric-ether* disputed those of the pastilles and a score of
drugs and perfume and soap scents. Our electric lights, set low down
in the windows before the tun-bellied Rosamund jars, flung inward
three monstrous daubs of red, blue, and green, that broke into kaleido-
scopic lights on the facetted knobs of the drug-drawers, the cut-glass
scent flagons, and the bulbs of the sparklet bottles.* They flushed the
white-tiled floor in gorgeous patches; splashed along the nickel-silver
counter-rails, and turned the polished mahogany counter-panels to
the likeness of intricate grained marbles—slabs of porphyry and mal-
achite. Mr. Shaynor unlocked a drawer, and ere he began to write, took
out a meagre bundle of letters. From my place by the stove, I could see
the scalloped edges of the paper with a flaring monogram in the corner
and could even smell the reek of chypre.* At each page he turned
toward the toilet-water lady of the advertisement and devoured her
with over-luminous eyes. He had drawn the Austrian blanket over his
shoulders, and among those warring lights he looked more than ever
the incarnation of a drugged moth—a tiger-moth as I thought.

He put his letter into an envelope, stamped it with stiff mechanical
movements, and dropped it in the drawer. Then I became aware of
the silence of a great city asleep—the silence that underlaid the even
voice of the breakers along the sea-front—a thick, tingling quiet of
warm life stilled down for its appointed time, and unconsciously
I moved about the glittering shop as one moves in a sick-room. Young
Mr. Cashell was adjusting some wire that crackled from time to time
with the tense, knuckle-stretching sound of the electric spark.
Upstairs, where a door shut and opened swiftly, I could hear his uncle
coughing abed.

'Here,' I said, when the drink was properly warmed, 'take some of this, Mr. Shaynor.'

He jerked in his chair with a start and a wrench, and held out his hand for the glass. The mixture, of a rich port-wine colour, frothed at the top.*

'It looks,' he said, suddenly, 'it looks—those bubbles—like a string of pearls winking at you—rather like the pearls round that young lady's neck.' He turned again to the advertisement where the female in the dove-coloured corset had seen fit to put on all her pearls before she cleaned her teeth.

'Not bad, is it?' I said.

'Eh?'

He rolled his eyes heavily full on me, and, as I stared, I beheld all meaning and consciousness die out of the swiftly dilating pupils. His figure lost its stark rigidity, softened into the chair, and, chin on chest, hands dropped before him, he rested open-eyed, absolutely still.

'I'm afraid I've rather cooked Shaynor's goose,' I said, bearing the fresh drink to young Mr. Cashell. 'Perhaps it was the chloric-ether.'

'Oh, he's all right.' The spade-bearded man glanced at him pityingly. 'Consumptives go off in those sort of doses very often. It's exhaustion . . . I don't wonder. I daresay the liquor will do him good. It's grand stuff,' he finished his share appreciatively. 'Well, as I was saying—before he interrupted—about this little coherer. The pinch of dust, you see, is nickel-filings. The Hertzian waves, you see, come out of space from the station that despatches 'em, and all these little particles are attracted together—cohere, we call it—for just so long as the current passes through them. Now, it's important to remember that the current is an induced current. There are a good many kinds of induction—'

'Yes, but what *is* induction?'

'That's rather hard to explain untechnically. But the long and the short of it is that when a current of electricity passes through a wire there's a lot of magnetism present round that wire; and if you put another wire parallel to, and within what we call its magnetic field—why then, the second wire will also become charged with electricity.'

'On its own account?'

'On its own account.'

'Then let's see if I've got it correctly. Miles off, at Poole, or wherever it is—'

'It will be anywhere in ten years.'

'You've got a charged wire—'

'Charged with Hertzian waves which vibrate, say, two hundred and thirty million times a second.' Mr. Cashell snaked his forefinger rapidly through the air.

'All right—a charged wire at Poole, giving out these waves into space. Then this wire of yours sticking out into space—on the roof of the house—in some mysterious way gets charged with those waves from Poole—'

'Or anywhere—it only happens to be Poole to-night.'

'And those waves set the coherer at work, just like an ordinary telegraph-office ticker?'

'No! That's where so many people make the mistake. The Hertzian waves wouldn't be strong enough to work a great heavy Morse instrument* like ours. They can only just make that dust cohere, and while it coheres (a little while for a dot and a longer while for a dash) the current from this battery—the home battery'—he laid his hand on the thing—'can get through to the Morse printing-machine to record the dot or dash. Let me make it clearer. Do you know anything about steam?'

'Very little. But go on.'

'Well, the coherer is like a steam-valve. Any child can open a valve and start a steamer's engines, because a turn of the hand lets in the main steam, doesn't it? Now, this home battery here ready to print is the main steam. The coherer is the valve, always ready to be turned on. The Hertzian wave is the child's hand that turns it.'

'I see. That's marvellous.'

'Marvellous, isn't it? And, remember, we're only at the beginning. There's nothing we shan't be able to do in ten years. I want to live—my God, how I want to live, and see it develop?'* He looked through the door at Shaynor breathing lightly in his chair. 'Poor beast! And he wants to keep company with Fanny Brand.'*

'Fanny *who*?' I said, for the name struck an obscurely familiar chord in my brain—something connected with a stained handkerchief, and the word 'arterial.'*

'Fanny Brand—the girl you kept shop for.' He laughed. 'That's all I know about her, and for the life of me I can't see what Shaynor sees in her, or she in him.'

'*Can't* you see what he sees in her?' I insisted.

'Oh, yes, if *that's* what you mean. She's a great, big, fat lump of a girl, and so on. I suppose that's why he's so crazy after her. She isn't his sort. Well, it doesn't matter. My uncle says he's bound to die before the year's out. Your drink's given him a good sleep, at any rate.' Young Mr. Cashell could not catch Mr. Shaynor's face, which was half turned to the advertisement.

I stoked the stove anew, for the room was growing cold, and lighted another pastille. Mr. Shaynor in his chair, never moving, looked through and over me with eyes as wide and lustreless as those of a dead hare.

'Poole's late,' said young Mr. Cashell, when I stepped back. 'I'll just send them a call.'

He pressed a key in the semi-darkness, and with a rending crackle there leaped between two brass knobs a spark, streams of sparks, and sparks again.

'Grand, isn't it? *That's* the Power—our unknown Power—kicking and fighting to be let loose,' said young Mr. Cashell. 'There she goes—kick—kick—kick into space. I never get over the strangeness of it when I work a sending-machine—waves going into space, you know. T. R. is our call. Poole ought to answer with L. L. L.'

We waited two, three, five minutes. In that silence, of which the boom of the tide was an orderly part, I caught the clear '*kiss—kiss—kiss*' of the halliards* on the roof, as they were blown against the installation-pole.

'Poole is not ready. I'll stay here and call you when he is.'

I returned to the shop, and set down my glass on a marble slab with a careless clink. As I did so, Shaynor rose to his feet, his eyes fixed once more on the advertisement, where the young woman bathed in the light from the red jar simpered pinkly over her pearls. His lips moved without cessation. I stepped nearer to listen. 'And threw—and threw—and threw,' he repeated, his face all sharp with some inexplicable agony.

I moved forward astonished. But it was then he found words —delivered roundly and clearly. These:—

And threw warm gules on Madeleine's young breast.*

The trouble passed off his countenance, and he returned lightly to his place, rubbing his hands.

It had never occurred to me, though we had many times discussed reading and prize-competitions as a diversion, that Mr. Shaynor ever read Keats, or could quote him at all appositely. There was, after all, a certain stained-glass effect of light on the high bosom of the highly-polished picture which might, by stretch of fancy, suggest, as a vile chromo* recalls some incomparable canvas, the line he had spoken. Night, my drink, and solitude were evidently turning Mr. Shaynor into a poet. He sat down again and wrote swiftly on his villainous note-paper, his lips quivering.

I shut the door into the inner office and moved up behind him. He made no sign that he saw or heard. I looked over his shoulder, and read, amid half-formed words, sentences, and wild scratches:—

> ——Very cold it was. Very cold
> The hare—the hare—the hare—
> The birds——

He raised his head sharply, and frowned toward the blank shutters of the poulterer's shop where they jutted out against our window. Then one clear line came:—

> The hare, in spite of fur, was very cold

The head, moving machine-like, turned right to the advertisement where the Blaudett's Cathedral pastille reeked abominably. He grunted, and went on:—

> Incense in a censer—*
> Before her darling picture framed in gold—
> Maiden's picture—angel's portrait—

'Hsh!' said Mr. Cashell guardedly from the inner office, as though in the presence of spirits. 'There's something coming through from somewhere; but it isn't Poole.' I heard the crackle of sparks as he depressed the keys of the transmitter. In my own brain, too, something crackled, or it might have been the hair on my head. Then I heard my own voice, in a harsh whisper: 'Mr. Cashell, there is something coming through here, too. Leave me alone till I tell you.'

'But I thought you'd come to see this wonderful thing—Sir,' indignantly at the end.

'Leave me alone till I tell you. Be quiet.'

I watched—I waited. Under the blue-veined hand—the dry hand of the consumptive—came away clear, without erasure:—

> And my weak spirit fails
> To think how the dead must freeze—

he shivered as he wrote—*

Beneath the churchyard mould.*

Then he stopped, laid the pen down, and leaned back.

For an instant, that was half an eternity, the shop spun before me in a rainbow-tinted whirl, in and through which my own soul most dispassionately considered my own soul as that fought with an overmastering fear. Then I smelt the strong smell of cigarettes from Mr. Shaynor's clothing, and heard, as though it had been the rending of trumpets, the rattle of his breathing. I was still in my place of observation, much as one would watch a rifle-shot at the butts, half-bent, hands on my knees, and head within a few inches of the black, red, and yellow blanket of his shoulder. I was whispering encouragement, evidently to my other self, sounding sentences, such as men pronounce in dreams.

'If he has read Keats, it proves nothing. If he hasn't—like causes *must* beget like effects. There is no escape from this law. *You* ought to be grateful that you know "St. Agnes' Eve" without the book; because, given the circumstances, such as Fanny Brand, who is the key of the enigma, and approximately represents the latitude and longitude of Fanny Brawne; allowing also for the bright red colour of the arterial blood upon the handkerchief, which was just what you were puzzling over in the shop just now; and counting the effect of the professional environment, here almost perfectly duplicated—the result is logical and inevitable. As inevitable as induction.'

Still, the other half of my soul refused to be comforted. It was cowering in some minute and inadequate corner—at an immense distance.

Hereafter, I found myself one person again,* my hands still gripping my knees, and my eyes glued on the page before Mr. Shaynor. As dreamers accept and explain the upheaval of landscapes and the resurrection of the dead, with excerpts from the evening hymn or the multiplication-table, so I had accepted the facts, whatever they might be, that I should witness, and had devised a theory, sane and plausible to my mind, that explained them all. Nay, I was even in advance of my facts, walking hurriedly before them, assured that they would fit my theory. And all that I now recall of that epoch-making theory are the lofty words: 'If he has read Keats it's the chloric-ether. If he hasn't, it's the identical bacillus, or Hertzian wave of tuberculosis, *plus* Fanny Brand and the professional status which, in conjunction with the main-stream of subconscious thought common to all mankind, has thrown up temporarily an induced Keats.'

Mr. Shaynor returned to his work, erasing and rewriting as before with swiftness. Two or three blank pages he tossed aside. Then he wrote, muttering:—

> The little smoke of a candle that goes out.

'No,' he muttered. 'Little smoke—little smoke—little smoke. What else?' He thrust his chin forward toward the advertisement, where-under the last of the Blaudett's Cathedral pastilles fumed in its holder. 'Ah!' Then with relief:—

> The little smoke that dies in moonlight cold.

Evidently he was snared by the rhymes of his first verse, for he wrote and rewrote 'gold—cold—mould' many times. Again he sought inspiration from the advertisement, and set down, without erasure, the line I had overheard:—

> And threw warm gules on Madeleine's young breast.

As I remembered the original it is 'fair'—a trite word—instead of 'young,' and I found myself nodding approval, though I admitted that the attempt to reproduce 'its little smoke in pallid moonlight died'* was a failure.

Followed without a break ten or fifteen lines of bald prose—the naked soul's confession of its physical yearning for its beloved—unclean as we count uncleanliness; unwholesome, but human exceedingly; the raw material, so it seemed to me in that hour and in that place, whence Keats wove the twenty-sixth, seventh, and eighth stanzas of his poem. Shame I had none in overseeing this revelation; and my fear had gone with the smoke of the pastille.

'That's it,' I murmured. 'That's how it's blocked out. Go on! Ink it in, man. Ink it in!'

Mr. Shaynor returned to broken verse wherein 'loveliness' was made to rhyme with a desire to look upon 'her empty dress'. He picked up a fold of the gay, soft blanket, spread it over one hand, caressed it with infinite tenderness, thought, muttered, traced some snatches which I could not decipher, shut his eyes drowsily, shook his head, and dropped the stuff. Here I found myself at fault, for I could not then see (as I do now) in what manner a red, black, and yellow Austrian blanket* coloured his dreams.

In a few minutes he laid aside his pen, and, chin on hand, considered the shop with thoughtful and intelligent eyes. He threw down the blanket, rose, passed along a line of drug-drawers, and read the names on the labels aloud. Returning, he took from his desk Christie's *New Commercial Plants* and the old Culpepper that I had given him, opened and laid them side by side with a clerkly* air, all trace of passion gone from his face, read first in one and then in the other, and paused with pen behind his ear.

'What wonder of Heaven's coming now?' I thought.

'Manna—manna—manna,' he said at last, under wrinkled brows. 'That's what I wanted. Good! Now then! Now then! Good! Good! Oh, by God, that's good!' His voice rose and he spoke rightly and fully without a falter:—

> Candied apple, quince and plum and gourd,
> And jellies smoother than the creamy curd,
> And lucent syrups tinct with cinnamon,
> Manna and dates in Argosy transferred
> From Fez; and spiced dainties, every one
> From silken Samarcand to cedared Lebanon.*

He repeated it once more, using 'blander' for 'smoother' in the second line, then wrote it down without erasure, but this time (my set eyes missed no stroke of any word) he substituted 'soother' for his atrocious second thought, so that it came away under his hand as it is written in the book—as it is written in the book.

A wind went shouting down the street, and on the heels of the wind followed a spurt and rattle of rain.

After a smiling pause—and good right had he to smile—he began anew, always tossing the last sheet over his shoulder:—

> The sharp rain falling on the window-pane,
> Rattling sleet—the wind-blown sleet.

Then prose: 'It is very cold of mornings when the wind brings rain and sleet with it. I heard the sleet on the window-pane outside, and thought of you, my darling. I am always thinking of you. I wish we could both run away like two lovers into the storm and get that little cottage by the sea which we are always thinking about, my own dear

darling. We could sit and watch the sea beneath our windows. It would
be a fairyland all of our own—a fairy sea—a fairy sea...'

He stopped, raised his head, and listened. The steady drone of the
Channel along the sea-front that had borne us company so long
leaped up a note to the sudden fuller surge that signals the change
from ebb to flood. It beat in like the change of step throughout an
army—this renewed pulse of the sea—and filled our ears till they,
accepting it, marked it no longer.

> A fairyland for you and me
> Across the foam—beyond...
> A magic foam, a perilous sea.

He grunted again with effort and bit his underlip. My throat dried, but
I dared not gulp to moisten it lest I should break the spell that was
drawing him nearer and nearer to the high-water mark but two of the
sons of Adam have reached. Remember that in all the millions permitted there are no more than five—five little lines—of which one can say:
'These are the pure Magic. These are the clear Vision. The rest is only
poetry.' And Mr. Shaynor was playing hot and cold with two of them!

I vowed no unconscious thought of mine should influence the
blindfold soul, and pinned myself desperately to the other three,
repeating and re-repeating:—

> A savage spot as holy and enchanted
> As e'er beneath a waning moon was haunted
> By woman wailing for her demon lover.*

But though I believed my brain thus occupied, my every sense hung
upon the writing under the dry, bony hand, all brown-fingered with
chemicals and cigarette-smoke.

> Our windows fronting on the dangerous foam,

(he wrote, after long, irresolute snatches), and then—

> Our open casements facing desolate seas
> Forlorn—forlorn—*

Here again his face grew peaked and anxious with that sense of loss
I had first seen when the Power snatched him. But this time the agony
was tenfold keener. As I watched it mounted like mercury in the tube.
It lighted his face from within till I thought the visibly scourged soul
must leap forth naked between his jaws, unable to endure. A drop of

sweat trickled from my forehead down my nose and splashed on the back of my hand.

> Our windows facing on the desolate seas
> And pearly foam of magic fairyland—

'Not yet—not yet,' he muttered, 'wait a minute. *Please* wait a minute. I shall get it then—

> Our magic windows fronting on the sea,
> The dangerous foam of desolate seas . . .
> For aye.

Ouh, my God!'

From head to heel he shook—shook from the marrow of his bones outwards—then leaped to his feet with raised arms, and slid the chair screeching across the tiled floor where it struck the drawers behind and fell with a jar. Mechanically, I stooped to recover it.

As I rose, Mr. Shaynor was stretching and yawning at leisure.

'I've had a bit of a doze,' he said. 'How did I come to knock the chair over? You look rather—'

'The chair startled me,' I answered. 'It was so sudden in this quiet.'

Young Mr. Cashell behind his shut door was offendedly silent.

'I suppose I must have been dreaming,'* said Mr. Shaynor.

'I suppose you must,' I said. 'Talking of dreams—I—I noticed you writing—before—'

He flushed consciously.

'I meant to ask you if you've ever read anything written by a man called Keats.'

'Oh! I haven't much time to read poetry, and I can't say that I remember the name exactly. Is he a popular writer?'

'Middling. I thought you might know him because he's the only poet who was ever a druggist. And he's rather what's called the lover's poet.'

'Indeed. I must dip into him. What did he write about?'

'A lot of things. Here's a sample that may interest you.'

Then and there, carefully, I repeated the verse he had twice spoken and once written not ten minutes ago.

'Ah! Anybody could see he was a druggist from that line about the tinctures and syrups. It's a fine tribute to our profession.'

'I don't know,' said young Mr. Cashell, with icy politeness, opening the door one half-inch, 'if you still happen to be interested in our trifling experiments. But, should such be the case—'

I drew him aside, whispering, 'Shaynor seemed going off into some sort of fit when I spoke to you just now. I thought, even at the risk of being rude, it wouldn't do to take you off your instruments just as the call was coming through. Don't you see?'

'Granted—granted as soon as asked,' he said, unbending. 'I *did* think it a shade odd at the time. So that was why he knocked the chair down?'

'I hope I haven't missed anything,' I said.

'I'm afraid I can't say that, but you're just in time for the end of a rather curious performance. You can come in too, Mr. Shaynor. Listen, while I read it off.'

The Morse instrument was ticking furiously. Mr. Cashell interpreted: '"*K.K.V. Can make nothing of your signals.*"' A pause. '"*M.M.V. M.M.V. Signals unintelligible. Purpose anchor Sandown Bay.* Examine instruments to-morrow.*" Do you know what that means? It's a couple of men-o'-war working Marconi signals off the Isle of Wight. They are trying to talk to each other. Neither can read the other's messages, but all their messages are being taken in by our receiver here. They've been going on for ever so long. I wish you could have heard it.'

'How wonderful!' I said. 'Do you mean we're overhearing Portsmouth ships trying to talk to each other—that we're eavesdropping across half South England?'

'Just that. Their transmitters are all right, but their receivers are out of order, so they only get a dot here and a dash there. Nothing clear.'

'Why is that?'

'God knows—and Science will know to-morrow. Perhaps the induction is faulty; perhaps the receivers aren't tuned to receive just the number of vibrations per second that the transmitter sends. Only a word here and there. Just enough to tantalise.'

Again the Morse sprang to life.

'That's one of 'em complaining now. Listen: "*Disheartening—most disheartening.*" It's quite pathetic. Have you ever seen a spiritualistic séance? It reminds me of that sometimes—odds and ends of messages coming out of nowhere—a word here and there—no good at all.'

'But mediums are all impostors,' said Mr. Shaynor, in the doorway, lighting an asthma-cigarette. 'They only do it for the money they can make. I've seen 'em.'

'Here's Poole, at last—clear as a bell. L.L.L. *Now* we shan't be long.' Mr. Cashell rattled the keys merrily. 'Anything you'd like to tell 'em?'

'No, I don't think so,' I said. 'I'll go home and get to bed. I'm feeling a little tired.'

MARY E. WILKINS FREEMAN

THE HALL BEDROOM

My name is Mrs. Elizabeth Jennings. I am a highly respectable woman. I may style myself a gentlewoman, for in my youth I enjoyed advantages. I was well brought up, and I graduated at a young ladies' seminary. I also married well. My husband was that most genteel of all merchants, an apothecary. His shop was on the corner of the Main Street in Rockton,* the town where I was born, and where I lived until the death of my husband. My parents had died when I had been married a short time, so I was left quite alone in the world. I was not competent to carry on the apothecary business by myself, for I had no knowledge of drugs, and had a mortal terror of giving poisons instead of medicines. Therefore I was obliged to sell at a considerable sacrifice, and the proceeds, some five thousand dollars, were all I had in the world. The income was not enough to support me in any kind of comfort, and I saw that I must in some way earn money. I thought at first of teaching, but I was no longer young, and methods had changed since my school days. What I was able to teach, nobody wished to know. I could think of only one thing to do: take boarders. But the same objection to that business as to teaching held good in Rockton. Nobody wished to board. My husband had rented a house with a number of bedrooms, and I advertised, but nobody applied. Finally my cash was running very low, and I became desperate. I packed up my furniture, rented a large house in this town and moved here. It was a venture attended with many risks. In the first place the rent was exorbitant, in the next I was entirely unknown. However, I am a person of considerable ingenuity, and have inventive power, and much enterprise when the occasion presses. I advertised in a very original manner, although that actually took my last penny, that is, the last penny of my ready money, and I was forced to draw on my principal to purchase my first supplies, a thing which I had resolved never on any account to do. But the great risk met with a reward, for I had several applicants within two days after my advertisement appeared in the paper. Within two weeks my boarding-house was well established, I became very successful, and my success would have been uninterrupted had it not been for the mysterious and bewildering occurrences which I am about to relate. I am now forced to leave the house and rent another. Some of my old boarders accompany me, some, with the most unreasonable nervousness, refuse to be longer associated in any way, however indirectly, with the terrible and uncanny happenings which I have to relate. It remains to be seen whether my ill luck in this house will follow me into another, and whether my whole prosperity in life will be forever shadowed by the Mystery of the Hall Bedroom. Instead of telling the strange story myself in my own words, I shall present the Journal of Mr. George H. Wheatcroft. I shall show you the portions beginning on January 18 of the present year, the date when he took up his residence with me. Here it is:

'January 18, 1883. Here I am established in my new boarding-house. I have, as befits my humble means, the hall bedroom,* even the hall bedroom on the third floor. I have heard all my life of hall bed-rooms, I have seen hall bedrooms, I have been in them, but never until now, when I am actually established in one, did I comprehend what, at once, an ignominious and sternly uncompromising thing a hall bedroom is. It proves the ignominy of the dweller therein. No man at thirty-six (my age) would be domiciled in a hall bedroom, unless he were himself ignominious, at least comparatively speaking. I am proved by this means incontrovertibly to have been left far behind in the race. I see no reason why I should not live in this hall bedroom for the rest of my life, that is, if I have money enough to pay the landlady, and that seems probable, since my small funds are invested as safely as if I were an orphan-ward in charge of a pillar of a sanctuary. After the valuables have been stolen, I have most care-fully locked the stable door. I have experienced the revulsion which comes sooner or later to the adventurous soul who experiences noth-ing but defeat and so-called ill luck. I have swung to the opposite extreme. I have lost in everything—I have lost in love, I have lost in money, I have lost in the struggle for preferment, I have lost in health and strength. I am now settled down in a hall bedroom to live upon my small income, and regain my health by mild potations of the min-eral waters here, if possible; if not, to live here without my health—for mine is not a necessarily fatal malady—until Providence shall take me out of my hall bedroom. There is no one place more than another where I care to live. There is not sufficient motive to take me away, even if the mineral waters do not benefit me. So I am here and to stay in the hall bedroom. The landlady is civil, and even kind, as kind as a woman who has to keep her poor womanly eye upon the main chance can be. The struggle for money always injures the fine grain of a woman; she is too fine a thing to do it; she does not by nature belong with the gold grubbers, and it therefore lowers her; she steps from heights to claw and scrape and dig. But she can not help it oftentimes, poor thing, and her deterioration thereby is to be condoned. The landlady is all she can be, taking her strain of adverse circumstances into consideration, and the table is good, even conscientiously so. It looks to me as if she were foolish enough to strive to give the boarders their money's worth, with the due regard for the main chance which is inevitable. However, that is of minor importance to me, since my diet is restricted.

'It is curious what an annoyance a restriction in diet can be even to a man who has considered himself somewhat indifferent to gastronomic delights. There was to-day a pudding for dinner, which I could not taste without penalty, but which I longed for. It was only because it looked unlike any other pudding that I had ever seen, and assumed a mental and spiritual significance. It seemed to me, whimsically no doubt, as if tasting it might give me a new sensation, and consequently a new outlook. Trivial things may lead to large results: why should I not get a new outlook by means of a pudding? Life here stretches before me most monotonously, and I feel like clutching at alleviations, though paradoxically, since I have settled down with the utmost acquiescence. Still one can not immediately overcome and change radically all one's nature. Now I look at myself critically, and search for the keynote to my whole self, and my actions, I have always been conscious of a reaching out, an overweening desire for the new, the untried, for the broadness of further horizons, the seas beyond seas, the thought beyond thought. This characteristic has been the primary cause of all my misfortunes. I have the soul of an explorer, and in nine out of ten cases this leads to destruction. If I had possessed capital, and sufficient push, I should have been one of the searchers after the North Pole. I have been an eager student of astronomy. I have studied botany with avidity, and have dreamed of new flora in unexplored parts of the world, and the same with animal life and geology. I longed for riches in order to discover the power and sense of possession of the rich. I longed for love in order to discover the possibilities of the emotions. I longed for all that the mind of man could conceive as desirable for man, not so much for purely selfish ends, as from an insatiable thirst for knowledge of a universal trend. But I have limitations, I do not quite understand of what nature—for what mortal ever did quite understand his own limitations, since a knowledge of them would preclude their existence?—but they have prevented my progress to any extent. Therefore behold me in my hall bedroom, settled at last into a groove of fate so deep that I have lost the sight of even my horizons. Just at present, as I write here, my horizon on the left, that is my physical horizon, is a wall covered with cheap paper. The paper is an indeterminate pattern in white and gilt. There are a few photographs of my own hung about, and on the large wall space beside the bed there is a large oil painting which belongs to my landlady. It has a massive, tarnished gold frame, and, curiously enough, the painting itself is rather good. I have no idea who the artist could have been. It is of the conventional landscape type in vogue some fifty years since, the type so fondly reproduced in chromos*—the winding river with the little boat occupied by a pair of lovers, the cottage nestled among trees on the right shore, the gentle slope of the hills and the church spire in the background—but still it is well done. It gives me the impression of an artist without the slightest originality of design, but much of technique. But for some inexplicable reason the picture frets me. I find myself gazing at it when I do not wish to do so. It seems to compel my attention like some intent face in the room. I shall ask Mrs. Jennings to have it removed. I will hang in its place some photographs which I have in a trunk.

'January 26. I do not write regularly in my journal. I never did. I see no reason why I should. I see no reason why any one should have the slightest sense of duty in such a matter. Some days I have nothing which interests me sufficiently to write out, some days I feel either too ill or too indolent. For four days I have not written, from a mixture of all three reasons. Now, to-day I both feel like it and I have something to write. Also I am distinctly better than I have been. Perhaps the waters are benefiting me, or the change of air. Or possibly it is something else more subtle. Possibly my mind has seized upon something new, a discovery which causes it to react upon my failing body, and serves as a stimulant. All I know is, I feel distinctly better and am conscious of an acute interest in doing so, which is of late strange to me. I have been rather indifferent, and sometimes have wondered if that were not the cause rather than the result of my state of health. I have been so continually balked that I have settled into a state of inertia. I lean rather comfortably against my obstacles. After all, the worst of the pain always lies in the struggle. Give up, and it is rather pleasant than otherwise. If one did not kick, the pricks would not in the least matter. However, for some reason, for the last few days, I seem to have awakened from my state of quiescence. It means future trouble for me, no doubt, but in the meantime I am not sorry. It began with the picture—the large oil painting. I went to Mrs. Jennings about it yesterday, and she, to my surprise—for I thought it a matter that could be easily arranged—objected to having it removed. Her reasons were two; both simple, both sufficient, especially since I, after all, had no very strong desire either way. It seems that the picture does not belong to her. It hung here when she rented the house. She says if it is removed, a very large and unsightly discoloration of the wall-paper will be exposed, and she does not like to ask for new paper. The owner, an old man, is traveling abroad, the agent is curt, and she has only been in the house a very short time. Then it would mean a sad upheaval of my room, which would disturb me. She also says that there is no place in the house where she can store the picture, and there is not a vacant space in another room for one so large. So I let the picture remain. It really, when I came to think of it, was very immaterial after all. But I got my photographs out of my trunk, and I hung them around the large picture. The wall is almost completely covered. I hung them yesterday afternoon, and last night I repeated a strange experience which I have had in some degree every night since I have been here, but was not sure whether it deserved the name of experience but was not rather one of those dreams in which one dreams one is awake. But last night it came again, and now I know. There is something very singular about this room. I am very much interested. I will write down for future reference the events of last night. Concerning those of the preceding nights since I have slept in this room, I will simply say that they have been of a similar nature, but, as it were, only the preliminary stages, the prologue to what happened last night.

'I am not depending upon the mineral waters here as the one remedy for my malady, which is sometimes of an acute nature, and indeed constantly threatens me with considerable suffering unless by medicines I can keep it in check. I will say that the medicine which I employ is not of the class commonly known as drugs. It is impossible that it can be held responsible for what I am about to transcribe. My mind last night and every night since I have slept in this room was in an absolutely normal state. I take this medicine, prescribed by the specialist in whose charge I was before coming here, regularly every four hours while awake. As I am never a good sleeper, it follows that I am enabled with no inconvenience to take any medicine during the night with the same regularity as during the day. It is my habit, therefore, to place my bottle and spoon where I can put my hand upon them easily without lighting the gas. Since I have been in this room, I have placed the bottle of medicine upon my dresser at the side of the room opposite the bed. I have done this rather than place it nearer, as once I jostled the bottle and spilled most of the contents, and it is not easy for me to replace it, as it is expensive. Therefore I placed it in security on the dresser, and, indeed, that is but three or four steps from my bed, the room being so small. Last night I wakened as usual, and I knew, since I had fallen asleep about eleven, that it must be in the neighborhood of three. I wake with almost clock-like regularity, and it is never necessary for me to consult my watch.

'I had slept unusually well and without dreams, and I awoke fully at once, with a feeling of refreshment to which I am not accustomed. I immediately got out of bed and began stepping across the room in the direction of my dresser, on which I had set my medicine-bottle and spoon.

'To my utter amazement, the steps which had hitherto sufficed to take me across my room did not suffice to do so. I advanced several paces, and my outstretched hands touched nothing. I stopped and went on again. I was sure that I was moving in a straight direction, and even if I had not been I knew it was impossible to advance in any direction in my tiny apartment without coming into collision either with a wall or a piece of furniture. I continued to walk falteringly, as I have seen people on the stage: a step, then a long falter, then a sliding step. I kept my hands extended; they touched nothing. I stopped again. I had not the least sentiment of fear or consternation. It was rather the very stupefaction of surprise. "How is this?" seemed thundering in my ears. "What is this?"

'The room was perfectly dark. There was nowhere any glimmer, as is usually the case, even in a so-called dark room, from the walls, picture-frames, looking-glass or white objects. It was absolute gloom. The house stood in a quiet part of the town. There were many trees about; the electric street lights were extinguished at midnight; there was no moon and the sky was cloudy. I could not distinguish my one window, which I thought strange, even on such a dark night. Finally I changed my plan of motion and turned, as nearly as I could estimate, at right angles. Now, I thought, I must reach soon, if I kept on, my writing-table underneath the window; or, if I am going in the opposite direction, the hall door. I reached neither. I am telling the unvarnished truth when I say that I began to count my steps and carefully measure my paces after that, and I traversed a space clear of furniture at least twenty feet by thirty—a very large apartment. And as I walked I was conscious that my naked feet were pressing something which gave rise to sensations the like of which I had never experienced before. As nearly as I can express it, it was as if my feet pressed something as elastic as air or water, which was in this case unyielding to my weight. It gave me a curious sensation of buoyancy and stimulation. At the same time this surface, if surface be the right name, which I trod, felt cool to my feet with the coolness of vapor or fluidity, seeming to overlap the soles. Finally I stood still; my surprise was at last merging into a measure of consternation. "Where am I?" I thought. "What am I going to do?" Stories that I had heard of travelers being taken from their beds and conveyed into strange and dangerous places, Middle Age stories of the Inquisition* flashed through my brain. I knew all the time that for a man who had gone to bed in a commonplace hall bedroom in a very commonplace little town such surmises were highly ridiculous, but it is hard for the human mind to grasp anything but a human explanation of phenomena. Almost anything seemed then, and seems now, more rational than an explanation bordering upon the supernatural, as we understand the supernatural. At last I called, though rather softly. "What does this mean?" I said quite aloud. "Where am I? Who is here? Who is doing this? I tell you I will have no such nonsense. Speak, if there is anybody here." But all was dead silence. Then suddenly a light flashed through the open transom* of my door. Somebody had heard me—a man who rooms next door, a decent kind of man, also here for his health. He turned on the gas in the hall and called to me. "What's the matter?" he asked, in an agitated, trembling voice. He is a nervous fellow.

'Directly, when the light flashed through my transom, I saw that I was in my familiar hall bedroom. I could see everything quite distinctly—my tumbled bed, my writing-table, my dresser, my chair, my little wash-stand, my clothes hanging on a row of pegs, the old picture on the wall. The picture gleamed out with singular distinctness in the light from the transom. The river seemed actually to run and ripple, and the boat to be gliding with the current. I gazed fascinated at it, as I replied to the anxious voice:

' "Nothing is the matter with me," said I. "Why?"

' "I thought I heard you speak," said the man outside. "I thought maybe you were sick."

' "No," I called back. "I am all right. I am trying to find my medicine in the dark, that's all. I can see now you have lighted the gas."

' "Nothing is the matter?"

' "No; sorry I disturbed you. Good-night."

' "Good-night." Then I heard the man's door shut after a minute's pause. He was evidently not quite satisfied. I took a pull at my medicine-bottle, and got into bed. He had left the hall-gas burning. I did not go to sleep again for some time. Just before I did so, some one, probably Mrs. Jennings, came out in the hall and extinguished the gas. This morning when I awoke everything was as usual in my room. I wonder if I shall have any such experience to-night.

'January 27. I shall write in my journal every day until this draws to some definite issue. Last night my strange experience deepened, as something tells me it will continue to do. I retired quite early, at half-past ten. I took the precaution, on retiring, to place beside my bed, on a chair, a box of safety matches, that I might not be in the dilemma of the night before. I took my medicine on retiring; that made me due to wake at half-past two. I had not fallen asleep directly, but had had certainly three hours of sound, dreamless slumber when I awoke. I lay a few minutes hesitating whether or not to strike a safety match and light my way to the dresser, whereon stood my medicine-bottle. I hesitated, not because I had the least sensation of fear, but because of the same shrinking from a nerve shock that leads one at times to dread the plunge into an icy bath. It seemed much easier to me to strike that match and cross my hall bedroom to my dresser, take my dose, then return quietly to my bed, than to risk the chance of floundering about in some unknown limbo either of fancy or reality.

'At last, however, the spirit of adventure, which has always been such a ruling one for me, conquered. I rose. I took the box of safety matches in my hand and started on, as I conceived, the straight course for my dresser, about five feet across from my bed. As before, I traveled and traveled and did not reach it. I advanced with groping hands extended, setting one foot cautiously before the other, but I touched nothing except the indefinite, unnameable surface which my feet pressed. All of a sudden, though, I became aware of something. One of my senses was saluted, nay, more than that, hailed, with imperiousness, and that was, strangely enough, my sense of smell, but in a hitherto unknown fashion. It seemed as if the odor reached my mentality first. I reversed the usual process, which is, as I understand it, like this: the odor when encountered strikes first the olfactory nerve, which transmits the intelligence to the brain. It is as if, to put it rudely, my nose met a rose, and then the nerve belonging to the sense said to my brain, "Here is a rose." This time my brain said, "Here is a rose," and my sense then recognized it. I say rose, but it was not a rose, that is, not the fragrance of any rose which I had ever known. It was undoubtedly a flower-odor, and rose came perhaps the nearest to it. My mind realized it first with what seemed a leap of rapture. "What is this delight?" I asked myself. And then the ravishing fragrance smote my sense. I breathed it in and it seemed to feed my thoughts, satisfying some hitherto unknown hunger. Then I took a step further and another fragrance appeared, which I liken to lilies for lack of something better, and then came violets, then mignonette. I can not describe the experience, but it was a sheer delight, a rapture of sublimated sense. I groped further and further, and always into new waves of fragrance. I seemed to be wading breast-high through flower-beds of Paradise, but all the time I touched nothing with my groping hands. At last a sudden giddiness, as of surfeit, overcame me. I realized that I might be in some unknown peril. I was distinctly afraid. I struck one of my safety matches, and I was in my hall bedroom, midway between my bed and my dresser. I took my dose of medicine and went to bed, and after a while fell asleep and did not wake till morning.

'January 28. Last night I did not take my usual dose of medicine. In these days of new remedies and mysterious results upon certain organizations, it occurred to me to wonder if possibly the drug might have, after all, something to do with my strange experience. I did not take my medicine. I put the bottle as usual on my dresser, since I feared if I interrupted further the customary sequence of affairs I might fail to wake. I placed my box of matches on the chair beside the bed. I fell asleep about quarter past eleven o'clock, and I waked when the clock was striking two—a little earlier than my wont. I did not hesitate this time. I rose at once, took my box of matches and proceeded as formerly. I walked what seemed a great space without coming into collision with anything. I kept sniffing for the wonderful fragrances of the night before, but they did not recur. Instead, I was suddenly aware that I was tasting something, some morsel of sweetness hitherto unknown, and, as in the case of the odor, the usual order seemed reversed, and it was as if I tasted it first in my mental consciousness. Then the sweetness rolled under my tongue. I thought involuntarily of "Sweeter than honey or the honeycomb" of the Scripture. I thought of the Old Testament manna.* An ineffable content as of satisfied hunger seized me. I stepped further, and a new savor was upon my palate. And so on. It was never cloying, though of such sharp sweetness that it fairly stung. It was the merging of a material sense into a spiritual one. I said to myself, "I have lived my life and always have I gone hungry until now." I could feel my brain act swiftly under the influence of this heavenly food as under a stimulant. Then suddenly I repeated the experience of the night before. I grew dizzy, and an indefinite fear and shrinking were upon me. I struck my safety match and was back in my hall bedroom. I returned to bed, and soon fell asleep. I did not take my medicine. I am resolved not to do so longer. I am feeling much better.

'January 29. Last night to bed as usual, matches in place; fell asleep about eleven and waked at half-past one. I heard the half-hour strike; I am waking earlier and earlier every night. I had not taken my medicine, though it was on the dresser as usual. I again took my match-box in hand and started to cross the room, and, as always, traversed strange spaces, but this night, as seems fated to be the case every night, my experience was different. Last night I neither smelled nor tasted, but I heard—my Lord, I heard! The first sound of which I was conscious was one like the constantly gathering and receding murmur of a river, and it seemed to come from the wall behind my bed where the old picture hangs. Nothing in nature except a river gives that impression of at once advance and retreat. I could not mistake it. On, ever on, came the swelling murmur of the waves, past and ever past they died in the distance. Then I heard above the murmur of the river a song in an unknown tongue, which I recognized as being unknown yet which I understood; but the understanding was in my brain, with no words of interpretation. The song had to do with me, but with me in unknown futures for which I had no images of comparison in the past; yet a sort of ecstasy as of a prophecy of bliss filled my whole consciousness. The song never ceased, but as I moved on I came into new sound-waves. There was the pealing of bells which might have been made of crystal, and might have summoned to the gates of heaven. There was music of strange instruments, great harmonies pierced now and then by small whispers as of love, and it all filled me with a certainty of a future of bliss.

'At last I seemed the centre of a mighty orchestra which constantly deepened and increased until I seemed to feel myself being lifted gently but mightily upon the waves of sound as upon the waves of a sea. Then again the terror and the impulse to flee to my own familiar scenes was upon me. I struck my match, and was back in my hall bedroom. I do not see how I sleep at all after such wonders, but sleep I do. I slept dreamlessly until daylight this morning.

'January 30. I heard yesterday something with regard to my hall bedroom which affected me strangely. I can not for the life of me say whether it intimidated me, filled me with the horror of the abnormal, or rather roused to a greater degree my spirit of adventure and discovery. I was down at the Cure,* and was sitting on the veranda sipping idly my mineral water, when somebody spoke my name. "Mr. Wheatcroft?" said the voice politely, interrogatively, somewhat apologetically, as if to provide for a possible mistake in my identity. I turned and saw a gentleman whom I recognized at once. I seldom forget names or faces. He was a Mr. Addison whom I had seen considerable of three years ago at a little summer hotel in the mountains. It was one of those passing acquaintances which signify little one way or the other. If never renewed, you have no regret; if renewed, you accept the renewal with no hesitation. It is in every way negative. But just now, in my feeble, friendless state, the sight of a face which beams with pleased remembrance is rather grateful. I felt distinctly glad to see the man. He sat down beside me. He also had a glass of the water. His health, while not as bad as mine, leaves much to be desired.

'Addison had often been in this town before. He had in fact lived here at one time. He had remained at the Cure three years, taking the waters daily. He therefore knows about all there is to be known about the town, which is not very large. He asked me where I was staying, and when I told him the street, rather excitedly inquired the number. When I told him the number, which is 240, he gave a manifest start, and after one sharp glance at me sipped his water in silence for a moment. He had so evidently betrayed some ulterior knowledge with regard to my residence that I questioned him.

'"What do you know about 240 Pleasant Street?" said I.

'"Oh, nothing," he replied, evasively sipping his water.

'After a little while, however, he inquired, in what he evidently tried to render a casual tone, what room I occupied. "I once lived a few weeks at 240 Pleasant Street myself," he said. "That house always was a boarding-house, I guess."

'"It had stood vacant for a term of years before the present occupant rented it, I believe," I remarked. Then I answered his question. "I have the hall bedroom on the third floor," said I. "The quarters are pretty straitened, but comfortable enough as hall bedrooms go."

'But Mr. Addison had showed such unmistakable consternation at my reply, that then I persisted in my questioning as to the cause, and at last he yielded and told me what he knew. He had hesitated both because he shrank from displaying what I might consider an unmanly superstition, and because he did not wish to influence me beyond what the facts of the case warranted. "Well, I will tell you, Wheatcroft," he said. "Briefly all I know is this: When last I heard of 240 Pleasant Street it was not rented because of foul play which was supposed to have taken place there, though nothing was ever proved. There were two disappearances, and—in each case—of an occupant of the hall bedroom which you now have. The first disappearance was of a very beautiful girl who had come here for her health and was said to be the victim of a profound melancholy, induced by a love disappointment. She obtained board at 240 and occupied the hall bedroom about two weeks; then one morning she was gone, having seemingly vanished into thin air. Her relatives were communicated with; she had not many, nor friends either, poor girl, and a thorough search was made, but the last I knew she had never come to light. There were two or three arrests, but nothing ever came of them. Well, that was before my day here, but the second disappearance took place when I was in the house—a fine young fellow who had overworked in college. He had to pay his own way. He had taken cold, had the grip, and that and the overwork about finished him, and he came on here for a month's rest and recuperation. He had been in that room about two weeks, a little less, when one morning he wasn't there. Then there was a great hullabaloo. It seems that he had let fall some hints to the effect that there was something queer about the room, but, of course, the police did not think much of that. They made arrests right and left, but they never found him, and the arrested were discharged, though some of them are probably under a cloud of suspicion to this day. Then the boarding-house was shut up. Six years ago nobody would have boarded there, much less occupied that hall bedroom, but now I suppose new people have come in and the story has died out. I dare say your landlady will not thank me for reviving it."

'I assured him that it would make no possible difference to me. He looked at me sharply, and asked bluntly if I had seen anything wrong or unusual about the room. I replied, guarding myself from falsehood with a quibble, that I had seen nothing in the least unusual about the room, as indeed I had not, and have not now, but that may come. I feel that that will come in due time. Last night I neither saw, nor heard, nor smelled, nor tasted, but I—*felt*. Last night, having started again on my exploration of, God knows what, I had not advanced a step before I touched something. My first sensation was one of disappointment. "It is the dresser, and I am at the end of it now," I thought. But I soon discovered that it was not the old painted dresser which I touched, but something carved, as nearly as I could discover with my unskilled finger-tips, with winged things. There were certainly long keen curves of wings which seemed to overlay an arabesque of fine leaf and flower work. I do not know what the object was that I touched. It may have been a chest. I may seem to be exaggerating when I say that it somehow failed or exceeded in some mysterious respect of being the shape of anything I had ever touched. I do not know what the material was. It was as smooth as ivory, but it did not feel like ivory; there was a singular warmth about it, as if it had stood long in hot sunlight. I continued, and I encountered other objects I am inclined to think were pieces of furniture of fashions and possibly of uses unknown to me, and about them all was the strange mystery as to shape. At last I came to what was evidently an open window of large area. I distinctly felt a soft, warm wind, yet with a crystal freshness, blow on my face. It was not the window of my hall bedroom, that I know. Looking out, I could see nothing. I only felt the wind blowing on my face.

'Then suddenly, without any warning, my groping hands to the right and left touched living beings, beings in the likeness of men and women, palpable creatures in palpable attire. I could feel the soft silken texture of their garments which swept around me, seeming to half infold me in clinging meshes like cobwebs. I was in a crowd of these people, whatever they were, and whoever they were, but, curiously enough, without seeing one of them I had a strong sense of recognition as I passed among them. Now and then a hand that I knew closed softly over mine; once an arm passed around me. Then I began to feel myself gently swept on and impelled by this softly moving throng; their floating garments seemed to fairly wind me about, and again a swift terror overcame me. I struck my match, and was back in my hall bedroom. I wonder if I had not better keep my gas burning to-night? I wonder if it be possible that this is going too far? I wonder what became of those other people, the man and the woman who occupied this room? I wonder if I had better not stop where I am?

'January 31. Last night I saw—I saw more than I can describe, more than is lawful to describe. Something which nature has rightfully hidden has been revealed to me, but it is not for me to disclose too much of her secret. This much I will say, that doors and windows open into an out-of-doors to which the outdoors which we know is but a vestibule. And there is a river; there is something strange with respect to that picture. There is a river upon which one could sail away. It was flowing silently, for to-night I could only see. I saw that I was right in thinking I recognized some of the people whom I encountered the night before, though some were strange to me. It is true that the girl who disappeared from the hall bedroom was very beautiful. Everything which I saw last night was very beautiful to my one sense that could grasp it. I wonder what it would all be if all my senses together were to grasp it? I wonder if I had better not keep my gas burning to-night? I wonder—'

This finishes the journal which Mr. Wheatcroft left in his hall bedroom. The morning after the last entry he was gone. His friend, Mr. Addison, came here, and a search was made. They even tore down the wall behind the picture, and they did find something rather queer for a house that had been used for boarders, where you would think no room would have been let run to waste. They found another room, a long narrow one, the length of the hall bedroom, but narrower, hardly more than a closet. There was no window, nor door, and all there was in it was a sheet of paper covered with figures, as if somebody had been doing sums. They made a lot of talk about those figures, and they tried to make out that the fifth dimension,* whatever that is, was proved, but they said afterward they didn't prove anything. They tried to make out then that somebody had murdered poor Mr. Wheatcroft and hid the body, and they arrested poor Mr. Addison, but they couldn't make out anything against him. They proved he was in the Cure all that night and couldn't have done it. They don't know what became of Mr. Wheatcroft, and now they say two more disappeared from that same room before I rented the house.

The agent came and promised to put the new room they discovered into the hall bedroom and have everything new—papered and painted. He took away the picture; folks hinted there was something queer about that, I don't know what. It looked innocent enough, and I guess he burned it up. He said if I would stay he would arrange it with the owner, who everybody says is a very queer man, so I should not have to pay much if any rent. But I told him I couldn't stay if he was to give me the rent. That I wasn't afraid of anything myself, though I must say I wouldn't want to put anybody in that hall bedroom without telling him all about it; but my boarders would leave, and I knew I couldn't get any more. I told him I would rather have had a regular ghost than what seemed to be a way of going out of the house to nowhere and never coming back again. I moved, and, as I said before, it remains to be seen whether my ill luck follows me to this house or not. Anyway, it has no hall bedroom.

H. G. WELLS

THE COUNTRY OF THE BLIND

THREE hundred miles and more from Chimborazo, one hundred from the snows of Cotopaxi, in the wildest wastes of Ecuador's Andes,* there lies that mysterious mountain valley, cut off from the world of men, the Country of the Blind. Long years ago that valley lay so far open to the world that men might come at last through frightful gorges and over an icy pass into its equable meadows; and thither indeed men came, a family or so of Peruvian half-breeds fleeing from the lust and tyranny of an evil Spanish ruler. Then came the stupendous outbreak of Mindobamba, when it was night in Quito for seventeen days, and the water was boiling at Yaguachi and all the fish floating dying even as far as Guayaquil;* everywhere along the Pacific slopes there were land-slips and swift thawings and sudden floods, and one whole side of the old Arauca crest* slipped and came down in thunder, and cut off the Country of the Blind for ever from the exploring feet of men. But one of these early settlers had chanced to be on the hither side of the gorges when the world had so terribly shaken itself, and he perforce had to forget his wife and his child and all the friends and possessions he had left up there, and start life over again in the lower world. He started it again but ill, blindness overtook him, and he died of punishment in the mines; but the story he told begot a legend that lingers along the length of the Cordilleras of the Andes to this day.

He told of his reason for venturing back from that fastness, into which he had first been carried lashed to a llama, beside a vast bale of gear, when he was a child. The valley, he said, had in it all that the heart of man could desire—sweet water, pasture, and even climate, slopes of rich brown soil with tangles of a shrub that bore an excellent fruit, and on one side great hanging forests of pine that held the avalanches high. Far overhead, on three sides, vast cliffs of grey-green rock were capped by cliffs of ice; but the glacier stream came not to them but flowed away by the farther slopes, and only now and then huge ice masses fell on the valley side. In this valley it neither rained nor snowed, but the abundant springs gave a rich green pasture, that irrigation would spread over all the valley space. The settlers did well indeed there. Their beasts did well and multiplied, and but one thing marred their happiness. Yet it was enough to mar it greatly. A strange disease had come upon them, and had made all the children born to them there—and indeed, several older children also—blind. It was to seek some charm or antidote against this plague of blindness that he had with fatigue and danger and difficulty returned down the gorge. In those days, in such cases, men did not think of germs and infections but of sins; and it seemed to him that the reason of this affliction must lie in the negligence of these priestless immigrants to set up a shrine so soon as they entered the valley. He wanted a shrine— a handsome, cheap, effectual shrine—to be erected in the valley; he wanted relics and such-like potent things of faith, blessed objects and mysterious medals and prayers. In his wallet he had a bar of native silver for which he would not account; he insisted there was none in the valley with something of the insistence of an inexpert liar. They had all clubbed their money and ornaments together, having little need for such treasure up there, he said, to buy them holy help against their ill. I figure this dim-eyed young mountaineer, sunburnt, gaunt, and anxious, hat-brim clutched feverishly, a man all unused to the ways of the lower world, telling this story to some keen-eyed, attentive priest before the great convulsion; I can picture him presently seeking to return with pious and infallible remedies against that trouble, and the infinite dismay with which he must have faced the tumbled vastness where the gorge had once come out. But the rest of his story of mischances is lost to me, save that I know of his evil death after several years. Poor stray from that remoteness! The stream that had once made the gorge now bursts from the mouth of a rocky cave, and the legend his poor, ill-told story set going developed into the legend of a race of blind men somewhere 'over there' one may still hear to-day.

And amidst the little population of that now isolated and forgotten valley the disease ran its course. The old became groping and purblind, the young saw but dimly, and the children that were born to them saw never at all. But life was very easy in that snow-rimmed basin, lost to all the world, with neither thorns nor briars, with no evil insects nor any beasts save the gentle breed of llamas they had lugged and thrust and followed up the beds of the shrunken rivers in the gorges up which they had come. The seeing had become purblind so gradually that they scarcely noted their loss. They guided the sightless youngsters hither and thither until they knew the whole valley marvellously, and when at last sight died out among them the race lived on. They had even time to adapt themselves to the blind control of fire, which they made carefully in stoves of stone. They were a simple strain of people at the first, unlettered, only slightly touched with the Spanish civilisation, but with something of a tradition of the arts of old Peru and of its lost philosophy. Generation followed generation. They forgot many things; they devised many things. Their tradition of the greater world they came from became mythical in colour and uncertain. In all things save sight they were strong and able, and presently the chance of birth and heredity sent one who had an original mind and who could talk and persuade among them, and then afterwards another. These two passed, leaving their effects, and the little community grew in numbers and in understanding, and met and settled social and economic problems that arose. Generation followed generation. Generation followed generation. There came a time when a child was born who was fifteen generations from that ancestor who went out of the valley with a bar of silver to seek God's aid, and who never returned. Thereabouts it chanced that a man came into this community from the outer world. And this is the story of that man.

He was a mountaineer from the country near Quito, a man who had been down to the sea and had seen the world, a reader of books in an original way, an acute and enterprising man, and he was taken on by a party of Englishmen who had come out to Ecuador to climb mountains, to replace one of their three Swiss guides who had fallen ill. He climbed here and he climbed there, and then came the attempt on Parascotopetl, the Matterhorn of the Andes,* in which he was lost to the outer world. The story of the accident has been written a dozen times. Pointer's narrative is the best. He tells how the little party worked their difficult and almost vertical way up to the very foot of the last and greatest precipice, and how they built a night shelter amidst the snow upon a little shelf of rock, and, with a touch of real dramatic power, how presently they found Nunez had gone from them. They shouted, and there was no reply; shouted and whistled, and for the rest of that night they slept no more.

As the morning broke they saw the traces of his fall. It seems impossible he could have uttered a sound. He had slipped eastward towards the unknown side of the mountain; far below he had struck a steep slope of snow, and ploughed his way down it in the midst of a snow avalanche. His track went straight to the edge of a frightful precipice, and beyond that everything was hidden. Far, far below, and hazy with distance, they could see trees rising out of a narrow, shut-in valley—the lost Country of the Blind. But they did not know it was the lost Country of the Blind, nor distinguish it in any way from any other narrow streak of upland valley. Unnerved by this disaster, they abandoned their attempt in the afternoon, and Pointer was called away to the war before he could make another attack. To this day Parascotopetl lifts an unconquered crest, and Pointer's shelter crumbles unvisited amidst the snows.

And the man who fell survived.

At the end of the slope he fell a thousand feet, and came down in the midst of a cloud of snow upon a snow slope even steeper than the one above. Down this he was whirled, stunned and insensible, but without a bone broken in his body; and then at last came to gentler slopes, and at last rolled out and lay still, buried amidst a softening heap of the white masses that had accompanied and saved him. He came to himself with a dim fancy that he was ill in bed; then realised his position with a mountaineer's intelligence, and worked himself loose and, after a rest or so, out until he saw the stars. He rested flat upon his chest for a space, wondering where he was and what had happened to him. He explored his limbs, and discovered that several of his buttons were gone and his coat turned over his head. His knife had gone from his pocket and his hat was lost, though he had tied it under his chin. He recalled that he had been looking for loose stones to raise his piece of the shelter wall. His ice-axe had disappeared.

He decided he must have fallen, and looked up to see, exaggerated by the ghastly light of the rising moon, the tremendous flight he had taken. For a while he lay, gazing blankly at that vast pale cliff towering above, rising moment by moment out of a subsiding tide of darkness. Its phantasmal, mysterious beauty held him for a space, and then he was seized with a paroxysm of sobbing laughter. . . .

After a great interval of time he became aware that he was near the lower edge of the snow. Below, down what was now a moonlit and practicable slope, he saw the dark and broken appearance of rock-strewn turf. He struggled to his feet, aching in every joint and limb, got down painfully from the heaped loose snow about him, went downward until he was on the turf, and there dropped rather than lay beside a boulder, drank deep from the flask in his inner pocket, and instantly fell asleep. . . .

He was awakened by the singing of birds in the trees far below.

He sat up and perceived he was on a little alp at the foot of a vast precipice, that was grooved by the gully down which he and his snow had come. Over against him another wall of rock reared itself against the sky. The gorge between these precipices ran east and west and was full of the morning sunlight, which lit to the westward the mass of fallen mountain that closed the descending gorge. Below him it seemed there was a precipice equally steep, but behind the snow in the gully he found a sort of chimney-cleft dripping with snow-water down which a desperate man might venture. He found it easier than it seemed, and came at last to another desolate alp, and then after a rock climb of no particular difficulty to a steep slope of trees. He took his bearings and turned his face up the gorge, for he saw it opened out above upon green meadows, among which he now glimpsed quite distinctly a cluster of stone huts of unfamiliar fashion. At times his progress was like clambering along the face of a wall, and after a time the rising sun ceased to strike along the gorge, the voices of the singing birds died away, and the air grew cold and dark about him. But the distant valley with its houses was all the brighter for that. He came presently to talus,* and among the rocks he noted—for he was an observant man—an unfamiliar fern that seemed to clutch out of the crevices with intense green hands. He picked a frond or so and gnawed its stalk and found it helpful.

About midday he came at last out of the throat of the gorge into the plain and the sunlight. He was stiff and weary; he sat down in the shadow of a rock, filled up his flask with water from a spring and drank it down, and remained for a time resting before he went on to the houses.

They were very strange to his eyes, and indeed the whole aspect of that valley became, as he regarded it, queerer and more unfamiliar. The greater part of its surface was lush green meadow, starred with many beautiful flowers, irrigated with extraordinary care, and bearing evidence of systematic cropping piece by piece. High up and ringing the valley about was a wall, and what appeared to be a circumferential water-channel, from which the little trickles of water that fed the meadow plants came, and on the higher slopes above this flocks of llamas cropped the scanty herbage. Sheds, apparently shelters or feeding-places for the llamas, stood against the boundary wall here and there. The irrigation streams ran together into a main channel down the centre of the valley, and this was enclosed on either side by a wall breast high. This gave a singularly urban quality to this secluded place, a quality that was greatly enhanced by the fact that a number of paths paved with black and white stones, and each with a curious little kerb at the side, ran hither and thither in an orderly manner. The houses of the central village were quite unlike the casual and higgledy-piggledy agglomeration of the mountain villages he knew; they stood in a continuous row on either side of a central street of astonishing cleanness; here and there their parti-coloured facade was pierced by a door, and not a solitary window broke their even frontage. They were parti-coloured with extraordinary irregularity, smeared with a sort of plaster that was sometimes grey, sometimes drab, sometimes slate-coloured or dark brown; and it was the sight of this wild plastering first brought the word 'blind' into the thoughts of the explorer. 'The good man who did that,' he thought, 'must have been as blind as a bat.'

He descended a steep place, and so came to the wall and channel that ran about the valley, near where the latter spouted out its surplus contents into the deeps of the gorge in a thin and wavering thread of cascade. He could now see a number of men and women resting on piled heaps of grass, as if taking a siesta, in the remoter part of the meadow, and nearer the village a number of recumbent children, and then nearer at hand three men carrying pails on yokes along a little path that ran from the encircling wall towards the houses. These latter were clad in garments of llama cloth and boots and belts of leather, and they wore caps of cloth with back and ear flaps. They followed one another in single file, walking slowly and yawning as they walked, like men who have been up all night. There was something so reassuringly prosperous and respectable in their bearing that after a moment's hesitation Nunez stood forward as conspicuously as possible upon his rock, and gave vent to a mighty shout that echoed round the valley.

The three men stopped, and moved their heads as though they were looking about them. They turned their faces this way and that, and Nunez gesticulated with freedom. But they did not appear to see him for all his gestures, and after a time, directing themselves towards the mountains far away to the right, they shouted as if in answer. Nunez bawled again, and then once more, and as he gestured ineffectually the word 'blind' came up to the top of his thoughts. 'The fools must be blind,' he said.

When at last, after much shouting and wrath, Nunez crossed the stream by a little bridge, came through a gate in the wall, and approached them, he was sure that they were blind. He was sure that this was the Country of the Blind of which the legends told. Conviction had sprung upon him, and a sense of great and rather enviable adventure. The three stood side by side, not looking at him, but with their ears directed towards him, judging him by his unfamiliar steps. They stood close together like men a little afraid, and he could see their eyelids closed and sunken, as though the very balls beneath had shrunk away. There was an expression near awe on their faces.

'A man,' one said, in hardly recognisable Spanish—'a man it is— a man or a spirit—coming down from the rocks.'

But Nunez advanced with the confident steps of a youth who enters upon life. All the old stories of the lost valley and the Country of the Blind had come back to his mind, and through his thoughts ran this old proverb, as if it were a refrain—

'In the Country of the Blind the One-eyed Man is King.'*

'In the Country of the Blind the One-eyed Man is King.'

And very civilly he gave them greeting. He talked to them and used his eyes.

'Where does he come from, brother Pedro?' asked one.

'Down out of the rocks.'

'Over the mountains I come,' said Nunez, 'out of the country beyond there—where men can see. From near Bogota,* where there are a hundred thousands of people, and where the city passes out of sight.'

'Sight?' muttered Pedro. 'Sight?'

'He comes,' said the second blind man, 'out of the rocks.'

The cloth of their coats Nunez saw was curiously fashioned, each with a different sort of stitching.

They startled him by a simultaneous movement towards him, each with a hand outstretched. He stepped back from the advance of these spread fingers.

'Come hither,' said the third blind man, following his motion and clutching him neatly.

And they held Nunez and felt him over, saying no word further until they had done so.

'Carefully,' he cried, with a finger in his eye, and found they thought that organ, with its fluttering lids, a queer thing in him. They went over it again.

'A strange creature, Correa,' said the one called Pedro. 'Feel the coarseness of his hair. Like a llama's hair.'

'Rough he is as the rocks that begot him,' said Correa, investigating Nunez's unshaven chin with a soft and slightly moist hand. 'Perhaps he will grow finer.' Nunez struggled a little under their examination, but they gripped him firm.

'Carefully,' he said again.

'He speaks,' said the third man. 'Certainly he is a man.'

'Ugh!' said Pedro, at the roughness of his coat.

'And you have come into the world?' asked Pedro.

'*Out* of the world. Over mountains and glaciers; right over above there, half-way to the sun. Out of the great big world that goes down, twelve days' journey to the sea.'

They scarcely seemed to heed him. 'Our fathers have told us men may be made by the forces of Nature,' said Correa. 'It is the warmth of things and moisture, and rottenness—rottenness.'

'Let us lead him to the elders,' said Pedro.

'Shout first,' said Correa, 'lest the children be afraid. This is a marvellous occasion.'

So they shouted, and Pedro went first and took Nunez by the hand to lead him to the houses.

He drew his hand away. 'I can see,' he said.

'See?' said Correa.

'Yes, see,' said Nunez, turning towards him, and stumbled against Pedro's pail.

'His senses are still imperfect,' said the third blind man. 'He stumbles, and talks unmeaning words. Lead him by the hand.'

'As you will,' said Nunez, and was led along, laughing.

It seemed they knew nothing of sight.

Well, all in good time he would teach them.

He heard people shouting, and saw a number of figures gathering together in the middle roadway of the village.

He found it tax his nerve and patience more than he had anticipated, that first encounter with the population of the Country of the Blind. The place seemed larger as he drew near to it, and the smeared plasterings queerer, and a crowd of children and men and women (the women and girls, he was pleased to note, had some of them quite sweet faces, for all that their eyes were shut and sunken) came about him, holding on to him, touching him with soft, sensitive hands, smelling at him, and listening at every word he spoke. Some of the maidens and children, however, kept aloof as if afraid, and indeed his voice seemed coarse and rude beside their softer notes. They mobbed him. His three guides kept close to him with an effect of proprietorship, and said again and again, 'A wild man out of the rocks.'

'Bogota,' he said. 'Bogota. Over the mountain crests.'

'A wild man—using wild words,' said Pedro. 'Did you hear that—*Bogota*? His mind is hardly formed yet. He has only the beginnings of speech.'

A little boy nipped his hand. 'Bogota!' he said mockingly.

'Ay! A city to your village. I come from the great world—where men have eyes and see.'

'His name's Bogota,' they said.

'He stumbled,' said Correa, 'stumbled twice as we came hither.'

'Bring him to the elders.'

And they thrust him suddenly through a doorway into a room as black as pitch, save at the end there faintly glowed a fire. The crowd closed in behind him and shut out all but the faintest glimmer of day, and before he could arrest himself he had fallen headlong over the feet of a seated man. His arm, outflung, struck the face of someone else as he went down; he felt the soft impact of features and heard a cry of anger, and for a moment he struggled against a number of hands that clutched him. It was a one-sided fight. An inkling of the situation came to him, and he lay quiet.

'I fell down,' he said; 'I couldn't see in this pitchy darkness.'

There was a pause as if the unseen persons about him tried to understand his words. Then the voice of Correa said: 'He is but newly formed. He stumbles as he walks and mingles words that mean nothing with his speech.'

Others also said things about him that he heard or understood imperfectly.

'May I sit up?' he asked, in a pause. 'I will not struggle against you again.'

They consulted and let him rise.

The voice of an older man began to question him, and Nunez found himself trying to explain the great world out of which he had fallen, and the sky and mountains and sight and such-like marvels, to these elders who sat in darkness in the Country of the Blind. And they would believe and understand nothing whatever he told them, a thing quite outside his expectation. They would not even understand many of his words. For fourteen generations these people had been blind and cut off from all the seeing world; the names for all the things of sight had faded and changed; the story of the outer world was faded and changed to a child's story; and they had ceased to concern themselves with anything beyond the rocky slopes above their circling wall. Blind men of genius had arisen among them and questioned the shreds of belief and tradition they had brought with them from their seeing days, and had dismissed all these things as idle fancies, and replaced them with new and saner explanations. Much of their imagination had shrivelled with their eyes, and they had made for themselves new imaginations with their ever more sensitive ears and finger-tips. Slowly Nunez realised this; that his expectation of wonder and reverence at his origin and his gifts was not to be borne out; and after his poor attempt to explain sight to them had been set aside as the confused version of a new-made being describing the marvels of his incoherent sensations, he subsided, a little dashed, into listening to their instruction. And the eldest of the blind men explained to him life and philosophy and religion, how that the world (meaning their valley) had been first an empty hollow in the rocks, and then had come, first, inanimate things without the gift of touch, and llamas and a few other creatures that had little sense, and then men, and at last angels, whom one could hear singing and making fluttering sounds, but whom no one could touch at all, which puzzled Nunez greatly until he thought of the birds.

He went on to tell Nunez how this time had been divided into the warm and the cold, which are the blind equivalents of day and night, and how it was good to sleep in the warm and work during the cold, so that now, but for his advent, the whole town of the blind would have been asleep. He said Nunez must have been specially created to learn and serve the wisdom they had acquired, and that for all his mental incoherency and stumbling behaviour he must have courage, and do his best to learn, and at that all the people in the doorway murmured encouragingly. He said the night—for the blind call their day night—was now far gone, and it behoved every one to go back to sleep. He asked Nunez if he knew how to sleep, and Nunez said he did, but that before sleep he wanted food.

They brought him food—llama's milk in a bowl, and rough salted bread—and led him into a lonely place to eat out of their hearing, and afterwards to slumber until the chill of the mountain evening roused them to begin their day again. But Nunez slumbered not at all.

Instead, he sat up in the place where they had left him, resting his limbs and turning the unanticipated circumstances of his arrival over and over in his mind.

Every now and then he laughed, sometimes with amusement, and sometimes with indignation.

'Unformed mind!' he said. 'Got no senses yet! They little know they've been insulting their heaven-sent king and master. I see I must bring them to reason. Let me think—let me think.'

He was still thinking when the sun set.

Nunez had an eye for all beautiful things, and it seemed to him that the glow upon the snowfields and glaciers that rose about the valley on every side was the most beautiful thing he had ever seen. His eyes went from that inaccessible glory to the village and irrigated fields, fast sinking into the twilight, and suddenly a wave of emotion took him, and he thanked God from the bottom of his heart that the power of sight had been given him.

He heard a voice calling to him from out of the village. 'Ya ho there, Bogota! Come hither!'

At that he stood up smiling. He would show these people once and for all what sight would do for a man. They would seek him, but not find him.

'You move not, Bogota,' said the voice.

He laughed noiselessly, and made two stealthy steps aside from the path.

'Trample not on the grass, Bogota; that is not allowed.'

Nunez had scarcely heard the sound he made himself. He stopped amazed.

The owner of the voice came running up the piebald path towards him.

He stepped back into the pathway. 'Here I am,' he said.

'Why did you not come when I called you?' said the blind man. 'Must you be led like a child? Cannot you hear the path as you walk?'

Nunez laughed. 'I can see it,' he said.

'There is no such word as *see*,' said the blind man, after a pause. 'Cease this folly, and follow the sound of my feet.'

Nunez followed, a little annoyed.

'My time will come,' he said.

'You'll learn,' the blind man answered. 'There is much to learn in the world.'

'Has no one told you, "In the Country of the Blind the One-eyed Man is King"?'

'What is blind?' asked the blind man carelessly over his shoulder.

Four days passed, and the fifth found the King of the Blind still incognito, as a clumsy and useless stranger among his subjects.

It was, he found, much more difficult to proclaim himself than he had supposed, and in the meantime, while he meditated his *coup d'état*, he did what he was told and learnt the manners and customs of the Country of the Blind. He found working and going about at night a particularly irksome thing, and he decided that that should be the first thing he would change.

They led a simple, laborious life, these people, with all the elements of virtue and happiness, as these things can be understood by men. They toiled, but not oppressively; they had food and clothing sufficient for their needs; they had days and seasons of rest; they made much of music and singing, and there was love among them, and little children.

It was marvellous with what confidence and precision they went about their ordered world. Everything, you see, had been made to fit their needs; each of the radiating paths of the valley area had a constant angle to the others, and was distinguished by a special notch upon its kerbing; all obstacles and irregularities of path or meadow had long since been cleared away; all their methods and procedure arose naturally from their special needs. Their senses had become marvellously acute; they could hear and judge the slightest gesture of a man a dozen paces away—could hear the very beating of his heart. Intonation had long replaced expression with them, and touches gesture, and their work with hoe and spade and fork was as free and confident as garden work can be. Their sense of smell was extraordinarily fine; they could distinguish individual differences as readily as a dog can. and they went about the tending of the llamas, who lived among the rocks above and came to the wall for food and shelter, with ease and confidence. It was only when at last Nunez sought to assert himself that he found how easy and confident their movements could be.

He rebelled only after he had tried persuasion.

He tried at first on several occasions to tell them of sight. 'Look you here, you people,' he said. 'There are things you do not understand in me.'

Once or twice one or two of them attended to him; they sat with faces downcast and ears turned intelligently towards him, and he did his best to tell them what it was to see. Among his hearers was a girl, with eyelids less red and sunken than the others, so that one could almost fancy she was hiding eyes, whom especially he hoped to persuade. He spoke of the beauties of sight, of watching the mountains, of the sky and the sunrise, and they heard him with amused incredulity that presently became condemnatory. They told him there were indeed no mountains at all, but that the end of the rocks where the llamas grazed was indeed the end of the world; thence sprang a cavernous roof of the universe, from which the dew and the avalanches fell; and when he maintained stoutly the world had neither end nor roof such as they supposed, they said his thoughts were wicked. So far as he could describe sky and clouds and stars to them it seemed to them a hideous void, a terrible blankness in the place of the smooth roof to things in which they believed—it was an article of faith with them that the cavern roof was exquisitely smooth to the touch. He saw that in some manner he shocked them, and gave up that aspect of the matter altogether, and tried to show them the practical value of sight. One morning he saw Pedro in the path called Seventeen and coming towards the central houses, but still too far off for hearing or scent, and he told them as much. 'In a little while,' he prophesied, 'Pedro will be here.' An old man remarked that Pedro had no business on path Seventeen, and then, as if in confirmation, that individual as he drew near turned and went transversely into path Ten, and so back with nimble paces towards the outer wall. They mocked Nunez when Pedro did not arrive, and afterwards, when he asked Pedro questions to clear his character, Pedro denied and outfaced him, and was afterwards hostile to him.

Then he induced them to let him go a long way up the sloping meadows towards the wall with one complacent individual, and to him he promised to describe all that happened among the houses. He noted certain goings and comings, but the things that really seemed to signify to these people happened inside of or behind the windowless houses—the only things they took note of to test him by—and of these he could see or tell nothing; and it was after the failure of this attempt, and the ridicule they could not repress, that he resorted to force. He thought of seizing a spade and suddenly smiting one or two of them to earth, and so in fair combat showing the advantage of eyes. He went so far with that resolution as to seize his spade, and then he discovered a new thing about himself, and that was that it was impossible for him to hit a blind man in cold blood.

He hesitated, and found them all aware that he had snatched up the spade. They stood alert, with their heads on one side, and bent ears towards him for what he would do next.

'Put that spade down,' said one, and he felt a sort of helpless horror. He came near obedience.

Then he thrust one backwards against a house wall, and fled past him and out of the village.

He went athwart one of their meadows, leaving a track of trampled grass behind his feet, and presently sat down by the side of one of their ways. He felt something of the buoyancy that comes to all men in the beginning of a fight, but more perplexity. He began to realise that you cannot even fight happily with creatures who stand upon a different mental basis to yourself. Far away he saw a number of men carrying spades and sticks come out of the street of houses, and advance in a spreading line along the several paths towards him. They advanced slowly, speaking frequently to one another, and ever and again the whole cordon would halt and sniff the air and listen.

The first time they did this Nunez laughed. But afterwards he did not laugh.

One struck his trail in the meadow grass, and came stooping and feeling his way along it.

For five minutes he watched the slow extension of the cordon, and then his vague disposition to do something forthwith became frantic. He stood up, went a pace or so towards the circumferential wall, turned, and went back a little way. There they all stood in a crescent, still and listening.

He also stood still, gripping his spade very tightly in both hands. Should he charge them?

The pulse in his ears ran into the rhythm of 'In the Country of the Blind the One-eyed Man is King!'

Should he charge them?

He looked back at the high and unclimbable wall behind—unclimbable because of its smooth plastering, but withal pierced with many little doors, and at the approaching line of seekers. Behind these others were now coming out of the street of houses.

Should he charge them?

'Bogota!' called one. 'Bogota! where are you?'

He gripped his spade still tighter, and advanced down the meadows towards the place of habitations, and directly he moved they converged upon him. 'I'll hit them if they touch me,' he swore; 'by Heaven, I will. I'll hit.' He called aloud, 'Look here, I'm going to do what I like in this valley. Do you hear? I'm going to do what I like and go where I like!'

They were moving in upon him quickly, groping, yet moving rapidly. It was like playing blind man's buff, with everyone blindfolded except one. 'Get hold of him!' cried one. He found himself in the arc of a loose curve of pursuers. He felt suddenly he must be active and resolute.

'You don't understand,' he cried in a voice that was meant to be great and resolute, and which broke. 'You are blind, and I can see. Leave me alone!'

'Bogota! Put down that spade, and come off the grass!'

The last order, grotesque in its urban familiarity, produced a gust of anger.

'I'll hurt you,' he said, sobbing with emotion. 'By Heaven, I'll hurt you. Leave me alone!'

He began to run, not knowing clearly where to run. He ran from the nearest blind man, because it was a horror to hit him. He stopped, and then made a dash to escape from their closing ranks. He made for where a gap was wide, and the men on either side, with a quick perception of the approach of his paces, rushed in on one another. He sprang forward, and then saw he must be caught, and *swish*! the spade had struck. He felt the soft thud of hand and arm, and the man was down with a yell of pain, and he was through.

Through! And then he was close to the street of houses again, and blind men, whirling spades and stakes, were running with a sort of reasoned swiftness hither and thither.

He heard steps behind him just in time, and found a tall man rushing forward and swiping at the sound of him. He lost his nerve, hurled his spade a yard wide at his antagonist, and whirled about and fled, fairly yelling as he dodged another.

He was panic-stricken. He ran furiously to and fro, dodging when there was no need to dodge, and in his anxiety to see on every side of him at once, stumbling. For a moment he was down and they heard his fall. Far away in the circumferential wall a little doorway looked like heaven, and he set off in a wild rush for it. He did not even look round at his pursuers until it was gained, and he had stumbled across the bridge, clambered a little way among the rocks, to the surprise and dismay of a young llama, who went leaping out of sight, and lay down sobbing for breath.

And so his *coup d'état* came to an end.

He stayed outside the wall of the valley of the Blind for two nights and days without food or shelter, and meditated upon the unexpected. During these meditations he repeated very frequently and always with a profounder note of derision the exploded proverb: 'In the Country of the Blind the One-Eyed Man is King.' He thought chiefly of ways of fighting and conquering these people, and it grew clear that for him no practicable way was possible. He had no weapons, and now it would be hard to get one.

The canker of civilisation had got to him even in Bogota, and he could not find it in himself to go down and assassinate a blind man. Of course, if he did that, he might then dictate terms on the threat of assassinating them all. But—sooner or later he must sleep!...

He tried also to find food among the pine trees, to be comfortable under pine boughs while the frost fell at night, and—with less confidence—to catch a llama by artifice in order to try to kill it—perhaps by hammering it with a stone—and so finally, perhaps, to eat some of it. But the llamas had a doubt of him and regarded him with distrustful brown eyes, and spat when he drew near. Fear came on him the second day and fits of shivering. Finally he crawled down to the wall of the Country of the Blind and tried to make terms. He crawled along by the stream, shouting, until two blind men came out to the gate and talked to him.

'I was mad,' he said. 'But I was only newly made.'

They said that was better.

He told them he was wiser now, and repented of all he had done.

Then he wept without intention, for he was very weak and ill now, and they took that as a favourable sign.

They asked him if he still thought he could '*see*.'

'No,' he said. 'That was folly. The word means nothing—less than nothing!'

They asked him what was overhead.

'About ten times ten the height of a man there is a roof above the world—of rock—and very, very smooth.' . . . He burst again into hysterical tears. 'Before you ask me any more, give me some food or I shall die.'

He expected dire punishments, but these blind people were capable of toleration. They regarded his rebellion as but one more proof of his general idiocy and inferiority; and after they had whipped him they appointed him to do the simplest and heaviest work they had for anyone to do, and he, seeing no other way of living, did submissively what he was told.

He was ill for some days, and they nursed him kindly. That refined his submission. But they insisted on his lying in the dark, and that was a great misery. And blind philosophers came and talked to him of the wicked levity of his mind, and reproved him so impressively for his doubts about the lid of rock that covered their cosmic casserole that he almost doubted whether indeed he was not the victim of hallucination in not seeing it overhead.

So Nunez became a citizen of the Country of the Blind, and these people ceased to be a generalised people and became individualities and familiar to him, while the world beyond the mountains became more and more remote and unreal. There was Yacob, his master, a kindly man when not annoyed; there was Pedro, Yacob's nephew; and there was Medina-saroté, who was the youngest daughter of Yacob. She was little esteemed in the world of the blind, because she had a clear-cut face, and lacked that satisfying, glossy smoothness that is the blind man's ideal of feminine beauty; but Nunez thought her beautiful at first, and presently the most beautiful thing in the whole creation. Her closed eyelids were not sunken and red after the common way of the valley, but lay as though they might open again at any moment; and she had long eyelashes, which were considered a grave disfigurement. And her voice was strong, and did not satisfy the acute hearing of the valley swains. So that she had no lover.

There came a time when Nunez thought that, could he win her, he would be resigned to live in the valley for all the rest of his days.

He watched her; he sought opportunities of doing her little services, and presently he found that she observed him. Once at a rest-day gathering they sat side by side in the dim starlight, and the music was sweet. His hand came upon hers and he dared to clasp it. Then very tenderly she returned his pressure. And one day, as they were at their meal in the darkness, he felt her hand very softly seeking him, and as it chanced the fire leapt then and he saw the tenderness of her face.

He sought to speak to her.

He went to her one day when she was sitting in the summer moonlight spinning. The light made her a thing of silver and mystery. He sat down at her feet and told her he loved her, and told her how beautiful she seemed to him. He had a lover's voice, he spoke with a tender reverence that came near to awe, and she had never before been touched by adoration. She made him no definite answer, but it was clear his words pleased her.

After that he talked to her whenever he could take an opportunity. The valley became the world for him, and the world beyond the mountains where men lived in sunlight seemed no more than a fairy tale he would some day pour into her ears. Very tentatively and timidly he spoke to her of sight.

Sight seemed to her the most poetical of fancies, and she listened to his description of the stars and the mountains and her own sweet white-lit beauty as though it was a guilty indulgence. She did not believe, she could only half understand, but she was mysteriously delighted, and it seemed to him that she completely understood.

His love lost its awe and took courage. Presently he was for demanding her of Yacob and the elders in marriage, but she became fearful and delayed. And it was one of her elder sisters who first told Yacob that Medina-saroté and Nunez were in love.

There was from the first very great opposition to the marriage of Nunez and Medina-saroté; not so much because they valued her as because they held him as a being apart, an idiot, incompetent thing below the permissible level of a man. Her sisters opposed it bitterly as bringing discredit on them all; and old Yacob, though he had formed a sort of liking for his clumsy, obedient serf, shook his head and said the thing could not be. The young men were all angry at the idea of corrupting the race, and one went so far as to revile and strike Nunez. He struck back. Then for the first time he found an advantage in seeing, even by twilight, and after that fight was over no one was disposed to raise a hand against him. But they still found his marriage impossible.

Old Yacob had a tenderness for his last little daughter, and was grieved to have her weep upon his shoulder.

'You see, my dear, he's an idiot. He has delusions; he can't do anything right.'

'I know,' wept Medina-saroté. 'But he's better than he was. He's getting better. And he's strong, dear father, and kind—stronger and kinder than any other man in the world. And he loves me—and, father, I love him.'

Old Yacob was greatly distressed to find her inconsolable, and, besides—what made it more distressing—he liked Nunez for many things. So he went and sat in the windowless council-chamber with the other elders and watched the trend of the talk, and said, at the proper time, 'He's better than he was. Very likely, some day, we shall find him as sane as ourselves.'

Then afterwards one of the elders, who thought deeply, had an idea. He was the great doctor among these people, their medicine-man, and he had a very philosophical and inventive mind, and the idea of curing Nunez of his peculiarities appealed to him. One day when Yacob was present he returned to the topic of Nunez.

'I have examined Bogota,' he said, 'and the case is clearer to me. I think very probably he might be cured.'

'That is what I have always hoped,' said old Yacob.

'His brain is affected,' said the blind doctor.

The elders murmured assent.

'Now, *what* affects it?'

'Ah!' said old Yacob.

'*This*,' said the doctor, answering his own question. 'Those queer things that are called the eyes, and which exist to make an agreeable soft depression in the face, are diseased, in the case of Bogota, in such a way as to affect his brain. They are greatly distended, he has eye-lashes, and his eyelids move, and consequently his brain is in a state of constant irritation and distraction.'

'Yes?' said old Yacob. 'Yes?'

'And I think I may say with reasonable certainty that, in order to cure him completely, all that we need do is a simple and easy surgical operation—namely, to remove these irritant bodies.'

'And then he will be sane?'

'Then he will be perfectly sane, and a quite admirable citizen.'

'Thank Heaven for science!' said old Yacob, and went forth at once to tell Nunez of his happy hopes.

But Nunez's manner of receiving the good news struck him as being cold and disappointing.

'One might think,' he said, 'from the tone you take, that you did not care for my daughter.'

It was Medina-saroté who persuaded Nunez to face the blind surgeons.

'*You* do not want me,' he said, 'to lose my gift of sight?'

She shook her head.

'My world is sight.'

Her head drooped lower.

'There are the beautiful things, the beautiful little things—the flowers, the lichens mong the rocks, the lightness and softness on a piece of fur, the far sky with its drifting down of clouds, the sunsets and the stars. And there is *you*. For you alone it is good to have sight, to see your sweet, serene face, your kindly lips, your dear, beautiful hands folded together. . . . It is these eyes of mine you won, these eyes that hold me to you, that these idiots seek. Instead, I must touch you, hear you, and never see you again. I must come under that roof of rock and stone and darkness, that horrible roof under which your imagination stoops. . . . No; you would not have me do that?'

A disagreeable doubt had arisen in him. He stopped, and left the thing a question.

'I wish,' she said, 'sometimes—' She paused.

'Yes,' said he, a little apprehensively.

'I wish sometimes—you would not talk like that.'

'Like what?'

'I know it's pretty—it's your imagination. I love it, but *now*—'

He felt cold. '*Now?*' he said faintly.

She sat quite still.

'You mean—you think—I should be better, better perhaps—'

He was realising things very swiftly. He felt anger, indeed, anger at the dull course of fate, but also sympathy for her lack of understanding—a sympathy near akin to pity.

'*Dear,*' he said, and he could see by her whiteness how intensely her spirit pressed against the things she could not say. He put his arms about her, he kissed her ear, and they sat for a time in silence.

'If I were to consent to this?' he said at last, in a voice that was very gentle.

She flung her arms about him, weeping wildly. 'Oh, if you would,' she sobbed, 'if only you would!'

For a week before the operation that was to raise him from his servitude and inferiority to the level of a blind citizen, Nunez knew nothing of sleep, and all through the warm sunlit hours, while the others slumbered happily, he sat brooding or wandered aimlessly, trying to bring his mind to bear on his dilemma. He had given his answer, he had given his consent, and still he was not sure. And at last work-time was over, the sun rose in splendour over the golden crests, and his last day of vision began for him. He had a few minutes with Medina-saroté before she went apart to sleep.

'To-morrow,' he said, 'I shall see no more.'

'Dear heart!' she answered, and pressed his hands with all her strength.

'They will hurt you but little,' she said; 'and you are going through this pain—you are going through it, dear lover, for *me*. . . . Dear, if a woman's heart and life can do it, I will repay you. My dearest one, my dearest with the tender voice, I will repay.'

He was drenched in pity for himself and her.

He held her in his arms, and pressed his lips to hers, and looked on her sweet face for the last time. 'Good-bye!' he whispered at that dear sight, 'good-bye!'

And then in silence he turned away from her.

She could hear his slow retreating footsteps, and something in the rhythm of them threw her into a passion of weeping.

He had fully meant to go to a lonely place where the meadows were beautiful with white narcissus, and there remain until the hour of his sacrifice should come, but as he went he lifted up his eyes and saw the morning, the morning like an angel in golden armour, marching down the steeps. . . .

It seemed to him that before this splendour he, and this blind world in the valley, and his love, and all, were no more than a pit of sin.

He did not turn aside as he had meant to do, but went on, and passed through the wall of the circumference and out upon the rocks, and his eyes were always upon the sunlit ice and snow.

He saw their infinite beauty, and his imagination soared over them to the things beyond he was now to resign for ever.

He thought of that great free world he was parted from, the world that was his own, and he had a vision of those further slopes, distance beyond distance, with Bogota, a place of multitudinous stirring beauty, a glory by day, a luminous mystery by night, a place of palaces and fountains and statues and white houses, lying beautifully in the middle distance. He thought how for a day or so one might come down through passes, drawing ever nearer and nearer to its busy streets and ways. He thought of the river journey, day by day, from great Bogota to the still vaster world beyond, through towns and villages, forest and desert places, the rushing river day by day, until its banks receded and the big steamers came splashing by, and one had reached the sea—the limitless sea, with its thousand islands, its thousands of islands, and its ships seen dimly far away in their incessant journeyings round and about that greater world. And there, unpent by mountains, one saw the sky—the sky, not such a disc as one saw it here, but an arch of immeasurable blue, a deep of deeps in which the circling stars were floating. . . .

His eyes scrutinised the great curtain of the mountains with a keener inquiry.

For example, if one went so, up that gully and to that chimney there, then one might come out high among those stunted pines that ran round in a sort of shelf and rose still higher and higher as it passed above the gorge. And then? That talus might be managed. Thence perhaps a climb might be found to take him up to the precipice that came below the snow; and if that chimney failed, then another farther to the east might serve his purpose better. And then? Then one would be out upon the amber-lit snow there, and half-way up to the crest of those beautiful desolations.

He glanced back at the village, then turned right round and regarded it steadfastly.

He thought of Medina-saroté, and she had become small and remote.

He turned again towards the mountain wall, down which the day had come to him.

Then very circumspectly he began to climb.

When sunset came he was no longer climbing, but he was far and high. He had been higher, but he was still very high. His clothes were torn, his limbs were blood-stained, he was bruised in many places, but he lay as if he were at his ease, and there was a smile on his face.

From where he rested the valley seemed as if it were in a pit and nearly a mile below. Already it was dim with haze and shadow, though the mountain summits around him were things of light and fire. The mountain summits around him were things of light and fire, and the little details of the rocks near at hand were drenched with subtle beauty—a vein of green mineral piercing the grey, the flash of crystal faces here and there, a minute, minutely-beautiful orange lichen close beside his face. There were deep mysterious shadows in the gorge, blue deepening into purple, and purple into a luminous darkness, and overhead was the illimitable vastness of the sky. But he heeded these things no longer, but lay quite inactive there, smiling as if he were satisfied merely to have escaped from the valley of the Blind in which he had thought to be King.

The glow of the sunset passed, and the night came, and still he lay peacefully contented under the cold clear stars.

E. M. FORSTER

THE MACHINE STOPS

PART I

THE AIR-SHIP

IMAGINE, if you can, a small room, hexagonal in shape, like the cell of a bee. It is lighted neither by window nor by lamp, yet it is filled with a soft radiance. There are no apertures for ventilation, yet the air is fresh. There are no musical instruments, and yet, at the moment that my meditation opens, this room is throbbing with melodious sounds. An arm-chair is in the centre, by its side a reading-desk—that is all the furniture. And in the arm-chair there sits a swaddled lump of flesh—a woman, about five feet high, with a face as white as a fungus. It is to her that the little room belongs.

An electric bell rang.

The woman touched a switch and the music was silent.

'I suppose I must see who it is,' she thought, and set her chair in motion. The chair, like the music, was worked by machinery, and it rolled her to the other side of the room, where the bell still rang importunately.

'Who is it?' she called. Her voice was irritable, for she had been interrupted often since the music began. She knew several thousand people; in certain directions human intercourse had advanced enormously.

But when she listened into the receiver, her white face wrinkled into smiles, and she said:

'Very well. Let us talk, I will isolate myself. I do not expect anything important will happen for the next five minutes—for I can give you fully five minutes, Kuno. Then I must deliver my lecture on "Music during the Australian Period".'

She touched the isolation knob, so that no one else could speak to her. Then she touched the lighting apparatus, and the little room was plunged into darkness.

'Be quick!' she called, her irritation returning. 'Be quick, Kuno; here I am in the dark wasting my time.'

But it was fully fifteen seconds before the round plate that she held in her hands began to glow. A faint blue light shot across it, darkening to purple, and presently she could see the image of her son, who lived on the other side of the earth, and he could see her.

'Kuno, how slow you are.'

He smiled gravely.

'I really believe you enjoy dawdling.'

'I have called you before, mother, but you were always busy or isolated. I have something particular to say.'

'What is it, dearest boy? Be quick. Why could you not send it by pneumatic post?'

'Because I prefer saying such a thing. I want—'

'Well?'

'I want you to come and see me.'

Vashti* watched his face in the blue plate.

'But I can see you!' she exclaimed. 'What more do you want?'

'I want to see you not through the Machine,' said Kuno. 'I want to speak to you not through the wearisome Machine.'

'Oh, hush!' said his mother, vaguely shocked. 'You mustn't say anything against the Machine.'

'Why not?'

'One mustn't.'

'You talk as if a god had made the Machine,' cried the other. 'I believe that you pray to it when you are unhappy. Men made it, do not forget that. Great men, but men. The Machine is much, but it is not everything. I see something like you in this plate, but I do not see you. I hear something like you through this telephone, but I do not hear you. That is why I want you to come. Come and stop with me. Pay me a visit, so that we can meet face to face, and talk about the hopes that are in my mind.'

She replied that she could scarcely spare the time for a visit.

'The air-ship* barely takes two days to fly between me and you.'

'I dislike air-ships.'

'Why?'

'I dislike seeing the horrible brown earth, and the sea, and the stars when it is dark. I get no ideas in an air-ship.'

'I do not get them anywhere else.'

'What kind of ideas can the air give you?'

He paused for an instant.

'Do you not know four big stars that form an oblong, and three stars close together in the middle of the oblong, and hanging from these stars, three other stars?'

'No, I do not. I dislike the stars. But did they give you an idea? How interesting; tell me.'

'I had an idea that they were like a man.'

'I do not understand.'

'The four big stars are the man's shoulders and his knees. The three stars in the middle are like the belts that men wore once, and the three stars hanging are like a sword.'*

'A sword?'

'Men carried swords about with them, to kill animals and other men.'

'It does not strike me as a very good idea, but it is certainly original. When did it come to you first?'

'In the air-ship—' He broke off, and she fancied that he looked sad. She could not be sure, for the Machine did not transmit *nuances* of expression. It only gave a general idea of people—an idea that was good enough for all practical purposes, Vashti thought. The imponderable bloom, declared by a discredited philosophy to be the actual essence of intercourse, was rightly ignored by the Machine, just as the imponderable bloom of the grape was ignored by the manufacturers of artificial fruit. Something 'good enough' had long since been accepted by our race.

'The truth is,' he continued, 'that I want to see these stars again. They are curious stars. I want to see them not from the air-ship, but from the surface of the earth, as our ancestors did, thousands of years ago. I want to visit the surface of the earth.'

She was shocked again.

'Mother, you must come, if only to explain to me what is the harm of visiting the surface of the earth.'

'No harm,' she replied, controlling herself. 'But no advantage. The surface of the earth is only dust and mud, no life remains on it, and you would need a respirator, or the cold of the outer air would kill you. One dies immediately in the outer air.'

'I know; of course I shall take all precautions.'

'And besides—'

'Well?'

She considered, and chose her words with care. Her son had a queer temper, and she wished to dissuade him from the expedition.

'It is contrary to the spirit of the age,' she asserted.

'Do you mean by that, contrary to the Machine?'

'In a sense, but—'

His image in the blue plate faded.

'Kuno!'

He had isolated himself.

For a moment Vashti felt lonely.

Then she generated the light, and the sight of her room, flooded with radiance and studded with electric buttons, revived her. There were buttons and switches everywhere—buttons to call for food, for music, for clothing. There was the hot-bath button, by pressure of which a basin of (imitation) marble rose out of the floor, filled to the brim with a warm deodorized liquid. There was the cold-bath button. There was the button that produced literature. And there were of course the buttons by which she communicated with her friends. The room, though it contained nothing, was in touch with all that she cared for in the world.

Vashti's next move was to turn off the isolation-switch, and all the accumulations of the last three minutes burst upon her. The room was filled with the noise of bells, and speaking-tubes. What was the new food like? Could she recommend it? Had she had any ideas lately? Might one tell her one's own ideas? Would she make an engagement to visit the public nurseries at an early date?—say this day month.

To most of these questions she replied with irritation—a growing quality in that accelerated age. She said that the new food was horrible. That she could not visit the public nurseries through press of engagements. That she had no ideas of her own but had just been told one—that four stars and three in the middle were like a man: she doubted there was much in it. Then she switched off her correspondents, for it was time to deliver her lecture on Australian music.

The clumsy system of public gatherings had been long since abandoned; neither Vashti nor her audience stirred from their rooms. Seated in her arm-chair she spoke, while they in their arm-chairs heard her, fairly well, and saw her, fairly well. She opened with a humorous account of music in the pre-Mongolian epoch, and went on to describe the great outburst of song that followed the Chinese conquest. Remote and primæval as were the methods of I-San-So and the Brisbane school, she yet felt (she said) that study of them might repay the musicians of to-day: they had freshness; they had, above all, ideas.

Her lecture, which lasted ten minutes, was well received, and at its conclusion she and many of her audience listened to a lecture on the sea; there were ideas to be got from the sea; the speaker had donned a respirator and visited it lately. Then she fed, talked to many friends, had a bath, talked again, and summoned her bed.

The bed was not to her liking. It was too large, and she had a feeling for a small bed. Complaint was useless, for beds were of the same dimension all over the world, and to have had an alternative size would have involved vast alterations in the Machine. Vashti isolated herself—it was necessary, for neither day nor night existed under the ground—and reviewed all that had happened since she had summoned the bed last. Ideas? Scarcely any. Events—was Kuno's invitation an event?

By her side, on the little reading-desk, was a survival from the ages of litter—one book. This was the Book of the Machine. In it were instructions against every possible contingency. If she was hot or cold or dyspeptic or at a loss for a word, she went to the book, and it told her which button to press. The Central Committee published it. In accordance with a growing habit, it was richly bound.

Sitting up in the bed, she took it reverently in her hands. She glanced round the glowing room as if some one might be watching her. Then, half ashamed, half joyful, she murmured 'O Machine! O Machine!' and raised the volume to her lips. Thrice she kissed it, thrice inclined her head, thrice she felt the delirium of acquiescence. Her ritual performed, she turned to page 1367, which gave the times of the departure of the air-ships from the island in the southern hemisphere, under whose soil she lived, to the island in the northern hemisphere, whereunder lived her son.

She thought, 'I have not the time.'

She made the room dark and slept; she awoke and made the room light; she ate and exchanged ideas with her friends, and listened to music and attended lectures; she made the room dark and slept. Above her, beneath her, and around her, the Machine hummed eternally; she did not notice the noise, for she had been born with it in her ears. The earth, carrying her, hummed as it sped through silence, turning her now to the invisible sun, now to the invisible stars. She awoke and made the room light.

'Kuno!'

'I will not talk to you,' he answered, 'until you come.'

'Have you been on the surface of the earth since we spoke last?'
His image faded.

Again she consulted the book. She became very nervous and lay
back in her chair palpitating. Think of her as without teeth or hair.
Presently she directed the chair to the wall, and pressed an unfamiliar
button. The wall swung apart slowly. Through the opening she saw
a tunnel that curved slightly, so that its goal was not visible. Should
she go to see her son, here was the beginning of the journey.

Of course she knew all about the communication-system. There
was nothing mysterious in it. She would summon a car and it would
fly with her down the tunnel until it reached the lift that communicated with the air-ship station: the system had been in use for many,
many years, long before the universal establishment of the Machine.
And of course she had studied the civilization that had immediately
preceded her own—the civilization that had mistaken the functions
of the system, and had used it for bringing people to things, instead
of for bringing things to people. Those funny old days, when men
went for change of air instead of changing the air in their rooms! And
yet—she was frightened of the tunnel: she had not seen it since her
last child was born. It curved—but not quite as she remembered; it
was brilliant—but not quite as brilliant as a lecturer had suggested.
Vashti was seized with the terrors of direct experience. She shrank
back into the room, and the wall closed up again.

'Kuno,' she said, 'I cannot come to see you. I am not well.'

Immediately an enormous apparatus fell on to her out of the ceiling, a thermometer was automatically inserted between her lips,
a stethoscope was automatically laid upon her heart. She lay powerless.
Cool pads soothed her forehead. Kuno had telegraphed to her doctor.

So the human passions still blundered up and down in the Machine.
Vashti drank the medicine that the doctor projected into her mouth,
and the machinery retired into the ceiling. The voice of Kuno was
heard asking how she felt.

'Better.' Then with irritation: 'But why do you not come to me
instead?'

'Because I cannot leave this place.'

'Why?'

'Because, any moment, something tremendous may happen.'

'Have you been on the surface of the earth yet?'

'Not yet.'

'Then what is it?'

'I will not tell you through the Machine.'

She resumed her life.

But she thought of Kuno as a baby, his birth, his removal to the public nurseries, her own visit to him there, his visits to her—visits which stopped when the Machine had assigned him a room on the other side of the earth. 'Parents, duties of,' said the book of the Machine, 'cease at the moment of birth. P.422327483.' True, but there was something special about Kuno—indeed there had been something special about all her children—and, after all, she must brave the journey if he desired it. And 'something tremendous might happen'. What did that mean? The nonsense of a youthful man, no doubt, but she must go. Again she pressed the unfamiliar button, again the wall swung back, and she saw the tunnel that curved out of sight. Clasping the Book, she rose, tottered on to the platform, and summoned the car. Her room closed behind her: the journey to the northern hemisphere had begun.

Of course it was perfectly easy. The car approached and in it she found arm-chairs exactly like her own. When she signalled, it stopped, and she tottered into the lift. One other passenger was in the lift, the first fellow creature she had seen face to face for months. Few travelled in these days, for, thanks to the advance of science, the earth was exactly alike all over. Rapid intercourse, from which the previous civilization had hoped so much, had ended by defeating itself. What was the good of going to Pekin when it was just like Shrewsbury? Why return to Shrewsbury when it would all be like Pekin? Men seldom moved their bodies; all unrest was concentrated in the soul.

The air-ship service was a relic from the former age. It was kept up, because it was easier to keep it up than to stop it or to diminish it, but it now far exceeded the wants of the population. Vessel after vessel would rise from the vomitories of Rye or of Christchurch* (I use the antique names), would sail into the crowded sky, and would draw up at the wharves of the south—empty. So nicely adjusted was the system, so independent of meteorology, that the sky, whether calm or cloudy, resembled a vast kaleidoscope whereon the same patterns periodically recurred. The ship on which Vashti sailed started now at sunset, now at dawn. But always, as it passed above Rheims, it would neighbour the ship that served between Helsingfors and the Brazils, and, every third time it surmounted the Alps, the fleet of Palermo would cross its track behind. Night and day, wind and storm, tide and earthquake, impeded man no longer. He had harnessed Leviathan.* All the old literature, with its praise of Nature, and its fear of Nature, rang false as the prattle of a child.

Yet as Vashti saw the vast flank of the ship, stained with exposure to the outer air, her horror of direct experience returned. It was not quite like the air-ship in the cinematophote.* For one thing it smelt—not strongly or unpleasantly, but it did smell, and with her eyes shut she should have known that a new thing was close to her. Then she had to walk to it from the lift, had to submit to glances from the other passengers. The man in front dropped his Book—no great matter, but it disquieted them all. In the rooms, if the Book was dropped, the floor raised it mechanically, but the gangway to the air-ship was not so prepared, and the sacred volume lay motionless. They stopped—the thing was unforeseen—and the man, instead of picking up his property, felt the muscles of his arm to see how they had failed him. Then someone actually said with direct utterance: 'We shall be late'—and they trooped on board, Vashti treading on the pages as she did so.

Inside, her anxiety increased. The arrangements were old-fashioned and rough. There was even a female attendant, to whom she would have to announce her wants during the voyage. Of course a revolving platform ran the length of the boat, but she was expected to walk from it to her cabin. Some cabins were better than others, and she did not get the best. She thought the attendant had been unfair, and spasms of rage shook her. The glass valves had closed, she could not go back. She saw, at the end of the vestibule, the lift in which she had ascended going quietly up and down, empty. Beneath those corridors of shining tiles were rooms, tier below tier, reaching far into the earth, and in each room there sat a human being, eating, or sleeping, or producing ideas. And buried deep in the hive was her own room. Vashti was afraid.

'O Machine! O Machine!' she murmured, and caressed her Book, and was comforted.

Then the sides of the vestibule seemed to melt together, as do the passages that we see in dreams, the lift vanished, the Book that had been dropped slid to the left and vanished, polished tiles rushed by like a stream of water, there was a slight jar, and the air-ship, issuing from its tunnel, soared above the waters of a tropical ocean.

It was night. For a moment she saw the coast of Sumatra edged by the phosphorescence of waves, and crowned by lighthouses, still sending forth their disregarded beams. These also vanished, and only the stars distracted her. They were not motionless, but swayed to and fro above her head, thronging out of one sky-light into another, as if the universe and not the air-ship was careening. And, as often happens on clear nights, they seemed now to be in perspective, now on a plane; now piled tier beyond tier into the infinite heavens, now concealing infinity, a roof limiting for ever the visions of men. In either case they seemed intolerable. 'Are we to travel in the dark?' called the passengers angrily, and the attendant, who had been careless, generated the light, and pulled down the blinds of pliable metal. When the air-ships had been built, the desire to look direct at things still lingered in the world. Hence the extraordinary number of skylights and windows, and the proportionate discomfort to those who were civilized and refined. Even in Vashti's cabin one star peeped through a flaw in the blind, and after a few hours' uneasy slumber, she was disturbed by an unfamiliar glow, which was the dawn.

Quick as the ship had sped westwards, the earth had rolled eastwards quicker still, and had dragged back Vashti and her companions towards the sun. Science could prolong the night, but only for a little, and those high hopes of neutralizing the earth's diurnal revolution had passed, together with hopes that were possibly higher. To 'keep pace with the sun,' or even to outstrip it, had been the aim of the civilization preceding this. Racing aeroplanes had been built for the purpose, capable of enormous speed, and steered by the greatest intellects of the epoch. Round the globe they went, round and round, westward, westward, round and round, amidst humanity's applause. In vain. The globe went eastward quicker still, horrible accidents occurred, and the Committee of the Machine, at the time rising into prominence, declared the pursuit illegal, unmechanical, and punishable by Homelessness.

Of Homelessness more will be said later.

Doubtless the Committee was right. Yet the attempt to 'defeat the sun' aroused the last common interest that our race experienced about the heavenly bodies, or indeed about anything. It was the last time that men were compacted by thinking of a power outside the world. The sun had conquered, yet it was the end of his spiritual dominion. Dawn, midday, twilight, the zodiacal path, touched neither

men's lives nor their hearts, and science retreated into the ground, to concentrate herself upon problems that she was certain of solving.

So when Vashti found her cabin invaded by a rosy finger of light,* she was annoyed, and tried to adjust the blind. But the blind flew up altogether, and she saw through the skylight small pink clouds, swaying against a background of blue, and as the sun crept higher, its radiance entered direct, brimming down the wall, like a golden sea. It rose and fell with the air-ship's motion, just as waves rise and fall, but it advanced steadily, as a tide advances. Unless she was careful, it would strike her face. A spasm of horror shook her and she rang for the attendant. The attendant too was horrified, but she could do nothing; it was not her place to mend the blind. She could only suggest that the lady should change her cabin, which she accordingly prepared to do.

People were almost exactly alike all over the world, but the attendant of the air-ship, perhaps owing to her exceptional duties, had grown a little out of the common. She had often to address passengers with direct speech, and this had given her a certain roughness and originality of manner. When Vashti swerved away from the sunbeams with a cry, she behaved barbarically—she put out her hand to steady her.

'How dare you!' exclaimed the passenger. 'You forget yourself!'

The woman was confused, and apologized for not having let her fall. People never touched one another. The custom had become obsolete, owing to the Machine.

'Where are we now?' asked Vashti haughtily.

'We are over Asia,' said the attendant, anxious to be polite.

'Asia?'

'You must excuse my common way of speaking. I have got into the habit of calling places over which I pass by their unmechanical names.'

'Oh, I remember Asia. The Mongols came from it.'

'Beneath us, in the open air, stood a city that was once called Simla.'*

'Have you ever heard of the Mongols and of the Brisbane school?'

'No.'

'Brisbane also stood in the open air.'

'Those mountains to the right—let me show you them.' She pushed back a metal blind. The main chain of the Himalayas was revealed. 'They were once called the Roof of the World, those mountains.'

'What a foolish name!'

'You must remember that, before the dawn of civilization, they seemed to be an impenetrable wall that touched the stars. It was supposed that no one but the gods could exist above their summits. How we have advanced, thanks to the Machine!'

'How we have advanced, thanks to the Machine!' said Vashti.

'How we have advanced, thanks to the Machine!' echoed the passenger who had dropped his Book the night before, and who was standing in the passage.

'And that white stuff in the cracks?—what is it?'

'I have forgotten its name.'

'Cover the window, please. These mountains give me no ideas.'

The northern aspect of the Himalayas was in deep shadow: on the Indian slope the sun had just prevailed. The forests had been destroyed during the literature epoch for the purpose of making newspaper-pulp, but the snows were awakening to their morning glory, and clouds still hung on the breasts of Kinchinjunga.* In the plain were seen the ruins of cities, with diminished rivers creeping by their walls, and by the sides of these were sometimes the signs of vomitories, marking the cities of to-day. Over the whole prospect air-ships rushed, crossing the inter-crossing with incredible *aplomb*, and rising nonchalantly when they desired to escape the perturbations of the lower atmosphere and to traverse the Roof of the World.

'We have indeed advanced, thanks to the Machine,' repeated the attendant, and hid the Himalayas behind a metal blind.

The day dragged wearily forward. The passengers sat each in his cabin, avoiding one another with an almost physical repulsion and longing to be once more under the surface of the earth. There were eight or ten of them, mostly young males, sent out from the public nurseries to inhabit the rooms of those who had died in various parts of the earth. The man who had dropped his Book was on the homeward journey. He had been sent to Sumatra for the purpose of propagating the race. Vashti alone was travelling by her private will.

At midday she took a second glance at the earth. The air-ship was crossing another range of mountains, but she could see little, owing to clouds. Masses of black rock hovered below her, and merged indistinctly into grey. Their shapes were fantastic; one of them resembled a prostrate man.

'No ideas here,' murmured Vashti, and hid the Caucasus behind a metal blind.

In the evening she looked again. They were crossing a golden sea, in which lay many small islands and one peninsula.

She repeated, 'No ideas here,' and hid Greece behind a metal blind.

PART II

THE MENDING APPARATUS

By a vestibule, by a lift, by a tubular railway, by a platform, by a sliding door—by reversing all the steps of her departure did Vashti arrive at her son's room, which exactly resembled her own. She might well declare that the visit was superfluous. The buttons, the knobs, the reading-desk with the Book, the temperature, the atmosphere, the illumination—all were exactly the same. And if Kuno himself, flesh of her flesh,* stood close beside her at last, what profit was there in that? She was too well-bred to shake him by the hand. Averting her eyes, she spoke as follows:

'Here I am. I have had the most terrible journey and greatly retarded the development of my soul. It is not worth it, Kuno, it is not worth it. My time is too precious. The sunlight almost touched me, and I have met with the rudest people. I can only stop a few minutes. Say what you want to say, and then I must return.'

'I have been threatened with Homelessness,' said Kuno.

She looked at him now.

'I have been threatened with Homelessness, and I could not tell you such a thing through the Machine.'

Homelessness means death. The victim is exposed to the air, which kills him.

'I have been outside since I spoke to you last. The tremendous thing has happened, and they have discovered me.'

'But why shouldn't you go outside?' she exclaimed, 'It is perfectly legal, perfectly mechanical, to visit the surface of the earth. I have lately been to a lecture on the sea; there is no objection to that; one simply summons a respirator and gets an Egression-permit. It is not the kind of thing that spiritually-minded people do, and I begged you not to do it, but there is no legal objection to it.'

'I did not get an Egression-permit.'

'Then how did you get out?'

'I found out a way of my own.'

The phrase conveyed no meaning to her, and he had to repeat it.

'A way of your own?' she whispered. 'But that would be wrong.'

'Why?'

The question shocked her beyond measure.

'You are beginning to worship the Machine,' he said coldly. 'You think it irreligious of me to have found out a way of my own. It was just what the Committee thought, when they threatened me with Homelessness.'

At this she grew angry. 'I worship nothing!' she cried. 'I am most advanced. I don't think you irreligious, for there is no such thing as religion left. All the fear and the superstition that existed once have been destroyed by the Machine. I only meant that to find out a way of your own was—Besides, there is no new way out.'

'So it is always supposed.'

'Except through the vomitories, for which one must have an Egression-permit, it is impossible to get out. The Book says so.'

'Well, the Book's wrong, for I have been out on my feet.'

For Kuno was possessed of a certain physical strength.

By these days it was a demerit to be muscular. Each infant was examined at birth, and all who promised undue strength were destroyed. Humanitarians may protest, but it would have been no true kindness to let an athlete live; he would never have been happy in that state of life to which the Machine had called him; he would have yearned for trees to climb, rivers to bathe in, meadows and hills against which he might measure his body. Man must be adapted to his surroundings, must he not? In the dawn of the world our weakly must be exposed on Mount Taygetus,* in its twilight our strong will suffer euthanasia, that the Machine may progress, that the Machine may progress, that the Machine may progress eternally.

'You know that we have lost the sense of space. We say "space is annihilated", but we have annihilated not space, but the sense thereof. We have lost a part of ourselves. I determined to recover it, and I began by walking up and down the platform of the railway outside my room. Up and down, until I was tired, and so did recapture the meaning of "Near" and "Far". "Near" is a place to which I can get quickly *on my feet*, not a place to which the train or the air-ship will take me quickly. "Far" is a place to which I cannot get quickly on my feet; the vomitory is "far", though I could be there in thirty-eight seconds by summoning the train. Man is the measure.* That was my first lesson. Man's feet are the measure for distance, his hands are the measure for ownership, his body is the measure for all that is lovable and desirable and strong. Then I went further: it was then that I called to you for the first time, and you would not come.

'This city, as you know, is built deep beneath the surface of the earth, with only the vomitories protruding. Having paced the platform outside my own room, I took the lift to the next platform and paced that also, and so with each in turn, until I came to the topmost, above which begins the earth. All the platforms were exactly alike, and all that I gained by visiting them was to develop my sense of space and my muscles. I think I should have been content with this—it is not a little thing,—but as I walked and brooded, it occurred to me that our cities had been built in the days when men still breathed the outer air, and that there had been ventilation shafts for the workmen. I could think of nothing but these ventilation shafts. Had they been destroyed by all the food-tubes and medicine-tubes and music-tubes that the Machine has evolved lately? Or did traces of them remain? One thing was certain. If I came upon them anywhere, it would be in the railway-tunnels of the topmost story. Everywhere else, all space was accounted for.

'I am telling my story quickly, but don't think that I was not a coward or that your answers never depressed me. It is not the proper thing, it is not mechanical, it is not decent to walk along a railway-tunnel. I did not fear that I might tread upon a live rail and be killed. I feared something far more intangible—doing what was not contemplated by the Machine. Then I said to myself, "Man is the measure", and I went, and after many visits I found an opening.

'The tunnels, of course, were lighted. Everything is light, artificial light; darkness is the exception. So when I saw a black gap in the tiles, I knew that it was an exception, and rejoiced. I put in my arm— I could put in no more at first--and waved it round and round in ecstasy. I loosened another tile, and put in my head, and shouted into the darkness: "I am coming, I shall do it yet," and my voice reverberated down endless passages. I seemed to hear the spirits of those dead workmen who had returned each evening to the starlight and to their wives, and all the generations who had lived in the open air called back to me, "You will do it yet, you are coming." '

He paused, and, absurd as he was, his last words moved her. For Kuno had lately asked to be a father, and his request had been refused by the Committee. His was not a type that the Machine desired to hand on.

'Then a train passed. It brushed by me, but I thrust my head and arms into the hole. I had done enough for one day, so I crawled back to the platform, went down in the lift, and summoned my bed. Ah what dreams! And again I called you, and again you refused.'

She shook her head and said:

'Don't. Don't talk of these terrible things. You make me miserable. You are throwing civilization away.'

'But I had got back the sense of space and a man cannot rest then. I determined to get in at the hole and climb the shaft. And so I exercised my arms. Day after day I went through ridiculous movements, until my flesh ached, and I could hang by my hands and hold the pillow of my bed outstretched for many minutes. Then I summoned a respirator, and started.

'It was easy at first. The mortar had somehow rotted, and I soon pushed some more tiles in, and clambered after them into the darkness, and the spirits of the dead comforted me. I don't know what I mean by that. I just say what I felt. I felt, for the first time, that a protest had been lodged against corruption, and that even as the dead were comforting me, so I was comforting the unborn. I felt that humanity existed, and that it existed without clothes. How can I possibly explain this? It was naked, humanity seemed naked, and all these tubes and buttons and machineries neither came into the world with us, nor will they follow us out, nor do they matter supremely while we are here. Had I been strong, I would have torn off every garment I had, and gone out into the outer air unswaddled. But this is not for me, nor perhaps for my generation. I climbed with my respirator and my hygienic clothes and my dietetic tabloids! Better thus than not at all.

'There was a ladder, made of some primæval metal. The light from the railway fell upon its lowest rungs, and I saw that it led straight upwards out of the rubble at the bottom of the shaft. Perhaps our ancestors ran up and down it a dozen times daily, in their building. As I climbed, the rough edges cut through my gloves so that my hands bled. The light helped me for a little, and then came darkness and, worse still, silence which pierced my ears like a sword. The Machine hums! Did you know that? Its hum penetrates our blood, and may even guide our thoughts. Who knows! I was getting beyond its power. Then I thought: "This silence means that I am doing wrong." But I heard voices in the silence, and again they strengthened me.' He laughed. 'I had need of them. The next moment I cracked my head against something.'

She sighed.

'I had reached one of those pneumatic stoppers that defend us from the outer air. You may have noticed them on the air-ship. Pitch dark, my feet on the rungs of an invisible ladder, my hands cut; I cannot explain how I lived through this part, but the voices still comforted me, and I felt for fastenings. The stopper, I suppose, was about eight feet across. I passed my hand over it as far as I could reach. It was perfectly smooth. I felt it almost to the centre. Not quite to the centre, for my arm was too short. Then the voice said: "Jump. It is worth it. There may be a handle in the centre, and you may catch hold of it and so come to us your own way. And if there is no handle, so that you may fall and are dashed to pieces—it is still worth it: you will still come to us your own way." So I jumped. There was a handle, and—'

He paused. Tears gathered in his mother's eyes. She knew that he was fated. If he did not die to-day he would die to-morrow. There was not room for such a person in the world. And with her pity disgust mingled. She was ashamed at having borne such a son, she who had always been so respectable and so full of ideas. Was he really the little boy to whom she had taught the use of his stops and buttons, and to whom she had given his first lessons in the Book? The very hair that disfigured his lip showed that he was reverting to some savage type. On atavism the Machine can have no mercy.*

'There was a handle, and I did catch it. I hung tranced over the darkness and heard the hum of these workings as the last whisper in a dying dream. All the things I had cared about and all the people I had spoken to through tubes appeared infinitely little. Meanwhile the handle revolved. My weight had set something in motion and I span slowly, and then—

'I cannot describe it. I was lying with my face to the sunshine. Blood poured from my nose and ears and I heard a tremendous roaring. The stopper, with me clinging to it, had simply been blown out of the earth, and the air that we make down here was escaping through the vent into the air above. It burst up like a fountain. I crawled back to it—for the upper air hurts—and, as it were, I took great sips from the edge. My respirator had flown goodness knows where, my clothes were torn. I just lay with my lips close to the hole, and I sipped until the bleeding stopped. You can imagine nothing so curious. This hollow in the grass—I will speak of it in a minute,—the sun shining into it, not brilliantly but through marbled clouds,—the peace, the nonchalance, the sense of space, and, brushing my cheek, the roaring fountain of our artificial air! Soon I spied my respirator, bobbing up and down in the current high above my head, and higher still were many air-ships. But no one ever looks out of air-ships, and in any case they could not have picked me up. There I was, stranded. The sun shone a little way down the shaft, and revealed the topmost rung of the ladder, but it was hopeless trying to reach it. I should either have been tossed up again by the escape, or else have fallen in, and died. I could only lie on the grass, sipping and sipping, and from time to time glancing around me.

'I knew that I was in Wessex,* for I had taken care to go to a lecture on the subject before starting. Wessex lies above the room in which we are talking now. It was once an important state. Its kings held all the southern coast from the Andredswald to Cornwall, while the Wansdyke protected them on the north,* running over the high ground. The lecturer was only concerned with the rise of Wessex, so I do not know how long it remained an international power, nor would the knowledge have assisted me. To tell the truth I could do nothing but laugh, during this part. There was I, with a pneumatic stopper by my side and a respirator bobbing over my head, imprisoned, all three of us, in a grass-grown hollow that was edged with fern.'

Then he grew grave again.

'Lucky for me that it was a hollow. For the air began to fall back into it and to fill it as water fills a bowl. I could crawl about. Presently I stood. I breathed a mixture, in which the air that hurts predominated whenever I tried to climb the sides. This was not so bad. I had not lost my tabloids and remained ridiculously cheerful, and as for the Machine, I forgot about it altogether. My one aim now was to get to the top, where the ferns were, and to view whatever objects lay beyond.

'I rushed the slope. The new air was still too bitter for me and I came rolling back, after a momentary vision of something grey. The sun grew very feeble, and I remembered that he was in Scorpio—*

I had been to a lecture on that too. If the sun is in Scorpio and you are in Wessex, it means that you must be as quick as you can, or it will get too dark. (This is the first bit of useful information I have ever got from a lecture, and I expect it will be the last.) It made me try frantically to breathe the new air, and to advance as far as I dared out of my pond. The hollow filled so slowly. At times I thought that the fountain played with less vigour. My respirator seemed to dance nearer the earth; the roar was decreasing.'

He broke off.

'I don't think this is interesting you. The rest will interest you even less. There are no ideas in it, and I wish that I had not troubled you to come. We are too different, mother.'

She told him to continue.

'It was evening before I climbed the bank. The sun had very nearly slipped out of the sky by this time, and I could not get a good view. You, who have just crossed the Roof of the World, will not want to hear an account of the little hills that I saw—low colourless hills. But to me they were living and the turf that covered them was a skin, under which their muscles rippled, and I felt that those hills had called with incalculable force to men in the past, and that men had loved them. Now they sleep—perhaps for ever. They commune with humanity in dreams. Happy the man, happy the woman, who awakes the hills of Wessex. For though they sleep, they will never die.'

His voice rose passionately.

'Cannot you see, cannot all you lecturers see, that it is we that are dying, and that down here the only thing that really lives is the Machine? We created the Machine, to do our will, but we cannot make it do our will now. It has robbed us of the sense of space and of the sense of touch, it has blurred every human relation and narrowed down love to a carnal act, it has paralysed our bodies and our wills, and now it compels us to worship it. The Machine develops—but not on our lines. The Machine proceeds—but not to our goal. We only exist as the blood corpuscles that course through its arteries, and if it could work without us, it would let us die. Oh, I have no remedy—or, at least, only one—to tell men again and again that I have seen the hills of Wessex as Ælfrid saw them when he overthrew the Danes.*

'So the sun set. I forgot to mention that a belt of mist lay between my hill and other hills, and that it was the colour of pearl.'

He broke off for the second time.

'Go on,' said his mother wearily.

He shook his head.

'Go on. Nothing that you say can distress me now. I am hardened.'

'I had meant to tell you the rest, but I cannot: I know that I cannot: good-bye.'

Vashti stood irresolute. All her nerves were tingling with his blasphemies. But she was also inquisitive.

'This is unfair,' she complained. 'You have called me across the world to hear your story, and hear it I will. Tell me—as briefly as possible, for this is a disastrous waste of time—tell me how you returned to civilization.'

'Oh—that!' he said, starting. 'You would like to hear about civilization. Certainly. Had I got to where my respirator fell down?'

'No—but I understand everything now. You put on your respirator, and managed to walk along the surface of the earth to a vomitory, and there your conduct was reported to the Central Committee.'

'By no means.'

He passed his hand over his forehead, as if dispelling some strong impression. Then, resuming his narrative, he warmed to it again.

'My respirator fell about sunset. I had mentioned that the fountain seemed feebler, had I not?'

'Yes.'

'About sunset, it let the respirator fall. As I said, I had entirely forgotten about the Machine, and I paid no great attention at the time, being occupied with other things. I had my pool of air, into which I could dip when the outer keenness became intolerable, and which would possibly remain for days, provided that no wind sprang up to disperse it. Not until it was too late did I realize what the stoppage of the escape implied. You see—the gap in the tunnel had been mended; the Mending Apparatus; the Mending Apparatus was after me.

'One other warning I had, but I neglected it. The sky at night was clearer than it had been in the day, and the moon, which was about half the sky behind the sun, shone into the dell at moments quite brightly. I was in my usual place—on the boundary between the two atmospheres—when I thought I saw something dark move across the bottom of the dell, and vanish into the shaft. In my folly, I ran down. I bent over and listened, and I thought I heard a faint scraping noise in the depths.

'At this—but it was too late—I took alarm. I determined to put on my respirator and to walk right out of the dell. But my respirator had gone. I knew exactly where it had fallen—between the stopper and the aperture—and I could even feel the mark that it had made in the turf. It had gone, and I realized that something evil was at work, and I had better escape to the other air, and, if I must die, die running towards the cloud that had been the colour of a pearl. I never started. Out of the shaft—it is too horrible. A worm, a long white worm, had crawled out of the shaft and was gliding over the moonlit grass.

'I screamed. I did everything that I should not have done, I stamped upon the creature instead of flying from it, and it at once curled round the ankle. Then we fought. The worm let me run all over the dell, but edged up my leg as I ran. "Help!" I cried. (That part is too awful. It belongs to the part that you will never know.) "Help!" I cried. (Why cannot we suffer in silence?) "Help!" I cried. Then my feet were wound together, I fell, I was dragged away from the dear ferns and the living hills, and past the great metal stopper (I can tell you this part), and I thought it might save me again if I caught hold of the handle. It also was enwrapped, it also. Oh, the whole dell was full of the things. They were searching it in all directions, they were denuding it, and the white snouts of others peeped out of the hole, ready if needed. Everything that could be moved they brought—brushwood, bundles of fern, everything, and down we all went intertwined into hell. The last things that I saw, ere the stopper closed after us, were certain stars, and I felt that a man of my sort lived in the sky. For I did fight, I fought till the very end, and it was only my head hitting against the ladder that quieted me. I woke up in this room. The worms had vanished. I was surrounded by artificial air, artificial light, artificial peace, and my friends were calling to me down speaking-tubes to know whether I had come across any new ideas lately.'

Here his story ended. Discussion of it was impossible, and Vashti turned to go.

'It will end in Homelessness,' she said quietly.

'I wish it would,' retorted Kuno.

'The Machine has been most merciful.'

'I prefer the mercy of God.'

'By that superstitious phrase, do you mean that you could live in the outer air?'

'Yes.'

'Have you ever seen, round the vomitories, the bones of those who were extruded after the Great Rebellion?'

'Yes.'

'They were left where they perished for our edification. A few crawled away, but they perished, too—who can doubt it? And so with the Homeless of our own day. The surface of the earth supports life no longer.'

'Indeed.'

'Ferns and a little grass may survive, but all higher forms have perished. Has any air-ship detected them?'

'No.'

'Has any lecturer dealt with them?'

'No.'

'Then why this obstinacy?'

'Because I have seen them,' he exploded.

'Seen *what*?'

'Because I have seen her in the twilight—because she came to my help when I called—because she, too, was entangled by the worms, and, luckier than I, was killed by one of them piercing her throat.'

He was mad. Vashti departed, nor, in the troubles that followed, did she ever see his face again.

PART III

THE HOMELESS

During the years that followed Kuno's escapade, two important developments took place in the Machine. On the surface they were revolutionary, but in either case men's minds had been prepared beforehand, and they did but express tendencies that were latent already.

The first of these was the abolition of respirators.

Advanced thinkers, like Vashti, had always held it foolish to visit the surface of the earth. Air-ships might be necessary, but what was the good of going out for mere curiosity and crawling along for a mile or two in a terrestrial motor? The habit was vulgar and perhaps faintly improper: it was unproductive of ideas, and had no connection with the habits that really mattered. So respirators were abolished, and with them, of course, the terrestrial motors, and except for a few lecturers, who complained that they were debarred access to their subject-matter, the development was accepted quietly. Those who still wanted to know what the earth was like had after all only to listen to some gramophone, or to look into some cinematophote. And even the lecturers acquiesced when they found that a lecture on the sea was none the less stimulating when compiled out of other lectures that had already been delivered on the same subject. 'Beware of first-hand ideas!' exclaimed one of the most advanced of them. 'First-hand ideas do not really exist. They are but the physical impressions produced by love and fear, and on this gross foundation who could erect a philosophy? Let your ideas be second-hand, and if possible tenth-hand, for then they will be far removed from that disturbing element—direct observation. Do not learn anything about this subject of mine—the French Revolution. Learn instead what I think that Enicharmon thought Urizen thought Gutch thought Ho-Yung thought Chi-Bo-Sing thought Lafcadio Hearn thought Carlyle thought Mirabeau said about the French Revolution.* Through the medium of these ten great minds,* the blood that was shed at Paris and the windows that were broken at Versailles* will be clarified to an idea which you may employ most profitably in your daily lives. But be sure that the intermediates are many and varied, for in history one authority exists to counteract another. Urizen must counteract the scepticism of Ho-Yung and Enicharmon, I must myself counteract the impetuosity of Gutch. You who listen to me are in a better position to judge about the French Revolution than I am. Your descendants will be even in a better position than you, for they will learn what you think I think, and yet another intermediate will be added to the chain. And in time'—his voice rose—'there will come a generation that has got beyond facts, beyond impressions, a generation absolutely colourless, a generation

> "seraphically free
> From taint of personality,"*

which will see the French Revolution not as it happened, nor as they would like it to have happened, but as it would have happened, had it taken place in the days of the Machine.'

Tremendous applause greeted this lecture, which did but voice a feeling already latent in the minds of men—a feeling that terrestrial facts must be ignored, and that the abolition of respirators was a positive gain. It was even suggested that air-ships should be abolished too. This was not done, because air-ships had somehow worked themselves into the Machine's system. But year by year they were used less, and mentioned less by thoughtful men.

The second great development was the re-establishment of religion.

This, too, had been voiced in the celebrated lecture. No one could mistake the reverent tone in which the peroration had concluded, and it awakened a responsive echo in the heart of each. Those who had long worshipped silently, now began to talk. They described the strange feeling of peace that came over them when they handled the Book of the Machine, the pleasure that it was to repeat certain numerals out of it, however little meaning those numerals conveyed to the outward ear, the ecstasy of touching a button, however unimportant, or of ringing an electric bell, however superfluously.

'The Machine,' they exclaimed, 'feeds us and clothes us and houses us; through it we speak to one another, through it we see one another, in it we have our being. The Machine is the friend of ideas and the enemy of superstition: the Machine is omnipotent, eternal; blessed is the Machine.' And before long this allocution was printed on the first page of the Book, and in subsequent editions the ritual swelled into a complicated system of praise and prayer. The word 'religion' was sedulously avoided, and in theory the Machine was still the creation and the implement of man. But in practice all, save a few retrogrades, worshipped it as divine. Nor was it worshipped in unity. One believer would be chiefly impressed by the blue optic plates, through which he saw other believers; another by the mending apparatus, which sinful Kuno had compared to worms; another by the lifts, another by the Book. And each would pray to this or to that, and ask it to intercede for him with the Machine as a whole. Persecution—that also was present. It did not break out, for reasons that will be set forward shortly. But it was latent, and all who did not accept the minimum known as 'undenominational Mechanism' lived in danger of Homelessness, which means death, as we know.

To attribute these two great developments to the Central Committee, is to take a very narrow view of civilization. The Central Committee announced the developments, it is true, but they were no more the cause of them than were the kings of the imperialistic period the cause of war. Rather did they yield to some invincible pressure, which came no one knew whither, and which, when gratified, was succeeded by some new pressure equally invincible. To such a state of affairs it is convenient to give the name of progress. No one confessed the Machine was out of hand. Year by year it was served with increased efficiency and decreased intelligence. The better a man knew his own duties upon it, the less he understood the duties of his neighbour, and in all the world there was not one who understood the monster as a whole. Those master brains had perished. They had left full directions, it is true, and their successors had each of them mastered a portion of those directions. But Humanity, in its desire for comfort, had over-reached itself. It had exploited the riches of nature too far. Quietly and complacently, it was sinking into decadence, and progress had come to mean the progress of the Machine.

As for Vashti, her life went peacefully forward until the final disaster. She made her room dark and slept; she awoke and made the room light. She lectured and attended lectures. She exchanged ideas with her innumerable friends and believed she was growing more spiritual. At times a friend was granted Euthanasia, and left his or her room for the homelessness that is beyond all human conception. Vashti did not much mind. After an unsuccessful lecture, she would sometimes ask for Euthanasia herself. But the death-rate was not permitted to exceed the birth-rate, and the Machine had hitherto refused it to her.

The troubles began quietly, long before she was conscious of them.

One day she was astonished at receiving a message from her son. They never communicated, having nothing in common, and she had only heard indirectly that he was still alive, and had been transferred from the northern hemisphere, where he had behaved so mischievously, to the southern—indeed, to a room not far from her own.

'Does he want me to visit him?' she thought. 'Never again, never. And I have not the time.'

No, it was madness of another kind.

He refused to visualize his face upon the blue plate, and speaking out of the darkness with solemnity said:

'The Machine stops.'

'What do you say?'

'The Machine is stopping, I know it, I know the signs.'

She burst into a peal of laughter. He heard her and was angry, and they spoke no more.

'Can you imagine anything more absurd?' she cried to a friend. 'A man who was my son believes that the Machine is stopping. It would be impious if it was not mad.'

'The Machine is stopping?' her friend replied. 'What does that mean? The phrase conveys nothing to me.'

'Nor to me.'

'He does not refer, I suppose, to the trouble there has been lately with the music?'

'Oh no, of course not. Let us talk about music.'

'Have you complained to the authorities?'

'Yes, and they say it wants mending, and referred me to the Committee of the Mending Apparatus. I complained of those curious gasping sighs that disfigure the symphonies of the Brisbane school. They sound like someone in pain. The Committee of the Mending Apparatus say that it shall be remedied shortly.'

Obscurely worried, she resumed her life. For one thing, the defect in the music irritated her. For another thing, she could not forget Kuno's speech. If he had known that the music was out of repair—he could not know it, for he detested music—if he had known that it was wrong, 'the Machine stops' was exactly the venomous sort of remark he would have made. Of course he had made it at a venture, but the coincidence annoyed her, and she spoke with some petulance to the Committee of the Mending Apparatus.

They replied, as before, that the defect would be set right shortly.

'Shortly! At once!' she retorted. 'Why should I be worried by imperfect music? Things are always put right at once. If you do not mend it at once, I shall complain to the Central Committee.'

'No personal complaints are received by the Central Committee,' the Committee of the Mending Apparatus replied.

'Through whom am I to make my complaint, then?'

'Through us.'

'I complain then.'

'Your complaint shall be forwarded in its turn.'

'Have others complained?'

This question was unmechanical, and the Committee of the Mending Apparatus refused to answer it.

'It is too bad!' she exclaimed to another of her friends. 'There never was such an unfortunate woman as myself. I can never be sure of my music now. It gets worse and worse each time I summon it.'

'I too have my troubles,' the friend replied. 'Sometimes my ideas are interrupted by a slight jarring noise.'

'What is it?'

'I do not know whether it is inside my head, or inside the wall.'

'Complain, in either case.'

'I have complained, and my complaint will be forwarded in its turn to the Central Committee.'

Time passed, and they resented the defects no longer. The defects had not been remedied, but the human tissues in that latter day had become so subservient, that they readily adapted themselves to every caprice of the Machine. The sigh at the crises of the Brisbane symphony no longer irritated Vashti; she accepted it as part of the melody. The jarring noise, whether in the head or in the wall, was no longer resented by her friend. And so with the mouldy artificial fruit, so with the bath water that began to stink, so with the defective rhymes that the poetry machine had taken to emit. All were bitterly complained of at first, and then acquiesced in and forgotten. Things went from bad to worse unchallenged.

It was otherwise with the failure of the sleeping apparatus. That was a more serious stoppage. There came a day when over the whole world—in Sumatra, in Wessex, in the innumerable cities of Courland* and Brazil—the beds, when summoned by their tired owners, failed to appear. It may seem a ludicrous matter, but from it we may date the collapse of humanity. The Committee responsible for the failure was assailed by complainants, whom it referred, as usual, to the Committee of the Mending Apparatus, who in its turn assured them that their complaints would be forwarded to the Central Committee. But the discontent grew, for mankind was not yet sufficiently adaptable to do without sleeping.

'Someone is meddling with the Machine—' they began.

'Someone is trying to make himself king, to reintroduce the personal element.'

'Punish that man with Homelessness.'

'To the rescue! Avenge the Machine! Avenge the Machine!'

'War! Kill the man!'

But the Committee of the Mending Apparatus now came forward, and allayed the panic with well-chosen words. It confessed that the Mending Apparatus was itself in need of repair.

The effect of this frank confession was admirable.

'Of course,' said a famous lecturer—he of the French Revolution, who gilded each new decay with splendour—'of course we shall not press our complaints now. The Mending Apparatus has treated us so well in the past that we all sympathize with it, and will wait patiently for its recovery. In its own good time it will resume its duties. Meanwhile let us do without our beds, our tabloids, our other little wants. Such, I feel sure, would be the wish of the Machine.'

Thousands of miles away his audience applauded. The Machine still linked them. Under the seas, beneath the roots of the mountains, ran the wires through which they saw and heard, the enormous eyes and ears that were their heritage, and the hum of many workings clothed their thoughts in one garment of subserviency. Only the old and the sick remained ungrateful, for it was rumoured that Euthanasia, too, was out of order, and that pain had reappeared among men.

It became difficult to read. A blight entered the atmosphere and dulled its luminosity. At times Vashti could scarcely see across her room. The air, too, was foul. Loud were the complaints, impotent the remedies, heroic the tone of the lecturer as he cried: 'Courage! courage! What matter so long as the Machine goes on? To it the darkness and the light are one.' And though things improved again after a time, the old brilliancy was never recaptured, and humanity never recovered from its entrance into twilight. There was an hysterical talk of 'measures,' of 'provisional dictatorship,' and the inhabitants of Sumatra were asked to familiarize themselves with the workings of the central power station, the said power station being situated in France. But for the most part panic reigned, and men spent their strength praying to their Books, tangible proofs of the Machine's omnipotence. There were gradations of terror—at times came rumours of hope—the Mending Apparatus was almost mended—the enemies of the Machine had been got under—new 'nerve-centres' were evolving which would do the work even more magnificently than before. But there came a day when, without the slightest warning, without any previous hint of feebleness, the entire communication-system broke down, all over the world, and the world, as they understood it, ended.

Vashti was lecturing at the time and her earlier remarks had been punctuated with applause. As she proceeded the audience became silent, and at the conclusion there was no sound. Somewhat displeased, she called to a friend who was a specialist in sympathy. No sound: doubtless the friend was sleeping. And so with the next friend whom she tried to summon, and so with the next, until she remembered Kuno's cryptic remark, 'The Machine stops'.

The phrase still conveyed nothing. If Eternity was stopping it would of course be set going shortly.

For example, there was still a little light and air—the atmosphere had improved a few hours previously. There was still the Book, and while there was the Book there was security.

Then she broke down, for with the cessation of activity came an unexpected terror—silence.

She had never known silence, and the coming of it nearly killed her—it did kill many thousands of people outright. Ever since her birth she had been surrounded by the steady hum. It was to the ear what artificial air was to the lungs, and agonizing pains shot across her head. And scarcely knowing what she did, she stumbled forward and pressed the unfamiliar button, the one that opened the door of her cell.

Now the door of the cell worked on a simple hinge of its own. It was not connected with the central power station, dying far away in France. It opened, rousing immoderate hopes in Vashti, for she thought that the Machine had been mended. It opened, and she saw the dim tunnel that curved far away towards freedom. One look, and then she shrank back. For the tunnel was full of people—she was almost the last in that city to have taken alarm.

People at any time repelled her, and these were nightmares from her worst dreams. People were crawling about, people were screaming, whimpering, gasping for breath, touching each other, vanishing in the dark, and ever and anon being pushed off the platform on to the live rail. Some were fighting round the electric bells, trying to summon trains which could not be summoned. Others were yelling for Euthanasia or for respirators, or blaspheming the Machine. Others stood at the doors of their cells fearing, like herself, either to stop in them or to leave them. And behind all the uproar was silence—the silence which is the voice of the earth and of the generations who have gone.

No—it was worse than solitude. She closed the door again and sat down to wait for the end. The disintegration went on, accompanied by horrible cracks and rumbling. The valves that restrained the Medical Apparatus must have been weakened, for it ruptured and hung hideously from the ceiling. The floor heaved and fell and flung her from the chair. A tube oozed towards her serpent fashion. And at last the final horror approached—light began to ebb, and she knew that civilization's long day was closing.

She whirled round, praying to be saved from this, at any rate, kissing the Book, pressing button after button. The uproar outside was increasing, and even penetrated the wall. Slowly the brilliancy of her cell was dimmed, the reflections faded from the metal switches. Now she could not see the reading-stand, now not the Book, though she held it in her hand. Light followed the flight of sound, air was following light, and the original void returned to the cavern from which it had so long been excluded. Vashti continued to whirl, like the devotees of an earlier religion, screaming, praying, striking at the buttons with bleeding hands.

It was thus that she opened her prison and escaped—escaped in the spirit: at least so it seems to me, ere my meditation closes. That she escapes in the body—I cannot perceive that. She struck, by chance, the switch that released the door, and the rush of foul air on her skin, the loud throbbing whispers in her ears, told her that she was facing the tunnel again, and that tremendous platform on which she had seen men fighting. They were not fighting now. Only the whispers remained, and the little whimpering groans. They were dying by hundreds out in the dark.

She burst into tears.

Tears answered her.

They wept for humanity, those two, not for themselves. They could not bear that this should be the end. Ere silence was completed their hearts were opened, and they knew what had been important on the earth. Man, the flower of all flesh, the noblest of all creatures visible, man who had once made god in his image, and had mirrored his strength on the constellations, beautiful naked man was dying, strangled in the garments that he had woven. Century after century had he toiled, and here was his reward. Truly the garment had seemed heavenly at first, shot with colours of culture, sewn with the threads of self-denial. And heavenly it had been so long as it was a garment and no more, so long as man could shed it at will and live by the essence that is his soul, and the essence, equally divine, that is his body. The sin against the body—it was for that they wept in chief; the centuries of wrong against the muscles and the nerves, and those five portals by which we can alone apprehend—glozing it over with talk of evolution, until the body was white pap, the home of ideas as colourless, last sloshy stirrings of a spirit that had grasped the stars.

'Where are you?' she sobbed.

His voice in the darkness said, 'Here.'

'Is there any hope, Kuno?'

'None for us.'

'Where are you?'

She crawled towards him over the bodies of the dead. His blood spurted over her hands.

'Quicker,' he gasped, 'I am dying—but we touch, we talk, not through the Machine.' He kissed her.

'We have come back to our own. We die, but we have recaptured life, as it was in Wessex, when Ælfrid overthrew the Danes. We know what they know outside, they who dwelt in the cloud that is the colour of a pearl.'

'But, Kuno, is it true? Are there still men on the surface of the earth? Is this—this tunnel, this poisoned darkness—really not the end?'

He replied:

'I have seen them, spoken to them, loved them. They are hiding in the mist and the ferns until our civilization stops. To-day they are the Homeless—to-morrow—'

'Oh, to-morrow—some fool will start the Machine again, to-morrow.'

'Never,' said Kuno, 'never. Humanity has learnt its lesson.'

As he spoke, the whole city was broken like a honeycomb. An airship had sailed in through the vomitory into a ruined wharf. It crashed downwards, exploding as it went, rending gallery after gallery with its wings of steel. For a moment they saw the nations of the dead, and, before they joined them, scraps of the untainted sky.

SIR ARTHUR CONAN DOYLE

THE TERROR OF BLUE JOHN GAP

THE following narrative was found among the papers of Dr. James Hardcastle, who died of phthisis* on February 4, 1908, at 36, Upper Coventry Flats, South Kensington.* Those who knew him best, while refusing to express an opinion upon this particular statement, are unanimous in asserting that he was a man of a sober and scientific turn of mind, absolutely devoid of imagination, and most unlikely to invent any abnormal series of events. The paper was contained in an envelope, which was docketed, 'A Short Account of the Circumstances which occurred near Miss Allerton's Farm in North-West Derbyshire in the Spring of Last Year.' The envelope was sealed, and on the other side was written in pencil—

'DEAR SEATON,

'It may interest, and perhaps pain you, to know that the incredulity with which you met my story has prevented me from ever opening my mouth upon the subject again. I leave this record after my death, and perhaps strangers may be found to have more confidence in me than my friend.'

Inquiry has failed to elicit who this Seaton may have been. I may add that the visit of the deceased to Allerton's Farm, and the general nature of the alarm there, apart from his particular explanation, have been absolutely established. With this foreword I append his account exactly as he left it. It is in the form of a diary, some entries in which have been expanded, while a few have been erased.

April 17.—Already I feel the benefit of this wonderful upland air. The farm of the Allertons lies fourteen hundred and twenty feet above sea-level, so it may well be a bracing climate. Beyond the usual morning cough I have very little discomfort, and, what with the fresh milk and the home-grown mutton, I have every chance of putting on weight. I think Saunderson will be pleased.

The two Miss Allertons are charmingly quaint and kind, two dear little hard-working old maids, who are ready to lavish all the heart which might have gone out to husband and to children upon an invalid stranger. Truly, the old maid is a most useful person, one of the reserve forces of the community. They talk of the superfluous woman,* but what would the poor superfluous man do without her kindly presence? By the way, in their simplicity they very quickly let out the reason why Saunderson recommended their farm. The Professor rose from the ranks himself, and I believe that in his youth he was not above scaring crows in these very fields.

It is a most lonely spot, and the walks are picturesque in the extreme. The farm consists of grazing land lying at the bottom of an irregular valley. On each side are the fantastic limestone hills, formed of rock so soft that you can break it away with your hands. All this country is hollow. Could you strike it with some gigantic hammer it would boom like a drum, or possibly cave in altogether and expose some huge subterranean sea. A great sea there must surely be, for on all sides the streams run into the mountain itself, never to reappear. There are gaps everywhere amid the rocks, and when you pass through them you find yourself in great caverns, which wind down into the bowels of the earth. I have a small bicycle lamp, and it is a perpetual joy to me to carry it into these weird solitudes, and to see the wonderful silver and black effects when I throw its light upon the stalactites which drape the lofty roofs. Shut off the lamp, and you are in the blackest darkness. Turn it on, and it is a scene from the Arabian Nights.*

But there is one of these strange openings in the earth which has a special interest, for it is the handiwork, not of nature, but of man. I had never heard of Blue John* when I came to these parts. It is the name given to a peculiar mineral of a beautiful purple shade, which is only found at one or two places in the world. It is so rare that an ordinary vase of Blue John would be valued at a great price. The Romans, with that extraordinary instinct of theirs, discovered that it was to be found in this valley, and sank a horizontal shaft deep into the mountain side. The opening of their mine has been called Blue John Gap, a clean-cut arch in the rock, the mouth all overgrown with bushes. It is a goodly passage which the Roman miners have cut, and it intersects some of the great water-worn caves, so that if you enter Blue John Gap you would do well to mark your steps and to have a good store of candles, or you may never make your way back to the daylight again. I have not yet gone deeply into it, but this very day I stood at the mouth of the arched tunnel, and peering down into the black recesses beyond, I vowed that when my health returned I would devote some holiday to exploring those mysterious depths and finding out for myself how far the Roman had penetrated into the Derbyshire hills.

Strange how superstitious these countrymen are! I should have thought better of young Armitage, for he is a man of some education and character, and a very fine fellow for his station in life. I was standing at the Blue John Gap when he came across the field to me.

'Well, doctor,' said he, 'you're not afraid, anyhow.'

'Afraid!' I answered. 'Afraid of what?'

'Of it,' said he, with a jerk of his thumb towards the black vault, 'of the Terror that lives in the Blue John Cave.'

How absurdly easy it is for a legend to arise in a lonely countryside! I examined him as to the reasons for his weird belief. It seems that from time to time sheep have been missing from the fields, carried bodily away, according to Armitage. That they could have wandered away of their own accord and disappeared among the mountains was an explanation to which he would not listen. On one occasion a pool of blood had been found, and some tufts of wool. That also, I pointed out, could be explained in a perfectly natural way. Further, the nights upon which sheep disappeared were invariably very dark, cloudy nights with no moon. This I met with the obvious retort that those were the nights which a commonplace sheep-stealer would naturally choose for his work. On one occasion a gap had been made in a wall, and some of the stones scattered for a considerable distance. Human agency again, in my opinion. Finally, Armitage clinched all his arguments by telling me that he had actually heard the Creature—indeed, that any one could hear it who remained long enough at the Gap. It was a distant roaring of an immense volume. I could not but smile at this, knowing, as I do, the strange reverberations which come out of an underground water system running amid the chasms of a limestone formation. My incredulity annoyed Armitage, so that he turned and left me with some abruptness.

And now comes the queer point about the whole business. I was still standing near the mouth of the cave, turning over in my mind the various statements of Armitage, and reflecting how readily they could be explained away, when suddenly, from the depth of the tunnel beside me, there issued a most extraordinary sound. How shall I describe it? First of all, it seemed to be a great distance away, far down in the bowels of the earth. Secondly, in spite of this suggestion of distance, it was very loud. Lastly, it was not a boom, nor a crash, such as one would associate with falling water or tumbling rock, but it was a high whine, tremulous and vibrating, almost like the whinnying of a horse. It was certainly a most remarkable experience, and one which for a moment, I must admit, gave a new significance to Armitage's words. I waited by the Blue John Gap for half an hour or more, but there was no return of the sound, so at last I wandered back to the farm-house, rather mystified by what had occurred. Decidedly I shall explore that cavern when my strength is restored. Of course, Armitage's explanation is too absurd for discussion, and yet that sound was certainly very strange. It still rings in my ears as I write.

April 20.—In the last three days I have made several expeditions to the Blue John Gap, and have even penetrated some short distance, but my bicycle lantern is so small and weak that I dare not trust myself very far. I shall do the thing more systematically. I have heard no sound at all, and could almost believe that I had been the victim of some hallucination, suggested, perhaps, by Armitage's conversation. Of course, the whole idea is absurd, and yet I must confess that those bushes at the entrance of the cave do present an appearance as if some heavy creature had forced its way through them. I begin to be keenly interested. I have said nothing to the Miss Allertons, for they are quite superstitious enough already, but I have bought some candles, and mean to investigate for myself.

I observed this morning that among the numerous tufts of sheep's wool which lay among the bushes near the cavern there was one which was smeared with blood. Of course, my reason tells me that if sheep wander into such rocky places they are likely to injure themselves, and yet somehow that splash of crimson gave me a sudden shock, and for a moment I found myself shrinking back in horror from the old Roman arch. A fetid breath seemed to ooze from the black depths into which I peered. Could it indeed be possible that some nameless thing, some dreadful presence, was lurking down yonder? I should have been incapable of such feelings in the days of my strength, but one grows more nervous and fanciful when one's health is shaken.

For the moment I weakened in my resolution, and was ready to leave the secret of the old mine, if one exists, for ever unsolved. But to-night my interest has returned and my nerves grown more steady. To-morrow I trust that I shall have gone more deeply into this matter.

April 22.—Let me try and set down as accurately as I can my extraordinary experience of yesterday. I started in the afternoon, and made my way to the Blue John Gap, I confess that my misgivings returned as I gazed into its depths, and I wished that I had brought a companion to share my exploration. Finally, with a return of resolution, I lit my candle, pushed my way through the briars, and descended into the rocky shaft.

It went down at an acute angle for some fifty feet, the floor being covered with broken stone. Thence there extended a long, straight passage cut in the solid rock. I am no geologist, but the lining of this corridor was certainly of some harder material than limestone, for there were points where I could actually see the tool-marks which the old miners had left in their excavation, as fresh as if they had been done yesterday. Down this strange, old-world corridor I stumbled, my feeble flame throwing a dim circle of light around me, which made the shadows beyond the more threatening and obscure. Finally, I came to a spot where the Roman tunnel opened into a water-worn cavern—a huge hall, hung with long white icicles of lime deposit. From this central chamber I could dimly perceive that a number of passages worn by the subterranean streams wound away into the depths of the earth. I was standing there wondering whether I had better return, or whether I dare venture farther into this dangerous labyrinth, when my eyes fell upon something at my feet which strongly arrested my attention.

The greater part of the floor of the cavern was covered with boulders of rock or with hard incrustations of lime, but at this particular point there had been a drip from the distant roof, which had left a patch of soft mud. In the very centre of this there was a huge mark—an ill-defined blotch, deep, broad and irregular, as if a great boulder had fallen upon it. No loose stone lay near, however, nor was there anything to account for the impression. It was far too large to be caused by any possible animal, and besides, there was only the one, and the patch of mud was of such a size that no reasonable stride could have covered it. As I rose from the examination of that singular mark and then looked round into the black shadows which hemmed me in, I must confess that I felt for a moment a most unpleasant sinking of my heart, and that, do what I could, the candle trembled in my outstretched hand.

I soon recovered my nerve, however, when I reflected how absurd it was to associate so huge and shapeless a mark with the track of any known animal. Even an elephant could not have produced it. I determined, therefore, that I would not be scared by vague and senseless fears from carrying out my exploration. Before proceeding, I took good note of a curious rock formation in the wall by which I could recognize the entrance of the Roman tunnel. The precaution was very necessary, for the great cave, so far as I could see it, was intersected by passages. Having made sure of my position, and reassured myself by examining my spare candles and my matches, I advanced slowly over the rocky and uneven surface of the cavern.

And now I come to the point where I met with such sudden and desperate disaster. A stream, some twenty feet broad, ran across my path, and I walked for some little distance along the bank to find a spot where I could cross dryshod. Finally, I came to a place where a single flat boulder lay near the centre, which I could reach in a stride. As it chanced, however, the rock had been cut away and made top-heavy by the rush of the stream, so that it tilted over as I landed on it, and shot me into the ice-cold water. My candle went out, and I found myself floundering about in utter and absolute darkness.

I staggered to my feet again, more amused than alarmed by my adventure. The candle had fallen from my hand, and was lost in the stream, but I had two others in my pocket, so that it was of no importance. I got one of them ready, and drew out my box of matches to light it. Only then did I realize my position. The box had been soaked in my fall into the river. It was impossible to strike the matches.

A cold hand seemed to close round my heart as I realized my position. The darkness was opaque and horrible. It was so utter that one put one's hand up to one's face as if to press off something solid. I stood still, and by an effort I steadied myself. I tried to reconstruct in my mind a map of the floor of the cavern as I had last seen it. Alas! the bearings which had impressed themselves upon my mind were high on the wall, and not to be found by touch. Still, I remembered in a general way how the sides were situated, and I hoped that by groping my way along them I should at last come to the opening of the Roman tunnel. Moving very slowly, and continually striking against the rocks, I set out on this desperate quest.

But I very soon realized how impossible it was. In that black, velvety darkness one lost all one's bearings in an instant. Before I had made a dozen paces, I was utterly bewildered as to my whereabouts. The rippling of the stream, which was the one sound audible, showed me where it lay, but the moment that I left its bank I was utterly lost. The idea of finding my way back in absolute darkness through that limestone labyrinth was clearly an impossible one.

I sat down upon a boulder and reflected upon my unfortunate plight. I had not told any one that I proposed to come to the Blue John mine, and it was unlikely that a search party would come after me. Therefore I must trust to my own resources to get clear of the danger. There was only one hope, and that was that the matches might dry. When I fell into the river, only half of me had got thoroughly wet. My left shoulder had remained above the water. I took the box of matches, therefore, and put it into my left armpit. The moist air of the cavern might possibly be counteracted by the heat of my body, but even so, I knew that I could not hope to get a light for many hours. Meanwhile there was nothing for it but to wait.

By good luck I had slipped several biscuits into my pocket before I left the farm-house. These I now devoured, and washed them down with a draught from that wretched stream which had been the cause of all my misfortunes. Then I felt about for a comfortable seat among the rocks, and, having discovered a place where I could get a support for my back, I stretched out my legs and settled myself down to wait. I was wretchedly damp and cold, but I tried to cheer myself with the reflection that modern science prescribed open windows and walks in all weather for my disease. Gradually, lulled by the monotonous gurgle of the stream and by the absolute darkness, I sank into an uneasy slumber.

How long this lasted I cannot say. It may have been for an hour, it may have been for several. Suddenly I sat up on my rock couch, with every nerve thrilling and every sense acutely on the alert. Beyond all doubt I had heard a sound—some sound very distinct from the gurgling of the waters. It had passed, but the reverberation of it still lingered in my ear. Was it a search party? They would most certainly have shouted, and vague as this sound was which had wakened me, it was very distinct from the human voice. I sat palpitating and hardly daring to breathe. There it was again! And again! Now it had become continuous. It was a tread—yes, surely it was the tread of some living creature. But what a tread it was! It gave one the impression of enormous weight carried upon sponge-like feet, which gave forth a muffled but ear-filling sound. The darkness was as complete as ever, but the tread was regular and decisive. And it was coming beyond all question in my direction.

My skin grew cold, and my hair stood on end as I listened to that steady and ponderous footfall. There was some creature there, and surely, by the speed of its advance, it was one which could see in the dark. I crouched low on my rock and tried to blend myself into it. The steps grew nearer still, then stopped, and presently I was aware of a loud lapping and gurgling. The creature was drinking at the stream. Then again there was silence, broken by a succession of long sniffs and snorts of tremendous volume and energy. Had it caught the scent of me? My own nostrils were filled by a low fetid odour, mephitic and abominable. Then I heard the steps again. They were on my side of the stream now. The stones rattled within a few yards of where I lay. Hardly daring to breathe, I crouched upon my rock. Then the steps drew away. I heard the splash as it returned across the river, and the sound died away into the distance in the direction from which it had come.

For a long time I lay upon the rock, too much horrified to move. I thought of the sound which I had heard coming from the depths of the cave, of Armitage's fears, of the strange impression in the mud, and now came this final and absolute proof that there was indeed some inconceivable monster, something utterly unearthly and dreadful, which lurked in the hollow of the mountain. Of its nature or form I could frame no conception, save that it was both light-footed and gigantic. The combat between my reason, which told me that such things could not be, and my senses, which told me that they were, raged within me as I lay. Finally, I was almost ready to persuade myself that this experience had been part of some evil dream, and that my abnormal condition might have conjured up an hallucination. But there remained one final experience which removed the last possibility of doubt from my mind.

I had taken my matches from my armpit and felt them. They seemed perfectly hard and dry. Stooping down into a crevice of the rocks, I tried one of them. To my delight it took fire at once. I lit the candle, and, with a terrified backward glance into the obscure depths of the cavern, I hurried in the direction of the Roman passage. As I did so I passed the patch of mud on which I had seen the huge imprint. Now I stood astonished before it, for there were three similar imprints upon its surface, enormous in size, irregular in outline, of a depth which indicated the ponderous weight which had left them. Then a great terror surged over me. Stooping and shading my candle with my hand, I ran in a frenzy of fear to the rocky archway, hastened up it, and never stopped until, with weary feet and panting lungs, I rushed up the final slope of stones, broke through the tangle of briars, and flung myself exhausted upon the soft grass under the peaceful light of the stars. It was three in the morning when I reached the farm-house, and to-day I am all unstrung and quivering after my terrific adventure. As yet I have told no one, I must move warily in the matter. What would the poor lonely women, or the uneducated yokels here think of it if I were to tell them my experience? Let me go to some one who can understand and advise.

April 25.—I was laid up in bed for two days after my incredible adventure in the cavern. I use the adjective with a very definite meaning, for I have had an experience since which has shocked me almost as much as the other. I have said that I was looking round for some one who could advise me. There is a Dr. Mark Johnson who practises some few miles away, to whom I had a note of recommendation from Professor Saunderson. To him I drove, when I was strong enough to get about, and I recounted to him my whole strange experience. He listened intently, and then carefully examined me, paying special attention to my reflexes and to the pupils of my eyes. When he had finished, he refused to discuss my adventure, saying that it was entirely beyond him, but he gave me the card of a Mr. Picton at Castleton, with the advice that I should instantly go to him and tell him the story exactly as I had done to himself. He was, according to my adviser, the very man who was preeminently suited to help me. I went on to the station, therefore, and made my way to the little town, which is some ten miles away. Mr. Picton appeared to be a man of importance, as his brass plate was displayed upon the door of a considerable building on the outskirts of the town. I was about to ring his bell, when some misgiving came into my mind, and, crossing to a neighbouring shop, I asked the man behind the counter if he could tell me anything of Mr. Picton. 'Why,' said he, 'he is the best mad doctor in Derbyshire, and yonder is his asylum.' You can imagine that it was not long before I had shaken the dust of Castleton from my feet and returned to the farm, cursing all unimaginative pedants who cannot conceive that there may be things in creation which have never yet chanced to come across their mole's vision. After all, now that I am cooler, I can afford to admit that I have been no more sympathetic to Armitage than Dr. Johnson has been to me.

April 27.—When I was a student I had the reputation of being a man of courage and enterprise. I remember that when there was a ghost-hunt at Coltbridge* it was I who sat up in the haunted house. Is it advancing years (after all, I am only thirty-five), or is it this physical malady which has caused degeneration? Certainly my heart quails when I think of that horrible cavern in the hill, and the certainty that it has some monstrous occupant. What shall I do? There is not an hour in the day that I do not debate the question. If I say nothing, then the mystery remains unsolved. If I do say anything, then I have the alternative of mad alarm over the whole country side, or of absolute incredulity which may end in consigning me to an asylum. On the whole, I think that my best course is to wait, and to prepare for some expedition which shall be more deliberate and better thought-out than the last. As a first step I have been to Castleton and obtained a few essentials—a large acetylene lantern* for one thing, and a good double-barrelled sporting rifle for another. The latter I have hired, but I have bought a dozen heavy game cartridges, which would bring down a rhinoceros. Now I am ready for my troglodyte* friend. Give me better health and a little spate of energy, and I shall try conclusions* with him yet. But who and what is he? Ah! there is the question which stands between me and my sleep. How many theories do I form, only to discard each in turn! It is all so utterly unthinkable. And yet the cry, the footmark, the tread in the cavern—no reasoning can get past these. I think of the old-world legends of dragons and of other monsters. Were they, perhaps, not such fairy-tales as we have thought? Can it be that there is some fact which underlies them, and am I, of all mortals, the one who is chosen to expose it?

May 3.—For several days I have been laid up by the vagaries of an English spring, and during those days there have been developments, the true and sinister meaning of which no one can appreciate save myself. I may say that we have had cloudy and moonless nights of late, which according to my information were the seasons upon which sheep disappeared. Well, sheep *have* disappeared. Two of Miss Allerton's, one of old Pearson's of the Cat Walk, and one of Mrs. Moulton's. Four in all during three nights. No trace is left of them at all, and the countryside is buzzing with rumours of gipsies and of sheep-stealers.

But there is something more serious than that. Young Armitage has disappeared also. He left his moorland cottage early on Wednesday night and has never been heard of since. He was an unattached man, so there is less sensation than would otherwise be the case. The popular explanation is that he owes money, and has found a situation in some other part of the country, whence he will presently write for his belongings. But I have grave misgivings. Is it not much more likely that the recent tragedy of the sheep has caused him to take some steps which may have ended in his own destruction? He may, for example, have lain in wait for the creature and been carried off by it into the recesses of the mountains. What an inconceivable fate for a civilized Englishman of the twentieth century! And yet I feel that it is possible and even probable. But in that case, how far am I answerable both for his death and for any other mishap which may occur? Surely with the knowledge I already possess it must be my duty to see that something is done, or if necessary to do it myself. It must be the latter, for this morning I went down to the local police-station and told my story. The inspector entered it all in a large book and bowed me out with commendable gravity, but I heard a burst of laughter before I had got down his garden path. No doubt he was recounting my adventure to his family.

June 10.—I am writing this, propped up in bed, six weeks after my last entry in this journal. I have gone through a terrible shock both to mind and body, arising from such an experience as has seldom befallen a human being before. But I have attained my end. The danger from the Terror which dwells in the Blue John Gap has passed never to return. Thus much at least I, a broken invalid, have done for the common good. Let me now recount what occurred as clearly as I may.

The night of Friday, May 3, was dark and cloudy—the very night for the monster to walk. About eleven o'clock I went from the farmhouse with my lantern and my rifle, having first left a note upon the table of my bedroom in which I said that, if I were missing, search should be made for me in the direction of the Gap. I made my way to the mouth of the Roman shaft, and, having perched myself among the rocks close to the opening, I shut off my lantern and waited patiently with my loaded rifle ready to my hand.

It was a melancholy vigil. All down the winding valley I could see the scattered lights of the farm-houses, and the church clock of Chapel-le-Dale* tolling the hours came faintly to my ears. These tokens of my fellow-men served only to make my own position seem the more lonely, and to call for a greater effort to overcome the terror which tempted me continually to get back to the farm, and abandon for ever this dangerous quest. And yet there lies deep in every man a rooted self-respect which makes it hard for him to turn back from that which he has once undertaken. This feeling of personal pride was my salvation now, and it was that alone which held me fast when every instinct of my nature was dragging me away. I am glad now that I had the strength. In spite of all that it has cost me, my manhood is at least above reproach.

Twelve o'clock struck in the distant church, then one, then two. It was the darkest hour of the night. The clouds were drifting low, and there was not a star in the sky. An owl was hooting somewhere among the rocks, but no other sound, save the gentle sough of the wind, came to my ears. And then suddenly I heard it! From far away down the tunnel came those muffled steps, so soft and yet so ponderous. I heard also the rattle of stones as they gave way under that giant tread. They drew nearer. They were close upon me. I heard the crashing of the bushes round the entrance, and then dimly through the darkness I was conscious of the loom of some enormous shape, some monstrous inchoate creature, passing swiftly and very silently out from the tunnel. I was paralyzed with fear and amazement. Long as I had waited, now that it had actually come I was unprepared for the shock. I lay motionless and breathless, whilst the great dark mass whisked by me and was swallowed up in the night.

But now I nerved myself for its return. No sound came from the sleeping countryside to tell of the horror which was loose. In no way could I judge how far off it was, what it was doing, or when it might be back. But not a second time should my nerve fail me, not a second time should it pass unchallenged. I swore it between my clenched teeth as I laid my cocked rifle across the rock,

And yet it nearly happened. There was no warning of approach now as the creature passed over the grass, Suddenly, like a dark, drifting shadow, the huge bulk loomed up once more before me, making for the entrance of the cave. Again came that paralysis of volition which held my crooked forefinger impotent upon the trigger. But with a desperate effort I shook it off. Even as the brushwood rustled, and the monstrous beast blended with the shadow of the Gap; I fired at the retreating form. In the blaze of the gun I caught a glimpse of a great shaggy mass, something with rough and bristling hair of a withered grey colour, fading away to white in its lower parts, the huge body supported upon short, thick, curving legs. I had just that glance, and then I heard the rattle of the stones as the creature tore down into its burrow. In an instant, with a triumphant revulsion of feeling, I had cast my fears to the wind, and uncovering my powerful lantern, with my rifle in my hand, I sprang down from my rock and rushed after the monster down the old Roman shaft.

My splendid lamp cast a brilliant flood of vivid light in front of me, very different from the yellow glimmer which had aided me down the same passage only twelve days before. As I ran, I saw the great beast lurching along before me, its huge bulk filling up the whole space from wall to wall. Its hair looked like coarse faded oakum;* and hung down in long, dense masses which swayed as it moved. It was like an enormous unclipped sheep in its fleece, but in size it was far larger than the largest elephant, and its breadth seemed to be nearly as great as its height. It fills me with amazement now to think that I should have dared to follow such a horror into the bowels of the earth, but when one's blood is up, and when one's quarry seems to be flying, the old primeval hunting-spirit awakes and prudence is cast to the wind. Rifle in hand, I ran at the top of my speed upon the trail of the monster.

I had seen that the creature was swift. Now I was to find out to my cost that it was also very cunning. I had imagined that it was in panic flight, and that I had only to pursue it. The idea that it might turn upon me never entered my excited brain. I have already explained that the passage down which I was racing opened into a great central cave. Into this I rushed, fearful lest I should lose all trace of the beast. But he had turned upon his own traces, and in a moment we were face to face.

That picture, seen in the brilliant white light of the lantern, is etched for ever upon my brain. He had reared up on his hind legs as a bear would do, and stood above me, enormous, menacing—such a creature as no nightmare had ever brought to my imagination. I have said that he reared like a bear, and there was something bear-like—if one could conceive a bear which was tenfold the bulk of any bear seen upon earth—in his whole pose and attitude, in his great crooked forelegs with their ivory-white claws; in his rugged skin, and in his red, gaping mouth, fringed with monstrous fangs. Only in one point did he differ from the bear, or from any other creature which walks the earth; and even at that supreme moment a shudder of hor-ror passed over me as I observed that the eyes which glistened in the glow of my lantern were huge, projecting bulbs, white and sightless. For a moment his great paws swung over my head. The next he fell forward upon me, I and my broken lantern crashed to the earth, and I remember no more.

When I came to myself I was back in the farm-house of the Allertons. Two days had passed since my terrible adventure in the Blue John Gap. It seems that I had lain all night in the cave insensible from con-cussion of the brain, with my left arm and two ribs badly fractured. In the morning my note had been found, a search party of a dozen farm-ers assembled, and I had been tracked down and carried back to my bedroom, where I had lain in high delirium ever since. There was, it seems, no sign of the creature, and no bloodstain which would show that my bullet had found him as he passed. Save for my own plight and the marks upon the mud, there was nothing to prove that what I said was true.

Six weeks have now elapsed, and I am able to sit out once more in the sunshine. Just opposite me is the steep hillside, grey with shaly rock, and yonder on its flank is the dark cleft which marks the open-ing of the Blue John Gap. But it is no longer a source of terror. Never again through that ill-omened tunnel shall any strange shape flit out into the world of men. The educated and the scientific, the Dr. Johnsons and the like, may smile at my narrative, but the poorer folk of the countryside had never a doubt as to its truth. On the day after my recovering consciousness they assembled in their hundreds round the Blue John Gap. As the *Castleton Courier* said—

'It was useless for our correspondent, or for any of the adventurous gentlemen who had come from Matlock, Buxton, and other parts, to offer to descend, to explore the cave to the end, and to finally test the extraordinary narrative of Dr. James Hardcastle. The country people had taken the matter into their own hands, and from an early hour of the morning they had worked hard in stopping up the entrance of the tunnel. There is a sharp slope where the shaft begins, and great boul-ders, rolled along by many willing hands, were thrust down it until the Gap was absolutely sealed. So ends the episode which has caused such excitement throughout the country. Local opinion is fiercely divided upon the subject. On the one hand are those who point to

Dr. Hardcastle's impaired health, and to the possibility of cerebral lesions of tubercular origin giving rise to strange hallucinations. Some *idée fixe*, according to these gentlemen, caused the doctor to wander down the tunnel, and a fall among the rocks was sufficient to account for his injuries. On the other hand, a legend of a strange creature in the Gap has existed for some months back, and the farmers look upon Dr. Hardcastle's narrative and his personal injuries as a final corroboration. So the matter stands, and so the matter will continue to stand, for no definite solution seems to us to be now possible. It transcends human wit to give any scientific explanation which could cover the alleged facts.'

Perhaps before the *Courier* published these words they would have been wise to send their representative to me. I have thought the matter out, as no one else has occasion to do, and it is possible that I might have removed some of the more obvious difficulties of the narrative and brought it one degree nearer to scientific acceptance. Let me then write down the only explanation which seems to me to elucidate what I know to my cost to have been a series of facts. My theory may seem to be wildly improbable, but at least no one can venture to say that it is impossible.

My view is—and it was formed, as is shown by my diary, before my personal adventure—that in this part of England there is a vast subterranean lake or sea, which is fed by the great number of streams which pass down through the limestone. Where there is a large collection of water there must also be some evaporation, mists or rain, and a possibility of vegetation. This in turn suggests that there may be animal life, arising, as the vegetable life would also do, from those seeds and types which had been introduced at an early period of the world's history, when communication with the outer air was more easy. This place had then developed a fauna and flora of its own, including such monsters as the one which I had seen, which may well have been the old cave-bear, enormously enlarged and modified by its new environment. For countless æons the internal and the external creation had kept apart, growing steadily away from each other. Then there had come some rift in the depths of the mountain which had enabled one creature to wander up and, by means of the Roman tunnel, to reach the open air. Like all subterranean life, it had lost the power of sight, but this had no doubt been compensated for by nature in other directions. Certainly it had some means of finding its way about, and of hunting down the sheep upon the hillside. As to its choice of dark nights, it is part of my theory that light was painful to those great white eyeballs, and that it was only a pitch-black world which it could tolerate. Perhaps, indeed, it was the glare of my lantern which saved my life at that awful moment when we were face to face. So I read the riddle. I leave these facts behind me; and if you can explain them, do so; or if you choose to doubt them, do so. Neither your belief nor your incredulity can alter them, nor affect one whose task is nearly over.

So ended the strange narrative of Dr. James Hardcastle.

JACK LONDON

THE RED ONE

THERE it was! The abrupt liberation of sound, as he timed it with his watch, Bassett likened to the trump of an archangel. Walls of cities, he meditated, might well fall down before so vast and compelling a summons.* For the thousandth time vainly he tried to analyze the tone-quality of that enormous peal that dominated the land far into the strongholds of the surrounding tribes. The mountain gorge which was its source rang to the rising tide of it until it brimmed over and flooded earth and sky and air. With the wantonness of a sick man's fancy, he likened it to the mighty cry of some Titan* of the Elder World vexed with misery or wrath. Higher and higher it arose, challenging and demanding in such profounds of volume that it seemed intended for ears beyond the narrow confines of the solar system. There was in it, too, the clamor of protest in that there were no ears to hear and comprehend its utterance.

—Such the sick man's fancy. Still he strove to analyze the sound. Sonorous as thunder was it, mellow as a golden bell, thin and sweet as a thrummed taut cord of silver—no; it was none of these, nor a blend of these. There were no words nor semblances in his vocabulary and experience with which to describe the totality of that sound.

Time passed. Minutes merged into quarters of hours, and quarters of hours into half hours, and still the sound persisted, ever changing from its initial vocal impulse yet never receiving fresh impulse—fading, dimming, dying as enormously as it had sprung into being. It became a confusion of troubled mutterings and babblings and colossal whisperings. Slowly it withdrew, sob by sob, into whatever great bosom had birthed it, until it whimpered deadly whispers of wrath and as equally seductive whispers of delight, striving still to be heard, to convey some cosmic secret, some understanding of infinite import and value. It dwindled to a ghost of sound that had lost its menace and promise, and became a thing that pulsed on in the sick man's consciousness for minutes after it had ceased. When he could hear it no longer, Bassett glanced at his watch. An hour had elapsed ere that archangel's trump had subsided into tonal nothingness.

Was this, then, *his* dark tower?—Bassett pondered, remembering his Browning* and gazing at his skeleton-like and fever-wasted hands. And the fancy made him smile—of Childe Roland bearing a slug-horn to his lips with an arm as feeble as his was. Was it months, or years, he asked himself, since he first heard that mysterious call on the beach at Ringmanu? To save himself he could not tell. The long sick-ness had been most long. In conscious count of time he knew of months, many of them; but he had no way of estimating the long intervals of delirium and stupor. And how fared Captain Bateman of the blackbirder* *Nari*? he wondered; and had Captain Bateman's drunken mate died of delirium tremens yet?

From which vain speculations, Bassett turned idly to review all that had occurred since that day on the beach of Ringmanu when he first heard the sound and plunged into the jungle after it. Sagawa had pro-tested. He could see him yet, his queer little monkeyish face eloquent with fear, his back burdened with specimen cases, in his hands Bassett's butterfly net and naturalist's shot-gun, as he quavered in Beche de mer English:* 'Me fella too much fright along bush. Bad fella boy too much stop'm along bush.'

Bassett smiled sadly at the recollection. The little New Hanover boy* had been frightened, but had proved faithful, following him without hesitancy into the bush in the quest after the source of the wonderful sound. No fire-hollowed tree-trunk, that, throbbing war through the jungle depths, had been Bassett's conclusion. Erroneous had been his next conclusion, namely, that the source or cause could not be more distant than an hour's walk and that he would easily be back by mid-afternoon to be picked up by the *Nari*'s whaleboat.

'That big fella noise no good, all the same devil-devil,' Sagawa had adjudged. And Sagawa had been right. Had he not had his head hacked off within the day? Bassett shuddered. Without doubt Sagawa had been eaten as well by the bad fella boys too much that stopped along the bush. He could see him, as he had last seen him, stripped of the shotgun and all the naturalist's gear of his master, lying on the narrow trail where he had been decapitated barely the moment before. Yes, within a minute the thing had happened. Within a minute, look-ing back, Bassett had seen him trudging patiently along under his burdens. Then Bassett's own trouble had come upon him. He looked at the cruelly healed stumps of the first and second fingers of his left hand, then rubbed them softly into the indentation in the back of his skull. Quick as had been the flash of the long-handled tomahawk, he had been quick enough to duck away his head and partially to deflect the stroke with his up-flung hand. Two fingers and a nasty scalp-wound had been the price he paid for his life. With one barrel of his ten-gauge shotgun* he had blown the life out of the bushman who had so nearly got him; with the other barrel he had peppered the bushmen bending over Sagawa, and had the pleasure of knowing that the major portion of the charge had gone into the one who leaped away with Sagawa's head. Everything had occurred in a flash. Only himself, the slain bushman, and what remained of Sagawa, were in the narrow, wild-pig run of a path. From the dark jungle on either side came no rustle of movement or sound of life. And he had suffered distinct and dreadful shock. For the first time in his life he had killed a human being, and he knew nausea as he contemplated the mess of his handiwork.

Then had begun the chase. He retreated up the pig-run before his hunters, who were between him and the beach. How many there were, he could not guess. There might have been one, or a hundred, for aught he saw of them. That some of them took to the trees and traveled along through the jungle roof he was certain; but at the most he never glimpsed more than an occasional flitting of shadows. No bow-strings twanged that he could hear; but every little while, whence discharged he knew not, tiny arrows whispered past him or struck tree-boles and fluttered to the ground beside him. They were bone-tipped and feather-shafted, and the feathers, torn from the breasts of humming-birds, iridesced like jewels.

Once—and now, after the long lapse of time, he chuckled gleefully at the recollection—he had detected a shadow above him that came to instant rest as he turned his gaze upward. He could make out nothing, but, deciding to chance it, had fired at it a heavy charge of number five shot. Squalling like an infuriated cat, the shadow crashed down through tree-ferns and orchids and thudded upon the earth at his feet, and, still squalling its rage and pain, had sunk its human teeth into the ankle of his stout tramping boot. He, on the other hand, was not idle, and with his free foot had done what reduced the squalling to silence. So inured to savagery had Bassett since become, that he chuckled again with the glee of the recollection.

What a night had followed! Small wonder that he had accumulated such a virulence and variety of fevers, he thought, as he recalled that sleepless night of torment, when the throb of his wounds was as nothing compared with the myriad stings of the mosquitoes. There had been no escaping them, and he had not dared to light a fire. They had literally pumped his body full of poison, so that, with the coming of day, eyes swollen almost shut, he had stumbled blindly on, not caring much when his head should be hacked off and his carcass started on the way of Sagawa's to the cooking fire. Twenty-four hours had made a wreck of him—of mind as well as body. He had scarcely retained his wits at all, so maddened was he by the tremendous inoculation of poison he had received. Several times he fired his shotgun with effect into the shadows that dogged him. Stinging day insects and gnats added to his torment, while his bloody wounds attracted hosts of loathsome flies that clung sluggishly to his flesh and had to be brushed off and crushed off.

Once, in that day, he heard again the wonderful sound, seemingly more distant, but rising imperiously above the nearer war-drums in the bush. Right there was where he had made his mistake. Thinking that he had passed beyond it and that, therefore, it was between him and the beach of Ringmanu, he had worked back toward it when in reality he was penetrating deeper and deeper into the mysterious heart of the unexplored island. That night, crawling in among the twisted roots of a banyan tree, he had slept from exhaustion while the mosquitoes had had their will of him.

Followed days and nights that were vague as nightmares in his memory. One clear vision he remembered was of suddenly finding himself in the midst of a bush village and watching the old men and children fleeing into the jungle. All had fled but one. From close at hand and above him, a whimpering as of some animal in pain and terror had startled him. And looking up he had seen her—a girl, or young woman, rather, suspended by one arm in the cooking sun. Perhaps for days she had so hung. Her swollen, protruding tongue spoke as much. Still alive, she gazed at him with eyes of terror. Past help, he decided, as he noted the swellings of her legs which advertised that the joints had been crushed and the great bones broken. He resolved to shoot her, and there the vision terminated. He could not remember whether he had or not, any more than could he remember how he chanced to be in that village or how he succeeded in getting away from it.

Many pictures, unrelated, came and went in Bassett's mind as he reviewed that period of his terrible wanderings. He remembered invading another village of a dozen houses and driving all before him with his shotgun save for one old man, too feeble to flee, who spat at him and whined and snarled as he dug open a ground-oven and from amid the hot stones dragged forth a roasted pig that steamed its essence deliciously through its green-leaf wrappings. It was at this place that a wantonness of savagery had seized upon him. Having feasted, ready to depart with a hind quarter of the pig in his hand, he deliberately fired the grass thatch of a house with his burning glass.

But seared deepest of all in Bassett's brain, was the dank and noisome jungle. It actually stank with evil, and it was always twilight. Rarely did a shaft of sunlight penetrate its matted roof a hundred feet overhead. And beneath that roof was an aerial ooze of vegetation, a monstrous, parasitic dripping of decadent life-forms that rooted in death and lived on death. And through all this he drifted, ever pursued by the flitting shadows of the anthropophagi,* themselves ghosts of evil that dared not face him in battle but that knew, soon or late, that they would feed on him. Bassett remembered that at the time, in lucid moments, he had likened himself to a wounded bull pursued by plains' coyotes too cowardly to battle with him for the meat of him, yet certain of the inevitable end of him when they would be full gorged. As the bull's horns and stamping hoofs kept off the coyotes, so his shotgun kept off these Solomon Islanders, these twilight shades of bushmen of the island of Guadalcanal.*

Came the day of the grass lands. Abruptly, as if cloven by the sword of God in the hand of God, the jungle terminated. The edge of it, perpendicular and as black as the infamy of it, was a hundred feet up and down. And, beginning at the edge of it, grew the grass—sweet, soft, tender, pasture grass that would have delighted the eyes and beasts of any husbandman and that extended, on and on, for leagues and leagues of velvet verdure, to the backbone of the great island, the towering mountain range flung up by some ancient earth-cataclysm, serrated and gullied but not yet erased by the erosive tropic rains. But the grass! He had crawled into it a dozen yards, buried his face in it, smelled it, and broken down in a fit of involuntary weeping.

And, while he wept, the wonderful sound had pealed forth—if by *peal*, he had often thought since, an adequate description could be given of the enunciation of so vast a sound so melting sweet. Sweet it was as no sound ever heard. Vast it was, of so mighty a resonance that it might have proceeded from some brazen-throated monster. And yet it called to him across that leagues-wide savannah, and was like a benediction to his long-suffering, pain-wracked spirit.

He remembered how he lay there in the grass, wet-cheeked but no longer sobbing, listening to the sound and wondering that he had been able to hear it on the beach of Ringmanu. Some freak of air pressures and air currents, he reflected, had made it possible for the sound to carry so far. Such conditions might not happen again in a thousand days or ten thousand days; but the one day it had happened had been the day he landed from the *Nari* for several hours' collecting. Especially had he been in quest of the famed jungle butterfly, a foot across from wing-tip to wing-tip, as velvet-dusky of lack of color as was the gloom of the roof, of such lofty arboreal habits that it resorted only to the jungle roof and could be brought down only by a dose of shot. It was for this purpose that Sagawa had carried the twenty-gauge shot-gun.

Two days and nights he had spent crawling across that belt of grass land. He had suffered much, but pursuit had ceased at the jungle-edge. And he would have died of thirst had not a heavy thunderstorm revived him on the second day.

And then had come Balatta. In the first shade, where the savannah yielded to the dense mountain jungle, he had collapsed to die. At first she had squealed with delight at sight of his helplessness, and was for beating his brain out with a stout forest branch. Perhaps it was his very utter helplessness that had appealed to her, and perhaps it was her human curiosity that made her refrain. At any rate, she had refrained, for he opened his eyes again under the impending blow, and saw her studying him intently. What especially struck her about him were his blue eyes and white skin. Coolly she had squatted on her hams, spat on his arm, and with her finger-tips scrubbed away the dirt of days and nights of muck and jungle that sullied the pristine whiteness of his skin.

And everything about her had struck him especially, although there was nothing conventional about her at all. He laughed weakly at the recollection, for she had been as innocent of garb as Eve before the fig-leaf adventure.* Squat and lean at the same time, asymmetrically limbed, string-muscled as if with lengths of cordage, dirt-caked from infancy save for casual showers, she was as unbeautiful a prototype of woman as he, with a scientist's eye, had ever gazed upon. Her breasts advertised at the one time her maturity and youth; and, if by nothing else, her sex was advertised by the one article of finery with which she was adorned, namely a pig's tail, thrust through a hole in her left ear-lobe. So lately had the tail been severed, that its raw end still oozed blood that dried upon her shoulder like so much candle-droppings. And her face! A twisted and wizened complex of apish features, perforated by upturned, sky-open, Mongolian nostrils,* by a mouth that sagged from a huge upper-lip and faded precipitately into a retreating chin, and by peering querulous eyes that blinked as blink the eyes of denizens of monkey-cages.

Not even the water she brought him in a forest-leaf, and the ancient and half-putrid chunk of roast pig, could redeem in the slightest the grotesque hideousness of her. When he had eaten weakly for a space, he closed his eyes in order not to see her, although again and again she poked them open to peer at the blue of them. Then had come the sound. Nearer, much nearer, he knew it to be; and he knew equally well, despite the weary way he had come, that it was still many hours distant. The effect of it on her had been startling. She cringed under it, with averted face, moaning and chattering with fear. But after it had lived its full life of an hour, he closed his eyes and fell asleep with Balatta brushing the flies from him.

When he awoke it was night, and she was gone. But he was aware of renewed strength, and, by then too thoroughly inoculated by the mosquito poison to suffer further inflammation, he closed his eyes and slept an unbroken stretch till sun-up. A little later Balatta had returned, bringing with her a half dozen women who, unbeautiful as they were, were patently not so unbeautiful as she. She evidenced by her conduct that she considered him her find, her property, and the pride she took in showing him off would have been ludicrous had his situation not been so desperate.

Later, after what had been to him a terrible journey of miles, when he collapsed in front of the devil-devil house* in the shadow of the breadfruit tree, she had shown very lively ideas on the matter of retaining possession of him. Ngurn, whom Bassett was to know after-ward as the devil-devil doctor, priest, or medicine man of the village, had wanted his head. Others of the grinning and chattering monkey-men, all as stark of clothes and bestial of appearance as Balatta, had wanted his body for the roasting oven. At that time he had not under-stood their language, if by *language* might be dignified the uncouth sounds they made to represent ideas. But Bassett had thoroughly understood the matter of debate, especially when the men pressed and prodded and felt of the flesh of him as if he were so much commodity in a butcher's stall.

Balatta had been losing the debate rapidly, when the accident happened. One of the men, curiously examining Bassett's shotgun, managed to cock and pull a trigger. The recoil of the butt into the pit of the man's stomach had not been the most sanguinary result, for the charge of shot, at a distance of a yard, had blown the head of one of the debaters into nothingness.

Even Balatta joined the others in flight, and, ere they returned, his senses already reeling from the oncoming fever-attack, Bassett had regained possession of the gun. Whereupon, although his teeth chattered with the ague and his swimming eyes could scarcely see, he held onto his fading consciousness until he could intimidate the bush-men with the simple magics of compass, watch, burning glass, and matches. At the last, with due emphasis of solemnity and awfulness, he had killed a young pig with his shotgun and promptly fainted.

Bassett flexed his arm-muscles in quest of what possible strength might reside in such weakness, and dragged himself slowly and totteringly to his feet. He was shockingly emaciated; yet, during the various convalescences of the many months of his long sickness, he had never regained quite the same degree of strength as this time. What he feared was another relapse such as he had already frequently experienced. Without drugs, without even quinine, he had managed so far to live through a combination of the most pernicious and most malignant of malarial and black-water fevers.* But could he continue to endure? Such was his everlasting query. For, like the genuine scientist he was, he would not be content to die until he had solved the secret of the sound.

Supported by a staff, he staggered the few steps to the devil-devil house where death and Ngurn reigned in gloom. Almost as infamously dark and evil-stinking as the jungle was the devil-devil house—in Bassett's opinion. Yet therein was usually to be found his favorite crony and gossip, Ngurn, always willing for a yarn or a discussion, the while he sat in the ashes of death and in a slow smoke shrewdly revolved curing human heads suspended from the rafters. For, through the months' interval of consciousness of his long sickness, Bassett had mastered the psychological simplicities and lingual difficulties of the language of the tribe of Ngurn and Balatta, and

Gngngn—the latter the addle-headed young chief who was ruled by Ngurn, and who, whispered intrigue had it, was the son of Ngurn.

'Will the Red One speak to-day?' Bassett asked, by this time so accustomed to the old man's gruesome occupation as to take even an interest in the progress of the smoke-curing.

With the eye of an expert Ngurn examined the particular head he was at work upon.

'It will be ten days before I can say "finish," ' he said. 'Never has any man fixed heads like these.'

Bassett smiled inwardly at the old fellow's reluctance to talk with him of the Red One. It had always been so. Never, by any chance, had Ngurn or any other member of the weird tribe divulged the slightest hint of any physical characteristic of the Red One. Physical the Red One must be, to emit the wonderful sound, and though it was called the Red One, Bassett could not be sure that red represented the color of it. Red enough were the deeds and powers of it, from what abstract clews he had gleaned. Not alone, had Ngurn informed him, was the Red One more bestial powerful than the neighbor tribal gods, ever a-thirst for the red blood of living human sacrifices, but the neighbor gods themselves were sacrificed and tormented before him. He was the god of a dozen allied villages similar to this one, which was the central and commanding village of the federation. By virtue of the Red One many alien villages had been devastated and even wiped out, the prisoners sacrificed to the Red One. This was true to-day, and it extended back into old history carried down by word of mouth through the generations. When he, Ngurn, had been a young man, the tribes beyond the grass lands had made a war raid. In the counter raid, Ngurn and his fighting folk had made many prisoners. Of children alone over five score living had been bled white before the Red One, and many, many more men and women.

The Thunderer, was another of Ngurn's names for the mysterious deity.* Also at times was he called The Loud Shouter, The God-Voiced, The Bird-Throated, The One with the Throat Sweet as the Throat of the Honey-Bird, The Sun Singer, and The Star-Born.

Why The Star-Born? In vain Bassett interrogated Ngurn. According to that old devil-devil doctor, the Red One had always been, just where he was at present, forever singing and thundering his will over men. But Ngurn's father, wrapped in decaying grass-matting and hanging even then over their heads among the smoky rafters of the devil-devil house, had held otherwise. That departed wise one had believed that the Red One came from out of the starry night, else why—so his argument had run—had the old and forgotten ones passed his name down as the Star-Born? Bassett could not but recognize something cogent in such argument. But Ngurn affirmed the long years of his long life, wherein he had gazed upon many starry nights, yet never had he found a star on grass land or in jungle depth—and he had looked for them. True, he had beheld shooting stars (this in reply to Bassett's contention); but likewise had he beheld the phosphorescence of fungoid growths and rotten meat and fireflies on dark nights, and the flames of wood-fires and of blazing candlenuts; yet what were flame and blaze and glow when they had flamed, and blazed and glowed? Answer: memories, memories only, of things which had ceased to be, like memories of matings accomplished, of feasts forgotten, of desires that were the ghosts of desires, flaring, flaming, burning, yet unrealized in achievement of easement and satisfaction. Where was the appetite of yesterday? the roasted flesh of the wild pig the hunter's arrow failed to slay? the maid, unwed and dead, ere the young man knew her?

A memory was not a star, was Ngurn's contention. How could a memory be a star? Further, after all his long life he still observed the starry night-sky unaltered. Never had he noted the absence of a single star from its accustomed place. Besides, stars were fire, and the Red One was not fire—which last involuntary betrayal told Bassett nothing.

'Will the Red One speak to-morrow?' he queried.

Ngurn shrugged his shoulders as who should say.

'And the day after?—and the day after that?' Bassett persisted.

'I would like to have the curing of your head,' Ngurn changed the subject. 'It is different from any other head. No devil-devil has a head like it. Besides, I would cure it well. I would take months and months. The moons would come and the moons would go, and the smoke would be very slow, and I should myself gather the materials for the curing smoke. The skin would not wrinkle. It would be as smooth as your skin now.'

He stood up, and from the dim rafters grimed with the smoking of countless heads, where day was no more than a gloom, took down a matting-wrapped parcel and began to open it.

'It is a head like yours,' he said, 'but it is poorly cured.'

Bassett had pricked up his ears at the suggestion that it was a white man's head; for he had long since come to accept that these jungle-dwellers, in the midmost center of the great island, had never had intercourse with white men. Certainly he had found them without the almost universal Beche de mer English of the west South Pacific. Nor had they knowledge of tobacco, nor of gunpowder. Their few precious knives, made from lengths of hoop-iron, and their few and more precious tomahawks, made from cheap trade hatchets, he had surmised they had captured in war from the bush-men of the jungle beyond the grass lands, and that they, in turn, had similarly gained them from the salt water men who fringed the coral beaches of the shore and had contact with the occasional white men.

'The folk in the out beyond do not know how to cure heads,' old Ngurn explained, as he drew forth from the filthy matting and placed in Bassett's hands an indubitable white man's head.

Ancient it was beyond question; white it was as the blond hair attested. He could have sworn it once belonged to an Englishman, and to an Englishman of long before by token of the heavy gold circlets still threaded in the withered ear-lobes.

'Now your head...' the devil-devil doctor began on his favorite topic.

'I'll tell you what,' Bassett interrupted, struck by a new idea. 'When I die I'll let you have my head to cure, if, first, you take me to look upon the Red One.'

'I will have your head anyway when you are dead,' Ngurn rejected the proposition. He added, with the brutal frankness of the savage: 'Besides, you have not long to live. You are almost a dead man now. You will grow less strong. In not many months I shall have you here turning and turning in the smoke. It is pleasant, through the long afternoons, to turn the head of one you have known as well as I know you. And I shall talk to you and tell you the many secrets you want to know. Which will not matter, for you will be dead.'

'Ngurn,' Bassett threatened in sudden anger. 'You know the Baby Thunder in the Iron that is mine.' (This was in reference to his all-potent and all-awful shotgun.) 'I can kill you any time, and then you will not get my head.'

'Just the same, will Gngngn, or some one else of my folk get it,' Ngurn complacently assured him. 'And just the same will it turn and turn here in the devil-devil house in the smoke. The quicker you slay me with your Baby Thunder, the quicker will your head turn in the smoke.'

And Bassett knew he was beaten in the discussion.

What was the Red One?—Bassett asked himself a thousand times in the succeeding week, while he seemed to grow stronger. What was the source of the wonderful sound? What was this Sun Singer, this Star-Born One, this mysterious deity, as bestial-conducted as the black and kinky-headed and monkey-like human beasts who worshiped it, and whose silver-sweet, bull-mouthed singing and commanding he had heard at the taboo distance for so long?

Ngurn had he failed to bribe with the inevitable curing of his head when he was dead. Gngngn, imbecile and chief that he was, was too imbecilic, too much under the sway of Ngurn, to be considered. Remained Balatta, who, from the time she found him and poked his blue eyes open to recrudescence of her grotesque, female hideousness, had continued his adorer. Woman she was, and he had long known that the only way to win from her treason to her tribe was through the woman's heart of her.

Bassett was a fastidious man. He had never recovered from the initial horror caused by Balatta's female awfulness. Back in England, even at best, the charm of woman, to him, had never been robust. Yet now, resolutely, as only a man can do who is capable of martyring himself for the cause of science, he proceeded to violate all the fineness and delicacy of his nature by making love to the unthinkably disgusting bushwoman.

He shuddered, but with averted face hid his grimaces and swallowed his gorge as he put his arm around her dirt-crusted shoulders and felt the contact of her rancid-oily and kinky hair with his neck and chin. But he nearly screamed when she succumbed to that caress so at the very first of the courtship and mowed and gibbered and squealed little, queer, pig-like gurgly noises of delight. It was too much. And the next he did in the singular courtship was to take her down to the stream and give her a vigorous scrubbing.

From then on he devoted himself to her like a true swain as frequently and for as long at a time as his will could override his repugnance. But marriage, which she ardently suggested, with due observance of tribal custom, he balked at. Fortunately, taboo rule was strong in the tribe. Thus, Ngurn could never touch bone, or flesh, or hide of crocodile. This had been ordained at his birth. Gngngn was denied ever the touch of woman. Such pollution, did it chance to occur, could be purged only by the death of the offending female. It had happened once, since Bassett's arrival, when a girl of nine, running in play, stumbled and fell against the sacred chief. And the girl-child was seen no more. In whispers, Balatta told Bassett that she had been three days and nights in dying before the Red One. As for Balatta, the bread-fruit was taboo to her. For which Bassett was thankful. The taboo might have been water.

For himself, he fabricated a special taboo. Only could he marry, he explained, when the Southern Cross* rode highest in the sky. Knowing his astronomy, he thus gained a reprieve of nearly nine months; and he was confident that within that time he would either be dead or escaped to the coast with full knowledge of the Red One and of the source of the Red One's wonderful voice. At first he had fancied the Red One to be some colossal statue, like Memnon,* rendered vocal under certain temperature conditions of sunlight. But when, after a war raid, a batch of prisoners was brought in and the sacrifice made at night, in the midst of rain, when the sun could play no part, the Red One had been more vocal than usual, Bassett discarded that hypothesis.

In company with Balatta, sometimes with men and parties of women, the freedom of the jungle was his for three quadrants of the compass. But the fourth quadrant, which contained the Red One's abiding place, was taboo. He made more thorough love to Balatta—also saw to it that she scrubbed herself more frequently. Eternal female she was, capable of any treason for the sake of love. And, though the sight of her was provocative of nausea and the contact of her provocative of despair, although he could not escape her awfulness in his dream-haunted nightmares of her, he nevertheless was aware of the cosmic verity of sex that animated her and that made her own life of less value than the happiness of her lover with whom she hoped to mate. Juliet or Balatta?* Where was the intrinsic difference? The soft and tender product of ultra-civilization, or her bestial prototype of a hundred thousand years before her?—there was no difference.

Bassett was a scientist first, a humanist afterward. In the jungle-heart of Guadalcanal he put the affair to the test, as in the laboratory he would have put to the test any chemical reaction. He increased his feigned ardor for the bushwoman, at the same time increasing the imperiousness of his will of desire over her to be led to look upon the

Red One face to face. It was the old story, he recognized, that the woman must pay, and it occurred when the two of them, one day, were catching the unclassified and unnamed little black fish, an inch long, half-eel and half-scaled, rotund with salmon-golden roe, that frequented the fresh water and that were esteemed, raw and whole, fresh or putrid, a perfect delicacy. Prone in the muck of the decaying jungle-floor, Balatta threw herself, clutching his ankles with her hands, kissing his feet and making slubbery noises that chilled his backbone up and down again. She begged him to kill her rather than exact this ultimate love-payment. She told him of the penalty of breaking the taboo of the Red One—a week of torture, living, the details of which she yammered out from her face in the mire until he realized that he was yet a tyro* in knowledge of the frightfulness the human was capable of wreaking on the human.

Yet did Bassett insist on having his man's will satisfied, at the woman's risk, that he might solve the mystery of the Red One's singing, though she should die long and horribly and screaming. And Balatta, being mere woman, yielded. She led him into the forbidden quadrant. An abrupt mountain, shouldering in from the north to meet a similar intrusion from the south, tormented the stream in which they had fished into a deep and gloomy gorge. After a mile along the gorge, the way plunged sharply upward until they crossed a saddle of raw limestone which attracted his geologist's eye. Still climbing, although he paused often from sheer physical weakness, they scaled forest-clad heights until they emerged on a naked mesa or tableland. Bassett recognized the stuff of its composition as black volcanic sand, and knew that a pocket magnet could have captured a full load of the sharply angular grains he trod upon.

And then, holding Balatta by the hand and leading her onward, he came to it—a tremendous pit, obviously artificial, in the heart of the plateau. Old history, the South Seas Sailing Directions,* scores of remembered data and connotations swift and furious, surged through his brain. It was Mendana who had discovered the islands and named them Solomon's, believing that he had found that monarch's fabled mines.* They had laughed at the old navigator's child-like credulity; and yet here stood himself, Bassett, on the rim of an excavation for all the world like the diamond pits of South Africa.

But no diamond this that he gazed down upon. Rather was it a pearl, with the depth of iridescence of a pearl; but of a size all pearls of earth and time welded into one, could not have totaled; and of a color undreamed of any pearl, or of anything else, for that matter, for it was the color of the Red One. And the Red One himself Bassett knew it to be on the instant. A perfect sphere, fully two hundred feet in diameter, the top of it was a hundred feet below the level of the rim. He likened the color quality of it to lacquer.* Indeed, he took it to be some sort of lacquer, applied by man, but a lacquer too marvelously clever to have been manufactured by the bush-folk. Brighter than bright cherry-red, its richness of color was as if it were red builded upon red. It glowed and iridesced in the sunlight as if gleaming up from underlay under underlay of red.

In vain Balatta strove to dissuade him from descending. She threw herself in the dirt; but, when he continued down the trail that spiraled the pit-wall, she followed, cringing and whimpering her terror. That the red sphere had been dug out as a precious thing, was patent. Considering the paucity of members of the federated twelve villages and their primitive tools and methods, Bassett knew that the toil of a myriad generations could scarcely have made that enormous excavation.

He found the pit bottom carpeted with human bones, among which, battered and defaced, lay village gods of wood and stone. Some, covered with obscene totemic figures and designs, were carved from solid tree trunks forty or fifty feet in length. He noted the absence of the shark and turtle gods, so common among the shore villages, and was amazed at the constant recurrence of the helmet motive. What did these jungle savages of the dark heart of Guadalcanal know of helmets? Had Mendana's men-at-arms worn helmets and penetrated here centuries before? And if not, then whence had the bush-folk caught the motive?

Advancing over the litter of gods and bones, Balatta whimpering at his heels, Bassett entered the shadow of the Red One and passed on under its gigantic overhang until he touched it with his finger-tips. No lacquer that. Nor was the surface smooth as it should have been in the case of lacquer. On the contrary, it was corrugated and pitted, with here and there patches that showed signs of heat and fusing. Also, the substance of it was metal, though unlike any metal or combination of metals he had ever known. As for the color itself, he decided it to be no application. It was the intrinsic color of the metal itself.

He moved his finger-tips, which up to that had merely rested, along the surface, and felt the whole gigantic sphere quicken and live and respond. It was incredible! So light a touch on so vast a mass! Yet did it quiver under the finger-tip caress in rhythmic vibrations that became whisperings and rustlings and mutterings of sound—but of sound so different; so elusive thin that it was shimmeringly sibillant; so mellow that it was maddening sweet, piping like an elfin horn,* which last was just what Bassett decided would be like a peal from some bell of the gods reaching earth-ward from across space.

He looked to Balatta with swift questioning; but the voice of the Red One he had evoked had flung her face-downward and moaning among the bones. He returned to contemplation of the prodigy. Hollow it was, and of no metal known on earth, was his conclusion. It was right-named by the ones of old-time as the Star-Born. Only from the stars could it have come, and no thing of chance was it. It was a creation of artifice and mind. Such perfection of form, such hollowness that it certainly possessed, could not be the result of mere fortuitousness. A child of intelligences, remote and unguessable, working corporally in metals, it indubitably was. He stared at it in amaze, his brain a racing wild-fire of hypotheses to account for this far-journeyer who had adventured the night of space, threaded the stars, and now rose before him and above him, exhumed by patient anthropophagi, pitted and lacquered by its fiery bath in two atmospheres.

But was the color a lacquer of heat upon some familiar metal? Or was it an intrinsic quality of the metal itself? He thrust in the blade-point of his pocket-knife to test the constitution of the stuff. Instantly the entire sphere burst into a mighty whispering, sharp with protest, almost twanging goldenly if a whisper could possibly be considered to twang, rising higher, sinking deeper, the two extremes of the registry of sound threatening to complete the circle and coalesce into the bull-mouthed thundering he had so often heard beyond the taboo distance.

Forgetful of safety, of his own life itself, entranced by the wonder of the unthinkable and unguessable thing, he raised his knife to strike heavily from a long stroke, but was prevented by Balatta. She upreared on her own knees in an agony of terror, clasping his knees and supplicating him to desist. In the intensity of her desire to impress him, she put her forearm between her teeth and sank them to the bone.

He scarcely observed her act, although he yielded atomatically* to his gentler instincts and withheld the knife-hack. To him, human life had dwarfed to microscopic proportions before this colossal portent of higher life from within the distances of the sidereal universe. As had she been a dog, he kicked the ugly little bushwoman to her feet and compelled her to start with him on an encirclement of the base. Part way around, he encountered horrors. Even, among the others, did he recognize the sun-shriveled remnant of the nine-years girl who had accidentally broken Chief Gngngn's personality taboo. And, among what was left of these that had passed, he encountered what was left of one who had not yet passed. Truly had the bush-folk named themselves into the name of the Red One, seeing in him their own image which they strove to placate and please with such red offerings.

Farther around, always treading the bones and images of humans and gods that constituted the floor of this ancient charnel house of sacrifice, he came upon the device by which the Red One was made to send his call singing thunderingly across the jungle-belts and grass-lands to the far beach of Ringmanu. Simple and primitive was it as was the Red One's consummate artifice. A great king-post, half a hundred feet in length, seasoned by centuries of superstitious care, carven into dynasties of gods, each superimposed, each helmeted, each seated in the open mouth of a crocodile, was slung by ropes, twisted of climbing vegetable parasites, from the apex of a tripod of three great forest trunks, themselves carved into grinning and grotesque adumbrations of man's modern concepts of art and god. From the striker king-post, were suspended ropes of climbers to which men could apply their strength and direction. Like a battering ram, this king-post could be driven end-onward against the mighty, red-iridescent sphere.

Here was where Ngurn officiated and functioned religiously for himself and the twelve tribes under him. Bassett laughed aloud, almost with madness, at the thought of this wonderful messenger, winged with intelligence across space, to fall into a bushman strong-hold and be worshiped by ape-like, man-eating and head-hunting savages. It was as if God's Word had fallen into the muck mire of the abyss underlying the bottom of hell; as if Jehovah's Commandments had been presented on carved stone to the monkeys of the monkey cage at the Zoo; as if the Sermon on the Mount had been preached in a roaring bedlam of lunatics.*

The slow weeks passed. The nights, by election, Bassett spent on the ashen floor of the devil-devil house, beneath the ever-swinging, slow-curing heads. His reason for this was that it was taboo to the lesser sex of woman, and, therefore, a refuge for him from Balatta, who grew more persecutingly and perilously loverly as the Southern Cross rode higher in the sky and marked the imminence of her nuptials. His days Bassett spent in a hammock swung under the shade of the great breadfruit tree before the devil-devil house. There were breaks in this program, when, in the comas of his devastating fever-attacks, he lay for days and nights in the house of heads. Ever he struggled to combat the fever, to live, to continue to live, to grow strong and stronger against the day when he would be strong enough to dare the grass-lands and the belted jungle beyond, and win to the beach, and to some labor-recruiting, black-birding ketch or schooner,* and on to civilization and the men of civilization, to whom he could give news of the message from other worlds that lay, darkly worshiped by beast-men, in the black heart of Guadalcanal's mid-most center.

On other nights, lying late under the breadfruit tree, Bassett spent long hours watching the slow setting of the western stars beyond the black wall of jungle where it had been thrust back by the clearing for the village. Possessed of more than a cursory knowledge of astronomy, he took a sick man's pleasure in speculating as to the dwellers on the unseen worlds of those incredibly remote suns, to haunt whose houses of light, life came forth, a shy visitant, from the rayless crypts of matter. He could no more apprehend limits to time than bounds to space. No subversive radium speculations* had shaken his steady scientific faith in the conservation of energy and the indestructibility of matter. Always and forever must there have been stars. And surely, in that cosmic ferment, all must be comparatively alike, comparatively of the same substance, or substances, save for the freaks of the ferment. All must obey, or compose, the same laws that ran without infraction through the entire experience of man. Therefore, he argued and agreed, must worlds and life be appanages* to all the suns as they were appanages to the particular sun of his own solar system.

Even as he lay here, under the breadfruit tree, an intelligence that stared across the starry gulfs, so must all the universe be exposed to the ceaseless scrutiny of innumerable eyes, like his, though grantedly different, with behind them, by the same token, intelligences that questioned and sought the meaning and the construction of the whole. So reasoning, he felt his soul go forth in kinship with that august company, that multitude whose gaze was forever upon the arras of infinity.

Who were they, what were they, those far distant and superior ones who had bridged the sky with their gigantic, red-iridescent, heaven-singing message? Surely, and long since, had they, too, trod the path on which man had so recently, by the calendar of the cosmos, set his feet. And to be able to send such a message across the pit of space, surely they had reached those heights to which man, in tears and travail and bloody sweat, in darkness and confusion of many counsels, was so slowly struggling. And what were they on their heights? Had they won Brotherhood? Or had they learned that the law of love imposed the penalty of weakness and decay? Was strife, life? Was the rule of all the universe the pitiless rule of natural selection? And, and most immediately and poignantly, were their far conclusions, their long-won wisdoms, shut even then in the huge, metallic heart of the Red One, waiting for the first earth-man to read? Of one thing he was certain: No drop of red dew shaken from the lion-mane of some sun in torment, was the sounding sphere. It was of design, not chance, and it contained the speech and wisdom of the stars.

What engines and elements and mastered forces, what lore and mysteries and destiny-controls, might be there! Undoubtedly, since so much could be inclosed in so little a thing as the foundation stone of public building, this enormous sphere should contain vast histories, profounds of research achieved beyond man's wildest guesses, laws and formulæ that, easily mastered, would make man's life on earth, individual and collective, spring up from its present mire to inconceivable heights of purity and power. It was Time's greatest gift to blindfold, insatiable, and sky-aspiring man. And to him, Bassett, had been vouchsafed the lordly fortune to be the first to receive this message from man's interstellar kin!

No white man, much less no outland man of the other bush-tribes, had gazed upon the Red One and lived. Such the law expounded by Ngurn to Bassett. There was such a thing as blood brotherhood, Bassett, in return, had often argued in the past. But Ngurn had stated solemnly no. Even the blood brotherhood was outside the favor of the Red One. Only a man born within the tribe could look upon the Red One and live. But now, his guilty secret known only to Balatta, whose fear of immolation before the Red One fast-sealed her lips, the situation was different. What he had to do was to recover from the abominable fevers that weakened him and gain to civilization. Then would he lead an expedition back, and, although the entire population of Guadalcanal be destroyed, extract from the heart of the Red One the message of the world from other worlds.

But Bassett's relapses grew more frequent, his brief convalescences less and less vigorous, his periods of coma longer, until he came to know, beyond the last promptings of the optimism inherent in so tremendous a constitution as his own, that he would never live to cross the grass lands, perforate the perilous coast jungle, and reach the sea. He faded as the Southern Cross rose higher in the sky, till even Balatta knew that he would be dead ere the nuptial date determined by his taboo. Ngurn made pilgrimage personally and gathered the smoke materials for the curing of Bassett's head, and to him made proud announcement and exhibition of the artistic perfectness of his intention when Bassett should be dead. As for himself, Bassett was not shocked. Too long and too deeply had life ebbed down in him to bite him with fear of its impending extinction. He continued to persist, alternating periods of unconsciousness with periods of semi-consciousness, dreamy and unreal, in which he idly wondered whether he had ever truly beheld the Red One or whether it was a night-mare fancy of delirium.

Came the day when all mists and cobwebs dissolved, when he found his brain clear as a bell, and took just appraisement of his body's weakness. Neither hand nor foot could he lift. So little control of his body did he have, that he was scarcely aware of possessing one. Lightly indeed his flesh sat upon his soul, and his soul, in its briefness of clarity, knew by its very clarity, that the black of cessation was near. He knew the end was close; knew that in all truth he had with his eyes beheld the Red One, the messenger between the worlds; knew that he would never live to carry that message to the world—that message, for aught to the contrary, which might already have waited man's hearing in the heart of Guadalcanal for ten thousand years. And Bassett stirred with resolve, calling Ngurn to him, out under the shade of the breadfruit tree, and with the old devil-devil doctor discussing the terms and arrangements of his last life effort, his final adventure in the quick of the flesh.

'I know the law, O Ngurn,' he concluded the matter. 'Whoso is not of the folk may not look upon the Red One and live. I shall not live anyway. Your young men shall carry me before the face of the Red

One, and I shall look upon him, and hear his voice, and thereupon die, under your hand, O Ngurn. Thus will the three things be satisfied: the law, my desire, and your quicker possession of my head for which all your preparations wait.'

To which Ngurn consented, adding:

'It is better so. A sick man who cannot get well is foolish to live on for so little a while. Also, is it better for the living that he should go. You have been much in the way of late. Not but what it was good for me to talk to such a wise one. But for moons of days we have held little talk. Instead, you have taken up room in the house of heads, making noises like a dying pig, or talking much and loudly in your own language which I do not understand. This has been a confusion to me, for I like to think on the great things of the light and dark as I turn the heads in the smoke. Your much noise has thus been a disturbance to the long-learning and hatching of the final wisdom that will be mine before I die. As for you, upon whom the dark has already brooded, it is well that you die now. And I promise you, in the long days to come when I turn your head in the smoke, no man of the tribe shall come in to disturb us. And I will tell you many secrets, for I am an old man and very wise, and I shall be adding wisdom to wisdom as I turn your head in the smoke.'

So a litter was made, and, borne on the shoulders of half a dozen of the men, Bassett departed on the last little adventure that was to cap the total adventure, for him, of living. With a body of which he was scarcely aware, for even the pain had been exhausted out of it, and with a bright clear brain that accommodated him to a quiet ecstasy of sheer lucidness of thought, he lay back on the lurching litter and watched the fading of the passing world, beholding for the last time the breadfruit tree before the devil-devil house, the dim day beneath the matted jungle roof, the gloomy gorge between the shouldering mountains, the saddle of raw limestone, and the mesa of black, volcanic sand.

Down the spiral path of the pit they bore him, encircling the sheening, glowing Red One that seemed ever imminent to iridesce from color and light into sweet singing and thunder. And over bones and logs of immolated men and gods they bore him, past the horrors of other immolated ones that yet lived, to the three-king-post tripod and the huge king-post striker.

Here Bassett, helped by Ngurn and Balatta, weakly sat up, swaying weakly from the hips, and with clear, unfaltering, all-seeing eyes gazed upon the Red One.

'Once, O Ngurn,' he said, not taking his eyes from the sheening, vibrating surface whereon and wherein all the shades of cherry-red played unceasingly, ever a-quiver to change into sound, to become silken rustlings, silvery whisperings, golden thrummings of cords, velvet pipings of elfland, mellow-distances of thunderings.

'I wait,' Ngurn prompted after a long pause, the long-handled tomahawk unassumingly ready in his hand.

'Once, O Ngurn,' Bassett repeated, 'let the Red One speak so that I may see it speak as well as hear it. Then strike, thus, when I raise my hand; for, when I raise my hand, I shall drop my head forward and make place for the stroke at the base of my neck. But, O Ngurn, I, who am about to pass out of the light of day forever, would like to pass with the wonder-voice of the Red One singing greatly in my ears.'

'And I promise you that never will a head be so well cured as yours,' Ngurn assured him, at the same time signaling the tribesmen to man the propelling ropes suspended from the king-post striker. 'Your head shall be my greatest piece of work in the curing of heads.'

Bassett smiled quietly to the old one's conceit, as the great carved log, drawn back through two-score feet of space, was released. The next moment he was lost in ecstasy at the abrupt and thunderous liberation of sound. But such thunder! Mellow it was with preciousness of all sounding metals. Archangels spoke in it; it was magnificently beautiful before all other sounds; it was invested with the intelligence of supermen of planets of other suns; it was the voice of God, seducing and commanding to be heard. And—the everlasting miracle of that interstellar metal! Bassett, with his own eyes, saw color and colors transform into sound till the whole visible surface of the vast sphere was a-crawl and titillant* and vaporous with what he could not tell was color or was sound. In that moment the interstices of matter were his, and the interfusings and intermating transfusings of matter and force.

Time passed. At the last Bassett was brought back from his ecstasy by an impatient movement of Ngurn. He had quite forgotten the old devil-devil one. A quick flash of fancy brought a husky chuckle into Bassett's throat. His shotgun lay beside him in the litter. All he had to do, muzzle to head, was press the trigger and blow his head into nothingness.

But why cheat him? was Bassett's next thought. Head-hunting, cannibal beast of a human that was as much ape as human, nevertheless

Old Ngurn had, according to his lights, played squarer than square. Ngurn was in himself a fore-runner of ethics and contract, of consideration, and gentleness in man. No, Bassett decided; it would be a ghastly pity and an act of dishonor to cheat the old fellow at the last. His head was Ngurn's, and Ngurn's head to cure it would be.

And Bassett, raising his hand in signal, bending forward his head as agreed so as to expose cleanly the articulation to his taut spinal cord, forgot Balatta, who was merely a woman, a woman merely and only and undesired. He knew, without seeing, when the razor-edged hatchet rose in the air behind him. And for that instant, ere the end, there fell upon Bassett the shadow of the Unknown, a sense of impending marvel of the rending of walls before the imaginable. Almost, when he knew the blow had started and just ere the edge of steel bit the flesh and nerves, it seemed that he gazed upon the serene face of the Medusa, Truth*—And, simultaneous with the bite of the steel on the onrush of the dark, in a flashing instant of fancy, he saw the vision of his head turning slowly, always turning, in the devil-devil house beside the breadfruit tree.

GERTRUDE BARROWS BENNETT
('FRANCIS STEVENS')

FRIEND ISLAND

A 'Different' Story.

Being the Veracious Tale of an Ancient Mariness,*
Heard and Reported in the Year A. D. 2100

IT was upon the water-front that I first met her, in one of the shabby little tea shops frequented by able sailoresses of the poorer type. The up-town, glittering resorts of the Lady Aviators' Union were not for such as she.

Stern of feature, bronzed by wind and sun, her age could only be guessed, but I surmised at once that in her I beheld a survivor of the age of turbines and oil engines—a true sea-woman of that elder time, when woman's superiority to man had not been so long recognized. When, to emphasize their victory, women in all ranks were sterner than to-day's need demands.

The spruce, smiling young maidens—engine-women and stokers of the great aluminum rollers,* but despite their profession, very neat in gold-braided blue knickers and boleros*—these looked askance at the hard-faced relic of a harsher day, as they passed in and out of the shop.

I, however, brazenly ignoring similar glances at myself, a mere male intruding on the haunts of the world's ruling sex, drew a chair up beside the veteran. I ordered a full pot of tea, two cups and a plate of macaroons, and put on my most ingratiating air. Possibly my unconcealed admiration and interest were wiles not exercised in vain. Or the macaroons and tea, both excellent, may have loosened the old sea-woman's tongue. At any rate, under cautious questioning, she had soon launched upon a series of reminiscences well beyond my hopes for color and variety.

'When I was a lass,' quoth the sea-woman, after a time, 'there was none of this high-flying, gilt-edged, leather-stocking luxury about the sea. We sailed by the power of our oil and gasoline. If they failed on us, like as not 'twas the rubber ring and the rolling wave for ours.'

She referred to the archaic practice of placing a pneumatic affair called a life preserver beneath the arms, in case of that dreaded disaster, now so unheard of, shipwreck.

'In them days there was still many a man bold enough to join our crews. And I've knowed cases,' she added condescendingly, 'where just by the muscle and brawn of such men some poor sailor lass has reached shore alive that would have fed the sharks without 'em. Oh, I ain't so down on men as you might think. It's the spoiling of them that I don't hold with. There's too much preached nowadays that man is fit for nothing but to fetch and carry and do nurse-work in big child-homes. To my mind, a man who hasn't the nerve of a woman ain't fitted to father children, let alone raise 'em. But that's not here nor there. My time's past, and I know it, or I wouldn't be setting here gossipin' to you, my lad, over an empty teapot.'

I took the hint, and with our cups replenished, she bit thoughtfully into her fourteenth macaroon and continued.

'There's one voyage I'm not likely to forget, though I live to be as old as Cap'n Mary Barnacle, of the *Shouter*.* 'Twas aboard the old *Shouter* that this here voyage occurred, and it was her last and likewise Cap'n Mary's. Cap'n Mary, she was then that decrepit, it seemed a mercy that she should go to her rest, and in good salt water at that.

'I remember the voyage for Cap'n Mary's sake, but most I remember it because 'twas then that I come the nighest in my life to committin' matrimony. For a man, the man had nerve; he was nearer bein' companionable than any other man I ever seed; and if it hadn't been for just one little event that showed up the—the *mannishness* of him, in a way I couldn't abide, I reckon he'd be keepin' house for me this minute.

'We cleared from Frisco with a cargo of silkateen* petticoats for Brisbane. Cap'n Mary was always strong on petticoats. Leather breeches or even half-skirts would ha' paid far better, they being more in demand like, but Cap'n Mary was three-quarters owner, and says she, land women should buy petticoats, and if they didn't it wouldn't be the Lord's fault nor hers for not providing 'em.

'We cleared on a fine day, which is an ill sign—or was, then when the weather and the seas o' God still counted in the trafficking of the humankind. Not two days out we met a whirling, mucking bouncer of a gale that well nigh threw the old *Shouter* a full point off her course in the first wallop. She was a stout craft, though. None of your featherweight, gas-lightened, paper-thin alloy shells, but toughened aluminum from stern to stern. Her turbine drove her through the combers at a forty-five knot clip, which named her a speedy craft for a freighter in them days.

'But this night, as we tore along through the creaming green billows, something unknown went 'way wrong down below.

'I was forward under the shelter of her long over-scoop, looking for a hairpin I'd dropped somewheres about that afternoon. It was a gold hairpin, and gold still being mighty scarce when I was a girl, a course I valued it. But suddenly I felt the old *Shouter* give a jump under my feet like a plane struck by a shell in full flight. Then she trembled all over for a full second, frightened like. Then, with the crash of doomsday ringing in my ears, I felt myself sailing through the air right into the teeth o' the shrieking gale, as near as I could judge. Down I come in the hollow of a monstrous big wave, and as my ears doused under I thought I heard a splash close by. Coming up, sure enough, there close by me was floating a new, patent, hermetic, thermo-ice-chest.* Being as it was empty, and being as it was shut up air-tight, that ice-chest made as sweet a life-preserver as a woman could wish in such an hour. About ten foot by twelve, it floated high in the raging sea. Out on its top I scrambled, and hanging on by a handle I looked expectant for some of my poor fellow-women to come floating by. Which they never did, for the good reason that the *Shouter* had blowed up and went below, petticoats, Cap'n Mary and all.'

'What caused the explosion?' I inquired curiously.

'The Lord and Cap'n Mary Barnacle can explain,' she answered piously. 'Besides the oil for her turbines, she carried a power of gasoline for her alternative engines, and likely 'twas the cause of her ending so sudden like. Anyways, all I ever seen of her again was the empty ice-chest that Providence had well-nigh hove upon my head. On that I sat and floated, and floated and sat some more, till by and by the storm sort of blowed itself out, the sun come shining—this was next morning—and I could dry my hair and look about me. I was a young lass, then, and not bad to look upon. I didn't want to die, any more than you that's sitting there this minute. So I up and prays for land. Sure enough toward evening a speck heaves up low down on the horizon. At first I took it for a gas liner, but later found it was just a little island, all alone by itself in the great Pacific Ocean.

'Come, now, here's luck, thinks I, and with that I deserts the ice-chest, which being empty, and me having no ice to put in it, not likely to have in them latitudes, is of no further use to me. Striking out I swum a mile or so and set foot on dry land for the first time in nigh three days.

'Pretty land it were, too, though bare of human life as an iceberg in the Arctic.

'I had landed on a shining white beach that run up to a grove of lovely, waving palm trees. Above them I could see the slopes of a hill so high and green it reminded me of my own old home, up near Couquomgomoc Lake in Maine.* The whole place just seemed to smile and smile at me. The palms waved and bowed in the sweet breeze, like they wanted to say, "Just set right down and make yourself to home. We've been waiting a long time for you to come." I cried, I was that happy to be made welcome. I was a young lass then, and sensitive-like to how folks treated me. You're laughing now, but wait and see if or not there was sense to the way I felt.

'So I up and dries my clothes and my long, soft hair again, which was well worth drying, for I had far more of it than now. After that I walked along a piece, until there was a sweet little path meandering away into the wild woods.

'Here, thinks I, this looks like inhabitants. Be they civil or wild, I wonder? But after traveling the path a piece, lo and behold it ended sudden like in a wide circle of green grass, with a little spring of clear water. And the first thing I noticed was a slab of white board nailed to a palm tree close to the spring. Right off I took a long drink, for you better believe I was thirsty, and then I went to look at this board. It had evidently been tore off the side of a wooden packing box, and the letters were printed in lead-pencil.

'"Heaven help whoever you be," I read. "This island ain't just right. I'm going to swim for it. You better too. Good-by. Nelson Smith." That's what it said, but the spellin' was simply awful. It all looked quite new and recent, as if Nelson Smith hadn't more than a few hours before he wrote and nailed it there.

'Well, after reading that queer warning I begun to shake all over like in a chill. Yes, I shook like I had the ague, though the hot tropic sun was burning down right on me and that alarming board. What had scared Nelson Smith so much that he had swum to get away? I looked all around real cautious and careful, but not a single frightening thing could I behold. And the palms and the green grass and the flowers still smiled that peaceful and friendly like. "Just make yourself to home," was wrote all over the place in plainer letters than those sprawly lead-pencil ones on the board.

'Pretty soon, what with the quiet and all, the chill left me. Then I thought, "Well, to be sure, this Smith person was just an ordinary man, I reckon, and likely he got nervous of being so alone. Likely he just fancied things which was really not. It's a pity he drowned himself before I come, though likely I'd have found him poor company. By his record I judge him a man of but common education."

'So I decided to make the most of my welcome, and that I did for weeks to come. Right near the spring was a cave, dry as a biscuit box, with a nice floor of white sand. Nelson had lived there too, for there was a litter of stuff—tin cans—empty—scraps of newspapers and the like. I got to calling him Nelson in my mind, and then Nelly, and wondering if he was dark or fair, and how he come to be cast away there all alone, and what was the strange events that drove him to his end. I cleaned out the cave, though. He had devoured all his tin-canned provisions, however he come by them, but this I didn't mind. That there island was a generous body. Green milk-coconuts, sweet berries, turtle eggs and the like was my daily fare.

'For about three weeks the sun shone every day, the birds sang and the monkeys chattered. We was all one big, happy family, and the more I explored that island the better I liked the company I was keeping. The land was about ten miles from beach to beach, and never a foot of it that wasn't sweet and clean as a private park.

'From the top of the hill I could see the ocean, miles and miles of blue water, with never a sign of a gas liner, or even a little government running-boat. Them running-boats used to go most everywhere to keep the seaways clean of derelicts and the like. But I knowed that if this island was no more than a hundred miles off the regular courses of navigation, it might be many a long day before I'd be rescued. The top of the hill, as I found when first I climbed up there, was a wore-out crater. So I knowed that the island was one of them volcanic ones you run across so many of in the seas between Capricorn and Cancer.*

'Here and there on the slopes and down through the jungly tree-growth, I would come on great lumps of rock, and these must have came up out of that crater long ago. If there was lava it was so old it had been covered up entire with green growing stuff. You couldn't have found it without a spade, which I didn't have nor want.

'Well, at first I was happy as the hours was long. I wandered and clambered and waded and swum, and combed my long hair on the beach, having fortunately not lost my sidecombs nor the rest of my gold hairpins. But by and by it begun to get just a bit lonesome. Funny thing, that's a feeling that, once it starts, it gets worse and worser so quick it's perfectly surprising. And right then was when the days begun to get gloomy. We had a long, sickly hot spell, like I never seen before on an ocean island. There was dull clouds across the sun from morn till night. Even the little monkeys and parrakeets, that had seemed so gay, moped and drowsed like they was sick. All one day I cried, and let the rain soak me through and through—that was the first rain we had—and I didn't get thorough dried even during the night, though I slept in my cave. Next morning I got up mad as thunder at myself and all the world.

'When I looked out the black clouds was billowing across the sky. I could hear nothing but great breakers roaring in on the beaches, and the wild wind raving through the lashing palms.

'As I stood there a nasty little wet monkey dropped from a branch almost on my head. I grabbed a pebble and slung it at him real vicious. "Get away, you dirty little brute!" I shrieks, and with that there come a awful blinding flare of light. There was a long, crackling noise like a bunch of Chinese fireworks, and then a sound as if a whole fleet of *Shouters* had all went up together.

'When I come to, I found myself way in the back of my cave, trying to dig further into the rock with my finger nails. Upon taking thought, it come to me that what had occurred was just a lightning-clap, and going to look, sure enough there lay a big palm tree right across the glade. It was all busted and split open by the lightning, and the little monkey was under it, for I could see his tail and his hind legs sticking out.

'Now, when I set eyes on that poor, crushed little beast I'd been so mean to, I was terrible ashamed. I sat down on the smashed tree and considered and considered. How thankful I had ought to have been. Here I had a lovely, plenteous island, with food and water to my taste, when it might have been a barren, starvation rock that was my lot. And so, thinking, a sort of gradual peaceful feeling stole over me. I got cheerfuller and cheerfuller, till I could have sang and danced for joy.

'Pretty soon I realized that the sun was shining bright for the first time that week. The wind had stopped hollering, and the waves had died to just a singing murmur on the beach. It seemed kind o' strange, this sudden peace, like the cheer in my own heart after its rage and storm. I rose up, feeling sort of queer, and went to look if the little monkey had came alive again, though that was a fool thing, seeing he was laying all crushed up and very dead. I buried him under a tree root, and as I did it a conviction come to me.

'I didn't hardly question that conviction at all. Somehow, living there alone so long, perhaps my natural womanly intuition was stronger than ever before or since, and so I *knowed*. Then I went and pulled poor Nelson Smith's board off from the tree and tossed it away for the tide to carry off. That there board was an insult to my island!'

The sea-woman paused, and her eyes had a far-away look. It seemed as if I and perhaps even the macaroons and tea were quite forgotten.

'Why did you think that?' I asked, to bring her back. 'How could an island be insulted?'

She started, passed her hand across her eyes, and hastily poured another cup of tea.

'Because,' she said at last, poising a macaroon in mid-air, 'because that island—that particular island that I had landed on—had a heart!

'When I was gay, it was bright and cheerful. It was glad when I come, and it treated me right until I got that grouchy it had to mope from sympathy. It loved me like a friend. When I flung a rock at that poor little drenched monkey critter, it backed up my act with an anger like the wrath o' God, and killed its own child to please me! But it got right cheery the minute I seen the wrongness of my ways. Nelson Smith had no business to say, "This island ain't just right," for it was a righter place than ever I seen elsewhere. When I cast away that lying board, all the birds begun to sing like mad. The green milk-coconuts fell right and left. Only the monkeys seemed kind o' sad like still, and no wonder. You see, their own mother, the island, had rounded on one of 'em for my sake!

'After that I was right careful and considerate. I named the island Anita, not knowing her right name, or if she had any. Anita was a pretty name, and it sounded kind of South Sea like.* Anita and me got along real well together from that day on. It was some strain to be always gay and singing around like a dear duck of a canary bird, but I done my best. Still, for all the love and gratitude I bore Anita, the company of an island, however sympathetic, ain't quite enough for a human being. I still got lonesome, and there was even days when I couldn't keep the clouds clear out of the sky, though I will say we had no more tornadoes.

'I think the island understood and tried to help me with all the bounty and good cheer the poor thing possessed. None the less my heart give a wonderful big leap when one day I seen a blot on the horizon. It drawed nearer and nearer, until at last I could make out its nature.'

'A ship, of course,' said I, 'and were you rescued?'

"'Tweren't a ship, neither,' denied the sea-woman somewhat impatiently. 'Can't you let me spin this yarn without no more remarks and fool questions? This thing what was bearing down so fast with the incoming tide was neither more nor less than another island!

'You may well look startled. I was startled myself. Much more so than you, likely. I didn't know then what you, with your book–learning, very likely know now—that islands sometimes float. Their under–parts being a tangled-up mess of roots and old vines that new stuff's growed over, they sometimes break away from the mainland in a brisk gale and go off for a voyage, calm as a old-fashioned, eight-funnel steamer. This one was uncommon large, being as much as two miles, maybe, from shore to shore. It had its palm trees and its live things, just like my own Anita, and I've sometimes wondered if this drifting piece hadn't really been a part of my island once—just its daughter like, as you might say.

'Be that, however, as it might be, no sooner did the floating piece get within hailing distance than I hears a human holler and there was a man dancing up and down on the shore like he was plumb crazy. Next minute he had plunged into the narrow strip of water between us and in a few minutes had swum to where I stood.

'Yes, of course it was none other than Nelson Smith!

'I knowed that the minute I set eyes on him. He had the very look of not having no better sense than the man what wrote that board and then nearly committed suicide trying to get away from the best island in all the oceans. Glad enough he was to get back, though, for the coconuts was running very short on the floater* what had rescued him, and the turtle eggs wasn't worth mentioning. Being short of grub is the surest way I know to cure a man's fear of the unknown.

'Well, to make a long story short, Nelson Smith told me he was a aeronauter.* In them days to be an aeronauter was not the same as to be an aviatress* is now. There was dangers in the air, and dangers in the sea, and he had met with both. His gas tank had leaked and he had dropped into the water close by Anita. A case or two of provisions was all he could save from the total wreck.

'Now, as you might guess, I was crazy enough to find out what had scared this Nelson Smith into trying to swim the Pacific. He told me a story that seemed to fit pretty well with mine, only when it come to the scary part he shut up like a clam, that aggravating way some men have. I give it up at last for just man-foolishness, and we begun to scheme to get away.

'Anita moped some while we talked it over. I realized how she must be feeling, so I explained to her that it was right needful for us to get with our kind again. If we stayed with her we should probably quarrel like cats, and maybe even kill each other out of pure human cussedness. She cheered up considerable after that, and even, I thought, got a little anxious to have us leave. At any rate, when we begun to provision up the little floater, which we had anchored to the big island by a cable of twisted bark, the green nuts fell all over the ground, and Nelson found more turtle nests in a day than I had in weeks.

'During them days I really got fond of Nelson Smith. He was a companionable body, and brave, or he wouldn't have been a professional aeronauter, a job that was rightly thought tough enough for a woman, let alone a man. Though he was not so well educated as me, at least he was quiet and modest about what he did know, not like some men, boasting most where there is least to brag of.

'Indeed, I misdoubt if Nelson and me would not have quit the sea and the air together and set up housekeeping in some quiet little town up in New England, maybe, after we had got away, if it had not been for what happened when we went. I never, let me say, was so deceived in any man before nor since. The thing taught me a lesson and I never got fooled again. This was the way of it.

'We was all ready to go, and then one morning, like a parting gift from Anita, come a soft and favoring wind. Nelson and I run down the beach together, for we didn't want our floater to blow off and leave us. As we was running, our arms full of coconuts, Nelson Smith, stubbed his bare toe on a sharp rock, and down he went. I hadn't noticed, and was going on.

'But sudden the ground begun to shake under my feet, and the air was full of a queer, grinding, groaning sound, like the very earth was in pain.

'I turned around sharp. There sat Nelson, holding his bleeding toe in both fists and giving vent to such awful words as no decent sea-going lady would ever speak nor hear to!

'"Stop it, stop it!" I shrieked at him, but 'twas too late.

'Island or no island, Anita was a lady, too! She had a gentle heart, but she knowed how to behave when she was insulted.

'With one terrible, great roar a spout of smoke and flame belched up out o' the heart of Anita's crater hill a full mile into the air!

'I guess Nelson stopped swearing. He couldn't have heard himself, anyways. Anita was talking now with tongues of flame and such roars as would have bespoke the raging protest of a continent.

'I grabbed that fool man by the hand and run him down to the water. We had to swim good and hard to catch up with our only hope, the floater. No bark rope could hold her against the stiff breeze that was now blowing, and she had broke her cable. By the time we scrambled aboard great rocks was falling right and left. We couldn't see each other for a while for the clouds of fine gray ash that filled the air and covered the sea.

'It seemed like Anita was that mad she was flinging stones after us, and truly I believe that such was her intention. I didn't blame her, neither!

'Lucky for us the wind was strong and we was soon out of range. After that it wasn't so long before my poor, outraged Anita was just a streak o' smoke on the horizon.

'"So!" says I to Nelson, after I'd got most of the ashes out of my mouth, and shook my hair clear of cinders. "So, that was the reason you up and left sudden when you was there before! You aggravated that island till the poor thing druv you out!"'

'"Well," says he, and not so meek as I'd have admired to see him, "how could I know the darn island was a lady?"'

'"Actions speak louder than words," says I. "You should have knowed it by her ladylike behavior!"'

'"Is volcanoes and slingin' hot rocks ladylike?" says he. "Is snakes ladylike? T'other time I cut my thumb on a tin can, I cussed a little bit. Say—just a li'l' bit! An' what comes at me out o' all the caves, and out o' every crack in the rocks, and out o' the very spring o' water where I'd been drinkin'? Why snakes! *Snakes*, if you please, big, little, green, red and sky-blue-scarlet! What'd I do? Jumped in the water, of course. Why wouldn't I? I'd ruther swim an' drown than be stung or swallered to death. But how was I t' know the snakes come outta the rocks because I cussed?"'

'"*You* couldn't," I agrees, sarcastic. "Some folks never knows a lady till she up and whangs 'em over the head with a brick. A real, gentle, kind-like warning, them snakes were, which you would not heed! Take shame to yourself, Nelly," says I, right stern, "that a decent, little island like Anita can't associate with you peaceable, but you must hurt her sacredest feelings with language no lady would stand by to hear!"

He give up his high manners then, for he knowed them words was true.

'I never did see Anita again. She may have blew herself right out of the ocean in her just wrath at the vulgar, disgustin' language of Nelson Smith. I don't know. We was took off the floater at last, and I lost track of Nelson just as quick as I could when we was landed at Frisco.

'He had taught me a lesson. A man is just full of mannishness, and the best of 'em ain't good enough for a lady to sacrifice her sensibilities to put up with.

'Nelson Smith, he seemed to feel real bad when he learned I was not for him, and then he apologized. But apologies weren't no use to me. I never could abide him, after the way he went and talked right in the presence of me and my poor, sweet lady friend, Anita!'

Now I am well versed in the lore of the sea in all ages. Through mists of time I have enviously eyed wild voyagings of sea rovers who roved and spun their yarns before the stronger sex came into its own, and ousted man from his heroic pedestal. I have followed—across the printed page—the wanderings of Odysseus. Before Gulliver I have burned the incense of tranced attention; and with reverent awe considered the history of one Munchausen, a baron.*

But alas, these were only men!

In what field is not woman our subtle superior?

Meekly I bowed my head, and when my eyes dared lift again, the ancient mariness had departed, leaving me to sorrow for my surpassed and outdone idols. Also with a bill for macaroons and tea of such incredible proportions that in comparison therewith I found it easy to believe her story!

W. E. B. DU BOIS

THE COMET

HE stood a moment on the steps of the bank, watching the human river that swirled down Broadway.* Few noticed him. Few ever noticed him save in a way that stung. He was outside the world—'nothing!' as he said bitterly. Bits of the words of the walkers came to him.

'The comet?'

'The comet—'

Everybody was talking of it. Even the president, as he entered, smiled patronizingly at him, and asked:

'Well, Jim, are you scared?'

'No,' said the messenger shortly.

'I thought we'd journeyed through the comet's tail once,' broke in the junior clerk affably.

'Oh, that was Halley's,'* said the president; 'this is a new comet, quite a stranger, they say—wonderful, wonderful! I saw it last night. Oh, by the way, Jim,' turning again to the messenger, 'I want you to go down into the lower vaults today.'

The messenger followed the president silently. Of course, they wanted *him* to go down to the lower vaults. It was too dangerous for more valuable men. He smiled grimly and listened.

'Everything of value has been moved out since the water began to seep in,' said the president; 'but we miss two volumes of old records. Suppose you nose around down there,—it isn't very pleasant, I suppose.'

'Not very,' said the messenger, as he walked out.

'Well, Jim, the tail of the new comet hits us at noon this time,' said the vault clerk, as he passed over the keys; but the messenger passed silently down the stairs. Down he went beneath Broadway, where the dim light filtered through the feet of hurrying men; down to the dark basement beneath; down into the blackness and silence beneath that lowest cavern. Here with his dark lantern he groped in the bowels of the earth, under the world.

He drew a long breath as he threw back the last great iron door and stepped into the fetid slime within. Here at last was peace, and he groped moodily forward. A great rat leaped past him and cobwebs crept across his face. He felt carefully around the room, shelf by shelf, on the muddied floor, and in crevice and corner. Nothing. Then he went back to the far end, where somehow the wall felt different. He sounded and pushed and pried. Nothing. He started away. Then something brought him back. He was sounding and working again when suddenly the whole black wall swung as on mighty hinges, and blackness yawned beyond. He peered in; it was evidently a secret vault—some hiding place of the old bank unknown in newer times. He entered hesitatingly. It was a long, narrow room with shelves, and at the far end, an old iron chest. On a high shelf lay the two missing volumes of records, and others. He put them carefully aside and stepped to the chest. It was old, strong, and rusty. He looked at the vast and old-fashioned lock and flashed his light on the hinges. They were deeply incrusted with rust. Looking about, he found a bit of iron and began to pry. The rust had eaten a hundred years, and it had gone deep. Slowly, wearily, the old lid lifted, and with a last, low groan lay bare its treasure—and he saw the dull sheen of gold!

'Boom!'

A low, grinding, reverberating crash struck upon his ear. He started up and looked about. All was black and still. He groped for his light and swung it about him. Then he knew! The great stone door had swung to. He forgot the gold and looked death squarely in the face. Then with a sigh he went methodically to work. The cold sweat stood on his forehead; but he searched, pounded, pushed, and worked until after what seemed endless hours his hand struck a cold bit of metal and the great door swung again harshly on its hinges, and then, striking against something soft and heavy, stopped. He had just room to squeeze through. There lay the body of the vault clerk, cold and stiff. He stared at it, and then felt sick and nauseated. The air seemed unaccountably foul, with a strong, peculiar odor. He stepped forward, clutched at the air, and fell fainting across the corpse.

He awoke with a sense of horror, leaped from the body, and groped up the stairs, calling to the guard. The watchman sat as if asleep, with the gate swinging free. With one glance at him the messenger hurried up to the sub-vault. In vain he called to the guards. His voice echoed and re-echoed weirdly. Up into the great basement he rushed. Here another guard lay prostrate on his face, cold and still. A fear arose in the messenger's heart. He dashed up to the cellar floor, up into the bank. The stillness of death lay everywhere and everywhere bowed, bent, and stretched the silent forms of men. The messenger paused and glanced about. He was not a man easily moved; but the sight was appalling! 'Robbery and murder,' he whispered slowly to himself as he saw the twisted, oozing mouth of the president where he lay half-buried on his desk. Then a new thought seized him: If they found him here alone—with all this money and all these dead men—what would his life be worth? He glanced about, tiptoed cautiously to a side door, and again looked behind. Quietly he turned the latch and stepped out into Wall Street.

How silent the street was! Not a soul was stirring, and yet it was high-noon—Wall Street? Broadway? He glanced almost wildly up and down, then across the street, and as he looked, a sickening horror froze in his limbs. With a choking cry of utter fright he lunged, leaned giddily against the cold building, and stared helplessly at the sight.

In the great stone doorway a hundred men and women and children lay crushed and twisted and jammed, forced into that great, gaping doorway like refuse in a can—as if in one wild, frantic rush to safety, they had crushed and ground themselves to death. Slowly the messenger crept along the walls, wetting his parched mouth and trying to comprehend, stilling the tremor in his limbs and the rising terror in his heart. He met a business man, silk-hatted and frock-coated, who had crept, too, along that smooth wall and stood now stone dead with wonder written on his lips. The messenger turned his eyes hastily away and sought the curb. A woman leaned wearily against the signpost, her head bowed motionless on her lace and silken bosom. Before her stood a street car, silent, and within—but the messenger but glanced and hurried on. A grimy newsboy sat in the gutter with the 'last edition' in his uplifted hand: 'Danger!' screamed its black headlines. 'Warnings wired around the world. The Comet's tail sweeps past us at noon. Deadly gases expected. Close doors and windows. Seek the cellar.' The messenger read and staggered on. Far out from a window above, a girl lay with gasping face and sleevelets on her arms. On a store step sat a little, sweet-faced girl looking upward toward the skies, and in the carriage by her lay—but the messenger looked no longer. The cords gave way—the terror burst in his veins, and with one great, gasping cry he sprang desperately forward and ran,—ran as only the frightened run, shrieking and fighting the air until with one last wail of pain he sank on the grass of Madison Square* and lay prone and still.

When he arose, he gave no glance at the still and silent forms on the benches, but, going to a fountain, bathed his face; then hiding himself in a corner away from the drama of death, he quietly gripped himself and thought the thing through: The comet had swept the earth and this was the end. Was everybody dead? He must search and see.

He knew that he must steady himself and keep calm, or he would go insane. First he must go to a restaurant. He walked up Fifth Avenue to a famous hostelry and entered its gorgeous, ghost-haunted halls. He beat back the nausea, and, seizing a tray from dead hands, hurried into the street and ate ravenously, hiding to keep out the sights.

'Yesterday, they would not have served me,'* he whispered, as he forced the food down.

Then he started up the street,—looking, peering, telephoning, ringing alarms; silent, silent all. Was nobody—nobody—he dared not think the thought and hurried on.

Suddenly he stopped still. He had forgotten. My God! How could he have forgotten? He must rush to the subway—then he almost laughed. No—a car; if he could find a Ford. He saw one. Gently he lifted off its burden, and took his place on the seat. He tested the throttle. There was gas. He glided off, shivering, and drove up the street. Everywhere stood, leaned, lounged, and lay the dead, in grim and awful silence. On he ran past an automobile, wrecked and over-turned; past another, filled with a gay party whose smiles yet lingered on their death-struck lips; on past crowds and groups of cars, pausing by dead policemen; at 42nd Street he had to detour to Park Avenue to avoid the dead congestion. He came back on Fifth Avenue at 57th and flew past the Plaza and by the park* with its hushed babies and silent throng, until as he was rushing past 72nd Street he heard a sharp cry, and saw a living form leaning wildly out an upper window. He gasped. The human voice sounded in his ears like the voice of God.

'Hello—hello—help, in God's name!' wailed the woman. 'There's a dead girl in here and a man and—and see yonder dead men lying in the street and dead horses—for the love of God go and bring the officers—' And the words trailed off into hysterical tears.

He wheeled the car in a sudden circle, running over the still body of a child and leaping on the curb. Then he rushed up the steps and tried the door and rang violently. There was a long pause, but at last the heavy door swung back. They stared a moment in silence. She had not noticed before that he was a Negro. He had not thought of her as white. She was a woman of perhaps twenty-five—rarely beautiful and richly gowned, with darkly-golden hair, and jewels. Yesterday, he thought with bitterness, she would scarcely have looked at him twice. He would have been dirt beneath her silken feet. She stared at him. Of all the sorts of men she had pictured as coming to her rescue she had not dreamed of one like him. Not that he was not human, but he dwelt in a world so far from hers, so infinitely far, that he seldom even entered her thought. Yet as she looked at him curiously he seemed quite commonplace and usual. He was a tall, dark working-man of the better class, with a sensitive face trained to stolidity and a poor man's clothes and hands. His face was soft and slow and his manner at once cold and nervous, like fires long banked, but not out.

So a moment each paused and gauged the other; then the thought of the dead world without rushed in and they started toward each other.

'What has happened?' she cried. 'Tell me! Nothing stirs. All is silence! I see the dead strewn before my window as winnowed by the breath of God,—and see—' She dragged him through great, silken hangings to where, beneath the sheen of mahogany and silver, a little French maid lay stretched in quiet, everlasting sleep, and near her a butler lay prone in his livery.

The tears streamed down the woman's cheeks and she clung to his arm until the perfume of her breath swept his face and he felt the tremors racing through her body.

'I had been shut up in my dark room developing pictures of the comet which I took last night; when I came out—I saw the dead!'

'What has happened?' she cried again.

He answered slowly:

'Something—comet or devil—swept across the earth this morning and—many are dead!'

'Many? Very many?'

'I have searched and I have seen no other living soul but you.'

She gasped and they stared at each other.

'My—father!' she whispered.

'Where is he?'

'He started for the office.'

'Where is it?'

'In the Metropolitan Tower.'*

'Leave a note for him here and come.'

Then he stopped.

'No,' he said firmly—'first, we must go—to Harlem.'*

'Harlem!' she cried. Then she understood. She tapped her foot at first impatiently. She looked back and shuddered. Then she came resolutely down the steps.

'There's a swifter car in the garage in the court,' she said.

'I don't know how to drive it,' he said.

'I do,' she answered.

In ten minutes they were flying to Harlem on the wind. The Stutz* rose and raced like an airplane. They took the turn at 110th Street on two wheels and slipped with a shriek into 135th.

He was gone but a moment. Then he returned, and his face was gray. She did not look, but said:

'You have lost—somebody?'

'I have lost—everybody,' he said, simply—'unless—'

He ran back and was gone several minutes—hours they seemed to her.

'Everybody,' he said, and he walked slowly back with something film-like in his hand which he stuffed into his pocket.

'I'm afraid I was selfish,' he said. But already the car was moving toward the park among the dark and lined dead of Harlem—the brown, still faces, the knotted hands, the homely garments, and the silence—the wild and haunting silence. Out of the park, and down Fifth Avenue they whirled. In and out among the dead they slipped and quivered, needing no sound of bell or horn, until the great, square Metropolitan Tower hove in sight. Gently he laid the dead elevator boy aside; the car shot upward. The door of the office stood open. On the threshold lay the stenographer, and, staring at her, sat the dead clerk. The inner office was empty, but a note lay on the desk, folded and addressed but unsent:

Dear Daughter:

I've gone for a hundred mile spin in Fred's new Mercedes.* Shall not be back before dinner. I'll bring Fred with me.

J. B. H.

'Come,' she cried nervously. 'We must search the city.'

Up and down, over and across, back again—on went that ghostly search. Everywhere was silence and death—death and silence! They hunted from Madison Square to Spuyten Duyvel; they rushed across the Williamsburg Bridge; they swept over Brooklyn; from the Battery and Morningside Heights* they scanned the river. Silence, silence everywhere, and no human sign. Haggard and bedraggled they puffed a third time slowly down Broadway, under the broiling sun, and at last stopped. He sniffed the air. An odor—a smell—and with the shifting breeze a sickening stench filled their nostrils and brought its awful warning. The girl settled back helplessly in her seat.

'What can we do?' she cried.

It was his turn now to take the lead, and he did it quickly.

'The long distance telephone—the telegraph and the cable—night rockets and then—flight!'

She looked at him now with strength and confidence. He did not look like men, as she had always pictured men; but he acted like one and she was content. In fifteen minutes they were at the central telephone exchange. As they came to the door he stepped quickly before her and pressed her gently back as he closed it. She heard him moving to and fro, and knew his burdens—the poor, little burdens he bore. When she entered, he was alone in the room. The grim switchboard flashed its metallic face in cryptic, sphinx-like immobility. She seated herself on a stool and donned the bright earpiece. She looked at the mouthpiece. She had never looked at one so closely before. It was wide and black, pimpled with usage; inert; dead; almost sarcastic in its unfeeling curves. It looked—she beat back the thought—but it looked,—it persisted in looking like—she turned her head and found herself alone. One moment she was terrified; then she thanked him silently for his delicacy and turned resolutely, with a quick intaking of breath.

'Hello!' she called in low tones. She was calling to the world. The world *must* answer. Would the world *answer*? Was the world—

Silence!

She had spoken too low.

'Hello!' she cried, full-voiced.

She listened. Silence! Her heart beat quickly. She cried in clear, distinct, loud tones: 'Hello—hello—hello!'

What was that whirring? Surely—no—was it the click of a receiver?

She bent close, she moved the pegs in the holes, and called and called, until her voice rose almost to a shriek, and her heart hammered.

It was as if she had heard the last flicker of creation, and the evil was silence. Her voice dropped to a sob. She sat stupidly staring into the black and sarcastic mouthpiece, and the thought came again. Hope lay dead within her. Yes, the cable and the rockets remained; but the world—she could not frame the thought or say the word. It was too mighty—too terrible! She turned toward the door with a new fear in her heart. For the first time she seemed to realize that she was alone in the world with a stranger, with something more than a stranger,—with a man alien in blood and culture—unknown, perhaps unknowable. It was awful! She must escape—she must fly; he must not see her again. Who knew what awful thoughts—

She gathered her silken skirts deftly about her young, smooth limbs—listened, and glided into a side-hall. A moment she shrank back: the hall lay filled with dead women; then she leaped to the door and tore at it, with bleeding fingers, until it swung wide. She looked out. He was standing at the top of the alley,—silhouetted, tall and black, motionless. Was he looking at her or away? She did not know—she did not care. She simply leaped and ran—ran until she found herself alone amid the dead and the tall ramparts of towering buildings.

She stopped. She was alone. Alone! Alone on the streets—alone in the city—perhaps alone in the world! There crept in upon her the sense of deception—of creeping hands behind her back—of silent, moving things she could not see,—of voices hushed in fearsome conspiracy. She looked behind and sideways, started at strange sounds and heard still stranger, until every nerve within her stood sharp and quivering, stretched to scream at the barest touch. She whirled and flew back, whimpering like a child, until she found that narrow alley again and the dark, silent figure silhouetted at the top. She stopped and rested; then she walked silently toward him, looked at him timidly; but he said nothing as he handed her into the car. Her voice caught as she whispered:

'Not—that.'

And he answered slowly: 'No—not that!'

They climbed into the car. She bent forward on the wheel and sobbed, with great, dry, quivering sobs, as they flew toward the cable office on the east side, leaving the world of wealth and prosperity for the world of poverty and work. In the world behind them were death and silence, grave and grim, almost cynical, but always decent; here it was hideous. It clothed itself in every ghastly form of terror, struggle, hate, and suffering. It lay wreathed in crime and squalor, greed and lust. Only in its dread and awful silence was it like to death everywhere.

Yet as the two, flying and alone, looked upon the horror of the world, slowly, gradually, the sense of all-enveloping death deserted them. They seemed to move in a world silent and asleep,—not dead. They moved in quiet reverence, lest somehow they wake these sleeping forms who had, at last, found peace. They moved in some solemn, world-wide *Friedhof*,* above which some mighty arm had waved its magic wand. All nature slept until—until, and quick with the same startling thought, they looked into each other's eyes—he, ashen, and she, crimson, with unspoken thought. To both, the vision of a mighty beauty—of vast, unspoken things, swelled in their souls; but they put it away.

Great, dark coils of wire came up from the earth and down from the sun and entered this low lair of witchery. The gathered lightnings of the world centered here, binding with beams of light the ends of the earth. The doors gaped on the gloom within. He paused on the threshold.

'Do you know the code?' she asked.

'I know the call for help—we used it formerly at the bank.'

She hardly heard. She heard the lapping of the waters far below,—the dark and restless waters—the cold and luring waters, as they called. He stepped within. Slowly she walked to the wall, where the water called below, and stood and waited. Long she waited, and he did not come. Then with a start she saw him, too, standing beside the black waters. Slowly he removed his coat and stood there silently. She walked quickly to him and laid her hand on his arm. He did not start or look. The waters lapped on in luring, deadly rhythm. He pointed down to the waters, and said quietly:

'The world lies beneath the waters now—may I go?'*

She looked into his stricken, tired face, and a great pity surged within her heart. She answered in a voice clear and calm, 'No.'

Upward they turned toward life again, and he seized the wheel. The world was darkening to twilight, and a great, gray pall was falling mercifully and gently on the sleeping dead. The ghastly glare of reality seemed replaced with the dream of some vast romance. The girl lay silently back, as the motor whizzed along, and looked half-consciously for the elf-queen to wave life into this dead world again. She forgot to wonder at the quickness with which he had learned to drive her car. It seemed natural. And then as they whirled and swung into Madison Square and at the door of the Metropolitan Tower she gave a low cry, and her eyes were great! Perhaps she had seen the elf-queen?*

The man led her to the elevator of the tower and deftly they ascended. In her father's office they gathered rugs and chairs, and he wrote a note and laid it on the desk; then they ascended to the roof and he made her comfortable. For a while she rested and sank to dreamy somnolence, watching the worlds above and wondering. Below lay the dark shadows of the city and afar was the shining of the sea. She glanced at him timidly as he set food before her and took a shawl and wound her in it, touching her reverently, yet tenderly. She looked up at him with thankfulness in her eyes, eating what he served. He watched the city. She watched him. He seemed very human,—very near now.

'Have you had to work hard?' she asked softly.

'Always,' he said.

'I have always been idle,' she said. 'I was rich.'

'I was poor,' he almost echoed.

'The rich and the poor are met together,' she began, and he finished:

'The Lord is the Maker of them all.'*

'Yes,' she said slowly; 'and how foolish our human distinctions seem—now,' looking down to the great dead city stretched below, swimming in unlightened shadows.

'Yes—I was not—human, yesterday,' he said.

She looked at him. 'And your people were not my people,'* she said; 'but today—' She paused. He was a man,—no more; but he was in some larger sense a gentleman,—sensitive, kindly, chivalrous, everything save his hands and—his face. Yet yesterday—

'Death, the leveler!'* he muttered.

'And the revealer,' she whispered gently, rising to her feet with great eyes. He turned away, and after fumbling a moment sent a rocket into the darkening air. It arose, shrieked, and flew up, a slim path of light, and, scattering its stars abroad, dropped on the city below. She scarcely noticed it. A vision of the world had risen before her. Slowly the mighty prophecy of her destiny overwhelmed her. Above the dead past hovercd the Angel of Annunciation.* She was no mere woman. She was neither high nor low, white nor black, rich nor poor. She was primal woman; mighty mother of all men to come and Bride of Life. She looked upon the man beside her and forgot all else but his manhood, his strong, vigorous manhood—his sorrow and sacrifice. She saw him glorified. He was no longer a thing apart, a creature below, a strange outcast of another clime and blood, but her Brother Humanity incarnate, Son of God and great All-Father of the race to be.

He did not glimpse the glory in her eyes, but stood looking outward toward the sea and sending rocket after rocket into the unanswering darkness. Dark-purple clouds lay banked and billowed in the west. Behind them and all around, the heavens glowed in dim, weird radiance that suffused the darkening world and made almost a minor music. Suddenly, as though gathered back in some vast hand, the great cloud-curtain fell away. Low on the horizon lay a long, white star—mystic, wonderful! And from it fled upward to the pole, like some wan bridal veil, a pale, wide sheet of flame that lighted all the world and dimmed the stars.

In fascinated silence the man gazed at the heavens and dropped his rockets to the floor. Memories of memories stirred to life in the dead recesses of his mind. The shackles seemed to rattle and fall from his soul. Up from the crass and crushing and cringing of his caste leaped the lone majesty of kings long dead. He arose within the shadows, tall, straight, and stern, with power in his eyes and ghostly scepters hovering to his grasp. It was as though some mighty Pharaoh lived again, or curled Assyrian lord.* He turned and looked upon the lady, and found her gazing straight at him.

Silently, immovably, they saw each other face to face—eye to eye. Their souls lay naked to the night. It was not lust; it was not love—it was some vaster, mightier thing that needed neither touch of body nor thrill of soul. It was a thought divine, splendid.

Slowly, noiselessly, they moved toward each other—the heavens above, the seas around, the city grim and dead below. He loomed from out the velvet shadows vast and dark. Pearl-white and slender, she shone beneath the stars. She stretched her jeweled hands abroad. He lifted up his mighty arms, and they cried each to the other, almost with one voice, 'The world is dead.'

'Long live the—'

'Honk! Honk!' Hoarse and sharp the cry of a motor drifted clearly up from the silence below. They started backward with a cry and gazed upon each other with eyes that faltered and fell, with blood that boiled.

'Honk! Honk! Honk! Honk!' came the mad cry again, and almost from their feet a rocket blazed into the air and scattered its stars upon them. She covered her eyes with her hands, and her shoulders heaved. He dropped and bowed, groped blindly on his knees about the floor. A blue flame spluttered lazily after an age, and she heard the scream of an answering rocket as it flew.

Then they stood still as death, looking to opposite ends of the earth.

'Clang—crash—clang!'

The roar and ring of swift elevators shooting upward from below made the great tower tremble. A murmur and babel of voices swept in upon the night. All over the once dead city the lights blinked, flickered, and flamed; and then with a sudden clanging of doors the entrance to the platform was filled with men, and one with white and flying hair rushed to the girl and lifted her to his breast. 'My daughter!' he sobbed.

Behind him hurried a younger, comelier man, carefully clad in motor costume, who bent above the girl with passionate solicitude and gazed into her staring eyes until they narrowed and dropped and her face flushed deeper and deeper crimson.

'Julia,' he whispered; 'my darling, I thought you were gone forever.'

She looked up at him with strange, searching eyes.

'Fred,' she murmured, almost vaguely, 'is the world—gone?'

'Only New York,' he answered; 'it is terrible—awful! You know,—but you, how did you escape—how have you endured this horror? Are you well? Unharmed?'

'Unharmed!' she said.

'And this man here?' he asked, encircling her drooping form with one arm and turning toward the Negro. Suddenly he stiffened and his hand flew to his hip. 'Why!' he snarled. 'It's—a—nigger—Julia! Has he—has he dared—'

She lifted her head and looked at her late companion curiously and then dropped her eyes with a sigh.

'He has dared—all, to rescue me,' she said quietly, 'and I—thank him—much.' But she did not look at him again. As the couple turned away, the father drew a roll of bills from his pockets.

'Here, my good fellow,' he said, thrusting the money into the man's hands, 'take that,—what's your name?'

'Jim Davis,' came the answer, hollow-voiced.

'Well, Jim, I thank you. I've always liked your people. If you ever want a job, call on me.' And they were gone.

The crowd poured up and out of the elevators, talking and whispering.

'Who was it?'

'Are they alive?'

'How many?'

'Two!'

'Who was saved?'

'A white girl and a nigger—there she goes.'

'A nigger? Where is he? Let's lynch the damned—'

'Shut up—he's all right—he saved her.'

'Saved hell! He had no business—'

'Here he comes.'

Into the glare of the electric lights the colored man moved slowly, with the eyes of those that walk and sleep.

'Well, what do you think of that?' cried a bystander; 'of all New York, just a white girl and a nigger!'

The colored man heard nothing. He stood silently beneath the glare of the light, gazing at the money in his hand and shrinking as he gazed; slowly he put his other hand into his pocket and brought out a baby's filmy cap, and gazed again. A woman mounted to the platform and looked about, shading her eyes. She was brown, small, and toil-worn, and in one arm lay the corpse of a dark baby. The crowd parted and her eyes fell on the colored man; with a cry she tottered toward him.

'Jim!'

He whirled and, with a sob of joy, caught her in his arms.

EXPLANATORY NOTES

MARY SHELLEY, *The Mortal Immortal*

Mary Wollstonecraft Godwin (1797–1851) was the daughter of radical parents famous, and infamous, throughout Britain. Her father, William Godwin (1756–1836) was a philosopher and novelist, author of, among other fictions, a political novel of terror, *Things As They Are; or, The Adventures of Caleb Williams* (1794) and the tale of earthly immortality, *St Leon* (1799) (very likely an influence on his daughter's tale, 'The Mortal Immortal'). Her mother, Mary Wollstonecraft (1759–97), was a writer on politics, a novelist, and the author of a classic travel book, *Letters Written in Sweden, Norway, and Denmark* (1796). Both her parents authored radical texts of political theory furthering the ideas of the French Revolution, Godwin producing the proto-anarchist work *Enquiry Concerning Political Justice* (1793) and Wollstonecraft writing the foundational feminist treatise *A Vindication of the Rights of Woman* (1792). Young Mary's mother died some eleven days after giving birth to her. Consequently, Mary Godwin grew up with her father in London; in 1801, he remarried—Mary's relationship with her stepmother, Mary Jane Clairmont (1766–1841), was notably frosty. In May 1814, Mary began a relationship with the young married poet, the aristocratic radical Percy Bysshe Shelley (1793–1822). Soon after meeting, the two lovers left for the Continent, accompanied by Mary's stepsister, Claire (Jane) Clairmont (1798–1879). In London, the following February, Mary gave birth to a daughter, two months premature, who died some ten days later, while Mary slept. The couple had a son, William, in January 1816. With the baby and Claire Clairmont, the couple travelled again to the Continent, in that Year Without a Summer. (Following the eruption of Mount Tambora in what is now Indonesia, there was major disruption to the climate across much of the world.) While staying at the Villa Diodati by Lake Geneva with Lord Byron (1788–1824), following long conversations about the possibility that human science might create life, she came up with the idea for her classic philosophical Gothic tale, *Frankenstein; or, The Modern Prometheus* (1818), often taken to be the first true science fiction novel. Some few months after their return to England, Shelley's wife, Harriet, drowned herself in the Serpentine. Nineteen days later, on 29 December 1816, Mary married Percy Shelley, with her father and stepmother acting as witnesses. In September 1817, Mary gave birth to a second daughter, Clara; a year later in Venice, Clara died of dysentery; the couple's son, William, died in Rome of malaria on 7 June 1819. Later that year, Mary gave birth to Percy Florence Shelley, the couple's only surviving child, who would, some twenty-five years later, become heir to his grandfather's (Sir Timothy Shelley's (1753–1844)) title and estate. In 1822, Percy Shelley drowned while out sailing in a storm in the sea off La Spezia in Italy. Mary saw through the publication of his *Posthumous Poems* (1824) and edited an edition of his poetical works, including a series of fascinating critical and biographical notes (1839).

After *Frankenstein*, Mary Shelley went on to write a series of other novels: *Mathilda* (written 1819, but only published in 1959), the tale of an incestuous relationship between father and daughter, expressing perhaps some of the author's own troubled feelings about her relationship with Godwin; *Valperga* (1823), a historical novel set in medieval Italy; another historical novel, *The Fortunes of Perkin Warbeck* (1830); *Lodore* (1835); and *Falkner* (1837). Aside from *Frankenstein*, her most important work, and another major contribution to the birth of science fiction, was *The Last Man* (1826), an apocalyptic novel set in the twenty-first century delineating a world destroyed by plague. Her influence both on later science fiction and on Gothic and 'horror' has been immense. Shelley wrote many short stories, of which 'The Mortal Immortal', a tale occupying (as *Frankenstein* does) the borderland between Gothic and science fiction, is probably the most well known. After some twelve years of illness, she died in 1851 in London.

The copy-text used here is based on Mary Wollstonecraft Shelley, *Tales and Stories of Mary Wollstonecraft Shelley*, ed. Richard Garnett (London: William Paterson & Co., 1891), 148–64. The story was first published in the Christmas 1833 edition of Frederic Mansel Reynolds (1800–50) (ed.), *The Keepsake for MDCCCXXXIV* (London: Longman, Rees, Orme, Brown, Green, and Longman, 1833), 71–87. Here the story was credited to 'the Author of Frankenstein', and was illustrated with a coy and prettified plate entitled 'Bertha', showing the story's heroine with her mother, as drawn by the portraitist Henry Perronet Briggs (1791–1844), and engraved by Frederick Bacon (1803–87), a former pupil of Henry Fuseli's. The story reappeared in Charles Gibbon (1843–90) and Mary Elizabeth Christie (1847–1906) (eds), *The Casquet of Literature: Being a Selection of Prose and Poetry from the Most Admired Authors* (London: Blackie & Son, 1877).

1 *The Wandering Jew*: a legendary figure, sometimes named as Ahasuerus, and less frequently as Cartaphilus, who was said to have insulted Jesus Christ while he was carrying the cross to Calvary, and in punishment would wander the earth, deathlessly, until Judgement Day. This anathematized character was of strong interest to writers in the early nineteenth century. To take only the most obvious examples: William Wordsworth (1770–1850) wrote a 'Song for the Wandering Jew' (1800); his fate informs that of the titular protagonist of Charles Maturin's (1780–1824) Gothic novel, *Melmoth the Wanderer* (1820); and the myth connects likewise to another set of individuals under a curse, the crew of *The Flying Dutchman*. Before going up to Oxford University, Percy Bysshe Shelley (1793–1822) wrote a narrative poem, *The Wandering Jew* (1810; pub. 1877), in part with his friend, Thomas Medwin (1788–1869), and Thomas Carlyle (1795–1881) makes mention of the myth in his *Sartor Resartus* (1834), to name only a few of the ways in which the character acted as a touchstone of the times.

the Seven Sleepers: this alludes to a legend of seven persecuted Christians who, around AD 250, took refuge in a cave outside the Ionian city of Ephesus, falling asleep there for some 300 years. The story was popularized by Gregory of Tours (538–94) and appears in Jacobus de Varagine's *Golden Legend* (*c.*1260), as well as the Qur'an. There was a revival of interest in the story in the nineteenth century.

the fabled Nourjahad: a reference to Frances Sheridan's (1723–66) 'oriental novel', *The History of Nourjahad* (1767), in which the Sultan Schemzeddin apparently permits his friend, Nourjahad, to enjoy all the sensual pleasures he desires while enjoying eternal life; with each sleep he falls into lasting years, only for it to be revealed that his supposed immortality is a mere trick. In 1812, the tale was incorporated into vol. ii of Henry Weber's (1783–1818) compilation, *Tales of the East: Comprising the Most Popular Romances of Oriental Origin* (Edinburgh: John Ballantyne) (with the Sultan renamed Schemerzad); in 1813, a play version of the novel, entitled *Illusion; or, The Trances of Nourjahad*, appeared at Drury Lane, and was wrongly attributed to Lord Byron (1788–1824) (in 1788, it had been previously dramatized by Sophia Lee (1750–1824)); and in July 1834, just a year after Shelley published her tale, an opera by Edward Loder, *Nourjahad*, based on the story successfully premiered in London.

Cornelius Agrippa: physician, cabbalist, and occultist (1486–1535), the author of (among other works) *De occulta philosophia* (1531–3). In Mary Shelley's *Frankenstein*, the eponymous protagonist enthusiastically responds to his discovery of the 'wild fancies' contained in Agrippa's writings, though his father dismisses them as 'sad trash' (chapter 1). As an alchemical writer Agrippa is in a paradoxical position, and might be placed either as a magician or a natural philosopher, an occultist or a scientist. When Frankenstein attends Ingoldstadt University, his teacher M. Krempe is less dismissive than his father had been: ' "these were men to whose indefatigable zeal modern philosophers were indebted for most of the foundations of their knowledge" '(chapter 2). In this way, Agrippa's presence in the tale places 'The Mortal Immortal' both as a Gothic fable and as an engagement with scientific possibilities. Particularly relevant to his appearance in this story is the legend (absorbed into Christopher Marlowe's (1564–93) *Doctor Faustus* (1589–92?) that after secretly looking through Agrippa's books, his apprentice inadvertently conjured up the Devil. The story appears in a ballad written by Robert Southey (1774–1843), 'Cornelius Agrippa' (1799), in which after examining 'the Conjuror's books' the hapless apprentice summons up the horned Devil.

3 *alembics*: an apparatus used for the distillation of a liquid in alchemical experiments, consisting largely of a gourd-shaped cucurbit with a tube that deposits the condensed fluid into a receiving flask.

7 *'a prophet is least regarded in his own country'*: a reference to Jesus' return to the town where he grew up, Nazareth, and the sceptical and mocking response that he received there, as set out in different forms in all four Gospels: 'And they were offended in him, But Jesus said unto them, A prophet is not without honour, save in his own country, and in his own house' (Matthew 1:57), and also in Mark 6:4; Luke 4:16–30 (though without explicitly stating the phrase paraphrased by Shelley); and John 4:44.

8 *the Nestors of our village*: a reference to Nestor, King of Pylos, one of the Achaeans or Argives in Homer's *The Iliad* and *The Odyssey*, and in both poems an old man known to be experienced, wise, and a source of good counsel.

12 *a Cain*: another biblical reference, this time to the eldest son of Adam and Eve, as described in Genesis 4. Out of envy, Cain, 'a tiller of the ground', murders his younger brother, Abel, 'a keeper of sheep'. God curses Cain for his deed, telling him 'When thou tillest the ground, it shall not henceforth yield unto thee her strength; a fugitive and a vagabond shalt thou be in the earth' (4:12).

benefactor of the human species: the word 'benefactor' echoes throughout Mary Shelley's novel, *Frankenstein; or, The Modern Prometheus* (1818/1831), though interestingly it is not used to refer to Victor Frankenstein himself, but rather to his friend Clerval ('The busy stage of life, the virtues of heroes, and the actions of men were his theme; and his hope and his dream was to become one among those whose names are recorded in story as the gallant and adventurous benefactors of our species' (chapter 2 and again in chapter 21)), to Frankenstein's father in relation to the serving-girl Justine (chapter 9), by the creature to Mr De Lacey (chapter 15), and to the mutinous sailors on Walton's ship (chapter 24).

EDGAR ALLAN POE, *The Conversation of Eiros and Charmion*

Within three years of his birth in 1809 in Boston, both of Edgar Poe's travelling-actor parents were dead. Poe was taken in by a Virginian tobacco merchant, John Allan, and his wife, Frances Allan. Brought up to follow his foster-father into the world of business, Poe dreamt of a life of writing and adventure. Poe quit the University of Virginia, largely due to the fact that Allan deprived him of sufficient money. Breaking with his foster-father, Poe left home, published his first book, *Tamerlane and Other Poems* (1827), and joined the army. He dropped out of West Point after eight months. Thereafter he maintained a precarious financial existence, writing poems, short stories, and reviews. He also acted as editor of a series of periodicals, from December 1835 to December 1836 with the *Southern Literary Messenger*, based in Richmond, and, after a move north to Philadelphia, in 1839–40 with *Burton's Gentleman's Magazine*, and then in 1841–2 with *Graham's Magazine*. In January 1845, in New York, he started up his own magazine, the *Broadway Journal*; it folded in the January of the following year. In May 1836, Poe married his cousin, Virginia Clemm; she was at the time 13 years old. In 1842, she contracted tuberculosis; she died in

January 1847, leaving Poe inconsolable. Sanguine, sensitive, and prone to intense melancholia, Poe had always been a drinker, and his waywardness and drunkenness perpetually wrecked every opportunity he received. On 7 October 1849, he died on polling day in Baltimore; his last words were 'God help my poor soul!'

Poe stands as one of the greatest writers of mid-nineteenth-century America, the author of a compelling and resonant novel of the sea, *The Narrative of Arthur Gordon Pym of Nantucket* (1838). He was one of the most influential writers of Gothic (the author of such short-story masterpieces as 'The Fall of the House of Usher', 'William Wilson' (both 1839), and 'The Black Cat' (1843)), the inventor of the detective story, with his 'The Murders in the Rue Morgue' (1841) and 'The Purloined Letter' (1844), arguably America's first great poet, and an inspired and foundational critic. To writers such as Baudelaire, he was the ragged incarnation of the *poète maudit*, an orphan, a wastrel, a grand refuser of the compromises of respectable life. As such, he was central to the development of the symbolist movement in France. He likewise has, by common critical agreement, proved central to the development of 'science fiction', through hoaxes such as 'The Unparalleled Adventure of One Hans Pfaal' (1835) (concerning a voyage to the moon by hot-air balloon), pastiches like 'The Thousand-and-Second Tale of Scheherazade' (1845), and the astonishing treatise/monograph/rhapsody *Eureka: A Prose Poem* (1848). In a famous essay written in 1926, Hugo Gernsback declared, 'By "scientifiction" I mean the Jules Verne, H. G. Wells, and Edgar Allan Poe type of story'.

The copy-text for 'The Conversation of Eiros and Charmion' is based on its appearance in Edgar A. Poe, *Tales* (London: Wiley and Putnam, 1845), 110–19, appearing between 'The Colloquy of Monos and Una' and 'The Murders in the Rue Morgue'. The story first appeared in *Burton's Gentleman's Magazine* (Philadelphia), 5 (December 1839), 321–3 (while Poe was editor). The story subsequently appeared in Poe's classic collection, *Tales of the Grotesque and Arabesque* (1840), ii. 213–22, and later in the Philadelphia *Saturday Museum* (1 April 1843), where it was retitled 'The Destruction of the World. (A Conversation between two Departed Spirits.)'. Isabelle Meunier translated the piece into French, as 'Le Colloque d'Eiros et Charmion', *Démocratie pacifique* (3 July 1847) (Paris).

13 *EIROS AND CHARMION*: these names reference, though without exactly reproducing, the names of two of Cleopatra's women-attendants, Iras and Charmion, in Plutarch's 'The Life of Marcus Antonius', trans. Sir Thomas North (1579), where they die alongside Cleopatra, and Charmion speaks, as it were, from beyond the grave, uttering her last words as the poison takes effect. They reappear under those same names in John Dryden's play *All For Love* (1677); in William Shakespeare's *Antony and Cleopatra* (1607?), Charmion becomes Charmian. Shakespeare's play also has a male attendant, named 'Eros', whose name may be crossed with 'Iras' here, so as to come to 'Eiros'. Poe had earlier used the names 'Eiros

and Charmion' in his unfinished verse drama, *Politiun* (1835–6) (scene iv, lines 24–6).

13 Πυρ σοι προσισω . . . *Euripides—Androm*: This motto (which can be transliterated as 'Pyr soy prosyso') comes from line 257 of Euripides' (*c*.480–*c*.406 BC) tragedy, *Andromache* (*c*.428–425 BC). The epigraph was first introduced when Poe republished the story in the Philadelphia *Saturday Museum* version (1843). The play's setting, after the destruction of Troy, may be intended to echo this tale that takes place after the end of the world. In the quote, during a long rhetorical dispute (or *agôn*), Hermione, the wife of Andromache's master, taunts the Trojan widow.

'voice of many waters': in this tale of latter days, Poe here quotes the Bible's last book, Revelation, the 'Apocalypse of John': 'And I heard a voice from heaven, as the voice of many waters, and as the voice of a great thunder: and I heard the voice of harpers harping with their harps: / And they sung as it were a new song before the throne, and before the four beasts, and the elders: and no man could learn that song but the hundred and forty and four thousand, which were redeemed from the earth' (Revelation 14:1–2).

Aidenn: from the Qu'ranic word *Adn*, meaning 'everlasting bliss', 'Eden' or 'paradise'. The word also appears in Poe's poem 'The Raven' (1845) ('Tell this soul with sorrow laden if, within this distant Aidenn, | It shall clasp a sainted maiden whom the angels name Lenore' (lines 93–4), and also in Poe's later colloquy, 'The Power of Words' (1845), where another spirit, Agathos tells the newly dead Oinos, 'There are *no* dreams in Aidenn'.

14 *the most holy writings which speak of the final destruction of all things by fire*: another reference to a biblical text concerning apocalypse and the end of the world, in this case 2 Peter 3:7 and 10: 'But the heavens and the earth, which are now, by the same word are kept in store, reserved unto fire against the day of judgment and perdition of ungodly men . . . / . . . But the day of the Lord will come as a thief in the night; in the which the heavens shall pass away with a great noise, and the elements shall melt with a fervent heat, the earth also and the works that are therein shall be burned up.'

15 *the announcement by astronomers of a new comet*: it is rather likely that in August 1835 Poe would have seen and read about Halley's Comet (named after Sir Edmond Halley (1656–1742), the astronomer and author of *Synopsis of the Astronomy of Comets* (1705), who had worked out the periodicity of the comet in question). Anxieties regarding the destructive potential of such a comet proliferated in the mid-1830s. In 1835, Henry Walker published a song, 'The Great Comet! A Fearful Tragedy', a ditty that begins, 'When Mister Bupps was first inform'd that one of these fine days, | A Comet's tail would strike the earth and set it in a blaze'. In June 1832, 'Encke's Comet' had similarly aroused interest on its periodic return to the night skies; at that time, the astronomer François Arago (1786–1853) had reassuringly calculated the chances of the comet striking the earth as 281,000,000 to 1 (*Tract on Comets* (1832)). In his discussion of the comet, Poe may have been influenced by S. Austin Jr's tale 'The Comet'

(published in *The Token and Atlantic Souvenir. A Christmas and New Year Present* (Boston: Otis, Broaders, and Company 1839), 174–213). The tale is something of an exploration through a dialogue of the meaning of suffering and apocalypse, and how the destruction of the earth could be reconciled to a sense of God's care and goodness. In the course of the discussion, some speculations arise as to the nature of the Lunarians, the hypothetically serene inhabitants of the moon, and how they might be affected by witnessing humanity's demise, bound as we are to the earth, which might be 'the abode of outcasts, perhaps . . . the purgatory of the solar system' (205). The tale closes with the loss of all life on earth.

perihelion: the point in the comet's orbit when it is closest to the sun.

17 *a compound of oxygen and nitrogen gases . . . every one hundred of the atmosphere*: Poe's science here is not far out: the earth's atmosphere is about 78 parts nitrogen, 21 parts oxygen, about 0.9 per cent argon, 0.04 per cent carbon dioxide, and various other gases in trace amounts. This composition was only scientifically established in the first half of the nineteenth century.

a total extraction of the nitrogen . . . the prophecies of the Holy Book: in this idea, scholars have concurred that Poe was likely impressed by Thomas Dick's (1774–1857) *The Christian Philosopher; or The Connection Between Science and Philosophy* (first published in 1823). In a section cheerily entitled 'The Discoveries of Science Tend to Illustrate the Doctrine of GENERAL CONFLAGRATION', Dick entertains the entire feasibility of the earth being consumed by fire:

> It was formerly stated . . . that the atmosphere, or the air we breathe, is a compound substance, composed of two very different and opposite principles, termed *oxygen* and *nitrogen*. The oxygen, which forms about a fifth part of the atmosphere, is now ascertained to be the principle of flame . . . The modern infidel, like the scoffers of old, scouts the idea of the dissolution of the world, and of the restitution of the universe, 'because all things continue as they were from the beginning of creation' . . . For should the Creator issue forth his Almighty Fiat—'Let the nitrogen of the atmosphere be completely separated from the oxygen, and let the oxygen exert its native energies without control, wherever it extends;'—from what we know of its nature, we are warranted to conclude, that instantly a universal conflagration would commence throughout all the kingdom of nature (from the 2nd American edn, New York: G. and C. Carvill, 1827), 326).

NATHANIEL HAWTHORNE, *Rappaccini's Daughter*

Nathaniel Hawthorne was born in Salem, Massachusetts, in 1804, the son of Nathaniel (1775–1808), a sea captain, and Elizabeth Hathorne (née Manning) (1780–1849). In 1808, his father died while on a voyage to Surinam, and his mother with her son and two daughters moved in with her Manning relatives. From 1821 to 1825, Hawthorne attended Bowdoin College in Maine (befriending his fellow student, the poet Henry Wadsworth Longfellow (1807–82) there). On graduating, Hawthorne moved back home, where he devoted himself to writing; a debut novel, *Fanshawe* (1828) would later prove a source of embarrassment to its author. From 1830, his stories began to appear in periodicals, and were collected in the volume *Twice-Told Tales* (1837). His fictions belong to a European tradition that merges Gothic and the fantastic, merging irony and the uncanny, the macabre and the fabulous. Touching on alchemy and magic, and on the pernicious desire to know both the secrets of another person and of nature itself, it was in these ways that some of Hawthorne's speculative tales form part of the origins of science fiction. Between 1839 and 1840, the young author worked as Measurer at the Boston Custom House. In 1841, for six months, Hawthorne joined the utopian socialistic and transcendentalist community at Brook Farm; the experience forms the background to his novel, *The Blithedale Romance* (1852). In 1842, he married the shy and sickly Sophia Peabody (1809–71); the couple settled in the Old Manse in Concord, while Hawthorne worked as Surveyor and Inspector of the Revenue at the port of Salem, until he lost that job in 1849, following a change in administration due to the Republican electoral victory. The couple had three children: the troubled and fragile Una (1844–77), Julian (1846–1934) (who would become a writer), and Rose (1851–1926) (who, under the name of Mother Mary Alphonsa, would become a Dominican nun). A second collection of stories, *Mosses from an Old Manse*, came out in 1846.

Fired from his job at Salem, Hawthorne returned after a hiatus to writing. His first novel, the astonishing *The Scarlet Letter* (1850), tells a story of adultery in puritan New England. Hawthorne himself was intrigued and troubled about his descent from puritans, his first American ancestor William Hathorne (1606–81) being notorious for his persecution of the Quakers, and his great-great-grandfather, John Hathorne (1641–1717) acting in 1692 as one of the judges in the Salem witch trials. A second novel, *The House of the Seven Gables*, followed in 1851, beginning with a preface justifying Hawthorne's decision to write not realistic novels, but 'romances'. That same year, another volume of stories appeared, *The Snow-Image*. Between 1853 and 1857, Hawthorne was American consul at Liverpool, his experience of England being described in his book, *Our Old Home* (1863); he then spent two years resident in Italy. His Italian sojourn inspired his last great romance, *The Marble Faun* (1860). He died in May 1864, leaving a further four romances unfinished.

The copy-text of 'Rappaccini's Daughter' is based on the story's first appearance in a book, as one of the short stories in *Mosses from an Old Manse* (London: Wiley and Putnam, 1846), Pt I, pp. 85–118. It is the fifth story in this particular volume, placed between 'Young Goodman Brown' and 'Mrs Bullfrog'. The story had previously been published in the *United States Magazine, and Democratic Review*, 15/78 (December 1844), 545–60, under the title 'Writings of Aubépine:—Rappaccini's Daughter'; the running heads for the story are 'Writings of Aubépine' on the left-hand page and 'Rappaccini's Daughter' on the right. Aptly, and most likely coincidentally, a poem by R. S. S. Andros

(1817–68), titled 'The Prisoner', about a woman kept captive precedes the tale. In 1844, Hawthorne prefaces the story with the following text, which does not appear in the first book publication or the subsequent edition of *Mosses* in 1851, but was restored to stand alongside the tale in the 1854 edition and other later editions:

We do not remember to have seen any translated specimens of the productions of M. de l'Aubépine; a fact the less to be wondered at, as his very name is unknown to many of his own country-men, as well as to the student of foreign literature. As a writer, he seems to occupy an unfortunate position between the Transcendentalists (who, under one name or another, have their share in all the current literature of the world), and the great body of pen-and-ink men who address the intellect and sympathies of the multitude. If not too refined, at all events too remote, too shadowy and unsubstantial in his mode of development, to suit the taste of the latter class, and yet too popular to satisfy the spiritual or metaphysical requisitions of the former, he must necessarily find himself without an audience; except here and there an individual, or possibly an isolated clique. His writings, to do them justice, are not altogether destitute of fancy and originality; they might have won him a greater reputation but for an inveterate love of allegory, which is apt to invest his plots and characters with the aspect of scenery and people in the clouds, and to steal away the warmth of his conceptions. His fictions are sometimes historical, sometimes of the present day, and sometimes, so far as can be discovered, have little or no reference either to time or space. In any case, he generally contents himself with a very slight embroidery of outward manners,—the faintest possible counterfeit of real life,—and endeavors to create an interest by some less obvious peculiarity of the subject. Occasionally, a breath of nature, a rain-drop of pathos and tenderness or a gleam of humor will find its way into the midst of his fantastic imagery, and make us feel as if, after all, we were yet within the limits of our native earth. We will only add to this very cursory notice, that M. de l'Aubépine's productions, if the reader chance to take them in precisely the proper point of view, may amuse a leisure hour as well as those of a brighter man; if otherwise, they can hardly fail to look excessively like nonsense.

Our author is voluminous; he continues to write and publish with as much praiseworthy and indefatigable prolixity, as if his efforts were crowned with the brilliant success that so justly attends those of Eugene Sue. His first appearance was by a collection of stories, in a long series of volumes, entitled '*Conte deux fois racontées.*' The titles of some of his more recent works (we quote from memory) are as follows:— '*Le Voyage Céleste à Chemin de Fer,*' 3. tom. 1838. '*Le nouveau père Adam et la nouvelle mère Eve,*' 2 tom. 1839. '*Roderic; ou le Serpent à l'estomac,*' 2 tom. 1840. '*Le Culte du Feu,*' a folio volume of ponderous research into the religion and ritual of the old Persian Ghebers, published in 1841, '*La Soirée du Chateau en Espagne,*' 1 tom. 8vo. 1842; and '*L'Artiste du Beau; ou le Papillon Mécanique,*' 5 tom. 4to. 1843. Our somewhat wearisome perusal of this startling catalogue of volumes has left behind it a certain personal affection and sympathy, though by no means admiration, for M. de l'Aubépine; and we would fain do the little in our power towards introducing him favorably to the American public. The ensuing tale is a translation of his '*Beatrice; ou La Belle Empoisonneuse*,' recently published in '*La Revue Anti-Aristocratique*.' This journal, edited by the Comte de Bearhaven, has, for some years past, led the defence of liberal principles and popular rights, with a faithfulness and ability worthy of all praise. (545)

Hawthorne characteristically packs this text with in-jokes and ruses, offering a self-conscious and slyly self-deprecatory introduction to his tale. *L'Aubépine* is French for the hawthorn, the writer thereby marking himself as another, foreign and strange. As part of the spoof, he renders his recent short stories as French texts: *Conte deux fois racontées* transforms his previous collection of short stories, *Twice-Told Tales* (1837); 'Le Voyage céleste à Chemin de Fer' refers to 'The Celestial Rail-Road' (1843); 'Le Nouveau Père Adam et la nouvelle mère Eve' doubles 'The New Adam and Eve' (1843); 'Roderic; ou Le Serpent à l'estomac' alters 'Egotism; or, The Bosom-Serpent' (1843) (though the snake in question has slipped down from the bosom to the stomach); 'Le Culte du feu' (literally 'The Fire Cult') translates the tale 'Fire-Worship' (1843); 'La Soirée du château en Espagne', meaning 'Evening at a Castle in Spain', the last phrase being another way of suggesting a 'castle in the air' (that is, a daydream or unrealizable project), disguises the tale 'A Select Party' (1844); while, finally, 'L'Artiste du beau; ou Le Papillon mécanique' translates and expands upon 'The Artist of the Beautiful' (1844). All these tales, like 'Rappaccini's Daughter', appeared in the *United States Magazine, and Democratic Review*. The present tale's Frenchified title, 'Beatrice; ou La Belle Empoisonneuse', removes the stress on the heroine's status as a daughter and instead suggests that she is rather a poisoner (*une empoisonneuse*) than the poisoned one. The journal's reimagining as '*La Revue anti-aristocratique*' stresses the oppositional aspect implicit in the concept of the 'democratic'. The journal was founded and edited by John Louis O'Sullivan (1813–95), infamous for coining in 1845 the phrase 'manifest destiny'. O'Sullivan was a good friend of Hawthorne and his family; entangled in O'Sullivan's 'Democratic' and Irish-American contradictions, he properly claimed (in a way that Hawthorne appears to have taken semi-comically) hereditary rights to a Spanish countship—one of his ancestors (Donal Cam O'Sullivan Beare (1561–1618) having been elevated by Philip III of Spain to Grandee of Spain and Earl of Bearhaven (or Berehaven).

19 *University of Padua*: founded in 1222, this university in the northern city of Padua was at the time of writing the story in Lombardy, a region under Austrian control. The university was well known for its strengths in natural philosophy, was home to a famous anatomical theatre, and is notable for the fact that Galileo Galilei (1564–1642) lectured there from 1592 to 1610.

Dante . . . immortal agonies of his Inferno: Dante Aligheri (1265–1321) was the author of *The Divine Comedy* (*Divina Commedia*) (1320), an allegorical journey through Hell, Purgatory, and Heaven. The first part, *Inferno*, is famous for its encounters with real individuals known to Dante and his contemporaries, all of whom undergo eternal tortures of grotesque inventiveness. The mention of Dante is apt for a tale where a young man falls in love, as Dante did, with a woman named Beatrice.

20 *one of those botanic gardens, which were of earlier date in Padua than elsewhere in Italy, or in the world*: as part of its status as a centre for research, the university was renowned for the Orto Botanico di Padova, founded in 1545, which was, as Hawthorne informs us, the first-ever botanical garden, a scientific institution devoted in part to growing medicinal plants.

Vertumnus: the Roman god of the seasons, gardens, and the growth of plants. In Book XIV of Ovid's (43 BC–AD 18) *Metamorphoses*, disguised as an old woman, Vertumnus enters the garden of Pomona, goddess of fruit trees and orchards, and seduces the goddess, who chooses to marry him.

21 *Was this garden, then, the Eden of the present world? . . . was he the Adam?*: the allusion here to the second and third chapters of Genesis places Rappaccini's property as a prelapsarian garden, home, it would seem, to a solitary man.

'Are you in the garden!': in the version of the text printed in *Mosses from an Old Manse*, this is printed with an exclamation mark, as here; however, in the first printing in the *United States Magazine, and Democratic Review*, the sentence ends instead with a question mark; the change shifts a note of interrogation to one of surprise.

25 *Lacryma*: an Italian wine, from the slopes of Mount Vesuvius in Campania in the south; its full name, Lacryma Christi, refers to the tears of Christ. It is possible that in choosing this wine, Hawthorne also alludes to another kind of *lacrima*, which is a medicinal gum exuded from trees and shrubs, or the exuded sap of a vine.

27 *rather a Grecian than an Italian head*: in other words, his profile resembles the type commonly found on Greek statues; in Hawthorne's later novel, *The Marble Faun* (1860), there's another young Italian, Donatello, whose features and appearance are closer to the Greek than to the Italian type.

33 *the maiden of a lonely island*: there are tacit allusions here to William Shakespeare's (1564–1616) *The Tempest* (1611?), and to the situation of Miranda, the lonely daughter of the magus Prospero. In the course of the play, she meets for the first time a human being (Ferdinand) from the world beyond the Mediterranean island where she and her father have long lived in isolation. In both *The Tempest* and in 'Rappaccini's Daughter', the young woman noticeably lacks a mother.

36 *an old classic author . . . a story that strangely interested me*: the origins of such narratives hail originally from India, with tales of the 'Visha Kanya', the 'poison girl', a legendary figure from Sanskrit literature, though it is possible that real practices regarding assassination are alluded to in such characters. In Vishakhadatta's Sanskrit play *Mudrarakshasa*, the king Parvata is slain by contact with a Visha Kanya. However, the classic author in question is certainly Robert Burton (1577–1640), author of the compendious,

profuse, and endlessly fascinating *The Anatomy of Melancholy* (1621), a trove of curious tales much admired by early nineteenth-century writers, such as Charles Lamb and John Keats (whose tale of a serpent-woman, 'Lamia' (1820), is borrowed from Burton). In Part I, section ii, member 2, subsection 3, 'Custom of Diet, Delight, Appetite, Necessity, how they cause or hinder', Burton informs us: 'Mithridates, by often use, which Pliny wonders at, was able to drink poison; and a maid, as Curtius records, sent to Alexander from King Porus, was brought up with poison from her infancy'. (Parvata is taken by some scholars to be based on King Porus.) At the time of Alexander's invasion of the country, Porus was an Indian king (he likely died around 324 BC). Burton alludes to Quintus Curtius Rufus' *Histories of Alexander the Great* (*Historiae Alexandri Magni*) (first century AD), but the tale he describes does not in fact as such appear there.

36 *Alexander the Great*: Alexander III of Macedon (356–323 BC), king and military leader, who established an empire stretching from the eastern Mediterranean to north-west India. See note to p. 70.

37 *Araby*: though 'Arabia' was the earlier term, by the 1840s 'Araby' had become the more archaic expression; the word signalled the exotic, the mysterious, the paradisal. It also particularly suggests a rich incense, scent, or perfume.

38 *alembic*: see note to p. 3.

Benvenuto Cellini: the vase was made by Benvenuto Cellini (1500–71), the Italian sculptor and goldsmith, author of a hugely popular *Autobiography* (first published in 1728).

the most powerful poisons of the Borgias: the House of Borgia was a noble and aristocratic family originally from Aragon in north-eastern Spain, and who in the sixteenth and seventeenth centuries were a dominating force in Italian politics and the Church (producing two popes), and notable cultural patrons. They were also scandalous figures, infamous for their taste for intrigue, assassination, and sexual licence. In particular, Lucrezia Borgia (1480–1519) was rumoured to have been a notorious poisoner, supposedly in possession of a hollow ring wherein she concealed her potions.

39 *vile empiric*: 'a physician or medical practitioner of a school of thought originating in ancient Greece and Rome and holding that treatment should be based on observation and experience rather than on deduction from theoretical principles' (*OED*).

41 *outgush*: this word is hyphenated in the version of the text in *Mosses from an Old Manse*, where it straddles a line, but is written thus as one word in the magazine publication.

EDGAR ALLAN POE, *The Facts in the Case of M. Valdemar*

For a biographical introduction to Poe, see the headnote to Poe, 'The Conversation of Eiros and Charmion', p. 13.

This story draws on the pseudoscience of mesmerism, as first framed by Friedrich Anton Mesmer (1734–1815), in which the skilled mesmerist can induce a hypnotic state in the subject by the harnessing of 'animal magnetism', a force or influence that supposedly exists between all animate and inanimate bodies. Poe went to some lengths to present his fiction as though it were a genuine empirical account of a mesmeric experiment. His ruse worked, and some readers took the story straight, or were confused as to whether it were a documentary account or a tall tale.

The copy-text for the story is based on its second publication, in Poe's *Broadway Journal*, 2/24 (20 December 1845), 365–8, where after an opening poem ('To "The Lady Geraldine"' by Frances S. Osgood) it forms the lead story. Leaning on Thomas Ollive Mabbott's edition of *The Collected Works of Edgar Allan Poe*, iii. *Tales and Sketches* (Cambridge, MA: Belknap Press of Harvard University Press, 1978), the text here draws on some changes made in Sarah Helen Whitman's copy of the periodical, incorporating manuscript revisions by Poe made in 1848. Whitman (1803–78) was herself a poet and essayist, and a spiritualist, and someone who took a great deal of interest in mesmerism. Though they had already encountered each other in 1845, it was after Poe's wife's death that the two writers became romantically involved. They were soon engaged to be married, though, following a falling-out, the wedding never took place. The slightly revised version in Whitman's possession corrects some misprints in the periodical publication, and alters 'putrescence' to 'putridity' in the concluding sentence of the story. Previous to its appearance in the *Broadway Journal*, the story had appeared in George Hooker Colton's (1818–47) *American Review: A Whig Journal of Politics, Literature, Art and Science*, 2/6 (December 1845), 561–5). In the *Broadway Journal*, the following note prefaces the tale:

> An article of ours, thus entitled, was published in the last number of Mr. Colton's 'American Review,' and has given rise to some discussion— especially in regard to the truth or falsity of the claims made. It does not become *us*, of course, to offer one word on the point at issue. We have been requested to reprint the article, and do so with pleasure. We leave it to speak for itself. We may observe, however, that there are a certain class of people who pride themselves upon Doubt, as a profession. *Ed. B. J.*

As well as a number of reprintings in the press, it was subsequently published as a separate pamphlet, *Mesmerism 'in articulo mortis'. Astounding & Horrifying Narrative, shewing the extraordinary power of mesmerism in arresting the Progress of Death* (London: Short & Co., 1846).

46 M. *VALDEMAR*: although the character is apparently of Polish origin, the name derives from Old Germanic sources, and, sometimes spelt 'Waldemar', is particularly associated with Denmark. Some critics have suggested that Monsieur Valdemar's name puns on *val de mort* (French), meaning 'valley of death'.

in articulo mortis: literally, in the article of death (and expressed as such in English some time before the Latin phrase entered the language), meaning at the very point of dying.

46 *'Bibliotheca Forensica,'* . . . *Marx* . . . *'Wallenstein' and 'Gargantua'*: the 'Bibliotecha Forensica' is a fictitious work, whose title suggests a forensic library or compilation, dealing with matters (including possibly medical matters) pertaining to courts of law. 'Issacher' is one of the twelve tribes of Israel; 'Marx' is similarly a Jewish-German surname. Friedrich Schiller's (1759–1805) *Wallenstein* (1799) is a trilogy of plays that relates the tragic history of the German general Albrecht von Wallenstein (1583–1634) during the Thirty Years War (1618–48). François Rabelais's (1483–94?–1553) *La Vie de Gargantua et Pantagruel* was published in five books between 1532 and 1564, though Poe may be referring not to the complete work but specifically to the second volume, *La Vie très horrifique du grand Gargantua, père de Pantagruel* (1534). The cultured and intellectual Valdemar, who will end by speaking from beyond the borders of mortality, is a man of letters, and clearly something of a polyglot with a curiously hybrid and diverse identity, a resident of a formerly Dutch district of New York City, perhaps Danish, masquerading as Jewish, and conversant with Latin, German, French, English, and Polish.

Harlaem, N. Y.: though more usually spelt 'Harlem', Poe's spelling is not unusual in the mid-nineteenth century as a way of referring to the district at the upper end of the island of Manhattan. Originally a seventeenth-century settlement, New Harlem Village (named after Haarlem in the Netherlands), in the mid-nineteenth century, when it was connected by rail to 'the city of New York' to the south, the locale was effectively a suburban town.

John Randolph: John Randolph of Roanoke (1773–1833) was a Congressman and Senator from Virginia, Poe's adopted state. He was known to be melancholic, a consumptive, a heavy drinker, and (as his first biographer put it), an 'opium eater'; when he was dying he declared to his physician, 'I have been an idiosyncrasy all my life' (Hugh A. Garland, *The Life of John Randolph of Roaknoke* (New York: D. Appleton and Company, 1850), ii. 371). A full-length sketch prefacing the second volume of Garland's biography shows that his legs were remarkably thin and bony; contemporaries were agreed that in appearance he was tall, slender, and altogether lofty.

47 *phthisis*: tuberculosis.

P—— . . . *D——and F——*: editors have speculated that these initials are intended to draw living contemporaries into the tale. 'P' is likely, of course, to suggest Poe, in keeping with the story's provenance as hoax. Similarly, 'D' might refer to Dr John William Draper (1811–82), a professor at the Medical School of New York University. Though Poe seems to have been on friendly terms with Draper in 1845, he later came to dislike him. He has a glancing dig at Draper in his story, 'Von Kempelen and His Discovery' (1849); in a letter to his friend, George Washington Eveleth (1819–1908), dated 26 June 1849, he puts him down as a 'merely perceptive man . . . a pompous nobody', and indicates that *Eureka* might (among other things) be a way to send him up. 'F' has been taken to allude to the ebullient and vivacious Dr John Wakefield Francis (1789–1861), the doctor who tended both Poe and his wife during the couple's time in New York. (Both Valdemar and Virginia Poe were mortally sick with tuberculosis.) From 1847, Francis was the second president of the New York Academy of Medicine.

48 *pocket-book*: a term particularly prevalent in North America at this time, this simply means a notebook.

Theodore L——l: editors have not been able to link this character to anyone known by Poe.

49 *I commenced the passes*: the mesmeric pass was intended to bring on a trance in the subject. There were various methods of making the pass, sometimes consisting of the mesmerist several times moving the right hand downwards over the hands or otherwise close to the face of the person to be mesmerized, or moving the hands from the subject's hands up to the head or to the shoulders, and then down from the face to the stomach, and so on to the knees, usually without touching or making actual physical contact, keeping a 1- or 2-inch distance. A long pass could move from the subject's head down to their feet. It was sometimes customary to shake one's figures out after making each pass. The word suggests a glancing movement but also a transition within the self and a moment of exchange, the transference of energies from one to another.

sleep-waking: not a misprint for 'sleep-walking', but a precise designation of a state in-between sleep and wake, being both and neither. In the Romantic period, as set out, for instance, in Robert MacNish's *The Philosophy of Sleep* (2nd edn, Glasgow: W. R. M'Phun, 1834), this half-waking state was seen to be especially productive for permitting the self to fall into a 'reverie', 'in which the mind is nearly divested of all ideas, and approximates closely to the state of sleep' (288). Talking of 'night-mair', Samuel Taylor Coleridge saw it as 'not a mere dream', but something that 'takes place when the waking state of the brain is recommencing, and most often during a rapid alternation, a twinkling, as it were, of sleeping and waking' (*The Literary Remains of Samuel Taylor Coleridge* (London: William Pickering, 1836), i. 201). In this fugitive state of being, therefore, images came to the mind freely and without censorship by the rational self.

53 *rapport*: a French term derived from mesmerism, meaning that the narrator has established connection with Valdemar, and can now exercise mesmeric influence upon him. To establish a community of sensation between the mesmerizer, the subject, and the attending others, they would need to touch, usually by linking hands.

FITZ-JAMES O'BRIEN, *The Diamond Lens*

Born in Cork, Ireland, Michael Fitz-James O'Brien (1828–62) was the son of James O'Brien, a coroner and lawyer. His father died when he was young (around 12 years old); his mother, Eliza (reputedly a great beauty), after a decent interval married again. After studying at Trinity College Dublin (or at least that was what O'Brien later claimed), he moved to London in 1849, where he rapidly frittered away his inheritance (the rather large sum of £8,000), and so, in the early 1850s, after an unhappy love affair, he decided to emigrate to America and make his fortune in New York. He threw himself into the charmingly dissipated, bohemian life of the city. He earned a precarious living as an all-purpose man of letters, or literary hack, crafting small theatrical pieces, burlesques, and comedies, and spinning out essays, poems, articles, and stories for *Harper's Weekly*, *Harper's Magazine*, and *Putnam's Magazine*, writing theatre reviews for the *Saturday Press* and a regular column in *Vanity Fair*. *Harper's* published 'What Was It?', his famously unnerving tale of an invisible spirit discovered in residence in a Manhattan lodging house, while his other two most famous stories of the strange and unaccountable—'The Wondersmith' (October 1859) and 'The Diamond Lens' (January 1858)—both saw the light in the *Atlantic Monthly*. Somewhat worn down by the erratic rigours of bohemia (as well as the ups and downs of his own unstable spirits), it was perhaps with some relief that on the outbreak of the Civil War in 1861, he enlisted in the Seventh Regiment of the National Guard of New York. In 1862, he joined the staff of General Frederick W. Lander (a fellow poet) as a lieutenant. Around Valentine's Day of that year, he fought at the skirmish of Bloomery Gap in West Virginia. A couple of days later, during another skirmish, he was wounded in the shoulder and died of tetanus some weeks later on 6 April.

The inspiration for 'The Diamond Lens', according to his friend George Arnold, came either from his fellow bohemian artist, Frank T. Bellew (1828–88), or from another friend, Dr A. L. Carroll, 'respecting the wonders concealed in a drop of water'. When the story appeared, there was a controversy in the press that perhaps O'Brien had stolen the idea for the story from William North (born in 1825 in England), a writer who had committed suicide on 13 November 1854, and whose lost story, 'Microcosmos', was supposed to be the uncredited origin of O'Brien's idea. The two men did know each other, and were enemies.

The copy-text derives from *The Poems and Stories of Fitz-James O'Brien*, ed. William Winter (Boston: James R. Osgood and Co., 1881), 145–76. The story was first published in *Atlantic Monthly*, 1/3 (January 1858), 354–67.

55 *capillary attraction*: 'the phenomenon whereby a fluid is drawn up a narrow channel by the intermolecular forces existing between the fluid and the sides of the channel; the intermolecular forces responsible for this phenomenon' (*OED*).

glass containing those oblate spheroidal knots familiarly known as 'bull's-eyes': at the centre of a sheet of blown glass, there sits a round thick boss or protuberance, somewhat flattened at the poles of the sphere ('oblate').

Field's simple microscope: perhaps the cheap 'school microscope', but perhaps more likely the highly popular prize-winning 'student microscope', still affordable at 3 guineas, designed in 1854–5 by the manufacturers R. [Robert] Field and Son, based in Birmingham, England.

56 *'Arabian Nights' Entertainments'*: the collection of fables, folk-tales, comic and fantastic stories, also known as *The Thousand and One Nights*, first translated into English (from a French translation by Antoine Galland (1646–1715)) in 1706–21. Here, as elsewhere in nineteenth-century European and North American culture, the text stands for mystery and enchantment.

Leeuwenhoek, Williamson, Spencer, Ehrenberg, Schultz, Dujardin, Schact, and Schleiden: all these men were notable microscopists. Born in Delft, the Dutchman Antonie Philips van Leeuwenhoek (1632–1723) is one of the pioneers of the microscope, and, as the discoverer of microbes (which he named *kleine diertjes*, 'little animals') a founding figure in the history of microbiology. The Yorkshireman, William Crawford Williamson (1816–95), was a physiologist, natural historian, and palaeobotanist, most famous in the 1850s for his studies of microscopic organisms, as in his monograph on the wheel-animacule, *Melicerta* (1853). Charles Achilles Spencer (1813–81) was a prominent and internationally successful American maker of microscopes, based in New York State, where he worked alongside his cousin, Hamilton Spencer, as C. A. and H. Spencer. Christian Gottfried Ehrenberg (1795–1876) was a professor of medicine in Berlin and an eminent microbiologist and geologist, and the first micropalaeontologist; in the 1820s, he explored North Africa with the naturalist Wilhelm Hemprich, amassing an enormous collection of specimens and artefacts. Karl Heinrich Schultz-Schultzenstein (1798–1871) was a botanist and physiologist based in Berlin, and in 1843, following Jan Purkyně (1787–1869), a pioneer of the idea that medical and scientific study required well-equipped laboratories so that staff and students could conduct microscopic research. In the 1820s, he studied the circulation of sap in plants, and using the microscope showed that the processes involved were analogous to the circulation of the blood in animals (as set out in his *Der Lebensprocess im Blute: Eine mikroscopischen Entdeckungen gegründete Untersuchung* ('The Life-Process in the Blood: A Microscopic Disovery founded on Investigation') (1822)). Félix Dujardin (1801–60) was an autodidact French biologist, from 1840 a professor at Toulouse, known for his groundbreaking analysis and description of single-cell organisms, named by him as 'Rhizopoda'. In 1835, he was likely the first scientist to discern 'protoplasm' (which he named 'sarcode'). The botanist Hermann Schacht (1814–64), the youngest of the scientists listed by O'Brien, was the author of *Das Mikroskop und seine Anwendung insbesondere für Pflanzen-Anatomie und Physiologie* (1851) (translated as *The Microscope and its Application to Vegetable Anatomy and Physiology* (1855)). A doctor's son from Hamburg, Matthias Jakob Schleiden (1804–81) was a founder of cell theory (that all living creatures are made from living cells) and an early exponent of evolutionary theory. In 1848, he published *Die Pflanze und ihr Leben*, a work translated that same year by the British botanist Arthur Henfry. This book begins with a rhapsodic consideration of the relation between the eye and the microscope, the spiritual and the corporeal worlds, and an exploration of the arbitrary facts of measurement and magnitude.

56 *cryptogamia*: as set out in the Linnæan taxonomy, one of the two major divisions of plants.

57 *common wheel animalcule (Rotifera vulgaris)*: the rotifer is a class of microscopic organism, first discovered in the 1690s by the English natural philosopher and Anglican priest, John Harris (1666–1719). 'Animalcule' was the standard English equivalent for Leeuwenhoek's *kleine diertjes* (Dutch), and a generic term for micro-organisms.

New York Academy: the New York Academy of Medicine was founded in 1847.

58 *Pike, the celebrated optician*: Benjamin Pike and Sons (headed by the British-born Benjamin Pike, Sr (1777–1863)) was a notable New York-based optician and manufacturer of mathematical and scientific instruments. One of his sons, Benjamin Pike, Jr (1809–64), also set up in business on his own as a manufacturer of such instruments (for surveying, navigation, metereology, astronomy, and optics, among other things) from 1843 to 1867 at a store at 294 Broadway, as his catalogue stated it, 'a few doors above the park'.

Field's Compound, Hingham's, Spencer's, Nachet's Binocular, (that founded on the principles of the stereoscope,) . . . Spencer's Trunnion Microscope: for Field and Spencer, see notes to pp. 55 and 56. I have been unable to locate any manufacturer of microscopes named Hingham. However, Camille Sébastien Nachet (1799–1881) was an eminent and celebrated Parisian optician, at the time when O'Brien was writing his tale based at 16, Rue Serpente. Invented by Sir Charles Wheatstone (1802–75) in 1832, the stereoscope was a two-lensed (hence 'binocular') instrument that produced the impression of a solid object by simultaneously presenting in one single image the combined different perspectives of the left and right eyes. The stereoscope was transformed by Sir David Brewster (1781–1868), who created a machine, first displayed at the Great Exhibition of 1851, that turned the combined picture formed by two adjacent photographs into an in-depth image. Spencer's Large Trunnion Microscope was first produced in 1849; as described by the enthusiastic microscopist Charles E. West, it had a double mirror, a plain stage, a movable stage, and a polarizer.

draw-tubes, micrometers, a camera-lucida, lever-stage, achromatic condensers, white cloud illuminators, prisms, parabolic condensers, polarizing apparatus, forceps, aquatic boxes, fishing-tubes: all these are accessories for the keen microscopist. A 'draw-tube' is the compound tube, sliding within the body of the microscope, which holds the object-glass and eyepiece—by drawing it out, you enlarge the image without needing to adjust the eyepiece; the micrometer is a slide that can be placed on another slide to enable the measurement of an object; in the context of microscopy, a 'camera lucida' is an aid to drawing the image seen through the microscope, consisting of a prism (or a mirror with a hole in it) that can be fixed to the eyepiece to enable the viewer to see both the magnified object and the surface on which it is to be drawn; the 'lever-stage' was a device used to enable the microscopist to follow a moving organism; an 'achromatic condenser' is an object-glass or set of lenses that condenses the light source reflected from the mirror so that the viewer can better focus on the area of the object, shutting out all extraneous light; a 'white cloud illuminator', invented by the British watercolourist and optician Cornelius Varley (1781–1873), is a device that by means of a reflector made from plaster of Paris (rather than a mirror) converts direct sunlight into the kind of white light produced by a white cloud, as this was deemed the best kind of light for examining objects; in this context, a 'prism' is a transparent object used to refract light; a 'parabolic condenser' gathers light from the light source and concentrates it into a cone of light that illumines the specimen; the 'polarising apparatus' consists of two plates of either the pyroelectric mineral, tourmaline or of two prisms that allow the transmission of otherwise obscured aspects of the specimen; the 'aquatic box' was, as the name suggests, a 'live' box container, originally made from wood or ivory and often later made of brass or sometimes of glass, that could be fitted into the stage (or base) of the microscope, and used for examining live aquatic creatures; a 'fishing-tube' is an open-ended glass tube used for selecting a specimen held in a fluid, or otherwise such a tube used for examining the capillary action in a small fish or marine creature.

59 *Ehrenberg's theory that the Volvox globator was an animal, and proved that his 'monads'*: for Christian Gottfried Ehrenberg, see note to p. 56; in *Die Infusionsthierchen als volkommene Organismen* (1838), Ehrenberg had promulgated the since disproved idea that 'infusoria' (protozoa) were animals with an internal circulatory, gastric, and nervous system. A 'monad' in this context is a single-cell creature. The 'volvox' is just such a creature, a spherical freshwater organism that uses cilia to roll in the water.

the assertions of Mr. Wenham: the young microscopist Francis Herbert Wenham (1824–1908) was a notable figure in the sciences in the mid-1850s, and had written controversial articles in 1854–6 on 'cell development', the vegetable cell, and on the circulation of sap in plants, as well as on the angular aperture of object-glasses in the *Quarterly Journal of Microscopical Sciences* (January 1854).

spherical and chromatic aberrations: the deviation of rays of light leading to an indistinct image, so that not all the colours converge in a single point, either caused by the defects in the lens or a mirror (spherical aberration) or by the differing 'refrangibility' (the ability to be refracted) of rays of light (chromatic aberration).

60 *Argus had eyes*: in Greek myth, Argus was a 100-eyed giant, employed by Hera to keep watch over the transformed Io, so that Zeus could not seduce her.

60 *Mexican caballero*: simply a gentleman, the Mexican version of that courtly gallant, the 'cavalier'.

Cellini: see note to p. 38.

the Upper Ten: the 'upper ten thousand' richest people in New York City, as first described in a newspaper article in the *Evening Mirror* by Nathanael Parker Willis (1806–67) in 1844. The phrase quickly caught on, and was popularized in 1852 in a series of articles, 'The Upper Ten Thousand: Sketches of American Society' in *Fraser Magazine* by Charles Astor Bristed (1820–74) (collected that same year in volume form); the anonymous play *The Startling Confessions of Eleanor Burton* (1852), described as 'exhibiting a dark page in the manners, customs, and crimes of the "Upper Ten"'; and in George Lippard's (1822–54) book, *New York: Its Upper Ten and Lower Million* (Cincinnati: H. M. Rulison, 1853).

61 *le renard*: (French) fox.

Bernard Palissy: Palissy (*c*.1510–*c*.1589) was a French ceramicist and potter, famous in particular for his colourful 'rustic' pieces (especially plates, but also vases) that feature in highly realistic relief small animals, notably lizards and snakes, but also butterflies, fish, frogs, and so on, among shells or flowers, foliage, flowers and moss. Palissy enjoyed an enormous vogue in the mid-nineteenth century, at a time when imitation 'Palissy ware' was manufactured for the Great Exhibition of 1851.

63 *It may have been biology*: that is, the explanation for this apparent communication with a spirit of the dead may have a biological and materialist explanation.

64 *rapport*: see note to p. 53.

carcel lamp: patented in 1800 by the French horologist Bernard Guillaume Carcel (1750–1818), this was a mechanical oil-lamp that used a clockwork pump to move the colza-oil (coleseed, or rape oil) up to the wick and thereby feed the flame.

65 *Malay creese*: a 'kris' or 'keris' is a Malay dagger, which though it can on occasion have a straight blade, more often (and more famously) had a wavy one.

66 *Lausseure's Clos Vougeot . . . Côte d'Or*: Joseph-Jules Lausseure (1789–1892) was a distinguished wine-merchant, renowned for applying the techniques of champagne making to Burgundy wine. 'Clos [de] Vougeot' is a walled vineyard in the Burgundy region of France, and hence also a red wine that comes from this vineyard. A major wine-producing region in the eastern centre of France, 'Côte d'Or' is one of the administrative departments created during the French Revolution, and is part of what had been the province of Burgundy.

a famous vintage, that of 1848: though not a bad year, in fact the great recent vintage year was not 1848, but very famously 1846. In linking his wine to 1848, O'Brien references the recent year of revolutions in Europe, a time of enormous social upheaval and political change throughout much of the Continent, and notably in France.

chansons: (French) songs.

69 *ANIMULA*: (Latin) 'little soul', but also containing echoes of the 'animal-cule', meaning the micro-organisms found by the microscopist.

galvanic battery, composed of nearly two thousand pairs of plates: named in honour of the Italian natural philosopher Luigi Galvani (1737–98), the discoverer of animal electricity and experimenter in the field of bioelec-tricity. The battery stored electricity, and was constructed from alternat-ing plates of usually (negative plates of) copper and (positive plates of) zinc, connected by a liquid (such as dilute sulphuric acid).

70 *Alexander's famous wish*: in the essay 'On Tranquillity of Mind' in Plutarch's *Moralia*, Alexander the Great (356–323 BC) hears the philoso-pher Anaxarchus (*c*.380–320 BC) describe how there may be an infinite number of worlds, and weeps, saying that it was worth crying when there are an infinite number of worlds, that he was not yet lord of a single one.

infusoria and protozoa, down to the original gaseous globule: see note to p. 59.

72 *the bees of Hybla*: Hybla is a region of Sicily, where the wild bees were par-ticularly famous for the sweetness of their honey. There are two allusions to the sweetness of Hybla's honey in Shakespeare, in *Henry IV Part One*, I.ii and in *Julius Caesar*, V.i. It is possible that this can therefore be seen as the first of a set of Shakespearean and classical allusions that begin to enter the text at this point, with the arrival of the mysterious female presence.

naiad: in ancient Greek and Roman mythology, a freshwater or river nymph and a spirit of place.

Beethoven the divine: Ludwig van Beethoven (1770–1827), the last of the great exponents of the classical tradition, a quintessential Romantic genius and a composer of some of the most powerful nineteenth-century music, including nine extraordinary symphonies.

Neptune: though observed far earlier (most famously by Galileo Galilei (1564–1642)) and mathematically predicted (by the astronomer Urbain Le Verrier (1811–77), Neptune was effectively 'discovered' at the Berlin Observatory by Johann Gottfried Galle (1812–1910) in 1846. It was Le Verrier who proposed the name 'Neptune' for the new planet. It was then, and, after a long spell of being dethroned by Pluto, is now again, the most distant planet from the sun.

the sylph: invented by the astrologer and alchemist Paracelsus (Theophrastus von Hohenheim) (1493/4–1541), a sylph was an elemental being who inhabited the air, and typically taken later to be winged, delicate, fey.

74 *Salmacis . . . Hermaphroditus*: in Ovid's *Metamorphoses*, Book IV, the naiad Salmacis attempts the seduction and rape of the reluctant Hermaphroditus. In the struggle between them in a pool, in answer to her prayer, the gods make the two of them one united person.

Adonaïs: a reference to the beautiful youth Adonis in Greek mythology, and likely an allusion too to Percy Bysshe Shelley's pastoral elegy for the poet John Keats (1795–1821), *Adonaïs* (1821). It may be significant that, due to the influence in particular of William Shakespeare's *Venus and Adonis* (1593), Adonis, like Hermaphroditus, is a man who resists and refuses a sexual advance from a woman.

74 *Count de Gabalis*: Abbé Nicolas-Pierre-Henri de Montfaucon de Villars's (1635–73) *Comte de Gabalis* (1670) is an occultist text (or perhaps a parody of occult texts). It presents the eponymous Comte, a 'Rosicrucian' (a member of a supposed secret society of occult initiates, that first came to public light in the early seventeenth century) who unveils to the author hidden knowledge concerning the spirit world, among other matters, concerning the four kinds of elemental being: the Sylphs of the air; the Gnomes of the earth; the Salamanders of fire; and the Nymphs, or Undines, of water. In this regard, the work derives from an earlier occult text, Paracelsus' *Liber de Nymphis, sylphis, gnomes et salamandris et de caeteris spiritibus* (1658).

75 *Niblo's*: built in 1834, burnt down in 1846, and reopened in 1849, 'Niblo's Garden', owned by the coffee-house proprietor, the Irishman William Niblo (1790–1878), was a large, rather refined and fashionable Broadway theatre, on the corner with Prince Street, on the site of what had previously been the Columbian Gardens. O'Brien himself was a habitué of Niblo's.

Caradolce: a fictional ballerina, her name a portmanteau composed of two Italian words: *cara*, meaning 'dear', and *dolce*, meaning 'sweet'. There is a famous piece by the Italian composer Alessandro Scarlatti (1660–1725) for singer and keyboard accompaniment, called 'Cara e dolce'.

pas-de-fascination: literally, a 'step (or a brief dance) of fascination' (French), and clearly connected to various forms of ballet step and dance (such as 'pas de deux' (a dance for two), 'pas de chat' (a step like the leap of a cat), or 'pas de cheval' (a step like a horse pawing the ground)). However, I cannot find any such step or dance as a 'pas de fascination'. It is likely also that O'Brien is making a pun here, as 'pas-de-fascination' could also be a way of saying that there is no fascination there at all.

GEORGE ELIOT, *The Lifted Veil*

George Eliot is a central and towering figure in the history of nineteenth-century fiction. She was born as Mary Anne (later Marian) Evans in 1819 on the Arbury Estate near Nuneaton in Warwickshire, where her father worked as agent to the Newdigate family. She was particularly close as a child to her older brother, Isaac. At school, she converted to Evangelicalism, but as a young woman lost this faith, causing great sadness to her family. Prodigiously bright, she studied hard and produced in 1846 an anonymous translation of David Friedrich Strauss's (1808–74) *Das Leben Jesu, kritisch bearbeitet* (*The Life of Jesus, Critically Examined*) (1835–6). In 1849, following her father's death, she spent six months in Geneva, and on her return moved into lodgings at 142 Strand, in London, as the paying guest of John Chapman (1821–94) and his much older wife. On Chapman's purchase of the *Westminster Review*, she became both assistant editor of and a regular contributor to this periodical. In 1851, she found herself strongly (and very likely unrequitedly) attached to a friend, the philosopher and advocate for evolutionary theory, Herbert Spencer (1820–1903). In 1854, she published a translation of Ludwig Feuerbach's (1804–72) *Das Wesen des Christentums* (*The Essence of Christianity*) (1841), a work that offers a broadly sympathetic sociological account of the Christianity which it disbelieves. At this time, she began a passionate and mutually supportive relationship with the writer and critic George Henry Lewes (1817–78), a married man unable to divorce his estranged wife, having condoned her adulterous relationship with the journalist and editor Thornton Leigh Hunt (1810–73). The scandal of Evans's cohabiting with Lewes led to ostracism by many in society, including most hurtfully her favourite brother, Isaac. In the late 1850s, adopting the pen name 'George Eliot', Evans began writing fiction, producing in a few short years the masterpieces *Scenes of Clerical Life* (1857), *Adam Bede* (1859), *The Mill on the Floss* (1860), and *Silas Marner* (1861). In Florence, she planned a historical novel on the Italian Renaissance, *Romola* (1862–3), and in 1866 published *Felix Holt, The Radical*. In 1871–2 appeared her greatest novel, *Middlemarch, A Study of Provincial Life*, one of the pinnacles of European prose fiction. Her last novel, *Daniel Deronda* (1874–6), explored the position of the Jews in nineteenth-century Britain. In 1878, she was devastated by the death of G. H. Lewes. Two years later, she married John Walter Cross, a man twenty-one years younger than herself; after a silence of some twenty years, her brother sent a note to congratulate them both. Seven months after the marriage ceremony, Marian Evans died.

Eliot's 'The Lifted Veil' is an anomalous work for a writer so usually committed to realism, probabilities, and the troubles and consolations of ordinary life. Written quickly before she began work on *The Mill on the Floss*, it was for many decades taken to be a slight, sinister, and melancholy tale, and not to be granted the high seriousness summoned up by *Adam Bede* or *Middlemarch*. In a letter to John Blackwood (31 March 1859), Eliot herself presented it as 'a slight story of an outré kind—not a *jeu d'esprit*, but a *jeu de melancolie*'; when she finally sent him the completed manuscript on 29 April 1859, she declared, 'Herewith the dismal story'. In another letter to Blackwood, G. H. Lewes described the story as being 'of an imaginative philosophical kind, quite new and piquant' (21 April 1859). Sending the proofs back on 18 May 1859, Blackwood himself, though impressed by the tale, clearly did not find it much to his taste: 'I wish the theme had been a happier one, and I think you must have been worrying and disturbing yourself about something when you wrote. Still, others are not so fond of sweets as I am'. (He paid her £37 and 10 shillings for the tale.) The story was well received ('All admire the excellence and power of the writing, lovers of the painful are thrilled and delighted', Blackwood told her by letter on 8 July 1859), but he continued to wish she would write again in a 'happier frame of mind'. For some time, critics shared this lack of enthusiasm.

Critical interest in the story became stronger in the late twentieth century, and now the work stands as a fine Gothic tale, suffused with anxieties about the scientific character, and involving an uncanny examination of contemporary science. It is precisely this speculative engagement with actual science that establishes 'The Lifted Veil' as a precursor of science fiction.

The copy-text used here is based on the tale's republication in the 1878 Cabinet Edition, *The Works of George Eliot*, lightly revised and copy-edited by Eliot herself. The volume in question contains *Silas Marner, The Lifted Veil*, and *Brother Jacob* (London and Edinburgh: William Blackwood and Sons, 1878), 275–341. The story had first appeared, anonymously, in *Blackwood's Edinburgh Magazine* 86/525 (July 1859), 24–48. Blackwood insisted on the anonymity, believing the tale would damage Eliot's prestige following the success of *Adam Bede*; given her fame at this point, suppressing Eliot's authorship is a strong indication of how ambivalent about the tale Blackwood felt. In 1866, he advised against including it in a collected edition of Eliot's works. Coincidentally, in the same issue of *Blackwood's Edinburgh Magazine*, there also appeared G. H. Lewes's important critical assessment of those great masterpieces of everyday realism, 'The Novels of Jane Austen' (99–113).

77 THE LIFTED VEIL: the notion that truth, or life, or the true self was veiled was, of course, time-honoured and an inherited one. There may, however, be specific literary allusions at work here: to Percy Bysshe Shelley's sonnet beginning, 'Lift not the painted veil which those who live | Call Life' (published posthumously in 1824); to Nathaniel Hawthorne's macabre masterpiece, the short story 'The Minister's Black Veil' (first published 1832, collected in *Twice-Told Tales* (1837)); or to the gnomic deferral that closes the doubting and anxious poem LVI in Tennyson's *In Memoriam* (1850) (a poem most famous for its line, 'Tho' Nature, red in tooth and claw'):

> O life as futile, then, as frail!
> O for thy voice to soothe and bless!
> What hope of answer, or redress?
> Behind the veil, behind the veil.

In the 1850s, the Italian sculptor Giovanni Strazza (1818–75) had carved a marble bust of a veiled Virgin Mary.

Give me no light . . . completer manhood: this epigraph first appears in the Cabinet Edition version of the tale. Eliot wrote the little text in 1873, though she held back at that point from republishing the story. The insistence on 'manhood' here perhaps connects to the ways in which the story might be seen to examine different modes of presenting masculinity, whether in the patriarchal father, the poet, the sportsman, or the scientist.

angina pectoris: a syndrome in which the sufferer experiences sudden severe chest pains, extending to the left shoulder and down the arm, and sometimes causing a numbness in the jaw. The origin of this pain is in fact due to impaired flow of blood to the heart, but at the time, no one yet understood what caused the condition. Anxiety, breathing difficulties, and a sense of suffocation were also seen as characteristic of angina, as was fainting (the story's protagonist will faint several times during its course). It was sometimes noted that men were far more often prone to the syndrome; in George Wyld's (1821–1906) *Diseases of the Heart* (1860), he remarks that of eighty-eight cases collected by Sir John Forbes (1787–1861), eighty occurred in men.

78 *ubi sæva indignatio ulterius cor lacerare nequit*: as Eliot's footnote informs us, this is the Latin motto written on a marble inscription memorializing the Irish poet and satirist Jonathan Swift (1667–1745) in St Patrick's Cathedral, Dublin. Penned by Swift himself, it means that in the grave he lies 'where savage indignation can no longer lacerate his heart'.

80 *Eton*: founded in 1440, Eton College is one of the four most famous of British 'public schools' for boys (with Winchester, Radley, and Harrow); it is located by the Thames near Windsor, to the west of London. In the nineteenth century, the education at such schools centred on the learning of Latin and Greek.

'those dead but sceptred spirits': this is a misquoted reference to some lines from Lord Byron's 'metaphysical drama' *Manfred, A Dramatic Poem* (1817). Manfred reminisces about a trip to the Colosseum and the effect of the moonlight that night:

> Leaving that beautiful which still was so,
> And making that which was not, till the place
> Became religion, and the heart ran o'er
> With silent worship of the great of old!
> The dead, but sceptered sovereigns, who still rule
> Our spirits from their urns.—
>
> (III.iv.36–41)

Potter's 'Æschylus' ... *Francis's 'Horace'*: Revd Robert Potter's (1721–1804) translation of the Greek dramatist Aeschylus' (*c*.525/4–456/5 BC) tragedies were first printed in 1777, and remained popular throughout the nineteenth century; similarly the Irish translator Revd Philip Francis's (1708–73) deftly done *A Poetical Translation of the Works of Horace* (published in four volumes, 1742–6) was still being reprinted in the early decades of the century.

81 *Plutarch, and Shakspere, and Don Quixote*: the Greek biographer Plutarch produced most notably a collection of lives of famous Greeks and Romans, some of which form the basis of plays by Shakespeare. ('Shakspere' is spelt thus in the Cabinet Edition versions of the text, though spelt in the more usual way in the *Blackwood's* magazine publication.) Miguel de Cervantes is the author of the greatest Spanish comic novel, *Don Quixote* (Pt I pub. 1605; Pt II pub. 1615).

81 *Geneva*: in the second half of 1849, following her father's death, Eliot had stayed in Geneva, the Swiss capital, for some six months. The setting of Geneva inevitably also recalls Mary Shelley's novel *Frankenstein, or The Modern Prometheus* (1818), where the city is Victor Frankenstein's hometown. Only a couple of months after completing 'The Lifted Veil', Eliot and Lewes travelled together to Switzerland, though they did not go on this occasion as far as Geneva. Eliot lamented in a letter to François D'Albert-Durade (18 October 1859) that she had not had the chance then 'to revisit the dear old scene'. In describing the city, Eliot's art is one of memory here, while Latimer himself, as protagonist, recalls that which he has not yet seen, projecting himself both into a future and another locale.

the Jura: a range of mountains, north of the western Alps, along the border between France and Switzerland.

as Jean Jacques did: as Jean-Jacques Rousseau (1712–78), the Geneva-born *philosophe* and writer, describes doing on Lake Bienne in the fifth of his *Rêveries du promeneur solitaire* (*Reveries of a Solitary Walker*) (1782), as well as in Book XII of his classic autobiography, *Confessions* (1782). Taken together, these two books are central expressions of the proto-Romantic self. Rousseau's first name is not hyphenated in either *Blackwood's* or the Cabinet Edition.

82 *the prophet's chariot of fire*: a biblical reference to the chariot of the prophet Elisha, who asks God to open the eyes of his servant, before a battle with the much-better equipped Syrians: 'And he answered, Fear not,: for they that be with us are more than they that be with them. / And Elisha prayed, and said, LORD, I pray thee, open his eyes, that he may see. And the LORD opened the eyes of the young man; and he saw; and, behold, the mountain was full of horses and chariots of fire round about Elisha' (2 Kings 6:16–17).

gamins: a word of mid-nineteenth-century French origin, meaning street urchins and streetwise boys.

Salève . . . Vevay: the Salève is a mountain in the Jura; Vevay, which Eliot visited in July 1849, is a small town on the far side of Lake Geneva.

83 *Prague*: Eliot and Lewes had visited Prague, the capital of Bohemia, then part of the Austrian Empire, in July 1858.

84 *that Homer saw the plain of Troy . . . Dante saw the abodes of the departed . . . Milton saw the earthward flight of the Tempter*: Latimer brings together three of the greatest expressions of the poetic imagination: Homer's *Iliad*, Dante's *Divine Comedy*, and John Milton's (1608–74) *Paradise Lost* (1667). The 'Tempter' refers to Satan.

Novalis . . . consumption: pen name of the visionary German poet and writer Georg Philipp Friedrich Freiherr von Hardenberg (1772–1801); he died young from tuberculosis.

85 *Canaletto*: Giovanni Antonio Canal (1697–1768), a Venetian painter famous for his serene paintings of the city and its canals.

86 *a Water-Nixie,—for my mind was full of German lyrics*: this may be a reference to a tale (in prose), 'Die Wassernixie', collected by Jakob Ludwig
Karl Grimm (1785–1863) and Wilhelm Carl Grimm (1786–1859), concerning a water sprite who captures two children who fall into her well.
The most famous 'nixie' is 'Die Lorelei', in Heinrich Heine's (1797–1856)
poem of that name, and set by Franz Liszt (1811–86) in 1841, and then in
a second version in 1854–6. It is very likely that this is the lyric to which
Latimer refers, as Eliot and Lewes were friends with Liszt, and we know
that he played for her.

'Monsieur ne se trouve pas bien?': (French) 'Are you not feeling well, sir?'

Hôtel des Bergues: an elegant hotel on the banks of the Rhône before the
river flows into Lake Geneva.

88 *a microscopic vision*: Eliot's partner, G. H. Lewes, had a profound interest
in science, and had worked alongside the comparative anatomist and
palaeontologist Professor Richard Owen (1804–92) in his laboratory at the
Hunterian, while researching Goethe's similar passion for scientific studies. While she was writing 'The Lifted Veil', Lewes was vivisecting frogs in
their shared house, and during that summer and autumn of 1859, Lewes
was busy using a newly acquired microscope.

90 *sylphs*: fragile and beautiful creatures in the vein of Friedrich de la Motte
Fouqué's (1777–1843) *Undine* (1811). See note to p. 73.

bonne et brave femme: (French) a good-hearted and honest woman.

92 *making audible to one a roar of sound where others find perfect stillness*: a fore-
runner to a more famous statement of the same idea in chapter 20 of
Eliot's later novel, *Middlemarch*, as her heroine realizes that her marriage
is a trap: 'If we had a keen vision and feeling of all ordinary human life, it
would be like hearing the grass grow and the squirrel's heart beat, and we
should die of that roar which lies on the other side of silence. As it is, the
quickest of us walk about well wadded with stupidity.'

energumen: someone believed to be possessed by a demon; Eliot would use
the term again in her later historical novel, *Romola*.

the Lichtenberg Palace: Eliot likely means the Liechtenstein Garden Palace
in Vienna, the home of the Princely House of Liechtenstein's extensive
collection of paintings.

93 *Giorgione's picture of the cruel-eyed woman, said to be a likeness of Lucrezia
Borgia*: the painting in question was in fact wrongly attributed to Giorgione,
the Italian painter (1477/8–1510), and is likely a copy of Lorenzo Lotto's
(c.1480–1556/7) *A Lady with a Drawing of Lucretia*. It is curious how, as in
'Rappaccini's Daughter', the tale here draws on the sensation of being poisoned. For more information regarding the Borgias, see note to p. 38.

Belvedere Gallery: in the Belvedere Palace in Vienna; home to paintings,
and collections of armour and jewellery.

the dogs for the wood-fire: these are andirons, that is, a pair of iron bars
in a fireplace 'sustained horizontally at one end by an upright pillar or

support usually ornamented or artistically shaped, at the other end by a short foot' to support the burning wood (*OED*).

93 *dying Cleopatra*: this allusion to the ancient Egyptian queen Cleopatra occurs twice in the text, bringing in a woman monarch famous for dying of poison to match the poisonous Lucrezia Borgia, mentioned earlier in the story. For 'Cleopatra', see also note to p. 13.

94 *sign a bond with their blood*: this suggests a relationship to the 'old story' of the legend of Doctor Faustus, who sold his soul to the Devil in return for knowledge.

95 *no patent tram-road*: tramways were becoming a feature of European cities in the 1850s. In 1856, William Joseph Curtis patented a new kind of tram-road, based on Alphonse Loubet's (1799–1866) designs for similar tramways in Paris. The first tracks in Britain were laid in Liverpool in 1860.

double consciousness: used three times in the tale, this phrase is never hyphenated by Eliot.

96 *the old synagogue*: demolished in 1867, this was at the time of Eliot's writing, the oldest synagogue in the city, known as the 'Altshul' or 'Altschule'.

cicerone: (Italian) a guide.

98 *old Cæsar, a Newfoundland*: the 'Newfoundland' is a large breed of working dog, originally from the island of Newfoundland off the East Coast of Canada. This dog's name, Cæsar, may have been suggested by the tale's interest in Cleopatra.

99 *an another direction:* this strange expression, likely but not definitely a misprint, is given here as Eliot has it in the text; the Blackwood's text has it as 'in another direction'.

Tasso: the Italian poet Torquato Tasso (1544–95), author of the romantic epic *Gerusalemme Liberata* (*Jerusalem Delivered*) (1581). Tasso struggled with persecution mania and was declared insane and imprisoned for some seven years by Alfonso II d'Este of Ferrara (1533–97). Tasso's story was celebrated in dramas and poems by Goethe (*Torquato Tasso* (1790)), Shelley ('Song for Tasso'), and Byron ('The Lament of Tasso'); these Romantic writers believed that Tasso's imprisonment was due to his passionate love for Alfonso's sister, Eleonora (Leonora) d'Este (1537–81).

100 *syren melody*: in Homer's *The Odyssey*, Odysseus ties himself to the mast so he can hear the enchanting song sung by the sirens, beautiful and grotesque female creatures, part-woman, part-bird, who lured men to their doom through their songs.

102 *adytum*: the inner sanctum of a temple, the most sacred precincts reserved for the oracles, the priests and priestesses.

badinage: (originally French), humorous banter and witty talk.

hashish: a narcotic drug derived from Indian hemp. In a letter to her friend, Barbara Bodichon, in December 1860, George Eliot declared:

'The highest "calling and election" is to *do without opium* and live through all our pain with conscious, clear-eyed endurance.' The critic A. D. Harvey has suggested that this phrase likely draws on the German poet Novalis's earlier formulation in his book *Blüthenstaub* (1798): 'Your so-called religion acts just like an opiate: stimulating, numbing, soothing pain from weakness' ('Ihre sogenannte Religion wirkt bloss wie ein Opiat: reizend, betäubend, Schmerzen aus Schwäche stillend').

104 *tête-à-tête*: (French) face to face. There is a curious insistence on this phrase in the tale, which Eliot uses on three occasions. The idea of being *tête-à-tête* in relation to the theme of clairvoyance and mind-reading acts as a kind of theme, almost a joke.

111 *peritonitis*: inflammation of the peritoneum, the lining of the abdominal cavity and the underside of the diaphragm.

transfusing blood: while Eliot was thinking up and writing 'The Lifted Veil', her partner, G. H. Lewes was writing and publishing his rather successful work, *The Physiology of Common Life* (Edinburgh: William Blackwood and Sons, 1859). Lewes's book was a popular scientific study of anatomy and physiology aimed at both students and 'the common reader'. In a chapter on 'The Structure and Uses of Our Blood', among other matters, Lewes sets out the history of transfusion, from the first transfusion performed by the physician and anatomist Richard Lower (1631–91) in February 1665, infusing blood into a dog, to the first transfusion into a man, conducted in 1667 by 'Denis' (actually Jean-Baptiste Denys (1643–1704)), who injected blood into a 'madman', who, according to Lewes, awoke 'sane'—only to become mad again some days later, dying shortly after. Most apropos to Eliot's tale, Lewes records how the 'ancients, indeed, thought that by infusing new blood into an old and failing organism, new life would be infused; and wild dreams of a sort of temporal immortality were entertained' (277). In a review of the story in 1878, Henry James suggested that the transfusion has no real relation to the second sight, which is the true focus of the tale (published in *Nation* (April 1878)). This is an uncharacteristically obtuse assertion, as, much like clairvoyance, transfusion clearly also intrudes on the boundaries of the self, the medical procedure acting as an analogy for other ways of penetrating into the being of another person.

113 *peignoir*: (French) from the mid-nineteenth century, this was a woman's light dressing-gown or negligée.

GRANT ALLEN, *Pausodyne: A Great Chemical Discovery*

Grant Allen was a scientific writer, a hack on New Grub Street, and the author of an array of stories and novels, embracing realism as well as the fantastic, but always allied to the radical and the progressive—as one of Allen's sisters declared of her family, 'there was much protesting blood in us'. He was born in Kingston, Ontario in Canada, on 24 February 1848, the son of a Church of

Ireland clergyman and the partly Scottish daughter of a French baron. In 1861, Allen's family left Canada first for the USA and then, after a year, on to France. The young man's undergraduate studies at Merton College, Oxford, were interrupted for a few desperate years by a marriage to Caroline Boothway, a labourer's daughter, a union rendered brief by her early death. In 1873, Allen married again, very happily, to the dowerless Ellen Jerrard; they would have one son together. Strapped for cash, after a short time spent schoolmastering (including at Brighton College), the couple moved to Jamaica for a few years while Allen taught philosophy at a college in Spanish Town. There he studied excitedly the works of the evolutionary philosopher and man of letters Herbert Spencer (1820–1903). In 1876, on the college's closure, Allen returned to Britain, and he began his life as an author. He started with scientific essays and books, but soon learnt that fiction was a more lucrative branch of writing, and so churned out a series of tales and novels (including some innovative works of detective fiction). His scientific works include *The Colour Sense* (1879), the essay collection *The Evolutionist at Large* (1881) (which prompted a fan letter from Charles Darwin), *Force and Energy* (1889), and *The Evolution of the Idea of God* (1897). Andrew Lang praised him as the most versatile man of his age (high praise from a man as versatile as Lang), and indeed Allen wrote on Anglo-Saxon Britain, anthropology, and botany with equal felicity. He produced many novels, but his greatest success was *The Woman Who Did* (1895), a key text in the evolution of representations of the so-called 'New Woman', and a work that created a scandal on its first publication. The novel *The Type-Writer Girl* (1897), published under the pseudonym Olive Pratt Rayner, introduced a new social type into fiction, and further evidences Allen's support for the emancipation of women. In 1899, Allen died of liver cancer in Hindhead, Surrey. His impact on the development of science fiction depends principally on three short tales—'Pausodyne' (1881); the fantasy of a future society, 'The Child of the Phalanstery' (1884); the apocalyptic story 'The Thames Valley Catastrophe' (1897)—and the satirical novel *The British Barbarians* (1895), a tale set in the twenty-fifth century.

'Pausodyne' first appeared in the edition of the '*Christmas Annual*' of *Belgravia* magazine (December 1881), under the pseudonym J. Arbuthnot Wilson. The story was reprinted in the New York-based *Frank Leslie's Illustrated Newspaper*, 53/1372 (14 January 1882), 342, 360, under the title 'Was He a Madman?'. It was collected in Allen's key volume in the field of fantasy writing, *Strange Stories* (London: Chatto & Windus, 1884), 234–54—this version constitutes the copy-text used here. It later appeared again in a volume published in America, *The Desire of the Eyes and Other Stories* (New York: R. F. Fenno and Company, 1895), 297–320.

116 *the Strand . . . Pall Mall . . . Charing Cross Station . . . York*: Spottiswood, the narrator, walks westwards along one of the main thoroughfares in central London, past one of the great railway terminuses of the capital, first opened in 1864.

117 *Caspar Hauser*: Kasper Hauser (?–1833), a young adolescent, wandered into the centre of Nuremberg in May 1828, and after some time recounted a tale of how he had spent the first years of his life locked in a room and all but absolutely solitary. Hauser was celebrated around the world as a genuine child of nature, but also suspected by many as a desperate impostor. He died in mysterious circumstances after being stabbed (or wounding himself) in the gardens of Ansbach's abandoned palace.

the Seven Sleepers of Ephesus: see note to p. 1. Here, a connection to that other great sleeper, Washington Irving's Rip Van Winkle (1819), is clear.

Embankment to Adelphi Terrace: Adelphi Terrace is a street between the Strand and the River Thames, containing late eighteenth-century houses, built between 1768 and 1772, and designed by the Adam brothers: John (1721–92), Robert (1728–1792), and James (1732–94).

the Metropolitan line: the Metropolitan Railway refers to the central London train line, originally running from Farringdon to Paddington on its opening in 1863, but much expanded, underground and overground, in the next twenty years. Opening in 1870, the so-called Inner Circle extended the line from Westminster along the Embankment to Blackfriars, and one year later from Mansion House all the way to South Kensington.

118 *Australian . . . landed at the Tower*: in the 1770s, the word 'Australian' only referred to the native inhabitants of that continent; only later could it also denote a European colonist resident there. Ships from the Pacific would have docked in the Port of London downstream of the Tower of London and Tower Bridge, by St Katharine's Docks.

119 *Mr. Cavendish . . . Monsieur Lavoisier . . . Dr. Priestley . . . new theory of phlogiston*: Cavendish, Lavoisier, and Priestley are three of the most important and influential 'natural philosophers' of the late eighteenth century. Henry Cavendish (1731–1810) was a reticent, plainly dressed, and socially uncomfortable character, who carried out important work in the 1760s and 1770s on the chemical analysis of airs and liquids (including collecting hydrogen from water), the nature of heat, electricity, and examining 'fixed air' (carbon dioxide). Antoine-Laurent de Lavoisier (1743–94) was a hugely influential chemist and biologist. His achievements are numerous, and he named oxygen and hydrogen that Priestley and Cavendish had arguably first discovered. He was guillotined during the French Revolution, following accusations of financial treachery, tax fraud against the people, and adulterating the tobacco supply with water. Joseph Priestley (1733–1804) was a political radical, a religious dissenter, a polymathic experimenter in chemistry and electricity, and a great popularizer of what we would now call 'science'. From 1667, when first described by the alchemist Johann Joachim Becher (1635–1682), 'Phlogiston' was posited as a hypothetical element present in all combustible bodies, and released by combustion. In that sense, there was nothing particularly 'new' about phlogiston, but Priestley had been publishing innovative work on 'phlogiston' (actually oxygen) in the 1770s, most notably his *Experiments*

and Observations on Different Kinds of Air (1774–86). A belief in this mythical substance was at the centre of both Cavendish's and Priestley's chemical experiments; Lavoisier argued against the phlogiston theory, and his freedom from belief in this erroneous hypothesis undoubtedly helped him to be the first person accurately to describe the process of oxidation and to understand what takes place during combustion. Lavoisier's work in the 1770s eventually put paid to phlogiston, though some tenaciously held to the theory for another twenty or thirty years.

119 *fixed air*: the name given in 1754 by the notable British physician and chemist Joseph Black (1728–99) to carbonic dioxide (carbonic acid). In 1772, Priestley had published a text outlining the process by which using this gas, we can make soda-water.

carbonic acid gas: in the nineteenth century this was the name given to carbon dioxide.

Mr. Carl Linnæus . . . Alchemilla vulgaris: Carl Linnæus (also, from 1761, known as Carl von Linné) (1707–78) was, with Georges-Louis Leclerc, Comte de Buffon (1707–88), the most important natural historian of the eighteenth century, and the man who in his *Systema Naturæ* (10th edn, 1758) formalized the naming of living creatures (whether animal or vegetable) and minerals, according to a taxonomy according to genus and species. *Alchemilla vulgaris*, named such by Linnæus, is more commonly known as Lady's Mantle, and is supposed to have medicinal benefits, helping to regulate menstrual flow, as an anti-inflammatory, and to combat insomnia.

Pausodyne: a word perhaps formed by combining the Latin *pausa*, meaning cessation, respite, and the Greek suffix *-odynia*, meaning pain.

120 *Anegeiric*: it cannot be determined why the natural philosopher should consider this so appropriate a name.

121 *Mr. Walker*: though likely an invented miniaturist, there are several possible artists named 'Walker' at work in the period in question, but it seems possible that Allen here refers to one of the engravers with that surname: James Walker (1758?–1822?) or William Walker (bapt. 1729–93).

Sir Joshua: Sir Joshua Reynolds (1723–98), an artist most famous for his many portraits, marked by a studied informality, and for being instrumental in the foundation of the Royal Academy of Arts in 1768 (he was its first president).

Gainsborough: Thomas Gainsborough (1727–84), the hugely talented portrait painter and landscape artist.

Fellowship of the Royal Society: founded in 1660, and initially based at Gresham College, London, the Royal Society was central to the position of natural philosophy in the polite society of the late seventeenth and eighteenth centuries, promoting experimental philosophy. To be made a Fellow of the Royal Society was (and is) a prestigious sign of recognition as a significant worker in the field of science.

122 *Dr. Priestley . . . St. Giles's*: in the 1780s and 1790s Priestley's religious unorthodoxy and his revolutionary radicalism indeed led to his becoming a highly unpopular figure in some quarters, and in 1791, in Birmingham, he and his family had to flee their house to escape the violence threatened by rioters. 'St. Giles's' refers to an area of central London, between the Seven Dials and Great Russell Street, infamous as a violent slum; Spottiswood makes a standard connection here between the poor mob of the district and a supposed (and perhaps adventitious) and opportunistic adherence to socially conservative views.

124 *St. Mary le Bone*: now named Marylebone, an area of west London.

125 *Marribon*: a fair approximation of how Londoners pronounce 'Marylebone'.

milled edges: the ribbed edges around a coin's rim produced when the coin is made in a mill or press.

126 *gray powder*: a nineteenth-century term, referring to a chalk mixed with mercury and used medicinally (most often as a laxative).

atomic weight of chlorine: the concept of atomic weight (the average weight of an atom of a particular element, measured in relation to a standard atom—usually at first either oxygen or hydrogen) only arrived in the first decade of the nineteenth century in the work of John Dalton (1766–1844). Further important work was done in this area by Jöns Jakob Berzelius (1779–1848) and in the 1860s by Stanislao Cannizzarro (1826–1910).

130 *Kensal Green Cemetery*: since the 1830s, one of the main London cemeteries, located in west London, and modelled on Père-Lachaise cemetery in Paris.

FRANK R. STOCKTON, *The Water-Devil: A Marine Tale*

Frank [Francis] Richard Stockton was born in Philadelphia on 5 April 1834, the son of a Methodist preacher. He began working life in 1850 as an engraver, but (after patenting a new double engraver) in 1867 switched to journalism. He worked as the editor of *Hearth and Home* in New York, then joined *Scribner's Monthly*, before ending up as assistant editor of a magazine for children, *St Nicholas*. Stockton became a notable writer of children's literature, and also produced numerous short stories (including his most famous work, the fantastic, unresolved tale fable of 'The Lady, or the Tiger?' (1882)) and novels for adults. As punishment for an affair with the king's daughter, the protagonist in 'The Lady, or The Tiger?' must choose to open one of two doors; behind one is a tiger, and behind the other the beautiful lady-in-waiting he would marry. As he hesitates to decide which door he will choose, he sees the princess he once loved in the watching crowd; she gestures towards one of the two doors, and he starts to open it, unsure if she is jealously sending him to his death, or giving him up to her lady-in-waiting whom he now loves. Stockton found it hard to match this tale's immense success; he continued to receive letters speculating on the most appropriate resolution of this story until the end of his life—he himself claimed not to know the proper conclusion to the narrative. Utterly unlike the fantasy of this tale is *Rudder Grange* (1879), which offers realistic and quietly wholesome sketches of a married couple, their young family, and their life on a canal boat. Usually noted for his realism (Arthur Quiller Couch compared him to Daniel Defoe), Stockton nonetheless also wrote some tales of the grotesque, such as 'Spectral Mortgage' and 'Transferred Ghost'. In the field of science fiction, he produced such stories as 'A Tale of Negative Gravity' (1886), the whimsical tale of Americans taking a walk in Italy using an invention to lighten their journey; *The Great War Syndicate* (1889), a novel of a war in the near future between America and Britain; and *The Great Stone of Sardis* (1898), an adventure story of a submarine seeking the North Pole and then investigating the earth's core. Popular and successful, Stockton was accepted as a humorist in the Mark Twain vein; Robert Louis Stevenson was one notable fan of his tales. A gentle and witty man, in his last years Stockton retreated for part of each year to Charles Town, in the Shenandoah Valley of West Virginia and his yellow-brick house 'Claymont'. He died in 1902 in Washington DC, following a cerebral haemorrhage.

The copy-text for 'The Water-Devil' is based on its first publication in book form, in *The Rudder Grangers Abroad and Other Stories* (New York: C. Scribner's Sons, 1891), 146–95. The story appeared in two parts as 'The Water Devil: A Marine Tale' in *Scribner's Magazine* (New York), 9/1 (January 1891), 108–18, and 9/2 (February 1891), 157–64. The first number has an illustration above the title of a devilish pointed-eared head, whose long hair curls and entwines to left and right around over what may be parts of a ship. The number ends with a decorative motif of Mercury tying on a winged sandal. The first part of the tale ends with the phrase, 'I had never known that the Bay of Bengal was so desperately lonely'. The second number concludes with an image of a spar of wood tangled up in rope and seaweed. In 1900, 'The Water-Devil' was published again in an edition with *The Great Stone of Sardis*.

134 *the Royal George*: a Royal Navy ship, launched in 1756, she saw service during the Seven Years War (1756–63) and the Anglo-Spanish War (1776–83), during which Spain aided the Americans in their war of liberation against Britain. On 29 August 1782, the ship sank off Portsmouth while being loaded for its next voyage, with the loss of perhaps as many as 900 lives.

      the Bay of Bengal . . . Calcutta: the Bay of Bengal is the north-eastern part of the Indian Ocean; Calcutta (now Kolkata) is a major Indian city on the coast of the Bay of Bengal, the oldest port in India, in the 1870s (and until 1911) the capital of British-held territories in the subcontinent.

135 *square sails, fore-and-aft sails, jib sails*: Arthur Young's *Nautical Dictionary* (1863) declares that 'square sails' 'hang from yards athwartships', while 'fore-and-aft sails' are set 'upon gaffs, booms, or stays, lengthways of the vessel'. A 'jib sail' is a large triangular sail set on a stay running out from a vessel's bowsprit.

cutwater: this is a piece of hard wood at the forepart of the stem, the upper end of which supports the figurehead under the bowsprit, and is therefore, as *Patterson's Nautical Dictionary* (1891) informs us, 'the foremost part of the stern that divides the water when the vessel is sailing'.

137 *abaft*: coming from the direction of the stern.

from Negapatam to Jellasore on the west coast, and from Chittagong to Kraw on the other: these are indeed all coastal towns on the Bay of Bengal. Negapatam (now Nagapattinam) was then in the Tanjore district in the Madras Presidency; Jellasore (now Jaleswar) is in West Bengal; Chittagong (now officially Chattogram in south-eastern Bangladesh) is a coastal city and an ancient port to the north of Bay of Bengal and not really therefore 'on the other' coast; the Kra Isthmus, however, really is beyond the easternmost limit of the Bay of Bengal, by the Andaman Sea (then known as the Burma Sea), at the southern end of the Malay peninsula, and at the time of the story in the area of the Siamese–Malay border.

138 *a yawl-boat*: a yawl is the smallest size of fishing-boat.

141 *whole kit and boodle*: the whole set, the entire collection of them. This is likely the origin of the more familiar American slang phrase, 'caboodle'.

146 *a while*: written as 'awhile' in the 1878 book version of the story, but given thus in the original magazine publication.

148 *trump*: a 'brick', an excellent person.

157 *submarine suit*: in 1715, John Lethbridge (1675–1759) had designed and made the first full diving-suit, though this was a cumbersome apparatus; soon after Fréminet thought up his *Machine Hydrostatique*; in the late eighteenth century, the Prussian designer Karl Heinrich Klingert (1760–1828) constructed plans for a diving-dress, though it is not clear if this was ever put to use at sea. In the nineteenth century, other more workable designs followed for the so-called *scaphandre à casque* by such inventors as Joseph Martin Cabirol (1799–1874) and Augustus Siebe (1788–1872) (including the gloriously impractical designs of one Jobard). In America, in 1837, Captain William H. Taylor published a pamphlet setting out his plans for a 'submarine dress'. The Royal Navy was known for its use of divers, and in 1843 founded the first naval diving school, in part inspired by the attempts in 1839 to salvage the *Royal George* (see note to p. 134), carried out using a modified version of Siebe's helmet and canvas diving-suit. There also may well be memories here of the most famous underwater adventure of all, Jules Verne's (1828–1905) *Vingt mille lieues sous les mers: Tour du monde sous-marin* (*Twenty Thousand Leagues under the Sea: A World Tour Underwater*) (1869–70).

159 *telegraphic cable . . . Madras and Rangoon*: attempts to lay such a cable across the floor of the Atlantic Ocean commenced from 1854 onwards; one was successfully if temporarily laid in 1858, and lasting success was finally achieved in 1866. In Jules Verne's *Vingt mille lieues sous les mers*, the submariners in the *Nautilus* take a closer look at this underwater cable. The entrepreneur Sir John Pender (1816–96) organized a telegraph link (with

the encouragement of the British Government) between Britain and India. Other submarine cable links followed, including one that connected Australia to Bombay, via Singapore. The city of Rangoon (now Yangon) in what was then called Burma (now Myanmar) and the southern Indian city of Madras were connected by telegraph in 1877, though overland rather than on the ocean floor.

H. G. WELLS, *The Crystal Egg*

On 21 September 1866, Herbert George Wells was born in Bromley in Kent. His mother was an innkeeper's daughter and his father a shopkeeper and cricketeer, whose career was cut short by a broken leg. Wells spent much of his childhood in the basement of the family shop. When his father went bankrupt, Wells's mother moved to Uppark, a country house on the South Downs near Midhurst. In 1880, young Wells, despite being his school's star pupil, left school early and was by turns a draper's assistant, a pupil teacher, a pharmacist's assistant, and an apprentice at a department store in Southsea. Unhappy and frustrated, Wells left the store and took up a post as teaching assistant at Midhurst Grammar School. In 1884, he enrolled as a student at T. H. Huxley's (1825–95) biology class at the Normal School in South Kensington. A central figure in late nineteenth-century science and the great champion of Charles Darwin and evolutionary theory, Huxley strongly influenced young Wells. Wells took up socialism, attending William Morris's meetings in Hammersmith. In 1887, he became a teacher at Holt Academy in Wales, but after an injury he was diagnosed with suspected tuberculosis. He obtained his BSc in London in 1890, and married his cousin, Isabel Wells (*c.*1866–1930) a year later. Wells began his career as a writer in the early 1890s, producing scientific articles, short stories, and essays.

In the late 1890s, he produced a series of extraordinary and highly popular short stories and book-length scientific romances: *The Time Machine* (1895); *The Island of Doctor Moreau* (1896); *The Invisible Man* (1897); *The War of the Worlds* (1898); and *The First Men in the Moon* (1901). These great works of the scientific imagination remain central to the history of science fiction. Wells also produced a series of utopian fictions that proved influential on the development of science fiction and on political and social thinking in the early twentieth century. They include *The Sleeper Awakes* (1899); *The Food of the Gods* (1904); and *In the Days of the Comet* (1906). In this period, alongside (and sometimes in opposition to) George Bernard Shaw (1856–1950) and Beatrice (1858–1943) and Sidney Webb (1859–1947), he was involved in the socialist Fabian Society. In the 1900s, he also wrote a set of impressive realist novels, touched with comedy in the Dickensian vein: *Love and Mr Lewisham* (1900); *Kipps* (1905); and, his masterpiece, *The History of Mr Polly* (1910). Works such as *Tono Bungay* (1909) and *Ann Veronica* (1909) introduce a stronger vein of social satire and progressive politics.

Following the failure of his first marriage after two years, Wells lived with an ex-student of his, Catherine ('Jane') Robbins (1871/2–1927). Jane and Wells married in 1895, and the couple had two sons, George in 1901 and Frank in

1903. From now on, Wells's love life was notoriously complex, entangling him in many affairs and liaisons, including with a young graduate economist from Cambridge, Amber Reeves (1887–1981), and the novelists Dorothy Richardson (1873–1957), Elizabeth von Arnim (1866–1941), and Rebecca West (1892–1983). He had a daughter, Anna-Jane, with Reeves and a third son, Anthony, with West. After the war, he remained a dominant intellectual figure in Britain and elsewhere, especially through the influence of his bestselling texts, *An Outline of History* (1920) and *A Short History of the World* (1922). He grew increasingly disillusioned by the horrors of the twentieth century, as expressed in his final book, *Mind at the End of Its Tether* (1945). On 13 August 1946, he died at Hanover Terrace in London.

The copy-text of 'The Crystal Egg' is based on the story's appearance in *The Country of the Blind and Other Stories* (London: Thomas Nelson & Sons, 1911), 285–307. The story first appeared (alongside the latest instalment of Henry James's *What Maisie Knew*) in W. E. Henley's *New Review* (London), 16/96 (May 1897), 556–71.

162 *Seven Dials*: in the 1890s, previously a very down-at-heel area of central London, but now (as Charles Booth's poverty map of London reveals) fairly comfortable and averagely off. Seven Dials is in the Covent Garden area, between Shaftesbury Avenue and Long Acre, where six roads (Queen Street, Great St Andrew Street, Little St Andrew Street, Lion Street, Little Earl Street, Great Earl Street—all since renamed) meet at one junction, with seven turn-offs around its centre. See note to p. 122.

164 *dog-fish*: as a 'naturalist', Cave's shop caters for the trade in vivisection, providing specimens for experimentation and dissection. In 1896, Wells had published his astonishing and brutal scientific romance, *The Island of Doctor Moreau*, which had focused (among other matters) on the morality and moral consequences of vivisection.

165 *Richmond*: then a south-western suburb at the edge of London, on the River Thames, and known for the beautiful views from Richmond Hill and for boating expeditions on the river, so that the area was one of resort for inner-city dwellers.

amuck: originally, a reference to a Malay given to enacting a frenzied attack, and later to the state of murderous frenzy itself.

166 *St. Catherine's Hospital, Westbourne Street*: there is no such London hospital, though St Mary's Hospital was near this area, on Praed Street in Paddington.

167 *refracted by the crystal and coming to a focus in its interior, but this diffusion*: refracted light is deflected; it is then concentrated within; by 'diffusion' Cave means that the light emanates out from the crystal.

168 *Pasteur Institute*: founded and named after the great French biologist Louis Pasteur (1822–95), the Pasteur Institute came into being as a research institute in Paris in June 1887.

170 *dense red weeds*: 'red' is italicized in the first published version in the *New Review*, probably with the intention of suggesting that this is Mars, 'the red planet'.

172 *a diurnal species of bat*: 'diurnal' means belonging to the day, so here the bat is not a nocturnal creature, but one that is active during the day.

173 *en rapport*: (French) in harmony, in connection; a term with links to the language of mesmerism, where it refers to the close influence of the mesmerizer on their subject. See note to p. 53.

moons: '*like our moon*: in the first book printing, this is given as '*moons!* "like our moon', but this reads rather awkwardly, and therefore the reading given in the first publication in the *New Review* is used here.

174 *St. Martin's Church*: St Martin-in-the-Fields, the Anglican church designed by James Gibbs (1682–1754) at the north-east corner of Trafalgar Square, and only a few streets south, down St Martins Lane, of the Seven Dials area where Mr Cave has his shop.

175 *Highgate*: opened in 1839, Highgate Cemetery, in north-west London, was one of the major Victorian burial-grounds.

dumfounded: this is written as 'dumbfounded' in the *New Review*, but this alternative spelling is also perfectly correct.

176 *The Daily Chronicle and Nature*: set up in 1872 and brought to prominence by Edward Lloyd (1815–90), the *Daily Chronicle* was a liberal and left-of-centre paper. Established in 1869, *Nature* was (and is) a highly important scientific journal, known then for its progressive stance.

young Prince of Bosso-Kuni in Java: a fictional prince of a fictional princedom; the island of Java in Indonesia was at the time a Dutch colony.

RUDYARD KIPLING, *'Wireless'*

Rudyard Kipling (1865–1936) was one of the most popular and influential poets and writers of short stories and of children's fiction in the 1890s and 1900s, the author of, among other works, *The Jungle Book* (1894), *The Second Jungle Book* (1895), *Kim* (1901), *Just So Stories* (1902), *Puck of Pook's Hill* (1906), and *Rewards and Fairies* (1910). Born in Bombay, in 1871 Kipling was sent to England to be educated. His first years there, spent at Southsea with his younger sister, Alice ('Trix') (1868–1948), were marked by terrible unhappiness, due to the abuse meted out by his carers, Captain and Mrs Pryse Agar Holloway. From 1878 to 1882, he was educated at the United Service College at Westward Ho!, near Bideford in North Devon. On leaving school, he returned to join his family in India. There he began work as a journalist, and soon made a mark as a writer of Anglo-Indian short stories and poems. The stories were collected in a series of books, including *Plain Tales from the Hills* (1888), *The Phantom 'Rickshaw and Other Tales* (1890), and *Life's Handicap* (1891); his early verse was published in *Departmental Ditties* (1886) and *Barrack-Room Ballads* (1892). Kipling returned to England, settling in London in 1889, by now a hugely popular and feted author. After some months of world travel, in January 1892, on the news of the death of his close friend, Wolcott Balestier, Kipling hurriedly returned to London to marry Wolcott's sister, Caroline. After a globetrotting honeymoon, the couple moved to Vermont. There their two daughters, Josephine and Elsie, were born. In September 1896, the family returned to England. They settled in Rottingdean, East Sussex (also home to Kipling's uncle, the painter Sir Edward Burne-Jones (1833–98)). Here in 1897 their son, John, was born. In 1899, on a visit to New York, the Kiplings' daughter, Josephine, died. Kipling's unspeakable grief for her is reflected in his mysterious ghost story 'They' (1904). After some time in South Africa, in 1902 the Kiplings returned to Sussex, settling in 'Bateman's', their house in Burwash, Sussex. In September 1915, Kipling's son, John, died at the Battle of Loos. In 1917, he became a member of the Imperial War Graves Commission; among other duties, he wrote a series of moving 'Epitaphs of the War'. After 1914, his writing became less prolific, though its quality remained high. He died in January 1936 and was buried in Westminster Abbey. His fascinating and reticent autobiography, *Something of Myself*, was published posthumously in 1937.

In *The New Machiavelli* (1911), H. G. Wells tells of just how influential Kipling was on the culture of the 1890s, becoming a 'national symbol' and an inspiration for young writers (not least for his 'wonderful discovery of machinery'). Nine years later, in *The Outline of History* (1920), Wells detected in this popular figure marks of the sadism and authoritarian illegality that characterized the imperialist mentality. As these quotes show, for many years Kipling's reputation was a highly contentious one; there was a 'good' and 'bad' Kipling in the popular imagination: he stands as the author of some of the most moving and imaginative works written between the 1880s and the 1930s, but also as the symbol of a stoic and brutally pugnacious imperialism, the melancholy victim of his own hard and limited vision of the world. His faults seemed inextricably bound up with his genius. At their best, when (as he put it) his 'daemon' wrote with him, his poems and tales are remarkable, and his position as one of the best writers of short stories in the English language looks set to stand firm.

As part of his interest in machinery and the impact of technology, Kipling wrote a handful of stories that might be considered 'science fiction', certainly including 'A Matter of Fact' (1893) (collected in *Many Inventions* (1893)); 'With the Night Mail: A Story of 2000 A.D.' (from *Actions and Reactions* (1909)); and 'As Easy as A.B.C.' (in *A Diversity of Creatures* (1917)). Although his contributions to sci-fi are few, they are influential, and traces of Kipling's influence can be found impressed on the work of such later authors as Robert Heinlein and Poul Anderson (both of whom attempted to rewrite *Kim* as a science fiction novel, in *Citizen of the Galaxy* (1957) and *The Game of Empire* (1985) respectively).

The copy-text of ' "Wireless" ' is based on the story's first publication in book form in Rudyard Kipling, *Traffics and Discoveries* (London: Macmillan and Co., 1904), 211–39. It had previously appeared as the first piece in *Scribner's Magazine* (New York), 32/2 (August 1902), 129–43, with five illustrations by the American artist F. C. (Frederick Coffay) Yohn (1875–1933). (J. M. Barrie's *The Little White Bird, or Adventures in Kensington Gardens* (1902), the first published account of Peter Pan, was being serialized in the same edition.) Yohn was a book illustrator and a regular contributor to *Scribner's*, and also to *Collier's Weekly* and *Harper's Magazine*. The five illustrations are captioned: ' "I can't. I tell you I'm alone in the place" '; ' "Poor beast! And he wants to keep company with Fanny Brand" '; ' "Mr. Cashell, there is something coming through here, too" '; 'Again he sought inspiration from the advertisement' (showing Shaynor gazing up at the woman in the advertising image); ' "I've had a bit of a doze," he said' (showing the fully awakened Shaynor standing and stretching, and in the process blocking out much of the woman in the advertising poster behind him). In *Traffics and Discoveries*, ' "Wireless" ' takes its place between the stories 'Steam Tactics' and 'The Army of a Dream—Part I', the latter being a polemical account of a Spartan future Britain (a utopia or dystopia, as you please) where all boys undergo military training.

178 KASPAR'S SONG IN 'VARDA': there is no such Swedish poem as 'Kaspar's Song', and no such book as 'Varda'. Fittingly for this tale of poetic possession, the opening poem is not a translation, but a channelling of Stagnelius (see note below), without an original in mind. In an article, ' "Wireless" and "Kaspar's Song": A Kipling Problem', *English Studies*, 45 (January 1965), 249–56, C. A. Bodelson declares that the poem might be related to another lyric by Stagnelius, entitled 'Vårsånger I' (Spring Songs). Bodelson also suggests that 'Varda' might derive from the phrase 'Valda Skrifter', meaning in Swedish, 'Selected Writings'. When it was later collected in Kipling's *Songs from Books* (1913), this poem was renamed 'Butterflies'. In the Sussex edition of the story, the last stanza in this poem is separated off from the rest by a series of elliptical dots.

Stagnelius: the Swedish Romantic poet Erik Johan Stagnelius (1793–1823), more or less an exact contemporary of John Keats. Stagnelius was an archetypal Romantic solitary, an alcoholic (perhaps), a user of drugs, and a mystic condemned to a short life. In 1868, Henry Lockwood translated some of Stagnelius's lyrics; later, in 1886, Edmund Gosse, the notable man of letters and an acquaintance of Kipling's, followed his example. In his entry on 'Sweden' in the *Encyclopedia Britannica* (11th edn, 1911), Gosse asserted that Stagnelius may be compared, 'not improperly', to Shelley (xxvi. 218).

The children follow where Psyche flies: in the later version of this poem, in *Songs from Books*, the second line was revised so that it reads: 'The Children follow the butterflies.' There is a traditional link in philosophy and mythology between the butterfly and the soul (*psyche* in Greek meaning both things). Carl Gustav Carus' treatise, *Psyche* (1846), uses the 'psyche' to stand for the unconscious mind. There may be a link too, given what follows in the story, to John Keats's 'Ode to Psyche' (1820).

Marconi business: Guglielmo Marconi (1874–1937) was the Italian inventor of 'wireless telegraphy' and in 1894–6, he effected the first radio transmissions. The first demonstration of the new technology followed in 1896 in Britain where a year later the Wireless Telegraph and Signal Company (from 1900, Marconi's Wireless Telegraph Company) was established. In Cyril Clemens, 'A Chat with Rudyard Kipling' (in Harold Orel (ed.), *Rudyard Kipling: Interviews and Recollections*, ii (London: Macmillan Press, 1983), 239–45, Kipling recalls that in 1899, while living in Rottingdean, he had lunch with Marconi, who described how 'wireless' worked to him: 'During the talk I consciously or unconsciously was gathering material for my story, "Wireless", in which I carried the idea of etheric vibrations into the possibility of thought transference' (241).

179 *Poole*: a town on the south coast of England in the county of Devon, on the eastern side of Bournemouth.

Bitter cold, isn't it?: the first allusion within the story to John Keats's poem, 'The Eve of St Agnes' (1820), in this case to the poem's opening line, 'St Agnes' Eve—Ah, bitter chill it was!'

ammoniated quinine: a notoriously unpleasant tasting medicinal drug, originally in liquid form, but also taken from the early 1890s onwards as a capsule (which helped rob it of its foul taste), used as a preventative and a treatment for influenza or colds.

Apothecaries' Hall: based in Black Friars Lane, London, the headquarters of the Worshipful Society of Apothecaries of London, one of the livery companies, or trade guilds, of the City of London, founded in 1617, and from the Apothecaries' Act of 1815, a professional body licensing and regulating medical practitioners.

djinns: evoking *The Thousand and One Nights*, a spirit, a jinn or 'genie' able to exert influence over human beings.

180 *Pharmaceutical Formulary*: a text offering a compendium of medicines for medical practitioners, and perhaps specifically a reference to Henry Beasley's *The Pharmaceutical Formulary . . . Being the twelfth edition of Beasley's Pocket Formulary*, ed. J. O. Braithwaite (London: J. & A. Churchill, 1899).

Nicholas Culpepper: (1616–54), a physician and astrologer, and the author of *The English Physitian, or, An Astrologo-physical Discourse on the Vulgar Herbs of This Nation, Being a Compleat Method of Physick, Whereby a Man May Preserve his Body in Health, or Cure Himself, Being Sick* (1652), more succinctly known through the nineteenth century as *Culpeper's Complete Herbal*. This was an influential work of practical remedies and treatments. Culpeper (spelt thus) appears as a character in Kipling's story 'A Doctor of Medicine' (1909) in *Rewards and Fairies* (1910).

Kirby Moors: more usually known as Kirby Hill, a village in North Yorkshire.

Co-operative stores: profit-sharing shops mutually owned by a group or society of individuals. The first of these stores was the Rochdale Society of Equitable Pioneers, established in 1844; in 1850, the London Central Cooperative Store was founded. In the mid-1890s in the United Kingdom, it was estimated that there were around 1,700 such societies in existence.

180 *Christie's New Commercial Plants*: Thomas Christy's twelve-volume work, *New Commercial Plants and Drugs* (London: Christy and Co., 1878–97). Thomas Christy (1831–1905) was a botanist and a Fellow of the *Linnean* Society. Given as 'Christie' also in the first printing of the story in *Scribner's Magazine*, in the Sussex edition of *Traffics and Discoveries* (London: Macmillan & Co., 1936), 221, the name is correctly emended to 'Christy'.

Three superb glass jars . . . that led Rosamund to parting with her shoes: in Maria Edgeworth's (1767–1849) tale 'The Purple Jar' (first collected as the opening story in *Early Lessons* (1804)), the easily distracted heroine ('about seven years old') pleads with her mother to buy a coloured jar from a chemist's shop, rather than a new pair of shoes.

orris, Kodak films, vulcanite: both aromatic and medicinal, orris is the root of the iris flower, used in perfumery and as a fixative in making pot-pourri; Kodak films are the rolls of photographic film produced by the George Eastman company; vulcanite is rubber that has been hardened by being treated with sulphur.

cayenne-pepper jujubes and menthol lozenges: a jujube is a gelatine lozenge, used as a stimulant, whereas menthol is an analgesic and decongestant used to cool and soothe the throat and clear the airways.

181 *that old hare! The wind's nearly blowing the fur off him*: another allusion to Keats's 'The Eve of St Agnes': 'The hare limp'd trembling through the frozen grass' (line 3).

drugged moth's: another allusion perhaps to the idea of the psyche as a butterfly, and also, though rather remotely, to line 213 of 'The Eve of St Agnes': 'As are the tiger-moth's deep-damask'd wings'.

St. Agnes: the local church is dedicated to Agnes of Rome (*c.*291–*c.*304), martyr and patron saint of girls and of chastity. In the original magazine publication, the text gives this simply as 'the church', and a few lines later spells this out fully as 'only go round by St. Agnes church'.

182 *graduated glass*: a glass used in chemistry for the measurement of the volume of a liquid.

Hertzian waves: testing James Clerk Maxwell's theoretical description, the German physicist Heinrich Hertz (1857–1894) experimentally verified the existence of electromagnetic waves.

coherer: the first rudimentary version of a radio signal detector, first invented by Édouard Eugène Désiré Branly (1844–1940).

cubeb: a pungent, peppery, spicy Javanese berry (and sometimes called Java pepper) used as a medicine to treat dysentery, gonorrhea, and, here most appositely, bronchitis.

183 *grateful and comforting*: 'Grateful—Comforting' had been the advertising slogan for Epps's Cocoa since the late 1860s.

benzoin: benzoin, derived from the resin of a Javanese tree, when burnt was used for inhalations for people with upper chest infections; in the 1890s and 1900s it was a popular ingredient in skin lotions for women.

184 *Austrian jute blanket*: jute is a vegetable fibre used for making a coarse cloth. In 1882, the press were reporting the establishment of large-scale jute mills in Austria. The raw materials were shipped to Trieste from Calcutta.

chloric-ether: in this context, very likely a solution of chloroform in alcohol.

sparklet bottles: a trade name, derived from the products of the Sparklets Corporation, referring to bottles, sold in chemists' shops, that 'aerated' liquids, producing fizzy fruit-drinks, sparkling wine, or carbonated soda-water. They were supposedly recommended by doctors as a safe way to aerate drinks for 'invalids'.

chypre: a heavy perfume based on sandalwood perhaps from Cyprus (*OED*).

185 *rich port-wine colour, frothed at the top*: possibly an allusion to Keats's 'Ode to a Nightingale': 'O for a beaker full of the warm South, | Full of the true, the blushful Hippocrene, | With beaded bubbles winking at the brim, | And purple-stained mouth' (lines 15–18). Kipling's story picks up the word 'winking' from Keats in the next paragraph.

186 *Morse instrument*: Samuel Morse (1791–1872) contributed to the development of Morse code, a means of sending messages via pulses of electro-magnetic telegraphy.

I want to live—my God, how I want to live, and see it develop?: there may be a printer's error here, as the statement would perhaps better end with an exclamation mark, and not a question mark as in the text of the book. In the first magazine publication, this passage reads as follows: 'I want to live—my God, how I want to live, and see things happen!'

Fanny Brand: a name (as the text goes on to tell us) that flirts with the memory of Fanny Brawne (1800–65), the young woman with whom John Keats was in love, and whom his infection with tuberculosis prevented him from marrying.

'arterial': in February 1820, as famously recorded by his friend Charles Brown, Keats coughed up blood into a handkerchief. Looking at it, Brown quotes the poet as saying, 'I know the colour of that blood;—it is arterial blood;—I cannot be deceived in that colour;—that drop of blood is my death-warrant'.

187 *halliards*: most often used in a nautical setting, these are ropes used for hoisting a sail or a flag.

And threw warm gules on Madeleine's young breast: from line 218 of 'The Eve of St Agnes': 'And threw warm gules on Madeline's fair breast'. The fragments of verse are presented differently in different editions of Kipling's tale. In the first book printing in *Traffics and Discoveries*, the inset quotes, as in the original printing of *Scribner's*, are in a slightly smaller font, and are not separated off by quote marks; in the first Tauchnitz edition of *Traffics and Discoveries*, some of the inset quotes are also put in double quotation marks, though most are not. In the Sussex edition (London: Macmillan and Co., 1936), the verse fragments are given in the same size and font as the main text and yet are marked off from the text by single quotation marks.

188 *vile chromo*: from 1875, used as a shortening of 'chromolithograph', a picture printed in colour, and often used to mean a cheap reproduction of something, as well as a work put down and devalued because its origins lay in a mechanical process.

Incense in a censer—: 'Like pious incense from a censer old' (Keats, 'The Eve of St Agnes', stanza 1, line 7).

189 *he shivered as he wrote*—: in the printing in *Scribner's Magazine*, this phrase is incorporated into the indented quote, in the same size font as the fragment of poetry, but separated off in square brackets.

And my weak spirit fails . . . Beneath the churchyard mould: 'and his weak spirit fails | To think how they may ache in icy hoods and mails' (Keats, 'The Eve of St Agnes', lines 17–18).

I found myself one person again: another reminiscence of Keats's 'Ode to a Nightingale', that extraordinary poetic expression of the imaginative spirit, and a profound questioning of the origins of art: "Forlorn! the very word is like a bell | To toll me back from thee to my sole self!'

190 *'its little smoke in pallid moonlight died'*: from 'The Eve of St Agnes', line 200: 'Its little smoke, in pallid moonshine, died'.

191 *red, black, and yellow Austrian blanket*: 'A cloth of woven crimson, gold and jet', from 'The Eve of St Agnes', line 256.

clerkly: the text in *Traffics and Discoveries* has 'clerky', while the first published version in *Scribner's* has 'clerkly'.

Candied apple, quince and plum . . . to cedared Lebanon:

> Of candied apple, quince, and plum, and gourd;
> With jellies soother than the creamy curd,
> And lucent syrops, tinct with cinnamon;
> Manna and dates, in argosy transferr'd
> From Fez; and spiced dainties, every one,
> From silken Samarcand to cedar'd Lebanon.
> (stanza 30, lines 265–70 of 'The Eve of St Agnes')

The Sussex edition (1936) corrects 'syrups' to 'syrops'.

192 *A savage spot . . . demon lover*: 'A savage place! as holy and enchanted | As e'er beneath a waning moon was haunted | By woman wailing for her demon-lover!', lines 14–16 of Samuel Taylor Coleridge's (1772–1834) 'Kubla Khan', another poem purportedly written in a kind of automatic writing, while under the influence of that imported drug, opium.

Our open casements . . . forlorn—: Shaynor has been coming close to reproducing, without actually doing so, the last lines of stanza 7 of Keats's 'Ode to a Nightingale': 'The same that oft-times hath | Charm'd magic case-ments, opening on the foam | Of perilous seas, in faery lands forlorn'.

193 '*I suppose I must have been dreaming*': an allusion to the last two lines of 'Ode to a Nightingale': 'Was it a vision, or a waking dream? | Fled is that music:—Do I wake or sleep?'

194 *Sandown Bay*: a broad bay on the south-eastern shores of the Isle of Wight, in the Solent, south of Portsmouth and Southsea. In 1898, Kipling had sailed with the Channel Fleet, while they were experimenting with the new Marconi technology.

MARY E. WILKINS FREEMAN, *The Hall Bedroom*

Mary Eleanor (originally Ella) Wilkins Freeman (1852–1930) was a writer of novels and short stories of remarkable subtlety and quiet force. Born on Halloween in the small town of Randolph, Massachusetts, south of Boston, to Eleanor and Warren Wilkins, Mary's childhood was marked by illness and soli-tude, the death of two of her younger siblings (her brother died aged 3 in 1858, and her sister, Anna, in 1876, at the age of 17), and a strict religious upbringing imposed by her pious Congregationalist parents. In 1867, the family moved to Brattleboro, Vermont, where her father (previously a carpenter) ran a dry-goods store. Beginning in 1870, Freeman spent some years at Mount Holyoke Female Seminary, where she struck her contemporaries as an aloof and diffi-dent character. A crush on a local naval ensign, one Hanson Tyler, was unre-quited. When her father's business failed in 1876, the family moved into the house of a local clergyman, Hanson Tyler's invalid father, and here Freeman's mother earned their keep as housekeeper. Her mother died in 1880, and, after moving to Florida for his health, in 1883 her father also died; these losses (par-ticularly that of her mother) left Mary Wilkins grief-stricken and isolated. With only a small legacy to maintain herself, she began to write poems and stories for magazine publication. Her first books, *A Humble Romance and Other Stories* (1887) and *A New England Nun and Other Stories* (1891), are perhaps her strongest collections, the latter containing such tales of grim comfort and resistance as 'A New England Nun', 'The Revolt of "Mother"', and 'Old Woman Magoun'. Many other works followed, including her best novel, *Pembroke* (1894); she contributed, with Henry James and William Dean Howells (among others), to *The Whole Family, A Novel by Twelve Authors* (1908). Her volume of supernatural stories, *The Wind in the Rose-Bush* (1903), is a classic of the genre. In 1892, she met Dr Charles Freeman, and after a long and hesitant courtship they finally married a decade later. The marriage was a troubled one, rocked by the wayward Freeman's alcoholism and womanizing. Some years later he entered the New Jersey Hospital for the Insane, and the marriage ended soon afterwards. A prolific and nuanced writer, 'The Hall Bedroom' is Freeman's only excursion into something that can be classified as science fiction, a tale that draws together the mysterious and a speculative sci-entific explanation.

The copy-text for 'The Hall Bedroom' derives from its first publication in the rather up-market and stylish *Collier's* (New York and London), 30/26 (28 March 1903), 19, 22–3. The story was illustrated with a heading picture by Anna Whelan Betts (1873–1959) of a writing man turning with alarm from his paper to face a picture to one side of him, and a much more striking image by Anna's younger sister, Ethel Franklin Betts (1877–1959), of a perplexed young chap closely surrounded by mysterious *femme fatale*-like figures, with the caption 'My groping hands touched living beings'. Both sisters produced work for magazines and periodicals in the 1890s and 1900s; Ethel Franklin Betts is best known for her illustrations of children's books, including Frances Hodgson Burnett's (1849–1924) *The Little Princess* (1905). The story includes a number of subheadings in bold: 'The Diary of an Ill-Fated Man'; 'Diet and Psychology'; 'The Mystery of the First Night'; 'The Startled Neighbor'; 'Further Nocturnal Experiences'; 'The Story of Strange Disappearances'; 'Two Who Vanished'; 'The Last Night'; and 'The Secret Chamber'. The story was reprinted in William Patten (ed.), *Short Story Classics (American)*, iv (New York: P. F. Collier & Son, 1905), 1275–1302. (It is followed by another classic of the fantastic, Ambrose Bierce's (1842–1914?) 'The Damned Thing'.) The editor prefaces the story with the following note:

Mrs. Freeman (born in 1862, at Randolph, Mass.) achieved under her name of Mary Eleanor Wilkins a reputation as the foremost realist among our American short story writers, and now threatens to link in the public mind her married name with the highest order of imaginative fiction. In the present selection, a tale of the fourth dimension, by clever story-telling art, she causes that most contracted of habitable cells, a city hall bedroom, to expand into infinite vistas, not only of space, but of sight, sound, sense, and their other unnamed brothers of the family of sense-perceptions. (1273)

Despite its not really containing a ghost, much later the tale appeared again in *Collected Ghost Stories by Mary Wilkins Freeman*, ed. Edward Wagenknecht (Sauk City, WI: Arkham House, 1974), 21–38.

196 *Rockton*: there are a couple of real hamlets or villages named Rockton on the American East Coast, namely in New York State and in Pennsylvania.

197 *the hall bedroom*: a specifically American living arrangement, and it would seem particularly associated between the 1880s and the 1910s with New York. It consisted of a small bedroom area partitioned off in a hallway, and was therefore deemed a rather provisional and only semi-private living space. A 'hall bed-roomer', according to a citation in the *OED* from 1899, is marked down as a 'lonely' species of lodger.

199 *chromos*: see the note to p. 188.

202 *the Inquisition*: a reference, of course, to the various institutions set up by the Roman Catholic Church, beginning in the twelfth century, in order to root out religious heresy.

transom: an American word for a small window above the lintel of a door.

205 *Sweeter than honey . . . Old Testament manna*: the narrator here cites a verse from the Bible referring to the 'fear of the Lord' and 'the judgements of the Lord' that are 'More to be desired than gold, yea, than much fine gold: sweeter also than honey and the honeycomb' (Psalm 19:10). Taking another biblical story, the 'manna' is the miraculous (and mysterious) food provided in the wilderness for the Israelites fleeing slavery in Egypt, as described in Exodus 16. It is perhaps of significance that the manna is to be found in the dew of the morning when the Israelites wake from sleep.

206 *the Cure*: more usually, a 'cure' in this context refers to the treatment undertaken by the chronically ill, a medical regimen, or a residence at a health resort or sanatorium—here clearly it means the building where the treatment itself takes place.

209 *the fifth dimension*: in addition to the three known dimensions of length, breadth, and depth, from the 1870s, speculation began to flourish that there might be additional dimensions (initially only a fourth) that exist beyond our perceptions as part of the material world. Though the idea had been outlined earlier, notably by the seventeenth-century Cambridge Platonist Henry More, with his notion of 'spissitude', the concept of a fourth dimension was first theoretically introduced by the mathematician James Joseph Sylvester (1814–97), drawing on speculations of Professor William Kingdon Clifford. A later key text in this regard was the work of two Scottish physicists, Balfour Stewart (1828–87) and Peter Guthrie Tait's (1831–1901) *The Unseen Universe* (1875). Within the history of science, this posited additional space is of interest in that it can be described, inferred, mathematically mapped, and imagined, but cannot be empirically proved. Stewart and Guthrie were busy trying to reconcile Christianity and science; an article in the *Pall Mall Gazette* (22 June 1875) describes their approach as 'transcendental physics'. Later, ideas of a 'fourth dimension' became a place where spiritualist writers were prepared to find common ground with experimental physicists.

H. G. WELLS, *The Country of the Blind*

For a brief biography of H. G. Wells, see the headnote to his 'The Crystal Egg', p. 362.

The copy-text for the story is its first publication in book form, in H. G. Wells, *The Country of the Blind and Other Stories* (London: Thomas Nelson and Sons, 1911), 536–68. The story first appeared in *The Strand* (London), 27/160 (April 1904), 401–15. (In the same issue appeared Arthur Conan Doyle's latest Sherlock Holmes short story, 'The Adventure of Charles Augustus Milverton'.) In *The Strand* version, Nunez is consistently spelt 'Nuñez'. The story was illustrated with eight pictures by Claude Allin Shepperson (1867–1921) which are captioned as follows: 'They found Nuñez had gone from them'; 'Nuñez stood forward as conspicuously as possible upon his rock'; '"Carefully," he cried, with a finger in his eye'; 'The glow upon the snow-fields and glaciers was the most beautiful thing he had ever seen'; 'They were moving in upon him quickly'; 'He sat down at her feet'; '"His brain is affected," said the blind doctor'; and 'He had a few minutes with Medina-Saroté before she went apart to sleep'. Like Wells born in Kent, Shepperson was a landscape painter and illustrator, famous later for his *Punch* cartoons and his drawings of field hospitals, clearing stations, and convalescent homes commissioned by the Ministry of Information during the First World War. Shepperson had worked with Wells earlier, producing the illustrations for the first edition of *The First Men in the Moon* (London: George Newnes, Limited, 1901).

In 1939, Wells saw through the press a limited edition of an expanded version of the story, published by Golden Cockerel Press, with engravings by Clifford Webb (1894–1972). In an introduction to this volume, Wells wrote of the original tale:

The stress is upon the spiritual isolation of those who see more keenly than their fellows and the tragedy of their incommunicable appreciation of life. The visionary dies, a worthless outcast, finding no other escape from his gift but death, and the blind world goes on, invincibly self-satisfied and secure.

211 *Chimborazo, one hundred from the snows of Cotopaxi, in the wildest wastes of Ecuador's Andes*: Chimborazo is a dormant volcano in the Andes, and the highest mountain in the South American country of Ecuador. Cotopaxi is an active volcano, also in the Ecuadorean Andes, some 30 miles south of Quito.

the *stupendous outbreak of Mindobamba . . . Quito . . . Yaguachi . . . as far as Guayaquil*: Mindobamba is a fictional volcano. Cotopaxi had spectacularly erupted fairly recently, in 1877, when the mudflow from the volcano travelled over 60 miles to the Pacific Ocean, and the town of Latacunga was levelled. Yaguachi is a real town in the coastal province of Guayas, where Guayaquil is the capital of the province and Ecuador's largest port.

Arauca crest: the Arauca River rises in the Colombian Andes and flows down until it meets the Orinoco River in Venezuela, flowing eastwards away from the Pacific Ocean.

213 *Parascotopetl, the Matterhorn of the Andes*: a fictitious mountain, compared with one of the highest peaks in the Alps, that spans the border between Switzerland and Italy.

215 *talus*: this can mean the descending slope of a mountain, but in the context here refers to the scree and debris on a slope below a cliff and consisting of rocks and stones that have fallen from it. The second time this word recurs in the story, the other meaning of a slope might be intended.

217 '*In the Country of the Blind the One-eyed Man is King*': first recorded in Desiderius Erasmus's (1466–1536) *Adages* (1500), variations of this phrase proliferated as a standard proverb in English. James Wood's *Dictionary of Quotations* (London and New York: Warne, 1893) has 'Among the blind the one-eyed is king'.

Bogota: the capital city of Colombia; perhaps coincidentally, the president of Columbia in the 1880s and early 1890s shares the name, (Rafael) Núñez, with the story's hero.

E. M. FORSTER, *The Machine Stops*

Edward Morgan Forster (1879–1970) was one of the most admired and talented British novelists of the early twentieth century. His father died when he was only 1 year old, leaving an inheritance that assured his widow and their only child a comfortable middle-class life. He spent most of his childhood very happily at Rooksnest, a house in the Hertfordshire countryside. In 1890, he started school as a boarder at Eastbourne, and in 1893 he and his mother moved to Tonbridge, where he went to school as a day-boy, a period of his life that in retrospect he remembered as constricted and miserable. In 1897, he went up to King's College, Cambridge, the start of an ongoing connection to the college that would be his home again from the end of the Second World War until his death. After four years at King's, financially free from the necessity of earning his living, Forster travelled in Italy and Greece, journeys that informed his early short stories and novels. He published *Where Angels Fear to Tread* in 1905, followed by *The Longest Journey* (1907) and *A Room with A View* (1908). In late 1908, he wrote 'The Machine Stops', a dystopian vision of the future, in form quite unlike any of his other works of fiction, though imbued with the same ambivalence about 'progress' that permeates his novels and other short stories. In the 1940s, he himself would describe it as 'a reaction to one of the earlier heavens of H. G. Wells'. In 1910, *Howard's End* appeared, a 'condition of England' novel that includes a famous hope that we might 'only connect' the prose and passion of life. Between 1910 and 1913, he wrote a novel, *Maurice*, that would remain unpublished until his death; this was due to the fact that it explored his own love and desire for men, a subject that he deemed only likely to upset his ageing mother. (It finally appeared in 1971.) Forster had already had a passionate (and chaste) friendship with Hugh Owen Meredith (1878–1964), a Cambridge friend, and in 1906 he fell in love with Syed Ross Masood (1889–1937), an Indian student to whom he gave Latin lessons. Encouraged by Masood, in 1912, Forster travelled with friends to India, spending six months there. He spent part of the First World War in Alexandria, where he worked for the Red Cross tracing missing soldiers. In 1921, he travelled again to India, where he took up a job as private secretary to the maharaja of Dewas. In 1922, his masterpiece, *A Passage to India*, was published; it was to be his last novel. From then until his death, Forster lived as a 'good influence' on undergraduates at King's and on younger writers, a humane, agnostic, and liberal voice, and a miscellaneous writer, producing literary criticism and essays, broadcasting on the BBC, working on the short film *A Diary for Timothy* (1945) with Humphrey Jennings (1907–50), and collaborating on a libretto of *Billy Budd* (1951) for Benjamin Britten (1913–76). He formed a long-lasting relationship with Bob Buckingham (1904–75), a married policeman, and in 1970 he died at the Buckinghams' home in Coventry.

The copy-text for 'The Machine Stops' is based on its first book publication in *The Eternal Moment and Other Stories* (London: Sidgwick & Jackson, Ltd, 1928), 1–61. It had earlier been published in the Michaelmas Term issue of *The Oxford and Cambridge Review* (London), 8 (November 1909), 83–122.

235 *Vashti*: a Hebrew name; in the Book of Esther in the Bible, Vashti is the first wife of King Ahasuerus, who is banished when she refuses to display her beauty at the king's banquet.

air-ship: first coined in the early nineteenth century to apply to any hypothetical flying vehicle, in the 1900s this word came to stand for the new dirigibles, such as the Zeppelin.

236 *'The four big stars are the man's shoulders and his knees. The three stars in the middle are like the belts that men wore once, and the three stars hanging are like a sword'*: the story refers here, of course, to the constellation of Orion, one of the forty-eight Ptolemaic constellations, as set out by Claudius Ptolemy (AD *c*.100–*c*.170) in the *Almagest* (*c*.150), and supposed to represent a giant huntsman, able to hunt and kill any animal.

240 *vomitories of Rye or of Christchurch*: 'vomitories' is a word of Roman origin and therefore perhaps laden with suggestions of ancient Rome. It is used here to mean an opening or vent by which people and the airships can pass in and out of the underground world. Rye likely means the East Sussex coastal town, home at the time to the novelist Henry James, and Christchurch likely refers, of course, to the New Zealand city on the South Island of that country.

241 *He had harnessed Leviathan*: a reference to God's challenge to Job, saying precisely what human beings are unable to do: 'Canst thou draw out leviathan with a hook? or his tongue with a cord which thou lettest down? . . . Will he make a covenant with thee? wilt thou take him for a servant for ever?' (Job 41:1 and 4). In the Bible, Leviathan refers to a mythical sea-monster of enormous strength and power.

cinematophote: in a period where the designated word for methods of shooting and screening film was still in flux, this invented term forges a compound Greek word, combining *kinema*, root meaning 'motion' (as in the popular 'cinematoscope') with the suffix *phote*, meaning 'light', as in the late nineteenth-century term 'telephote'.

243 *a rosy finger of light*: a nod to one of Homer's most famous epithets, *rhododáktulos Ēōs*, most often translated as 'rosy-fingered dawn', and used in both *The Iliad* and *The Odyssey*.

Simla: now known more usually as Shimla, from 1864 this Indian city was the 'summer capital' of the Raj, a place of resort for the British to escape from the summer heat, on the cool south-western ranges of the Himalayas.

244 *Kinchinjunga*: now more usually known as Kangchenjunga, or Kanchenjunga, this Himalayan mountain is the third highest peak in the world.

245 *flesh of her flesh*: reversing the genders, and putting a son in place of a wife, this is a biblical allusion: 'And Adam said, This is now bone of my bones, and flesh of my flesh: she shall be called Woman, because she was taken out of Man. Therefore shall a man leave his father and his mother, and shall cleave unto his wife: and they shall be one flesh. And they were both naked, the man and his wife, and were not ashamed' (Genesis 2:23–5).

246 *In the dawn of the world our weakly must be exposed on Mount Taygetus*: a mountain on the Peloponnese peninsula in southern Greece, where, according to the Greek biographer Plutarch's 'Life of Lycurgus', the Spartans reputedly left weak, deformed, or sickly babies to die.

247 *Man is the measure*: this statement originates with the Greek philosopher and sophist Protagoras of Abdera (*c*.490–*c*.420 BC).

249 *showed that he was reverting to some savage type. On atavism the Machine can have no mercy*: the Edwardian period was much preoccupied with ideas of degeneracy, evolutionary recapitulation, and atavism, and the possibility that human beings might fall backwards in evolutionary terms or be stuck in earlier stages of evolutionary development. As was the fashion of the time, Forster himself sported a fine moustache.

250 *Wessex*: originally a Saxon kingdom in south-west England, and hardly used in any other sense for several hundred years, 'Wessex' had been recently revived by William Barnes and more especially by Thomas Hardy as a name for this region. (In *Aspects of the Novel* (London: Edward Arnold, 1927), Forster wrote, 'the work of Hardy is my home'.)

the southern coast from the Andredswald to Cornwall, while the Wansdyke protected them on the north: the 'Andredswald' refers to an ancient forest that once straddled the weald from Kent into Sussex; constructed in AD 400–700, the Wansdyke is a defensive earthwork in the west of southern England that stretches in two dykes from the Savernake Forest to Morgan's Hill in Wiltshire and from Monkton Combe to Maes Knoll in Somerset. Though the matter is still unclear, it was perhaps built by the Britons against the encroaching Saxon invaders.

Scorpio—: another of the Ptolemaic constellations, this is also the eighth astrological sign of the zodiac. The sun is in Scorpio from (approximately) 21 October to (approximately) 21 November. Aptly for the themes of his story, Forster may be picking up on his earlier mention of the constellation of Orion. The hunter was killed by a scorpion, as a punishment by Artemis and her mother Leto for his hubristic boast that he would hunt and kill every animal on earth. As a result, the constellations of Orion and of Scorpio never appear together in the night sky.

251 *as Ælfrid saw them when he overthrew the Danes*: 'Ælfrid' is the old English spelling of Alfred, rather self-consciously employed as a kind of linguistic atavism here, but used with some regularity in British history books of the late seventeenth and early eighteenth centuries. Alfred the Great (*c*.848–99) was king of Wessex from 871 to *c*.886 and king of all the Anglo-Saxons from *c*.886

to 899. Alfred defended his territory against the Danes for many years, and most famously defeated the Danish invaders at the Battle of Edington in 878.

255 *what I think that Enicharmon thought Urizen thought Gutch thought Ho-Yung thought Chi-Bo-Sing thought Lafcadio Hearn thought Carlyle thought Mirabeau said about the French Revolution:* 'Enicharmon' appears to be a mistake (deliberate or inadvertent) for the poet William Blake's (1757–1827) 'Enitharmon', the female emanation and wife of Los, the spirit of the imagination; 'Urizen' also derives from Blake's personal mythology, and stands for the embodiment of law and reason. 'Gutch' may refer to various minor authors of that name (such as the antiquary John Gutch (1746–1831) or the folklorist Eliza Gutch (1840–1931)), but most likely alludes to an invented author. Similarly Ho-Yung would appear to be an author of the future, as is Chi-Bo-Sing. However, Lafcadio Hearn (1850–1904) was an American writer, most famous for his long engagement with Japanese culture, and especially for his collections of Japanese ghost stories. The Scottish author and Victorian sage Thomas Carlyle (1795–1881) wrote *The French Revolution: A History* (London: Chapman and Hall, 1837), which quotes many apposite sayings of the Revolutionary leader and moderate Honoré Gabriel Riqueti, Comte de Mirabeau (1749–91).

ten great minds: the text says there are 'ten' great minds, but only lists eight. In later editions of the story, Forster corrected this mistake.

Versailles: the palace of Versailles was the main residence of the king of France from 1682 until the French Revolution. On 5 October 1789, a few thousand people, predominantly women, marched from Paris to nearby Versailles demanding that King Louis XVI and his wife, Marie Antoinette, return with them to Paris.

"seraphically free From taint of personality": a slightly mangled quote from George Meredith's (1828–1909) poem 'The Lark Ascending' (1881), first collected in *Poems and Lyrics of the Joy of Earth* (London: Macmillan and Co., 1883). Forster had an ambivalent relationship with Meredith's writing, being both rather indebted to him and rather impatient with him. Meredith died in May of 1909, the year when Forster wrote 'The Machine Stops', and was perhaps again on his mind for that reason. The lines describe how the bird's free song is better than our own:

> We want the key of his wild note
> Of truthful in a truthful throat,
> The song seraphically free
> Of taint of personality,
> So pure that it salutes the suns
> The voice of one for millions.
>
> (lines 91–8)

259 *Courland*: this is a region in western Latvia; at the time of Forster's writing the story, part of the Russian Empire. The region had been in the news in 1905–6, due to an epidemic of cholera and subsequent political and nationalistic unrest. Some few years earlier, under the pseudonym Carl

Joubert, the mysterious Tolstoyan Adolphus Waldorf Carl Grottey (?–1906) had published *The Tyranny of Faith: A Story of Courland* (London: Hurst and Blackett, 1906).

SIR ARTHUR CONAN DOYLE, *The Terror of Blue John Gap*

Arthur Conan Doyle was born in Edinburgh in 1859, the son of an alcoholic draughtsman and an Irish Catholic mother. With help from the family, Doyle attended Stonyhurst College, a Roman Catholic boarding school. He studied medicine at Edinburgh University, where he was taught by Joseph Bell, whose analytical methods with corpses inspired the deductive process applied by Doyle's most famous literary creation, the consulting detective Sherlock Holmes. After a period working as a ship's doctor, he settled in Southsea, where he wrote and set himself up in general practice. In 1885, he married Louisa Hawkins; their son, Alleyne Kingsley Conan Doyle, was born in 1892. In 1887, the first Sherlock Holmes novel was published, *A Study in Scarlet*. *The Sign of Four* followed in 1890, and from 1891, he published a highly lucrative and successful series of Holmes stories in the newly established *Strand Magazine*. Doyle's strong connection with *The Strand* would last until 1927, in the end Doyle produced four Holmes novels and fifty-six stories. He had an equivocal relationship with the mythic character he had created, and tried to kill him off in the story 'The Final Problem' (December 1893). Doyle resurrected the character, first of all in the excellent *The Hound of the Baskervilles* (1902), a tale set before Holmes's reputed demise, and then from the following year properly in a series of tales, collected in *The Return of Sherlock Holmes* (1905). Doyle put a higher estimate on his historical fictions, such as *The Exploits of Brigadier Gerard* (1896) or *Sir Nigel* (1903).

Doyle enjoyed enormous fame throughout his life, and was a highly regarded public figure, supporting the imperialist war against the Boers in South Africa (serving for a time as volunteer doctor), campaigning against the Belgian version of imperialism in the Congo, and inveighing against (and investigating) a number of miscarriages of justice at home in Britain. His first wife died of tuberculosis in 1906. Fifteen months later, after a long-standing passionate friendship, he married Jean Leckie; they would have three children together. Doyle's enduring interest in spiritualism was strengthened following the death of his son, Kingsley, in 1918, and he became a prominent advocate for the spiritualist cause. In *The Coming of the Fairies* (1922), he also wrote enthusiastically about supposed contact between fairies and two young girls in Cottingley, Yorkshire, a contact that had purportedly led to a series of photographs of these strange creatures. He died of a heart attack in 1930.

Doyle's position as a writer of science fiction rests largely on his Professor Challenger stories, including the short novels *The Lost World* (1912), a romance that describes the discovery of a lingering outpost of the prehistoric in contemporary South America, and *The Poison Belt* (1913), an apocalyptic tale, and such short stories as 'The Disintegration Machine' (1929). A later Professor Challenger novel, *The Land of Mist* (1926), saw the bluffly irascible and committed scientist peripherally entangled in the realm of spiritualism.

The copy-text for 'The Terror of Blue John Gap' is from the first printing of the story in book form, in *The Last Galley: Impressions and Tales* (London: Smith, Elder & Co., 1911), 273–98. The story is prefaced by an illustration by the New Zealander Harry Rountree (1878–1950), showing the moment where 'He had reared up on his hind legs as a bear would do, and stood above me, enormous, menacing'. The tale was first published (with five illustrations by Rountree) as the lead story in the *Strand Magazine* (London), 40/236 (August 1910), 131–41. The story was prefaced on the facing page with the same illustration that appeared in *The Last Galley*; the other four illustrations were captioned as follows: 'Suddenly from the depths of the tunnel behind me there issued a most extraordinary sound' (showing a rather dapper version of the protagonist in a white three-piece suit); 'Sheep have disappeared'; 'Rifle in hand, I ran at the top of my speed upon the trail of the monster'; 'I and my broken lantern crashed to the earth' (depicting the hero in the paws of the monster). The forthcoming story had been advertised in the previous month's magazine, with an accompanying photograph of Doyle. Then, after publication in book form, the story was also printed in *The Sun* (New York) magazine on 1 December 1912. Doyle had an established relationship with *The Sun*, which, among other pieces, had serialized the novels *The White Company* (in 1891) and *Rodney Stone* (in 1896), as well as several of the early Sherlock Holmes stories.

264 *phthisis*: tuberculosis (also the disease from which M. Valdemar dies in Poe's 'The Facts in the Case of M. Valdemar').

South Kensington: an area of London that is pertinently home to the Natural History Museum, opened in 1881, which houses, among other exhibits, a full-scale replica of a Diplodocus skeleton, given to the museum by Andrew Carnegie in 1905.

265 *superfluous woman*: a woman rendered socially unnecessary as, due to an imbalance regarding the sexes in the population, she finds that she cannot marry. The term became even more prevalent after the First World War, making the 1920s and 1930s an era of 'maiden aunts', but the phrase had first appeared in the 1850s. In 1894, Emma Frances Brooke (1844–1926) published anonymously a scandalous novel, titled *A Superfluous Woman*.

Arabian Nights: see note to p. 56.

Blue John: a variety of fluorite, a semi-precious stone, veined with bands of purplish-blue, found in Derbyshire (and also known as Derbyshire Drop), particularly in the region of the High Peak village of Castleton. From the mid-eighteenth century, it was used by lapidaries for decoration and ornaments.

273 *Coltbridge*: there is no village or town named Coltbridge in Derbyshire, and given the fact that Hardcastle is imagined to be a visitor to the district, it is most likely that this alludes to the Coltbridge area of Edinburgh, the town where Doyle was born and was a medical student.

acetylene lantern: a gas lantern, and a rather up-to-date technology for this tale, being first used in the middle of the 1890s, particularly as bicycle lamps.

troglodyte: a cave-dwelling person, or creature, and from the 1860s applied to our prehistoric ancestors.

try conclusions: to put to the proof, and a phrase that carries Shakespearean echoes, picking up *Hamlet* (III.iv.196) and even Launcelot Gobbo's 'I will try confusions with him' in *The Merchant of Venice*, II.i.

274 *Chapel-le-Dale*: there is a Chapel-le-Dale in Yorkshire, in what was then the West Riding; in Derbyshire, there is an Alsop-en-le-Dale, with a Norman church, St Michael and All Angels, though at quite some distance from the area of Castleton.

276 *oakum*: the light-brown coarse fibres separated from flax or hemp.

JACK LONDON, *The Red One*

Jack (John) Griffith London (1876–1916) was one of the early twentieth century's most successful and prolific American literary figures, a novelist, short-story writer, and memoirist who was part of the transformation of the image of the sedentary American man of letters into the character of a man of action. Born in San Francisco in poor circumstances, his parents were involved with esoteric philosophy and practices: his biological father (who deserted London's mother before their son's birth) was an itinerant astrologer and his mother a spiritualist medium. From the age of 13, London commenced a wandering and precarious life of adventure, working as an oyster pirate, a sailor on a voyage to Japan, a factory hand, and a hobo (he spent thirty days imprisoned for vagrancy). After returning to Oakland High School and briefly being an under-graduate at Berkeley (he left without graduating), in 1897 he joined the Klondike Gold Rush. These varied experiences formed the background of much of his fiction, including the powerful short story of the frailty of life, 'To Build a Fire' (1902, rev. 1908); *The Call of the Wild* (1903), his tale of a pet dog returning to his wolfish ancestral origins in the Yukon; and his Nietzschean novel *Martin Eden* (1909). After living voluntarily in the East End slums of London, he wrote *People of the Abyss* (1903) (London was a socialist of a pecu-liarly individualistic kind); *The Road* (1907) recalls his time living as a tramp; while his *John Barleycorn* (1913) is an autobiographical novel that records something of his own relationship with alcohol. In 1904 he was a war corres-pondent during the Russo-Japanese War and worked again in the same capacity in 1914 in Mexico.

In 1900, he married Bessie Maddern (1876–1947); the couple had two daughters, Joan (1901–71) and Becky (Bess) (1902–92). The marriage was always a fraught and difficult one; during its early years, he continued a pas-sionate friendship with the writer Anna Strunsky (1877–1964). In 1904, the Londons divorced, and in 1905, he married Charmian Kitteridge (1871–1955), herself a writer. From 1905, the couple lived on a ranch in the Sonoma Valley, California, though in 1907, they set off on *The Snark*, a 45-foot yacht, on a long (and disastrous) voyage around the Pacific, one plagued by ill health. During their two-year travels, among other places they visited the Solomon Islands, where London would set his science fiction story 'The Red One'. On their travels, in 1907, Jack and Charmian London also first visited the beach resort at Waikiki, by Honolulu, the capital of Hawaii; London spent more than half a year on the island in 1915–16, where he wrote 'The Red One'. After years of debilitating sickness, on 22 November 1916 London died of gastro-intestinal uraemic poisoning.

Alongside Edgar Rice Burroughs, London is the most influential and important writer of science fiction in early twentieth-century America. His works in the field include 'The Shadow and the Flash' (1903), a tale of invisibility; the dystopian novel *The Iron Heel* (1908) (an influence on George Orwell's (1903–50) *Nineteen Eighty-Four* (1949)); the Sinophobic story of biological warfare, 'The Unparalleled Invasion' (1909); the apocalyptic novella *The Scarlet Plague* (1912); and his short story 'The Red One'.

The copy-text is based on the story's first printing in a book, in *The Red One* (New York: The Macmillan Company, 1918), 1–50. The story first appeared earlier that year in *Cosmopolitan*, 65 (October 1918), 34–41, 132, 135–8. The book including the tale was published in Britain the following year (London: Mill & Boon, Ltd, 1919), 7–70. Some years later, on 10 October 1931, in a letter to Upton Sinclair, London's widow Charmian suggested that the idea of the fallen 'possible meteorite' came from London's friend, the poet and fellow bohemian George Sterling (1869–1926) (Dale L. Walker, *The Fiction of Jack London: A Chronological Bibliography* (El Paso, TX: Texas Western Press, 1972), 31).

280 *the trump of an archangel. Walls of cities ... might well fall down before so vast and compelling a summons*: two moments from the Bible merge here. The first obliquely alludes to the Second Coming of Jesus Christ: 'For the Lord himself shall descend from heaven, with the voice of the archangel, and with the trump of God' (1 Thessalonians 4:16). The second reference brings in the story of the fall of Jericho in Joshua 6:1–21, where the shouting of Joshua's army and the blowing of trumpets cause the walls of that city to collapse: 'So the people shouted when the priests blew with the trumpets: and it came to pass, when the people heard the sound of the trumpet, and the people shouted with a great shout, that the wall fell down flat, so that the people went up into the city, every man straight before him, and they took the city.'

Titan: a reference to Greek mythology, where, in Hesiod's (*c*.750–650 BC) *Theogony* (*c*.730–*c*.700 BC), the Titans are the pre-Olympian gods, the first children of Uranus (the sky god) and Gaia (the goddess of the earth) (or, in Homer, of Oceanus and Tethys). They were deposed by the children of Cronus, the Titan, led by Zeus.

281 *his dark tower?—Bassett pondered, remembering his Browning*: a reference to Robert Browning's (1812–89) 'Childe Roland to the Dark Tower Came' (1855), a mysterious and ineffable poem of knight-errantry. The poem ends with the narrator achieving his quest, in a typically obscure and indeterminate way:

There they stood, ranged about the hill-sides, met
To view the last of me, a living frame
For one more picture! in a sheet of flame
I saw them and I knew them all. And yet
Dauntless the slug-horn to my lips I set,
And blew. '*Childe Roland to the Dark Tower came.*'

(lines 199–204)

(The 'slug-horn' is a poeticism derived from the late eighteenth-century boy-poet Thomas Chatterton (1752–70).)

blackbirder: late nineteenth-century nautical slang for a slave trader, or, in this case, a slave-trading boat, at work in the South Pacific, abducting or press-ganging people to work in the sugar plantations.

Beche de mer English: bêche-de-mer (also called 'beach-la-mar' or 'biche-la-mar') is a jargon or 'pidgin' English used in the Western Pacific.

New Hanover boy: the partly mountainous New Hanover Island is found in the Bismarck Archipelago off the coast of Papua New Guinea in the Western Pacific.

282 *ten-gauge shotgun*: the gauge of a gun is measured according to the diameter of its bore, and therefore the size of the shot that can be fired from it; the smaller the gauge, the larger the bore diameter. Later, the protagonist describes having a twenty-gauge gun, which would be a lighter and more convenient weapon for hunting, and less explosive in its effects.

284 *anthropophagi*: literally, cannibals, from Latin and Greek; Latin *anthropophagus* is a human-eater.

Solomon Islanders, these twilight shades of bushmen of the island of Guadalcanal: the Solomon Islands are a scattered group of islands east of New Guinea in Oceania, in the Western Pacific. In 1887, Henry Brougham Guppy (1854–1926) remarked of travellers in this region that 'Day after day he skirts the shores of islands of which science has no "ken"'' (London: Swan Sonnenschein, 1887), 1). Guadalcanal is the largest of the Solomon Islands, and was in the latter nineteenth century a centre of the colonialist slave trade. See also note to p. 293.

285 *innocent of garb as Eve before the fig-leaf adventure*: a reference to the popular iconography of the story of Adam and Eve in Eden, who, becoming self-conscious and knowing good and evil, were supposed to have covered themselves after the Fall with a fig leaf: 'And the eyes of them both were opened, and they knew that they were naked; and they sewed fig-leaves together, and made themselves aprons' (Genesis 3:7). Such fig leaves were added to statues and paintings from the sixteenth century on in order to conceal nakedness.

286 *Mongolian nostrils*: in the racist theories of the late nineteenth and early twentieth centuries, the 'Mongolian' represented a supposedly more primitive version of humanity, and was associated with a low stage in human evolutionary development.

286 *devil-devil house*: specifically relating to Australian Aboriginal belief, the 'devil-devil' is an evil spirit.

287 *quinine . . . malarial and black-water fevers*: made from the cinchona bark, and native to South America, where it had long been used medicinally, quinine was used as a treatment for malaria by Europeans from the seventeenth century onwards. In the late nineteenth century, the drug was also used to treat the complicated form of malaria named 'blackwater fever'.

288 *The Thunderer, was another of Ngurn's names for the mysterious deity*: the term 'thunderer' had since the medieval period been applied to God and also to Jupiter or Jove.

292 *the Southern Cross*: the constellation Crux, only visible in the southern hemisphere, and, as the name suggests, perceived as forming the shape of a cross.

Memnon: the Colossi of Memnon, constructed in the fourteenth century, are two enormous statues showing seated figures, depicting the Egyptian Pharaoh Amenhotep III of the Eighteenth Dynasty, and once employed to guard the entrance to the Pharaoh's mortuary temple. The Greek hero Memnon became identified with the Egyptian figures, and turned somehow or other into a supposed Egyptian god. First mentioned by the Greek historian Strabo (65 BC–AD 23), and appearing too in writings by Pliny (23/24–79), Pausanias (*c.*110–*c.*180), Tacitus (*c.*56–*c.*120), and others, these statues were reported to be able to 'sing' or otherwise to produce sound on the coming of the dawn. As London's narrator suggests, this phenomenon, if true, was probably due to the effects of heat, and the dew drying in the cracks between the blocks from which the statues were made. The legend continued and appears in Oscar Wilde's (1854–1900) 'The Happy Prince' (1889) and in Act IV, scene xi of Henrik Ibsen's (1828–1906) *Peer Gynt* (1867) (though here in both cases the singing statue is of the reputed God Memnon).

Juliet or Balatta?: presumably a reference to the heroine of William Shakespeare's (1564–1616) *Romeo and Juliet* (1594/5?), and taken to be the epitome of a tragic lover.

293 *tyro*: a beginner, a novice.

the South Seas Sailing Directions: a book of charts and directions for sailors navigating coasts and ports. There does not seem to have been a specific text named 'South Seas Sailing Directions', but the American Government's Hydrographic Office published a series of such books, including most recently, *Pacific Islands Pilot*, i. *Western Groups* (Washington, DC: Government Printing Office, 1916). The United States Hydrographic Office was set up in 1866 in imitation of the United Kingdom's Hydrographic Department (established 1795).

Mendana who had discovered the islands and named them Solomon's, believing that he had found that monarch's fabled mines: indeed inspired by stories from South America that there were precious stones and gold in lands further to the west, in 1568 the Spanish navigator and explorer Álvaro de

Mendaña y Neira (or Neyra) (1542–95) went on a voyage of discovery in the Pacific and came upon what he then christened the Solomon Islands. As London informs us, the islands were indeed named as such in the belief that they were the place (perhaps even the biblical city of Ophir) from whence King Solomon had received his great riches: 'And the navy also of Hiram, that brought gold from Ophir, brought in from Ophir great plenty of almug trees, and precious stones' (1 Kings 10:12).

294 *lacquer*: a gold-coloured varnish.

295 *piping like an elfin horn*: perhaps a memory of the Scottish ballads 'Thomas the Rhymer', 'The Elfin Knight', or 'Lady Isabel and the Elf Knight', all of which feature enchanting elfin horns. Most famously, in one of the songs in Alfred Tennyson's *The Princess* (London: E. Moxon, 1847), 'The splendour falls on castle walls', we find: 'O sweet and far from cliff and scar | The horns of Elfland faintly blowing!'

atomatically: in the original text, this is written as 'atomatically', which may be a misprint for 'automatically'. However, the following sentence with its sense of life shrinking to microscopic proportions suggests that perhaps London was constructing a neologism here.

296 *as if God's Word had fallen . . . as if Jehovah's Commandments had been presented . . . as if the Sermon on the Mount had been preached in a roaring bedlam of lunatics*: at first, an allusion, perhaps, to the Parable of the Sower in Matthew 13:3–23, in which the word of God is scattered like seed on the ground. The Ten Commandments were given to Moses on Mount Sinai (Exodus 20–1). Jesus delivers the Sermon on the Mount in Matthew 5–7.

297 *labor-recruiting, black-birding ketch or schooner*: a ketch is a two-masted sailing ship. The 'labor-recruiting' vessel is rather euphemistically named, see note to p. 281.

subversive radium speculations: on 21 December 1898, the chemical element radium, an alkaline earth metal, was discovered by Marie Skłodowska Curie (1867–1934) and her husband, Pierre Curie (1859–1906). The element was found to emit detectable 'rays', even though no diminution in mass could be discovered in the element itself. As such, this challenged the theory of the conservation of energy, first proposed by Émilie du Châtelet (1706–49) in her 1756 translation into French of Isaac Newton's (1642–1726/7) *Principia Mathematica* (1687) and first fully theorized and demonstrated in 1841 by Julius Robert Mayer (1814–78), which posited that energy can neither be created or destroyed, but can only be transferred or transformed. A journalist in the *Manchester Guardian* (26 March 1903) put the puzzling properties of this new element starkly: 'All one's ideas about the conservation of energy are so rudely affronted by this impassively active substance, which persists in turning out heat without haste and without rest, without beginning and without end.'

appanages: here used either in the sense of being dependent territories or perhaps mere adjuncts.

301 *titillant*: a neologism of London's, meaning lightly touched or stimulated.

302 *the serene face of the Medusa, Truth*: Medusa was a female monster from Greek mythology, one of the three Gorgons, snake-haired sisters; anyone who met her gaze would turn into stone.

GERTRUDE BARROWS BENNETT, *Friend Island*

Gertrude Mabel (perhaps Myrtle?) Barrows was born in Minneapolis on 18 September 1884 (some say 1883). Her father, Charles Barrows, perhaps died in 1892. She left school after completing eighth grade, in order to help to support her family, and trained as a stenographer, in 1910 taking up an office job at a department store. Her first story, 'The Curious Experience of Thomas Dunbar', was published in the pulp magazine *The Argosy* in 1904; it was to be her last published story for some thirteen years. In 1909, she married Stewart Bennett, a British journalist; he died one year later, drowned while on a voyage seeking sunken treasure. That same year, Gertrude gave birth to their daughter, Josephine. Years of financial struggle followed, with Gertrude supporting her child and her invalid mother. From 1917, under the pseudonym Francis Stevens, she began publishing science fiction and 'weird' fantasy short stories in the pulps, beginning with 'The Nightmare' (*All-Story Weekly*, 14 April 1917), and including three masterpieces for *The Argosy*: 'The Citadel of Fear' (14 September–26 October 1918), a story of the discovery of a lost Aztec city; 'Claimed' (6–20 March 1920), an account of an ancient god summoned to modern New Jersey; and 'Serapion' (19 June–10 July 1920), a tale of possession. At this point, her writing career more or less ended, maybe because of her mother's death and her return to full-time work; her last published tale, 'Sunfire', perhaps written much earlier, appeared three years later in two issues of *Weird Tales* (July and September 1923). In 1948, she died in California.

Barrows Bennett is a key writer of the 1910s, a pioneer of what has been named 'dark fantasy', bringing a notably Gothic imagination to her fantastic tales. Her work also counts as a contribution to the development of science fiction, including the feminist utopian tale 'Friend Island' (1918), and the dystopian fiction 'The Heads of Cerberus' (serialized in *The Thrill Book*, 15 August–15 October 1919).

The copy-text for the tale derives from its first publication in *All-Story Weekly* (New York) (7 September 1918), 217–23. The tale was subtitled 'A "Different" Story'. Founded by Frank Munsey (1854–1924), *All-Story Weekly* was a 'pulp magazine' established in January 1905 as the *All-Story Magazine* (it became *All-Story Weekly* on 7 March 1914). As the name suggests, the periodical published fiction, including mystery tales, early science fiction, adventure stories, romances, Westerns, and verse. *All-Story Weekly* was particularly famed for its connection to Edgar Rice Burroughs; a glance at the letters columns in the periodical evidences just how popular he was with its readers. In September 1918, *All-Story Weekly* cost 10 cents per copy (or $4 for a year's subscription).

303 *Ancient Mariness*: an imagined female version of the outcast storyteller of Samuel Taylor Coleridge's (1772–1834) supernatural ballad of the sea, 'The Rime of the Ancyent Marinere' (1798).

aluminum rollers: though first produced in 1825, this metal was expensive to produce until the process of electrolysis was perfected in 1886. From the 1890s, aluminum (as it was called in the USA) or aluminium (as it was named in Britain) was seen as the metal of the future; the W. H. Mullins Company was making aluminum boats from the mid-1890s, and in 1894, Walter E. Wellman (1858–1934) made a voyage of discovery to the Arctic in one. A 'roller' is a ship, usually then a steamship, that pitches and rolls (*OED*).

boleros: (Spanish) short jackets reaching just above the waist.

304 *Shouter*: in the copy-text, the name of the ship is never italicized.

silkateen: developed first in the late 1890s, this was a textile thread made of mercerized cotton, used particularly for net darning, knitting, or crocheting.

305 *patent, hermetic, thermo-ice-chest*: an icebox, a refrigerator.

306 *Couquomgomoc Lake in Maine*: the Caucomgomoc Lake lies in the North Maine Woods, near the border with Canada.

307 *between Capricorn and Cancer*: between the tropic of Capricorn, the most southerly circle of latitude at which the sun can be directly overhead, and the tropic of Cancer, the most northerly such circle of latitude.

309 *Anita was a pretty name, and it sounded kind of South Sea like*: originally a Spanish diminutive of 'Ana', Anita became popular as a girl's name in the nineteenth century. Perhaps a slantwise element in what may be the allegory of the story, the name originally derives from 'Hannah', the Hebrew word for 'grace'.

310 *floater*: a cask or buoy left out at sea, containing a message (*OED*).

aeronauter: very likely a coinage of Bennett's, designed to sound futuristic, but derived from the term 'aeronaut', used first for balloonists, from the late eighteenth century onwards, but more recently on rare occasions applied to the fliers of planes.

aviatress: a fashionable figure of the 1910s, these women fliers were seen as glamorous and adventurous pioneers. Intrepid embracers of modernity, they likewise exemplified a specifically female independence. In 1909, Raymonde de Laroche (1882–1919) (the self-styled Baronesse de Laroche) became the first woman pilot, her first flight advertised as having been performed in defiance of her male instructors; Dorothy Levitt (1882–1922), the first woman racing-driver, was reputed to be the first British aviatress. In 1916, the American flier Ruth Law (1887–1970) flew non-stop from Chicago to New York; one year later, Katherine Stinson (1891–1977) completed the perilous flight over the Tehachapi Mountains in California. In 1919, a song by 'Will Curtis and Irving Bibo' (actually Irving Berlin (1888–1989)) describes how 'Since Katy the Waitress (Became an Aviatress)' 'all the boys are up in the air'.

313 *the wanderings of Odysseus . . . Gulliver . . . the history of one Munchausen, a baron*: references to three tales of male adventurers' wandering: from island to island in Homer's *The Odyssey* and Jonathan Swift's (1667–1745) *Gulliver's Travels* (1726); and all across Europe (and up to the moon) in the German author Rudolf Erich Raspe's (1736–1794) English-language tale of the epic liar, *Baron Munchausen's Narrative of His Marvellous Travels and Campaigns in Russia* (1785).

W. E. B. DU BOIS, The Comet

In 1868, William Edward Burghardt Du Bois was born in Great Barrington, Massachusetts, the son of Alfred Du Bois, a barber, and Mary Silvina Du Bois (née Burghardt), a domestic worker. In 1870, his father left his wife and son, and Mary moved with the child back to her parents' house. A bright pupil, Du Bois flourished at high school, in part under the mentorship of the principal, Frank Hosmer. Following his mother's death in March 1885, aided by a fund set up with Hosmer's help, Du Bois went to study at Fisk University in Nashville, Tennessee. In the summers of 1886 and 1887, he worked with black children as a schoolteacher in rural Tennessee. On graduating in 1888 (he was the valetudinarian), with the help of a Price-Greenleaf grant, he became a junior at Harvard, where he was taught by the historian Albert Bushnell Hart (1854–1943) and the philosopher William James (1842–1910), both of whom became his friends. In 1890, he graduated *cum laude*, staying on at the university as a graduate student in social sciences. After gaining an MA in 1891, he spent two years (1892–4) at the University of Berlin (Friedrich-Wilhelm III Universität). In 1895, he became the first black student to earn a PhD in history from Harvard. In 1896, he married Nina Gomer (a student at Wilberforce College, where he had been teaching classics since the summer of 1894), published his first book, based on his thesis *The Suppression of the African Slave-Trade to the United States of America, 1638–1870*, and took up a position at the University of Pennsylvania. His research at the university led to his book, *The Philadelphia Negro* (1899), a masterpiece of sociological study based on hundreds of hours of interviews in several thousand Philadelphia households. (Du Bois was anything but what he termed 'a car-window sociologist'.) After a year at the University of Pennsylvania, in 1897, Du Bois accepted a faculty position teaching economics and history at Atlanta University.

His son, Burghardt Gomer Du Bois, was born in 1897, and died less than two years later in Atlanta. His daughter, Nina Yolande Du Bois, was born in October 1900. His popular masterpiece *The Souls of Black Folk*, bringing together a number of articles, essays, memoir, and fiction, was published in 1903. Among other matters, the book dissected what it saw as the harmful influence of the African American leader Booker T. Washington (1856–1915), extolled the germinative impact of what Du Bois named 'the talented tenth' (the best and brightest of the African American community), and analysed 'the sorrow songs' of American slaves, exploring their potency, beauty, and influence. This book remains the most important analysis of 'the problem of the color-line' (Du Bois's phrase) of the early twentieth century.

In 1910, Du Bois left Atlanta to edit the newly founded National Association for the Advancement of Colored People's (NAACP) journal, *The Crisis: A Record of the Darker Races*. Living in New York, Du Bois became an influential figure in the emerging Harlem Renaissance. In 1911, he published his first novel, *The Quest of the Silver Fleece*; in 1915, his study of African culture and history, *The Negro*, appeared. Initially a supporter of the American effort in the First World War, Du Bois quickly came to see the war as the consequence of European colonialism. From this time, he was influenced by Marxist thought, visiting the Soviet Union in 1926, and became an enthusiast for Joseph Stalin (1878–1953) (even composing a eulogy for him after the Soviet leader's death). In 1920, *Darkwater: Voices from Within the Veil* was published, another book diversely composed of memoir, essay, poetry, and fiction (namely his venture into speculative fiction, 'The Comet').

In 1934, Du Bois resigned from the NAACP and from his editorship of *The Crisis*, and in 1935, he returned to work for a second time at Atlanta University, as chair of the Sociology Department. In 1944, he was compelled to retire, and took up a position as director of special research with the NAACP. He remained engaged through the post-war years as an activist and writer. In 1948, he was dismissed from the NAACP, and he joined the Council on African Affairs, where he was vice-chairman until 1956. In 1950, Nina, Du Bois's wife, died in Baltimore, and in 1961, his daughter died, also in Baltimore, of a heart attack. Later in 1961, at the invitation of President Kwame Nkrumah (1909–72), he moved to Ghana, where he died, a Ghanaian citizen, in 1963.

The copy-text of 'The Comet' is based on the tale's first publication in W. E. Burghardt Du Bois, *Darkwater: Voices from Within The Veil* (New York: Harcourt, Brace and Howe, 1920), 253–74. There, linked to the tale, a poem, titled 'The Hymn to the Peoples' (275–6), follows, a rhapsodic ode 'Foreshadowing the union of the World!' and ending with a plea to God to 'Help us, O Human God, in this Thy Truce, | To make Humanity Divine!'

314 *Broadway*: a central thoroughfare that diagonally crosses the length of Manhattan Island, and the first indication of the New York setting of Du Bois's tale. In August 1910, Du Bois moved to New York to take up the editorship of the NAACP's monthly magazine, *The Crisis*. From 1912, he lived with his family at 3059 Villa Avenue in the Bronx.

Halley's: on 19 May 1910, during the latest appearance of the short-period Halley's Comet, the earth passed through the comet's tail. From early in the year, there had been some alarm, expressed in the press, about the potential dangers of this imminent event, especially that some gas present in the tail might be poisonous to life on earth. In a letter to *The Times* on 10 February 1910, Sir Robert Ball (1840–1913), the Director of the Cambridge Observatory, reassured readers that passing through the tail of the comet was about as dangerous to us as a 'rhinoceros in full charge' would be endangered by 'collision with a cobweb'. In 1861, the earth had already passed through the tail of a comet, without much result. In January

1910, another comet had appeared, bright enough to be seen in the day-light sky. See also note to p. 15.

316 *Madison Square*: a small inner-city green square, on Fifth Avenue and Twenty-third Street, just north of the Flatiron Building.

317 *'Yesterday, they would not have served me'*: even where Jim Crow laws enshrining segregation were not in place, discrimination against African Americans in public places in northern cities was widespread in the 1910s (and indeed much later).

past the Plaza and by the park: opened in 1907, the Plaza Hotel stands in Grand Army Plaza at the intersection of Fifth Avenue and Fifty-ninth Street, on the corner of Central Park.

318 *the Metropolitan Tower*: the Metropolitan Life Insurance Company Tower, completed in 1913, stands on Madison Avenue and Twenty-fourth Street.

319 *Harlem*: beginning in 1904, despite opposition from some landlords and locals, there had been a move to rent properties to African Americans in this previously largely Irish, Jewish, and Italian district of upper Manhattan (with the Italians centred around Jefferson Park). By 1913, the area was acknowledged to be largely African American.

Stutz: Harry C. Stutz's (1876–1930) Ideal Motor Company, established in 1911, and known for making racing cars and luxurious sports cars. In 1913, it became the Stutz Motor Company. Having started with a mass-produced Ford, the male protagonist has traded up.

Mercedes: a luxury brand of car, originally named, in 1901, after the daughter of Emil Jellinek (1853–1918), the entrepreneur who helped transform the Daimler-Motoren-Gesellschaft into 'Mercedes-Benz'. Such cars were associated with the wealthy.

320 *from Madison Square to Spuyten Duyvel . . . Williamsburg Bridge . . . Brooklyn . . . the Battery and Morningside Heights*: the couple travel at random around New York City, from the intersection of Fifth Avenue and Broadway up to Spuyten Duyvil, a well-heeled area of the Bronx by where the Hudson and Harlem rivers meet; back down and across to the Lower East Side and the large suspension bridge (completed in 1903) that bridges the East River to Brooklyn, the large borough on the mainland opposite Manhattan; back across the bridge and over to the southern tip of the island by Battery Park; and then up along the Hudson River to Morningside Heights, to the west of Harlem.

322 *Friedhof*: (German) a cemetery, a graveyard.

'The world lies beneath the waters now—may I go?': the protagonist expresses a suicidal wish here. The phrase may also perhaps be an allusion to the story of Noah's flood, where God drowns most of the sinful world, though sparing Noah and his family. The phrase may also suggest the apocalyptic story of another island civilization than Manhattan: the tale of Atlantis, drowned by the sea, as first set out in Plato's *Timaeus* and *Critias*. Speculations about Atlantis were a feature of early twentieth-century

fantastic fiction, most influentially in Cutliffe Hynes's (1866–1944) *The Lost Continent* (1899). In Jules Verne's *Vingt mille lieues sous les mers: Tour du monde sous-marin*, the submarine *Nautilus* comes upon the submerged city.

323 *she had seen the elf-queen*: possibly a glance at the ballad of 'Thomas the Rymer', where the poet encounters the queen of Elfland, who shows him three roads, to Heaven, to Hell, and to her own country. It is also, more remotely, possibly a reference to the effect of being visited by Queen Mab, as described as Mercutio in Act I, scene iv of William Shakespeare's *Romeo and Juliet*, where such visitations lead to the distortion of reality in dream.

'The rich and the poor are met together,' . . . *'The Lord is the Maker of them all'*: the poor man and the rich woman here meet together also in sharing a tradition, and both knowing and quoting the same one Bible verse: 'The rich and the poor meet together: the Lord is the maker of them all' (Proverbs 22:2). There may be some level of glancing allusion here to the fact that these are words ascribed to King Solomon, who writes of a woman lover, who is, as she says herself, 'black, but comely' (Song of Solomon 1:5).

'And your people were not my people': another biblical cadence drawing on the moment when the widowed Ruth, a Moabite, tells Naomi, her Jewish mother-in-law, 'Intreat me not to leave thee, or to return from following after thee: for whither thou goest, I will go; and where thou lodgest, I will lodge: and thy people shall be my people, and thy God my God' (Ruth 1:16). Again, the biblical tale in question concerns the relationship of a people to a figure regarded as an outsider.

'Death, the leveler!': the phrase is proverbial, but originally derives from a line in Claudian's (*c.*370–*c.*404) *De Raptu Proserpinae* (*The Abduction of Proserpine*), 'omnia mors aequat' (ii. 302), meaning death makes all equal, or death levels or smooths out all things. Or, as Thomas Fuller's (1654–1734) *Gnomologia: adages and proverbs* (London: B. Barker, 1732) puts it, 'Death is the grand Leveller'.

324 *the Angel of Annunciation*: another biblical allusion, this time to the angel Gabriel's visit to Mary, telling her that she, blessed among women, will be the mother of Jesus (Luke 1:26–38). As Du Bois continues the analogy, the woman survivor becomes also a new Eve, ready to repopulate the earth with her Adam.

mighty Pharaoh lived again, or curled Assyrian lord: in relation to Du Bois's interests at the time, the story here evokes images of a noble African and Middle Eastern tradition of kingship, allied to and derived from 'the Negro' (as set out in his study, *The Negro* (New York: Henry Holt and Company, 1915)).